"Two eminent scholars and theologically-minded pastors bring together a survey of the latest source-based research and an analysis of contemporary issues for ancient Eastern Christian worship in the modern world. No other introduction combines the broad scope of liturgy—including texts of prayers and hymns, sacramental theology and ritual actions, art and architecture—and their myriad expressions in various Eastern Churches. This book will become the standard reference for anyone interested in the rites of the Christian East, whether scholars specializing in one of its many traditions or curious students and practitioners looking for an accessible introduction to a different ethos and form of spirituality."

— Daniel Galadza, Metropolitan Andrey Sheptytsky Institute of Eastern Christian Studies, University of Toronto

"This book is a cause for celebration! Study of eastern Christian liturgy has long been hampered by isolation of the scholarship into separate fields, often by linguistic category, prohibiting full appreciation of the rich, complex, and fertile intersections, diversifications, and developments that have enabled eastern liturgies to flourish across the centuries. Instead, here in one concise, eloquently crafted volume, is the presentation of eastern Christian liturgies in their full panoply of splendor. A monumental achievement, opening new frontiers for study and knowledge."

— Susan Ashbrook Harvey, Willard Prescott and Annie McClelland Smith Professor of Religion and History, Brown University

"This book could not be more relevant or necessary. *Introduction to Eastern Christian Liturgies* comes at a time when many foundational Christian traditions are threatened with extinction in the very lands of their origin. It deserves deep study and serious meditation."

— Joseph P. Amar, Professor of Syriac Christianity, University of Notre Dame

"This substantial volume provides the ideal reference work for Western Christians wanting to gain more than a superficial acquaintance with the liturgical practices of the Eastern Churches. It is detailed and comprehensive, covering much more than the Eucharist or the rites of the Orthodox Church. It incorporates the latest scholarship in tracing the history of the various traditions. And it intersperses tables and quotations of texts liberally throughout, to make the complexity much more easily intelligible."

— Paul F. Bradshaw, Emeritus Professor of Liturgy, University of Notre Dame

"Those who teach liturgy are well aware that hitherto there has been no single, up-to-date, and comprehensive study that covers both the history and the present *sitz im leben* of the classical Eastern liturgical rites. This timely volume by Stefanos Alexopoulos and Maxwell Johnson admirably fills the lacuna."

— Bryan D. Spinks, Bishop F. Percy Goddard Professor of Liturgical Studies and Pastoral Theology, Yale Institute of Sacred Music and Yale Divinity School

"The diversity of Eastern Christian rites is not only a rich inheritance from the past; it is also of increasing importance in a globalized world—and at the same time acutely endangered in some of its pristine homelands. In this situation, this comprehensive, clear, and accessible introduction is on the one hand of interest for scholars and students seeking reliable information and up-to-date bibliographies; on the other hand, it opens up the treasures of theology and spirituality transmitted in the liturgical life of the Eastern Christian churches."

— Harald Buchinger, Chair of Liturgical Studies, University of Regensburg, Germany

"The field of liturgical studies has long needed a manual like this. While the discipline affirms the fundamental importance of studying liturgy comparatively, students often find it difficult to access the Eastern rites. Alexopoulos and Johnson have helped fill a major void with this important introduction to the rich liturgies of the Christian East. It will be an important reference for scholars and students alike."

— Gabriel Radle, Assistant Professor of Liturgical Studies, University of Notre Dame

"Here is a new prowess and a great service rendered to Westerners interested in developing a genuine understanding of the Christian communities belonging to the churches of the East. Through state-of-the-art scholarship, the rites of the different churches (holy mysteries, liturgical year and divine office, funerals) are studied through a systematic comparative liturgy approach in a dynamic way which accounts for the historical development of each tradition placed in immediate parallel with all the others, even reflecting present-day questioning. The Introduction presents the domain, the methodological approaches, the mind of Eastern Christianity, while the ethos and spirituality of the Oriental Churches conclude a most informative volume."

— Fr. Emmanuel Fritsch, CSSp, pastor of the Byzantine-rite Catholic parish of Saint Irenaeus of Lyons, Lyons (France)

"At last, Eastern liturgies have a true academic manual, necessary for students as well as teachers. We have waited half a century, but the expectation has been amply rewarded."

— Stefano Parenti, University of Regensburg, Germany

## The Alcuin Club: Promoting the Study of Liturgy

Founded in 1897, the Alcuin Club seeks to promote the study of Christian liturgy and worship in general with special reference to worship in the Anglican Communion. The Club has published a series of annual Collections, including *A Companion to Common Worship*, volumes 1 and 2, edited by Paul F. Bradshaw; *The Origins of Feasts, Fasts and Seasons in Early Christianity* by Paul F. Bradshaw and Maxwell E. Johnson (SPCK 2011) and, by the same authors, *The Eucharistic Liturgies: Their Evolution and Interpretation* (SPCK 2012); and a new completely revised 4th edition of R. C. D. Jasper and G. J. Cuming, *Prayers of the Eucharist: Early and Reformed* (Liturgical Press Academic, 2019); also *The Cross and Creation in Christian Liturgy and Art* by Christopher Irvine (SPCK, 2013), *Eucharistic Epicleses Ancient and Modern* by Anne McGowan (SPCK, 2014), *Dean Dwelly of Liverpool: Liturgical Genius* by Peter Kennerley (Carnegie Publishing, 2015), *Ancient Christian Worship* by Andrew B. McGowan (Baker Academic, 2016), *The Rise and Fall of the Incomparable Liturgy: The Book of Common Prayer 1559–1906* by Bryan D. Spinks (SPCK, 2017) and, by the same author, *Scottish Presbyterian Worship* (St Andrew Press, 2020); and *The Pilgrimage of Egeria* by Anne McGowan and Paul F. Bradshaw (Liturgical Press Academic, 2018).

The Alcuin Liturgy Guide series aims to address the theology and practice of worship, and includes *The Use of Symbols in Worship*, edited by Christopher Irvine, two volumes covering the celebration of the Christian Year: *Celebrating Christ's Appearing: Advent to Christmas*; and *Celebrating Christ's Victory: Ash Wednesday to Trinity*, both by Benjamin Gordon-Taylor and Simon Jones, and most recently *Celebrating Christian Initiation* by Simon Jones.

The Club works in partnership with the Group for the Renewal of Worship (GROW) in the publication of the Joint Liturgical Studies series, with two studies being published each year.

In 2013 the Club also published a major new work of reference, *The Study of Liturgy and Worship: An Alcuin Guide*, edited by Juliette Day and Benjamin Gordon-Taylor (SPCK, 2013).

Members of the Club receive publications of the current year free and others at a reduced rate. The President of the Club is the Rt Revd Dr Stephen Platten, its Chairman is the Revd Canon Christopher Irvine, and the Secretary is the Revd Dr Gordon Jeanes. For details of membership and the annual subscription, contact The Alcuin Club, 5 Saffron Street, Royston, Herts, SG8 9TR United Kingdom; email: alcuinclub@gmail.com; or visit the Alcuin Club website at: www.alcuinclub.org.uk.

Alcuin Club Collections 96

# Introduction to Eastern Christian Liturgies

Stefanos Alexopoulos

*and*

Maxwell E. Johnson

LITURGICAL PRESS
ACADEMIC

Collegeville, Minnesota
www.litpress.org

Cover design by Monica Bokinskie.
Detail of *Keresztrefeszítés—A kenethozó asszonyok (Crucifixion—The Anointing Women)*, Rabbula kódex, 586, Firenze, Laurenziana, Plut. I. 56.
Image courtesy of Wikimedia Commons. Used under Creative Commons Attribution-Share Alike 4.0 International License.

The Translit Palatino fonts used in this work are available at www.linguistsoftware.com.



1 2 3 4 5 6 7 8 9

**Library of Congress Cataloging-in-Publication Data**

Names: Alexopoulos, Stefanos, author. | Johnson, Maxwell E., 1952– author.
Title: Introduction to Eastern Christian liturgies / Stefanos Alexopoulos and Maxwell E. Johnson.
Description: Collegeville, Minnesota : Liturgical Press Academic, [2021] | Series: Alcuin club collections ; 96 | Includes bibliographical references and index. | Summary: "A survey of the liturgical life of the Eastern Christian Churches within the seven distinct liturgical Eastern rites still in existence today: Armenian, Byzantine, Coptic, Ethiopic, East Syrian, West Syrian, and Maronite"— Provided by publisher.
Identifiers: LCCN 2021027570 (print) | LCCN 2021027571 (ebook) | ISBN 9780814663554 (paperback) | ISBN 9780814663806 (epub) | ISBN 9780814663806 (pdf)
Subjects: LCSH: Eastern churches—Liturgy.
Classification: LCC BX107 .A44 2021 (print) | LCC BX107 (ebook) | DDC 264/.015--dc23
LC record available at https://lccn.loc.gov/2021027570
LC ebook record available at https://lccn.loc.gov/2021027571

# Contents

# Abbreviations

| | |
|---|---|
| ACC | Alcuin Club Collections |
| AGLS | Alcuin/GROW Liturgical Study |
| ANF | Ante-Nicene Fathers |
| BAS | The Anaphoras of St. Basil of Caesarea (various versions: ArmBAS = Armenian BAS; ByzBAS = Byzantine Basil; EgBAS = Egyptian Basil; SyrBAS = Syriac Basil) |
| BEW | Robert Taft, *Beyond East and West: Problems in Liturgical Understanding*. Second revised and enlarged edition. Rome: Pontifical Oriental Institute, 1997. |
| CHR | The Anaphora of St. John Chrysostom |
| DBL | E. C. Whitaker, ed. *Documents of the Baptismal Liturgy*. Third revised and expanded edition, edited by Maxwell E. Johnson. ACC 79. Collegeville, MN: Liturgical Press, Pueblo, 2003. |
| ET | English Translation |
| GLS | Grove Liturgical Study |
| JAS | The Anaphora of St. James of Jerusalem |
| LWSS | Maxwell E. Johnson, ed. *Living Water, Sealing Spirit: Readings on Christian Initiation*. Collegeville, MN: Liturgical Press, Pueblo, 1995. |
| MFC | Message of the Fathers of the Church |
| MFC 5 | Thomas M. Finn, ed. *Early Christian Baptism and the Catechumenate: West and East Syria*. Message of the Fathers of the Church 5. Collegeville, MN: Michael Glazier, 1992. |

| | |
|---|---|
| MFC 6 | Thomas M. Finn, ed. *Early Christian Baptism and the Catechumenate: Italy, North Africa, and Egypt*. Message of the Fathers of the Church 6. Collegeville, MN: Michael Glazier, 1992. |
| NPNF | Nicene and Post-Nicene Fathers |
| OCA | Orientalia Christiana Analecta |
| OCP | *Orientalia Christiana Periodica* |
| PEER 4 | R. C. D. Jasper and G. J. Cuming, eds., *Prayers of the Eucharist: Early and Reformed*. Fourth Edition, edited by Paul F. Bradshaw and Maxwell E. Johnson. ACC 94. Collegeville, MN: Liturgical Press Academic, 2019. |
| PG | Migne, *Patrologia Graeca* |
| PL | Migne, *Patrologia Latina* |
| QL | *Questions Liturgiques* |
| SC | Sources chrétiennes |

# Acknowledgments

The authors wish to express here their gratitude for the use of previously copyrighted and other material from the following works in this study:

Parts of the introduction appear in German in Stefanos Alexopoulos, "Die Liturgie in den östlichen Kirchen," in the *Gottesdienst der Kirche - Handbuch der Liturgiewissenschaft*, vol. I.1.

The second half of chapter 4 appeared originally in Paul F. Bradshaw, *Rites of Ordination: Their History and Theology* (Collegeville, MN: Liturgical Press, Pueblo, 2013).

R. C. D. Jasper and G. J. Cuming, eds., *Prayers of the Eucharist: Early and Reformed*, 4th ed., ed. Paul F. Bradshaw and Maxwell E. Johnson, ACC 94 (Collegeville, MN: Liturgical Press Academic, 2019).

Paul F. Bradshaw and Maxwell E. Johnson, *The Origins of Feasts, Fasts, and Seasons in Early Christianity*, ACC 86 (Collegeville, MN: Liturgical Press, Pueblo, 2011).

An earlier version of chapter 2 appeared originally in Paul F. Bradshaw and Maxwell E. Johnson, *The Eucharistic Liturgies: Their Evolution and Interpretation*, ACC 87 (Collegeville, MN: Liturgical Press, Pueblo, 2012), 137–92.

Coptic Orthodox Diocese of Southern USA, "Coptic Reader," Apple App Store, Vers. 2.84 (2020), https://apps.apple.com/us/app/coptic-reader/id649434138.

The Right Reverend M. Daniel Findikyan, primate and bishop of the Eastern Diocese of the Armenian Apostolic Orthodox Church in

America, New York, New York, for the translation of the Armenian Anaphora of St. Athanasius, which appears in M. Daniel Findikyan, ed., *The Divine Liturgy of the Armenian Church with Modern Armenian and English Translations, Transliteration, Musical Notation, Introduction and Notes* (New York: St. Vartan Press, 1999), 28–39.

An earlier version of chapter 1 appeared in Maxwell E. Johnson, *The Rites of Christian Initiation: Their Evolution and Interpretation*, rev. and exp. ed. (Collegeville, MN: Liturgical Press, Pueblo, 2007), 269–308.

Kenneth Stevenson, *To Join Together: The Rite of Marriage*, Studies in the Reformed Rites of the Catholic Church 5 (New York: Pueblo Publishing Company, 1987).

Robert Taft, *The Liturgy of the Hours in East and West: The Origins of the Divine Office and Its Meaning for Today*, 2nd rev. ed. (Collegeville, MN: Liturgical Press, 1993).

E. C. Whitaker, ed., *Documents of the Baptismal Liturgy*, Third rev. and exp. ed., edited by Maxwell E. Johnson, ACC 79 (Collegeville, MN: Liturgical Press, 2003).

Where not otherwise acknowledged, translations are the work of the authors.

# INTRODUCTION

## The Rites of the Christian East

There is a growing awareness of and interest in Eastern Christianity among Western Christians, so much so that Pope John Paul II in a well-known quotation said, "Without the Christian East Western Christianity breathes with only one lung." And Sebastian Brock has recently noted that the liturgical traditions of the Syriac Orient constitute actually a "third lung," since Christianity is not made up only of Latin and Greek traditions.[1] This increased awareness is the result of contacts within the ecumenical movement over the last seventy years or so, the increasing presence of Eastern Christian communities in the West (originally immigrant communities but more and more integrated into mainstream society), and, more recently, new movements of immigration due to the plight of Eastern Christians in the Middle East, especially in Syria, Iran, and Iraq. Indeed, even some of the great classic centers of Eastern Christianity (e.g., Mosul) have been destroyed, and their communities are now part of Eastern Christian diasporas located in California, Detroit, and Chicago.

Although short studies of Eastern Christian liturgies have occasionally appeared,[2] these have often been limited either to one specific rite or ritual family, such as the Byzantine, or tend to be introductions

[1] Sebastian Brock, "Variety in Institution Narratives in the Syriac Anaphoras," in *The Anaphoral Genesis of the Institution Narrative in Light of the Anaphora of Addai and Mari*, ed. Cesare Giraudo, OCA 295 (Rome: Edizioni Orientalia Christiana, 2013), 65n1.

[2] Robert Taft, *The Byzantine Rite: A Short History*, American Essays in Liturgy (Collegeville, MN: Liturgical Press, 1992); and Edward Finn, *These Are My Rites: A Brief History of the Eastern Rites of Christianity*, American Essays in Liturgy (Collegeville, MN: Liturgical Press, 1980).

now rather out of date, based on scholarship long surpassed by the reigning experts in the field. In other words, really nothing of this sort of one-volume introduction to the liturgies of the Christian East has been produced within the last fifty years. Classic studies, such as Irénée-Henri Dalmais, *Eastern Liturgies*,[3] or Donald Attwater, *The Christian Churches of the East*,[4] while still helpful, were both written long before crucial developments in contemporary liturgical scholarship on the Christian East, exemplified by the work of scholars like Sebastian Brock (Syrian liturgies),[5] Gabriele Winkler (Armenian and Ethiopian),[6] and, of course, Robert Taft (Byzantine).[7] Even Hans-Joachim Schulz's excellent study, *The Byzantine Liturgy*,[8] was, again, limited to only one of the Eastern liturgical traditions. This study, then, seeks to fill this lacuna in the liturgical study of the Christian East.

It is not always remembered, especially among Western Christians, that Christianity originated as an Eastern religion. It was born in the East and saw its first communities established in Palestine, in Syria, in Cappadocia, and in Egypt. By the second century Christianity had reached Mesopotamia and India (evangelized, according to tradition, by the Apostle Thomas and his disciples), and by the fourth century Armenia and Ethiopia were Christian. Missionaries from Mesopotamia reached as far as China in the seventh century, and in the tenth

[3] Irénée-Henri Dalmais, *Eastern Liturgies*, Twentieth Century Encyclopedia of Catholicism, vol. 112 (New York: Hawthorn Books, 1960)

[4] Donald Attwater, *The Christian Churches of the East*, 2 vols. (Ann Arbor: University of Michigan Library, 1961).

[5] See Sebastian Brock, *Fire from Heaven: Studies in Syriac Theology and Liturgy*, Variorum Collected Studies Series 863 (Aldershot, England: Ashgate, 2006).

[6] See Gabriele Winkler, *Das armenische Initiationsrituale. Entwicklungsgeschichtliche und liturgievergleichende Untersuchung der Quellen des 3. bis 10. Jahrhunderts*, OCA 217 (Rome: Pontificio Istituto Orientale, 1982).

[7] See Robert Taft, *The Byzantine Rite: A Short History*; idem, *Beyond East and West: Problems in Liturgical Understanding*, 2nd rev. and enl. ed. (Rome: Pontifical Oriental Institute, 1997); idem, *A History of the Liturgy of St. John Chrysostom*, vol. 4, *The Diptychs*, OCA 238 (Rome: Pontifical Oriental Institute, 1991); idem, *A History of the Liturgy of St. John Chrysostom*, vol. 6: *The Communion, Thanksgiving, and Concluding Rites*, OCA 281 (Rome: Pontificio Istituto Orientale, 2008); idem, *The Great Entrance: A History of the Transfer of Gifts and Other Preanaphoral Rites of the Liturgy of St. John Chrysostom*, 2nd ed., OCA 200 (Rome: Pontificio Istituto Orientale, 1978); and idem, "The Liturgy of the Great Church: An Initial Synthesis of Structure and Interpretation on the Eve of Iconoclasm," *Dumbarton Oaks Papers* 34–35 (1980–1981): 45–75.

[8] Hans-Joachim Schulz, *The Byzantine Liturgy: Symbolic Structure and Faith Expression* (New York: Pueblo, 1986).

century missionaries from Byzantium Christianized the Rus and the Slavs. It is noteworthy that when the "Pentarchy" was established in the fourth and fifth centuries, four of the five patriarchates were (and still are) located in the East: Constantinople, Alexandria, Antioch, and Jerusalem (with only Rome belonging to the West). These indigenous Christians have been living in these countries for up to two millennia now, from the very beginning of Christianity, and they are still present among us today, living in countries that popular mentality often does not associate with Christianity, such as Israel, Palestine, Lebanon, Jordan, Syria, Turkey, Iraq, Iran, India, and Egypt. In other countries Eastern Christians are the majority (Ethiopia and Eritrea in Africa, Armenia and Georgia in the Caucasus, Greece, Cyprus, Bulgaria, Romania, Serbia, Montenegro, North Macedonia, Romania, Moldova, Belarus, Russia, Ukraine), whereas in others they are a historical minority (Albania, Kosovo, Bosnia, Czech Republic, Slovakia, Poland, Finland, Latvia). Because of financial reasons, geopolitical shifts, wars, and persecution, a large number of these Eastern Christians have been immigrating in the last two centuries to Western Europe, to the Americas, to Africa, to Asia, and to Oceania, thus establishing Eastern Christian communities throughout the world.[9]

All of these Eastern Christian families have long-standing and rich liturgical traditions, called "rites." A rite is a unique and integrated system of worship with its own rules and inner system conditioned by history, culture, theological outlook, and it embodies that tradition's official expression of its Christian faith, i.e., what Aidan Kavanagh has called a "distinct ecclesial way of being Christian."[10] And in the East there are today seven extant liturgical rites: Armenian, Byzantine, Coptic, Ethiopian, East Syrian, West Syrian, and Maronite. Broadly speaking, these liturgical rites represent four ecclesial communities: the Orthodox, the non-Ephesians, the Oriental Orthodox, and the Eastern Catholic. (1) The Orthodox (Chalcedonian Christians) follow the Byzantine Rite. They are a communion of independent (autocephalus) churches that recognize the Patriarch of Constantinople

[9] It is very difficult to assign numbers of adherents to each of the Eastern traditions; the study by Ronald Roberson, *The Eastern Christian Churches: A Brief Survey*, 7th ed. (Rome: Pontificio Istituto Orientale, 2010) has become the standard reference. See also Johannes Oeldemann, *Die Kirchen des christlichen Ostens: Orthodoxe, orientalische und mit Rom unierte Ostkirchen* (Kevelaer: Verlagsgemeinschaft Topos Plus, 2006).

[10] Aidan Kavanagh, *On Liturgical Theology* (New York: Pueblo, 1984), 100.

as first among equals (*primus inter pares*). (2) The non-Ephesians are those who rejected the Council of Ephesus in 431—they follow the East Syrian Rite and are called "Church of the East." (3) The Oriental Orthodox are those who rejected the Council of Chalcedon in 451. These are a communion of churches, each following their own rite: the Coptic Church, the Ethiopian Church, the Eritrean Church, the Armenian Church, the Syrian Orthodox Church. Finally, (4) the Eastern Catholics are communities of either Eastern Orthodox, Church of the East, or Oriental Orthodox that have entered into communion with Rome while maintaining their liturgical rites. A unique member of this group is the Maronite Church (follows the Maronite Rite) with no counterpart among the Orthodox or the Oriental Orthodox, which claims it has always been in communion with Rome.[11]

A note should be made here regarding the naming of these liturgical traditions or rites. Historically, there is no standard principle behind the naming of a liturgical tradition; there are different ways, sometimes even overlapping: some are based on confession (such as "Orthodox," "Chalcedonian," "non-Chalcedonian," "Monophysite," "Nestorian"); others are based on language ("Syrian," "Coptic," "Armenian"); others again are based on political labels ("Byzantine," "Armenian," "Ethiopian"); others are named after people ("Nestorian," "Maronite," "Jacobite"); others are geographical ("Byzantine," "Alexandrian," "Antiochene," "Hagiopolite"). In addition, as it is obvious from the short description above, the christological contro-

[11] For helpful introductions to these rites, see Ephrem Carr, "Liturgical Families in the East," in *Handbook for Liturgical Studies*, vol. 1: *Introduction to the Liturgy*, ed. Anscar J. Chupungco (Collegeville, MN: Liturgical Press, Pueblo, 1997), 11–24. See also Bryan D. Spinks, "Eastern Christian Liturgical Traditions: Oriental Orthodox," in *The Blackwell Companion to Eastern Christianity*, ed. Ken Parry (Oxford: Wiley-Blackwell, 2007), 339–67; Gregory Woolfenden, "Eastern Christian Liturgical Traditions: Eastern Orthodox," in ibid., 319–38; Christine Chaillot, "The Ancient Oriental Churches," in *The Oxford History of Christian Worship*, ed. Geoffrey Wainwright and Karen Westerfield Tucker (Oxford: Oxford University Press, 2006), 131–69; Lucas Van Rompay, "Excursus: The Maronites," in ibid., 170–74; and Alexander Rentel, "Byzantine and Slavic Orthodoxy," in ibid., 254–306. See also Paul Naaman, *The Maronites: The Origins of an Antiochene Church—A Historical and Geographical Study of the Fifth to the Seventh Centuries*, Cistercian Studies 243 (Collegeville, MN: Cistercian Publications, 2009). On Eastern Christianity in general, see Mahmoud Zibawi, *Eastern Christian Worlds* (Collegeville, MN: Liturgical Press, 1995); and for Egypt specifically, see Massimo Capuani, *Christian Egypt: Coptic Art and Monuments through Two Millennia* (Collegeville, MN: Liturgical Press, 2002).

versies of the fourth and fifth centuries gave rise to the first major divisions in Christianity, and particular rites came to be associated with this or that communion of churches. As a result, terms used until recently were colored by this history and oftentimes were inaccurate. For example, the Coptic, the Ethiopian, the Armenian, and the Syriac churches were labeled as "Monophysite." The Monophysitism condemned at the Council of Chalcedon in 451 was, however, that of Eutyches, one that these more accurately called "Miaphysite" churches also condemn! In the same vein, the use of the term "Nestorian" for the Church of the East is incorrect and misleading; it is the theology of Theodore of Mopsuestia and not that of Nestorius that defines the Church of the East. In addition, Eastern communities that have entered into communion with Rome (Eastern Catholics) were labeled as "Uniate" by the Orthodox, a term used in a derogatory manner. In fact, ecumenical dialogue between the Eastern and Oriental Orthodox Churches[12] and between many of these churches and the West has led to greater understanding and progress toward Christian unity. For example, the 1994 *Common Christological Declaration between the Catholic Church and the Assyrian Church of the East*, leading in 2001 to a document titled *Guidelines for Admission to the Eucharist between the Chaldean Church and the Assyrian Church of the East*,[13] is a hopeful

[12] Christine Chaillot, ed., *The Dialogue between the Eastern Orthodox and the Oriental Orthodox Churches* (Volos: Volos Academy Publications, 2016).

[13] Beginning in 1994 with a *Common Christological Declaration between the Catholic Church and the Assyrian Church of the East*, continued ecumenical dialogue and convergence led in 2001 to a document titled *Guidelines for Admission to the Eucharist between the Chaldean Church and the Assyrian Church of the East*. There is no question that this is one of the most significant liturgical-ecumenical developments ever in the history of the Church. What makes it so is that it now allows Chaldean Catholics to receive Holy Communion in liturgies celebrated in assemblies of the Assyrian Church of the East among whom that early Semitic eucharistic prayer called the Anaphora of Saints Addai and Mari is used, that famous third-century eucharistic prayer which, like other extant prayers from the pre-Nicene period, lacks the institution narrative, the Verba Christi! (For a text of the anaphora of Addai and Mari see R. C. D. Jasper and G. J. Cuming, eds., *Prayers of the Eucharist: Early and Reformed*, 3rd ed. [Collegeville, MN: Liturgical Press, Pueblo, 1987], 39–44). Hence, the Eucharistic Prayer of Addai and Mari, *even without the explicit recital of the words of institution*, is recognized by Rome as a valid prayer of eucharistic consecration; i.e., as constituting a Catholic Eucharist in the full sense of the word within the Assyrian Church of the East and Chaldean Catholics, those receiving Communion in such eucharistic celebrations are assured that they are indeed receiving the Body and Blood of Christ. The implications of this are mind-boggling on several levels, not the least of which is the now-official

ecumenical sign of things to come, including the recognition by Rome of the validity of the Anaphora of Addai and Mari, as used by the Church of the East still today, without a narrative of institution included or recited. And, indeed, christological and ecclesiological dialogues between Rome and the Oriental Orthodox Churches are quite promising along these same lines, as are the dialogues between the Orthodox and Oriental Orthodox Churches.

Modernity and the drastic changes occurring in our world today pose a new challenge to the Eastern Churches and their liturgical traditions. Through either immigration or forced expulsion, these Eastern communities find refuge in the West in a foreign cultural and intellectual milieu; we must not forget that the Eastern Churches have *not* experienced the Renaissance, the Reformation, and the Enlightenment and therefore face multifaceted tensions: between their culture and the culture of their new home, between their communities abroad and the communities in the "old" countries, between the past and the future. These new contexts are destined to have repercussions on the liturgical language used, on the length of services, on the texts used in the rituals, on liturgical architecture and iconography, and so on. Dealing with modernity, there are two major reactions, with many gradations in between: an extreme "conservatism" and rejection of modernity and all that it entails, on the one hand, and an extreme "liberalism" in which everything new is good and everything old is bad. The "old" countries also face these tensions now as they are more and more Westernized and are posed with the same issues and challenges. The Eastern Churches are at the crossroads, and it is their opportunity, through engaging modernity and all that it entails, to contribute to the modern world a worldview and a viewpoint that is rooted in history and tradition but is also fresh, vibrant, and prophetic; one of their major contributions is their liturgical traditions.

Before entering into an examination of these Eastern liturgical rites in the following chapters, it is important to give a framework and

recognition of what liturgical scholars have been saying for years—namely, that it is the entire eucharistic prayer itself, and not various "formulas" (whether institution narrative or epiclesis), that "consecrate" the Eucharist. On all of this, see Robert Taft, "Mass without the Consecration? The Historic Agreement on the Eucharist between the Catholic Church and the Assyrian Church of the East Promulgated 26 October 2001," *Worship* 77, no. 6 (2003): 482–509.

context for our study. Therefore, what follows are brief sections on the methodology of the study of the Eastern liturgical traditions, the phases of the evolution of liturgical rites, a discussion on the factors and forces in the development of these rites, some of the characteristics of these rites, and, not least, a description of each of the living rites themselves.

## Methodology

There are two traditional theories regarding the emergence of liturgical rites. The theory of "diversification," proposed by Ferdinand Probst,[14] argues that from the initial pristine liturgy of the apostolic times the various rites emerged, becoming quite distinct over time. Although Probst had a point in recognizing that Christian liturgical practice ultimately has its roots in apostolic times and practice, more recent scholarship has noted that the development of a multitude of liturgical usages were there from the very beginning and certainly continued during the first three centuries and beyond.[15] Anton Baumstark,[16] the father of comparative liturgy, recognized the Peace of Constantine in 312 as a major turning point in liturgical history. After the Peace, one observes an ongoing process of unification, moving not from unity to diversity but from original diversity toward unity, anchored around ecclesiastical centers and dependent on ecclesiastical and political influence, historical circumstances, and dogmatic disputes. There have been two primary methodological approaches in examining Eastern liturgies: (1) *philological* and (2) *Liturgiewissenschaft* or the approach of comparative liturgy. The *philological* approach

[14] Ferdinand Probst, *Liturgie der drei ersten christlichen Jahrhunderte* (Tübingen: H. Laupp, 1870); idem, *Liturgie des vierten Jahrhunderts und deren Reform* (Münster: Aschendorff, 1893).

[15] See Paul F. Bradshaw, *The Search for the Origins of Christian Worship*, 2nd ed. (London: SPCK, 2002), 1–20; and Andrew McGowan, *Ancient Christian Worship: Early Church Practices in Social, Historical, and Theological Perspective* (Grand Rapids: Baker, 2014).

[16] Anton Baumstark, *Vom geschichtlichen Werden der Liturgie* (Freiburg im Breisgau: Herder, 1923) = idem, *On the Historical Development of the Liturgy* (Collegeville, MN: Liturgical Press, 2011), introduction, translation, and annotation by Fritz West; and Anton Baumstark, *Liturgie comparée; principes et méthodes pour l'étude historique des liturgies chrétiennes*, 3rd ed. (Chevetogne: Éditions de Chevetogne, 1953) = idem, *Comparative Liturgy*, ed. Bernard Botte (Westminster, MD: Newman Press, 1958).

is centered primarily on the critical editions of original texts. This approach is absolutely necessary for the study of Eastern liturgies, as without the proper edition of the primary texts no serious further study can be made. And unless further primary texts are properly edited and published, the systematic study of the liturgical traditions of the East will lag.

The origins and the evolution of the liturgical rites are studied by the approach called *comparative liturgiology*, founded by Anton Baumstark and incarnated in the work of Juan Mateos, Robert Taft, Gabriele Winkler, Paul Bradshaw, and their students.[17] Robert Taft points out that comparative liturgy as a method is based on the fact that

> knowledge is not the accumulation of data, not even new data, but the perception of relationships in the data, the creation of hypothetical frameworks to explain new data, or to explain in new ways the old. For the sources alone do not tell us how they got the way they are, nor do later ones tell us why they are not the same as earlier ones. . . . The problems of liturgical history . . . arise from the appearance of changes in the sources themselves, be they additions, omissions, or aberrations, which constitute a departure from previously established patterns. The only way these problems can be solved, if only hypothetically, is by sifting and analyzing, classifying and comparing, liturgical texts and units within and across the traditions. . . . And since the evidence presents similarities and differences, its study is comparative.[18]

In the study of a particular rite of any liturgical tradition it is very important to identify and study the building blocks of that rite, which are called liturgical units.[19] These liturgical units form the founda-

[17] On the method of comparative liturgy, in addition to Bradshaw in note 15 above, see Robert Taft, "Comparative Liturgy Fifty Years after Anton Baumstark (d. 1948): A Reply to Recent Critics," *Worship* 73 (1999): 521–40; Fritz West, *The Comparative Liturgy of Anton Baumstark* (Nottingham: Grove Books, 1995). In 1998 a conference tribute to Baumstark and his methodology took place, where a large number of papers were delivered demonstrating the methodology "in action"; see Robert Taft and Gabriele Winkler, eds., *Comparative Liturgy Fifty Years after Anton Baumstark (1872–1948): Acts of the International Congress, Rome, 25–29 September 1998*, OCA 265 (Rome: Pontificio Istituto Orientale, 2001); and the preface by Robert Taft in Baumstark, *On the Historical Development of the Liturgy*, xv–xxiv.

[18] Taft, "Comparative Liturgy Fifty Years after Anton Baumstark (d. 1948)," 523.

[19] See, for example, Robert Taft, "The Structural Analysis of Liturgical Units: An Essay in Methodology," in BEW, 187–202.

tional structures on which or through which the rites are built. For example, we see in the Armenian liturgical tradition a persistence of a standard structural unit, called *"kanon"* in Armenian. It consists of a (1) psalm (hymn), (2) followed by a diaconal proclamation (invitation to prayer, expanded to a proleptic statement), and (3) concluded by a prayer. Another such liturgical unit with origins in Jerusalem but eventually appearing in almost all traditions (it can clearly be seen in the Byzantine and the Armenian Rites) is the following: (1) diaconal proclamation, (2) first prayer, (3) offering of peace and response, (4) invitation to inclination, and (5) second prayer (inclination prayer). Another important element in the study of liturgy is the identification of the "soft points"[20] in a rite; these are moments where in the original primitive structure one would have actions, usually of a practical nature, without words. These were then covered by chant and concluded by a prayer, thus forming a liturgical unit: action, covered by chant, concluding with prayer. For example, "soft points" can be identified in three places in the celebration of the Divine Liturgy across all traditions: (1) the entrance into the church/the beginning of the service; (2) the kiss of peace and transfer of gifts; and (3) the fraction, Communion, and dismissal rites. It is at these particular "soft points" that we observe the greatest diversity among liturgical rites and the multiplicity of layers of liturgical material deposited there over the centuries. At the same time, the contribution of the social sciences (such as anthropology, sociology) is recognized in the study of liturgy, even giving birth to a separate liturgical discipline called ritual studies. This methodological approach allows for the study of liturgy "from the bottom up"; in other words, it allows us to explore how people in a given time and place lived, experienced, and understood liturgy.

## Phases in the Evolution of Liturgical Rites[21]

Although each liturgical tradition of the East has its own history of evolution, growth, adoption, adaptation, and inculturation, the following phases can be discerned in almost all of the traditions, as

[20] See, for example, Robert Taft, "How Liturgies Grow: The Evolution of the Byzantine Divine Liturgy," in BEW, 203–32.

[21] The identification of the phases is of Robert Taft, as presented in his class lectures on Eastern liturgies.

they share the same broader geographical region and therefore are prone to live together through the watersheds of history. (1) The first phase is that of initial formation, from the very beginnings of Christianity to the time of Constantine the Great. Characteristic of this period is the considerable variety of ritual practice among Christian communities but also a certain synthesis around centers. (2) The second phase, lasting from the fourth to the seventh centuries, is the phase of growth and differentiation; greater unity is observed in particular areas but also differences between larger areas. It is during this phase that we can start to recognize and identify liturgical families. (3) The third phase, from the eighth century on, is characterized by the diffusion of liturgical families, where recognizable formed traditions are transplanted elsewhere. Such an example is the diffusion and expansion of the Byzantine Rite to the Balkans and Kievan Rus'. (4) The beginning of the fourth phase coincides with the invention of the printing press, which in liturgy has a drastic effect; as soon as liturgical books are printed (in the first centuries of printing mainly in Rome and Venice), the printing press in essence dramatically slows down the process of liturgical evolution, as the copy of the same original is diffused to a wide geographical area, thus eliminating local ritual expression and creativity. (5) Finally, the twentieth and twenty-first centuries have forced all the Eastern liturgical traditions, in varying levels and degrees, to face and engage modernity and its challenges.

## Factors and Forces of Influence in the Development of Eastern Liturgies

A variety of factors and forces played a larger or a smaller role in the development and evolution of the Eastern liturgical tradition, and their study provides us with a hermeneutical tool both in our examination of their history and in our understanding of their faith, life, liturgy, and spirituality. (1) Political structures without any doubt played an important role. The emergence, for example, of Constantinople in the fourth century as the new capital of the Roman Empire catapulted this city into the epicenter of events, displacing cities such as Alexandria and Antioch, which, nevertheless, continued to play a very important role as regional centers of finance, education, government, and theology. It is not a coincidence that these important cities were also significant ecclesiastical centers. (2) The dynamics in the relationship between states, such as the Byzantine Empire and the Persian Empire, or the Byzantine Empire, the Latin Crusader Kingdoms, and Armenia, were also an important factor. (3) Geography and geographical proximity certainly played a key role as well; trade routes enhanced liturgical exchange as liturgy and liturgical practices traveled together with people. For example, communication between Alexandria and Rome via the sea trade routes might explain some common elements between the two liturgical traditions. (4) The liturgical influence of Jerusalem after the fourth century as a center for Christian pilgrimage needs to be highlighted. Christians from all around the Christian world, of different languages and liturgical traditions, came to Jerusalem, and pilgrims brought liturgical practices back home from the Holy City. Jerusalem's liturgical stamp can be seen, in a greater or a lesser degree, on almost all liturgical traditions. (5) The Christianization of the Roman Empire changed how the empire viewed itself and influenced the development of liturgical art and practice (such as psalmody, architecture, iconography, public liturgical processions). (6) The christological controversies of the fifth century played an immensely important role in the history of the Eastern liturgical traditions. Combined with political tensions, they led to the first major schism in the Church, leading to the formation of the Church of the East and the non-Chalcedonian Churches (Oriental Orthodox), each developing its own liturgical tradition, colored by these dogmatic tensions and clashes. (7) The end of martyrdom with the Christianization of the Roman Empire gave rise to monasticism in places like Upper and Lower Egypt, Palestine, Caesarea, Antioch, Mount Sinai, and later Bithynia, Mount Athos, and Meteora, and this influenced, in varying degrees, the development and theological approach of liturgy in the various liturgical traditions. (8) One cannot underestimate the significant contributions of particular individuals and the effect they had on their liturgical traditions, such as Ephrem the Syrian, Basil the Great, John Chrysostom, Severus of Antioch, Theodore of Mopsuestia, Nersess the Gracious, and Išoʿyahb III, to name just a few. (9) Finally, the reality of an oppressive rule that almost all Christians of the East have experienced and many are still experiencing has also affected the way liturgy is practiced, its architecture, and its art, leading—and we are generalizing here—to a miniaturization of everything liturgical and related to liturgy in order not to be visible and thus provoke persecution, a reality that also affects spirituality and theology.

## The Characteristics of Eastern Liturgies

"Liturgy is the soul of the Christian East."[22] Liturgy is not just texts, rites, and rituals; it is encountering the mystery of God, the now-and-not-yet of the Christian experience; it is the visible expression of the faith of a community; the incarnation of the Christian message in a particular time, place, culture, and people. The history of liturgy is a story of people at prayer, and the different rites express particular cultural incarnations of a people at prayer. For liturgy is at their center as it expresses their faith, their life, their spirituality, their piety, their heritage, and their experience of God. Central to the identity, conscience, and liturgical practice of the Eastern Christian traditions is the celebration of the eucharistic liturgy. The Divine Liturgy (Byzantine), *Qurbana* (Syriac), *Badarak* (Armenian), *Prosfora* (Coptic), *Qedussah* (East Syrian), or *Keddase* (Ethiopian), and worship as a whole, is seen as the expression and the epitome of the faith of the Church. It is through worship that Scripture is taught, as Scripture permeates every aspect of Eastern worship, and the worship space is filled in many traditions with an iconic representation of the Divine Economy (scenes from the Old and the New Testament) and the life of the Church (martyrs and saints).

Among Eastern Christians there is a sense of ownership of their liturgical tradition that connects them with their historical, cultural, and theological roots as a community. There is also the awareness of the responsibility to hand their tradition down to the coming generations. In these communities clergy have a role of liturgical, spiritual, and communal leadership. Eastern Christians have a very strong sense of community, fostered by the communal liturgical celebrations. Liturgy has a sense of transcendence: "The liturgy is transcendent but not distant, hieratic but not clericalized, communal but not impersonal, traditional but not formalistic."[23] Finally, another characteristic of the Eastern Churches and their liturgical traditions is the fact that most of them have survived in contexts hostile to Christianity, and many still do. Hence, the notion and sense of martyrdom is very real for them. The martyrs of the early Church and the neo-martyrs of the recent centuries are sources of inspiration and courage, giving a strong eschatological flavor to their liturgy and spirituality.

[22] Taft, "Response to the Berakah Award," BEW, 286.

[23] Taft, "Sunday in the Byzantine Tradition," BEW, 67.

It is in this context where the Eastern Christian understanding of sacraments and sacramental theology should be placed. When Eastern Christians talk about sacraments, they usually use the term "mysteries," from the Greek word *mysterion*, and its equivalent in the other Eastern languages. They talk about participating in the sacramental life of the Church, not "receiving" the sacraments.[24] It is through the celebration of and participation in the sacraments that the faithful enter into communion with the triune God, where the community experiences the presence of God. Although most of the Eastern Churches will say that the sacraments are seven, this number has been superimposed on them through direct or indirect scholastic Western influence.[25] If one looks at the lists of sacraments of the Eastern Churches, one finds, other than the standard seven (baptism, chrismation, Eucharist, ordination, penance, marriage, unction), others counted as sacraments such as funerals, tonsure of monks, the blessing of waters on Epiphany, and consecration of a church, while chrismation sometimes is not considered separate from baptism. As a result, the total number of sacraments varies, even among authors within the same tradition.

## The Liturgical Rites of the Christian East

As we noted above, there are seven extant liturgical rites in the Christian East: Armenian, Byzantine, Coptic, Ethiopian, East Syrian, West Syrian, and Maronite. We begin here, however, with Jerusalem and Palestine, since, as we have also noted, Jerusalem's liturgical stamp can be seen, to a greater or lesser degree, on almost all of these

[24] Michael Fahey, "Sacraments in the Eastern Churches," in *The New Dictionary of Sacramental Worship*, ed. Peter Fink (Collegeville, MN: Liturgical Press, Michael Glazier, 1990), 1123–30, here at 1125.

[25] Thomas Hopko, as quoted by D. Smolarski, *Sacred Mysteries: Sacramental Principles and Liturgical Practice* (New York: Paulist Press, 1995), 1; Christiaan Kappes, "A New Narrative for the Reception of Seven Sacraments into Orthodoxy: Peter Lombard's *Sentences* in Nicholas Cabasilas and Symeon of Thessalonica and the Utilization of John Duns Scotus by the Holy *Synaxis*," *Nova et Vetera* 15, English ed. (2017): 383–419; see also Yury Avvakumov, "Sacramental Ritual in Middle and Later Byzantine Theology: Ninth-Fifteenth Centuries," in *The Oxford Handbook of Sacramental Theology*, ed. Hans Boersma and Matthew Levering (Oxford: Oxford University Press, 2015), 249–66, here 253–54; Evangelos Theodorou, «Τὸ ζήτημα τοῦ ἀριθμοῦ τῶν μυστηρίων ἐξ ἐπόψεως ὀρθοδόξου» in *Θεολογία* 57 (1986): 370–77.

liturgical traditions of the Christian East and, for that matter, in the various Western rites as well.

### 1. *The Liturgy of Jerusalem and Palestine*

Although Jerusalem is the birthplace of Christianity, it did not play any influential role in the first three centuries of Christian history. In the second and third centuries it existed as a small Roman garrison town called Aelia Capitolina and had a very small Christian population, ecclesiastically belonging to Caesarea Maritima, under Antioch. This dramatically changed in the fourth century with the discovery of sites associated with the life, death, and resurrection of Christ. With the help of imperial patronage, Jerusalem very quickly became a pilgrimage center, establishing its own liturgical identity by developing rituals for the newly constructed churches, shrines, and sites and attending to the religious and liturgical needs of thousands of Christian pilgrims coming from all over the empire. The liturgical tradition that emerged is called in the documents "Hagiopolite" (Jerusalem was now called *Hagia Polis*—Holy City, hence the term Hagiopolite). The liturgical life in Jerusalem thrived, grew, and developed between the fourth and the sixth centuries but was halted in the seventh century and later by the Persian and then Arab invasions and conquests. The ninth century marks the beginning of the Byzantinization of the Hagiopolite Rite, a process that was completed by the thirteenth century.[26] Although the language of the Hagiopolite Rite was Greek, its most important sources that have survived—beyond, of course, the *Baptismal Catecheses* of Cyril of Jerusalem in Greek (ca. 350), the *Mystagogical Catecheses* ascribed to Cyril and/or his successor John II,[27] also in Greek, and the Latin travel diary of the pilgrim Egeria[28]—are Armenian and Georgian translations of Greek, such as the *Armenian Lectionary*, reflecting Hagiopolite liturgical use

[26] On the Byzantinization of the Hagiopolite Rite, see Daniel Galadza, *Liturgy and Byzantinization in Jerusalem* (Oxford: Oxford University Press, 2018).

[27] See *Lectures on the Christian Sacraments: The Procatechesis and the Five Mystagogical Catecheses Ascribed to St. Cyril of Jerusalem: Text, Translation and Introduction*, trans. Maxwell E. Johnson, Popular Patristic Series 57 (Yonkers: St. Vladimir's Seminary Press, 2017).

[28] See Anne McGowan and Paul F. Bradshaw, *The Pilgrimage of Egeria: A New Translation of the* Itinerarium Egeriae *with Introduction and Commentary*, ACC 93 (Collegeville, MN: Liturgical Press, 2018).

of the fifth century, and the *Georgian Lectionary*, reflecting Hagiopolite liturgical use from the fifth to the eighth century, the homilies of Hesychios, and the Anastasis Typikon.[29] Although extinct today, elements of the Hagiopolite Rite are still present, in varying degrees, in almost all liturgical traditions of East and West, pointing to its significance, influence, and dissemination.

Parallel to the Holy City itself, monasticism thrived in the Judean desert, dotted by monastic communities and ascetics. These monastic communities also developed liturgical rites adapted to the liturgical needs of monks. This liturgical life of Palestinian monasticism, particularly that of the Monastery of St. Sabas,[30] influenced and was influenced by the Byzantine Rite and played a very important role in the evolution of Byzantine liturgy, particularly in the Liturgy of the Hours. In studying the liturgical traditions of the East (and the West) we see, in varying degrees, traces of the Hagiopolite Rite in the Liturgy of the Hours, the liturgical calendar, Holy Week, the lectionary cycle, and hymnody. As for the celebration of the eucharistic liturgy, the Hagiopolite Liturgy of St. James is still in use in the West Syrian liturgical tradition and was introduced in the nineteenth century in the Byzantine liturgical tradition and occasionally used (once or twice a year).[31]

[29] Athanase Renoux, *Le codex arménien Jérusalem 121*, vol. 1: *Introduction*, Patrologia Orientalis 35, no. 1 (Turnhout: Brepols, 1969); vol. 2: *Édition*, Patrologia Orientalis 36, no. 2 (Turnhout: Brepols, 1971); for the *Georgian Lectionary*, see Michel Tarchnischvili, *Le grand lectionnaire de l'Église de Jérusalem, Ve–VIIIe siècle*, Corpus Scriptorum Christianorum Orientalium (Louvain: Secrétariat du CSCO, 1959–1960); on the homilies of Hesychius of Jerusalem, see Michel Aubineau, *Les homélies festales d'Hesychius de Jérusalem*, vol. 1: *Les homélies I–XIV*, Subsidia hagiographica 59 (Brussels: Societé des Bollandistes, 1978); for the Anastasis Typikon, *Hagios Stauros 43*, see Juan Mateos, *Le typicon de la grande Église*, vol. 1: *Le cycle des douze mois*, OCA 165 (Rome: Pontifical Oriental Institute, 1962).

[30] Joseph Patrich, *Sabas, Leader of Palestinian Monasticism* (Washington, DC: Dumbarton Oaks Research Library and Collection, 1995).

[31] Heinzgerd Brakmann, "Divi Jacobi testimonium. Die Editio princeps der Jerusalemer Liturgie durch Jean de Saint-André und der Beitrag der Konstantinos Palaiokappa," in *Sion, mère des Églises: Mélanges liturgiques offerts au Père Charles Athanase Renoux*, ed. Michael Daniel Findikyan, Daniel Galadza, and André Lossky (Münster: Aschendorff Verlag, 2016), 49–77; idem, "'Retour sur une tradition inventée. Le développement de la Liturgie grecque moderne de Saint Jacques," in *60 Semaines liturgiques à Saint-Serge : bilans et perspectives nouvelles*, ed. André Lossky and Goran Sekulovski (Münster: Aschendorff Verlag, 2016), 73–91.

## 2. *The Armenian Rite*

Armenia is at a key geopolitical location, and this fact alone is enough to interpret the history and evolution of the Armenian liturgical rite. Evangelized, according to tradition, by the apostles Bartholomew and Thaddeus, the roots of Armenian liturgical history revolve around two different poles: that of Syria (Edessa) in the south and that of Cappadocia (Caesarea) in the west. Armenia became the first nation in history to become Christian, when, in 301, King Tiridates III was baptized by Gregory the Illuminator and made Christianity the official religion of his state, and Gregory the Illuminator, having been ordained a bishop in Caesarea, became the first head of the Armenian Church. The invention of the Armenian alphabet in the early fifth century and the subsequent translation of the Bible and Christian literature open the next phase of Armenian liturgical history.

The Armenian Rite itself, celebrated by both the Armenian Apostolic Orthodox Church and the Armenian Catholic Church, was long thought to be but a modified or even simplified version of the Byzantine Rite. Recent scholarship, however, especially on the *Badarak* (Divine Liturgy), has shown that Byzantine influence dates only from the turn of the first millennium.[32] More fundamental is an earlier Cappadocian-Caesarean stratum,[33] as well as, thanks to the work of Gabriele Winkler, a decidedly Syrian core.[34] Although later influences are certainly present in the current shape of the Armenian Rite, including both Byzantine and Latin (due to Dominican missionaries in the twelfth century), it is also becoming increasingly clear that the Armenians developed their earlier rites in close connection with Jerusalem, expressed, for example, in the fifth-century *Armenian Lectionary*,[35] widely viewed as related to late fourth-century Jerusalem practice. Byzantine liturgical influence can be seen in the structure and contents of the Liturgy of the Word, the Church Dedication Rite,

[32] See Charles Renoux, "Un bilan provisoire sur l'héritage grec du rite arménien," *Le Muséon* 116 (2003): 53–69.

[33] See M. Daniel Findikyan, *The Commentary on the Armenian Daily Office by Bishop Step'anos Siwnets'i (†735): Critical Edition and Translation with Textual and Liturgical Analysis*, OCA 270 (Rome: Pontificio Istituto Orientale, 2004), 511–15.

[34] See Winkler, *Das armenische Initiationsrituale.*

[35] See Charles Renoux, *Le lectionnaire de Jérusalem en Arménie: le Čašoc*, Patrologia Orientalis 44.4 (Turnhout: Brepols, 1989).

and the presence of numerous prayers of Byzantine provenance, preserved today in an earlier form than in the current Byzantine Rite. Finally, the presence of the Crusaders between the twelfth and the fifteenth centuries resulted in a very intriguing cultural exchange, especially in the Armenian Kingdom of Cilicia. The Latin influence can be seen, for example, in the very beginning (a Latin-type *Confiteor*) and end (the "Last Gospel") of the *Badarak* (stemming from the Dominican Missal), vestments, the ordination rites, and the penitential practice. By the fourteenth century the Armenian Rite had reached its final form.

This openness to outside influence is characterized by its eclectic nature, its creative spirit, and its ability to bridge traditions. It is within the Armenian Rite that we find East Syrian, Cappadocian, Hagiopolite, Byzantine, and Latin elements organically and creatively incorporated within the same liturgical tradition. At the same time, however, the Armenian Rite manages to preserve ancient liturgical uses and material now lost, such as elements of the now extinct Jerusalem Rite. Another characteristic of the Armenian liturgical tradition is that it is characterized by a strong incarnational theology with an emphasis on the divinity of Christ, bearing the stamp of the christological controversies of the fifth century and the Christology of Cyril of Alexandria.[36] An additional characteristic of the Armenian liturgical practice is that it uses prayers that ask only for the privilege to glorify and worship God; they ask for nothing else. This genre of prayer, also present in the East Syrian liturgical tradition, is of considerable antiquity and striking beauty. For example, upon the entrance of the clergy in the church for the celebration of the Eucharist, the priest prays: "In the midst of this temple and in the presence of these divine and bright holy signs and holy place, bowing down in fear we worship, we glorify thine holy marvelous and triumphant Resurrection and unto thee with the Father and the Holy Ghost we offer blessing and glory now and ever and world without end. Amen."[37] Finally, the Armenian liturgical literature boasts a very rich exegetical and

[36] Robert Taft, "The Armenian Liturgy: Its Origins and Characteristics," in *Treasures in Heaven: Armenian Art, Religion, and Society*, Papers Delivered at the Pierpont Morgan Library at a symposium organized by Thomas F. Mathews and Roger S. Wieck, May 21–22, 1994 (New York: Pierpont Morgan Library, 1998), 22–23.

[37] F. E. Brightman, *Liturgies Eastern and Western*, vol. 1: *Eastern* (London: Oxford University Press, 1965), 416.

mystagogical tradition, with a number of commentaries on the Divine Liturgy, with a number of commentaries on the Liturgy of the Hours, a commentary on the Lectionary, and three commentaries on the rite of the dedication of a church; it corresponds to a very rich biblical exegetical tradition that has not been studied.

Some mention here must also be made of the Orthodox Church of Georgia in the Caucasus Mountains on the east of the Black Sea. While the Orthodox Church of Georgia has followed the Byzantine Rite since the eleventh century, its earlier liturgical tradition, somewhat like that of Armenia, with whom it also shares an early relationship with Jerusalem, is more akin to East rather than West Syria.[38]

### *3. The Byzantine Rite*

"We knew not whether we were in heaven or on earth. For on earth there is no such splendor or such beauty, and we are at a loss how to describe it. We know only that God dwells there among men, and their service is fairer than the ceremonies of other nations. For we cannot forget that beauty."[39] This often-quoted excerpt from the report of the emissaries of Vladimir, the prince of Kiev, describing their experience of the celebration of the Divine Liturgy at the end of the tenth century in the Great Church of Hagia Sophia, the cathedral of Constantinople, reflects to a large measure the sumptuousness, the ceremonial, and the beauty of the Byzantine liturgical tradition. It also connects the experience of liturgy with a particular space, that of Hagia Sophia, and this is important for two reasons: first, it highlights the importance of this church edifice to the development of Byzantine liturgy; second, it points to the intimate connection between ritual action (liturgy), sacred space (architecture), sacred art (iconography), and its theological interpretation (liturgical commentaries-mystagogies) in the Byzantine liturgical tradition. The Byzantine Rite as it survives and is celebrated today is a hybrid rite, the result of the

[38] See Gabriele Winkler, "Baptism 2. Eastern Churches," in *The New Westminster Dictionary of Liturgy and Worship*, ed. Paul F. Bradshaw (Louisville: Westminster John Knox, 2002), 38.

[39] Samuel Cross and Olgerd Sherbowitz-Wetzor, eds. and trans., *The Russian Primary Chronicle: Laurentian Text* (Cambridge, MA: Medieval Academy of America, 1953), 110–11.

synthesis and fusion of the liturgy that was celebrated in the Great Church of Hagia Sophia with the liturgical tradition of Palestinian monasteries, in particular that of Hagios Sabas in the Judean desert and the liturgical tradition of the Anastasis Cathedral. The Byzantine Rite, in other words, the liturgy of the Orthodox Patriarchate of Constantinople, gradually came to be identified with the liturgy of the Eastern Chalcedonian Christianity, and thus during the Middle Ages the Chalcedonian Patriarchates of Alexandria, Antioch, and Jerusalem were "byzantinized" by adopting the Byzantine Rite.[40] As a result, the Byzantine Rite is the common liturgical expression of the Orthodox Churches, the largest communion among Eastern Churches, and their Eastern Catholic counterparts.

Five phases can be identified, sometimes overlapping, in the evolution of the Byzantine Rite.[41] These are as follows: (1) The paleo-Byzantine or pre-Constantinian era, about which we know very little; the city on the shores of Bosphorus, called Byzantium (hence the name Byzantine), was small in size and of negligible importance. Its bishop was dependent on the episcopal see of Herakleia. (2) The imperial phase, which dates from the fourth century up to the Latin conquest of Constantinople (1204–1261). Constantine the Great's selection of Byzantium as the place for the erection of the new Roman capital, Constantinople, drastically changed the destiny, the life, and the liturgical rites of the city. During the first decades of this phase the liturgy of Constantinople did not have any particular distinguishing characteristics, liturgically being under the influence of Antioch. But the end of the fourth century marks the beginning of what we may call the "Byzantine Rite," particularly with the emergence of liturgical processions taking place in the city,[42] a development that was an integral part of the liturgical life of Constantinople with its numerous liturgical processions throughout the city and was destined to leave its mark on the Byzantine Rite (for example, the Office of the Three Antiphons, the *Trisagion*, the *Ektenēs* Litany). A major turning point for the history of the Byzantine Rite was, however, the erection and

[40] See Galadza, *Liturgy and Byzantinization in Jerusalem*.

[41] Taft, *The Byzantine Rite: A Short History*, 18–20.

[42] John Baldovin, *The Urban Character of Christian Worship: The Origins, Development, and Meaning of Stational Liturgy*, OCA 228 (Rome: Pontificium Institutum Studiorum Orientalium, 1987), 167–226.

inauguration on December 27, 537, of the Cathedral of Hagia Sophia by Emperor Justinian I (527–565) on the ruins of the old Hagia Sophia (the second church on the site) destroyed during the "Nika" revolt in 532. The liturgy celebrated within the walls of the Great Church of Constantinople and the imperial ritual of Constantinople immensely influenced the Byzantine Rite. No other building has exerted so much influence in the development of liturgy as Hagia Sophia has on Byzantine liturgy. One could even dare the generalizing comment that the celebration of the Divine Liturgy in the Byzantine Rite today is a "miniaturization" of the Divine Liturgy as it was celebrated in the Great Church of Hagia Sophia, bearing, of course, the marks of a long evolution and history. Another important factor was that by the fifth century the Church of Constantinople, as the church of the capital of the Roman Empire, was elevated to the second place of honor, after only Rome, among the patriarchates of the Pentarchy (Rome, Constantinople, Alexandria, Antioch, and Jerusalem), destined to a role of leadership among the Orthodox in the centuries to come. (3) The third phase is called the "Dark Ages" and lasts from the seventh to the ninth centuries. It is from this period that the earliest euchology manuscript of the Byzantine Rite survives, dating from the middle to the end of the eighth century; the famous Barberini Codex gr. 336;[43] as well as the Byzantine Commentary on the Divine Liturgy authored by Patriarch Germanus of Constantinople (patriarch from 715–730, died in 733).[44] But more important, this period is marked by Iconoclasm (726–843) and the debate over the use of icons in worship as its major turning point. As far as history of liturgy is concerned, Iconoclasm led to the so-called Studite reform in which monks coming from Palestine inhabited the Studios Monastery in Constantinople under the leadership of Theodore the Studite and synthesized their monastic liturgy with the cathedral liturgy of Hagia Sophia. This leads us to (4) the Studite era from the beginning of the 800s to the sack of Constantinople by the Fourth Crusade in 1204, a period of synthesis of the two traditions, the Palestinian monastic

[43] Stefano Parenti and Elena Velkovska, *L'Eucologio Barberini gr. 336*, 2nd ed., Bibliotheca Ephemerides Liturgicae, Subsidia 80 (Rome: C.L.V.-Edizioni Liturgiche, 2000).

[44] Paul Meyendorff, *St. Germanus of Constantinople on the Divine Liturgy* (Crestwood, NY: St. Vladimir's Seminary Press, 1984).

tradition and the Constantinopolitan cathedral tradition, finding its ultimate codification in the Studite Typika.[45] In this process the local Constantinopolitan monastic practice of the *Akoimētoi* (sleepless ones) was supplanted by that of the Studite monks; in the liturgical synthesis of this period the Divine Liturgies and the sacraments remained Constantinopolitan (albeit with monastic influence) whereas the Liturgy of the Hours through the Palestinian monastic book *Horologion* became monastic. During this period the cathedral rite of Hagia Sophia lost ground but was still celebrated in Hagia Sophia until 1204, when the Latin rite was imposed in Hagia Sophia. It is also during this period that the Schism took place, traditionally given the date of 1054 when Cardinal Humbert and Patriarch Michael Cerularius excommunicated one another. The Schism, however, was more than just a moment; it was a four-centuries-long process of estrangement between East and West, sealed by the fall of Constantinople to the Crusaders of the Fourth Crusade in 1204. The restoration of Byzantine rule in Constantinople in 1261 did not lead to the restoration of the cathedral rite in Hagia Sophia; the Studite rite was now celebrated, even in Hagia Sophia of Constantinople, thus leading us to (5) the fifth phase in the history of Byzantine liturgy, that of the neo-Sabaitic synthesis. During this period the liturgy became even more monastic, through the synthesis of the Studite tradition with further monastic influence from the liturgical tradition of the Sabas monastery, hence the term "neo-Sabaitic," with its ultimate expression gaining dominance during the Hesychast period and the ascendancy of Athonite monasticism.[46] This neo-Sabaitic synthesis was codified in the liturgical Diataxis of Patriarch Philotheos Kokkinos,[47] the liturgical

[45] Miguel Arranz, *Le typicon du monastère du Saint-Sauveur à Messine. Codex Messinensis GR 115 A.D. 1131*, OCA 185 (Rome: Pontificium Institutum Orientalium Studiorum, 1969). Other such examples are David Petras, *The Typicon of the Patriarch Alexis the Studite: Novgorod—St. Sophia 1136*, Excerpta ex dissertatione ad Doctoratum, Pontificium Institutum Orientalium Studiorum (Cleveland, 1991); Robert Jordan, *The Synaxarion of the Monastery of the Theotokos Evergetis*, vol. 1: *September to February*; vol. 2 *March to August: The Moveable Cycle*, Belfast Byzantine Texts and Translations 6.5/6.6 (Belfast: Institute of Byzantine Studies the Queen's University of Belfast, 2000–2005).

[46] Robert Taft, "Mount Athos: A Late Chapter in the History of the Byzantine Rite," *Dumbarton Oaks Papers* 42 (1988): 179–94.

[47] Panayiotis Trempelas, *Αἱ τρεῖς λειτουργίαι κατὰ τοὺς ἐν Ἀθήναις κώδικας*, 2nd ed. (Athens: Soter, 1982).

commentary of Nicholas Cabasilas,[48] and the Typikon of Hagios Sabas.[49] It is this liturgical tradition that is now normative in the Orthodox Church, although various adjustments are made by each local Orthodox Church. In the Greek-speaking Orthodox world, for example, the Typikon of Hagios Sabas has been amended for parish use in the effort to adjust the monastic liturgy reflected in this Typikon in the context of urban parishes.[50]

### *4. The Coptic Rite*

Christianity in Egypt traces itself back to the New Testament times, claiming that it was the evangelist St. Mark who brought the good news of Christ to Egypt. Initially, Christianity grew among the Hellenistic Jewish communities and the Greek-speaking coastal area of Egypt, but it quickly spread in the south among the Coptic-speaking indigenous population. Already by the third century, Scripture and liturgical books were translated from Greek into Coptic, and by the fourth century original compositions were made in Coptic. During the christological controversies of the fifth century the Greek-speaking coastline, centered around Alexandria, accepted Chalcedon while the Coptic-speaking hinterlands, the narrow slip of land on both sides of the Nile, refused Chalcedon and were persecuted, and the Coptic patriarch took refuge at the monastery of St. Macarius while the Greek-speaking Chalcedonians gradually became Byzantinized. With the Arab conquest in 640 and the Arabization of the population the

[48] Nicholas Cabasilas, *A Commentary on the Divine Liturgy*, trans. J. M. Hussey and P. A. McNulty (London: SPCK, 1983).

[49] Editio princeps: *Τυπικὸν τῆς ἐκκλησιαστικῆς ἀκολουθίας τῆς ἐν Ἱεροσολύμοις Ἁγίας Λαύρας τοῦ Ὁσίου καὶ Θεοφόρου πατρὸς ἡμῶν Σάββα* (Venice, 1545). Later editions were printed in 1577, 1643, 1685, 1738, all in Venice. See Stefanos Alexopoulos and Dionysios Bilalis Anatolikiotes, "Towards a History of Printed Liturgical Books in the Modern Greek State: An Initial Survey," *Ecclesia Orans* 34 (2017): 421–60, here 429–33.

[50] Constantinos Byzantios, *Τυπικὸν Ἐκκλησιαστικὸν κατὰ τὸ ὕφος τῆς τοῦ Χριστοῦ Μεγάλης Ἐκκλησίας* (Constantinople, 1838), reprinted with corrections and additions in Constantinople in 1868, and finally in Venice in 1881, superseded by George Violakis, *Τυπικὸν τῆς τοῦ Χριστοῦ Μεγάλης Ἐκκλησίας* (Constantinople, 1888), and since then with numerous reprints in Athens from the Saliveros publishing house. The adoption of the Gregorian calendar in 1923 in Greece and its effects on the liturgical year led to the annual publication of the liturgical ordo by the Church of Greece: *Ἐκκλησιαστικὸν Ἡμερολόγιον* 1924–1951, *Ἡμερολόγιον τῆς Ἐκκλησίας τῆς Ἑλλάδος* 1952–1988, and *Δίπτυχα τῆς Ἐκκλησίας τῆς Ἑλλάδος* 1989–today.

Coptic language has remained in liturgical use but has ceased to be a spoken language. Naturally, then, as the Coptic patriarchate was located at the monastery of St. Macarius and the monks were the only educated ones among the peasants of the Egyptian hinterlands, the Coptic Rite is marked by a strong monastic influence.

> This monastic culture—concrete, popular, ascetic—created the liturgy and offices of the Coptic Church. It is a highly penitential, contemplative rite, long, solemn, even monotonous, with much less speculative poetry, symbolic splendor and sumptuous ceremonial than, for example, the Byzantine tradition.[51]

The Coptic Rite today is built on this monastic foundation, modified by two liturgical reforms, that of Patriarch Gabriel II Ibn Turayk (1131–1145), who reduced the numbers of anaphoras used to the ones used today (see our chapter below on the Eucharist), and that of Patriarch Gabriel V (1409–1427), who unified the various liturgical practices in Egypt into one.

*Nubian Liturgy*. The now-extinct Christianity in Nubia flourished for almost a millennium in the Nile Valley between Egypt and Ethiopia, from roughly the sixth to the fifteenth centuries. From the little we know, we can assume that Nubian Christians had their own particular liturgical rite, the Nubian Rite, which was a synthesis of Coptic, Byzantine, and local elements. Our major sources for the Nubian liturgical traditions are inscriptions and fragments of manuscripts in the remains of churches (such as Faras[52] and Q'asr Ibrim[53]) and monasteries (such as Old Dongola). There is evidence that the Nubian liturgical tradition employed Greek, Nubian, and Coptic in its worship.[54]

[51] Robert Taft, *The Liturgy of the Hours in East and West: The Origins of the Divine Office and Its Meaning for Today*, 2nd rev. ed. (Collegeville, MN: Liturgical Press, 1993), 250–51.

[52] See J. Kubínska, "Prothesis de la Cathédrale de Faras. Documents et recherches," *Revue des Archéologues et Historiens d'Art de Louvain* 9 (1976): 7–37.

[53] William Frend, "A Eucharistic Sequence from Qasr Ibrim," *Jahrbuch für Antike und Christentum* 30 (1987): 90–98.

[54] Heinzgerd Brakmann, "Defunctus adhuc loquitur. Gottesdienst und Gebetsliteratur der untergegangenen Kirche in Nubien," *Archiv für Liturgiewissenschaft* 48 (2006): 283–333; Gawdat Gabra and Hany Takla, *Christianity and Monasticism in Aswan and Nubia* (Cairo: The American University of Cairo Press, 2013).

## *5. The Ethiopian Rite*

Although closely related to the Coptic Rite, the Ethiopian Rite is not a variant of the Coptic Rite, as it was considered until recently; it is a distinct rite with a distinct history and development.[55] In spite of the close connection of the Ethiopian Church with the Coptic Church, as the former was dependent on the latter for its patriarch from the fourth century up to the twentieth century, research has shown that the roots of the Ethiopian liturgical tradition should be sought not only with the Coptic heritage but also with the Syriac tradition, as there is more and more evidence of a strong Syriac influence, especially in the formative years of the Ethiopian Rite.

According to tradition, Christianity reached Ethiopia through the Ethiopian eunuch mentioned in Acts (8:27-39), and it is possible that by the fourth century Christian communities were already present in Ethiopia. Frumentius and Edesius are, however, considered the apostles to Ethiopia who in the fourth century, being in the servitude of the emperor, converted the emperor's son, and by 330 Christianity was declared the imperial religion. Frumentius was ordained a bishop by Athanasius of Alexandria, thus establishing a centuries-long tradition and link with Alexandria according to which the head of the Ethiopian Church was ordained and appointed by the Coptic patriarch of Alexandria, to be broken only in the twentieth century. Certain aspects of the Ethiopian Rite bear the marks of the Coptic influence, such as the structure of the anaphoral prayers, the baptismal rites (and for this reason are not examined below in our chapter on Christian initiation), the ordination rites, and the vestments. On the other hand, the link with Syria can be seen in the tradition of the nine Syrian monks who arrived in Ethiopia from Syria toward the end of the fifth century as a result of the christological controversies and the ensuing upheaval. According to this tradition, these monks spread the non-Chalcedonian Christology, translated sacred literature into Geʿez and instituted monasticism. Contacts, however, with Syriac Christianity

[55] On Ethiopian Christianity, see Habtemichael Kidane, "Ethiopian (Geʿez) Worship," in *The New Westminster Dictionary of Liturgy and Worship*, ed. Bradshaw, 169–72; Aziz S. Atiya, *History of Eastern Christianity* (Notre Dame, IN: University of Notre Dame Press, 1968), 146–66; Adrian Hastings, *The Church in Africa: 1450–1950* (Oxford: Clarendon Press, 1994), chaps. 1, 4, and 6; Elizabeth Isichei, *A History of Christianity in Africa from Antiquity to the Present* (London: SPCK, 1995).

are highly probable also through trading routes that spanned the Arabic peninsula and the Horn of Africa.

Another strain of influence and a unique characteristic of the Ethiopian Rite is the strong presence of Old Testament practices in the Ethiopian liturgical traditions, such as circumcision, observance of the Sabbath, and a ritual dance around the ark of the covenant. We do not know where this Jewish influence comes from, although we know there was a significant Jewish community in Ethiopia in the first century. At the same time, the Ethiopian Rite is marked by a number of interesting native features, such as instrumental music, liturgical umbrellas and liturgical dance; it has a highly refined system of hymnography and hymnology, comprised of twelve hymnographic forms, including one called *Qene*, where the *däbtära*, the trained professional musicians of the Ethiopian liturgical tradition, spontaneously compose and sing hymns. The city of Axum is considered to be the cradle of Christianity in Ethiopia. The Eritrean Church also follows the Ethiopian Rite. Originally part of the Ethiopian Church, it received autocephaly after Eritrea received independence from Ethiopia in 1993.

## 6. *The East Syrian Rite*

The East Syrian Rite, centered originally in the region of Nisibis (Nusyabin, Syria) and in Edessa (Urfa, Turkey), beyond the borders and influence of the dominant Roman Empire, is also sometimes referred to as "The Assyro-Chaldean Rite," the "Assyrian" or "Chaldean Rite," or part of the "Persian Family" of rites. More properly, it is the rite celebrated by the Ancient (Assyrian) Church of the East, the Chaldean Catholic Church, and the Syro-Malabar Catholic Church in India. The East Syrian Rite is the ritual expression of Mesopotamian Christianity. Its theological and intellectual center since the second century was the city of Edessa (Urfa), the location of a Syrian-speaking school that, after the Council of Ephesus, was forced to flee to Nisibis within the Persian Empire.

Because the Ancient Assyrian Church of the East at the Synod of Seleucia-Ctesiphon (c. 410) was believed to have adopted the Christology of Nestorius, a split between this Church and the rest of both Eastern and Western Christianity resulted after the Council of Ephesus (431) and has remained for centuries, with members of this ancient tradition often called in the past by the pejorative term "Nestorian." Isolated from Byzantium, it developed its unique liturgy with ancient features. It is a liturgical tradition that does not have a Greek foundation; rather, it is clearly Semitic, and this displays several ancient Syrian features in broad continuity with the witness of early Syrian documents like the mid-third-century *Didascalia Apostolorum* and the Syrian *Acts*, both of which are essential for the rites of Christian initiation in this tradition, and with the great East Syrian fathers, Aphrahat, Ephrem, and Narsai. Further, the ancient Eucharistic Prayer of Addai and Mari, dated by most scholars to the third century, remains in contemporary use without the narrative of institution within the eucharistic liturgy of the Church of the East. It is this anaphora, with some medieval additions, that was codified in the mid-seventh-century liturgical reforms of Patriarch Išoʿyahb III (ca. 650–660).

Important figures for this tradition are Theodore of Mopsuestia (d. 428), Mar Aba (d. 552), a hymnographer, and Patriarch Išoʿyahb III (d. 657), who is credited with a vast liturgical reform that standardized, united, and enriched the East Syrian Rite, which, with some medieval additions, defines its use today.

One of the characteristics of the East Syrian Rite is its emphasis on the glory and praise of God with an eschatological outlook. An expression of this is found in a number of East Syrian prayers that their main objective is solely praising and worshiping God; nothing is asked for, as this prayer from the Liturgy of the Word demonstrates: "Thou, O my Lord, art in truth the quickener of our bodies and thou art the good savior of our souls and the constant preserver of our lives: thee, O Lord, we are bound to confess and adore and glorify at all times, Lord of all, Father and Son and Holy Ghost, for ever."[56]

### 7. *The West Syrian Rite*

The West Syrian Rite, sometimes also called "Antiochene" or "Syro-Antiochene," is celebrated by the Syrian Orthodox Church and its Catholic counterpart, the Syrian Catholic Church, and in India by the

[56] F. E. Brightman, *Liturgies Eastern and Western*, vol. 1: *Eastern* (London: Oxford University Press, 1965), 255.

Malankara Orthodox Church and its Catholic counterpart, the Syro-Malankara Church. The West Syrian Rite is the liturgical expression of the Christians of the geographical region of Syria who rejected the Council of Chalcedon. Ephrem Carr summarizes West Syrian Christianity as follows:

> Syrian Christians became divided by reason of the council of Chalcedon [451] into Melkites, who were loyal to the council and the emperor (*malko* = "ruler" or "king"), and the anti-chalcedonians. The Melkites gradually accepted also the liturgy of the imperial capital and became by the twelfth century part of the Byzantine rite. The Syrian faithful who rejected the council slowly formed their own church, a move fostered by Jacob Baradai (†578) and his establishment of an independent hierarchy from 543 onward. Thus the Syrian church came to be called Jacobite. During the upheavals over Christology in the fifth and sixth centuries the Antiochene liturgy was revised and augmented. An important role was played by Patriarch Severus (512–518, †538), who reformed the ritual of baptism and composed a Hymn Book (ὀκτώηχος) with some of his own liturgical poetry.[57]

In its earlier stages, the West Syrian Rite is reflected in documents such as the *Apostolic Constitutions*, the homilies of John Chrysostom during his tenure as presbyter in Antioch, and the catechesis of Theodore of Mopsuestia. Although West Syrian Christians' theological center was Greek-speaking Antioch, their strength lay in the Syriac-speaking hinterlands and were massively influenced by the liturgical tradition of Jerusalem; in other words, they may claim Antioch and Jerusalem as the parent cities of the rite. As a result, the West Syrian Rite was initially a bilingual tradition, but very quickly Syriac dominated and liturgical texts were translated from Greek into Syriac, while others were composed in Syriac. It was during the sixth century under the leadership of Jacob Baradeus (d. 578) that a separate hierarchy was established and therefore the non-Chalcedonians of Syria gradually formed their own church (thus also called Jacobites). Significant personalities that influenced the West Syrian Rite in a variety of ways are Severus of Antioch, Jacob Baradeus, Jacob of Serug, and Philoxenus of Mabbug.

[57] Ephrem Carr, "Liturgical Families in the East," in *Handbook for Liturgical Studies*, ed. Chupungco, 1: 15.

## *8. The Maronite Rite*

Within the overall West Syrian family of rites the Maronite Rite might also be placed, though today it is usually recognized as a rite in itself.[58] It reflects not only West Syrian but East Syrian and Jerusalem influence as well. It is named after St. Maron, an ascetic who lived in the fourth and early fifth centuries. Its roots are associated with the Monastery of St. Maron, which became a center for the defense of Chalcedonian Christianity. The Monothelite controversy, however, in the seventh century led to their becoming an independent church by the eighth century. After the destruction of the Monastery of St. Maron in the tenth century their ecclesiastical center was moved to Mount Lebanon. Their contact with the Crusades and the ensuing relationship with the Roman Catholic Church resulted in massive Latin influence, especially during the sixteenth century, to the point that one can speak of a Latinization of the liturgy. An important person in Maronite history is Patriarch Stephan Douaihy (1670–1704),[59] who revitalized and consolidated the Maronite liturgical tradition, managing to keep a balance between Latinization and maintenance of the Syriac character of the Maronite Rite. It is only recently, after Vatican II, that there is a move to discover the Syrian origins of this rite, thus moving toward a restoration of Maronite liturgy, architecture, and iconography.[60]

Each of these rites will be presented in the following chapters within our discussion of the various liturgical-sacramental rites themselves. That is, using Irénée-Henri Dalmais's structure as an overall guide, chapter 1 will focus on Christian initiation and reconciliation; chapter 2, on the eucharistic liturgies; chapter 3, on the liturgical year and Liturgy of the Hours; chapter 4, on marriage and holy orders; chapter 5, on the rites of anointing of the sick and burial; and chapter 6,

[58] It was William Macomber who first made the strong case that the Maronite Rite is a distinct rite. See William Macomber, "A Theory on the Origins of the Syrian, Maronite, and Chaldean Rites," OCP 39 (1973): 235–42. See also Naaman, *The Maronites*.

[59] Lucas Van Rompay, "Excursus: The Maronites," in *The Oxford History of Christian Worship*, ed. Wainwright and Westerfield Tucker, 170–74, here 171; Georg Graf, *Geschichte der christlichen arabischen Literatur*, vol. 3, Studi e Testi 118 (Vatican: Biblioteca apostolica vaticana, 1944–1954), 361–62.

[60] Abdo Badwi, *The Liturgical Year Iconography of the Syro-Maronite Church* (Kaslik: Publications de l'Université Saint-Esprit de Kaslik, 2006).

a conclusion centering on the Eastern ethos of Christian liturgy and liturgical spirituality. In addition, a preliminary bibliography is included, providing pointers for further research and organized according to the seven distinct Eastern liturgical traditions so that one may read further in a tradition of particular interest without trying to sort through materials for all seven each time. It is hoped that this study will be of interest to an educated general audience as well as for the university and seminary context where it will serve as a general introduction for courses in Eastern Christianity in general and Eastern liturgies in particular, from the undergraduate to the graduate level.

Thanks are due to several people who have supported and assisted us during this process: colleagues at both the University of Notre Dame (especially Professors Gabriel Radle, Nina Glibetić, and Paul Bradshaw, who gave us his kind permission to use his chapter on Eastern ordination rites from his recent study[61]) and at The Catholic University of America (especially Fr. Mark Morozowich, dean of the School of Theology and Religious Studies, and Professors Robin Darling Young, Aaron Butts, and Monica Blanchard). We are also grateful to our colleagues, scholars, and professors for their assistance at various stages of writing this book (mentioned alphabetically): Tinatin Chronz, Fr. Armando Elkoury, Fr. Aphram Faham, Fr. Claude Franklin, Fr. Emmanuel Fritsch, Stig Simeon Frøyshov, Deacon Daniel Galadza, Fr. Hovsep Karapetian, Deacon Arsenius (Ramez) Mikhail, Alex Neroth van Vogelpoel, Fr. Damaskinos Olkinuora, and Vitaly Permiakov. Thanks go also to our graduate assistant, Fr. Lucas Christensen, for his help with proofreading and indexing. And, finally, we wish to express our profound thanks to Hans Christoffersen of Liturgical Press for undertaking this project with us and for his great patience in working with us toward its completion and publication.

Stefanos Alexopoulos<br>
Maxwell E. Johnson<br>
December 13, 2020<br>
Saint Lucy of Syracuse, Martyr

[61] Paul F. Bradshaw, *Rites of Ordination: Their History and Theology* (Collegeville, MN: Liturgical Press, Pueblo, 2013), 82–105.

# *Chapter 1*

# Christian Initiation and Reconciliation

The Rites of Initiation in the Christian East, generally speaking, have kept their original unity as one integral rite with three key sacramental moments. Postbaptismal chrismation has remained an inseparable part of the baptismal rites. The baptized, no matter their age, are chrismated and immediately communed either from the reserved Eucharist or at the subsequent eucharistic liturgy, although, as we shall see below, this is not always the case in practice everywhere today, especially among Eastern Catholics. Chrismation is administered by a priest with the chrism itself consecrated by a bishop, or even by the patriarch or catholicos. Historically, especially in Syrian and Armenian baptismal practices, there was originally only one anointing, namely, a *pre*baptismal anointing, representing a theology of baptism of birth, imitation, and adoption closer to John 3 and Jesus's own baptism in the Jordan by John, rather than a Romans 6 theology of dying and rising with Christ. Baptism is seen more as the incorporation of a new member into the Church, the Body of Christ, rather than a cleansing from original sin, an Augustinian-Latin concept actually rather foreign to the Christian East in general. The ritual process of initiation remains, by and large, faithful to the shape of the ritual process of Christian initiation of the fourth and fifth centuries, known to us from the homilies and writings of the great mystagogues, Cyril (or John) of Jerusalem, John Chrysostom, and Theodore of Mopsuestia.[1]

[1] For patristic antecedents, see Maxwell E. Johnson, *The Rites of Christian Initiation: Their Evolution and Interpretation*, rev. and exp. ed. (Collegeville, MN: Liturgical Press, Pueblo, 2007), 41–82, and 115–57; Bryan Spinks, *Early and Medieval Rituals and Theologies of Baptism: From the New Testament to the Council of Trent* (Aldershot, England:

In this chapter we present, not a detailed study of the initiation rites in each of the seven Eastern liturgical traditions,[2] but a study of those

Ashgate, 2006), 3–70; and Edward Yarnold, *The Awe-Inspiring Rites of Initiation: The Origins of the R.C.I.A.*, 2nd ed. (Collegeville, MN: Liturgical Press, 2001).

[2] In addition to Spinks, *Early and Medieval Rituals*, 71–108, for the Byzantine Rite, see Alexander Schmemann, *Of Water and the Spirit: A Liturgical Study of Baptism* (Crestwood, NY: St. Vladimir's Seminary Press, 1974); Miguel Arranz, "Les Sacrements de l'ancien Euchologe constantinopolitain" (9 articles): 1, OCP 48 (1982): 284–335; 2, OCP 49 (1983): 42–90; 3, OCP 49 (1983): 284–302; 4, OCP 50 (1984): 43–64; 5, OCP 50 (1984): 372–97; 6, OCP 51 (1985): 60–86; 7, OCP 52 (1986): 145–78; 8, OCP 53 (1987): 59–106; and 9, OCP 55 (1989): 33–62; idem, "Evolution des rites d'incorporation et de réadmission dans l'église selon l' Euchologe byzantin," in *Gestes et paroles dans les diverses familles liturgiques : Conférences Saint-Serge, XXIVe Semaine d'études liturgiques, Paris, 28 juin-1er juillet 1977*, ed. A. Pistoia and A. Triacca (Rome: Centro liturgico vincenciano, 1978), 31–75; and Stefano Parenti, "Christian Initiation in the East," in *Handbook for Liturgical Studies*, vol. 4: *Sacraments and Sacramentals*, ed. Anscar Chupungco (Collegeville, MN: Liturgical Press, Pueblo, 2000), 29–48. For other initiation rites, see as follows. *Armenian, Syrian, Maronite:* Sebastian Brock, "The Consecration of the Water in the Oldest Manuscripts of the Syrian Orthodox Baptismal Liturgy," OCP 37 (1971): 317–32; idem, "The Epiklesis in the Antiochene Baptismal *Ordines*," *Symposium Syriacum*, OCA 197 (Rome: Pontificium Institutum Orientalium Studorium, 1974): 183–218; idem, *The Holy Spirit in the Syrian Baptismal Tradition*, Syrian Churches Series 9 (Kottayam, India: Anita Printers, 1979); idem, "Studies in the Early History of the Syrian Orthodox Baptismal Liturgy," *Journal of Theological Studies* 23 (1972): 16–64; idem, "The Syrian Baptismal Ordines," *Studia Liturgica* 12 (1977): 177–83; idem, "The Syrian Baptismal Rites," *Concilium* 122 (1979): 98–104; idem, "The Transition to a Post-Baptismal Anointing in the Antiochian Rite," *Bibliothecha Ephemerides Liturgicae, Subsidia* 19 (1981): 215–25; Joseph Chalassery, *The Holy Spirit and Christian Initiation in the East Syrian Tradition*, (Rome: Mar Thoma Yogam, 1995); Augustin Mouhanna, "Le symbolisme dans les rites de l'initiation de l'Église Maronite," *Studia Anselmiana* 87 (1983): 105–21; Baby Varghese, *Les onctions baptismales dans la tradition syrienne*, CSCO, Subsidia 82 (Louvain: Peeters, 1989); Winkler, *Das armenische Initiationsrituale*; idem, "The Blessing of Water in the Oriental Liturgies," *Concilium* 178 (1985), 53-61; idem, "The History of the Syriac Prebaptismal Anointing in the Light of the Earliest Armenian Sources," *Symposium Syriacum 1976*, OCA 205 (Rome: Pontificio Istituto Orientale 1978): 317–24; and idem, "The Original Meaning of the Prebaptismal Anointing and Its Implications," *Worship* 52 (1978): 24–45 (= LWSS, 58–81). *Coptic and Ethiopic:* Paul Bradshaw, "Baptismal Practice in the Alexandrian Tradition," LWSS, 82–100; Heinzgerd Brakmann, "Neue Funde und Forschungen zur Liturgie der Kopten 1992–1996," in *Ägypten und Nubien in spatäntiker und christlicher Zeit. Akten des 6. Internationalen Koptologenkongresses, Münster, 20.–26. 1996*, ed. Stephen Emmel (Weisbaden: Reichert, 1999), 451–64; O. H. E. Khs-Burmester, "The Baptismal Rite of the Coptic Church: A Critical Study," *Bulletin de la Société d'Archéologie Copte* 11 (1945): 27–68; Georg Kretschmar, "Beiträge zur Geschichte der Liturgie, insbesondere der Taufliturgie, in Ägypten," *Jahrbuch für Liturgik und Hymnologie* 8 (1963): 1–54; and Habtemichael Kidane, "Ethiopian (or Geʿez) Worship," in *The New Westminster Dictionary of Liturgy and Worship*, ed. Paul F. Bradshaw (Louisville: Westminster John Knox, 2002),

baptismal, chrismation, and First Communion rites in the Christian East organized by what is a common overall pattern in all of the rites. That is, our presentation is organized into the four parts or sections of the rites themselves: (1) the making of catechumens, (2) prebaptism and baptism, (3) chrismation, and (4) Communion. In each case, attention will be given to specific texts in context.

Because the rites of confession, penance, or reconciliation have been often interpreted from very early on as a repentant return to baptism and the catechumenate, we include a brief description of this sacrament in the various Eastern rites at the end of this chapter.

## 1.1 The Making of Catechumens

Because infant initiation would become the regular and dominant practice in both East and West, the rites of the ancient catechumenate were ultimately reduced to a series of lengthy ceremonies taking place at the beginning of the initiation rites in all of the Eastern liturgical traditions. As table 1.1 illustrates, however, the provision of specific prayers for infants on the eighth and fortieth (eightieth for females in the Coptic and Ethiopic Rites) days after birth (all rites except Armenian, East Syrian, and West Syrian) is a clear indication that, unlike in the medieval West, infants in the East were never really baptized *quamprimum* (as soon as possible after birth), except in danger of death or for some other serious reason. Rather, at least some vestiges or remnants of the overall catechumenal process remained in effect as they still do in many of these churches today. One of those catechumenal remnants appears in the introductory rubric in the ninth- or tenth-century Armenian rite of baptism and a pertinent rubric in the *Georgian Lectionary*, which represents Hagiopolite liturgical practices between the fifth and eighth centuries. The Armenian baptismal rubric reads in part:

> The Canon of Baptism when they make a Christian. Before which it is not right to admit him into the church. But he shall have hands laid on beforehand, *three weeks or more* before the baptism, in time sufficient for him to learn from the Wardapet [Instructor] both the faith and the baptism of the church.[3]

---

169–72; and Maxwell E. Johnson, *Liturgy in Early Christian Egypt*, AGLS 33 (Bramcote, Nottingham: Grove Books, 1995).

[3] DBL, 74.

## Table 1.1: The Making of Catechumens

| Armenian | Byzantine | Coptic | Ethiopian | East Syrian | West Syrian | Maronite |
|---|---|---|---|---|---|---|
| | Rite of the first day | | | | | |
| | Rite of the eighth day | | | | | Rite of the eighth day |
| | Rite of the fortieth day | Rite of the fortieth and eightieth day | Rite of the fortieth or eightieth day | | | Rite of the fortieth day |
| Psalm 130 (131)<br>Blessing of *Narawt* (ribbon/crown)<br>Prayer | | | | | | |
| Pss 3, 25, 26 50 (51)<br>Deacon's Proclamation | Facing East<br>Consignation and Exsufflation | Psalm 50 (51) | Psalm 50 (51) | | Chants and Readings | Chants and Readings |
| Prayer<br>Psalm 90 (91) | | Prayer<br>Name of Child | Prayer<br>Name of Child | | | |
| Imposition of Hands | Inscription: Imposition of Hands and Prayer | Inscription:<br>Prayer x2<br>Prayer over Oil | | Inscription: Imposition of Hands<br>Prayer | Priestly Prayer<br>Inscription: Prayer | Inscription: Prayer |
| Signation | Exorcistic Prayers (3) | Consignation with Oil<br>Prayers (everyone kneeling) | Consignation with Oil<br>Prayers (everyone kneeling) | Consignation with Oil | Consignation x3 | Consignation |

| | | | | | | |
|---|---|---|---|---|---|---|
| | | | | Psalms | | Hymns |
| | | | | | | Priestly Prayer |
| | | | | | | Exsufflation |
| | Exorcism with Exsufflation and Consignation | | Imposition of Hands and Prayer | Imposition of Hands and Prayer | Exorcism with Consignations | Exorcism with Consignations |
| Renunciation of Devil | Facing West: Renunciation of Devil Spit and Blow | Facing West: Renunciation of Devil Spit and Blow | Facing West: Renunciation of Devil Spit and Blow | Renunciation of Devil Spit | Renunciation of Devil Spit | Renunciation of Devil Spit |
| Profession of Faith | Facing East: Adherence to Christ Profession of Faith | Facing East: Adherence to Christ Profession of Faith | Facing East: Adherence to Christ Profession of Faith | Facing East: Profession of Faith | Facing East: Adherence to Christ Profession of Faith | Facing East: Adherence to Christ Profession of Faith |
| Matt 28:16-20 Nicene Creed Deacon's Proclamation Prayer | Prayer: Call to Baptism | Prayer | Prayer | Consecration of and Anointing with Oil | Prayer | |
| | | Renunciation Anointing Imposition of Hands with Two Prayers | Renunciation Anointing Imposition of Hands with Two Prayers | | | |

And the *Georgian Lectionary*, while listing the same nineteen catechetical readings as the prebaptismal catecheses of Cyril of Jerusalem and the *Armenian Lectionary*, specifically directs that catechesis is to begin with these readings on the Monday of the Fifth Week in Lent, that is, exactly *nineteen* days (or approximately three weeks) before paschal baptism.[4]

It is also important to note, perhaps not surprisingly, given the patristic witness of John Chrysostom and Theodore of Mopsuestia,[5] that it is the Byzantine and West Syrian prebaptismal rites that have tended to become the most exorcistic in orientation.

### *1.1.1 Byzantine*

> Today you are to publish before Christ the contract of faith: for our pen and ink we use our understanding, our tongue and our behaviour. Watch therefore how you write your confession: make no mistake, lest you be deceived. When men are about to die, they make a will and assign someone else as the heir of their possessions: tomorrow night, you are to die unto sin: now you make and ordain a will, namely your renunciation, and you assign the devil as the heir of your sins, and you dispose of your sins as a patrimony (to him). So if any of you has anything belonging to the devil in his heart, throw it to him. He that dies no longer has power over his possessions: let none of you therefore preserve in your hearts anything that is the devil's. That is why you stand and hold up your hands when I command, as though being searched lest anyone has hidden upon him anything belonging to the devil. Let no one harbour enmity or anger, let no one behave with deceit, let no one listen with hypocrisy. Throw to the devil all *filthiness and superfluity of naughtiness* [Jas 1:21]. Conduct yourselves as prisoners, for as such Christ purchases you. Each of you shall look at the devil and hate him, and thus you shall blow upon him. Each of you must enter into his conscience, search his heart, and see what he has done. If after you have blown upon the devil there is still anything evil in you, spit it out. Let no Jewish hypocrisy dwell in any one; have no doubts about the sacrament. *The Word of God* searches your hearts, *being*

[4] See above, p. 3.

[5] See DBL, 43–49; Yarnold, *Awe-Inspiring Rites*, 156–61, 168–79.

*sharper than any two-edged sword* [Heb 4:12]. The devil stands now to the west, gnashing his teeth, tearing his hair, wringing his hands, biting his lips, crazed, bewailing his loneliness, disbelieving your escape to freedom. For this cause Christ sets you opposite the devil, that having renounced him and having blown upon him you may take up the warfare against him. The devil stands to the west because it is from there that darkness comes: renounce him, blow upon him, and then turn to the east and join yourselves unto Christ. Be not contemptuous. Behave with reverence: all that is happening is most awful and horrifying. All the powers of the heavens are there, all angels and archangels. Unseen, the Cherubim and Seraphim record your voices: at this moment they look down from heaven to receive your vows and carry them to the Master. Take care therefore how you renounce the enemy and accept the Creator.[6]

### *1.1.2 West Syrian*

*On pronouncing each of the following invocations, the priest draws the sign of the cross upon the face of the child who is facing East.*

Upon You do we call, O Lord God, maker of heaven and earth, and of all things visible and invisible, while we lay our hand upon this Your creature whom we seal in Your Holy Name, from whom restrain all the devils, demons, and unclean spirits that they may be driven away from Your creature who is formed by Your holy hands. Hear us, O Lord, rebuke them and cleanse this Your servant from the instigation of the adversary.

A. Hearken unto me, you perverter and rebellious one who oppresses this creature of God ✠

B. Enemy of righteousness who violates the holy and divine law, I do adjure you by the glory of the great King, and command you to depart hence with dread, and be subject under the authority of the almighty Lord by Whose command the earth is firmly founded on the waters, and the sand is an established boundary for the seas ✠

[6] DBL, 110.

C. I adjure you by God, Who has authority in heaven and on earth, by Him Who created all things and by Whose providence they are preserved ☩

D. I adjure you in the name of the Redeemer Who sent the legion of demons into the swine and drowned them in the water. I adjure you by the name of God Who drowned the hard-hearted Pharoah, his horsemen, and chariots in the depth of the sea ☩

E. I adjure you by Jesus Christ, Who with power and divine authority ordered the mute and inarticulate spirit saying: "Get out of the man, O you unclean spirit, and dare not to attach him again" ☩

F. Stand in awe of God's dreadful name of Whom the creation of angels and archangels tremble; in Whose presence all the powers and ministers stand in fear; Whom the cherubim and seraphim dare not behold; the heavenly hosts worship Him with reverence, and the whole universe declares His glory ☩

G. Stand in awe of God's dreadful name Who fastened the first rebellious ones in chains of darkness and sent them to the pit of perdition ☩

H. Stand in fear of the judgment to come; tremble and depart. Do not approach or afflict God's creation. Dwell not in God's creation for it is not the dwelling place of demons, but the temple and dwelling place of the Living God Who said: "I shall dwell among them and walk with them; I shall be their God and they will be My people." As to you, He made you detestable, void of virtues, and fuel for the unquenchable fire ☩

I. I adjure you by God Who is victorious and holy, the Father, the Son, and the Holy Spirit, depart from this servant of God and go to the pathless deserted lands where there is no water, where your dwelling place should be ☩

Be uprooted and dispersed. Be vanished from God's creation, O you accursed one, unclean spirit, spirit of deception, and fuel for the unquenchable flames. Make haste and do not resist. God, the Father, the Son, and the Holy Spirit shall extirpate you and drive you out from His creation that you may be destroyed and tormented in the tormenting fire; whereas this, who is the creation of His hands, shall be redeemed until the day of salvation. For to Him is the kingdom, the power, and the glory for evermore.[7]

At the same time, those rites that include anointing as part of the catechumenal or baptismal preparation process (Coptic/Ethiopian and East Syrian), as the following texts demonstrate, tend to conflate an exorcistic orientation with an "oil of gladness" theology (Coptic/Ethiopic) or show no signs of an exorcistic motif at all (East Syrian).

### *1.1.3 Coptic and Ethiopian*

First Prebaptismal Anointing: *Anoint his forehead, saying:* You are anointed, child of N., in the Name of the Father and of the Son and of the Holy Spirit, One God, with oil of catechumens in the holy only catholic and apostolic Church of God. *Amen. Anoint his breast and his hands and his back, saying:* May this oil render of none effect all assaults of the adversary. *Amen.*[8]

Second Prebaptismal Anointing: *Take the agallielaion of the oil of exorcism. Anoint him who is to be baptized on his breast and his arms and over his heart behind and between his two hands in the sign of the cross, saying:* You are anointed, child of N., with the oil of gladness, availing against all the workings of the adversary, unto your grafting into the sweet olive tree of the holy catholic Church of God. Amen.[9]

### *1.1.4 East Syrian*

First Prebaptismal Anointing: *He signs in the air above them all, and then signs them on their foreheads with the Sign of the Cross with the oil in the Horn with his forefinger from below upward and from right to left, saying:* So and so is signed (with the Oil of Anointing) in

[7] DBL, 84–85.
[8] DBL, 134.
[9] DBL, 136.

> the name of the Father, and of the Son, and of the Holy Spirit for ever. *And they respond:* Amen.[10]

The Coptic/Ethiopian Rites appear to have conflated what may be interpreted as an earlier non-exorcistic "oil of gladness" with the "oil of exorcism" itself ("the agallielaion of the oil of exorcism"). Such a conflation, according to Paul Bradshaw, may well have resulted from the influence of the *Apostolic Tradition* within Egyptian Christianity.[11] Finally, elements such as spitting at or blowing against the devil at the time of the renunciation are certainly related to the increase in what might be called the flair for the dramatic in the immediate aftermath of Constantine in the fourth century.[12]

Following the west-facing *apotaxis*, or renunciation of Satan (including a literal spitting at Satan), and an east-facing *syntaxis*, or "act of adherence to Christ," expressing "a change of allegiance" for the candidate, first testified to in the catechetical lectures of the great fourth-century Eastern mystagogues (John Chrysostom, Theodore of Mopsuestia, and Cyril [John] of Jerusalem), all Eastern rites today have the profession of faith using a declarative form ("I believe") of the Nicene Creed. There is some scholarly debate, however, as to whether earlier forms of the Eastern rites, especially the Coptic, may once have known instead an interrogatory form of the profession (i.e., "Do you believe in God the Father?" etc.) within the context of the baptismal immersions, which only later became declaratory.[13]

## 1.2 Prebaptismal Rites and Baptism

Within the baptismal rites themselves, especially in those rites immediately before the baptismal washing, i.e., the consecration of the baptismal waters and the prebaptismal anointing(s),[14] the clearest

[10] The Order of Holy Baptism that was composed by Mar Išoʿyahb of Kh'dayab, catholicos, and was later explained by Mar Eliya, catholicos-patriarch, translated by M. J. Birnie, and used with permission.

[11] See Bradshaw, "Baptismal Practice" 94.

[12] Yarnold, *Awe-Inspiring Rites*, 59–66.

[13] See Paul Bradshaw, "The Profession of Faith in Early Christian Baptism," *Evangelical Quarterly* 78, no. 2 (2006): 107ff.

[14] The best guide to the anointings in the Eastern liturgical traditions is Gabriele Winkler. See her essays, "History of the Syriac Prebaptismal Anointing," 317–24; and

indications of the overall theology of baptism in the various rites are to be located. Here we will look in particular at the anointing(s), the blessing of the waters prayers, and the baptismal formulae employed in the rites. The overall shape of "baptism proper" is indicated in table 1.2.

### *1.2.1 Prebaptismal Anointing(s)*

As indicated in table 1.2 the Armenian Rite has a consecration of the prebaptismal oil at the very location where both the West Syrian and Maronite Rites have a simple anointing of the baptismal candidate on the forehead. The full-body anointing, characteristic of the East Syrian, West Syrian, Maronite, and Byzantine Rites, is separated from this initial anointing by the consecration of the water with its own attendant ceremonies. The Byzantine Rite is a notable exception here with no break between anointings but with the full-body anointing flowing directly from that of the anointing of the forehead, breast, and back. At this point the Byzantine Rite may well have preserved a vestige of how it was that a full-body anointing resulted from an earlier anointing of the head only. The second prebaptismal anointing in the West Syrian Rite provides somewhat of a parallel to the Byzantine Rite in this regard.

It is important to look briefly at the texts of these various prayers and anointings:

#### *1.2.1.1 Armenian*

*Prayer Over the Oil:* Blessed are you, O Lord our God, who chose for yourself a people, unto priesthood and kingship, *for a holy race and for a chosen people* [1 Pet 2:9]. As of old you anointed priests and kings and prophets with such all-holy oil, so now also, we pray you, beneficent Lord, send the grace of your Holy Spirit into this oil: to the end that it shall be for him who is anointed with it unto holiness of spiritual wisdom, that he may courageously fight and triumph over the adversary, unto strength of virtuous actions, and unto his perfect instruction and exercise

"The Original Meaning of the Prebaptismal Anointing and Its Implications," 24–45 (= LWSS, 58–81).

## Table 1.2: Baptism

| Armenian | Byzantine | Coptic | Ethiopian | East Syrian | West Syrian | Maronite |
|---|---|---|---|---|---|---|
| Procession to Font with Ps 117<br>Hymn<br>Deacon's Proclamation<br>Prayer<br>Ps 99 (100)<br>Deacon's Proclamation<br>Prayer<br>Hymn | Procession to Font | Procession to Font | Procession to Font | Procession to Font | Procession to Font | Procession to Font |
| Blessing of Oil | | | | | Consignation with Oil | Consignation with Oil |
| Pouring of the Water in the Font | Incensation | Pouring Oil in the Font | Pouring Oil in the Font | | Prayer | Prayer |
| Readings | Petitions | Liturgy of the Word until after the Readings | Liturgy of the Word until after the Readings | Liturgy of the Word until after the Readings | Prayer | Prayer |
| Intercessions | Prayer of Priest | | | Prayer of Priest | Chant | |
| Blessing of the Water | Blessing of the Water with Consignations and Exsufflations | Prayer over the Font<br>Prayer of Priest<br>Creed<br>Pouring of Oil in the Font with Exsufflations and Consignations | Prayer over the Font<br>Prayer of Priest<br>Creed<br>Pouring of Oil in the Font with Exsufflations and Consignations | Placing of Oil on Altar<br>Creed | Blessing of the Water with Consignations and Exsufflations | Blessing of the Water with Consignations and Exsufflations |

| | | | | | | |
|---|---|---|---|---|---|---|
| | Blessing of the Oil | | | Consecration of the Oil | | |
| Pouring Oil in the water with Alleluia | Pouring Oil in the water with Alleluia | Pouring Chrism in the Water with Alleluia | Pouring Chrism in the Water with Alleluia | Pouring the Oil in the Water | Pouring Chrism in the water with Alleluia | Pouring Chrism in the water with Alleluia |
| | | | | | | Lord's Prayer |
| | | | | | Prayer | |
| | Anointing of the Body | | | Anointing of the Body with chant | Anointing of the Body with chant | Anointing of the Body with chant |
| Three immersions with Formula | Three Immersions with Formula | Three Immersions with Formula | Three Immersions with Formula | Three Immersions with Formula and Imposition of Hands | Three Immersions with Formula | Three Immersions with Formula |
| Ps 33 (34) | Ps 31 | | | | Chant and Ps 31 | |
| Hymn<br>Rom 6:3-11<br>Matt 3:13-17<br>Lord's Prayer<br>Hymn | | | | | | |
| | Dressing with Formula | The "Release" of Water | The "Release" of Water | Dressing with Formula | | |

in the worship of God. To the end that enlightened in his understanding he may pass through the life of this world, unto the salvation of his soul, to the honour and glory of the all-holy Trinity, to become worthy of and to attain to the lot and heritage of those who love the name of Jesus Christ our Lord, with whom to you, Father, and to the Holy Spirit, are due glory, rule, and honor.[15]

*1.2.1.2 Byzantine*

*Such a one* is anointed with the oil of gladness, in the Name of the Father and of the Son and of the Holy Spirit. . . . *And then his whole body is anointed by the deacon.*[16]

*1.2.1.3 East Syrian*

Second Prebaptismal Anointing: *The faces of the candidates for baptism being to the east, the priest anoints each one of them on his breast with his three middle fingers from above downward and from right to left—not from below upward—with the Sign of the Cross, saying:* N. is anointed in the name of the Father, and of the Son, and of the Holy Spirit for ever, *showing by this that the knowledge of the Trinity is fixed in his heart, which is imparted from above. Then such as are preparers anoint the whole body of one who has been anointed by the priest, discreetly and in an orderly fashion (except for a mature woman or a mature man). And they turn him again upon his back in the previous manner without omission.*[17]

*1.2.1.4 West Syrian*

First Prebaptismal Anointing: *The priest moistens his right thumb with the anointing oil in the vase of ointment and signs the child upon his forehead. At each invocation he draws the sign of the cross upon the child's forehead and says:* N . . . is signed with ointment of spiritual rejoicing that he might confront the satanic influence and be en-

[15] DBL, 76. See Maxwell E. Johnson and M. Daniel Findikyan, "Toward the Restoration of Pre-baptismal Anointing in the Armenian Rite of Baptism," in *Eastern Christian Studies*, ed. Nina Glibetić and Gabriel Radle (Leuven: Peeters, forthcoming).

[16] DBL, 122.

[17] DBL, 68–69.

grafted into the cultivated olive tree in Your Holy, Catholic, and Apostolic Church. *Deacons: Barekhmore (Bless, my lord). Priest:* In the name of the Father, ✠ *Deacon: Amen.* And of the Son, ✠ *Deacon: Amen.* And of the Holy Spirit ✠ for everlasting life. *Deacon: Amen.*[18]

Second Prebaptismal Anointing: *The deacon presents the child to the priest who moistens his right thumb with the anointing oil, and as he says the following prayer, he draws the sign of the cross upon the child's forehead at every invocation: Priest:* N . . . is anointed with the oil of gladness wherewith to be armed against the operations of the adversary. *Priest:* In the name of the Father, ✠ *Deacon:* Amen. And of the Son, ✠ *Deacon:* Amen. And of the living Holy Spirit ✠ for life eternal. *Deacon:* Amen. *The priest pours out a sufficient quantity of the anointing oil into the palm of his hand and anoints the child's body completely, head downwards. If there be more than one child, the same act of anointing is to be followed for each one. During the anointing, the deacons chant the following hymn (Tune: Moray d'Ramsho—Second):* God said: "Let Aaron be anointed with the oil of holiness and henceforth be consecrated." Now this innocent lamb, who has come for baptism, is being anointed likewise. Aaron was made perfect by receiving the oil of holiness, a sacrament of consecration which was declared by the prophet David. Now the new lamb who has come to be baptized is being anointed in the Church.[19]

*1.2.1.5 Maronite*

N. is signed a member of the Christian community with the holy life-giving oil in the name of the Father ✠ and of the Son, and of the Holy Spirit. ℟. Amen.[20]

In light of the various political, social, and religious shifts in the fourth- and fifth-century Christian East noted in our introduction,

[18] DBL, 87–88.

[19] DBL, 93–94.

[20] DBL, 106. An alternative translation appears in Diocese of St. Maron—USA, *Mysteries of Initiation: Baptism, Confirmation, Communion, According to the Maronite Antiochene Church* (Washington, DC: Diocesan Office of Liturgy, 1987), 45: "N. is anointed as a member of the flock of Christ with the living oil of the divine anointing. In the name of the Father. . . ." Our thanks to Jorge Perales of Miami, Florida, for providing us with this text.

even with the shift toward exorcism in the prebaptismal rites of the Eastern Churches, the prebaptismal anointing(s) still retain the strong remnant of what scholars such as Sebastian Brock and Gabriele Winkler[21] have identified as the earlier stratum and theology of the Eastern rites. That is, although the prebaptismal anointing itself ultimately disappeared from the Armenian Rite, the following images from the consecration of the oil prayer still point in that ancient Syrian direction focused on the Holy Spirit's assimilation of the candidate to the messianic priesthood and kingship of Christ: "Blessed are you, O Lord our God, who chose for yourself a people, unto priesthood and kingship, *for a holy race and for a chosen people* [1 Pet 2:9]. As of old you anointed priests and kings and prophets with such all-holy oil, so now also, we pray you, beneficent Lord, send the grace of your Holy Spirit into this oil: to the end that it shall be for him who is anointed with it unto holiness of spiritual wisdom." What is most interesting here is that, currently, the Armenian Rite has this blessing prayer for the prebaptismal oil in the rite, but, even if used today, this oil is merely set aside and there is, as noted, no prebaptismal anointing at all. Since the Synod of the Armenian Apostolic Church has recently taken up the question of the reform of the Rite of Baptism as an item of high priority, it is possible that even this prayer will disappear from the prebaptismal rites, since it is regularly omitted already. This possibility has led some to argue not only for the retention of this prayer but for the restoration of the rite of the prebaptismal anointing itself.[22]

The simple formulae in the East Syrian Rite show no trace of an exorcistic understanding just as, surprisingly, neither does the Byzantine anointing: "*Such a one* is anointed with the oil of gladness, in the Name of the Father and of the Son and of the Holy Spirit."[23] With regard to the West Syrian or Antiochene Rites, Brock himself has demonstrated on the basis of the earliest manuscripts that the formula, "N . . . is signed with ointment of spiritual rejoicing that he might confront the satanic influence and be engrafted into the culti-

[21] See note 14 above.

[22] See Maxwell E. Johnson and M. Daniel Findikyan, "Toward the Restoration of Pre-baptismal Anointing in the Armenian Rite of Baptism," in *Eastern Christian Studies*, ed. Glibetić and Radle.

[23] The prayer of consecration of the oil, of course, *does* contain a reference to the exorcistic power of the oil. See DBL, 122.

vated olive tree in Your Holy, Catholic, and Apostolic Church," was originally, "N is signed (*rsm*) with the oil of gladness, *that he may be made worthy of the adoption of rebirth*, in the name . . ."[24] The references in these formulae (West Syrian, and the Coptic and Ethiopic prayers included in the previous section) to fighting against the adversary and to being grafted into the "sweet" or "cultivated olive tree" is a sure sign of Jerusalem influence, going back to Cyril (John) of Jerusalem's description of the prebaptismal anointing in MC II.3.[25]

### *1.2.2 The Consecration of the Baptismal Waters*

The prayers for the consecration of the baptismal waters in the various Eastern rites, with their attendant hymns and ceremonies of exorcisms, consignations, exsufflations, and infusions of chrism, also offer an important window by which to view the theology of baptism in the Christian East.[26] While the following texts are both abbreviated and selective, they will suffice in order to demonstrate their particular theological orientation.

#### *1.2.2.1 Armenian*

> You have also decreed by your unfailing word that they who are not born of water and of the spirit shall not enter into the kingdom of God. So this your servant, standing in awe of your word and desiring everlasting life, has willingly come for the baptism of this spiritual water. We now therefore pray, O Lord, send your Holy Spirit into this water and sanctify the same as you sanctified the river Jordan by descending thereinto and prefiguring thereby this font of baptism for the regeneration of all people.[27]

[24] Brock, "Studies in the Early History of the Syrian Orthodox Baptismal Liturgy," 32; emphasis added.

[25] Ibid., 38–39.

[26] On the consecration of waters, see Brock, "The Epiklesis in the Antiochene Baptismal *Ordines*," in *Symposium Syriacum 1972*, 183–218; and Gabriele Winkler, "The Blessing of Water in the Oriental Liturgies," 53–61.

[27] Adapted from Tiran Nersoyan, *The Order of Baptism According to the Rite of the Armenian Apostolic Orthodox Church* (Evanston, IL: Saint Nersess Publications, 1964), 47. This prayer, unfortunately, does not appear in DBL.

*1.2.2.2 Byzantine*

You have set free the children of our race. You sanctified a virgin's womb by your birth: the whole creation hymns your appearing. For you, our God, looked upon the earth and dwelt among men. For you sanctified the waves of Jordan, you sent down your Holy Spirit from heaven and crushed down the heads of the serpents that lurked there. *Therefore, our loving king, be present now in the visitation of your Holy Spirit and sanctify this water. Give it the grace of redemption, the blessing of Jordan.* Make it a fount of purity, a gift of sanctification, a way of deliverance from sins, a protection against disease, a destruction to demons, unapproachable to the power of the enemy, filled with angelic power. Let all who seek the overthrow of this your child flee away from it, that we may praise your name, O Lord, which is wondrous and glorious and fearful to the enemy. *And he breathes into the water three times and signs it with his finger three times, and says:* May all the enemy powers be crushed down by the sign of the type of the cross of your Christ. May all aerial and unseen shapes depart from us, may no dark demon lie hidden in this water: and, we pray you, Lord, let no evil spirit go down with him at his baptism to bring darkness of counsel and confusion of mind. But, maker of all things, declare this water to be a water of rest, water of redemption, water of sanctification, a cleansing of the pollution of the body and soul, a loosening of chains, forgiveness of sins, enlightenment of souls, washing of rebirth, grace of adoption, raiment of immortality, renewal of spirit, fount of life.[28]

*1.2.2.3 Coptic and Ethiopian*

And now, O our Master, lord of hosts, king of the armies of heaven; look, you who sit upon the Cherubim; sow forth yourself, and look upon this your creature, this water; give unto it the grace of the Jordan, and the power and strength of heaven; and by the descent of your Holy Spirit upon it, bestow upon it the blessing of the Jordan. *Amen.* Give it power to become water of life. *Amen.*

[28] DBL, 120–21; emphasis added.

Holy water. *Amen.* Water washing away sins. *Amen.* Water of the laver of new birth. *Amen.* Water of sonship. *Amen.*[29]

### *1.2.2.4 East Syrian*

By your grace, O our Maker, *repeat,* which is a fountain of living water, the need of your creation is filled, and manifold petitions are offered to you, after which generous gifts come, and from the great riches of your mercifulness assistance is rendered for the refreshment and support of our nature. For you, in your incomprehensible knowledge, brought us into this world corruptible at the beginning, and in the time which was pleasing to you proclaimed to us the good news of renewal and restoration through our Lord Jesus Christ, who by the type of his baptism pre-figured our resurrection from the dead, and he commissioned us to make, by the Mystery of his baptism, a new and spiritual birth for those who believe. For the Holy Spirit, who is from the glorious Being of your Trinity, through visible water makes new as he wills the worn out condition of our fashioning, placing in us by his grace an incorruptible earnest, who also descended upon our Savior and remained on him, when he delineated the type and image of this holy baptism. And may there come, O my Lord, the same Spirit upon this water as well, that those who are baptized in it may receive power for their help and salvation, that being perfected in body and soul they may lift up to you glory, honor, confession, and worship, now, always, and for ever and ever. *And he signs over the water. Also one should know this: when the priest comes to the phrase which says,* "And may there come, O my Lord, the same," *he kneels, and the archdeacon says,* In silence and fear remain as you are. Peace be with us. *And all who are there kneel, and when the priest rises they rise. And at the end of the Canon they respond*: Amen. *Then the priest takes the Horn of the Oil of Anointing and signs the water with the oil which is in it, pouring it over it in the form of a cross and saying*: This water is signed, consecrated, and mingled with the Holy Oil, that it may be a new womb, giving birth spiritually through absolving baptism, in the

[29] Adapted from Reginald Maxwell Woolley, *Coptic Offices* (London: SPCK, 1930), 37.

name of the Father, and of the Son, and of the Holy Spirit for ever.[30]

*1.2.2.5 West Syrian*

Hymn (Tune: *Quqoyo*): The voice of the Lord is over the waters, Halleluiah. John mixed the water of the baptistery, which Christ sanctified and went into the river to be baptized in it. At the moment when He came out from the water, heaven and earth gave honor to Him. The sun submitted its dazzling light and the stars did obeisance to Him Who sanctified all the rivers and springs, Halleluiah, Halleluiah. You gave gifts to people, Halleluiah. Who has ever seen two noble sisters such as the pure baptistery and the Holy Church; the one gives birth to the new and spiritual children and the other nurtures them; whomsoever the baptistery bears from the water, the Holy Church receives and presents to the altar, Halleluiah, Halleluiah. *Priest:* Glory be to the Father. . . . *Here the priest uncovers the baptismal font and waves the veil above the water.* How miraculous is the time when the priest stretches out his hands and opens the baptismal font! The heavenly hosts are astounded to behold the mortal standing above the flame. He calls upon the Holy Spirit to descend from above. His desire is hastily fulfilled when the Holy Spirit sanctifies the baptistery for the remission of sins, Halleluiah, Halleluiah. *Deacons:* From eternity to eternity. Amen. When the baptistery was sanctified by the Father, the Son, and the Holy Spirit it became a fountain of life. The Father's voice was heard saying: "This is My beloved Son," the Son was bending His head to be baptized and the Holy Spirit descending upon Him like a dove: Holy Trinity by whom the worlds gained life. Halleluiah, Halleluiah. . . . *Priest:* You did establish the seas firmly with Your might. You did break the heads of the dragons that lay hidden in the waters. You are awe-inspiring. Who dares to stand against You? We beseech You, O Lord, to look upon this water which is Your creation; grant to it the grace of Your salvation, the blessings of the Jordan River, and the holiness of Your Holy Spirit.[31]

[30] DBL, 67.
[31] DBL, 89–90.

### *1.2.2.6 Maronite*

> Bestow upon them [the waters] the power of the Holy Spirit. As the womb of our mother, Eve, gave birth to mortal and corruptible children, so may the womb of this baptismal font give birth to heavenly and incorruptible children. And as the Holy Spirit hovered over the waters at the work of creation, and gave birth to living creatures and animals of all kinds, may he hover over this baptismal font which is a spiritual womb. May he dwell in it and sanctify it. Instead of an earthly Adam, may it give birth to a heavenly Adam. May those who enter it to be baptized be permanently changed and receive a spiritual nature, instead of a corporal one, a participation in the invisible reality, instead of the visible one, and instead of the weakness of their spirit, may the Holy Spirit abide in them.[32]

As should be obvious from the above texts, the various prayers for the consecration of the baptismal waters illustrate beyond the shadow of a doubt that the overall theology of baptism in the Christian East was based on Jesus's own baptism in the Jordan with its related focus on adoption, new birth, and new creation in the Holy Spirit. While it is also clear that an exorcistic emphasis on preparing the one about to be baptized for the subsequent *postbaptismal* gift of the Spirit is present as well, it never replaced what is surely the more traditional emphasis in these traditions. With specific regard to anointing and baptism in the Syrian Rites—East, West, and Maronite—Sebastian Brock has written that:

> The anointing and baptism are . . . intimately tied up with each other as far as the meaning of the early Syrian baptismal rite was concerned. Baptism was seen primarily as rebirth to something new (John 3); it is the conferring of a new mode of existence on the baptismal candidate, a mode of existence that had originally belonged to [hu]man[ity] before the Fall. Syriac writers are particularly fond of expressing this idea by means of the imagery (Jewish in origin) of the "robe of glory," which Adam and Eve possessed in Paradise, but which had been lost at the Fall; Christ brings back the robe for [hu]mankind, and leaves it in the

[32] Diocese of St. Maron—USA, *Mysteries of Initiation*, 41. See the alternative translation in DBL, 104–5.

> Jordan waters for [hu]mankind to put on again in baptism. Significantly this robe of glory which Adam wore in Paradise was already understood in Jewish tradition as being both priestly and royal. Baptism is thus regarded as the means of recovery of the proper relationship between [hu]man[ity] and God, in whose image they are created. . . . Two points here will strike the western Christian at once; there is little or no hint in the early Syrian rite of the Pauline teaching of baptism as death, burial, and rising with Christ (Romans 6); and the pre-baptismal anointing is essentially charismatic in character, in total contrast to the cathartic and exorcistic role that the pre-baptismal anointing has in other rites.[33]

It is for this reason that liturgical scholars such as Gabriele Winkler have claimed that it is especially the Maronite Rite, with its references to "mother Eve," the baptismal "womb," and "Adam," that has best preserved here the ancient Syrian baptismal theology. Winkler writes:

> Those baptismal liturgies which remained firmly grounded in the creation account (in particular Gen. 1.2, with the hovering of the Spirit over the primordial waters) and in Jesus' own baptism in the river Jordan (with the center of gravity in the descent of the Spirit upon Jesus), combined with the inclusion of being born through the Spirit (John 3.5), tend not to favor the expansion of exorcisms.[34]

Of equal interest here is that consistent with the witness of the third-century Syrian *Acts* (Judas Thomas and John)[35] a maternal emphasis both on baptism as a *womb* and the Holy Spirit as "Mother" remains at least in the background of these later baptismal rites. But it survives as well in various baptismal hymns in some of these traditions. Again it is Winkler who has noted:

> We know that the Holy Spirit as Mother was once a widespread theologoumenon in Syria. This idea of God's Spirit as Mother can also be demonstrated in the early Armenian sources and the Armenian baptismal hymns (many of which are also sung at Epiphany and Pente-

[33] Brock, "Syrian Baptismal Rites," 100.

[34] Gabriele Winkler, "Baptism 2. Eastern Churches," in *The New Westminster Dictionary of Liturgy and Worship*, ed. Bradshaw, 38. See also idem, "The Blessing of Water," 53–61.

[35] See DBL, 15–22.

> cost!). In the oldest Armenian history (*Agathangeli Historia*) we read of the *womb of the maternal Spirit* of God; here the morning of creation and birth by water and the Spirit (John 3:5) are woven into a unity: "And just as he separated the first earth from the waters . . . [and] by water made all animals fruitful . . . in like manner he caused the womb of the baptismal water to bring forth, once again opening *the womb of the invisible Spirit* by visible water. . . ." Elsewhere there is an allusion to baptism "by water and *the womb of the Spirit*." As far as I know, this archaic approach, originating in Syria, has only survived in a few Syrian sources, as, e.g., in the Maronite and West Syrian orders of baptism. . . . We find in a Syrian baptismal hymn ". . . outspread your wings, Holy Church and receive the perfect sheep, *born by the Holy Spirit* in the water of baptism. . . ." But the idea has also survived in the Armenian baptismal hymns: "Today the birth-pangs of the first Mother come to an end, for those who were born unto death *are reborn by the Spirit* to be sons of light. . . . Thou (= Holy Spirit) who art co-Creator like the Father and the Son, by whom creatures are born to life in water, today dost Thou *give birth* to sons of God from the water. Spirit of God, have mercy. . . . Thou who didst fashion all creations, brooding over the waters, now, descending into the water-basin, *Thou bringest sons of God to birth*."[36]

The use of feminine imagery for the Holy Spirit, coming from the baptismal practice and theology of the Syrian churches, is something rooted in an ancient and classic tradition of Christianity!

While this sort of emphasis is more obvious in the Syrian-based baptismal liturgies, however, it is also clear that a Jordan-based theology of baptism remains a characteristic of all of the rites. The water consecration prayer in the more exorcistic Byzantine Rite, for example, also includes the following: "For you sanctified the waves of Jordan, you sent down your Holy Spirit from heaven and crushed down the heads of the serpents that lurked there. Therefore, our loving king, be present now in the visitation of your Holy Spirit and sanctify this water. Give it the grace of redemption, the blessing of Jordan." And the Coptic/Ethiopic prayer also underscores the Jordan as well as baptismal regeneration and the reception of "sonship."

Another important element, expressed especially again in the consecration prayers of the Syrian rites is that of the language of the

[36] Winkler, "The Blessing of Water," 56–57.

epiclesis of the Holy Spirit. In an important 1972 study of the Syrian baptismal rites, "The Epiklesis in the Antiochene Baptismal *Ordines*," Sebastian Brock convincingly argues for the antiquity of the imperative form of the verb "to come" and the later development of the verb "to send" in the epiclesis of the Holy Spirit upon the baptismal waters. Brock notes further that, along with changes in verb form, there is also a change in the divine person addressed. That is, in the earliest layers of the tradition the epiclesis with the imperative form "come" was addressed directly to Christ. A later stage asks Christ either that he "let His Spirit come" or, simply, that his Spirit "may come." At a still later stage of development God (the Father) was asked that the Spirit "may come," until, finally, through (fifth-century) Greek influence, the imperative form of the verb "to send" was adopted and addressed directly to God, i.e., that he now "send the Holy Spirit."[37] While it is this later form that is characteristic of most epicletic prayer in Eastern and Western liturgy in general, both the above East Syrian prayer in its epiclesis of the Holy Spirit over the baptismal waters (also in the consecration of the oil)[38] and, again, the Maronite prayer have retained, at least, the intermediate stage in this development with the use of the hortatory "let . . . come." In a particular way, then, these rites put us in touch with some of the earliest forms of liturgical prayer in Christian history.

### *1.2.3 Formulae for Baptism*

The various formulae for baptism employed in the Eastern rites, which still traditionally accompany the full submersion of the candidate in the font, can be presented here with only minimal comment.

[37] Brock, "The Epiklesis in the Antiochene Baptismal *Ordines*," in *Symposium Syriacum 1972*, 183–218. In her studies on the Sanctus and Epiclesis in liturgical prayer Gabriele Winkler has built on Brock's scholarship. See her essays, "Further Observations in Connection with the Early Form of the Epiklesis," in *Le Sacrement de l'initiation: Origines et Prospective, Patrimoine Syriaque Actes du colloque III* (Antelias, Lebanon, 1996), 66–80; "Nochmals zu den Anfängen der Epiklese und des Sanctus im Eucharistischen Hochgebet," *Theologisches Quartalschrift* 174, no. 3 (1994): 214–31; and "Weitere Beobachtungen zur frühen Epiklese (den Doxologien und dem Sanctus). Über die Bedeutung der Apokryphen für die Erforschung der Entwicklung der Riten," *Oriens Christianus* 80 (1996): 177–200.

[38] See DBL, 65.

Consistent with the theological interpretation of John Chrysostom and Theodore of Mopsuestia, the Armenian, Byzantine, East Syrian, and West Syrian Rites all employ a passive formula, and the Coptic, Ethiopian, and, traditionally, Maronite Rites use an indicative formula. While it might be tempting to view the Coptic, Ethiopian, and traditional Maronite Rites as having been influenced here by Western Latinization, Egypt already knew the use of the indicative formula in the early fourth century (*Canons of Hippolytus* 19). And, based on the use of the indicative in the third-century Syrian *Acts*,[39] it appears as though it is the use of the passive formula as interpreted by John and Theodore that represents the later usage.

#### *1.2.3.1 Armenian*

N. is baptized in the name of the Father, Son, and Holy Spirit, redeemed by the blood of Christ from the slavery of sin, receiving the freedom of adoption as son of the heavenly Father, having become a co-heir with Christ, and a temple of the Holy Spirit. Now and ever and for eternity [repeated at each of the three immersions].[40]

#### *1.2.3.2 Byzantine*

Such a one [or N.] is baptized in the name of the Father, Amen [first immersion] and of the Son, Amen [second immersion] and of the Holy Spirit, Amen [third immersion].[41]

#### *1.2.3.3 Coptic and Ethiopian*

I baptize you, son of N., in the Name of the Father [first immersion]. And of the Son [second immersion]. And of the Holy Spirit [third immersion].[42]

[39] See DBL, 15–22.

[40] DBL, 77.

[41] DBL, 122.

[42] DBL, 137.

## Table 1.3: Chrismation

| Armenian | Byzantine | Coptic | Ethiopian | East Syrian | West Syrian | Maronite |
|---|---|---|---|---|---|---|
| Prayer | Prayer | Prayer | Prayers | Prayer<br>Hymns | Prayer | |
| Chrismation with Formula | Chrismation with Formula | Chrismation with Formula | Chrismation with Formula | Imposition of Hands with Two Prayers | Chrismation with Formula | Chrismation with Formula |
| | | Imposition of Hands with Prayer | Imposition of Hands with Formula | Chrismation with Formula | | |
| | | Exsufflation with Formula | | | | |
| Dressing | | Dressing | Dressing | | Dressing | Dressing |
| | | Prayer | Prayer | | Prayer | Prayer |
| Prayer and Hymn | | Crowning with Prayer and Hymns | Crowning with Prayers | Crowning with Prayer | Crowning with Formula | Crowning with Hymn |

*1.2.3.4 East Syrian*

N. is baptized in the name of the Father, Amen [first immersion]. And of the Son, Amen [second immersion]. And of the Holy Spirit, Amen [third immersion].[43]

*1.2.3.5 West Syrian*

N. is baptized for holiness, salvation, a blameless life, and for the blessed resurrection from among the dead in the hope of life and the forgiveness of sins . . .
In the name of the Father, Amen [first immersion]. And of the Son, Amen [second immersion]. And of the Holy Spirit for life eternal, Amen [3rd immersion].[44]

*1.2.3.6 Maronite*

I baptize you, N., lamb in the flock of Christ, in the name of the Father and of the Son and of the Holy Spirit for eternal life.[45]

## 1.3 Chrismation

In the aftermath of Constantine's ascendancy to the imperial throne the rites of Christian initiation in the East underwent a transformation from the period of catechetical preparation all the way through postbaptismal mystagogy. One of those transformations, witnessed clearly in Cyril (John) of Jerusalem's *Mystagogical Catecheses*, was the inclusion of a postbaptismal anointing with chrism associated with the gift of the Holy Spirit. Not surprisingly, this has become a very important sacramental event in all of the Eastern rites. Table 1.3 provides a structural outline of this part of the baptismal rite:

What is absolutely crucial to note is that the Eastern rites knew—and still know (!)—only *one* postbaptismal anointing or chrismation,

[43] DBL, 69.

[44] DBL, 94.

[45] Recent Maronite baptismal liturgies in the United States use the passive formula: "N. is baptized a member of the Christian community [or lamb in the flock of Christ] in the name of the Father, Amen. And of the Son, Amen. And of the Holy Spirit for everlasting [eternal] life. Amen." DBL, 106, and *Mysteries of Initiation*, 46–47.

administered by bishops or presbyters using chrism that was consecrated by the bishop, the ecumenical patriarch, or the catholicos. Whether that chrismation included only the five signings of the Byzantine Rite, the nine of the Armenian (the five of the Byzantine plus the hands, the heart, the backbone, and the feet), the thirty-six (!) of the Coptic Rite, or didn't even enter the East Syrian liturgical tradition until the seventh century, the churches of the Christian East are unanimous in their interpretation of this anointing as associated with the gift of the Holy Spirit. The following formulae for chrismation illustrate this quite clearly.

### *1.3.1 Armenian*

*Forehead:* A fragrant oil poured out in the name of the Christ, the seal of heavenly gifts.

*Eyes:* This seal which is in the name of Christ, may it enlighten your eyes, that you may not ever sleep in death.

*Ears:* May the anointing of holiness be for you unto hearing of the divine commandments.

*Nostrils:* May this seal of Christ be to you for the sweet smell from life to life.

*Mouth:* May this seal be to you a watch set before your mouth and a door to keep your lips.

*Palms of the Hands:* May this seal of Christ be for you a means of doing good, of virtuous actions and living.

*Heart:* May this seal of divine holiness establish in you a holy heart, and renew an upright spirit within your interior.

*Backbone:* May this seal which is in the name of Christ be for you a shield and buckler, whereby you may be able to quench all the fiery darts of the evil one.

*Feet:* May this divine seal guide your steps aright unto life immortal.[46]

[46] DBL, 78–79.

### *1.3.2 Byzantine*

The Seal of the Gift of the Holy Spirit (with signing of the cross on forehead, eyes, nostrils, mouth, and both ears).[47]

### *1.3.3 Coptic and Ethiopian*

[With thirty-six signings of the cross on various parts of the neophyte's body:] In the name of the Father and the Son and the Holy Spirit. An unction of the grace of the Holy Spirit. An unction of the pledge of the kingdom of heaven. An unction of participation in eternal and immortal life. A holy unction of Christ our God, and a seal that should not be loosed. The perfection of the grace of the Holy Spirit, and the breastplate of the faith and the truth. You are anointed, son/daughter of N., with holy oil, in the Name of the Father and the Son and the Holy Spirit. Amen.[48]

### *1.3.4 East Syrian*

[With signing of the forehead alone:] N. is baptized and completed [or, perfected] in the name of the Father and of the Son and of the Holy Spirit for ever. [49]

### *1.3.5 West Syrian*

[With sealing the forehead of the neophyte three times with the cross:] By the holy myron which is Christ's fragrance, the seal of the true faith, and perfection of the Holy Spirit's gifts, N. is sealed in the name of the Father, Amen. And of the Son, Amen. And of the Holy Spirit for life eternal. Amen. *The priest pours the holy myron on his palm and anoints the child first on his (her) forehead, then his (her) right ear, arm, shoulder, and all his (her) right side, including the fingers of his (her) right hand and the toes of his (her) right foot. He then anoints the child's left side, his (her) arm, shoulder, ear, the fingers of his (her) left hand, and the toes of his (her) left foot. He returns to the*

[47] DBL, 123. On chrismation, especially in the Byzantine Rite, see the recent excellent study of Nicholas E. Denysenko, *Chrismation: A Primer for Catholics* (Collegeville, MN: Liturgical Press, Pueblo, 2014).

[48] DBL, 138.

[49] DBL, 71.

> *child's forehead, head, eyes, chest, and back until the child's body is completely anointed.*[50]

### 1.3.6 *Maronite*

> [With sealing the forehead of the neophyte three times with the cross:] With this Holy Myron (Chrism) of Jesus Christ, symbol of the true faith, the seal and fullness of the gifts of the Holy Spirit, this servant of God, N., is signed in the name of the Father ✠ and of the Son ✠ and of the Holy Spirit. ✠ Amen. N., you have been clothed by the Father, you have received the Son, you have put on the Holy Spirit, you have been given the glorious robe which Adam lost.[51]

As the "seal of the Holy Spirit," or "seal" and/or "perfection" of the Holy Spirit's gifts, this postbaptismal chrismation has remained intimately connected to baptism itself in the Christian East and, as such, should never simply be equated with Western "confirmation." If anything, this *single* anointing in the Eastern rites corresponds to the *first* postbaptismal anointing of the Roman Rite and not to the second anointing administered traditionally in the Roman Rite by the bishop alone (or by his delegate), a second postbaptismal anointing that none of the Eastern rites contain. In fact, the churches of the Christian East only came to call their single postbaptismal anointing "the *sacrament* of chrismation," because of encounters with the West and the influence of Western Scholastic theology. In the words of Thomas Hopko:

> The practice of counting the sacraments was adopted in the Orthodox Church from the Roman Catholics. It is not an ancient practice of the Church and, in many ways, it tends to be misleading since it appears that there are just seven specific rites which are "sacraments" and that all other aspects of the life of the Church are essentially different from these traditional actions. The more ancient and traditional practice of the Orthodox Church is to consider everything which is in and of the Church as sacramental or mystical.[52]

[50] DBL, 96.

[51] DBL, 107.

[52] Thomas Hopko, as quoted by Smolarski, *Sacred Mysteries*, 1.

While it is true that a form of *anointing* is used apart from baptism in the Eastern churches—somewhat like confirmation in the Roman Rite as well—to receive into their membership persons baptized within other Christian traditions,[53] the close and inseparable connection between the postbaptismal chrismation and baptism has never been lost. As Paul Turner summarizes:

> In the east, chrismation is offered to adults, children, and infants alike. When adults are baptized and chrismated, they symbolize their conversion and commitment to Christ. When children are baptized and chrismated, they enter the mystery of Christ which will continue to unfold throughout their lives. *Chrismation* is not so much the second mystery, as it is the very fulfillment of baptism. While baptism incorporates us into Christ's new risen existence, *chrismation* makes us partakers of his Spirit, the very source of this new life and of total illumination.[54]

Two additional postbaptismal rites stand out in this context as well. First, the Coptic and Ethiopian Rites contain a hand-laying prayer after the chrismation, which can only be interpreted pneumatically:

> May you be blessed with the blessing of the heavenly ones, and the blessing of the angels. May the Lord Jesus Christ bless you: and in his name (*here he shall breathe in the face of him that has been baptized and say*), receive the Holy Spirit and be a purified vessel; through Jesus Christ our Lord, whose is the glory, with his good Father and the Holy Spirit, now and ever.

[53] See, however, John Klentos, "Rebaptizing Converts into the Orthodox Church: Old Perspectives on a New Problem," *Studia Liturgica* 29 (1999): 216–34. Klentos surveys the variety of ways that people have been received into Orthodoxy and demonstrates by a comparative analysis of texts in the Greek euchologia that, at least in the classic *Greek* Orthodox tradition, the *anointing* administered as part of the rite is actually *distinct* from the postbaptismal *chrismation* of the initiation rites. Caution, therefore, must be urged in attempting to compare the rite of anointing at the reception into Orthodoxy as the same as Roman confirmation.

[54] Paul Turner, *Confirmation: The Baby in Solomon's Court* (New York: Paulist Press, 1993), 34.

And during the clothing with a white garment, the priest continues:

> Master, Lord God Almighty, who alone are eternal, the Father of our Lord and our God and our Saviour Jesus Christ; who commanded that your servants should be born through the laver of the new birth, and have bestowed upon them forgiveness of their sins and the garment of incorruption and the grace of sonship. Now again, O our Master, send down upon them the grace of your Holy Spirit the Paraclete; make them partakers of life eternal and immortality, in order that, according as your Only-Begotten Son, our Lord and our God and our Saviour Jesus Christ promised, being born again by water and spirit, they may be able to enter into the kingdom of heaven. Through the Name and the power and the grace of your Only-Begotten Son Jesus Christ our Lord.[55]

The second of these two prayers appears to have some affinity with the hand-laying "confirmation" prayer in the *Gelasian Sacramentary* and so might suggest Latin influence in these rites.[56] A postbaptismal hand-laying prayer associated with the Holy Spirit, however, is already present in Egypt in the early fourth-century *Canons of Hippolytus* and may simply be therefore based on influence of the so-called *Apostolic Tradition* in Egyptian liturgical practice, since the *Canons* themselves are viewed as the earliest derived document from the *Apostolic Tradition*.[57]

The second postbaptismal rite, common to all Eastern rites except for the Armenian[58] and Byzantine, is a "crowning" of the head of the neophyte, although in modern Greek practice the baby's head is now frequently covered by a linen cap. Such a crowning, obviously symbolic of baptismal royalty, joy, and celebration, may make use of a literal crown (Coptic and Ethiopian) or even a cloth headband called a *klilo* (East and West Syrian and Maronite).[59] Such "crowns" actually

[55] DBL, 138.

[56] See Johnson, *The Rites of Christian Initiation*, 222–29.

[57] See Paul Bradshaw, Maxwell Johnson, and L. Edward Phillips, *The Apostolic Tradition: A Commentary*, Hermeneia (Minneapolis: Fortress Press, 2002).

[58] In the Armenian Rite, a blessing of the *narawt* (ribbons or crown with red and white ribbons), which is used in other rites besides baptism, occurs near the beginning of the rite and may somehow be connected with the taking of an oath or consecration to God.

[59] See Christine Chaillot, "The Ancient Oriental Churches," in *The Oxford History of Christian Worship*, ed. Geoffrey Wainwright and Karen Westerfield Tucker (Oxford: Oxford University Press, 2006), 131–69; Lucas Van Rompay, "Excursus: The Maronites," in ibid., 170–74.

function as a way simply to cover the head after chrismation as a kind of chrismal cloth or "veiling" seen also in the West.[60] As rubrics in the Maronite Rite direct: "He may bind him/her with a headband, as a crown (to protect the myron)."[61] While the origins of such a widespread Eastern practice are obscure, one wonders whether it was suggested by the practice of the linen cloth being worn on the head originally after the *prebaptismal* anointing, adapted from the surrounding culture as a sign of being a free person in Mopsuestia during the time of its illustrious bishop Theodore,[62] or suggested even earlier by documents such as *The Odes of Solomon*.[63]

## 1.4 First Communion

All of the rites of initiation in the Christian East culminate theoretically in the neophyte's reception of First Communion usually today from the reserved Eucharist, according to the following structures. Of these rites, only the Ethiopian has retained the additional use of milk and honey, consistent with what was once a component of communion rites more widely in early Christianity.[64]

It is interesting to note, however, that while the immediate postbaptismal reception of First Communion is *theoretically* the case, as is indicated by table 1.4, praxis does not always follow theory. Irénée-Henri Dalmais wrote in 1960 that "under Latin influence the Maronites have abolished infant communion" and that First Communion of infants at baptism had fallen into disuse among the Assyro-Chaldeans.[65] Similarly, Stefano Parenti has written of contemporary Byzantine practice:

> It often happens, contrary to common sense, that initiation is celebrated on Sunday afternoon. In such celebration the congregational and symbolic aspects, otherwise well expressed in the ancient rituals, are notably lacking. Among the many models for Byzantine celebration of

[60] For the Western evidence, see J. Michael Joncas, "'Mystic Veiling,' of the Head of One Newly Baptized: A Baptismal Ritual in the Carolingian West," *Ecclesia Orans* 16 (1999): 519–46.

[61] *Mysteries of Initiation*, 48.

[62] See DBL, 49.

[63] See Johnson, *The Rites of Christian Initiation*, 47–49.

[64] See ibid., 48–49, 70–71, 84–85, and 168–69.

[65] Irénée-Henri Dalmais, *Eastern Liturgies*, Twentieth Century Encyclopedia of Catholicism, vol. 112 (New York: Hawthorne Books, 1960), 74.

## Table 1.4: First Communion

| Armenian | Byzantine | Coptic | Ethiopian | East Syrian | West Syrian | Maronite |
|---|---|---|---|---|---|---|
| Baptized kisses altar 3 times | *Trisagion* and Procession | | | | | Procession |
| Prayer of Inclination | | | | | | |
| | Readings | | | | | |
| Communion | Communion | Communion | Communion | Communion | Communion | Communion |
| Procession with Ps 31 (32) | | Prayer and Imposition of Hands | Milk and Honey | | | Final Prayer |
| Prayer | | Blessing | Imposition of Hands and Prayer | Procession | | |
| | | Procession with Hymns | Procession with Hymns | "Release" of Waters | Hymns | |
| Prayer for Eighth Day | Rites of the Eighth Day | Rites of the Eighth Day | Rites of the Eighth Day | Rites of the Eighth Day | Rites of the Eighth Day | Rites of the Eighth Day |
| Baptismal kiss | | | | | | |
| Hymn | | | | | | |
| Dismissal Prayer | | | | | | |
| Lord's Prayer | | | | | | |

> initiation that have appeared throughout its long history, the present one is certainly the least traditional. There have been attempts—in Greece, for example—to return to a more ecclesial vision by conferring baptism and chrismation on Sunday, immediately before the Divine Liturgy, during which the neophyte receives communion for the first time. These, of course, are private initiatives by individual priests. But they deserve attention and support. . . . With regard to Catholic Eastern Churches, since the eighteenth century some of them have followed the Roman model of initiation completely, substituting infusion for immersion, reserving the anointing with myron to the bishop and postponing "first communion." In most cases these things were not imposed by Rome but were autonomous decisions made by the synods of the particular churches. . . . The practice today, officially confirmed not long ago, is to return to the authentic Eastern discipline in all things. But the actual situation of individual Churches, coupled with a clergy whose formation has been weak, as well as a mistaken desire to be liturgically different from their Orthodox counterparts—all these are obstacles to an immediate, albeit desirable, restoration.[66]

In Greece it also happens on occasion that baptism and chrismation take place on Saturdays with First Communion postponed until the Divine Liturgy the next day, and in the Syro-Malabar tradition, under Latin influence, First Communion is usually delayed until the candidate is older.

The Armenian and Byzantine Rites, with the short Liturgy of the Word (with the reading of Romans 6:3-11 and Matthew 3:13-17 [Armenian] and Matthew 28:16-20 [Byzantine]) prior to the reception of Communion, have best preserved a vestige of the ancient tradition once characteristic of all of these rites, wherein baptism and chrismation led immediately into the celebration of the eucharistic liturgy itself. At the same time, the intriguing location of the chrismation *after* the short Liturgy of the Word in the Armenian Rite may well underscore that such a chrismation was again a later development in the rite.[67] While a complete restoration of baptism and chrismation to the Divine Liturgy and a closer association with the feasts and seasons of the liturgical year would be a very difficult task in the

[66] Parenti, "Christian Initiation in the East," in *Handbook for Liturgical Studies*, ed. Chupungco, 4:46–47.

[67] See Winkler, *Das armenische Initiationsrituale*, 439–41.

Christian East, it would not be impossible, and the Armenian and Byzantine Rites do provide a beginning model on which to build. For it is unfortunately the case, as is often the situation in the Latin West as well, that the Eastern rites of Christian initiation tend to be private or familial events separate from the Sunday and festal liturgies of the Church.

Reference in table 1.4 in all of the Eastern baptismal liturgies to "Rites of the Eighth Day" is also a remnant or vestige of the week of mystagogical catechesis. Today, these rites, including the ritual offering of small cuts of the neophyte's hair, a "Christianization of an ancient custom of offering the first fruits to the divinity,"[68] often take place at the conclusion of the baptismal rite rather than eight days later.

## 1.5 Conclusion

While one must be careful not to romanticize the initiation rites of the Christian East, the fact remains—as is at least reflected in the Eastern and Oriental Orthodox Churches still today—that by keeping baptism, the postbaptismal rites associated with the Holy Spirit, and the reception of First Communion together within a single, unitive, and integrated process of Christian initiation, including the retention of some elements of the prebaptismal catechumenate even for infants, the Christian East was able to avoid the problems associated with "confirmation" as a separate sacrament of strength and maturity for those at the "age of discretion" in the West. With the retention of such an integral pattern, catechesis itself becomes, essentially, "mystagogy" rather than preliminary instruction and preparation for the reception of sacraments. That is, through life-long postbaptismal catechesis the baptized, chrismated, and communed are continually formed to live out the "mysteries" that they have already received and in which they were sealed from the beginning. In such a way the churches of the Christian East continued to *initiate* infants rather than simply *baptize* them and, as in the West, postpone their full initiation until a later age through confirmation and First Communion, even

[68] Parenti, "Christian Initiation in the East," in *Handbook for Liturgical Studies*, ed. Chupungco, 4:43.

if, as we have seen, this process often today takes place outside the Church's corporate Sunday and festal liturgy.

## 1.6 Reconciliation

One's participation in the sacraments of initiation demanded of that person a particular way of life, faithful to the Gospel. Falling into grave sin (murder, adultery, apostasy) would bar that person from participating in the celebration of and participation in the Eucharist, voluntarily or involuntarily being excluded from the eucharistic community (excommunication). The process of reconciliation of these grave sinners, particularly the *lapsi*, those who under pressure during the persecutions of the third century had denied their faith (apostasy), posed a great challenge to the early Church. A lengthy process of ecclesial penance for those wishing to be reincorporated into the life of the Church emerged in the third century. The first phase of this process could be called the "penance of isolation," when the grave sin is confessed and the person is cut off from the ecclesial community. This was a period of fasting, prayer, and spiritual direction, so that the penitent realized the gravity of his or her sin. Then the "penance of segregation" would follow, an intermediate stage of penance where the penitents were assigned a special place in the church building but they could not attend the Eucharist nor partake of it. Prayers as well as exorcisms would be read over them during this period. In this context a public confession of the sin(s) committed and expression of repentance would take place. Finally, the reconciliation of the penitent with the ecclesial community would publicly take place, where the bishop would lay his hands on the penitent and possibly also anoint him or her.[69] Generally, this could take place only once in one's lifetime.

By the fourth century there is evidence that the penitents would be subdivided into further groups, their place in the church building

[69] Joseph Favazza, *The Order of Penitents: Historical Roots and Pastoral Future* (Collegeville, MN: Liturgical Press, 1988), 121–70. The author uses the terms "penance of isolation" and "penance of segregation" when describing penance in Origen, but we borrow these and apply them to this very brief summary of penitential practices of the third century.

and the level of their participation in the liturgical life of the ecclesial community depending on their place in the process of repentance:

> At the first level, the sinner is outside the church, shedding tears and weeping. Next, he is allowed to stand apart from the congregation inside the doors to the atrium, to hear the readings and the sermon, but he must leave before the prayers. At the third level, the sinner stands just inside the entrance of the church, falls down to receive the prayers of the congregation and the blessing of the bishop, but again leaves, together with the catechumens, before the celebration of the mysteries. At the fourth level, the sinner joins the congregation and stands together with them in the church during the readings and congregation prayers. Finally, the sinner's full readmission is sealed and confirmed by participation in the Eucharist.[70]

This process of reconciliation was often called "second baptism," as it gave the sinner the chance to be readmitted in the ecclesial community. It also strongly resembled the baptismal process, with its various stages of the catechumenate culminating in baptism, involving not only the ecclesial leadership but also the whole community. But while this process of public reconciliation gradually declined and eventually disappeared by the sixth or seventh centuries (as did the organized adult catechumenate), the link between reconciliation and baptism remained. In fact, in the Byzantine tradition the spiritual father or confessor of the sinner in the now-private context of reconciliation is called a "sponsor" who accompanies the sinner on the road to reconciliation, as the baptismal sponsor accompanies the catechumen to his journey to baptism.[71] With the growth of the monastic movement, a fertile synthesis took place between the public ecclesial process of reconciliation, on the one hand, and repentance as a spiritual art that assists in one's growing in the likeness of Christ.[72] While individual private reconciliation became the norm in

[70] Claudia Rapp, "Spiritual Guarantors at Penance, Baptism, and Ordination in the Late Antique East," in *A New History of Penance*, ed. Abigail Firey (Leiden: Brill, 2008), 121–48, here 127.

[71] Ibid., 127–33; Stefano Parenti, "Confessione, penitenza e perdono nelle chiese orientali," *Rivista Liturgia* 104 (2017): 114–41, here 125.

[72] Alexis Torrance, *Repentance in Late Antiquity: Eastern Asceticism and the Framing of the Christian Life c. 400–650 CE* (Oxford: Oxford University Press, 2013).

almost all Eastern Christian Churches (with the exception of the Church of the East), communal rites of reconciliation remained in the practice of many Eastern Christian traditions.

The Syrian traditions in particular have maintained, in various degrees, communal reconciliation, in parallel with private reconciliation (West Syrian, Maronite), or in the absence of private reconciliation (East Syrian tradition as practiced by the Church of the East).

### *1.6.1 West Syrian*

The West Syrian liturgical tradition in its current practice knows of both private and communal reconciliation. Public reconciliation fell out of use by the eighth century, while the first rite of private reconciliation that we know of appeared in the twelfth century.[73] While this reconciliation rite was composed at a time of strong Latin political and ecclesial influence, its use of the divine office of the West Syrian tradition as its liturgical framework helped it achieve a fine balance "between theocentric, christological, and ecclesiological elements,"[74] maintaining a therapeutic rather than a juridical approach to the confession of sins and a broader understanding of confession as an ecclesial event.

In current practice, reconciliation takes place privately and involves two prayers: a prayer said by the penitent before the priest at confession, and the absolution prayer read over the penitent by the priest. The first prayer is a general confession of faith, a confession of sinfulness, and a request to be absolved; the second prayer is a prayer of absolution with the Latin formula "I absolve you . . . ," clearly a Western influence in today's practice:[75]

> I make my confession to God, the Father Almighty, and to His beloved Son, Jesus Christ, and to the Holy Spirit. I confess the holy faith of the three Ecumenical Councils of Nicea, Constantinopolis and Ephesus, in the most noble priesthood ascribed unto you, Father Priest, by which

[73] Brian Gogan, "Penance Rites of the West Syrian Liturgy: Some Liturgical and Theological Implications," *The Irish Theological Quarterly* 42 (1975): 182–96, here 187–92. This is preserved in Vatican syr. 51, dated to 1171; Gogan, "Penance Rites," 187n18.

[74] Ibid., 192.

[75] Ibid., 193.

> you set loose and bind. I have sinned through all my senses, both inwardly and outwardly, in word, in deed and in thought. My sin is great, very great, and I repent of it most sincerely, purposing not to fall again into the same ever. Preferring death rather than embrace sin. And I ask you, by the authority of the sacred priesthood, that you absolve me of my sins, asking God to pardon me through His grace. Amen.
>
> May God have mercy upon you and guide you to eternal life. By the authority of the sacred priesthood, which was entrusted by our Lord, Jesus Christ, to His disciples, who, in turn, handed it to their successors, until it was given to my humble person. I absolve you, my brother, from all sins that you have confessed and repented of them, as well as all the transgressions that have escaped your memory, in the name of the Father, Son and Holy Spirit for ever-lasting life. Amen.[76]

In addition to this private form of reconciliation, the West Syrian tradition has a communal reconciliation embedded in all of its Divine Liturgies, attached to the "Canon of the Faithful Departed," the last section of the intercessions of the anaphora in the West Syrian liturgical rite. In praying for the departed and the forgiveness of their sins, the prayer transitions to petitioning the forgiveness of the sins of those present at the celebration of the Divine Liturgy. The two examples below are from the Anaphora of St. Philoxenus of Mabbug and the Anaphora of the Twelve Apostles.

As a response to the intercessions for the dead, the people petition that the sins of both the dead and theirs are forgiven: "O God, remove, pardon and forgive. . . ." This short prayer is a feature that goes back to Palestinian monastic communion practices.[77] The priest responds to this petition by repeating it almost word for word and then completing the prayer by asking God to forgive the sins of all present.

[76] https://dss-syriacpatriarchate.org/church-rites/penance-rites/?lang=en.

[77] Higoumène André (Wade), "La prière ἄνες, ἄφες, συγχώρησον. La pratique palestinienne de demander l'absolution pour la communion solitaire et quotidienne. *Lex orandi* pour une orthopraxis perdue?," Θυσία αἰνέσεως. *Mélanges liturgiques offerts à la mémoire de l'archevêque Georges Wagner (1930–1993)*, ed. Job Getcha and André Lossky, Analecta Sergiana 2 (Paris: Presses Saint-Serge, 2005), 431–35; Louis Ligier, "Pénitence et Eucharistie en Orient: Théologie sur une interférence de prières et de rites," OCP 29 (1963): 5–78, here 19–20, note 1.

| Anaphora of St. Philoxenus of Mabbug | Anaphora of the Twelve Apostles |
|---|---|
| *Priest:*<br>We beseech You, O God of abundant mercy, that You accept their souls in the Jerusalem mansions and Abraham's bosom. Remember not the sins that they committed in this world full of offenses, for no one among those born of women is free from sin except our Lord and our God and our Savior Jesus Christ through Whom we also hope to find mercy and forgiveness of sins for His sake, both for us and for them. | *Priest:*<br>In the true hope of Your resurrection, all the departed have rested, awaiting Your mercies, O Adorable God. Make them worthy of the life-giving word which calls and invites them to be guests in Your kingdom, and, by Your grace, grant us a peaceful departure; by Your loving-kindness, blot out our transgressions because only One is He Who appeared on earth sinless, Your Only-begotten Son, through Whom we hope to find mercy and forgiveness of sins for His sake and for both us and for them. |
| *People:*<br>O God, remove, pardon and forgive the offenses of ours and theirs which we have committed before You willingly and unwillingly, wittingly and unwittingly. | *People:*<br>O God, remove, pardon and forgive the offenses of ours and theirs which we have committed before You willingly and unwillingly, wittingly and unwittingly. |
| *Priest:*<br>O God, remove and pardon our offenses committed in thought, word and deed, those that are manifest and those that are concealed, yet are evident to You. | *Priest:*<br>O God, remove and pardon our offenses committed in thought, word and deed, those that are manifest and those that are concealed, yet are evident to You. |
| Put to an end and quench from us, O Lord, all the passions of sins, the willing and unwilling, the witting and unwitting. Lead us and our departed ones to the everlasting delight so that, herein as in all things, Your all Honored and Blessed Name be glorified and exalted with that of our Lord Jesus Christ and of Your Holy Spirit, now, always and forever.[78] | Relieve us and them, O Lord, from the burdens of sin. Pardon, by Your mercy, our transgressions and be, O Lord, Absolver and Forgiver of sins for us and for them so that through us, for us and for the sake of us Your All-respected and most Blessed Name be glorified, praised and extolled with that of our Lord Jesus Christ and that of Your Holy Spirit, now, always and forever.[79] |

78 http://syriacorthodoxresources.org/Liturgy/Anaphora/Philoxenus.html.
79 http://syriacorthodoxresources.org/Liturgy/Anaphora/12Apostles.html.

### 1.6.2 Maronite

The Maronite tradition has adopted the Latin form of private reconciliation that is used any time confession is practiced. It has, however, preserved a form of public reconciliation, celebrated once every year on Holy Saturday, and is titled "Prayer of Forgiveness." This service is structured around the *Husoyo* (Prayer of Absolution), a standard liturgical unit in the Syrian liturgical tradition:

- Opening Doxology
- Opening Prayers
- *Qolo* (Hymn)
- Psalm 50 (51)
- *Husoyo* (Prayer of Absolution)
    - *Proemion* (Preface)
    - *Sedro* (Prayer)
    - *Qolo* (Hymn)
    - *Etro* (Prayer of Incense)
- Readings
    - Jeremiah 31:31-35
    - Zechariah 1:1-6
    - 2 Corinthians 6:16-21
    - Matthew 18:15-22
- Supplication of St. James
- *Trisagion* and Resurrectional Response
- Lord's Prayer
- Concluding Prayer
- Resurrectional Acclamation[80]

The supplication of St. James is a beautiful exhortation to the faithful to change their ways, and a great example of practical ethics: it

[80] *Qurbono: The Book of Offering; The Service of the Holy Mysteries according to the Antiochene Syriac Maronite Church; Season of Great Lent and Passion Week* (Brooklyn, NY: St. Maron Publications, 1994), 213–28; Augustin Mouhanna, "Le rite du pardon dans l'Église Maronite," *Parole de l'Orient* 6–7 (1975–1976): 309–24.

identifies the vice, anger in this instance, as the root cause of divisiveness among people. It then brings in Christ as the paradigm of forgiveness, humility, and love and calls for a radical transformation of oneself, not out of fear of punishment (in fact, the supplication makes no mention of punishment), but by living out the Gospel:

> Come, you who are angry, and make peace with your enemies.
> Bow your head before them and embrace them.
> Engrave in yourself the sign of the Son of God—
> as he humbled himself before the brethren,
> so humble yourself!
>
> O disciple who show anger toward your neighbor,
> look for another Lord than the crucified One.
> Those who show anger, not love, toward their neighbor
> are against the Lord.
>
> O disciple who seek to imitate the Lord,
> come and see how Christ humbled himself
> and, like him, seek humility.
> He gave you the command of pardon
> and gave the keys of pardon
> to the head of the disciples.
> O merciful One, you destroyed anger;
> Through your blood you established peace
> between the inhabitants of heaven and earth.
> By your good news,
> you made all people brothers and sisters.
> Glory and praise to the Trinity.[81]

In fact, there is no mention at all of the threat of eternal punishment or damnation throughout the service. Quite the contrary! While sinfulness is clearly acknowledged, the prayers and the hymns express a solid confidence in Christ's love for the sinner and Christ's assured forgiveness. In the *Sedro*, forgiveness of sin is understood through the prism of the incarnation through which forgiveness is granted to humanity: "you took the image of a servant in order to give forgiveness to your servant."[82] The *Etro* places forgiveness of sins in the

[81] *Qurbono*, 225.
[82] Ibid., 219.

context of the crucifixion: "O heavenly High Priest, you died to redeem us from our faults. O forgiving Oblation, you offered yourself as a pleasing sacrifice to your Father. O pure Hyssop, you washed the wounds of our souls in your compassion. O Christ . . . by you our faults are forgiven and our souls protected."[83] And the concluding prayer highlights that penance is not so much about forgiveness but restoration and reconciliation:

> O Christ, our Lord, accept the penance we now offer to you and one another. May the grace and power of your Spirit come to purify, sanctify, and save us. May your life be a model for our own life so that we may live imitating your life, your death, and your resurrection. May we reach that day which will unite us to you and each other, and give you thanks and glory, now and forever. Amen.[84]

### *1.6.3 East Syrian*

The East Syrian liturgical tradition is unique in that it is the only tradition that does not have private reconciliation in its practice. This does not mean that spiritual advice and guidance in private do not take place; rather, communal reconciliation is part of the eucharistic liturgy and takes place before Communion.[85] The section between the epiclesis and Communion contains a number of penitential elements. For example, after the epiclesis Psalm 50 (51) is recited with two alternating responses: "O Christ the King, have mercy on me," and "O Christ the King, glory to your name." At the incense offering that follows, the priest prays:

> May our prayer and petition please you, our Lord and our God, and the fragrance of our pleasant censer be for your satisfaction, as the censer of Aaron the priest within the tabernacle. Restore our souls with our bodies, and be reconciled to your creation because of your many mercies, O Creator of pleasant roots and sweet spices, Lord of all, Father, Son, and Holy Spirit for ever.[86]

[83] Ibid., 221.

[84] Ibid., 227.

[85] Parenti, "Confessione," 131; Ligier, "Pénitence et Eucharistie en Orient," 24–32.

[86] https://web.archive.org/web/20071026094008/http://www.cired.org/, 22–23. Translated by Corbishop Michael J. Birnie. We owe the link and the information to Alex Neroth van Vogelpoel. We disagree with Ligier who argues that the intention of the prayer is the appeasement of God; Ligier, "Pénitence et Eucharistie en Orient," 28.

After the fraction, the priest recites a prayer, a sort of mini-anaphora, which resembles the anamnesis section of an anaphora: After mentioning the incarnation, the cross, the resurrection, the ascension, he continues:

> And he committed to us his holy Mysteries, that by them we might recall all his grace toward us. Let us, then, with overflowing love and a lowly will, receive the gift of eternal life, and with pure prayer and manifold sorrow, partake of the Mysteries of the church in the hope of repentance, turning from our offenses and sorrowing for our sins, and asking for mercy and forgiveness from God, the Lord of all.[87]

A dialogue then follows between the deacon and the people, sealed by a prayer. Both the exchange between the deacon and the people and the prayer that follows highlight the collective and public nature of this reconciliation rite embedded in the Divine Liturgy:

*Deacon:* We overlook the offenses of our fellow-servants.

*People:* Lord, pardon the sins and offenses of your servants.

*Deacon:* We purify our consciences from divisions and strife.

*People:* Lord, pardon the sins and offenses of your servants.

*Deacon:* Our souls being cleared of wrath and enmity.

*People:* Lord, pardon the sins and offenses of your servants.

*Deacon:* Let us take the sacrament and be sanctified by the Holy Spirit.

*People:* Lord, pardon the sins and offenses of your servants.

*Deacon:* In unity and with a mingling of our minds let us receive in mutual agreement the communion of the Mysteries.

*People:* Lord, pardon the sins and offenses of your servants.

*Deacon:* That they may be to us, O my Lord, for the resurrection of our bodies and for the salvation of our souls.

*People:* And for eternal and unending life.

[87] https://web.archive.org/web/20071026094008/http://www.cired.org/, 25.

*Priest:* Pardon in your compassion, O my Lord, the sins and offenses of your servants, and hallow our lips in your lovingkindness, that they may yield the fruits of glory to your exalted Godhead with all your saints in your kingdom.[88]

The Lord's Prayer then follows.

In the case of serious sins that bar a person from receiving the Eucharist, there is a different reconciliation service, also communal and public, called *Taxa d'Hoosâya* (Order of Pardon).[89] This service, which can also include the anointing with baptismal oil, especially for apostates, occurs before the Morning Prayers of the day one would receive Communion.[90] This public form of reconciliation opens with a doxology and Psalms 24 (25) and 129 (130), continues with a series of hymns, and concludes with a prayer. The hymns acknowledge one's sinfulness, appeal to God's mercy, and express the hope that God will extend his mercy so that the baptismal grace is restored, recalling the parable of the prodigal son (Luke 15:11-32):

> O Lord, upon the foundation of the rock of Simon Peter's faith Thou hast set me up, and in baptism Thou didst promise me the gift of adoption; but by my life I have likened myself to the heir who squandered away all his living, and now like him I pray and say: I have sinned against heaven and before Thee, and am no more worthy to be called Thy son. O merciful Lord, have mercy on me.
>
> The sinner who repents and comes unto Thee, O Lord God, Thou wilt not cast out from Thy presence, and from Thine everlasting benefits, but wilt stretch forth to him Thy helping hand, and address him in Thy love, saying: This is he who was dead and is alive again, was lost and is found. Therefore, O Thou lover of mankind, in Thy compassion have pity upon me also, and have mercy upon me.[91]

[88] https://web.archive.org/web/20071026094008/http://www.cired.org/, 26.

[89] Jacques Isaac, *Taksa D-Hussaya. Le rite du Pardon dans l'Église syriaque orientale*, OCA 233 (Rome: Pontificio Istituto Orientale, 1989); Bryan Spinks, "The East Syrian Rite of Penance," in *Seeking the Favor of God*, vol. 3: *The Impact of Penitential Prayer beyond Second Temple Judaism*, ed. Mark Boda, Daniel Falk, and Rodney Werline (Atlanta: Society of Biblical Literature, 2008), 213–23.

[90] George Badger, *The Nestorians and Their Rituals*, vol. 2 (London: Joseph Masters, 1852), 155.

[91] Ibid., 156.

The prayer that follows the hymnody does not grant absolution; rather, it affirms God's mercy, speaks of renewal in baptismal terms, and points to one's participation in the Eucharist as that which forgives sins, a point shared with all Eastern Christian traditions:

> Pour out Thy loving compassion upon this Thy servant [*or* servants], change him through the hope of a fresh renovation, and renew in him Thy Holy Spirit, whereby he was sealed unto the day of redemption. Confirm the hope of his faith by the help of Thy grace, direct the steps of his going in the way of righteousness, and make him finally to rejoice with the saints in Thy kingdom, by establishing in him the confidence of his faith in his adoption through the participation of Thy sin-forgiving sacraments.[92]

### *1.6.4 Coptic*

While the Coptic tradition practices private reconciliation, where both the confession of sins takes place and the absolution is granted, there is yet no official formulary; the ritual of reconciliation as currently practiced is structured around the "Three Absolutions,"[93] a set of three prayers that are recited at the end of every Coptic liturgical service, right after the Lord's Prayer.[94] What seems to emerge as the structure of the reconciliation rites in current practice would involve the Thanksgiving Prayer[95] (another prayer that is found in the beginning of almost every Coptic liturgical service), Psalm 50 (51), the Litany of the Sick, and the Three Absolution Prayers,[96] although the use of just the last of the Three Absolution Prayers is not unusual.

[92] Ibid., 156–57.

[93] *The Coptic Liturgy of St. Basil* (Cairo: St. John the Beloved Publishing House, 1993), 171–79; "Three Absolutions," in Coptic Orthodox Diocese of Southern USA, "Coptic Reader," Apple App Store, Vers. 2.84 (2020), https://apps.apple.com/us/app/coptic-reader/id649434138.

[94] For a discussion of these prayers, see Ligier, "Pénitence et Eucharistie en Orient," 32–48.

[95] *The Coptic Liturgy of St. Basil*, 7–8.

[96] John Paul Abdelsayed, "Liturgy: Heaven on Earth," in *The Coptic Christian Heritage: History, Faith, and Culture*, ed. Lois Farag (London: Routledge, 2014), 143–59, here 152; Archbishop Basilios, "Absolution," in *Claremont Coptic Encyclopedia*, https://ccdl.claremont.edu/digital/collection/cce/id/32/rec/1; O. H. E. Khs-Burmester, *The Egyptian or Coptic Church: A Detailed Description of Her Liturgical Services and the Rites and Ceremonies Observed in the Administration of Her Sacraments* (Cairo: Publications de la Société d'Archéologie Copte, 1967), 126–28.

This third prayer is titled "The Prayer of Absolution to the Son" and reads as follows:

> O Master, Lord Jesus Christ, the only-begotten Son and Logos of God the Father, who has broken every bond of our sins through His saving, life-giving, sufferings; who breathed into the face of His saintly disciples and holy apostles, and said to them, "Receive the Holy Spirit. If you forgive the sins of any, they are forgiven; if you retain the sins of any, they are retained." Now, also, O our Master, You have given grace through Your holy apostles to those who for a time labor in the priesthood in Your holy Church to forgive sin upon the earth and to bind and to loose every bond of iniquity. Now we also ask and entreat Your goodness, O Lover of Mankind, for Your servants, my fathers and my brethren, and my weakness, those who bow their heads before Your holy glory. Dispense to us Your mercy and loose every bond of our sins, and if we have committed any sin against You knowingly or unknowingly, or through anguish of heart, whether in deed or word or from faint-heartedness, O Master who knows the weakness of men as the Good One and Lover of Mankind, O God, grant us the forgiveness of sins, bless us, purify us, absolve us, and all Your people. Fill us with Your fear and strengthen us for Your holy good will.[97]

This structure of absolution prayers is also found in the celebration of the Eucharist. The Divine Liturgies of the Coptic Church (St. Basil, St. Gregory, St. Cyril) have each a set of three absolution prayers right after the recitation of the Lord's Prayer.[98] In each case the third prayer is the one that petitions for the forgiveness and absolution of the sins of the celebrants and the people. The third prayer in the Divine Liturgy of St. Gregory is titled "The Prayer of Absolution to the Son" and is the same prayer as the one quoted above. The anamnesis section of the prayer refers to John 20:22-23 (the giving of the Holy Spirit to the disciples and their power to forgive sins), and the epiclesis makes petitions that the sins of the celebrants and the people are forgiven. The Divine Liturgies of St. Basil and St. Cyril share the third prayer, titled "The Prayer of Absolution Addressed to the Father."

[97] "Three Absolutions," in Coptic Orthodox Diocese of Southern USA, "Coptic Reader"; *The Coptic Liturgy of St. Basil*, 175–77.

[98] For a discussion of these prayers, see Ligier, "Pénitence et Eucharistie en Orient," 32–48.

The anamnesis section of the prayer refers to Matthew 16:18-19 (Peter and the keys of heaven, binding and loosing sins) and Matthew 18:18-19 (binding and loosing sins), and in the epiclesis the following request is made:

> Therefore, O Lord, let Your servants, my fathers and my brethren and my own weakness, be absolved by my mouth, through Your Holy Spirit . . . hasten to accept the repentance of Your servants, for the light of knowledge and forgiveness of sins. . . . If we have sinned against You, either by word or by deeds, pardon and forgive us. . . . O God, absolve us and absolve all Your people from every sin, and from every curse, and from every denial, and from every false oath, and from every encounter with the heretics and the heathen. . . . Inscribe our names with all the choir of Your saints in the Kingdom of heaven, in Christ Jesus our Lord.[99]

An older practice, known as the "confession to the censer" has left its mark on the Divine Liturgy of the Coptic Church. While the priest would cense the church at the beginning of the Divine Liturgy, the people would each one confess their sins, and upon his return to the altar, the priest would recite the following prayer still in use, titled "The Prayer of Confession": "O God, who received the confession of the thief upon the honorable Cross, accept the confession of Your people and forgive them all their sins for the sake of Your holy name which is called upon us. According to Your mercy, O Lord, and not according to our sins."[100]

### *1.6.5 Ethiopian*

The Ethiopian tradition knows both private reconciliation and communal reconciliation as in the Coptic tradition. The modern practice includes three separate stages: the confession of sins, the imposition of penance and its accomplishment, and the absolution after the

[99] "St. Basil—Liturgy of the Faithful" in Coptic Orthodox Diocese of Southern USA, "Coptic Reader."

[100] "St. Basil—Liturgy of the Word," in Coptic Orthodox Diocese of Southern USA, "Coptic Reader."

accomplishment of the imposed penance.[101] A unique practice of communal penance takes places on Palm Sunday, after the conclusion of the Divine Liturgy, when a general absolution is given to all present in case they die during Holy Week because the priests are not allowed to do any service other than the designated Holy Week services.[102]

### *1.6.6 Armenian*

The Armenian tradition knows of a ritual of public reconciliation for penitents,[103] but it is no longer in use. Private reconciliation follows a form attributed to St. Gregory the Illuminator,[104] but its present form is most likely a later development. While a private reconciliation, the penitent acknowledges that his or her reconciliation is taking place not only before God but also before the Mother of God and the saints and, of course, the priest, making his or her confession of sin public in the sense that he or she is standing before the whole church, in an ecclesial sense. The general confession that follows is inclusive of all sins that are acknowledged as failing to keep the baptismal promises and uphold the Christian way of life:

*Priest:* In the name of the Father and of the Son and of the Holy Spirit, Amen.

*People:* I have sinned against the all-Holy Trinity, the Father, the Son and the Holy Spirit. I have sinned against God.

I confess before God, and before the Holy Mother of God, and before all the saints and before you, holy father, all the sins which I have committed; for I have sinned in thought, word, and deed, willingly and unwillingly. I have sinned against God. I have sinned against God.

[101] Emmanuel Fritsch, "Penance," in *Encyclopaedia Aethiopica*, vol. 4 (Wiesbaden: Harrassowitz Verlag, 2010), 131–33, here 131–32.

[102] Ibid., 132.

[103] Alphonse Raes, "Les Rites de la Pénitence chez les Arméniens," OCP 13 (1947): 648–55; for texts, see F. C. Conybeare, *Rituale Armenorum, Being the Administration of the Sacraments and the Breviary Rites of the Armenian Church* (Oxford: Clarendon Press, 1905), 190–220, 294–95.

[104] James Issaverdens, *The Sacred Rites and Ceremonies of the Armenian Church* (Venice: Armenian Monastery of St. Lazzaro, 1876), 405.

*Priest:* May God forgive you.

*People:* I have sinned by the seven transgressions of the deadly sins and all their forms, namely by pride, envy, anger, laziness, covetousness, gluttony and lust. I have sinned against God. I have sinned against God.

*Priest:* May God forgive you.

*People:* I have also sinned against all the commandments of God, both positive and prohibitive; for I have neither performed the positive commands, nor abstained from those things that are prohibited. I accepted the laws, but was slothful in keeping them. I was called to the profession of Christianity but was found unworthy of it by my deeds. While knowing the evil, I willingly gave in to it, and I purposely kept away from good deeds. Woe to me. Woe to me. Woe to me. Which of my misdeeds shall I recount? Which shall I confess? For my sins are innumerable. I have sinned against God. I have sinned against God.

*Priest:* May God forgive you.

*People:* Reverend Father, I hold you as reconciler and intercessor with the only-begotten Son of God, that by the authority given to you, you will release me of the bond of my sins, I ask you.

**Absolution**

*Priest:* Lord have mercy. Lord have mercy. Lord have mercy.

May God who loves humankind have mercy on you and forgive all of your sins, both those which you have confessed, as well as those which you have forgotten. Therefore, with the priestly authority committed to me and by the Lord's command that "Whatever you forgive on earth shall be forgiven in heaven," by his very word, I absolve you of all participation in sin, in thought, in word, and in deed, in the name of the Father and of the Son and of the Holy Spirit. And I reinstate you in the sacraments of the holy Church, that whatever you may do may be accounted

to you for good and for the glory of the life to come.
Amen.[105]

An interesting shift taking place in this ritual is that while the penitent makes his or her confession of sins, the priest encourages him or her by repeating, "May God forgive you," but when he moves to the prayer of absolution he shifts to "I absolve you . . . I reinstate you . . ." appealing to his priestly authority. The use of the "I absolve you . . ." formula must be a Latin influence and therefore reflect a later date of composition of this prayer. Absolution prayers in all the public rites of reconciliation for penitents do not use this Latin formula. Instead, they use expressions such as "Lord . . . do remit this man's trespasses; and bless him . . . and release him"[106] or "Lord . . . accept their repentance . . . forgive them"[107] or "let the sins . . . confessed be remitted"[108] or "Lord . . . give unto him room for repentance and pardon all his sins. . . . Welcome his return . . . and vouchsafe remission . . . and blot out his sins."[109]

### *1.6.7 Byzantine*

Private reconciliation gradually emerges in the Byzantine tradition already from the fifth to sixth centuries, but it is neither widespread nor obligatory among the laity.[110] The earliest Constantinopolitan

[105] Translation kindly provided by Fr. Hovsep Karapetian. For an older translation, see Issaverdens, *The Sacred Rites*, 405–7.

[106] Conybeare, *Rituale Armenorum*, 197; although in the following prayer the priest apparently has the power to forgive the sins committed against people of this world, while God forgives sins committed against heaven: "But howsoever he shall have sinned in the transgressions of this world . . . I have according to thy commandment remitted on earth; and in heaven has God remitted the sins of this man and of us all." Conybeare, *Rituale Armenorum*, 198–99.

[107] Ibid., 201.

[108] Ibid., 203.

[109] Ibid., 295.

[110] Robert Barringer, "Ecclesiastical Penance in the Church of Constantinople: A Study of the Hagiographical Evidence to 983 A.D." (PhD diss., University of Oxford, 1979). This dissertation is available at https://ora.ox.ac.uk/objects/uuid:8992f857-b13b-4429-86d7-ceccb1490a4e; for the Greek, see Stefano Parenti and Elena Velkovska, *L'Eucologio Barberini gr. 336*, Bibliotheca Ephemerides Liturgicae. Subsidia 80, 2nd ed. (Rome: C.L.V.-Edizioni Liturgiche, 2000), 194–95, no. 201.

penitential prayers are preserved in the eighth-century Euchologion Barberini gr. 336. Both their titles and contents point to two different moments of the reconciliation process, repentance and confession,[111] but the manuscript itself does not provide a ritual context for these prayers, so we are not sure when and how they were used.

| "Prayer for Those Who Are Repenting" | "Prayer of Those Who Are Confessing" |
|---|---|
| O God our savior, who through your prophet Nathan granted remission to David who repented for his own faults, and accepted Manasseh's prayer of repentance, | Lord our God, who granted remission of sins to Peter and the prostitute through their tears and who justified the tax collector who recognized the transgressions of his way of life, |
| also the very same, your servant N., who repents of his own transgressions, accept him according to your habitual love of humanity, ignoring his offenses. For you are Lord, the one who calls out to forgive seventy times seven those who have fallen into sins, for such is your magnanimity as well as your mercy, and you are the God of those who repent, while repenting of all our iniquities. | also accept the confession of your servant N., as you are the Good One, forgive the sins he has committed, voluntarily or involuntarily, in word, deed, or thought, because you alone have the authority to remit sins. |
| For you are our God and to you are due glory.[112] | For you remain a merciful God, one of tenderness and of love for humanity, and we send up glory.[113] |

Both prayers follow the same classic structure of anamnesis–epiclesis; they both appeal to biblical figures known for their repentance and proceed forward to the petition. The first prayer asks that God accept the person's repentance, while the second asks that God

[111] Parenti, "Confessione," 128.

[112] Translation from Robert Phoenix Jr. and Cornelia Horn, "Prayer and Penance in Early and Middle Byzantine Christianity: Some Trajectories from the Greek- and Syriac-Speaking Realms," in *Seeking the Favor of God*, vol. 3: *The Impact of Penitential Prayer beyond Second Temple Judaism*, ed. Mark Boda et al., 225–54, here 231.

[113] Translation from Phoenix and Horn, "Prayer and Penance," 235; for the Greek, see Parenti and Velkovska, *L'Eucologio Barberini gr. 336*, 195, no. 202.

accept the confession and forgive the person confessing. The hypothesis has been made that the first prayer might be a prayer used by the patriarch in his ministry in the royal court of Constantinople, because of its appeal to the example of the repentance of two biblical kings, David and Manasseh.[114]

A possible moving force behind the eventual emergence of private reconciliation rites is the appearance of the *Kanonarion*, a manual of confession attributed to Patriarch John IV the Faster (582–595).[115] Other than providing us with a list of sins and the necessary penance of each, this *Kanonarion* provides a short reconciliation rite. It opens with Psalm 69 (LXX) and the *Trisagion*, and then the one who hears the confession is encouraged to pray with the penitent, followed by the confession. A short prayer seals the end of confession, followed by the assignment of the proper penance.[116] The text does not specify the ecclesiastical status of the one hearing the confession and thus leaves open the possibility that a nonordained person might hear the confession.[117] The author identifies himself as John the monk and deacon. In fact, the tradition of having a spiritual director among the nonordained monastics is not unknown, even in current practice.[118] The spiritual director here assumes the role of the sponsor (as at baptism) who shares with the sinner the responsibility and the burden of the latter's sins.[119]

The earliest private reconciliation rites appear in the tenth and eleventh centuries in South Italian manuscripts. These are characterized by the presence of multiple prayers for reconciliation, many

[114] Phoenix and Horn, "Prayer and Penance," 233.

[115] Frans van de Paverd, *The Kanonarion by John, Monk and Deacon, and Didascalia Patrum*, Kanonika 12 (Rome: Pontificio Istituto Orientale, 2006).

[116] The prayer reads as follows: "God, who for our sake became man and bears the sins of the whole world, he himself, in his all-good kindness, brother, will take upon him all to what you now in his sight have confessed to my unworthiness, forgiving you all in this and the future world. He who wishes, awaits and dispenses the salvation of all. 'He who is blessed forever' (2 Cor 11:31)." See (for the whole rite and this prayer) van de Paverd, *The Kanonarion*, 54–55.

[117] Neither is the ecclesiastical status of the confessor mentioned, nor is there any indication of clerical vestments (priestly stole) used, leaving the possibility open of a non-ordained confessor.

[118] Rapp, "Spiritual Guarantors," 124, citing Paul Meyendorff, "Penance in the Orthodox Church Today," *Studia Liturgica* 18 (1988): 108–11, here 110.

[119] Parenti, "Confessione," 125.

having their origin in the Middle East and some bearing the marks of contemporary Western usage.[120] The variety of reconciliation prayers in the manuscript tradition[121] came to an abrupt end with the emergence of the printing press, which standardized texts. The current rite of reconciliation has the form of a short office: opening blessing, petitions, the *Trisagion*, Psalm 50, penitential hymns, and an expanded version of the "Prayer for Those Who Are Repenting" that we saw above. After the prayer, the actual confession of sins takes place, accompanied by ritualized words of encouragement by the confessor such as "Brother (Sister), be not ashamed that you have come to God and to me: for it is not to me that you confess, but to God, before whom you stand." After the confession of sins, the following two prayers are read:

> My spiritual child, who did confess to my lowliness: it is not I, lowly and sinful, who have the power to forgive sins upon the earth, but God. But through that divine voice which spoke to the Apostles after the resurrection of our Lord Jesus Christ, saying: "If you forgive the sins of any, they are forgiven; if you retain the sins of any, they are retained," taking confidence from this we also say: Whatsoever you have confessed to my abject lowliness, and whatsoever you did not mention, whether from ignorance or from forgetfulness, may God forgive you, both in the present age and in that to come.
>
> O God, who did forgive David the sins which he confessed through the prophet Nathan, and Peter the denial he bitterly bewailed, and the sinful woman who wept at Your feet, and the publican, and the prodigal son: may the same God forgive you all through me a sinner, in this age and in that to come; and may He present you blameless before His fearful judgement-seat. Take no thought for the sins which have been forgiven you, but go in peace.[122]

[120] Ibid., 128–29.

[121] Miguel Arranz has collected the manuscript evidence in Miguel Arranz, "Les prières pénitentielles de la tradition byzantine. Les sacrements de la restauration de l'ancien euchologe constantinopolitain II-2," OCP 57 (1991); 87–143, 309–29; 58 (1992): 23–82; Miguel Arranz, "Les formulaires de confession dans la tradition byzantine. Les sacrements de la restauration de l'ancien euchologe constantinopolitain II-3," OCP 58 (1992): 423–59; 59 (1993): 63–89, 357–86. For a critique of Arranz's methodology, see Parenti, "Confessione," 115.

[122] John Chryssavgis, *Repentance and Confession in the Orthodox Church* (Brookline, MA: Holy Cross Orthodox Press, 1996), 95–100. While this is the given ritual, many

In both prayers, the priest confesses his own sinfulness and inadequacy, presenting himself as a sojourner in the struggle against sin. In fact, the relationship between the confessor and the one confessing is supposed to be a lifelong relationship of spiritual direction,[123] an ongoing conversation assisting in the lifelong process of repentance, sharing the burden of sin, listening, cosuffering, and prayer with the penitent. It is a relationship of companionship,[124] whose emphasis is on healing rather than punishing.[125] By appealing to God's forgiveness in the cases of David (a king), Peter (a disciple), the sinful woman, the publican, and the prodigal son, the prayer is inclusive of all walks of life, pointing to the reality of sin, on the one hand, no matter who one is, but also to the reality of God's forgiving love and acceptance.

### *1.6.8 Conclusion*

The sacrament of repentance is in crisis in the current practice of Eastern Christian churches. The comments of John Chryssavgis are applicable not only to the Byzantine tradition but to all Eastern traditions:

> Confession is in decline and repentance is misapprehended. The decline and misapprehension cannot be easily qualified, but they are unmistakable at least inasmuch as they are considered to be no more than incidental practices in the life of the Church today. The "traditional" way of thinking of sin and forgiveness has collapsed among a growing number of Christians. Nothing less than a theological and pastoral renewal is necessary in order to rediscover the living meaning of repentance and confession. . . . There is a need to appeal to the deepening of repentance and confession as spiritual realities rather

---

priests today amend the ritual by abbreviating it or adding prayers of their choosing; the ritual is understood more as a guideline rather than prescriptive. Confession of sins usually takes place within the context of spiritual guidance in dialogue with the person confessing, although the use of questionnaires is not unknown.

[123] John Chryssavgis, *Soul Mending: The Art of Spiritual Direction* (Brookline, MA: Holy Cross Orthodox Press, 2000).

[124] Nicholas Denysenko, "Orthodox Confession: Receiving Forgiveness for the Life of the World," *Liturgy* 34 (2019): 3–11, here 8.

[125] Enrico Mazza, "La celebrazione della penitenza nella liturgia bizantina e in Occidente: due concezioni a confronto," *Ephemerides Liturgicae* 115 (2001): 385–440.

than their imposition as obligatory customs. It is only in a realization of the nature of sacramental life that repentance acquires its significance as a way of renewal and reconciliation in Christ.[126]

[126] Chryssavgis, *Repentance and Confession*, 3.

# *Chapter 2*

# The Eucharistic Liturgies

The eucharistic liturgies of the Churches of the Christian East are known by a variety of different titles, each title emphasizing a particular liturgical understanding of the Mystery being celebrated.[1] The Byzantine Rite uses the terminology of *Theia Leitourgia*, "the Divine Liturgy." Among the Syrians, Armenians, and Copts the title of the liturgy underscores its sacrificial or offering character with the use of *Qurbana* (Syriac), *Surb Patarag* (Armenian), or *Prosfora* (Coptic). For the East Syrians and Ethiopians the titles *Qedussah* or *Keddase* reflect the overall influence of the Sanctus and the process of the sanctification of the eucharistic gifts and communicants.[2] In our introduction we presented the concept of liturgical "soft spots" and their propensity to attract various additional elements to themselves, often with the result of making the earlier liturgical units at the entrance, transfer of the eucharistic gifts to the altar, and the time of Communion (all actions accompanied by chants and concluded by collects) difficult to uncover or discern. Stefano Parenti has noted that in comparison with Western liturgies, particularly that of the Roman Rite, the Eastern liturgies differ primarily in the various verbal elements added to these "soft spots."[3] With the addition of the Liturgies of the Word

[1] See the classic study of Irénée-Henri Dalmais, *Eastern Liturgies*, Twentieth Century Encyclopedia of Catholicism, vol. 112 (New York: Hawthorne Books, 1960), 75–95.

[2] For the Ethiopian title especially, see Gabriele Winkler, *Das Sanctus: Über den Ursprung und die Anfänge des Sanctus und sein Fortwirken*, OCA 267 (Rome: Pontificio Istituto Orientale, 2002), 196ff.

[3] Stefano Parenti, "The Eucharistic Liturgy in the East: The Various Orders of Celebration," in *Handbook for Liturgical Studies*, vol. 3: *The Eucharist*, ed. Anscar J. Chupungco (Collegeville, MN: Liturgical Press, Pueblo, 1999), 62. Parenti's essay has served here as a guide for portions of this chapter. Another very helpful resource is Bryan D. Spinks, *Do This in Remembrance of Me: The Eucharist from the Early Church to the Present Day* (London: SCM Press, 2013), 68–189.

and the various Eastern anaphoras, our presentation of the Eastern rites here will follow those "soft spots" primarily. Because the Byzantine Rite is the dominant, largest, and most influential liturgical tradition of and in the Christian East, it will often be our point of reference and model for our comparative presentation.

Before proceeding, however, we want to draw attention to some of the unique characteristics of the eucharistic liturgy within each of the rites. And a major characteristic that needs to be noted immediately is that with regard to the eucharistic liturgies the particular eucharistic prayers (anaphoras or prosphoras) used in those rites often give their names to the entire liturgy itself (e.g., the "Divine Liturgy of St. John Chrysostom or St. Basil," or "The Liturgy of St. James"). Similarly, these various anaphoras themselves are structured according to patterns called "West Syrian," "Antiochene," or "Syro-Byzantine," along with "East Syrian" and "Alexandrian," although many of these types, through cross-fertilization and influence, can be found in more than one tradition. The following chart outlines these structures and their representative anaphoras:

## Table 2.1: Anaphoral Structure (East)

| ***Antiochene/ West Syrian*** | ***East Syrian*** | ***Alexandrian*** |
|---|---|---|
| Preface | Preface | Preface |
| Sanctus/Benedictus | Sanctus/Benedictus | *Offering-Intercessions* |
| Post-Sanctus | Post-Sanctus | Sanctus (no Benedictus) |
| Institution Narrative | Institution Narrative[4] | *Epiclesis I (Fill . . .)* |
| Anamnesis | Anamnesis | Institution Narrative (*For . . .*) |
| Epiclesis | *Intercessions* | Anamnesis |
| Intercessions | *Epiclesis* | *Epiclesis II* |
| Doxology | Doxology | Doxology |

[4] The earliest text of Addai and Mari, most scholars would claim today, did not have an institution narrative. See below, 68–69.

**Eastern Anaphoras According to Types**

| | | |
|---|---|---|
| Apostolic Tradition | Addai and Mari | Strasbourg Papyrus |
| St. Basil (all versions) | St. Peter (*Sharar*) | Louvain Coptic Papyrus |
| St. James | | John Rylands Papyrus |
| Cyril of Jerusalem (?) | | Cyril of Jerusalem (?) |
| Apostolic Constitutions, Bk 8 | | Deir Balizeh Papyrus |
| Twelve Apostles | | Sarapion of Thmuis |
| St. John Chrysostom | | St. Mark<br>St. Cyril (= Coptic Mark)<br>St. Gregory Nazianzen |

**Eastern Anaphoras According to Rites**

| | | |
|---|---|---|
| Armenian | East Syrian | Coptic |
| Byzantine | Maronite | Ethiopian |
| West Syrian | | |
| (Coptic) | | |
| (Maronite) | | |

## 2.1 Characteristics of the Individual Rites

### *2.1.1 The Armenian Rite*

The Divine Liturgy (*Surb Patarag*) in the Armenian Rite is celebrated today using only one eucharistic prayer, that of the Anaphora of Athanasius (Patriarch of Alexandria),[5] but historically that was not always the case. The oldest Armenian anaphora is the Anaphora of Gregory the Illuminator, which, as has been demonstrated, is an Armenian translation from the beginning of the fifth century of an early version of the Anaphora of Basil that actually predates both the Byzantine and the Coptic versions of the Anaphora of Basil.[6] By the

[5] For text see below, 81–85.

[6] Hieronymus Engberding, *Das eucharistische Hochgebet der Basileiosliturgie. Textgeschichtliche Untersuchungen und kritische Ausgabe*, Theologie des christlichen Ostens 1 (Münster: Aschendoff, 1931); and Gabriele Winkler, *Die Basilius-Anaphora: Edition der*

end of the same century other anaphoras were translated or composed, such as the Anaphora of Sahak, the Anaphora of Gregory of Nazianzen, the Anaphora of Cyril, along with Athanasius. It is this last one that by the end of the ninth century became the dominant one in the Armenian Rite, and today it is the only one used. A study of this anaphora reveals that (1) it is dependent on the oldest Armenian redaction of the Anaphora of Basil; (2) it bears the signs of significant Syrian influence; and (3) it reflects a secondary Byzantine influence.[7] Later translations of other anaphoras appear in the manuscript tradition, such as the Anaphora of Ignatius, the Anaphora of James, the Anaphora of Chrysostom, the Anaphora of Basil (an Armenian translation of the Byzantine version of Basil), and the Roman *Ordo Missae*, as well as the Byzantine Lenten Liturgy of the Presanctified Gifts. It is doubtful, however, that all of these were actually used.

A unique characteristic of the celebration of the Eucharist in the Armenian liturgical tradition is that it uses unleavened bread. This practice is not due to Latin influence; on the contrary, the Armenian liturgical tradition is the only Christian tradition that has been doing so from the very beginning; there is documentation of the Armenian use of unleavened bread centuries before its introduction in the Latin Rite. In addition, the wine it uses in the celebration of the Divine Liturgy is unmixed wine. Both of these usages possibly reflect the Armenian cultural context. Another particularly unique Armenian characteristic is that the Liturgy of the Word (i.e., the first part of the Divine Liturgy) was, up to the twelfth century, associated more with the Liturgy of the Hours than with the beginning of the Divine Liturgy. Not only is this part absent or underrepresented in manuscripts of the Divine Liturgy predating the twelfth century; it is actually dealt with in liturgical commentaries of the Liturgy of the Hours such as that of Bishop Step'anos Siwnec'i (†735).[8]

---

*beiden armenischen Redaktionen und der relevanten Fragmente, Übersetzung und Zusammenschau aller Versionen im Licht der orientalischen Überlieferungen*, Anaphorae Orientales 2, Anaphorae Armeniacae 2 (Rome: Pontificio Istituto Orientale, 2005). And see below, 86–90, 96–99.

[7] Hans-Jürgen Feulner, *Die armenische Athanasius-Anaphora. Kritische Edition, Übersetzung und liturgievergleichender Kommentar*, Anaphorae Orientales 1, Anaphorae Armeniacae 1 (Rome: Pontificio Istituto Orientale, 2001), 189, 209.

[8] Michael Daniel Findikyan, *The Commentary on the Armenian Daily Office by Bishop Step'anos Siwnec'i (†735): Critical Edition and Translation with Textual and Liturgical Analysis*, OCA 270 (Rome: Pontificio Istituto Orientale, 2004), 437–69.

### 2.1.2 The Byzantine Rite

As in all of the Eastern rites, the celebration of the Divine Liturgy (*Theia Leitourgia*) is central to the faith, life, and spirituality of the Byzantine liturgical tradition. In current practice the Anaphora of St. John Chrysostom is celebrated most often,[9] with the Anaphora of Byzantine Basil (ByzBAS)[10] reserved for ten days a year: the five Sundays of Lent, Holy Thursday, Easter Vigil, the eve of Christmas, the eve of Epiphany, and January 1, the feast of St. Basil. Before the tenth century, however, the Anaphora of Basil was the dominant one, with that of Chrysostom (CHR) reserved for Saturdays and weekdays. It was in the tenth century that this important shift took place, with the anaphora of CHR displacing that of BAS.[11] ByzBAS, reflecting Basil's own theological work, is rich in theology and ecclesiology; "the petition for the building up of the church by 'the one bread and the one cup into the koinonia of the Holy Spirit' shows how a pneumatological ecclesiology and eucharistic ecclesiology inseparably condition one another."[12] The importance of ByzBAS is also highlighted by the fact that it is present, in various versions, in virtually all languages and liturgical traditions of the Christian East and is indicative of its central place in the history and theology of the Eucharist.[13] As with ByzBAS it has also been claimed by Robert Taft that authorship attribution in CHR reflects a historical reality, that is, that CHR is the end result of the editorial work of John Chrysostom himself.

[9] See the recent and long-awaited study by Stefano Parenti, *L'Anafora di Crisostomo: Testo e contesti*, Jerusalemer Theologisches Forum 36 (Münich: Aschendorff Verlagen, 2020).

[10] For texts of Basil and Chrysostom anaphoras, see below, 86–93.

[11] On the possible reasons behind this shift, see Stefanos Alexopoulos, "The Influence of Iconoclasm on Byzantine Liturgy: A Case Study," in *Worship Traditions in Armenia and the Neighboring Christian East*, ed. Roberta Ervine, AVANT: Treasures of the Armenian Christian Tradition 3 (Crestwood, NY: St. Vladimir's Seminary Press/ St. Nersess Armenian Seminary, 2006), 127–37; and Stefano Parenti, "La 'vittoria' nella chiesa di Costantinopoli della liturgia di Crisostomo sulla liturgia di Basilio," in *Comparative Liturgy Fifty Years After Anton Baumstark*, ed. Taft and Winkler, 907–28.

[12] Hans-Joachim Schulz, *The Byzantine Liturgy: Symbolic Structure and Faith Expression* (New York: Pueblo, 1986), 150.

[13] See above, footnote 6. See also Achim Budde, *Die ägyptische Basilios-Anaphora, Text-Kommentar Geschichte* (Münster: Aschendorff, 2004); and Anne Vorhes McGowan, "The Basilian Anaphoras: Rethinking the Question," in *Issues in Eucharistic Praying in East and West: Essays in Liturgical and Theological Analysis*, ed. Maxwell E. Johnson (Collegeville, MN: Liturgical Press, Pueblo, 2010), 219–62.

While Taft's comparative study of CHR and the Syriac Anaphora of the Twelve Apostles argues that both share a common underlying text,[14] phrases and stylistic features found in CHR are also found *only* in works of Chrysostom and hence it was Chrysostom himself who reworked Twelve Apostles into CHR.[15] Stefano Parenti's recent work, however, *L'Anafora di Crisostomo*,[16] challenges Taft's conclusions that Chrysostom himself is responsible for reworking Twelve Apostles, pointing out that the attribution to Chrysostom likely occurred significantly after his life (between the mid-sixth and eighth centuries), and suggests that alternative theories could likewise explain the various concurrences noted by Taft (e.g., later insertion of quotations from Chrysostom into CHR). At the same time, whether this text had anything to do with Chrysostom or not, from a stylistic point of view, CHR remains an example of a very carefully executed work of Christian literary art.[17]

Oftentimes, the so-called Liturgy of the Presanctified Gifts is numbered among the liturgies celebrated in the Byzantine liturgical tradition. Reserved for the weekdays of Great Lent, when the eucharistic celebration is not allowed, people have the opportunity to receive Holy Communion in the context of the Presanctified. This service is not a Divine Liturgy *per se* as it lacks an anaphora; it is a communion office attached to Vespers, in the context of which Holy Communion reserved from the previous Sunday celebration is distributed. Originally it could be used for *all* fasting days, including Wednesdays and Fridays of the year, but in current practice it is reserved for Wednesdays and Fridays of Great Lent and for Holy Monday, Tuesday, and Wednesday of Holy Week.[18]

The Byzantine celebration of the Divine Liturgy bears the marks of Constantinople, the city in which it was celebrated, and Hagia Sophia, the church in which it grew and was formed. For example,

[14] John Fenwick, *'The Missing Oblation': The Contents of the Early Antiochene Anaphora*, AGLS 11 (Bramcote, Nottingham: Grove Books, 1989).

[15] Robert Taft, "The Authenticity of the Chrysostom Anaphora Revisited: Determining the Authorship of Liturgical Texts by Computer," OCP 56 (1990): 5–51.

[16] Parenti, *L'Anafora di Crisostomo*.

[17] See Daniel Sheerin, "The Anaphora of the Liturgy of St. John Chrysostom: Stylistic Notes," in *Language and the Worship of the Church*, ed. David Jasper and R. C. D. Jasper (London: Macmillan Press, 1990), 44–81.

[18] Stefanos Alexopoulos, *The Presanctified Liturgy in the Byzantine Rite: A Comparative Analysis of Its Origins, Evolution, and Structural Components*, Liturgia Condenda 21 (Leuven: Peeters, 2009).

the opening of the Byzantine liturgy, i.e., the office of the three antiphons and the so-called Little Entrance in current practice (that is, the procession of the clergy with the Gospel book out of the altar, through the church, and back into the altar), has its origins in the liturgical processions in Constantinople and the original entrance of clergy and people in the church that would signify the beginning of the Divine Liturgy.[19] The other procession in the celebration of the Byzantine liturgy is the so-called Great Entrance, or the transfer of the gifts of bread and wine from the *Prothesis* (preparation table) within the altar, through the church, in the altar again and their placement on the altar table. This transfer of gifts has its origins in the church plan of Hagia Sophia, where the gifts were prepared in a building adjacent to Hagia Sophia and at the proper time were brought from outside *into* the church and placed on the altar for the celebration of the Eucharist to take place.[20] In both cases we are dealing with "soft" points (see the introduction), and in both cases the terminology for these processions used today, Small *Entrance* and Great *Entrance*, reveal their original function; both were real entrances into the church: the first of the clergy and people to celebrate the Divine Liturgy, and the second of the gifts of bread and wine to be offered in the celebration of the Divine Liturgy.

### *2.1.3 The Coptic Rite*

In the current liturgical practice of the Coptic Church three anaphoras are in use: the anaphora called Egyptian Basil (EgBAS), the Anaphora of Gregory Nazianzen, and the Anaphora of Cyril (Mark in Greek). In current practice, however, EgBAS is predominantly used, with Gregory, used during the Easter season and on other christological feasts; the anaphora of Cyril is rarely used. EgBAS

[19] Juan Mateos, *La célébration de la parole dans la liturgie byzantine: Étude historique*, OCA 191 (Rome: Pontificium Institutum Studiorum Orientalium, 1971), 29–31. ET by Steven Hawkes-Teeples, *A History of the Liturgy of St. John Chrysostom*; vol. 1: *The Liturgy of the Word* (Fairfax: Eastern Christian Publications, 2016). See also John Baldovin, *The Urban Character of Christian Worship: The Origins, Development, and Meaning of Stational Liturgy*, OCA 228 (Rome: Pontificium Institutum Studiorum Orientalium, 1987), 167–226.

[20] See Robert Taft, *A History of the Liturgy of St. John Chrysostom*, vol. 2: *The Great Entrance: A History of the Transfer of Gifts and Other Pre-anaphoral Rites*, 4th ed., OCA 200 (Rome: Pontificio Istituto Orientale, 1975).

is regarded as an earlier version of ByzBAS. The current hypothesis is that Basil possibly brought with him the anaphora used in Cappadocia while he was in Egypt (thus the Egyptian version is attributed to Basil), and later Basil himself reworked and expanded that same Cappadocian anaphora, thus giving rise to ByzBAS. The Anaphora of Gregory is unique in that it is addressed to the Son. It is a lengthy anaphora, in which various phases of editing can be discerned. In its original form it was an anti-Arian anaphora from Cappadocia, which explains why it is addressed to the Son. In the next stage, an editor expanded it with anti-Nestorian statements, and, finally, in the third stage, the anaphora was indigenized in Egypt, thus giving to it local character. The Anaphora of Cyril (Mark), on the other hand, follows the Egyptian anaphoral structure. This unique anaphoral structure has its roots in the indigenous Egyptian tradition of anaphoral prayers, as seen in documents that reflect either an earlier version of the Anaphora of Cyril (Mark) or other Egyptian anaphoras or remnants of anaphoras; such documents are the Strasbourg Papyrus, the Louvain Coptic Papyrus, the John Rylands Papyrus, the Deir Balizeh Papyrus, the Barcelona Papyrus,[21] and the anaphora in the Euchologion of Sarapion of Thmuis; others yet see an anaphoral relationship between the liturgical tradition of Alexandria and Rome.[22]

### 2.1.4 The Ethiopian Rite

Unlike the Coptic liturgical tradition, the Ethiopian liturgical tradition knows no fewer than twenty anaphoras.[23] These are (1) the

[21] For the recent discussion on this text, see Michael Zheltov, "The Anaphora and the Thanksgiving Prayer from the Barcelona Papyrus: An Underestimated Testimony to the Anaphoral History in the Fourth Century," *Vigiliae Christianae* 62 (2008): 467–504; Paul Bradshaw's response, "The Barcelona Papyrus and the Development of Early Eucharistic Prayers," in *Issues in Eucharistic Praying*, ed. Johnson, 129–38; and especially Nathan Chase, "Rethinking Anaphoral Development in Light of the Barcelona Papyrus" (PhD diss., University of Notre Dame, 2020).

[22] Walter Ray, "Rome and Alexandria: Two Cities, One Anaphoral Tradition," in *Issues in Eucharistic Praying*, ed. Johnson, 99–127. On the Anaphora of St. Gregory of Nazianzen see Nicholas Newman, *The Liturgy of Saint Gregory the Theologian: Critical Text with Translation and Commentary* (Belleville, IL: Saint Dominic's Media, 2019).

[23] For texts in English, see *The Liturgy of the Ethiopian Church*, trans. Marcos Daoud and revised by H. E. Blatta Marsie Hazen (originally published in 1959; repr. Kingston, Jamaica: Ethiopian Orthodox Church, 1991, reedited 2006). For a recent study,

Anaphora of the Apostles, (2) the Anaphora of our Lord, Jesus Christ, (3) the Anaphora of Our Lady Mary by Cyriacus, (4) the Anaphora of Dioscorus, (5) the Anaphora of John Chrysostom, (6) the Anaphora of John the Evangelist, (7) the Anaphora of James, the Brother of the Lord, (8) the Hosanna-Liturgy of Gregory, (9) the Christmas Liturgy of Gregory, (10) the Anaphora of Our Lady Mary by Gregory, (11) the alternative Anaphora of Our Lady Mary by Gregory, (12) the Anaphora of the 318 Orthodox, (13) the Anaphora of Basil, (14) the Anaphora of Athanasius, (15) the Anaphora of Epiphanius, (16) the longer Anaphora of Cyril, (17) the shorter Anaphora of Cyril, (18) the Anaphora of James of Serug, (19) the Anaphora of Mark, and (20) the Anaphora of Our Lady Mary. According to the study of E. Hammerschmidt, only five of these anaphoras have a very clear structure: the Anaphora of the Apostles and the Anaphora of Mark clearly have the Alexandrian-type structure, while the Anaphora of Our Lord, Jesus Christ, the Anaphora of Basil, and the Anaphora of James have the West-Syrian type of anaphoral construction. In addition, while the anaphoras of the Apostles and of Our Lord are of considerable antiquity and are related to the so-called *Apostolic Tradition*, ascribed to Hippolytus and the *Testamentum Domini*,[24] the anaphoras of Basil, James, and Mark are clearly the product of translations of the above anaphoras into Geᶜez. Regarding the other anaphoras, the "poetical element predominates and often conceals the clearness of structure."[25] An example of the unique creativity of the Ethiopian anaphoras is the Anaphora of Our Lady Mary by Cyriacus. This anaphora "exceeds all proportions and violates the normal structure of classical liturgy. The Eucharistic Thanksgiving consists mainly of praise of Mary, put in the framework of a Eucharistic Liturgy."[26] Additional striking

---

see Emmanuel Fritsch, "The Anaphoras of the Geᶜez Churches: A Challenging Orthodoxy," in *The Anaphoral Genesis of the Institution Narrative in Light of the Anaphora of Addai and Mari*, ed. Cesare Giraudo, OCA 295 (Rome: Edizioni Orientalia Christiana, 2013), 275–315.

[24] E. Hammerschmidt, *Studies in the Ethiopic Anaphoras*, 2nd rev. ed., Äthiopistische Forschungen 25 (Stuttgart: Franz Steiner Verlag Wiesbaden, 1987), 75. On the *Apostolic Tradition*, see Paul Bradshaw, Maxwell Johnson, and L. Edward Phillips, *The Apostolic Tradition: A Commentary*, Hermeneia (Minneapolis: Fortress Press, 2002). On the *Testamentum Domini*, see Grant Sperry-White, *The Testamentum Domini: A Text for Students, with Introduction, Translation, and Notes*, AGLS 19, GLS 66 (Bramcote, Nottingham: Grove Books, 1991).

[25] Hammerschmidt, *Studies in the Ethiopic Anaphoras*, 58.

[26] Ibid., 75.

characteristics of this particular anaphora are the double appearance of the Sanctus and the Creed.

### *2.1.5 The East Syrian Rite*

The East Syrian Rite currently uses three anaphoras: the Anaphora of Nestorius, the Anaphora of Theodore the Interpreter (Mopsuestia), and the Anaphora of Addai and Mari. The origins of the first two are not certain but were possibly compiled or edited in the sixth century by Mar Aba I. The Anaphora of Nestorius bears some literary relationship with the anaphoras of CHR and BAS and is used five times a year: on Epiphany, the Friday of St. John the Baptist, the feast of the Greek Fathers, the Wednesday of the fast of the Ninevites, and Holy Thursday. The Anaphora of Theodore was possibly inspired by that of Nestorius, Addai and Mari, and the liturgical homilies of Theodore of Mopsuestia. It is used from the first Sunday of the Annunciation/Nativity period until the Sunday of Hosanna. These two anaphoras follow the distinct East Syrian anaphoral structure.

The Anaphora of Addai and Mari is the main anaphora used and it is attributed to the Apostle Addai and his disciple Mari, who according to tradition evangelized Edessa. A unique characteristic of this anaphora is that it lacks the institution narrative, and, from after the Sanctus on, it is addressed directly to Christ. Although earlier scholarship argued that originally there must have been an institution narrative that was later taken out (possibly during the reforms of Išoʿyahb III in the seventh century), the current scholarly consensus points to the fact that the absence of the institution narrative is one of the archaic features, characteristic of very early anaphoras, as the institution narrative is a later embolism to the anaphoral structure. Dated to the beginning of the third century, it is the earliest extant anaphora and the earliest still in actual use.[27] The words of institution have been inserted in liturgical use of the Chaldean and the Syro-Malabar Churches. Related to the Anaphora of Addai and Mari is the Anaphora of Peter III or "Sharrar" of the Maronite Rite where the third section of the anaphora is reworked to include an institution

[27] In addition to A. Gelston, *The Eucharistic Prayer of Addai and Mari* (Oxford: Clarendon Press, 1992), 65–76, and Bryan Spinks, *Addai and Mari—The Anaphora of the Apostles: A Text for Students*, GLS 24 (Cambridge: Grove Books, 1980), see the recent collection of essays on precisely this topic in *Anaphoral Genesis*, ed. Giraudo.

narrative. In a historic agreement sealed by the 2001 document titled "Guidelines for the Admission to the Eucharist between the Chaldean Church and the Assyrian Church of the East," the Roman Catholic Church recognized the Anaphora of Addai and Mari as a valid and full eucharistic prayer, even without the explicit recital of the institution narrative.[28]

A unique liturgical tradition of the East Syrian Rite is that of the *Malka*, or the Mystery of the Holy Leaven.[29] The *Malka* is a special dough powder, a portion of which is added to the dough of the eucharistic bread before it is baked (it should be noted that the preparation and the baking of the eucharistic bread is the responsibility of the priest). The *Malka* is believed to originate from the Last Supper, where a portion of the bread broken and distributed by Christ to the apostles was saved, and since that time a portion of that must be part of the bread prepared for the *Holy Qurbana*, the Eucharist. The *Malka* is renewed every Holy Thursday and is considered a sacrament. It acts both as a sign of continuity and unity with Christ and the apostles and as a visible sign of unity within the Church of the East. Characteristically, one of the prayers recited at the renewal of the *Malka* says:

> Signed and sanctified and mixed is this new leaven with this holy and old leaven of our Lord Jesus Christ, which has been handed down to us from our spiritual fathers, Mar Mari and Mar Addai and Mar Thoma, the blessed Apostles, teachers of this Eastern Country, and has been carried from place to place and from country to country for the perfecting and the mixing of the living Bread of the life-giving mysteries, as often as reason of necessity requires, in the name of the Father and of the Son, and of the Holy Ghost. [30]

[28] Robert Taft, "Mass Without the Consecration? The Historic Agreement on the Eucharist between the Catholic Church and the Assyrian Church of the East Promulgated 26 October 2001," *Worship* 77, no. 6 (2003): 482–509. See also Nicholas Russo, "The Validity of the Anaphora of *Addai and Mari:* Critique of the Critiques," in *Issues in Eucharistic Praying*, ed. Johnson, 21–62.

[29] In addition to Bryan Spinks, "The Mystery of Holy Leaven (*Malkā*) in the East Syrian Tradition," in *Issues in Eucharistic Praying*, ed. Johnson, 63–70, see Mar Awa Royel, "The Sacrament of the Holy Leaven (*Malka*) in the Assyrian Church of the East," in *Anaphoral Genesis*, ed. Giraudo, 363–86. See also See Alex C. J. Neroth van Vogelpoel, "Known in the Baking of the Bread: The Preparation of the Eucharistic Gifts in the East Syriac Tradition" (PhD diss., University of Notre Dame, anticipated 2021).

[30] Spinks, "The Mystery of Holy Leaven," 68–69.

### *2.1.6 The West Syrian Rite*

For the celebration of the *Qurbona* (the Eucharist) the West Syrian Rite has displayed a remarkable creativity: more than eighty different anaphoras are attested to in the manuscript tradition, dating from the seventh to the fifteenth century, others translated from Greek and others originally written in Syriac. Two of the most important anaphoras are the Anaphora of James (SyrJAS) and the Anaphora of the Twelve Apostles. SyrJAS, which functions as the major anaphora, is a translation of the Greek Anaphora of James (GrJAS) made sometime between the fifth and the seventh centuries, reflecting the strong influence of Jerusalem, whose liturgy was known as the "Liturgy of St. James" and is still celebrated in Greek on the Feast of St. James (October 23) by the Church of Greece. A significant difference between the GrJAS and the SyrJAS is that in the latter the intercessions are arranged in a structure of six units, each dedicated to a particular group: (1) Orthodox Hierarchs; (2) the Living; (3) Kings and Rulers; (4) the Virgin Mary, Apostles, and Saints; (5) Fathers of the Church; and (6) the Departed, whereas in GrJAS the intercessions are just one prayer. Each unit consists of one prayer said silently by the priest, one prayer said audibly by the deacon, followed by a prayer said audibly by the priest. The Anaphora of the Twelve Apostles is the Syriac counterpart to the Byzantine Anaphora of CHR. It is much less elaborate, but their relationship is complex: most likely both are dependent on an earlier form now lost.[31] SyrJAS and Twelve Apostles have functioned as sources for the numerous other anaphoras.

### *2.1.7 The Maronite Rite*

An anaphora currently being restored to use, and a traditional part of the Maronite tradition, is that of St. Peter (III), more commonly referred to by its first word in Syriac, "Sharar."[32] This anaphora is the

[31] Robert Taft, "Some Structural Problems in the Syriac Anaphora of the Twelve Apostles I," in *A Festschrift for Dr. Sebastian P. Brock, ARAM Periodical* 5 (1993): 505–20.

[32] See Augustin Mouhanna, "La troisième anaphore de Saint Pierre Apôtre, dite *Šarrar*, en usage dans l'Église Maronite," in *Anaphoral Genesis*, ed. Giraudo, 237–58; and Bryan Spinks, "A Tale of Two Anaphoras: Addai and Mari and Maronite Sharar," in *Anaphoral Genesis*, ed. Giraudo, 259–74. For the text of Addai and Mari, see below, 104–7.

Maronite version of the Anaphora of Addai and Mari but includes, after the Sanctus, an institution narrative and anamnesis. Thanks to the initial work of William Macomber,[33] liturgical scholars now see this text as sharing a common source with Addai and Mari[34] and reflecting not a West Syrian but an East Syrian structure, with the epiclesis of the Holy Spirit coming after rather than before the intercessions. After the Sanctus, *Sharar*, like Addai and Mari throughout, is addressed directly to Christ, a sure sign of its antiquity, and it may actually preserve in some instances (e.g., in the epiclesis) an earlier version of the text than does Addai and Mari. Scholars have also noted in *Sharar* the influence of another East Syrian anaphora called Theodore the Interpreter.[35]

The current anaphoras are fourteen in number and include the Anaphora of the Twelve Apostles, another Anaphora of Peter (I), JAS, the Anaphora of the Roman Church (the Roman *canon missae*),[36] and, increasingly, the use of *Sharar*. On the one hand, an example of the Latinization that the Maronite Rite has undergone is the emphasis on the words of institution as the moment of consecration, both in the bold print in the euchology and in the manual acts of the priest, but, on the other, these same words of institution are usually recited in Aramaic. This binary relationship expresses the tension and the effort of the Maronite Church to recover and underscore its Syriac heritage while remaining faithful to Roman norms.

## 2.2 Preliminary Rites and the Liturgy of the Word

Before the liturgies proper begin with elements such as opening blessings, hymns, and litanies immediately before the Liturgy of the Word, all of the Eastern rites have elaborate rites of preparation (called the *Prothesis* in the Byzantine Rite) of the eucharistic gifts of

[33] William Macomber, "The Maronite and Chaldean Versions of the Anaphora of the Apostles," OCP 37 (1971), 55–84; and idem, "A Theory on the Origins of the Syrian, Maronite, and Chaldean Rites," OCP 39 (1973): 235–42.

[34] See Spinks, *Addai and Mari*; and Gelston, *The Eucharistic Prayer of Addai and Mari*.

[35] See Bryan Spinks, *Mar Nestorius and Mar Theodore the Interpreter: The Forgotten Eucharistic Prayers of East Syria*, AGLS 45 (Cambridge: Grove Books, 1999).

[36] See *Anaphora Book of the Syriac-Maronite Church of Antioch*, trans. Joseph P. Amar (Youngstown, OH: The Liturgical Commission, Diocese of St. Maron, USA, 1978).

bread (leavened bread, except for the Armenians and Maronites) and wine as well as for the ministers (prayers for vesting and private prayers of unworthiness similar to the various *apologiae* often noted with regard to Gallican influence on the Roman Rite). In the Coptic and Ethiopian Rites the bread and wine are prepared at the altar, and the East Syrian Rite includes a presentation of the bread and wine at the altar during the entrance rite of the liturgy itself.[37] The East Syrians even include as part of these rites the baking of the bread, into which is added, as noted above, the *Malka*, or holy leaven. In the Armenian, Byzantine, and West Syrian (Maronite, at least) Rites, the bread and wine are prepared at a side table (behind the *iconostasis* or "icon screen" for the Byzantines) and are solemnly transferred to the altar after the Liturgy of the Word during what is called (for Armenians and Byzantines) the "Great Entrance." In Constantinople at Hagia Sophia, the eucharistic gifts were prepared in a separate building altogether—the *Skeuophylakion*—from where they were transferred to the altar with a high degree of solemnity during the Great Entrance.[38] Of particular interest is the fact that in many of these rites the bread that has been prepared is referred to even at this point as the "Lamb of God who takes away the sins of the world."

The rites of entrance or the beginning of the liturgy in the Byzantine Rite (called the *Enarxis*), as table 2.2 below shows, consists now of an opening blessing ("Blessed is the kingdom of the Father and of the Son and of the Holy Spirit now and forever and unto the ages of ages. Amen"), a long litany called the "Grand Synaptē" or "Synaptē of Peace"[39] (beginning "In peace, let us pray to the Lord," with the response "Kyrie Eleison"), followed by a prayer and antiphon, a short litany (*Mikra* or "Little Synaptē"), followed by a prayer and antiphon,

[37] See Neroth van Vogelpoel, *Known in the Baking of the Bread.*

[38] See Thomas F. Mathews, *The Early Churches of Constantinople: Architecture and Liturgy* (University Park: Pennsylvania State University Press, 1971); Taft, *The Great Entrance;* and Nina Glibetić, "An Early Balkan Testimony of the Byzantine Prothesis Rite: The Nomocanon of St. Sava of Serbia (†1236)," in *CYNAΞIC KAΘOΛIKH. Beiträge zu Gottesdienst und Geschichte der fünf altkirchlichen Patriarchate für Heinzgerd Brakmann zum 70. Geburtstag,* ed. Diliana Atanassova and Tinatin Chronz (Wien: Lit Verlag, 2014), 239–48.

[39] The "Grand Synaptē" was originally attached to the prayers of the faithful after the readings and homily. See Mateos, *La célébration de la parole,* 29–31.

and, finally, another "Little Synaptē," followed by a prayer and antiphon to which has been attached the hymn, *Ho Monogenēs*:

> Only-Begotten Son and Word of God, immortal as you are, You condescended for our salvation to be incarnate from the Holy Theotokos and ever-virgin Mary, and without undergoing change, You became Man; You were crucified, O Christ God, and you trampled death by your death; You are One of the Holy Trinity; equal in glory with the Father and the Holy Spirit: save us!

Juan Mateos demonstrated several years ago, however, that the original beginning of the Byzantine Divine Liturgy is to be seen in what is now called "the Little Entrance," where the presiding minister takes the Gospel book from the altar and processes out the north door of the iconostasis (icon screen), through the body of the church, and back to the altar through the central gates in front of the altar.[40] Originally, claimed Mateos, this procession would have taken place as the opening procession of the liturgy from the entrance of the church itself to the altar during the chanting of the *Trisagion* as the entrance antiphon: "Holy God, Holy Mighty One, Holy Immortal One, have mercy on us!"[41] In fact, it is still only during this chant that a bishop actually enters the church and goes to the altar, thus underscoring Mateos's point. The "Prayer of the Entrance" in the Byzantine Rite demonstrates this clearly:

> Master Lord our God, who established in the heavens the orders and hosts of angels and archangels to minister to your glory: Make our entrance to be united with the entrance of the holy angels, that together we may serve and glorify your goodness. For to you belong all glory, honor, and worship, to the Father and to the Son and to the Holy Spirit, now and forever and to the ages of ages. Amen.[42]

[40] Ibid, 71–90.

[41] On the *Trisagion*, in addition to ibid, 91–110, see Sebastià Janeras, "Les byzantins et le *trisagion* christologique," in *Miscellanea liturgica in onore di Sua Eminenza il Cardinale Giacomo Lercaro*, vol. 2 (Rome: Desclée, 1967), 469–99; and idem, "Le trisagion: Une formule brève en liturgie comparée," in *Comparative Liturgy Fifty Years after Anton Baumstark (1872–1948)*, ed. Taft and Winkler, 495–562.

[42] Greek text in C. E. Hammond and F. E. Brightman, *Liturgies Eastern and Western: Being the Texts, Original or Translated, of the Principal Liturgies of the Church*, vol. 1: *Eastern* (Oxford: Clarendon Press, 1896, repr. 1965), 312.

## Table 2.2: Liturgy of the Word

| Armenian | Byzantine | Coptic |
|---|---|---|
| -blessing | initial blessing *enarxis*<br>long litany, prayer, and antiphon | -incensation of altar three times with prayers |
| | -short litany, prayer, and antiphon<br>-2nd short litany, prayer, and antiphon | |
| -*Ho Monogenēs*<br>or seasonal hymn | *Ho Monogenēs* | |
| -blessing | -Little Entrance | |
| -four prayers said by priest while choir sings the proper psalm and hymn | -seasonal hymns | |
| -***Trisagion*** | -***Trisagion*** | |
| -litany | | |
| -epistle reading | -epistle reading | reading from Paul + prayer<br>reading from Catholic epistles + prayer<br>reading from Acts + prayer<br>petitions, reverences, and processions around altar<br>offering of incense<br>***Trisagion*** |
| -Gospel reading | -Gospel reading | Gospel and procession |
| -creed | | |
| -litany | -litany | prayer of the Gospel |
| -blessing | | |
| -dismissal of catechumens | -prayer for and dismissal of catechumens | |

Hence, the *Trisagion*, originating at Constantinople during the reign of Proclus in the fifth century, was moved to its present location only after other seasonal hymns or entrance antiphons related to various feasts were added, a process beginning there already in the sixth century.

But if the original function of the *Trisagion* is masked by its current location and other seasonal hymns and antiphons, so also is the actual beginning of the Byzantine Divine Liturgy at the Little Entrance obscured by the three litanies, prayers, and antiphons that now precede it. This "Office of the Three Antiphons," as it is called, has its

| Ethiopian | East Syrian | West Syrian |
|---|---|---|
| invitation to stand<br>-peace | -*Lakho Mara* prayer of praise to Christ the Lord | |
| -invitation to worship of Trinity | | |
| Epistle readings | -***Trisagion***<br>-two readings (Malabar) or four readings (Chaldean) | -***Trisagion*** (in Aramaic)<br>-*mazmooro* a psalm chanted by the assembly and priest<br>-one or two readings |
| Praises of Mary | | |
| ***Trisagion*** | | |
| Gospel reading | [Gospel reading included]<br>-[prayer of the faithful (Malabar)]<br>-Creed | -Gospel reading<br>-brief seasonal response<br>-Creed |

origins, according to Mateos,[43] in the various stational liturgies of Constantinople during the reign of Justinian. That is, this reflects various processions from stational churches to Hagia Sophia, during which psalms and litanies and, later, nonbiblical refrains or antiphons were sung, one of which is the *Ho Monogenēs* added in the year 528) described above. Hence, the "Office of the Three Antiphons" appears

[43] In addition to Mateos, *La celebration de la parole*, 34–45, see also idem, "The Evolution of the Byzantine Liturgy," in *John XXIII Lectures*, vol. 1 (New York: John XXIII Center For Eastern Christian Studies, Fordham University, 1965), 76–112.

as a vestige of liturgical processions from elsewhere in Constantinople now moved indoors and codified as a part of Byzantine liturgy.

Because the *Trisagion* appears also in every other Eastern eucharistic liturgy, scholars have customarily interpreted its presence therein as functioning originally in the same way as it did in the Byzantine Rite, namely, as an introit or entrance chant. This is not, however, self-evident. M. Daniel Findikyan has argued[44] that because the Armenian and East Syrian Rites already had their own entrance psalms (Ps 92 for the Armenians and the hymn *Laku Mara*, "To You, Lord," for the East Syrians)[45] *before* they adopted the *Trisagion* from Constantinople, the chant has a different function in those rites and is not part of a now deteriorated entrance rite. According to Findikyan, that function in the Armenian and East Syrian Rites is in relation to the Liturgy of the Word and precisely in connection to the reading and procession of the Gospel. The very location of the *Trisagion* in the Coptic and Ethiopian Rites in relation to the Gospel would tend to support Findikyan's conclusion. Hence, if the *Trisagion* were part of the original beginning of the Byzantine Rite, it is connected more closely to the Liturgy of the Word in all other Eastern rites.

The location and function of the *Trisagion* is not the only difference between the Byzantine Rite and the others: its theological interpretation is also a key distinction. In the Byzantine Rite the *Trisagion* is interpreted as a trinitarian hymn, while in all of the other rites it is viewed christologically, especially with the addition of the clause "who was crucified for us" added to its conclusion by Patriarch Peter the Fuller at Antioch in 468.[46] Viewed by the Byzantines as a heretical (i.e., Monophysite) insertion, this so-called Theopaschite clause underscored the christological interpretation of the *Trisagion* and contributed to its function as one of a "solemnization of the gospel reading, the high point of the Eucharistic Synaxis."[47]

[44] Findikyan, *Commentary*, 456ff.

[45] "You, Lord of all, we confess; you, Jesus Christ, we glorify; for you are the lifegiver of our bodies and you are the Savior of our souls." ET adapted from Hammond and Brightman, *Liturgies Eastern and Western*, 1:249. See Sarhad Jammo, *La structure de la Messe chaldéene du début jusqu'à l'Anpaphore; Étude historique*, OCA 207 (Rome: Pontificium Institutum Orientalium Studiorum, 1979), 97–99.

[46] See the discussion of this in Schulz, *The Byzantine Liturgy*, 22–25; and see the work of Janeras in note 41 above.

[47] Findikyan, *Commentary*, 456. On the Theopaschite controversy, see Schulz above, note 46.

With regard to the biblical readings themselves, as table 2.2 above also shows, the Copts, Ethiopians, and East and West Syrians have retained the older pattern of several readings before the gospel, while the Armenians and Byzantines have only an epistle reading.[48] In comparison with earlier centuries, however, the Eastern rites as well as those of the West will see the further development of complete lectionaries for the eucharistic liturgies. One of the most prominent of these is included in the tenth-century *typikon* of Constantinople, edited by Juan Mateos,[49] which still functions in the Byzantine Rite today. Finally, while both the Armenian and Byzantine Rites still keep prayers for and dismissals of catechumens at the end of the Liturgy of the Word, the initiation of infants (baptism, chrismation, and communion) became the norm in all of the Eastern rites, and, hence, there are seldom any real catechumens present to be dismissed from the liturgical assembly.

## 2.3 Pre-anaphoral Rites

The term "pre-anaphoral rites" is customary in Eastern Christian liturgical study for describing the various rites and ceremonies that take place between the Liturgy of the Word and the anaphora itself. As table 2.3 shows, these rites include elements such as the transfer of the eucharistic gifts (with the exception of the Coptic[50] and Ethiopian Rites), the recitation of the creed (with the exception of the Armenians and Syrians, where it occurs earlier), and the kiss of peace, still in its classic Eastern (and originally Western) position before the Eucharist proper.

In the Byzantine Rite the transfer of the eucharistic gifts to the altar, the "Great Entrance," became and has remained clearly one of the more visible and dramatic moments of the entire Divine Liturgy. This action, including a solemn procession through the church with candles and incense among both the Byzantines and Armenians, is accompanied by the chant known as the *Cherubic Hymn*:

[48] For details on the Liturgy of the Word in general, see Mateos, *La célébration de la parole*, 127–47.

[49] Juan Mateos, *Le Typicon de la Grande Église*, 2 vols., OCA 165, 166 (Rome: Pontificio Istituto Orientale, 1962–1963).

[50] On the Coptic preanaphoral rites, see Maxwell E. Johnson, *Liturgy in Early Christian Egypt*, AGLS 33 (Bramcote, Nottingham: Grove Books, 1995), 17–21.

## Table 2.3: Pre-Anaphoral Rites

| Armenian | Byzantine | Coptic |
|---|---|---|
| | -prayer of access to the altar<br>-prayer of the faithful | -prayer of veil (prayer of access) intercessions |
| -proclamation "The Body of our Lord, and the Blood of our Redeemer are about to be present . . ."<br>-*hagiology* of the day<br>-removal of vestments of honor from clergy<br>-transfer of gifts with Cherubic hymn with corresponding prayer | -"Great Entrance" with Cherubic hymn | |
| -incensation of gifts<br>-diaconal admonition<br>-prayer of oblation<br>-benediction<br>-peace greeting | -incensation<br><br>-litany of offering<br><br>-kiss of peace<br>-Creed | -incensation<br><br><br><br>-Creed<br>-peace |

> We who mystically represent the Cherubim, who sing to the life-giving Trinity the thrice-holy hymn, let us now lay aside all earthly care that we may welcome the king of All, invisibly escorted by angel hosts. Alleluia! Alleluia! Alleluia![51]

Anton Baumstark, the father of "comparative liturgiology," articulated as one of his "laws of liturgical development" that "certain actions which are purely utilitarian by nature may receive a symbolic meaning either from their function in the liturgy as such or from factors in the liturgical texts which accompany them."[52] There is probably no better example of this than the rite of the Great Entrance. The utilitarian action of transferring the bread and wine from either

[51] For the Greek Text see Hammond and Brightman, *Liturgies Eastern and Western*, 1:377–79.

[52] Anton Baumstark, *Comparative Liturgy* (Westminster, MD: The Newman Press, 1958), 59–60, 130.

| Ethiopian | East Syrian | West Syrian |
|---|---|---|
| | -access to the altar | -prayer of access to the altar |
| -prayer of blessing and intercession<br>-Creed<br>-prayer of purification<br>-doxology | | |
| | -transfer of gifts (Chaldean) or presentation and preparation of gifts (Malabar)<br>-prayer of gratitude on the part of the ministers | -transfer of gifts to the altar<br>-prayer of offering<br>-general incensation |
| -kiss of peace | -greeting of peace<br>-unveiling of gifts<br>-incensing of gifts | -peace |

the old Constantinopolitan *Skeuophylakion* or from a side table, from the time of Maximus the Confessor (580–662) through Symeon of Thessalonica in the fourteenth century, became interpreted as related symbolically or allegorically either to heavenly spiritual realities or to various moments in Christ's passion (e.g., being carried to his burial) or other events in his life, even his Palm Sunday entrance into Jerusalem or his second coming (see table 2.5 below). While the Armenians and Maronites do have offertory prayers at this point in their rites, probably under Latin influence, Robert Taft, in his definitive study of this rite,[53] has demonstrated that the Great Entrance is in no way equivalent to Western "offertory" rites. Rather, the eucharistic offering takes place within the "anaphora"—the "prayer of offering"—itself! The Great Entrance and other pre-anaphoral rites, in other words, are entirely preparatory for that event.

[53] Taft, *The Great Entrance*.

The entrance of the Nicene-Constantinopolitan Creed into Eastern eucharistic liturgies is dated to the patriarchate of Timothy (511–517) at Constantinople,[54] from where it spread elsewhere throughout the Christian East, though, as we see in table 2.3, its location in those rites varies. In the Armenian Rite, for example, the location of the creed immediately following the gospel has its only close parallel with the Roman Rite. While this has sometimes been interpreted as the result of Latin influence, Findikyan has shown that it was already there prior to the time of Latinization in the twelfth century.[55]

The exchange or kiss of peace in its traditional location has remained a characteristic liturgical element in all of the Eastern rites. Until only recently, however, with contemporary attempts at its restoration in various places,[56] that action, as in the Roman Rite before the reforms of the Second Vatican Council, had been either suppressed altogether or had become shared only among the clergy and other liturgical ministers at the altar.

## 2.4 The Anaphoras

A characteristic of eucharistic praying in the East, as also in the West, is that beginning in the sixth century (East) we begin to get references to the anaphora being prayed silently during the liturgy. While the reasons for this are not clear, this tendency would become a characteristic of all of the Eastern rites, with the anaphora being prayed behind the central gates of the iconastasis (Byzantine) or behind a veil drawn across the front of the altar (Syrian). At the same time, it is often the case that both the narrative of institution and the *epiclesis* of the Holy Spirit are recited or sung aloud so that, unlike the West, the anaphora itself is never completely in silence.[57]

[54] See Parenti, "The Eucharistic Liturgy in the East," 68. See also the work of Gabriele Winkler on the Eastern Creeds, *Über die Entwicklungsgeschichte des armenische Symbolums: Ein Vergleich mit dem syrischen und griechischen Formelgut unter Einbezug der relevanten georgischen und äthiopischen Quellen*, OCA 262 (Rome: Pontificio Istituto Orientale, 2000).

[55] Findikyan, *Commentary*, 466.

[56] See *The Divine Liturgy: An Anthology for Worship*, ed. Peter Galadza, et al. (Ottawa: Metropolitan Andrey Sheptytsky Institute of Eastern Christian Liturgical Studies, 2004), 138.

[57] See Robert Taft, "Was the Eucharistic Anaphora Recited Secretly or Aloud? The Ancient Tradition and What Became of It," in *Worship Traditions in Armenia and the Neighboring Christian East*, ed. Ervine, 15–58.

### *2.4.1 The Armenian Anaphora of St. Athanasius*[58]

While it is certainly true that the Armenian Rite at one time did know and use versions of BAS—and, according to Gabriele Winkler,[59] versions that reflect Syriac sources and predate EgBAS—the only anaphora used in the Armenian Rite today, as noted above, is known as "St. Athanasius," also sometimes referred to as the "Liturgy of St. Gregory the Illuminator," and is dependent in part on those earlier Armenian versions of BAS.[60]

*The Priest:* The grace, the love and the divine sanctifying power of the Father and of the Son and of the Holy Spirit be with you all.

*The Choir:* Amen. And with your spirit.

*The Deacon:* The doors, the doors! With all wisdom and good heed lift up your minds in the fear of God.

*The Choir:* We have them lifted up to you, O Lord almighty.

*The Deacon:* And give thanks to the Lord with the whole heart.

*The Choir:* It is proper and right.

*The Priest:* It is truly proper and right with most earnest diligence always to adore and glorify you, Father almighty, who did remove the hindrance of the curse by your imponderable Word, your co-creator, who, having taken the Church to be a people to himself, made his own those who believe in you, and was pleased to dwell among us in a ponderable nature, according to the dispensation through the Virgin, and as the divine master-builder building a new work, he thereby made this earth into heaven. For he, before whom the companies

[58] ET is from PEER 4, 183–91, adapted from *The Divine Liturgy of the Armenian Church with Modern Armenian and English Translations, Transliteration, Musical Notation, Introduction and Notes*, ed. M. Daniel Findikyan (New York: St. Vartan Press, 1999), 28–39.

[59] See G. Winkler, *Die Basilius-Anaphora;* idem, "Armenia's Liturgy at the Crossroads of Neighbouring Traditions," OCP 74, no. 2 (2008): 363–87; and idem, "On the Formation of the Armenian Anaphoras: A Completely Revised and Updated Overview," *Studi sull'Oriente Cristiano* 11, no. 2 (2007): 97–130.

[60] The critical edition of this anaphora with commentary is H.-J. Feulner, *Die armenische Athanasius-Anaphora.*

of vigilant angels could not bear to stand, being amazed at the resplendent and unapproachable light of his divinity, even he, becoming man for our salvation, granted to us that we should join the heavenly ones in spiritual choirs, and in one voice with the seraphim and the cherubim, we should sing holy songs and make melodies and, boldly crying out, shout with them and say:

*The Choir:* Holy, holy, holy Lord of hosts; Heaven and earth are full of your glory. Praise in the highest. Blessed are you who did come and are to come in the name of the Lord. Hosanna in the highest. Blessed [are] you who did come and are to come in the name of the Lord. Hosanna in the highest.

*The Priest:* Holy, holy, holy are you truly and all-holy; and who is he that will presume to contain in words the outpouring of your infinite loving kindness to us? From the very beginning you did care for him who had fallen into sin and did comfort him in diverse manners by the prophets, by the giving of the law, by the priesthood and by the prefigurative offering of animals. And at the end of these days, tearing up the sentence of condemnation for all our debts, you gave us your only-begotten Son, both debtor and debt, immolation and anointed, lamb and heavenly bread, high priest and sacrifice; for he is distributor and he himself is distributed always in our midst without ever being consumed. For having become man truly and without illusion, and having become incarnate, through union without confusion, through the Mother of God, the holy Virgin Mary, he journeyed through all the passions of our human life without sin and came willingly to the world-saving cross, which was the occasion of our redemption.

Taking the bread in his holy, divine, immortal, spotless and creative hands, he blessed it, gave thanks, broke it and gave it to his chosen, holy disciples, who were seated, saying: Take, eat; this is my body, which is distributed for you and for many, for the expiation and remission of sins.

*The Choir:* Amen.

*The Priest:* Likewise taking the cup, he blessed it, gave thanks, drank and gave it to his chosen, holy disciples, who were seated, saying: Drink this all of you. This is my blood of the new covenant, which is shed for you and for many for the expiation and remission of sins.

*The Choir:* Amen.

*The Choir:* Heavenly Father, who did give your Son to death for us, debtor for our debts, by the shedding of his blood, we beseech you, have mercy upon your rational flock.

*The Priest:* And your only-begotten beneficent Son gave us the commandment that we should always do this in remembrance of him. And descending into the lower regions of death in the body which he took of our kinship, and mightily breaking asunder the bolts of hell, he made you known to us the only true God, the God of the living and of the dead. And now, O Lord, in accordance with this commandment, bringing forth the saving mystery of the body and blood of your Only-begotten, we remember his redemptive sufferings for us, his life-giving crucifixion, his burial for three days, his blessed resurrection, his divine ascension and his enthronement at your right hand, O Father; his awesome and glorious second coming, we confess and praise. And we offer to you yours of your own from all and for all.

*The Choir:* In all things blessed are you, O Lord. We bless you, we praise you; We give thanks to you; We pray to you, O Lord our God.

*The Priest:* We do indeed praise you and give thanks to you at all times, O Lord our God, who, having overlooked our unworthiness, have made us ministers of this awesome and ineffable mystery. Not by reason of any good works of our own, of which we are always altogether bereft and at all times find ourselves void, but ever taking refuge in your overflowing forbearance, we make bold to approach the ministry of the body and blood of your Only-begotten, our Lord and Savior Jesus Christ, to whom is befitting glory, dominion and honor, now and always and unto the ages of ages. Amen.

*The Priest:* ☩ Peace to all.

*The Choir:* And with your spirit.

*The Deacon:* Let us bow down to God.

*The Choir:* Before you, O Lord.

*The Choir:* Son of God, who are sacrificed to the Father for reconciliation, bread of life distributed among us, through the shedding of your holy blood, we beseech you, have mercy on your flock saved by your blood.

*The Priest:* We bow down and beseech and ask you, beneficent God, send to us and to these gifts set forth, your co-eternal and co-essential Holy Spirit.

*The Deacon:* Amen. Bless, Lord.

*The Priest:* Whereby blessing this bread, make it truly the body of our Lord and Savior Jesus Christ. *[He repeats this three times.]* And blessing this cup, make it truly the blood of our Lord and Savior Jesus Christ. *[He repeats this three times.]* Whereby blessing this bread and this wine, make them truly the body and blood of our Lord and Savior Jesus Christ, changing them by your Holy Spirit. *[He repeats this three times.]* So that for all of us who approach it, this may be for acquittal, for expiation and for remission of sins.

*The Choir:* Spirit of God, who, descending from heaven, accomplishes through us the mystery of him who is glorified with you, by the shedding of his blood, we beseech you, grant rest to the souls of those of ours who have fallen asleep.

*The Priest:* Through this grant love, stability and desirable peace to the whole world, to the holy Church and to all orthodox bishops, to priests, to deacons, to kings, to the princes of the world, to peoples, to travelers, to seafarers, to prisoners, to those who are in danger, to the weary and to those who are at war with barbarians. Through this grant also seasonableness to the weather and fertility to the fields and a speedy recovery to those who are afflicted with diverse diseases. Through this give rest to all who long ago have fallen asleep in Christ: to the forefathers, the patriarchs, the prophets, the apostles, martyrs, bishops, presbyters, deacons and the whole company of your holy Church and to all the laity, men and women, who have ended their life in faith. With whom, O beneficent God, visit us also, we beseech you. . . .

*[The intercessions continue.]*

*The Priest:* . . . And having cleansed our thoughts, make us temples fit for the reception of the Body and Blood of your Only-begotten and our Lord and Savior Jesus Christ, with whom to you, O Father almighty, together with the life-giving and liberating Holy Spirit, is befitting glory, dominion and honor, now and always and unto the ages of ages. Amen.

### *2.4.2 Byzantine Rite*

The Byzantine Rite, of course, uses those anaphoras called Byzantine Basil (ByzBAS) and John Chrysostom (CHR) together with, on rare occasions, Greek James (GrJAS)[61] and another called St. Gregory,

[61] On JAS see below, 107–112.

which is the only Byzantine anaphora addressed directly to Christ. The texts of both ByzBAS and CHR follow here.

*2.4.2.1 ByzBAS*[62]

*Priest:* The grace of our Lord Jesus Christ and the love of the God and Father, and the communion of the Holy Spirit be with you all.

*People:* And with your spirit.

*Priest:* Let us lift up our hearts.

*People:* We have them with the Lord.

*Priest:* Let us give thanks to the Lord.

*People:* It is fitting and right <to worship the Father, the Son, and the Holy Spirit, the consubstantial and undivided Trinity>.

*And the priest begins the holy anaphora:*

I AM, Master, Lord God, Father almighty, reverend it is truly fitting and right and befitting the magnificence of your holiness to praise you, to hymn you, to bless you, to worship you, to give you thanks, to glorify you, the only truly existing God, and to offer to you with a contrite heart and a humble spirit this our reasonable service. For it is you who granted us the knowledge of your truth; and who is sufficient to declare your powers, to make all your praises to be heard, or to declare all your wonders at all times? [Master], Master of all, Lord of heaven and earth and all Creation, visible and invisible, you sit on the throne of glory and behold the depths, without beginning, invisible, incomprehensible, infinite, unchangeable, the Father of our Lord Jesus Christ the Great God and savior of our hope, who is the image of your goodness, the identical seal, manifesting you the Father in himself, living Word, true God, before all ages wisdom, life, sanctification, power, the true Light by whom the Holy Spirit was revealed, the spirit of truth, the grace of sonship, the pledge of the inheritance to come, the first fruits of eternal good things,

[62] PEER 4, 171–80. On the Byzantine anaphoras, see also Spinks, *Do This in Remembrance of Me*.

lifegiving power, the fountain of sanctification, by whose enabling the whole rational and spiritual Creation does your service and renders you the unending doxology; for all things are your servants. For angels, archangels, thrones, dominions, principalities, powers, virtues, and the cherubim with many eyes praise you, the seraphim stand around you, each having six wings, and with two covering their own faces, and with two their feet, and with two flying, and crying one to the other with unwearying mouths and never-silent doxologies, (aloud) singing the triumphal hymn, crying aloud and saying:

*People:* Holy, <holy, holy, Lord of Sabaoth; heaven and earth are full of your glory. Hosanna in the highest. Blessed is he who comes in the name of the Lord. Hosanna in the highest.>

*The priest says privately:* With these blessed powers, Master, lover of men, we sinners also cry and say: you are truly holy and all-holy, and there is no measure of the magnificence of your holiness, and you are holy in all your works, for in righteousness and true judgment you brought all things upon us. For you took dust from the earth and formed man; you honored him with your image, O God, and set him in the paradise of pleasure, and promised him immortality of life and enjoyment of eternal good things in keeping your commandments. But when he had disobeyed you, the true God who created him, and had been led astray by the deceit of the serpent, and had been subjected to death by his own transgressions, you, O God, expelled him in your righteous judgment from paradise into this world, and turned him back to the earth from which he was taken, dispensing to him the salvation by rebirth which is in your Christ. For you did not turn away finally from your creature, O good one, nor forget the works of your hands, but you visited him in many ways through the bowels of your mercy. You sent forth prophets; you performed works of power through your saints who were pleasing to you in every generation; you spoke to us through the mouths of your servants the prophets, foretelling to us the salvation that should come; you gave the Law for our help; you set angels as guards over us.

But when the fullness of time had come, you spoke to us in your Son himself, through whom also you made the ages, who, being the reflection of your glory and the impress of your substance, and bearing all things by the word of his power, thought it not robbery to be equal with you, the God and Father, but he who was God before the ages was seen on earth and lived among men; he was made flesh from a holy virgin and humbled himself, taking the form of a slave; he was conformed to the body of our humiliation that he might conform us to the image of his glory. For since through man sin had entered into the world, and through sin death, your only-begotten Son, who is in your bosom, O God and Father, being born of a woman, the Holy Mother of God and ever-Virgin Mary, born under the law, was pleased to condemn sin in his flesh, that those who died in Adam should be made alive in him, your Christ. And having become a citizen of this world, he gave us commandments of salvation, turned us away from the error of the idols, and brought us to the knowledge of you, the true God and Father; he gained us for himself, a peculiar people, a royal priesthood, a holy nation; and when he had cleansed us with water and sanctified us by the Holy Spirit, he gave himself as a ransom to death, by which we were held, having been sold under sin. By means of the cross he descended into hell, that he might fill all things with himself, and loosed the pains of death; he rose again on the third day, making a way to resurrection from the dead for all flesh, because it was not possible for the prince of life to be conquered by corruption, and became the first fruits of those who had fallen asleep, the first-born from the dead, so that he might be first in all ways among all things. And ascending into the heavens, he sat down at the right hand of the[63] majesty in the highest, and will also come to reward every one according to their works. And he left us memorials of his saving passion, these things which we have set forth[64] according[65] to his commandments.

For when he was about to go out to his voluntary and laudable and life-giving death, in the night in which he gave himself up for the life of the world, he took bread in his holy and undefiled hands and showed it to you, the God and Father, gave thanks, blessed, sanctified, and broke it, and gave it to his holy disciples

[63] Now "your."

[64] Perfect tense.

[65] The Barberini MS breaks off here.

and apostles, saying, "Take, eat; this is my body, which is broken for you for the forgiveness of sins."

*People:* Amen.

Likewise also he took the cup of the fruit of the vine and mixed it, gave thanks, blessed, sanctified, and gave it to his holy disciples and apostles, saying, "Drink from this, all of you; this is my blood, which is shed for you and for many for the forgiveness of sins. <*People:* Amen.> Do this for my remembrance. For as often as you eat this bread and drink this cup, you proclaim my death, you confess my resurrection."

Therefore, Master, we also, remembering his saving Passion, his lifegiving cross, his three-day burial, his resurrection from the dead, his ascension into heaven, his session at your right hand, God and Father, and his glorious and fearful second coming; (*aloud*) offer[-ing] you your own from your own, in all and through all,

*People:* we hymn you, <we bless you, we give you thanks, O Lord, and pray to you, our God.>

Therefore, Master all-Holy, we also, your sinful and unworthy servants, who have been held worthy to minister at your holy altar, not for our righteousness, for we have done nothing good upon earth, but for your mercies and compassions which you have poured out richly upon us, with confidence approach your holy altar. And having set forth[66] the likeness of the holy body and blood of your Christ, we pray and beseech you, O holy of holies, in the good pleasure of your bounty, that your [all-]Holy Spirit may come upon us and upon these gifts set forth, and bless them and sanctify and show[67] (*he signs the holy gifts with the cross three times, saying:*) this bread the precious body of our Lord and God and Savior Jesus Christ. Amen. And this cup the precious blood of our Lord and God and Savior Jesus Christ, [Amen.] which is shed for the life of the world <and salvation>. Amen <*thrice*>.

[66] Aorist.

[67] Greek: *anadeixai*.

*Prayer:* Unite with one another all of us who partake of the one bread and the cup into fellowship with the one Holy Spirit; and make none of us to partake of the holy body and blood of your Christ for judgment or for condemnation, but that we may find mercy and grace with all the saints who have been well-pleasing to you from of old, forefathers, fathers, patriarchs, prophets, apostles, preachers, evangelists, martyrs, confessors, teachers, and every righteous spirit perfected in faith; (*aloud*) especially our all-holy, immaculate highly blessed <glorious> Lady, Mother of God and ever-Virgin Mary; (*while the diptychs are read by the deacon, the priest says the prayer:*) Saint John the <prophet,> forerunner and Baptist, <the holy and honored apostles,> this saint *N.* whose memorial we are keeping, and all your saints: at their entreaties, visit us, O God.

And remember all those who have fallen asleep in hope of resurrection to eternal life, and grant them rest where the light of your countenance looks upon them.

Again we pray you, Lord, remember your holy, catholic, and apostolic Church from one end of the world to the other, and grant it the peace which you purchased by the precious blood of your Christ, and [e]stablish this holy house until the consummation of the age, and grant it peace.

Remember, Lord, those who presented these gifts, and those for whom, and through whom, and on account of whom they presented them.

Remember, Lord, those who bring forth fruit and do good work in your holy churches and remember the poor. Reward them with rich and heavenly gifts. Grant them heavenly things for earthly, eternal things for temporal, incorruptible things for corruptible.

*The intercessions continue*

*Concluding doxology*

. . . and grant us with one mouth and one heart to glorify and hymn your all-honorable and magnificent name, the Father and the Son and the Holy Spirit, now <and always and to the ages of ages.>

*People*: Amen.

2.4.2.2 *CHR*[68]

*The priest says:* The grace of our Lord Jesus Christ, and the love of the God and Father, and the communion of the Holy Spirit be with you all.

*People:* And with your spirit.

*Priest:* Let us lift up our hearts.

*People:* We have them with the Lord.

*Priest:* Let us give thanks to the Lord.

*People:* It is fitting and right <to worship the Father, the Son, and the Holy Spirit, the consubstantial and undivided Trinity>.

*The priest begins the holy anaphora:* It is fitting and right to hymn you, <to bless you, to praise you,> to give you thanks, to worship you in all places of your dominion. For you are God, ineffable, inconceivable, invisible, incomprehensible, existing always and in the same way, you and your only-begotten Son and Your Holy Spirit. You brought us out of non-existence into existence; and when we had fallen, you raised us up again, and did not cease to do everything until you had brought us up to heaven, and granted us the kingdom that is to come. For all these things we give thanks to you and to your only-begotten Son and to your Holy Spirit, for all that we know and do not know, your seen and unseen benefits that have come upon us.

We give you thanks also for this ministry; vouchsafe to receive it from our hands, even though thousands of archangels and ten thousands of angels stand before you, cherubim and seraphim, with six wings and many eyes, flying on high, (*aloud*) singing the triumphal hymn <proclaiming, crying, and saying>:

*People:* Holy, <holy, holy, Lord of Sabaoth; heaven and earth are full of your glory. Hosanna in the highest. Blessed is he who comes in the name of the Lord. Hosanna in the highest>.

*The priest, privately:* With these powers, Master, lover of humanity, we also cry and say: holy are you and all-holy, and your only-begotten Son, and your Holy Spirit; holy are you and all-holy

[68] PEER 4, 164–71.

and magnificent is your glory; for you so loved the world that you gave your only-begotten Son that all who believe in him may not perish, but have eternal life.

When he had come and fulfilled all the dispensation for us, on the night in which he handed himself over, he took bread in his holy and undefiled and blameless hands, gave thanks, blessed, broke, and gave it to his holy disciples and apostles, saying, (*aloud*) "Take, eat; this is my body, which is <broken> for you <for forgiveness of sins." *People:* Amen>. <*privately*> Likewise the cup also after supper, saying, (*aloud*) "Drink from this, all of you; this is my blood of the new covenant, which is shed for you and for many for the forgiveness of sins."

*People:* Amen.

*The priest, privately:* We therefore, remembering this saving commandment and all the things that were done for us: the cross, the tomb, the resurrection on the third day, the ascension into heaven, the session at the right hand, the second and glorious coming again; (*aloud*) offering you your own from your own, in all and for all,

*People:* we hymn you, <we bless you, we give you thanks, Lord, and pray to you, our God>.

*The priest* says *privately:* We offer you also this reasonable and bloodless service, and we pray and beseech and entreat you, send down your Holy Spirit on us and on these gifts set forth; and make this bread the precious body of your Christ, [changing it by your Holy Spirit] Amen; and that which is in this cup the precious blood of your Christ, changing it by your Holy Spirit, Amen; so that they may become to those who partake for vigilance of soul, for communion with the Holy Spirit, for the fullness of the kingdom (of heaven), for boldness toward you, not for judgment or condemnation.

We offer you this reasonable service also for those who rest in faith, <forefathers,> fathers, patriarchs, prophets, apostles, preachers, evangelists, martyrs, confessors, ascetics, and all the righteous <spirits> perfected in faith; (*aloud*) especially our all-holy, immaculate, highly glorious, Blessed Lady, Mother of God and ever-Virgin Mary; <*diptychs of the dead;*> Saint John the <prophet,> forerunner, and Baptist, and the holy, <glorious,> and honored Apostles; and this saint whose memorial we are keeping; and all your saints: at their entreaties, look on us, O God.

And remember all those who have fallen asleep in hope of resurrection to eternal life, <*he remembers them by name*> and grant them rest where the light of your own countenance looks upon them.

Again we beseech you, remember, Lord, all the orthodox episcopate who rightly divide the word of your truth, all the priesthood, the diaconate in Christ, and every order of the clergy.

We offer you this reasonable service also for the (whole) world, for the holy, catholic, and apostolic Church, for those who live in a chaste and reverend state, [for those in mountains and in dens and in caves of the earth,] for the most faithful Emperor, the Christ-loving Empress, and all their court and army: grant them, Lord, a peaceful reign, that in their peace we may live a quiet and peaceful life in all godliness and honesty.

Remember, Lord, the city in which we dwell, and all cities and lands, and all who dwell in them in faith.

(*aloud*) Above all, remember, Lord, our Archbishop N.

<*Diptychs of the living.*>

Remember, Lord, those at sea, travelers, the sick, those in adversity, prisoners, and their salvation.

Remember, Lord, those who bring forth fruit and do good works in your holy churches and remember the poor; and send out your mercies upon us all, (*aloud*) and grant us with one mouth and one heart to glorify and hymn your all-honorable and magnificent name, the Father, the Son, and the Holy Spirit, <now and always and to the ages of ages>.

*People:* Amen.

### *2.4.3 Coptic Rite*

As previously noted, the Coptic Rite employs anaphoras of both the Alexandrian and Syro-Byzantine types. The primary anaphora used is EgBAS with Coptic Mark (also known as "St. Cyril") used on occasion and another later, and less-used, West Syrian imported text named for St. Gregory Nazianzus. Both Coptic Mark (Cyril) and EgBAS follow here, though due to its length Coptic Mark (Cyril) includes only pertinent sections.

*2.4.3.1 Coptic Mark (Cyril)*[69]

*Within the preface:*

You have made all things through Your wisdom, Your true light, your only begotten Son, our Lord and our God and our Savior and the king of us all, Jesus Christ, through whom we give thanks, we offer unto you with him and the Holy Spirit, the holy consubstantial undivided Trinity, this reasonable sacrifice and this unbloody service which all nations offer unto you from the rising of the sun unto the going down of the same and from the north to the south, for Your name is great, O Lord, among all the Gentiles and in every place incense is offered unto Your holy name and a purified sacrifice.

*The intercessions begin with the following:*

And over this sacrifice and this offering we pray and beseech Your goodness, O lover of man. Remember, O Lord, the peace of Your one only holy catholic and apostolic church. . . .

*Introduction to the Sanctus and the Sanctus*

For You are God who are above every principality and every power and every virtue and every dominion and every name that is named not only in this world but also in that which is to come: for before You stand the thousand thousands and the ten thousand times ten thousand of the angels and archangels serving you: for before You stand Your two living creatures exceedingly honourable, the six winged and many eyed, seraphim and cherubim, with two wings covering their face by reason of thy Godhead which none can gaze upon nor comprehend, and with two covering their feet, with two also flying for at all times all things hallow You. But with them that hallow You, receive our hallowing, O Lord, at our hands also, praising You with them and saying:

[69] The translation is adapted from Hammond and Brightman, *Liturgies Eastern and Western*, 1:164–80.

Holy, holy, holy, Lord Sabaoth: full are the heaven and the earth of your holy glory.

*Epiclesis I*
Truly heaven and earth are full of Your holy glory through Your only-begotten Son our Lord and our God and our Savior and the king of us all Jesus Christ. Fill this also Your sacrifice, O Lord, with the blessing that is from You, through the descent upon it of Your Holy Spirit, and in blessing bless and in purifying purify these Your precious gifts *which have been set before Your face, this bread and this cup.*

*Narrative of Institution and Anamnesis*
For Your only begotten Son our Lord and our God and our Savior and the king of us all Jesus Christ in the same night in which he gave Himself up to undergo the passion in behalf of our sins and the death which he accepted of his own will himself to undergo the passion and the death which he accepted of his own will himself in behalf of us all took bread upon his holy spotless and undefiled and blessed and life giving hands. . . . For as often as you shall eat of this Bread and drink of this Cup you show my death, you confess my resurrection, you make my memorial until I come.

(*The People:*) Your death, O Lord we acclaim and your holy resurrection and ascension we confess.

Now also, O God the Father almighty, showing the death of Your only begotten Son our Lord and our God and our Savior and the king of us all Jesus Christ, confessing his holy resurrection and his ascension into the heavens and his session at Your right hand, O Father, looking for his second advent, coming from the heavens, fearful and glorious at the end of this world, wherein he will come to judge the world in righteousness to render to every man according to his works whether it be good or bad. Before Your holy glory we have set Your own gift of Your own, O our holy Father,

(*The People:*) We praise You, we bless You, we give thanks to You, Lord and we ask you our God.

*Epiclesis II*

Have mercy upon us, O God the Father almighty, and send down from Your holy height and from heaven Your dwelling place and from Your infinite bosom, from the throne of the kingdom of Your glory, him, the Paraclete, Your Holy Spirit, who is hypostatic, the indivisible, the unchangeable, who is the Lord, the giver of life, who spoke in the law and the prophets and the apostles, who is everywhere, who fills all places and no place contains him: and of his own will after Your good pleasure working sanctification on those in whom he delights, not ministerially: simple in his nature, manifold in his operation, the fountain of the graces of God, who is of one substance with You, who proceeds from You, the sharer of the throne of the kingdom of Your glory with Your only begotten Son our Lord and our God and our Savior and the king of us all Jesus Christ: send him down upon us Your servants and upon these Your precious gifts *which have been set before You*, upon this bread and upon this cup that they may be hallowed and changed and that he may make this bread the holy body of Christ and this cup also his precious blood of the New Testament even of our Lord and our God and our Saviour and the king of us all Jesus Christ. . . .

*2.4.3.2 EgBAS*[70]

*The bishop:*[71] The Lord be with you all.

*People:* And with your spirit.

*Bishop:* Let us lift up our hearts.

*People:* We have them with the Lord.

*Bishop:* Let us give thanks to the Lord.

*People:* It is fitting and right.

*Bishop:* It is fitting and right, fitting and right, truly it is fitting and right, I AM, truly Lord God, existing before the ages, reigning until the ages; you dwell on high and regard what is low; you made heaven and earth and the sea and all that is in them. Father of our Lord and God and Savior Jesus

[70] PEER 4, 115–23.

[71] Greek: *Hiereus*.

Christ, through whom you made all things visible and invisible, you sit on the throne of your glory; you are adored by every holy power. Around you stand angels and archangels, principalities and powers, thrones, dominions, and virtues; around you stand the cherubim with many eyes and the seraphim with six wings, forever singing the hymn of glory and saying:

*People:* Holy, holy, holy Lord (etc.)

*Bishop:* Holy, holy, holy you are indeed, Lord our God. You formed us and placed us in the paradise of pleasure; and when we had transgressed your commandment through the deceit of the serpent, and had fallen from eternal life, and had been banished from the paradise of pleasure, you did not cast us off for ever, but continually made promises to us through your holy prophets; and in these last days you manifested to us who sat in darkness and the shadow of death your only-begotten Son, our Lord and God and Savior, Jesus Christ. He was made flesh of the Holy Spirit and of the holy Virgin Mary, and became man; he showed us the ways of salvation, granted us to be reborn from above by water and the Spirit, and made us a people for [his] own possession, sanctifying us by his Holy Spirit. He loved his own who were in the world, and gave himself for our salvation to death who reigned over us and held us down because of our sins.

. . . by his blood.[72] From the cross he descended into hell and rose from the dead and the third day, he ascended into heaven and sat at the right hand of the Father; he appointed a day on which to judge the world with justice and render to each according to his works.

And he left us this great mystery of godliness for when he was about to hand himself over to death for the life of the world, he took bread, blessed, sanctified, broke, and gave it to his holy disciples and apostles, saying, "Take and eat from this, all of you; this is my body, which is given for you and for many for forgiveness of your sins. Do this for my remembrance.

[72] The earliest Coptic (Sahidic) text begins here.

Likewise also the cup after supper: he mixed wine and water, blessed, sanctified, gave thanks, and again gave it to them, saying, "Take and drink from it, all of you; this is my blood which shall be shed for you and for many for the forgiveness of your sins. Do this for my remembrance. For as often as you eat this bread and drink this cup, you proclaim my death until I come."

We therefore, remembering his holy sufferings, and his resurrection from the dead, and his ascension into heaven, and his session at the right hand of the Father, and his glorious and fearful coming to us (again), have set forth before you your own from your own gifts, this bread and cup. And we, sinners and unworthy and wretched, pray you, our God, in adoration that in the good pleasure of your goodness your Holy Spirit may descend upon us and upon these gifts that have been set before you, and may sanctify and make them holy of holies.

Make us all worthy to partake of your holy things for sanctification of soul and body, that we may become one body and one spirit, and may have our portion with all the saints who have been pleasing to you from eternity.

Remember, Lord, also your one, holy, catholic, and apostolic Church; give it peace, for you purchased it with the precious blood of Christ; and (remember) all the orthodox bishops in it.

Remember first of all your servant Archbishop Benjamin and his colleague in the ministry holy Bishop Colluthus, and all who with him dispense the word of truth; grant them to feed the holy churches, your orthodox flocks, in peace.

Remember, Lord, the priests and all the deacons who assist, all those in virginity and chastity, and all your faithful people; and have mercy on them all.

Remember, Lord, also this place, and those who live in it in the faith of God.

Remember, Lord, also mildness of climate and the fruits of the earth.

Remember, Lord, those who offer these gifts to you, and those for whom they offered them; and grant them all a heavenly reward.

Since, Master, it is a command of your only-begotten Son that we should share in the commemoration of your saints, vouchsafe to remember, Lord, those of our fathers who have been pleasing to you from eternity: patriarchs, prophets, apostles, martyrs, confessors, preachers, evangelists, and all the righteous perfected in faith; especially at all times the holy and glorious Mary, Mother of God; and by her prayers have mercy on us all, and save us through your holy name which has been invoked upon us.

Remember likewise all those of the priesthood who have already died, and all those of lay rank; and grant them rest in the bosom of Abraham, Isaac, and Jacob, in green pastures, by waters of comfort, in a place whence grief, sorrow, and sighing have fled away.

(*To the deacon*) Read the names. (*The deacon reads the diptychs.*)

*Bishop*: Give them rest in your presence; preserve in your faith us who live here, guide us to your kingdom, and grant us your peace at all times; through Jesus Christ and the Holy Spirit.

The Father in the Son, the Son in the Father with the Holy Spirit, in your holy, one, catholic, and apostolic Church.[73]

### *2.4.4 Ethiopian Rite*

As noted above, the Ethiopian Rite uses at least twenty different anaphoras, generally of the Alexandrian type, the most commonly used being a version of St. Mark closely resembling the one used on occasion in the Coptic Rite. Another of these, called the Anaphora of

[73] On the various versions of BAS, see G. Winkler, *Die Basilius-Anaphora*. See also idem, "Zur Erforschung orientalischer Anaphoren in liturgievergleichender Sicht II: Das Formelgut der Oratio post Sanctus und Anamnese sowie Interzessionen und die Taufbekenntnisse," in *Comparative Liturgy Fifty Years after Anton Baumstark (1872–1948)*, ed. Taft and Winkler, 407–93. For the state of the question on this prayer, see McGowan, "The Basilian Anaphoras: Rethinking the Question," in *Issues in Eucharistic Praying*, ed. Johnson (Collegeville, MN: Liturgical Press, Pueblo, 2011), 219–62.

Mary of Hereyaqos of Behensa, is addressed directly to the Virgin Mary,[74] underscoring the high Mariology of the Ethiopian Church, although the rich and poetic text is quite clear in not ascribing attributes to Mary belonging to God alone. We present a portion of this prayer from its post-Sanctus section:

> O Virgin, full of glory, with whom and with what likeness shall we liken you? You are the loom from which Emmanuel took his ineffable garment of flesh. He made the warp from the same flesh as that of Adam, and the woof is your flesh. The shuttle is the Word himself, Jesus Christ. The length of the warp is the shadow of God the Most High. The weaver is the Holy Spirit. How marvelous and wonderful is this thing! O bridge over which the ancient fathers crossed from death to life! O ladder from earth to heaven, through you the first creation was renewed!
>
> [. . .]
>
> O Virgin, you were not wed to Joseph for coming together, but in order that he might keep you in purity, and so was it fulfilled. When God the Father saw your purity he sent to you his radiant angel, whose name is Gabriel, and he said to you: The Holy Spirit shall come upon you, and the power of the Most High shall overshadow you. The Word came to you without being separated from the bosom of his Father; you conceived him without his being limited, and he stayed in your womb without making subtraction from above or addition from beneath. In your womb there dwelt inestimable and unsearchable fire of the Godhead. It is not just to compare him with earthly fire. Fire has measurement and volume, but of the Deity it cannot be said that it is like this, or even seems to be like this. . . .
>
> O Virgin, when there dwelt in your womb the fire of the Godhead, whose face is fire, whose clothes are fire, whose covering is fire, how did it not burn you? In what part of your womb were the

[74] See David K. Glenday, "Mary in the Liturgy: An Ethiopian Anaphora," *Worship* 47 (1973): 222–26; Getatchew Haile, "A Hymn to the Blessed Virgin from Fifteenth-Century Ethiopia," *Worship* 65 (1991): 445–50; idem, "On the Identity of Silondis and the Composition of the Anaphora of Mary Ascribed to Hereyaqos of Behensa," OCP 49 (1983): 366–89; and idem, "On the Writings of Abba Giyorgis Saglawi from Two Unedited Miracles of Mary," OCP 48 (1982): 65–91.

> seven curtains of the flame of the fire prepared and spread? Were they in the right or the left side while you were a but a child? In what part of your womb was the glittering cherubic throne, compassed by the flame of fire, prepared and planted while you were a young bride? How wonderful it is! A mother and a maid; the narrowness of the womb and the infinite; conception without intercourse, as a bee conceives, from the voice of a word; milk with virginity! When I think of this my mind likes to swim in the depth of your Son's seas, and the billows from the hiding-place of your Beloved seep across it . . . .
>
> O Virgin who give the fruit that can be eaten, and the spring which can be drunk: O Bread got from you, that gives life and salvation to those who eat of it in faith. O Bread got from you, that is as hard as the stone of "Admas," which cannot be chewed, to those who do not eat of it in faith. O Cup got from you, that helps those who drink of it in faith to incline to wisdom, and that gives them life. O Cup got from you, that intoxicates those who do not drink of it in faith and causes them to stumble and fall and adds sin to them instead of the remission of sin![75]

What has captured the attention of recent liturgical scholarship, however, is the Ethiopian Anaphora of the Apostles, a fourteenth-century text that includes an Ethiopian translation of the anaphora of chapter 4 of the so-called *Apostolic Tradition*, as well as a concluding Benedictus doxology from the Ethiopic version of the late fourth- or early fifth-century church order, the *Testamentum Domini*. While the overall pattern appears to reflect a more Alexandrian structure with intercessions in the preface and the post-Sanctus connected to the Sanctus by means of "full," there is no explicit post-Sanctus epiclesis of the Holy Spirit upon the gifts but, rather, a consecratory epiclesis in the Syro-Byzantine position after the anamnesis. Recent work on the Sanctus and Benedictus in this anaphora also suggests early Syrian influence by means of a document of Syrian origin, but in its Geʿez translation, namely, the Book of Enoch. So, while the text in its

[75] ET adapted from *Liturgy of the Ethiopian Church*, trans. Daoud, rev. Hazen, 134–36, 141–42.

present shape may be from the fourteenth century, it is quite plausible that some very early elements are represented within it.[76]

### 2.4.4.1 *The Ethiopian Anaphora of the Apostles*[77]

*Preface*

*Priest:* We give thanks to you, O Lord, through your beloved Son our Lord Jesus, who in the last days you sent to us, your Son, the Savior and Redeemer, the messenger of your counsel. This Word is he, who is from you, and through whom you made all things according to your will.

*[Intercessions]*

*Introduction to the Sanctus and Sanctus*

*Priest:* There stand before you a thousand thousands and ten thousand times ten thousand, both the holy angels and archangels and your honorable beasts, each with six wings. [*Deacon:* Look to the east.] With two of their wings they cover their face, with two of their wings they cover their feet, and with two of their wings they fly from end to end of the world. [*Deacon:* Let us be attentive.] And they all constantly hallow and praise you, with all of those who hallow and praise you. Receive also our hallowing, which we utter to you: Holy, holy, holy, perfect Lord of hosts. [*Deacon:* Answer you all.]

*People:* Holy, holy, holy, perfect Lord of hosts, heaven and earth are full of the holiness of your glory.

[76] See Winkler, *Das Sanctus*, 96ff., 143ff. See also Maxwell Johnson, "Recent Research on the Anaphoral *Sanctus*: An Update and Hypothesis," in *Issues in Eucharistic Praying*, ed. Johnson, 161–88. For recent work on the *Testamentum Domini*, see Gabriele Winkler, "Über das christliche Erbe Henochs und einige Probleme des *Testamentum Domini*," *Oriens Christianus* 93 (2009): 201–47.

[77] PEER 4, 123–32. ET adapted from Daoud, *Liturgy of the Ethiopian Church*, 69–76. A critical edition of the Ethiopian text is in process by Reinhard Meßner and Martin Lang. See their study, "Ethiopian Anaphoras: Status and Tasks in Current Research Via an Edition of the Ethiopian Anaphora of the Apostles," in *Jewish and Christian Liturgy and Worship: New Insights into its History and Interaction*, ed. Albert Gerhards and Clemens Leonhard, Jewish and Christian Perspectives 15 (Leiden: Brill, 2007), 185–206.

*Post-Sanctus*

*Priest:* Truly heaven and earth are full of the holiness of your glory, through our Lord, God and Savior Jesus Christ, your holy Son. He came and was born of a virgin, so that he might fulfill your will and make a people for yourself.

*People:* Remember us all in your kingdom; remember us, Lord, Master, in your kingdom; remember us, Lord, in your kingdom, as you remembered the thief on the right hand when you were on the tree of the holy cross.

*Priest:* He stretched out his hands in the passion, suffering to save the sufferers that trust in him; he, who was delivered to the passion that he might destroy death, break the bonds of Satan, tread down hell, lead forth the saints, establish a covenant and make known his resurrection.

*Institution Narrative*

*Priest:* In the same night that they betrayed him. . . . As often as you do this, do it in remembrance of me.

*People:* We proclaim your death, Lord, and your holy resurrection; we believe in your ascension and your second advent. We glorify you, and confess you, we offer our prayer to you and supplicate you, our Lord and our God.

*Anamnesis*

*Priest:* Now, Lord, we remember your death and your resurrection. We confess you and we offer to you this bread and this cup, giving thanks to you; and thereby you have made us worthy of the joy of standing before you and ministering to you.

*Epiclesis*

*Priest:* We pray and beseech you, O Lord, that you would send the Holy Spirit and power upon this bread and upon this cup. May he make them the body and blood of our Lord, God, and Savior Jesus Christ, unto the ages of ages.

*People:* Amen. Lord pity us, Lord spare us, Lord have mercy on us.

*Deacon:* With all our heart let us beseech the Lord our God that he grant to us the good communion of the Holy Spirit.

*People:* As it was, is, and shall be unto generations of generations, world without end.

*Priest:* Grant it together to all of them that partake of it, that it may be to them for sanctification and for filling with the Holy Spirit and for strengthening of the true faith, that they may hallow and praise you and your beloved Son, Jesus Christ with the Holy Spirit.

*People:* Amen.

*Priest:* Grant us to be united through your Holy Spirit, and heal us by this oblation, that we may live in you for ever. *[The people repeat his words.]*

*Priest:* Blessed be the Name of the Lord, and blessed be he that comes in the Name of the Lord, and let the Name of the Lord, and let the Name of his glory, be blessed. So be it. So be it. So be it blessed. *[The people repeat his words.]*

*Priest:* Send the grace of the Holy Spirit upon us. *[The people repeat his words.]*

### *2.4.5 East Syrian Rite*

As we have already noted, the most famous anaphora used by the East Syrian Rite is that of Addai and Mari. It is still used by the Ancient (Assyrian) Church of the East without the narrative of institution, though in the versions used by the Chaldean Catholics and by the Syro-Malabars in India the narrative appears.

#### *2.4.5.1 Addai and Mari*[78]

*And the priest says:* The grace of our Lord, etc.

*And they reply:* Amen.

[78] PEER 4, 64–69, originally from Bryan Spinks, *Addai and Mari*. For what may have been an earlier version of *Addai and Mari*, before the insertion of explicit trinitarian language, the Sanctus, and narrative of institution, see Paul F. Bradshaw and Maxwell E. Johnson, *The Eucharistic Liturgies: Their Evolution and Interpretation*, ACC 87 (Collegeville, MN: Liturgical Press, Pueblo, 2012), 39–41.

*And the priest says:* Lift up your minds.

*And they reply:* Towards you, O God.

*And the priest says:* The oblation is offered to God, the Lord of all.

*And they reply:* It is fit and right.

*And the deacon says:* Peace be with us.

*And the priest recites quietly:* Worthy of praise from every mouth, and thanksgiving from every tongue is the adorable and glorious name of the Father and of the Son and of the Holy Spirit, who created the world by his grace and its inhabitants in his compassion, and redeemed humankind in his mercy, and has effected great grace towards mortals.

Your majesty, Lord, a thousand thousand heavenly beings worship; myriad myriads of angels, hosts of spiritual beings, ministers of fire and of spirit, with cherubim and holy seraphim, glorify your Name.

*Qanona:*[79] crying out and glorifying

*And they reply:* Holy, holy . . .

*And the priest recites quietly:* And with these heavenly powers we give thanks to you, O Lord, even we, your lowly, weak, and miserable servants, because you have effected in us a great grace which cannot be repaid, in that you put on our humanity so as to quicken us by your divinity. And you lifted up our poor estate, and righted our fall. And you raised up our mortality. And you forgave our debts. You justified our sinfulness and you enlightened our understanding. And you, our Lord and our God, vanquished our enemies and made triumphant the lowliness of our weak nature through the abundant compassion of your grace.

*Qanona:* And for all . . .

*And they reply:* Amen.

*And the deacon says:* in your minds.

[79] An audible conclusion to a prayer recited quietly.

*The priest says privately:* You, O Lord, in your unspeakable mercies make a gracious remembrance for all the upright and just fathers who have been pleasing before you, in the commemoration of the body and blood of your Christ which we offer to you upon the pure and holy altar, as you have taught us. And grant us your tranquility and your peace all the days of the world. [Repeat.]

*And they reply:* Amen.

That all the inhabitants of the earth may know that you alone are God, the true Father, and you have sent our Lord Jesus Christ, your Son and your beloved, and he, our Lord and our God, taught us on his life-giving gospel all the purity and holiness of the prophets, apostles, martyrs and confessors and bishops and priests and deacons, and of all the children of the holy catholic church who have been marked with the mark of holy baptism.

And we also, Lord, *[three times]* your lowly, weak, and miserable servants who are gathered together and stand before you at this time have received tradition of the example which is from you rejoicing, and glorifying, and magnifying, and commemorating, and praising, and performing this great and dread mystery of the passion and death and resurrection of our Lord Jesus Christ.

May he come, O Lord, your Holy Spirit, and rest upon this oblation. . . .

*And the deacon says:* Be in silence.

. . . of your servants, and bless and hallow it, that it may be to us, O Lord, for the pardon of debts and the forgiveness of sins, and a great hope of resurrection from the dead and a new life in the kingdom of heaven with all who have been pleasing before you.

And for all your marvelous economy towards us we give you thanks and praise you without ceasing in your Church, redeemed by the precious blood of your Christ, with open mouths and with uncovered faces.

*Qanona:* As we offer up

*And they say:* Amen.

In addition to Addai and Mari, the East Syrians, with the exception of the Syro-Malabars, also make use of two other anaphoras, namely, Mar Nestorius, named, of course, for the fifth-century patriarch whose views against the term *Theotokos* were condemned by the Council of Ephesus, and Mar Theodore the Interpreter, named for Theodore of Mopsuestia. These two anaphoras, called by Bryan Spinks "the forgotten Eucharistic prayers of East Syria," are often claimed to be but "compilations based on the two Byzantine anaphoras"[80] (i.e., ByzBAS and CHR). They are actually, however, both mid-sixth-century redactions, probably by Mar Aba (†553), catholicos (i.e., patriarch) of the East Syrians from 540 to 552, making use of earlier Greek liturgical sources such as BAS and CHR, as well as earlier East Syrian anaphoral traditions (Addai and Mari) and other sources, and reflecting the strongly Antiochene theology of Theodore of Mopsuestia himself.[81]

### *2.4.6 West Syrian Rite*

Like that of the Ethiopian Rite, the West Syrians employ several different anaphoras, including a Syriac version of JAS,[82] and several others in current usage.[83] JAS is connected to early Jerusalem liturgy, especially to the *Mystagogical Catecheses* of Cyril (John) of Jerusalem and the text also bears some relationship to the anaphoral tradition of BAS. Following Geoffrey Cuming, John R. K. Fenwick argues, in fact, that the core of JAS was the result of an amalgamation made in the late fourth century between the prayer described in the *Mystagogical Catecheses* and EgBAS, and was then subject to several considerable

[80] Enzo Lodi, "The Oriental Anaphoras," in *Handbook for Liturgical Studies*, vol. 3: *The Eucharist*, ed. Chupungco, 95.

[81] For texts of these prayers and commentary, see Spinks, *Mar Nestorius and Mar Theodore the Interpreter*.

[82] On Syriac JAS see Baby Varghese, *The Syriac Version of the Liturgy of St. James: A Brief History for Students*, AGLS 49 (Cambridge: Grove Books, 2001). See also Phillip Tovey, *The Liturgy of St. James as Presently Used*, AGLS 40 (Cambridge: Grove Books, 1998).

[83] For current texts in Syriac and English translation, see *Anaphoras: The Book of the Divine Liturgies According to the Rite of the Syrian Orthodox Church of Antioch*, trans. Murad Saliba Barsom, ed. Mar Athanasius Yeshue Samuel (Lodi, NJ: Mar Athanasius Yeshue Samuel, 1991).

later influences.[84] More recently, while noting some relationship between JAS and EgBAS, Gabriele Winkler has suggested in a preliminary way a much closer relationship with the first Armenian version of BAS, a relationship noted above also with the Anaphora of St. Athanasius.[85] We present the anaphora of JAS here with what have been identified to be the later Greek insertions in brackets.

*2.4.6.1 Anaphora of Saint James*[86]

*The bishop:*[87] The love of God the Father, the grace of our Lord [and] God and Savior Jesus Christ, and the fellowship [and the gift] of the [all-]Holy Spirit be with you all.

*People:* And with your spirit.

*The Bishop:* Let us lift up our minds and hearts.

*People:* We have them with the Lord.

*The Bishop:* Let us give thanks to the Lord.

*People:* It is fitting and right.

*The bishop, bowing, says:*

It is truly fitting and right, suitable and profitable, to praise you, [to hymn you,] to bless you, to worship you, to glorify you, to give thanks to you, the creator of all creation, visible and invisible, [the treasure of eternal good things, the fountain of life and immortality, the God and Master of all]. You are hymned by [the heavens and] the heavens of heavens and all their powers; the sun and moon and all the choir of stars; earth, sea, and all that is in them; the heavenly Jerusalem, [the assem-

[84] See J. R. K. Fenwick, *The Anaphoras of St. Basil and St. James: An Investigation into Their Common Origin*, OCA 240 (Rome: Pontificium Institutum Orientale, 1992); John Witvliet, "The Anaphora of St. James," in *Essays on Early Eastern Eucharistic Prayers*, ed. Paul F. Bradshaw (Collegeville, MN: Liturgical Press, Pueblo, 1997), 153–72.

[85] Gabriele Winkler, "Preliminary Observations about the Relationship between the Liturgies of St. Basil and St. James," OCP 76 (2010): 5–55. See also idem, *Die Jakobus-Liturgie in ihren Überlieferungssträngen. Edition des Cod. arm 17 von Lyon, Übersetzung und Liturgievergleich*, Anaphorae Orientales 4, Anaphorae Armeniacae 4 (Rome: Pontificio Istituto Orientale, 2013).

[86] PEER 4, 139–53.

[87] Greek: *hiereus.*

bly of the elect,] the church of the first-born written in heaven, [the spirits of the righteous and prophets, the souls of martyrs and apostles;] angels, archangels, thrones, dominions, principalities and powers, and awesome virtues. The cherubim with many eyes and seraphim with six wings, which cover their own faces with two wings, and their feet with two, and fly with two, cry one to the other with unwearying mouths and never-silent hymns of praise, (*aloud*) [*singing*] with clear voice the triumphal hymn of your magnificent glory, proclaiming, praising, crying, and saying:

*People:* Holy, holy, holy, Lord of Sabaoth; heaven and earth are full of your glory. Hosanna in the highest. Blessed is he that comes[88] and will come in the name of the Lord. Hosanna in the highest.

*And the bishop, standing up, seals the gifts, saying privately:* Holy you are, King of the ages and [Lord and] Giver of all holiness; holy too is your only-begotten Son, our Lord Jesus Christ, [through whom you made all things;] and holy too is your [all-]Holy Spirit, who searches out all things, even your depths, O God and Father. (*He bows and says:*) Holy you are, almighty, omnipotent, awesome, good, [compassionate,] with sympathy above all for what you fashioned.

You made humankind from the earth [after your image and likeness,] and granted them the enjoyment of paradise; and when they transgressed your commandment and fell, you did not despise or abandon them, for you are good, but you chastened them as a kindly father, you called them through the law, you taught them through the prophets.

Later you sent your only-begotten Son, [himself, our Lord Jesus Christ,] into the world to renew [and raise up] your image [by coming himself.] He came down [from heaven] and was made flesh from the Holy Spirit and Mary, the Holy [ever-] Virgin Mother of God. He dwelt among men and ordered everything for the salvation of our race.

[88] Syriac: came and comes.

And when he was about to endure his voluntary [and life-giving] death [on the cross], the sinless for us sinners, in the night when he was betrayed,[89] [or rather handed himself over,] for the life and salvation of the world. (*He stands up, takes the bread, seals it, and says:*) he took bread in his holy, undefiled, blameless, [and immortal] hands, [looked up to heaven, and] showed it to you, his God and Father; he gave thanks, blessed, sanctified, and broke it, and gave it to his [holy and blessed] disciples and apostles, saying, (*he puts the bread down, saying aloud:*) "Take, eat; this is my body, which is broken and distributed for you for the forgiveness of sins." *People:* Amen.

(*He takes the cup, seals it, and says privately:*) "Likewise after supper [he took] the cup, he mixed wine and water, [he looked up to heaven and showed it to you, his God and Father; he gave thanks,] blessed, and sanctified it, [filled it with the Holy Spirit,] and gave it to his [holy and blessed] disciples and apostles, saying, (*he puts it down, saying aloud:*) "Drink from it, all of you; this is my blood of the new covenant, which is shed and distributed for you and for many for forgiveness of sins." *People:* Amen.

(*Then he stands and says privately:*) "Do this for my remembrance; for as often as you eat this bread and drink this cup, you proclaim the death of the Son of Man and confess his Resurrection, until he comes."[90]

(*And the deacons present answer:*) We believe and confess.

*People:* Your death, Lord, we proclaim and your Resurrection we confess.

*Then he makes the sign of the cross, bows, and says:*[91] We [sinners,] therefore, [also] remembering [his life-giving suffering and his saving cross and] his death [and his burial] and his Resurrection from the dead on the third day and his return to heaven and his session at your right hand, his God and Father, and his glorious and awesome second coming, when he [comes with

[89] Greek: *paredidoto* and *paredidou*.

[90] Syriac: my death and confess my resurrection until I come.

[91] From this point onward the Syriac version is addressed to Christ.

glory to] judge the living and the dead, when he will reward each according to his works [—spare us, Lord our God (*thrice*)—or rather according to his compassion], we offer you, [Master,] this awesome and bloodless sacrifice, [asking you] that you "deal not with us after our sins nor reward us according to our iniquities," but according to your gentleness and [unspeakable] love for man to [pass over and] blot out [the handwriting that is against us][92] your suppliants, [and grant us your heavenly and eternal gifts, "which eye has not seen nor ear heard nor have entered into the heart of man, which you, O God, have prepared for those who love you." And do not set at naught your people on account of me and my sins, O Lord, lover of men (*thrice*),] (*aloud*) for your people and your Church entreats you.

*People:* Have mercy on us, [Lord, God,] Father, the almighty.

*And the bishop stands up and says privately:* Have mercy on us, [Lord,] God the Father, almighty; [have mercy on us, God, our Savior. Have mercy on us, O God, according to your great mercy,] and send out upon us and upon these [holy] gifts set before you your [all-]Holy Spirit, (*he bows*) the Lord and giver of life, who shares your throne and the kingdom with you, God the Father and your [only-begotten] Son, consubstantial and co-eternal, who spoke in the law and the prophets and in your new covenant, who descended in the likeness of a dove upon our Lord Jesus Christ in the river Jordan [and remained upon him,] who descended upon your holy apostles in the likeness of fiery tongues [in the Upper Room of the holy and glorious Zion on the day of the holy Pentecost; (*he stands up and says privately:*) send down, Master, your all-Holy Spirit himself upon us and upon these holy gifts set before you,] (*aloud*) that he may descend upon them, [and by his holy and good and glorious coming may sanctify them,] and make this bread the holy body of Christ, (*People:* Amen.) and this cup the precious blood of Christ.[93] (*People:* Amen.)

[92] Syriac: the sins of.

[93] This passage is greatly enlarged in the Syriac.

*The bishop stands up and says privately:* that they may become to all who partake of them [for forgiveness of sins and for eternal life] for sanctification of souls and bodies, for bringing forth good works, for strengthening your holy, [catholic, and apostolic] Church, which you founded on the rock of faith, that the gates of hell should not prevail against it, rescuing it from heresy and from the stumbling-blocks of those who work lawlessness, [and from the enemies who rose and rise up] until the consummation of the age.

*The clerics alone answer:* Amen.

*Then he makes the sign of the cross, bows, and says:* We offer to you, [Master,] for your holy places also, which you glorified by the theophany of your Christ [and the descent of your all-Holy Spirit;] principally for [holy and glorious] Zion, the mother of all the churches, and for your holy, [catholic, and apostolic] Church throughout the world: even now, Master, grant it richly the gifts of your [all-]Holy Spirit.

Remember, Lord, also our holy [fathers and] bishops [in the Church,] who [in all the world] divide the word of truth [in orthodoxy]; principally our holy Father N., [all his clergy and priesthood]: grant him an honorable old age; preserve him to shepherd your flock in all piety and gravity for many years.

Remember, Lord, the honorable presbytery here and everywhere, the diaconate in Christ, all the other ministers, every ecclesiastical order, [our brotherhood in Christ, and all the Christ-loving people. . . .]

*[The intercessions continue]*

*The bishop says aloud:* Through whom, [as a good God and a Master that loves people,] to us and them (*People:*) remit, forgive, pardon, O God, our transgression, voluntary and involuntary, witting and unwitting.

*The bishop alone says:* By the grace and compassion and love for people of your Christ, with whom you are blessed and glorified, with your all-Holy and life-giving Spirit, now and always and to the ages of ages. Amen.

### *2.4.7 Maronite Rite*

As noted above, the Maronites are often associated with the West Syrian Rite, but several of their liturgies—including their rites of Christian initiation, as we saw in the previous chapter—also have close affinities with East Syrian liturgy. One of these, as discussed above, is the anaphora called the Third Anaphora of St. Peter, or *Sharar*, that text sharing a common ancestor with Addai and Mari and possibly reflecting even an earlier version of Addai and Mari in part.

#### *2.4.7.1 Third Anaphora of Saint Peter* (Sharar)[94]

*Deacon:* Let us stand aright.

*Priest:* We offer to you, God, our Father, Lord of all, an offering and a commemoration and a memorial in the sight of God, living and from the beginning holy from eternity, for the living and the dead, for the near and for the far, for the poor and for travelers, for the churches and monasteries, which are here and in every place and in all regions; and for me, unworthy and a sinner, whom you have made worthy to stand before you (remember me in your heavenly kingdom); and for the souls and spirits whom we commemorate before you, Lord, mighty God, and for this people which is in the true faith and awaits your abundant mercy; and for the sins, faults and defects of us all, we offer this pure and holy offering.

*People:* It is fitting and right.

*Priest:* It is fitting and right, our duty and our salvation, natural and good. Let our minds ever be lifted up to heaven, and all our hearts in purity.

*People:* To you, Lord, God of Abraham, Isaac, and Israel, O King glorious and holy forever.

*Priest:* To you, Lord, God of Abraham, savior of Isaac, strength of Israel, O king glorious and holy forever. The Lord is worthy to be confessed by us and adored and praised.

[94] PEER 4, 69–76.

(*Here the priest blesses the people, and says a prayer relating to the incense and a number of commemorations, after which he begins the anaphora.*)

*Priest (bowing):* Glory to you, adorable and praiseworthy name of the Father and of the Son and of the Holy Spirit. You created the world through your grace and all its inhabitants by your mercy and made redemption for mortals by your grace.

Your majesty, O Lord, a thousand thousand heavenly angels adore; myriad myriads of hosts, ministers of fire and spirit, praise you in fear. With the cherubim and seraphim, who in turn bless, glorify, proclaim, and say, let us also, Lord, become worthy of your grace and mercy, to say with them thrice, "Holy, holy, holy. . ."

(*bowing*) We give thanks to you, Lord, we your sinful servants, because you have given your grace which cannot be repaid. You put on our human nature to give us life through your divine nature; you raised our lowly state; you restored our Fall; you gave life to our mortality; you justified our sinfulness; you forgave our debts; you enlightened our understanding, conquered our enemies, and made our weak nature to triumph.

(*aloud*) And for all your grace towards us, let us offer you glory and honor, in your holy Church before your altar of propitiation. . . .

(*bowing*) You, Lord, through your great mercy, be graciously mindful of all the holy and righteous Fathers, when we commemorate your body and blood, which we offer to you on your living and holy altar, as you, our hope, taught us in your holy gospel and said, "I am the living bread who came down from heaven that mortals may have life in me."

(*aloud*) We make the memorial of your Passion, Lord, as you taught us. In the night in which you were betrayed to the Jews, Lord, you took bread in your pure and holy hands, and lifted your eyes to heaven to your glorious Father; you blessed, sealed, sanctified, Lord, broke, and gave it to your disciples the blessed Apostles, and said to them, "This bread is my body, which is broken and given for the life of the world, and will be to those who take it for the forgiveness of debts and pardon of sins; take and eat from it, and it will be to you for eternal life."

(*He takes the cup*) Likewise over the cup, Lord, you praised, glorified, and said, "This cup is my blood of the new covenant, which is shed for many for forgiveness of sins; take and drink from it, all of you, and it will be to you for pardon of debts and forgiveness of sins, and for eternal life." Amen.

"As often as you eat from this holy body, and drink from this cup of life and salvation, you will make the memorial of the death and resurrection of your Lord, until the great day of his coming."

*People:* We make the memorial, Lord, of your death. . . .

*Priest:* We adore you, only begotten of the Father, first born of creation, spiritual Lamb, who descended from heaven to earth, to be a propitiatory sacrifice for all men and to bear their debts voluntarily, and to remit their sins by your blood, and sanctify the unclean through your sacrifice.

Give us life, Lord, through your true life, and purify us through your spiritual expiation; and grant us to gain life through your life-giving death, that we may stand before you in purity and serve you in holiness and offer that sacrifice to your Godhead, that it may be pleasing to the will of your majesty, and that your mercy, Father, may flow over us all. . . .

We ask you, only-begotten of the Father, through whom our peace is established; Son of the Most High, in whom highest things are reconciled with lower; Good Shepherd, who laid down your life for your sheep and delivered them from ravening wolves; merciful Lord, who raised your voice on the cross and gathered us from vain error; God, the god of spirits and of all flesh; may our prayers ascend in your sight, and your mercy descend on our petitions, and let that sacrifice be acceptable before you; we offer it as a memorial of your Passion on your altar of propitiation.

> May it please your Godhead, and may your will be fulfilled in it; by it may our guilt be pardoned and our sins forgiven; and in it may our dead be remembered. Let us praise you and adore you, and the father who sent you for our salvation, and your living and Holy Spirit now. . . .
>
> By it may the glorious Trinity be reconciled, by the thurible and the sacrifice and the cup; by it may the souls be purified and the spirits sanctified of those for whom and on account of whom it was offered and sanctified; and for me, weak and sinful, who offered it, may the mercy of the glorious Trinity arise, Father. . . .

(*The priest bows and says a prayer to the Mother of God.*)

> We offer before you, Lord, this sacrifice in memory of all righteous and pious fathers, of prophets, apostles, martyrs, confessors, and all our patriarchs, and the pope of the city of Rome and metropolitan bishops, area bishops, visitors, priests, deacons, deaconesses, young men, celibates, virgins, and all the children of the holy Church who have been sealed with the sign of saving baptism, and whom you have made partakers of your holy body.

(*privately*) First and especially we commemorate the holy and blessed and saintly Virgin, the Blessed Lady Mary.

*Deacon:* Remember her, Lord God, and us through her pure prayers.

*Priest (bowing):* Remember, Lord God, at this time the absent and the present, the dead and the living, the sick and the oppressed, the troubled, the afflicted, and those who are in various difficulties.

Remember, Lord God, at this time our fathers and brothers in spirit and in body; and forgive their offences and sins.

Remember, Lord God, at this time, those who offer sacrifices, vows, firstfruits, memorials; grant to their petitions good things from your abundant store.

Remember, Lord God, at this time, those who join in commemorating your mother and your saints; grant them recompense for all their good works; and for all who communicated in this eucharist which was offered on this holy altar; grant them, Lord God, a reward in your kingdom; and for all who have said to us, "pray for us in your prayers before the Lord." Remember them, Lord God, and purge their iniquities.

Remember, Lord God, at this time, my miserableness, sinfulness, importunity, and lowliness; I have sinned and done evil in your sight consciously or not, voluntarily or not. Lord God, in your grace and mercy pardon me and forgive whatever I have sinned against you; and may this eucharist, Lord, be as a memorial of our dead and for the reconciliation of our souls.

Remember, Lord God, at this time, your weak and sinful servant George, who wrote this, and pardon him and forgive him his offences and sins, and forgive his fathers. Amen.

(*kneeling*) Hear me, Lord (*thrice*), and let your living and Holy Spirit, Lord, come and descend upon this offering of your servants, and may it be to those who partake for remission and forgiveness of sins, for a blessed resurrection from the dead, and for new life in the kingdom of heaven for ever.

(*aloud*) And because of your praiseworthy dispensation towards us, we give thanks to you, we your sinful servants redeemed by your innocent blood, with eloquent mouth in your holy Church before your altar of propitiation.

## 2.5 Communion and Dismissal Rites

Many of the rites often referred to as post-anaphoral or precommunion, culminating in the distribution and reception of Holy Communion itself, were already in place by the end of the fourth and beginning of the fifth centuries. *Mystagogical Catechesis* 5.11-20 of Cyril (John) of Jerusalem describes the recitation of the Lord's Prayer immediately after the eucharistic prayer, followed by an invitation to communion ("Holy things for the holy") coupled with the elevation of the gifts, as table 2.4 shows, and with the congregational response, "One is holy, one Lord, Jesus Christ"—what Robert Taft calls the "ancient communion call and its response" of Eastern liturgies.[95] Early references to this also appear in Egypt with the earliest being the *De Trinitate* 3.13 of Didymus the Blind and *In Johannis Evangelium* 4.7, 12 of Cyril of Alexandria. There was also a prayer of thanksgiving after communion in *Mystagogical Cathechesis* 5.22, the equivalent of Western post-communion prayers. These elements are paralleled in some other early Eastern sources. Theodore of Mopsuestia, for example, already makes reference to a "fraction" rite, as well as describing a commixture or commingling of the bread and wine before communion (*Baptismal Homily* 5.15-20), a similar invitation to communion ("Holy things for the holy"), and a prayer of thanksgiving after communion (*Baptismal Homily* 5.22-23, 29). A prayer of inclination before communion, a thanksgiving prayer after communion, and a final inclination prayer at the dismissal were becoming characteristic structures in the late fourth century among the Copts (including the *Prayers of Sarapion of Thmuis*) and the East and West Syrians (including *Apostolic Constitutions* 8).[96]

While all of the Eastern rites, with the exception of the Armenians, regularly use a mixed chalice containing both wine and water prepared earlier in the liturgy, only the Byzantine Rite maintains in current usage the addition of hot water (the *zeon*) poured into the chalice immediately after the fraction and the commixture (the comingling of the Body and Blood of Christ). According to Robert Taft,[97] however, evidence from the Byzantine liturgical manuscripts demonstrates that beginning in the sixth century this action took place during the

[95] See Robert Taft, *A History of the Liturgy of St. John Chrysostom*, vol. 5: *The Precommunion Rites*, OCA 261 (Rome: Pontificio Istituto Orientale 2000), 231ff. See also his essay, "'Holy Things for the Saints': The Ancient Call to Communion and Its Response," in *Fountain of Life*, ed. Gerard Austin (Washington, DC: Pastoral Press, 1991), 87–102.

[96] See Taft, *The Precommunion Rites*, 231ff. On the development of the fraction rites in the Syrian East, see the essay by Bryan D. Spinks, "From Functional to Artistic? The Development of the Fraction in the Syrian Orthodox Tradition," *Anaphora* 10, no. 2 (2016): 89–114. On the development of post-communion prayers in East and West see Harald Buchinger, "Die Postcommunio. Zur Frügeschichte und Character eienes eucharistischen Gebetes," *Ecclesia Orans* 38 (2021): 45–94.

[97] Ibid., 441–502.

preparation of the bread and wine before the liturgy (at the *Prothesis*). Later in history, in order to have a warm chalice for communion, the *zeon* began to be added immediately before the Great Entrance. But it was not until the eleventh century that the current practice developed and became normative. By that time, various theological interpretations had arisen as to the meaning of this action. As Alex Rentel has noted:

> Byzantine liturgical commentators will . . . see what transpires at the epiclesis, with the descent of the Holy Spirit, as completed only at the addition of hot water, the *zeon*, to the chalice directly after the fraction and commixture. This ritual vividly portrays Christ's resurrected body and blood being enlivened by the warmth and "fullness of the Holy Spirit" [Barberini gr. 336].[98]

Together with this resurrection imagery others began to interpret the *zeon* as indicative of Christ's living *warm* blood (and water) flowing from his side after his death on the cross.[99]

With regard to the distribution and reception of Holy Communion itself, while every Eastern rite came to have a stylized fraction (*melismos*) and commixture, and every rite distributes Communion (*comminution*) under both bread and wine, only the Copts and East Syrians have retained the practice of distributing the bread and cup separately, while the other rites use forms of intinction, with the Byzantines since the eleventh century using a spoon.[100] Again it is Taft who has argued that:

> the distinction between melismos and comminution [has] validity only in the later stages of liturgical development, when the ritualization of the manual acts symbolizing the rejoining of Christ's body and blood

[98] Alexander Rentel, "Byzantine and Slavic Orthodoxy," in *The Oxford History of Christian Worship*, ed. Geoffrey Wainwright and Karen Westerfield Tucker (Oxford: Oxford University Press, 2006), 295.

[99] On this, as well as controversies with the Armenians over the use of a mixed chalice or wine alone and its christological arguments, see Schulz, *The Byzantine Liturgy*, 39–43.

[100] Robert Taft, *A History of the Liturgy of St. John Chrysostom*, vol. 6: *The Communion, Thanksgiving, and Concluding Rites*, OCA 281 (Rome: Pontificio Istituto Orientale, 2008), 281–315.

> (intinction, consignation, commixture) forces a distinction in the fraction between the "symbolic" melismos that precedes these rites, and the "practical" comminution that follows.[101]

He notes further:

> Just when and how this comminution took place is not indicated in the early sources. Van de Paverd has suggested "that a piece of bread was broken off for each individual communicant so that for all practical purposes the fraction took place during communion." This solution seems to fit the evidence best. First, the main celebrant at the altar broke off particles for himself and his fellow ministers. Then the gifts were brought out and a piece was broken off and placed in the hand of each communicant as he or she approached in the communion procession. Communion is still given this way in the Coptic Orthodox service.[102]

All of the Eastern rites also have one or more prayers of preparation for the worthy reception of Communion called "inclination" prayers. In the Byzantine and Armenian Rites, however, this prayer probably functioned originally in the time of John Chrysostom as a prayer for the solemn "dismissal" of non-communing faithful who, in the context of the post-Constantinian influx of converts and the gradual decline in the reception of communion in general, were leaving the Eucharist at this point. This type of "dismissal prayer" seems to be related as well to the discipline of public penance. In some places (e.g., Asia Minor and Constantinople), certain penitents known as "bystanders without offering" were dismissed from the Eucharist with a special blessing, before Communion was then distributed.[103] In this context, we might also note the penitential character of many of the Eastern pre-communion rites, including prayers of absolution in some rites, especially among the Copts and Ethiopians.

All of the Eastern rites have some form of communion antiphon, called the *koinōnikon* in the Byzantine Rite, that is, a chant sung dur-

[101] Robert Taft, "Melismos and Comminution: The Fraction and Its Symbolism in the Byzantine Tradition," *Studia Anselmiana* 95 (1988): 531–52, here at 541.

[102] Ibid., 538–39.

[103] On all of this, see Robert Taft, "The Inclination Prayer before Communion in the Byzantine Liturgy of St. John Chrysostom: A Study in Comparative Liturgy," *Ecclesia Orans* 3 (1986): 29–60, here at 42–48.

ing the reception of Communion, a characteristic also of Western rites. Together with *Apostolic Constitutions* 8.13.16-17 and the witness of John Chrysostom, the *Mystagogical Catechesis* 5.20, ascribed to Cyril of Jerusalem, offers our earliest evidence for the use of responsorial psalmody at this point in the liturgy (i.e., Psalm 33 (34), "Taste and see that the Lord is good," at Jerusalem), from which the communion antiphon, or *koinōnikon*, will eventually develop.[104]

In addition to a final inclination prayer of blessing and dismissal at some point in all of the rites, the Armenians and Byzantines distribute to all in attendance the bread that is known in the churches of the Byzantine Rite as *antidoron* ("instead of the gift"). This is the remainder of the bread prepared at the *Prothesis* but not consecrated or used for Communion. Having its origins in early Christian customs, perhaps even as the vestige of a full Christian meal, such distribution of unconsecrated leftover bread was a common practice at one time in churches of both the West[105] and the East. It appears that the *antidoron* grew in importance, at least among the Byzantines, at a time in which both frequent communion was in decline and the *Prothesis* itself was developing into a more elaborate rite.[106]

Of all the Eastern rites, only the West Syrians and the Maronites have a prayer of "farewell" addressed to the altar by the priest. The Maronite version reads:

> Remain in peace, O altar of God, and I hope to return to you in peace. May the sacrifice which I have offered upon you forgive my sins, help me to avoid faults, and prepare me to stand blameless before the throne of Christ. I know not whether I will be able to return to you again to offer sacrifice. Guard me, O Lord, and protect your holy Church, so that she may remain the way of salvation and the light of the world.[107]

[104] See Thomas Schattauer, "The Koinonikon of the Byzantine Liturgy: An Historical Study," OCP 49 (1983): 91–129, here at 116–17; Frans van de Paverd, *Zur Geschichte der Messliturgie in Antiocheia und Konstantinopel gegen Ende des vierten Jahrhunderts*, OCA 187 (Rome: Pontificium Institutum Orientalium Studorium, 1970), 395; and Taft, *The Communion, Thanksgiving, and Concluding Rites*, 281–315.

[105] See Joseph Jungmann, *The Mass of the Roman Rite* (New York: Benziger, 1955), 2:453–55.

[106] See Taft, *The Communion, Thanksgiving, and Concluding Rites*, 699–719.

[107] *Anaphora Book of the Syriac-Maronite Church of Antioch*, 30–31.

## Table 2.4: Communion and Dismissal Rites

| Armenian | Byzantine | Coptic |
|---|---|---|
| | -litany of supplication | |
| -Lord's prayer | -Lord's prayer | -Lord's prayer |
| | | -several prayers of remembrance |
| | | -prayer of absolution |
| | preparation prayer | |
| -incensation | | |
| -prayer of penitence addressed to Holy Spirit | | |
| -elevation | -elevation | -elevation |
| -fraction | -fraction | -fraction |
| | -*Zeon* | |
| -priest's communion with accompanying prayers | -communion of clergy | |
| -communion of people | -communion of people | -preparation prayers and communion |
| | -litany | |
| -thanksgiving prayer | -thanksgiving prayer | -thanksgiving prayer |
| | -dismissal | |
| | -Prayer behind the Ambo | |
| -"last gospel" (John 1:1-14) | | |
| -prayer for peace | | |
| -final blessing and distribution of *antidoron* | -final blessing and distribution of *antidoron* | -blessing |
| | | -dismissal |

While this prayer undoubtedly originates in Jerusalem and/or Palestinian usage, it is clearly an addition to an earlier Antiochene-type concluding rite that would have ended the liturgy with a simple prayer of blessing and dismissal.

To the Byzantine Rite was added a final prayer called the *Opisthambonos*, "prayer behind the ambo."[108] Originally prayed by the clergy at Hagia Sophia in Constantinople during the recession to the *Skeuophylakion*, with another prayer said therein at their arrival, this prayer behind the ambo was moved to its current location *after* the dismissal by the tenth century. And only the Armenians, under the influence of the Dominican Order in the twelfth century, have incorporated the "Last Gospel," John 1:1-14, a characteristic of various Latin medieval, eventually including the Tridentine, rites of the mass.

[108] On dismissal and final prayers, especially in Byzantine usage, see Taft, *The Communion, Thanksgiving, and Concluding Rites*, 565–644.

| Ethiopian | East Syrian | West Syrian |
|---|---|---|
| -thanksgiving prayer | | |
| -Lord's Prayer | -proclamation of faith in the life-giving bread of heaven | |
| -prayers of blessing, absolution and remembrance | | |
| | -fraction and signing | -fraction and signing |
| | -elevation | |
| | -litany prayer for forgiveness | |
| -fraction | | |
| -elevation | -Lord's prayer | -Lord's prayer |
| | | -penitential rite |
| | | -elevation |
| -preparation prayers | communion | -communion |
| -communion | -thanksgiving prayer | -prayer of thanksgiving |
| | -blessing | -final blessing |
| -thanksgiving prayer | -dismissal | |
| | | -"farewell" prayer addressed to the altar |
| -blessing of people | | |
| -final blessing and dismissal | | |

## 2.6 Liturgy of the Presanctified

As noted earlier, several of the Eastern liturgical traditions also have a rite for the distribution of communion separate from the eucharistic liturgy, known as the Liturgy of the Presanctified (PRES). Technically speaking, the PRES is not a "liturgy"—a term often reserved in the East for the Divine Liturgy—but an office of communion attached to vespers; therefore, its central prayer is *not* an anaphora, but it is structured around and combines various pre-communion and other elements from ByzBAS.[109] Its origins lay in the fourth and fifth centuries, within the context of incidents of abuse of, and eventual suppression of, private reservation of the Eucharist and private Communion; fears of heresy; a move toward liturgical uniformity; and increased clericalization of the liturgy. It should also be noted

109 Alexopoulos, *Presanctified Liturgy in the Byzantine Rite*.

that the PRES appears in places where the celebration of the full Eucharist was prohibited on fasting days, while in places where the full Eucharist was allowed on fasting days, the PRES either never appeared or appeared only momentarily in history.

The earliest manuscript evidence for the Byzantine PRES comes from Barberini gr. 336, where the PRES already appears in a rather developed form. Our first reference to a PRES in the Byzantine Rite, however, comes from the beginning of the seventh century. The original simple form of the PRES would have included the reservation of the gifts from a previous full liturgy, the transfer of the gifts to the altar, and Communion. It is on this basic structure that the PRES expanded. Three dynamics fueled its development: (1) imitation, as the communion part of the PRES grew copying structures, actions, and elements of the full liturgy; (2) conservatism, as the PRES preserved elements of the cathedral office of daily prayer otherwise lost, or elements that were dropped from the full liturgy; and (3) differentiation, in that we see in the PRES an effort to halt the imitation of the full liturgy and the attempt to create its own identity.[110]

Currently the PRES in the Byzantine liturgical tradition is celebrated on Wednesdays and Fridays of Lent and Holy Monday, Holy Tuesday, and Holy Wednesday in Great Week. Originally it could be celebrated on every Wednesday and Friday of the year, Wednesday and Friday of Cheesefare Week (the week before the beginning of Lent), all weekdays of Lent, Holy Monday, Tuesday, Wednesday, and Friday, and possibly September 14, as well as in the context of coronations, appointments of civil servants, and weddings. The PRES, however, is not unique to the Byzantine liturgical tradition. In fact, there are three other types in the Christian East: Syrian (i.e., West Syrian and Maronite), Jerusalem (e.g., Armenian), and Nubian (a variation of the Ethiopian Rite). With the exception of the Nubian tradition, each of these types can be further divided into two categories: cathedral and monastic.[111] In all Eastern liturgical traditions originally only consecrated bread was reserved, the cup being sanctified by the signing of the chalice/commingling; that is, the adding

[110] Ibid., 294.
[111] Ibid., 95–127.

of the consecrated bread to unconsecrated wine. In the Syrian tradition, in fact, the PRES is called "The Signing of the Chalice."[112]

Not all of the Eastern Churches today, however, have the practice either of the PRES or even of reserving the Eucharist.[113] The Coptic Orthodox, Ethiopian Orthodox, and the Ancient (Assyrian) Church of the East still do not reserve the Eucharist, though, as we have seen, the East Syrians have the practice of reserving and adding the *Malka* to the eucharistic bread during its preparation.[114] And what is fascinating about this is that these churches are all recognized by Rome as having authentically *Catholic* eucharistic doctrine and practice. Hence, to reserve or not to reserve the Eucharist cannot be the question or litmus test with regard to individual churches and their theology of the Real Presence of Christ in the Eucharist. Together with this it should also be noted that, unlike the later Western medieval period wherein devotion to the Eucharist outside of the liturgy became a popular practice (including, for example, the development of the feast of Corpus Christi in the thirteenth century), the Christian East never developed any equivalent devotional practices separate from its liturgical context. Where the Eucharist is reserved in the Christian East, as in early Christianity, it is for the communion of the sick or for the PRES during Lent.[115] Many Eastern Christians greet and venerate icons when they enter a church building, not the eucharistic host reserved in a tabernacle on a main or side altar.

## 2.7 Eastern Eucharistic Theology

Within the Christian East there appears to be a rather consistent theological-historical continuity with the previous centuries, especially the fourth and fifth centuries. Nathan Mitchell has noted that "medieval Latin theology's preoccupation with the sacrificial aspects

[112] For examples of this rite, see ibid., 95–107.

[113] On Eastern practices of reservation and veneration of the Eucharist apart from the liturgy, see Taft, *The Communion, Thanksgiving, and Concluding Rites*, 415–53.

[114] See above, p. 69.

[115] See Robert Taft, "Reservation and Veneration of the Eucharist in the Orthodox Traditions," in *Inquiries into Eastern Christian Worship: Selected Papers of the Second International Congress of the Society of Oriental Liturgy, Rome, 17–21 September 2008*, ed. Bert Groen, Steven Hawkes-Teeples, and Stefanos Alexopoulos, Eastern Christian Studies 12 (Leuven: Peeters, 2012), 99–120.

of Eucharist developed in part from a tendency to separate 'sacrifice' from 'sacrament,' and 'consecration' from the church's 'offering' and communion."[116] But such separation and compartmentalization of the Eucharist does not take place in the Eastern liturgical traditions. With particular reference to the anaphoral oblation in the Byzantine Rite, Taft has noted:

> There is one single offering of the Church within which several things happen. These things are expressed in various ways and moments according to the several pre-reformation traditions of East and West, all of which agree on the basic ritual elements of their traditions. These classical anaphoras express that the Eucharist is a sacrifice, the sacramental memorial of Christ's own sacrifice on the cross, in which the Church, repeating what Jesus did at the Last Supper, invokes God's blessing on bread and wine so that it might become Jesus' body and blood, our spiritual food and drink. . . . All attempts to squeeze more out of the words of the prayer . . . [are] an inference that can only be made by imposing on the text the results of later theological reflection and/or polemics. . . . So the most one can say is that the "offering" expressions that fall between institution and epiclesis in BAS and CHR neither confirm nor exclude any particular theological thesis of when or by what particular part of the anaphoral prayer the consecration is effected, or just *what*, beyond the Eucharistic service in its most general sense of the Church's offering of the memorial Jesus is believed to have commanded the Church to repeat, is offered: bread and wine, body and blood, the "reasonable and unbloody sacrifice" of the Church, the sacrifice of Christ represented in its sacrament. . . . My own view is that later precisions, in the sense in which they are sometimes posed today as the result of confessional disputes, are sterile and pointless. . . . I would prefer that the earlier liturgical language, which is metaphorical and evocative, not philosophical and ontological, includes *all these "offerings,"* if implicitly and not self-consciously.[117]

[116] Nathan Mitchell, "Eucharistic Theologies," in *The New Westminster Dictionary of Liturgy and Worship*, ed. Paul F. Bradshaw (Louisville: Westminster John Knox, 2002), 200.

[117] Robert Taft, "Understanding the Byzantine Anaphoral Oblation," in *Rule of Prayer, Rule of Faith: Essays in Honor of Aidan Kavanagh, O.S.B.*, ed. Nathan D. Mitchell and John F. Baldovin (Collegeville, MN: Liturgical Press, Pueblo, 1996), 32–55, here at 53–54.

This does not mean, however, that various positions on when and how consecration takes place did not develop in the Christian East. To that we now turn.

### *2.7.1 Eucharistic Consecration*

It is often assumed by Western Christians, though not exclusively by them, that as the West came to focus on the narrative of institution as the "moment" of eucharistic consecration of the bread and wine into the Body and Blood of Christ, so the Eastern rites focused and continue to focus that "moment" on the epiclesis of the Holy Spirit following that narrative. And it is certainly true that a variety of liturgical texts and commentaries could be listed as supporting such a view. This becomes especially the case, for example, in the liturgical writings of the fourteenth-century Byzantine lay theologian and mystic Nicholas Cabasilas (†ca. 1363), who in his influential *Commentary on the Divine Liturgy* claims:

> When these words have been said [i.e., the words of the epiclesis], the whole sacred rite is accomplished, the offerings are consecrated, the sacrifice is complete; the splendid Victim, the Divine oblation, slain for the salvation of the world, lies upon the altar. For it is no longer the bread, which until now has represented the Lord's Body, nor is it a simple offering, bearing the likeness of the true offering, carrying as if engraved on it the symbols of the Savior's Passion; it is the true Victim, the most holy Body of the Lord, which really suffered the outrages, insult and blows; which was crucified and slain, which under Pontius Pilate bore such splendid witness; that Body which was mocked, scourged, spat upon, and which tasted gall. In like manner the wine has become the blood which flowed from that Body. It is that Body and Blood formed by the Holy Spirit, born of the Virgin Mary, which was buried, which rose again on the third day, which ascended into heaven and sits on the right hand of the Father.[118]

Cabasilas claimed that the Roman *canon missae* could be brought to bear here as well since he interpreted the post–institution narrative

[118] Cabasilas, *Commentary on the Divine Liturgy*, chap. 27, as quoted in Schulz, *The Byzantine Liturgy*, 129. On Cabasilas's theology, see Schulz, *The Byzantine Liturgy*, 124–32.

*Supplices te rogamus* portion of the Canon, in which the angel is asked to take the offerings to God's altar in heaven and the faithful receive Christ's Body and Blood, as an equivalent consecratory epiclesis.

The view of Cabasilas and other theologians on the importance of the epiclesis of the Holy Spirit was seriously challenged at the Council of Florence (1438–1445), called initially to bring about union between the Church at Constantinople, needing assistance against the invading Turks, and Rome, together with other Eastern rites (Coptic, Armenian, and, eventually, West Syrians). With regard to eucharistic theology the representatives of the Byzantine East, with the notable exception of Mark Eugenikos, metropolitan of Ephesus, all signed an agreement (*Laetetus Coeli*, 1439) that asserted—among other controversial things like acceptance of the *filioque* clause in the Nicene Creed and the doctrine of purgatory—that it is the narrative of institution alone that consecrates the Eucharist. It was, however, the position of Mark of Ephesus (now venerated by the Orthodox as *Saint* Mark of Ephesus), in agreement with that of Cabasilas, that eventually won the day in the Byzantine East after the ill-fated Florentine attempt at union fell apart.[119]

Even so, however, eucharistic consecration by means of the epiclesis of the Holy Spirit is not the only Eastern Christian position on the transformation of the bread and wine into the Body and Blood of Christ. In a recent essay, Russian Orthodox scholar Michael Zheltov has demonstrated that, at least for the Byzantines, a variety of differing opinions has existed historically and even today still exists on this question.[120] These positions include the narrative of institution; the elevation of the gifts with the invitation "Holy things for the holy," as the moment when the Holy Spirit descends; the dropping of the consecrated bread into the unconsecrated wine in the PRES (= consecration without an *epiclesis*); the *Prothesis* rite at the beginning of the Divine Liturgy; and other acts of the priest during the liturgy (e.g., priestly blessings). Zheltov's conclusion is important in drawing attention to the *why* of eucharistic consecration in the first place:

[119] See Michael Zheltov, "The Moment of Eucharistic Consecration in Byzantine Thought," in *Issues in Eucharistic Praying*, ed. Johnson, 263–306, here at 276–81.

[120] See ibid. See also the important essay by Robert Taft, "Ecumenical Scholarship and the Catholic-Orthodox Epiclesis Dispute," *Ostkirchliche Studien* 45 (1996): 201–26.

> [W]ith respect to a "moment" of the Eucharistic consecration, the Byzantines by no means limited themselves to the epiclesis. But the most distinct feature of their approach seems to be not their preference for one set of words over another but their reverence toward the manual acts of the Eucharistic celebration—be it the priestly blessing, the elevation, or the immersion of the Lamb into the chalice. However strange this attitude may seem, there is some logic behind it. It stresses the unity of the liturgical text and ritual action behind it and, in the case of the elevation, the importance of experiencing the whole Divine Liturgy in its entirety—the gifts are not "complete" until they are needed for communion. Such a perception of the liturgy reveals its holistic and integral character and does not allow its reduction to the recitation of a "sacramental formula."[121]

Along similar lines Alexander Rentel has written of the internal logic of the Divine Liturgy:

> The ritual of the Divine Liturgy . . . already in the preparatory rites, points to the bread as the "Lamb of God who takes away the sins of the world" and who is "sacrificed for the life of the world and its salvation" and whose side is pierced where "straightway there came forth blood and water and he who saw bore witness and his witness is true." The theme of the lamb being sacrificed is only resumed again later, right before communion at the fraction, when the priest says, "Broken and divided is the Lamb of God, who is broken, but not disunited, who is ever-eaten, but never consumed, but sanctifies all the faithful." Here there is no movement, no intervening climax; the liturgy began where it ends. Obviously, according to the Orthodox Church, something does happen in the liturgy that changes the bread and wine into the body and blood of Christ, but this something cannot be reduced to an efficacious word or phrase or a single moment or even the arc of a series of moments. It is simply a mystery effected by the power of God. If there is an overarching unidirectional moment, it is intended to be on the part of believers, who in one unitary contemplation of salvation offered by God, with many voices proclaiming it and many layers enriching it and giving it depth, move toward union with him.[122]

[121] Zheltov, "Moment of Eucharistic Consecration," 305–6.

[122] Rentel, "Byzantine and Slavic Orthodoxy," 294.

The purpose of the consecration of the Eucharist into the Body and Blood of Christ is for the communion of the faithful. *When* and *where* this occurs in the liturgy matters less in the East than *why*—the reason for which this occurs!

Before leaving this section on eucharistic consecration, one more point is especially important to make, particularly for Western readers. That is, while there is no question about Eastern Christian belief in the real presence of Christ in the Eucharist, including even at times apparition conversion stories with a little child (Lamb of God) seen as being sacrificed and divided on the *diskos* (paten), rivaling Western stories of bleeding hosts for their realism,[123] Eastern eucharistic theology, with the exception of those churches in full communion with Rome, does not accept the terminology of *transubstantiation*.[124] Even so, words like "transformation," "conversion," "change," and others are used to speak of what happens at the consecration. But the East does not appeal to the Aristotelian framework used by Western Scholastic theology, in terms of substance and accidents, to explain or undergird this reality. In other words, as the Christian East demonstrates clearly, neither terms like "transubstantiation" nor practices like the reservation of the Eucharist are necessary in order to demonstrate a belief in or theology of the real presence of Christ in the Eucharist.

### *2.7.2 Liturgical Commentaries*

Liturgical theology of the Eucharist in the Christian East is based not only on the rites themselves but also on the numerous liturgical commentaries that have been produced over the ages. Five liturgical commentaries on the Divine Liturgy survive from the Byzantine era: (1) the *Mystagogy* of Maximus the Confessor from the seventh century; (2) the *Ecclesiastical History and Mystical Contemplation* of Germanus of Constantinople from the eighth century; (3) the *Protheoria* of Nicholas and Theodore of Andida from the eleventh century; (4) the *Commentary on the Divine Liturgy* of Nicholas Cabasilas from the fourteenth century; and (5) the works *Explanation of the Divine Temple* and *On the*

[123] See Schulz, *The Byzantine Liturgy*, 66–67.

[124] See John A. McGuckin, *The Orthodox Church: An Introduction to Its History, Doctrine, and Spiritual Culture* (Oxford: Blackwell Publishing, 2008), 291.

*Sacred Liturgy* of Symeon of Thessaloniki from the fifteenth century. In these commentaries we see a shift from the earlier eschatological and allegorical approach, influenced by the *Ecclesiastical Hierarchy* of pseudo-Dionysios the Areopagite, to a more historical approach where each element, movement, or action in the context of the Divine Liturgy corresponds to an event in the life of Christ.[125] This symbolic approach reached its apogee with the *Protheoria* but was later reigned in with Cabasilas in the fourteenth century who brought forth a more balanced approach. With Symeon of Thessaloniki we observe a shift toward the eschatological and allegorical approach:

> Therefore in the sanctuary the divine temple represents the Master of heaven through the awe-inspiring, that is to say, the sacred altar, which is also called 1) the holy of holies, 2) the seat, 3) the place of God and the repose, 4) the mercy seat and 5) the workshop of the great sacrifice, 6) the tomb of Christ, and 7) the abode of His glory. By means of the curtain in the sanctuary it typifies the heavenly tabernacle round about God, where the hosts of angels and the repose of saints are. By means of the chancel screen, or the pillars, it represents the difference between sensible and spiritual realities.[126]

Such approaches to liturgical theology are certainly in harmony and continuity with the great Eastern mystagogues of the fourth and fifth centuries, namely, Cyril (John) of Jerusalem, John Chrysostom, and Theodore of Mopsuestia. The particular style of those commentaries, however, is often seen as beginning with the description of Theodore, who viewed the whole eucharistic liturgy as a ritual allegory reenacting the events of Jesus's passion, death, burial, and resurrection, with the bringing up of the bread and wine by the deacons symbolizing Christ being led to his passion, the cloths on the altar as his burial cloths in the tomb, and the climax of the rite occurring at the epiclesis of the Holy Spirit when the bread and wine become Christ's *risen* body.[127] While what began with Theodore continued in

[125] R. Bornert, *Les commentaires byzantins de la Divine Liturgie du VIIe au XVe siècle*, Archives de l'Orient Chrétien 9 (Paris: Institut Français d'Études Byzantines, 1966).

[126] Bornert, *Les commentaires byzantins*.

[127] See Edward Yarnold, *The Awe-Inspiring Rites of Initiation: The Origins of the R.C.I.A.*, 2nd ed. (Collegeville, MN: Liturgical Press, 1994; repr. 2001), 233–34.

## Table 2.5: "Life of Christ" Symbolism in the Liturgy: Comparative Table*

| | Prothesis | Enarxis | First Entrance | Ascent to Throne | Epistle | Gospel |
|---|---|---|---|---|---|---|
| **Maximus the Confessor** | | | First coming of Christ in the flesh, Passion and Resurrection | The Ascension of Christ | Instruction in the Christian life | The end of the world and the Second Coming of Christ to judge the world |
| **Germanus** | The sacrifice of Christ: Passion and Death | Prophetic foretelling of the Incarnation | Coming of the Son of God into the world | Completion of salvation and Ascension | Prokeimenon (psalm or canticle) and Alleluia = Prophecies of the coming of Christ | Revelation of God brought by Christ Bishop's blessing after Gospel = Second Coming |
| **Nicholas of Andida** | The Virgin Birth and hidden life of Christ before his baptism | Prophetic foretelling of the Incarnation and the ministry of John the Baptist | Manifestation of Christ at his Baptism in the Jordan | Passage from the Law and the Old Covenant to the beginning of divine grace | The calling of the Apostles | The teaching of Christ |
| **Nicholas Cabasilas** | The Incarnation and early years of Christ; his Passion and Death fore-shadowed | Prophetic witness to the coming of Christ: the time before the Baptist | Manifestation of Christ to the crowds at his Baptism | | Manifestation of Christ in his teach-ing to the Apostles | Manifestation of Christ in his teach-ing to the crowds |
| **Symeon of Thessalonike** | The Incarnation of Christ; his Passion and Death fore-shadowed | The Incarnation and the work of the incarnate Word | The resurrection and ascension of Christ<br>The coming of the Spirit | Christ's sitting at the right hand of the Father | Mission of the Apostles to the Gentiles | Proclamation of the Gospel in all the world |

| | Dismissal of Catechumens | Great Entrance | Placing of Gifts on Holy Table | Anaphora | Elevation | After Communion |
|---|---|---|---|---|---|---|
| **Maximus the Confessor** | The entrance of those worthy into the bridal chamber of Christ | Revelation of the mystery of salvation hidden in God | | Our future union with the spiritual powers of heaven | The union of all the faithful with God in the age to come | |
| **Germanus** | | Christ proceeding to his mystical sacrifice | The burial of Christ in the tomb | The Resurrection of Christ | | |
| **Nicholas of Andida** | | The Lord's journey to Jerusalem on Palm Sunday | The upper room made ready | The Last Supper | Christ's Crucifixion, Death and Resurrection | The Ascension of Christ and the coming of the Spirit |
| **Nicholas Cabasilas** | | Christ's journey to Jerusalem and his entry on Palm Sunday | | Christ's Death, Resurrection, and Ascension | The Zeon = The coming of the Holy Spirit | |
| **Symeon of Thessalonike** | The end of the world and final consummation | The final coming of Christ | | | The elevation of Christ on the Cross | The Ascension of the Lord and the proclamation of the Gospel in all the world |

*This comparative table is adapted from Hugh Wybrew, *The Orthodox Liturgy: The Development of the Eucharistic Liturgy in the Byzantine Rite* (Crestwood, NY: St. Vladimir's Seminary Press, 1990), 182–83.

all of the Eastern traditions to some extent,[128] and Theodore himself, of course, is representative of early *Syrian* rather than Byzantine theology, table 2.5 shows that one can actually trace the historical development of the Divine Liturgy by means of these mystagogical commentaries, all the way from Maximus the Confessor in the sixth century until Symeon of Thessalonica in the fourteenth.

There was already in the fourth and fifth centuries a tendency toward the dramatic, the development of what Alexander Schmemann called a "mysteriological piety" divorced increasingly from true liturgical symbolism toward making Christianity a "Mystery Religion,"[129] infrequent reception of Communion, and the liturgy increasingly viewed as an object of devotion to be gazed on from afar. That tendency has clearly continued in the Eastern rites. As Stefano Parenti concludes succinctly:

> The process of development was . . . marked in both East and West by regressive features . . .; for example, the shortening of the biblical readings, the atrophy or elimination of the psalmody, the decline in the prayer of the faithful, the suppression or clericalization of the sign of peace, and the recitation of the celebrant's prayers, including the anaphora, in a low voice. . . . The gradual loss of a clear understanding of the structure of the liturgical action led to compositions in

[128] The primary study for the Byzantine commentaries is Bornert, *Les commentaires byzantins de la Divine Liturgie du VIIe au XVe siècle*. For East Syrian commentaries, see Sebastian Brock, "An Early Syriac Commentary on the Liturgy," 387–403, and "Gabriel of Qatar's Commentary on the Litrugy," 1–25, both in Sebastian Brock, *Fire from Heaven: Studies in Syriac Theology and Liturgy*, Variorum Collected Studies Series 863 (Aldershot, England: Ashgate, 2006). See also Pauly Maniyattu, "East Syriac Theology of Eucharist," in *East Syriac Theology: An Introduction*, ed. Pauly Maniyattu (Satna, India: Ephrem's Publications, 2007), 320–44. For Armenian commentaries, see A. Renoux, "Les commentaires liturgiques arméniens," in *Mystagogie: pensée liturgique d'aujourd'hui et liturgie ancienne: Conferénces Saint-Serge XXXIXe semaine d'études liturgiques*, ed. A. M. Triacca and A. Pistoia (Rome: C.L.V.-Edizioni Liturgiche, 1993), 276–308; and Michael Daniel Findikyan, "Christology in Early Armenian Liturgical Commentaries," in *The Place of Christ in Liturgical Prayer: Trinity, Christology, and Liturgical Theology*, ed. Bryan D. Spinks (Collegeville, MN: Liturgical Press, Pueblo, 2008), 197–221. For some Ethiopic sources, see Habtemichael Kidane, "The Holy Spirit in the Ethiopian Orthodox *Täwaḥədo* Church Tradition," in *The Spirit in Worship—Worship in the Spirit*, ed. Teresa Berger and Bryan Spinks (Collegeville, MN: Liturgical Press, Pueblo, 2009), 179–205.

[129] Alexander Schmemann, *Introduction to Liturgical Theology*, 2nd ed. (Crestwood: St. Vladimir's Seminary Press, 1975), 81–86.

> the genre seen in the medieval liturgical commentaries. The Eucharistic celebration which is a *re-presentation* to the Father of the redemptive economy of Christ, this being rendered actual by the action of the Holy Spirit, becomes in the literary genre of the liturgical commentaries, a *representation* of the life of Christ for the sake of the faithful.[130]

This is precisely what we have seen.

[130] Parenti, "The Eucharistic Liturgy in the East," 62.

# *Chapter 3*

# The Liturgical Year and the Liturgy of the Hours

This chapter is concerned with the relationship between liturgy and time in the Christian East as that reality is expressed in the feasts and seasons of what has come to be called the "liturgical year" and in that daily cycle of liturgical prayer known as the Divine Office or the Liturgy of the Hours. In the two sections that follow, after a general introduction to the liturgical year or Liturgy of the Hours in each, the pertinent contents of the seven living traditions are described according to the various extant rites themselves, beginning, as in previous chapters with the Armenian and ending with the West Syrian and Maronite.

## 3.1 The Liturgical Year

The liturgical year in the Christian East provides the rhythm, the color, and the theological tone of the various liturgical ritual celebrations. In the liturgical year the faith of the Church is proclaimed; the events of Divine Economy are celebrated in a remembrance (*anamnesis*) that is not just a commemoration of things past but a grace-filled encounter with the saving reality of these events in the present, making them relevant and personal to each and every one. Characteristic is the word "today" in opening hymns and prayers commemorating events of the Divine Economy. For example, the dismissal hymn for the feast of the Annunciation in the Byzantine Rite reads: "*Today* is the crown of our salvation and the manifestation of the mystery that is from all eternity. The Son of God becomes Son of the Virgin, and Gabriel announces the good tidings of grace. Therefore, let us also join him and cry aloud to the Theotokos: Hail, thou who art full of grace: the Lord is with Thee."[1]

This cycle of fasting and feasting, of penitence and celebration provides a constant opportunity for worshiping the triune God, for reflection, for one's renewal of Christian life, and for deepening one's relationship to Christ. This is not supposed to be an individualistic endeavor, as it is sometimes seen, but takes place within the communal worship of the Church. The celebration of feasts within the liturgical year is not simply a devotional act of piety but theology: a constant source for the understanding of faith, a constant reminder of the significance of the Divine Economy, a constant renewal of one's relationship with Christ in and through the common worship of the Church. Thus, the liturgical year permeates the lives of the faithful, is the grid upon which one lives and grows in their faith. This is eloquently expressed in the Byzantine *doxastikon* hymn of Easter:

> It is the day of Resurrection; let us be radiant for the festival, and let us embrace one another. Let us say, O brethren, even to those that hate us: Let us forgive all things on the Resurrection; and thus let us cry: Christ is risen from the dead, by death hath He trampled down death, and on those in the graves hath He bestowed life.[2]

### *3.1.1 The Armenian Rite*

The liturgical year of the Armenian Rite is rooted in the now-extinct ancient liturgical tradition of Jerusalem and has maintained some unique and remarkably ancient characteristics no longer present in the other Eastern rites. The most well-known of these characteristics is that the Armenians still celebrate the Nativity of the Lord (Christmas) on January 6, along with Jesus's Baptism and the Blessing of Water, while all other Eastern traditions, starting in the fourth century, gradually adopted the December 25 date as the date for Christmas and dedicated January 6 to the Baptism of Jesus alone. According to

[1] Mother Mary and Archimandrite Kallistos Ware, trans., *The Festal Menaion* (London: Faber and Faber, 1969), 445–46.

[2] Mother Mary and Archimandrite Kallistos Ware, trans., *The Pentecostarion* (Boston: Holy Transfiguration Monastery, 1990) 36.

the travel diary of Egeria, a fourth-century pilgrim to Jerusalem, the celebration of the Nativity on January 6 included an early morning procession from elsewhere, chanting Matthew 21:9 ("Blessed is he who comes in the name of the Lord . . ."), to Jerusalem for the principal celebrations of the day, which began an eight-day celebration of the feast, but she tells us nothing more other than giving us a description of the stations for the octave and the sumptuous decorations and candles in the church.[3] Further, everything leading up to her reference to the early morning procession is missing from the manuscript. The *Armenian Lectionary* would seem to fill up this lacuna by noting that on the night of January 5 there was a celebration at "The Place of the Shepherds," near Bethlehem. This included the gospel reading from Luke 2:8-20, followed by a vigil in Bethlehem itself, and the principal liturgy the next day on January 6 at the Martyrium (Church of the Holy Sepulcher), in Jerusalem with Matthew 2:1-12 as the assigned gospel reading.[4] But, in spite of the evidence from the *Armenian Lectionary*, the fact remains that we really have no idea what was actually being celebrated on the January 6 feast in Jerusalem at the time of Egeria's visit. If we take, naturally, the contents of the *Armenian Lectionary* as representing the late fourth-century Jerusalem celebration of Epiphany and its octave, we would be led to conclude that it is Christ's birth, including the visit of the Magi (Matt 2:1-12), which was the focus. But the *Georgian Lectionary* assigns Matthew 3:1-17, the baptism of Jesus, a text appearing nowhere in the *Armenian Lectionary*, as the gospel reading for Epiphany at the Martyrium, complete with a January 5 baptismal-oriented vigil, including a blessing of water.[5] Does this merely reflect an adjustment made after the Jerusalem liturgy came to accept the December 25 date for the Nativity?

[3] For text of Egeria, see Anne McGowan and Paul F. Bradshaw, *The Pilgrimage of Egeria: A New Translation of the* Itinerarium Egeriae *with Introduction and Commentary*, ACC 93 (London: SPCK; Collegeville, MN: Liturgical Press, Pueblo, 2018).

[4] See Athanase Renoux, *Le codex arménien Jérusalem 121*, vol. 1: *Introduction*, Patrologia Orientalis 35, no. 1 (Turnhout: Brepols, 1969); vol. 2: *Édition*, Patrologia Orientalis 36, no. 2 (Turnhout: Brepols, 1971), [75] 211–[77] 215; and McGowan and Bradshaw, *The Pilgrimage of Egeria*, 156–59.

[5] For the *Georgian Lectionary*, see Michel Tarchnischvili, *Le grand lectionnaire de l'Église de Jérusalem, Ve-VIIIe siècle*, Corpus Scriptorum Christianorum Orientalium, 1 (Louvain: Secrétariat du CSCO, 1959), 188–89, 204–5.

It is well known that the Armenian Church never accepted the "new" December 25 date for Christ's Nativity and, instead, has maintained the January 6 date until the present day. But what is celebrated by the Armenians on January 6 today is both the birth of Christ with Matthew 1:18-25 (*not* Matthew 2:1-12) being read at the *Surb Patarag* and a concluding blessing of waters rite focused on the baptism of Jesus with Matthew 3:1-17 assigned as the gospel text. Scholars, such as Athanase Renoux and Thomas Talley, have argued that this Armenian connection between birth and baptism on January 6 represents a later synthesis based on Monophysite doctrinal concerns and polemics against a focus on a separate "bodily" nativity celebration.[6] Gabriele Winkler, however, has challenged this argument, seeing the Armenian connection of these feasts as reflecting a very early stage in the development of the January 6 feast of the Epiphany itself in Eastern Christianity:

> The further development of the celebration of Epiphany in the fourth century and the introduction of the feast of Christmas at this time in several regions of the East has to be tied . . . to the evolution and change in the christological debates. The initial tension between the baptism of Jesus and his birth in Bethlehem, which lay behind the Gospels and also seems most closely to affect the feast of Epiphany at its beginnings, is thereby gradually resolved: from the one feast on Epiphany, which in its oldest eastern form apparently understood the baptism of Jesus as his birth, there first developed a celebration on January 6 which linked Jesus' baptism with his birth in Bethlehem (as, for example, in Syria, Armenia, and Egypt). Then, the emphasis shifted either to Jesus' birth in Bethlehem (as was the case above all in Jerusalem for a considerable length of time), or else a new feast was introduced.[7]

[6] See Charles (Athanase) Renoux, "L'Épiphanie á Jérusalem au IVe et au Ve siècle d'après le lectionnaire arménien de Jérusalem," *Revue des études arméniennes* 2 (1965): 343–59; Thomas J. Talley, *The Origins of the Liturgical Year*, 2nd ed. (Collegeville, MN: Liturgical Press, Pueblo, 1991), 139–40; and J. Neil Alexander, *Waiting for the Coming: The Liturgical Meaning of Advent, Christmas, Epiphany* (Washington, DC: Pastoral Press, 1993), 88–90.

[7] Gabriele Winkler, "Die Licht-Erscheinung bei der Taufe Jesu und der Ursprung des Epiphaniefestes," *Oriens Christianus* 78 (1994): 177–229 = "The Appearance of the Light at the Baptism of Jesus and the Origins of the Feast of Epiphany: An Investigation of Greek, Syriac, Armenian, and Latin Sources," in *Between Memory and Hope: Readings on the Liturgical Year*, ed. Maxwell E. Johnson (Collegeville, MN: Liturgical Press, Pueblo, 2000), 294–95.

Abraham Terian, in his recent study and edition, *The Letter of Macarius I to the Armenians*, claims that in 335, almost fifty years earlier than Egeria's visit, the Jerusalem church was celebrating baptisms on Epiphany. If correct, this would confirm Winkler's hypothesis.[8]

The feast of the Nativity of the Lord on January 6 is one of only six feasts with fixed dates, another unique characteristic of the Armenian Rite. The other five all have origins in Jerusalem, namely, the Presentation of the Lord in the Temple (February 14), the Annunciation (April 7), the Birth of the Mother of God (September 8), together with the August 15 Dormition, as the earliest Marian feast,[9] the Presentation of Mary to the Temple (November 21), and the Conception of Mary by Joachim and Anna (December 9). Hence, the primary emphasis is on Sunday, often referred to today as the "original Christian feast," and the liturgical year is thus structured around the weekly cycle. Sunday is highlighted, then, as a symbol of the totality of the mystery of Christ in full eschatological reality.

Most other feasts on the liturgical calendar are moveable, and a directory (the *Tōnacʿoycʿ*) provides the formulae for each particular case for calculating the date of the feast in a particular year. Some of the principles guiding this process are as follows: (1) Major feasts are celebrated on Sundays. For example, the Dormition of the Virgin Mary is celebrated not on August 15, but on the Sunday closest to this date. In a similar way, the feast of the Holy Cross on September 14 is not celebrated on that day but on the closest Sunday, together with anniversary of the Dedication of the Holy Sepulchre in Jerusalem.[10] (2) Saints are celebrated on Mondays, Tuesdays, Thursdays, and Saturdays, never on Wednesdays, Fridays, and Sundays. (3) Prominent

[8] Abraham Terian, *Macarius of Jerusalem: Letter to the Armenians, AD 335*, AVANT: Treasures of the Armenian Christian Tradition 4 (Crestwood, NY: St. Vladimir's Seminary Press/St. Nersess Armenian Seminary, 2008), 83–85.

[9] See Maxwell E. Johnson, "*Sub Tuum Praesidium:* The *Theotokos* in Christian Life and Worship Before Ephesus," in *The Place of Christ in Liturgical Prayer: Christology, Trinity and Liturgical Theology*, ed. Bryan D. Spinks (Collegeville, MN: Liturgical Press, Pueblo, 2008), 243–67. See also Walter Ray, "August 15 and the Development of the Jerusalem Calendar" (PhD diss., University of Notre Dame, 2000); and Stephen J. Shoemaker, *Mary in Early Christian Faith and Devotion* (New Haven: Yale University Press, 2016), 178–86.

[10] On the importance of this feast of the Holy Cross in the Armenian tradition and its relationship to the early fourth-century Dedication of the Holy Sepulchre in Jerusalem, see M. Daniel Findikyan, "Armenian Hymns of the Church and the Cross," *St. Nersess Theological Review* 11 (2006): 63–105; and idem, "Armenian Hymns of the Holy Cross and the Jerusalem *Encaenia*," *Revue des études armeniennes* 32 (2010): 25–58.

saints are celebrated on Saturdays. (4) The commemoration of a saint is not attached to a date but is based on a formula that has two components: the day of the week to be celebrated and the "anchor" week nearby. For example, the feast of Constantine and Helen is celebrated on the Tuesday of the fourth week after Pentecost. (5) Wednesday and Friday are exclusively devoted to fasting and therefore the Divine Liturgy is not celebrated (with the exception of the six major feasts). These days lose their fasting and penitential character after Easter, during the period of Pentecost. (6) Because the period between the Nativity and Easter is variable, depending on the date of Easter, some feasts are celebrated one year within the months of January and February and another year within the months of June and July. (7) Because Sundays are reserved for dominical feasts, feasts of the Virgin Mary, and feasts of the cross, the primacy of Sunday eucharistic celebrations is maintained in the liturgical year.

One recent development of a new feast merits brief mention here, namely, the transformation into a liturgical feast of the traditional April 24 commemoration of the 1915 Armenian Genocide in Turkey, called by President Theodore Roosevelt the greatest crime of World War I.[11] The victims of this genocide were canonized as martyrs by the Armenian Apostolic Orthodox Church on April 23, 2015. No longer a commemoration of the genocide, April 24 is now a date on the liturgical calendar titled *The Commemoration of the Holy Martyrs who gave their lives during the Genocide of the Armenians for faith and for the homeland*.[12] Such a contemporary updating of the calendar of especially martyrs to account for twentieth- and twenty-first-century persecution of Christians, especially in the Eastern Christian world, is, as we shall see below, by no means limited to the Armenian Church.

### *3.1.2 The Byzantine Rite*

The liturgical year of the Byzantine liturgical tradition is defined by three cycles: (1) the annual cycle of fixed feasts, commencing on

[11] See *Holy Women, Holy Men: Celebrating the Saints* (New York: Church Publishing, Inc., 2010), 342–43.

[12] On this new feast, see M. Daniel Findikyan, *From Victims to Victors: The Holy Martyrs of the Armenian Genocide* (New York: Diocese of the Armenian Church of America [Eastern], 2015). See also Maxwell E. Johnson, "The Blood of the Martyrs, Still the 'Seed of the Church': The Holy Martyrs of the Armenian Genocide," in Stefano Parenti, ed., *Gedankschrift for Robert Taft, SJ*, Orientalia Christiana Analecta (Rome: Pontificio Istituto Orientale). Forthcoming.

September 1, the beginning of the liturgical year; (2) the annual cycle of moveable feasts, centered on Easter, which is also the starting point of the annual Lectionary, marking the beginning of the epistle and gospel readings and the cycle of the eleven resurrection gospel readings read at *Orthros* (matins) every Sunday (together with their accompanying hymnody, called the *exaposteilarion* and the *eothinon doxastikon*); and (3) the weekly cycle of the eight tones (*oktōēchos*), which also begins with Easter.[13] In the experience of Byzantine worship, these three cycles are combined and superimposed on one another, giving a constant and unfailing variety.[14]

Among all feasts on the Byzantine liturgical calendar, Easter, the "feast of feasts," occupies without any doubt the very center of the liturgical year, and it is important to note that among the Orthodox churches its calculation depends on the Julian, rather than Gregorian, calendar for determining its date each year, which is why there is often a difference of dates between East and West and even within the Eastern rites themselves. Preceded by a pre-Lenten period of three weeks (including the last two Sundays, known as Cheesefare and Meatfare, related to the approaching Lenten fast that includes abstinence from all dairy products and meat), Great Lent itself, Holy or Great Week, followed by the period of fifty days culminating on the fiftieth-day feast of Pentecost, and this post-Easter season sealed by the feast of All Saints on the Sunday after Pentecost, the Easter cycle dominates more than one-third of the liturgical year.[15] The spirit and centrality of Easter throughout the Byzantine liturgical year are well expressed in the following Hymn of the Resurrection sung every Saturday evening, after the gospel reading, at *Orthros* of the resurrection vigil:

> Having beheld the resurrection of Christ, let us adore the Holy Lord Jesus, the only sinless one. Your cross do we adore, O Christ, and your holy resurrection we praise and glorify: for you are our God and we know no other besides you; it is your name that we proclaim. Come all you faithful, let us adore Christ's holy resurrection. For lo, through the cross has joy come into all the world. Ever blessing the Lord, let

[13] On the *Oktōēchos* and their history and development, see Stig Simeon R. Frøyshov, "The Early Development of the Liturgical Eight-Mode System in Jerusalem," St. Vladimir's *Theological Quarterly* 51 (2007): 139–78.

[14] *The Festal Menaion*, 40–41.

[15] See Mother Mary and Archimandrite Kallistos Ware, *The Lenten Triodion* (Boston: Faber and Faber, 1978).

us sing his resurrection; for, having endured the cross for us, he has by his death trampled death.[16]

The celebration of Great Lent and Holy Week in particular bears the stamp of a long evolution and reflects significant Hagiopolite influence, as well as synthesis of that influence with Antiochene and older Constantinopolitan practices.[17] To give but one example of this synthesis, the old Constantinopolitan Easter Vigil, vespers with the vigil readings and the Liturgy of St. Basil, is now celebrated on Holy Saturday morning with Easter Sunday *Orthros* then celebrated at midnight, followed by the Light Service (originating in Jerusalem at the Holy Sepulchre) and concluding with the Liturgy of St. John Chrysostom.[18] With the Easter Vigil itself actually anticipated on Holy Saturday morning today, the Byzantine Rite finds itself in a situation analogous to the Roman Rite before the Holy Week reforms of Pope Pius XII in 1951 and 1955 and the liturgical reforms of Vatican II expressed in the Missal of Pope Paul VI. Because of this, there have been various suggestions and attempts among some Eastern Christians, both Eastern Catholic and Orthodox, to reform this rite, most notably by the monks of the Orthodox Monastery of New Skete in Cambridge, New York.[19]

[16] Text as quoted by Robert Taft, "The Spirit of Eastern Christian Worship," BEW, 159.

[17] Mark Morozowich, "A Palm Sunday Procession in the Byzantine Tradition? A Study of the Jerusalem and Constantinopolitan Evidence," OCP 75 (2009): 359–83; idem, "Jerusalem Celebration of Great Week Evening Services from Monday to Wednesday in the First Millennium," *Studi sull'Oriente Cristiano* 14 (2010): 99–126; and idem, *Holy Thursday in Jerusalem and Constantinople: The Liturgical Celebrations from the Fourth to the Fourteenth Centuries*, OCA (Rome: Pontificio Istituto Orientale, forthcoming). See the description and interpretation of Great or Holy Week in Robert Taft, "Holy Week in the Byzantine Tradition," in *Between Memory and Hope: Readings on the Liturgical Year*, ed. Johnson, 155–82. On the meaning and spirituality of Lent in the Byzantine tradition, see Alexander Schmemann, *Great Lent: Journey to Pascha*, rev. ed. (Crestwood, NY: St. Vladimir's Seminary Press, 1974).

[18] See Miguel Arranz, "Les sacrements de l'ancien Euchologe constantinopolitain (9) IVe partie: L'illumination de la nuit de Pâques," OCP 55 (1989): 33–62; and Taft, "Holy Week in the Byzantine Tradition," in *Between Memory and Hope*, ed. Johnson, 178–81.

[19] See *Passion and Resurrection* (Cambridge, NY: New Skete, 1995). See also Robert Taft, "In the Bridegroom's Absence: The Paschal Triduum in the Byzantine Church," in *La celebrazione del Triduo pasquale: anamnesis e mimesis. Atti del III Congresso Internazionale di Liturgia, Roma, Pontificio Istituto Liturgico, 9–13 maggio 1988*, Analecta Liturgica 14, Studia Anselmiana 102 (Rome: Pontificio Ateneo S. Anselmo, 1990), 71–97.

Connected to Easter are the twelve great feasts, including the dominical feasts of Palm Sunday (the Sunday before Easter) and Ascension (the fortieth day of Easter). Other fixed dominical feasts are Christmas on December 25 (Nativity of Christ); Epiphany or Theophany on January 6 (Baptism of Christ), with a solemn blessing of water both for a sprinkling rite and for the blessing of homes by the priest during the following week;[20] the Transfiguration (August 6); and the Exaltation of the Cross (September 14). Dependent on the date of Christmas are both the Annunciation (March 25) and the Presentation or Meeting of Our Lord (February 2), both of which, as we have seen, are among the oldest "Marian" feasts, although they are more properly viewed as feasts of the Lord. Other Marian feasts on the calendar are the Dormition of the Mother of God (August 15), the Nativity of the Mother of God (September 8), and the Entry of the Mother of God into the Temple (November 21). With regard to the date of Christmas, it should be noted that within various Slavic Byzantine traditions, including the Russian and Ukrainian Orthodox Churches, it is the Julian calendar that is followed not only for the calculation of Easter but for other feasts as well, with the celebration of Christmas appearing on January 7 in the Gregorian calendar. But there is nothing special about January 7, and this should never be confused with the Armenian tradition of celebrating the Nativity (and Baptism) of Christ on January 6 of the Gregorian calendar. January 7 on the Gregorian calendar is simply December 25 on the Julian calendar.

A characteristic of these twelve great feasts is a period of preparation before the feast and an after-feast, a period of continued celebration until its *apodosis*, "leave taking," the last day of celebration of this after-feast, as the following list makes clear:

*The Twelve Great Feasts of the Byzantine Rite*

September 8: Nativity of the Mother of God; leave-taking, September 12 (five days of the feast)

September 14: Exaltation of the Holy and Life-giving Cross; leave-taking, September 21 (eight days of the feast)

[20] On this, see Nicholas Denysenko, *The Blessing of Waters and Epiphany: The Eastern Liturgical Tradition* (Farnham, Surrey, England; Burlington, VT: Ashgate, 2012).

November 21: Entry (Presentation) of the Mother of God into the Temple; leave-taking, November 25 (five days of the feast)

December 25: Nativity of the Lord; leave-taking, December 31 (seven days of the feast)

January 6: The Epiphany or Theophany of the Lord; leave-taking, January 14 (nine days of the feast)

February 2: The Meeting (Presentation) of Christ in the Temple; leave-taking, February 9 (eight days of the feast)

March 25: The Annunciation of the Most Holy Mother of God (takes precedence over *all* Lenten and/or fast days); leave-taking, March 26 (two days of the feast)

Palm Sunday (the Sunday before Easter)

Ascension of the Lord (fortieth day of Easter)

Pentecost (fiftieth day of Easter)

August 6: The Transfiguration of the Lord; leave-taking, August 13 (eight days of the feast)

August 15: The Dormition of the Mother of God; leave-taking, August 23 (nine days of the feast)

Some of these feasts are also accompanied by a *synaxis*, a celebration on the next day of the feast of a person closely related to the feast. December 26, for example, is the synaxis of the Mother of God; January 7 is the synaxis of John the Baptist; and March 26 is the synaxis of Archangel Gabriel, who "announced" Christ's conception to Mary.

As noted, various seasons of preparation and fasting appear before some of these major feasts as well. The forty days of Lent begin on Monday, seven weeks before Easter, and end on the Friday evening before Palm Sunday, with neither the next day, Lazarus Saturday, nor Palm Sunday counted as part of Lent. A fast known as the Fast of the Apostles, of variable length, begins on the Monday, eight days after Pentecost, and culminates with the feast of Saints Peter and Paul on June 29. The feast of the Dormition of the Mother of God is preceded by a fasting period of preparation from August 1 to 14. And the December feast of the Nativity of the Lord has its own "Lent," a forty-day "Christmas Fast," beginning on November 15 and ending on

Christmas Eve. What is most interesting about this "Christmas Fast" is that, while it is not called by the Western term "Advent," it is clearly parallel to that Western season of Christmas preparation, with some Western traditions (e.g., the Ambrosian and Mozarabic Rites) still keeping a season of forty days (or six weeks) as well.[21] What is more, this season in the Byzantine tradition has a distinct Marian emphasis. In fact, beginning with the November 21 feast of the Presentation of Mary in the Temple, multiple Marian images associated with the ark of the covenant, the tabernacle, and even as the heavenly temple appear in the various *troparia* and prayers throughout the season.[22] And two Sundays before Christmas "The Holy Ancestors of Christ" are commemorated, culminating, of course, in Mary, and on the Sunday before Christmas "all the Fathers who down the centuries have been pleasing to God, from Adam to Joseph, husband of the Most Holy Mother of God" are celebrated.[23] In addition, on December 26, the day after Christmas, Mary's divine maternity as Theotokos, a feast already in existence at Constantinople by the time of the Nestorian controversy in the middle of the fifth century, is celebrated.[24]

As important as fasting is in preparation for these feasts, including the individual fast days of September 14 (Exaltation of the Holy Cross), August 29 (the Beheading of St. John the Baptist), January 5 (the Eve of the Epiphany), along with every Wednesday and Friday in continuity with early Christian practice, fasting is balanced by times when it is strictly forbidden. These times include the period from Christmas

[21] See Paul F. Bradshaw and Maxwell E. Johnson, *The Origins of Feasts, Fasts, and Seasons in Early Christianity*, ACC 86 (Collegeville, MN: Liturgical Press, Pueblo, 2011), 158–68.

[22] See *The Festal Menaion*, 164–98.

[23] Pierre Jounel, "The Christmas Season," in *The Church at Prayer*, vol. 4: *The Liturgy and Time*, ed. A. G. Martimort, new ed. (Collegeville, MN: Liturgical Press, 1986), 93.

[24] See Johnson, "*Sub Tuum Praesidium*," 262ff. See also Shoemaker, *Mary in Early Christian Faith and Devotion*, 178–86. On Mary in the Byzantine tradition, see Robert Taft, "'What Shall We Call You?' Marian Liturgical Veneration in the Byzantine Tradition," in *Úcta ku presvätej Bohorodičke na kresťanskom Východe*. Medzinárodná vedecká konferencia 25.–26. novembra 2005, Teologická fakulta Trnavskej univerzity/Centrum spirituality Východ-Západ Michala Lacka, vedeckovýskukmné prackovisko Teologickej fakulty TU (Košice, 2005), 121–40; and idem, "Marian Liturgical Veneration: Origins, Meaning, and Contemporary Catholic Renewal," in *Orientale Lumen III Conference. Proceedings—1999. June 15–18, 1999, at The Catholic University of America, Washington, DC* (Fairfax, VA: Eastern Churches Publications 1999), 91–112.

to Theophany or Epiphany, during the tenth week before Easter, during the last week before Lent (although abstaining from meat since it is after Meatfare Sunday), during the Easter or "Bright" Week, during the week after Pentecost, and, with the exception of the Exaltation of the Cross, on all of the twelve great feasts. As our colleague John Klentos of the Athenagoras Institute in Berkeley, California, notes: "These are not times when you *should* not fast; these are times when you *must* not fast!"[25] While what we have presented here with regard to the rhythm of feasting and fasting is according to the Byzantine Rite, a similar pattern is generally characteristic of all the Eastern rites as well.

Finally, like the Armenians in canonizing the victims of the Armenian Genocide as martyrs, so within the various churches of the Byzantine tradition there has been a similar phenomenon taking place. The Russian Orthodox Church, for example, has canonized "new martyrs," like St. Elizabeth, the Grand Duchess and later an Orthodox abbess, martyred with her sisters by the Bolsheviks on July 18, 1918.[26] Likewise, the Greek Orthodox Church canonized in 1992 Bishops Chrysostom of Smyrna, Gregory of Cydoniai, Ambrosios of Moschonisia, Procopius of Iconium, Euthymius of Zelon, and the clergy and laity who were martyred with them for their faith in Asia Minor in 1922.[27]

### *3.1.3 The Coptic Rite*

The Coptic Churches employ the Alexandrian calendar, which is the continuation of the ancient Egyptian calendar. Accordingly, the year is divided into twelve months of thirty days each, with an additional "month" that is five days long (or six days long every four years). The year opens on the first of the month Thôout (in Coptic or Tût in Arabic), equivalent to August 29 (or 30 in a leap year) in the Julian calendar or September 11 (or 12 in a leap year) in the Gregorian

[25] John Klentos, private conversation.

[26] Eirene Kasapi, *Οι Ανακηρύξεις Αγίων στη Ρωσικὴ Εκκλησία* (Athens, 2009).

[27] Stefanos Alexopoulos, "The Canonization of the Greek Martyrs of 1922: Is It a Novelty?," paper delivered at the Sixth International Congress of the Society of Oriental Liturgy in Armenia, Holy Etchmiadzin, September 11–16, 2016, to be published in the acta of the congress.

calendar. One peculiar characteristic of the Coptic liturgical calendar is the monthly celebration of three feasts: the first, on the twelfth day of the month, is the feast of Archangel Michael. The second feast, on the twenty-first, is the feast of the Virgin Mary. And the third feast, celebrated on the twenty-ninth day, celebrates together the annunciation, the nativity, and the resurrection.[28]

Another unique characteristic of the Coptic liturgical calendar is its division into three seasons based on the annual weather patterns and the flooding of the Nile, demonstrating the historic importance of the Nile to the life of the people of Egypt. Each season comes with its own prayers that are inserted into the liturgical services. The first season is the flooding season, from the middle of June to October. During this period, the following prayers are recited in the liturgy:

*Priest:* O graciously, Lord, please grant Thy blessings to the waters of the River.

*Deacon:* Pray that the waters of the river may rise this year, that Christ, our Lord, may bless it, raise it to its normal level, and gladden the face of the earth; that He will help us, humankind, protect our cattle, and forgive us our sins.

*Congregation:* Lord, have mercy (3x).

The second season is the sowing season, from October to the middle of January. During this period the following prayers for the crops are recited at the liturgy:

*Priest:* Graciously, O Lord, grant Thy blessings to the plants, the herbs, and vegetables of the fields.

*Deacon:* Pray for the plants, the herbs, and vegetables of the fields this year that Christ, our Lord, may grant them His blessings, that they may grow and bring forth plentiful fruit; that He may have compassion for the creatures of His hands, and forgive us our sins.

*Congregation:* Lord, have mercy (3x).

[28] On the Coptic liturgical year in general, see Samir Khalil Samir, "L'année liturgique copte," *Prôche-Orient chrétien* 39 (1989): 26–34.

Finally, the third season is the harvest season, from the middle of January to the middle of June. During this period the following prayers for the harvest are recited at the liturgy:

*Priest:* O Lord, please grant Thy blessings this year to the winds of the sky and the fruits of the earth.

*Deacon:* Pray for the winds of the sky and the fruits of the earth, the trees and vines, and every fruit-bearing tree so that Christ, our Lord, may grant them His blessings, bring them to harvesting without damage, and forgive our sins.

*Congregation:* Lord, have mercy (3x).[29]

In addition to these unique emphases, the Coptic Rite celebrates seven major holy feasts and seven minor holy feasts.[30] The seven major feasts, not surprisingly, are:

The Annunciation (Baramhat 29; April 7)

The Nativity of Christ (Christmas) (Kayhk 29; January 7); preceded by a fast of forty-three days

The Epiphany or the Baptism of Christ (Tobah 11; January 19), including a blessing of water and a blessing of the people by the water on their foreheads and hands as a renewal of baptism

Palm Sunday

Easter, preceded by Great Lent (fifty-five days, including Holy Week) and, like the Byzantines, is considered by the Coptic Church to be the "Feast of feasts"

Ascension (the fortieth day of Easter)

Pentecost (the fiftieth day of Easter)

[29] Wissa Wassef, "Calendar, Seasons, and Coptic Liturgy" in *The Coptic Encyclopedia*, ed. Aziz Atiya (New York: Macmillan, 1991), 2:443–44.

[30] An excellent online resource for general introductions to the feasts and fasts of the Coptic Rite is the *Encyclopedia Coptica* at http://www.coptic.net/EncyclopediaCoptica. The following lists and descriptions of Coptic feasts and fasts are dependent on these resources.

The seven minor holy feasts include some of those ranked among the Byzantine Rite as part of the twelve great feasts:

The Circumcision of Our Lord, on the eighth day after Christmas (Tobah 6; January 14)

The Entrance (or Presentation) of Our Lord in the Temple (Amshir 8; February 15)

The Escape of the Holy Family to Egypt (Bashans 24; June 1)

The First Miracle of Our Lord Jesus at Cana (Tobah 13; January 12)

The Transfiguration of Christ (Musra 13; August 19)

Maundy Thursday, Thursday of Holy Week, including the washing of feet and the only day in Holy Week when the eucharistic liturgy is celebrated

Thomas Sunday, the Second Sunday of Easter

In addition to these major and minor dominical feasts, the Coptic Church also celebrates several common and indigenous feasts of the Theotokos:

The Annunciation of her birth (Misra 7; August 13)

Her Nativity (Paschans 1; May 9)

Her Presentation in the Temple (Kyahk 3; December 12)

Her Dormition (Tobah 21; January 29)

The Assumption of her body (Paoni 21; June 28)

Her Apparition over the Church of Zeitoon in 1968 (Baramhat 24; April 2)

The Apparition of her body to the apostles (Mesra 16; August 22)

Other important feasts include the Apostles' Feast (Abib 5; July 12), which celebrates the martyrdom of Sts. Peter and Paul and includes a water blessing and *pedilavium* (foot washing rite); The Nayrouz Feast (1st of Tout; September 11), celebrating the beginning of the Coptic year; and two Feasts of the Cross on Tout 17 (September 27) and Barmahat 10 (March 19), celebrating, respectively, the

Dedication of the Holy Sepulchre in Jerusalem and the discovery of the Holy Cross by Empress Helena.

The Coptic calendar of saints is full of other feasts usually commemorating the martyrdom of popular saints from Coptic history.[31] As a persecuted Church even today, the calendar of Coptic martyrs continues to grow, including the February 2015 martyrdom in Libya of twenty-one Coptic construction workers by the Islamic State of Iraq and the Levant (ISIS) now commemorated on Ashmir 8 (February 15), and victims of terrorist bombings of Coptic churches in Egypt, as recent as Palm Sunday 2017, and, in May 2017, a busload of Coptic pilgrims on their way to the Monastery of St. Samuel attacked, with twenty-nine people, including children, martyred, and twenty-five others injured.[32]

Including the ancient Christian fast days of Wednesdays and Fridays, Coptic Christians fast for over 210 days each year, during which no animal products (meat, poultry, fish, milk, eggs, butter, etc.) are allowed. And, similar to the Muslim practice of Ramadan, no food or drink is permitted during these fasting periods between sunrise and sunset. Lent, known as "the Great Fast," begins with a pre-Lenten fast of one week, followed by the forty-day fast itself leading to the Paschal Fast of Holy Week. Other fasting seasons include the Fast of the Nativity (parallel to Advent), the Fast of the Apostles (before Abib 5; July 12), the Fast of the Theotokos, and the Fast of Nineveh, a three-day fast commemorating the repentance of the Ninevites in the time of Jonah, occurring three weeks before the start of Lent. This particular fast is shared with the Armenians, the Ancient Church of the East, and the Ethiopians.

Finally, we would be remiss if we did not note three of the great contributions of Egyptian-Coptic Christianity to the development and content of the liturgical year in general, in both East and West, namely: (1) the celebration of Jesus's baptism on Theophany or Epiphany, already witnessed to by Clement of Alexandria in the late second century;[33] (2) the origins of Lent as, originally in Egypt, a beginning-

[31] See the *Coptic Synaxarium: Lives of Saints* (London: Oxford Publishing House, 2006).

[32] See https://www.dw.com/en/gunmen-kill-coptic-christians-on-pilgrimage-to-egypts-st-samuel-monastery/a-46135832.

[33] *Stromateis* 1.2.1. See Bradshaw and Johnson, *The Origins of Feasts, Fasts, and Seasons*, 137ff.

of-the-year, forty-day fast following the celebration of the Theophany leading to the celebration of baptism at the end of that six-week period, which, after the Council of Nicaea in 325, was adopted elsewhere but placed before what appears to have been the newly emerging emphasis on paschal baptism;[34] and (3) the wide acceptance of the Egyptian calculation of the date of Pascha itself as the first Sunday after the first full moon after the vernal equinox.[35]

### *3.1.4 The Ethiopian Rite*

The liturgical year of the Ethiopian Rite follows the Coptic calendar in that the year begins on September 1 (September 11 or 12 on the Gregorian calendar) and is divided into twelve months of thirty days each with an additional five-day-long (or six-day-long if a leap year) month. Peculiar to the Ethiopian liturgical tradition is the monthly cycle of daily commemorations; several days of the month are dedicated to fixed liturgical commemorations, and these commemorations are repeated every month on the same day.[36] That is, the Nativity of the Virgin Mary is commemorated on the first day of the month; the Apostle (Jude) Thaddeus and Abba Guba, one of those known as the Nine Saints (fifth-century missionaries) in Ethiopia, on the second; the Presentation of the Virgin Mary in the Temple on the third; Gäbrä Mänfäs Qeddus (a popular fourteenth-/fifteenth-century hermit and monastic founder) on the fifth; the Holy Trinity on the seventh; St. Michael the Archangel on the twelfth; Abba Za-Mikael Arägawi (another of the Nine Saints) on the fourteenth; *Kidanä Mehrät* (the Covenant of Mercy), commemorating a promise Jesus made from his

[34] In addition to ibid., 99–108, see also Nicholas Russo, "The Origins of Lent" (PhD diss., University of Notre Dame, 2009). A recent challenge to contemporary scholarship on the Egyptian origins of Lent appears in Magid S. A. Mikhail, "The Evolution of Lent in Alexandria and the Alleged Reforms of Patriarch Demetrius," in *Copts in Context: Tradition and Modernity*, ed. Nelly van Doorn-Harder (South Carolina: University of South Carolina Press, 2017): 169–80, 252–58.

[35] See Bradshaw and Johnson, *The Origins of Feasts, Fasts, and Seasons*, 48–59.

[36] See Emmanuel Fritsch, *The Liturgical Year of the Ethiopian Church*, Ethiopian Review of Cultures, Special Issue 9 and 10 (Addis Ababa, Ethiopa: Master Printing Press, 2001); idem, "The Liturgical Year and the Lectionary of the Ethiopian Church," *Warszawskie Studia Teologiczne* 12, no. 2 (1999): 71–116; and Habtemichael Kidane, "Ethiopian (or Geʿez) Worship," in *The New Westminster Dictionary of Liturgy and Worship*, ed. Paul F. Bradshaw (Louisville: Westminster John Knox, 2002), 169–72.

cross to the Virgin Mary that he would forgive the sins of those who sought her intercession, on the sixteenth; St. Gabriel the Archangel on the nineteenth; the Assumption of the Virgin Mary on the twenty-first; Täklä Haymanot (thirteenth-century monk and monastic founder) on the twenty-fourth; the death of Christ on the twenty-seventh; and the incarnation of Christ on the twenty-ninth.

As for the liturgical seasons of the Ethiopian liturgical year, there are three overlapping divisions:

(1) division according to the four seasons of the year: the windy season, the dry season, the sowing season, and the rainy season; this division is obviously based on the climate and the agricultural rhythm of life in Ethiopia

(2) division into three seasons according to the chantbook *Maṣḥafa Deggwā*, following the Coptic division, but with different names and themes: *Yoḥannes* (John), from the beginning of the year, the first of Maskaram (September 11 or 12 [if a leap year]), to the beginning of December; *Astämḥero* (supplication), from the beginning of December to April, where the theme centers on God's mercy and forgiveness; and *Fasikā*, from Easter to the end of the year, where the theme centers on the resurrection for the first part and the transformation of nature and the glorification of the Creator for the second, coinciding with the rainy season

(3) division into four periods and a total of thirty liturgical seasons, twenty fixed and ten mobile, depending on the date of Easter; some of these seasons last only for a day. The first period, of the beginning of the year, has seven fixed liturgical seasons. The second period, of the Nativity and Epiphany, has eight fixed liturgical seasons and one mobile. The third period, of Easter, has nine mobile liturgical seasons and one fixed that begins on the 17 of Sane (the 25 or the 26 [in leap year] of June) and marks the end of the mobile cycle. The fourth period, of the rainy season, has four fixed liturgical seasons and leads to the end of the year.[37]

[37] Fritsch, *The Liturgical Year of the Ethiopian Church*, 73–74.

Within these various liturgical seasons nine major and six minor feasts of the Lord are celebrated in addition to a host of Marian feasts and those of martyrs, angels, and saints from both Old and New Testaments, as well as Ethiopian kings and monks.[38] According to Emmanuel Fritsch's listing,[39] the nine major feasts of the Lord are:

The Annunciation (Maggabit 29; April 7)

The Nativity of the Lord (Tahsas 29; January 7)

Epiphany (the baptism of Jesus, including the carrying of the ark of the covenant to the river and an all-night vigil, with blessing of water) (Terr 11; January 19) and the Miracle at Cana (Terr 12; January 20)

The Transfiguration (Nahase 13; August 19)

Holy Week (moveable)

Easter (moveable)

The Appearance of the Risen Lord to Thomas (Second Sunday of Easter)

Ascension (the fortieth day of Easter)

Paracletos or Pentecost (the fiftieth day of Easter)

The six minor feasts of the Lord, including two feasts of the cross as in the Coptic tradition above, always take precedence over Sundays in the Ethiopian Rite.[40] These feasts are:

The (Exaltation of the) Cross (Maskaram 17; September 27)

The Circumcision of the Lord (Terr 6; January 14)

The Multiplication of the Loaves (Terr 28; February 5)

[38] For the lives of these saints and their feast days, see the classic *The Book of the Saints of the Ethiopian Church; A Translation of the Ethiopic Synaxarion Made from the Manuscripts Oriental 660 and 661 in the British Museum*, trans. E. A. Wallis Budge, 4 vols. (Cambridge: Cambridge University Press, 1928). On the Ethiopian sanctoral cycle, see M. De Fenoyl, *Le Sanctoral Copte*, Recherches publiées sous la Direction de l'Institut de Lettres Orientales de Beyrouth, vol. 15 (Beyrouth, Lebanon: Imprimerie Catholique, 1960).

[39] Fritsch, "The Liturgical Year and the Lectionary of the Ethiopian Church," 94.

[40] Ibid., 95.

The Presentation of the Lord in the Temple (Yakkatit 8; February 15)

The Finding of the True Cross (Maggabit 10; March 19)

The Flight into Egypt (Genbot 24; June 1)

To these are sometimes added the first three Sundays in the season of preparation for Christ's nativity (Advent), known, respectively, as *Sebkät* ("Preaching," commemorating the Old Testament prophecies concerning Christ's coming), *Berhan* ("Light"), and *Nolawi* ("Good Shepherd"), together with Christmas Eve on January 6 and what is known as the Sunday of *Däbrä Zäyt* ("Mount of Olives," on the Fifth Sunday of Lent, focused on Christ's parousia).[41]

One of the most unique characteristics in relationship to other Eastern rites is that the Ethiopian liturgical calendar contains *thirty-three feasts* of the Theotokos, in addition to her four monthly commemorations (Nativity, Presentation in the Temple, the *Kidanä Mehrät* [Covenant of Mercy], and Assumption). Recall from chapter 2 above that the Ethiopian Rite also uniquely has an anaphora addressed directly to the Theotokos herself, thus underscoring, together with these feasts, the important role she plays in this rite. These thirty-three feasts are divided into four categories with five feasts related to her life (i.e., Presentation in the Temple, Dormition, Nativity, St. Anne's Conception of Mary, and Assumption), two feasts honoring one of her names or titles, three commemorating Marian miracles, and four dedicated to Marian sanctuaries, together with several other commemorations. Emmanuel Fritsch notes:

> Emperor Zar'a Ya`eqob (1434–1468) instituted the celebration of a total of 33 annual feasts in honour of Our Lady, "to be kept like Sundays." However, the Ethiopian tradition holds that Mary told St. John that, should someone be unable to entirely satisfy this precept, she asks that everyone should faithfully keep her five main commemorations. She promises those who venerate her in this way, as well as by writing her praises, commenting, learning and teaching them, to stand by when they die and to assist them in every trouble.[42]

[41] See Kidane, "Ethiopian (or Geʿez) Worship," 171.

[42] Fritsch, "The Liturgical Year and the Lectionary of the Ethiopian Church," 96.

These five feasts, perhaps surprisingly, are not simply equivalent to those listed above under the category of Mary's life but are her Dormition (Terr 21; January 30), the Covenant of Mercy (Yakkatit 16; February 24), her Nativity (Genbot 1; May 9), the consecration of her church at Philippi (Sane 21; June 28), and her Assumption (Nahase 16–21; August 22–27, a six-day festival).

Given, perhaps, the monastic hegemony of both traditions, the Ethiopian Rite shares with the Coptic Rite a very strong ascetic emphasis on fasting, with the faithful obligated to 180 days of fasting and priests and monks to 250 days each year. According to the collection of Ethiopian canon and civil law, the *Fetha Nagást* ("Law of the Kings"),[43] together with the tradition of fasting on Wednesdays and Fridays (called the Fast of Salvation) outside of the Easter Season, there are six periods of fasting incumbent on all Ethiopian Rite Christians: the Fast of the Prophets, *Tsome Nebiyat* (or *Soma Ledat* "of the Nativity"), a forty-three day fast equivalent to Advent from Hedar 15 to Tahsas 29 (November 25–January 7); the Gehad Fast on the eves of the Nativity and the Epiphany; the Fast of Nineveh (a three-day fast during the tenth week before Easter); the Great Fast of Lent (fifty-five days total, including Holy Week); the Fast of the Apostles, from the Monday after Pentecost to Hamle 5 (July 12), the Feast of Sts. Peter and Paul; and the Fast of the Assumption from Nahase 1 through Nahase 16 (August 1–16).[44]

Finally, while the Ethiopian Churches have not yet officially canonized any contemporary martyrs, together with the contemporary Christian East in general they certainly know violent persecution, including the burning of over sixty of their churches in 2011.[45] Indeed, shortly after the February 2015 martyrdom of the twenty-one Coptic Christians referred to above, ISIS also executed approximately twenty-eight Ethiopian Orthodox Christians in Libya, quite possibly

[43] *The Fetha Nagást—The Law of the Kings Translated from the Geʿez*, by Abba Paulos Tzadua (Addis-Ababa, Ethiopia: Faculty of Law, Haile Sellassie I University, 1968).

[44] On the above fasting seasons, see Fritsch, "The Liturgical Year and the Lectionary of the Ethiopian Church," 110–11.

[45] Jayson Casper, "More Martyrs: ISIS Executes Dozens of Ethiopian Christians in Libya," *Christianity Today* (April 20, 2015), online version at https://www.christianitytoday.com/news/2015/april/more-martyrs-isis-executes-ethiopian-christians-libya.html.

migrant workers, as "worshippers of the cross belonging to the hostile Ethiopian church."[46]

### *3.1.5 The East Syrian Rite*

The structure of the liturgical year in its present form among the East Syrian Churches dates back to the seventh-century liturgical reform initiated by Patriarch, or Catholicos, Išoʿyahb III. Within this tradition, the year is divided into nine liturgical seasons,[47] centered on the seven major feasts of the Nativity of Christ, the Epiphany (as the baptism of Jesus), the Resurrection of Christ, Pentecost, the Transfiguration, the Glorious Cross, and the Parousia.[48]

1. *Subara-Yalda*, Annunciation-Nativity, which begins on the Sunday between November 27 and December 4 and concludes on the Sunday before *Denha*, Epiphany (January 6), with an overall length of seven weeks[49]
2. *Denha*, Epiphany, which covers the period from Epiphany to the beginning of Lent
3. *Sawma Raba*, Great Lent, including Holy Week
4. *Qyamta*, Resurrection,[50] which covers the period from Easter to Pentecost

[46] Ibid.

[47] See Pauly Maniyattu, "East Syrian Worship," in *The New Westminster Dictionary of Liturgy and Worship*, ed. Bradshaw, 160.

[48] For the Church of the East, see Thoma Darmo, ed., *Ktābā da-qdām wad-bātar wad-ḥudrā wad-kaškōl wad-gazzā w-qālē d-ʿudrānē ʿam ktābā d-mazmorē* (in Syriac), 3 vols. (Trichur, India: Mar Narsai Press, 1960–1962); for the Assyro Chaldeans, see Paulus Bedjan, ed., *Breviarium iuxta ritum Syrorum Orientalium id est Chaldaeorum* (in Syriac), 3 vols. (Paris, 1886–1887); and for the Syro-Malabars, the Liturgical Commission conveniently publishes a calendar every year in Malayalam and English; the liturgical calendar in English for 2016–2017 is here: http://www.syromalabarchurch.in/pdf/Liturgical%20calendar%202017_English.pdf. See also Sebastian P. Brock, "A Concordance to Bedjan's Breviarium Chaldaicum and Darmo's Hudra," *The Harp* 19 (2006): 117–36.

[49] See J. Moolan, *The Period of Annunciation-Nativity in the East Syrian Calendar* (Kottayam: Paurastya Vidyapitham, 1985). See also P. Kuruthukulangara, *The Feast of the Nativity of Our Lord in the Chaldean and Malabar Liturgical Year* (Kottayam: Oriental Institute of Religious Studies, 1989).

[50] See V. Pathikulangara, *Resurrection, Life, and Renewal* (Bangalore: Dharmararam Publications, 1982).

5. *Sliha*, Pentecost
6. *Kaita*, Summer
7. *Eliah-Sliba*, Elijah and the Cross
8. *Moses*
9. *Qudash Etta*, Dedication of the Church, which lasts for four weeks and closes the liturgical year (in contrast to the West Syrian and Maronite traditions, below, where this feast begins the liturgical year), in which the emphasis is on the parousia of Christ

Apart from the seasons of Annunciation-Nativity and the Dedication of the Church, the other liturgical seasons last approximately seven weeks each.

Among the Syrian Christian traditions in general, both East and West, the assigned gospel readings on the Sundays for the season of Christmas preparation, that is, Annunciation-Nativity, include, in order, the annunciation to Zechariah, the annunciation to Mary, the visitation of Mary to Elizabeth, the nativity of John the Baptist, and, finally, the annunciation to Joseph. Indeed, for these reasons, including the overall Byzantine focus during the season of preparation for Christmas, what Western Christians refer to as "Advent" is often referred to as a "Marian" season in the Christian East.

With regard to particular feasts of the Blessed Virgin Mary, however, a distinction has to be made between the Church of the East and those East Syrian Churches in full communion with Rome, that is, the Assyro-Chaldean and Syro-Malabar Churches, which keep many of the Marian feasts common throughout the Christian East as well as some indigenous celebrations and other feasts displaying a decisive process of Latinization:

The Immaculate Conception (or the Conception of Mary without Natural Sin), December 8

Divine Maternity of Mary; Last Friday in the Season of Nativity (Friday before Epiphany)

Presentation of the Lord and Purification of Mary, February 2 (Syro-Malabar)

Our Lady of Lourdes (Day of the Sick), February 11 (Syro-Malabar)

The Annunciation to the Holy Virgin Mary, March 25

Our Lady of the Fields, May 15 (Chaldean)[51]

Our Lady of Perpetual Help, June 27 (Chaldean)

The Visitation, May 31 (Syro-Malabar)

Our Lady of Mount Carmel, July 16 (Syro-Malabar)

The Assumption of Mary, August 15

The Nativity of Mary, September 8

Our Lady of the Rosary, October 7 (Chaldean)

Dedication (Presentation) of Mary in the Temple, November 21 (Syro-Malabar)

The Church of the East, as we have seen, however, never accepted the title of Theotokos from the Council of Ephesus and celebrates only *three* feasts of Mary during the liturgical year, namely, the Friday before Epiphany (the equivalent to December 26 in the Byzantine and West Syrian traditions), usually occurring on either the Friday or second Friday after the Nativity; "the Memorial of My Lady Mary for the Preservation of Seeds" on May 15 (equivalent to "Our Lady of the Fields" above); and her Dormition (*šunaya*, transitus, death) on August 15, along with a weekly commemoration of her on Wednesdays.[52] But even if there is no official acceptance of the Theotokos decree of Ephesus in the Church of the East, Sebastian Brock has drawn attention to the presence of that very title in East Syrian liturgical texts and to the rich poetic imagery regarding Mary in the authentic hymns of St. Ephrem the Syrian.[53] Two examples of this, clearly reflecting the ancient patristic Eve-Mary typology, follow:

[51] This feast already appears in Syriac lectionaries in the nineteenth century. See Ray, "August 15 and the Development of the Jerusalem Calendar," 112–61.

[52] See Othottil Ulakarran Jincy, "The Commemoration of Blessed Marth Maryam in the Church of the East: A Study Based on Ḥudra Ms. dt 1598 Alkaya," *The Harp* 25 (2010): 273–89. On the early origins of these three feasts, see Shoemaker, *Mary in Early Christian Faith and Devotion*, 134–45.

[53] Sebastian Brock, "Mary in Syriac Tradition," in *Mary's Place in Christian Dialogue*, ed. A. Stacpoole (Wilton: Morehouse-Barlow Co., Inc., 1982), 182–91.

The virgin earth of old gave birth to the Adam who is lord of the earth,
But today another virgin has given birth to the Adam who is Lord of heaven.
(*H. Nativ.* 1.16)[54]

Adam brought forth travail upon the woman who sprang from him,
But today she [Mary], who bore him a Saviour, has redeemed that travail.
A man [Adam] who himself knew no birth, bore Eve the mother:
How much more should Eve's daughter [Mary] be believed to have given birth
without the aid of a man. (*H. Nativ.* 1.14-15)[55]

Of special interest as well, Ephrem relates the baptismal womb of the Jordan with the womb of Mary in giving birth to Christ and even views the incarnation of Christ as Mary's own baptism:

O Christ, you have given birth to your own mother
in the second birth that comes from water. . . .
The Son of the Most High came and dwelt in me,
And I became his mother. As I gave birth to him,
—his second birth—so too he gave birth to me
a second time. He put on his mother's robe
—his body; I put on his glory. (*H. Nativ.* 16.9, 11)[56]

Fire and Spirit are in the womb of her who bore you,
Fire and Spirit are in the river in which you were baptized,
Fire and Spirit are in our baptism,
And in the Bread and Cup is Fire and Holy Spirit.
(*H. Fid.* 10.17)[57]

It is on the basis of such Marian imagery, clearly reflecting an incarnational-sacramental-liturgical context, that Brock can conclude, saying:

[54] Ibid., 186.
[55] Ibid., 187.
[56] Ibid., 190.
[57] Ibid., 190.

> In actual fact, the Christological differences that separate the Syrian Orthodox, Greek Orthodox (Chalcedonian) Churches and the Church of the East do not appear to have had much effect on their attitudes to Mary. . . . Thus those who are familiar with the Byzantine tradition will find much of what Syriac writers say on the subject of Mary not unfamiliar.[58]

Traditionally, saints in the East Syrian tradition are commemorated on Fridays, in relation to the passion of Christ, as the first saints were martyrs. The celebration of saints on other days of the week has, however, been introduced, and some, albeit important saints to the local church, have fixed dates.[59]

Compared, for example, with the Coptic and Ethiopian Rites, East Syrian Christians spend considerably less time in fasting periods during the liturgical year. Together with the seven-week *Sawma Rabba*, the Great Fast (Lent), including the first four days of Holy Week among the Chaldeans and Syro-Malabars in order to have forty days of fasting, and, of course, the traditional fasting days of Wednesday and Friday, there are five additional lesser fasts among East Syrian Christians. These are the Fast of Mar Zaya (late fourth-, early fifth-century mystic and missionary) in September, the three days after the second Sunday of the Nativity; the Fast of the Virgins, after the first Sunday of the Epiphany; the Fast of the Ninevites, seventy days before Easter; and the pre-Dormition Fast, the Fast of *Mart Mariam* (Our Lady), from August 1 to 14.

Finally, as we noted in our introduction, it is precisely from among East and West Syrian Churches that new movements of immigration have arisen in our own day due to the plight of these Eastern Christians in the Middle East, especially in Syria, Iran, and Iraq. Indeed, even some of the great classic centers of Eastern Christianity (e.g., Mosul) have been destroyed, including the destruction of numerous churches, especially East Syrian, in Iraq from before the Gulf Wars up to the current persecution of Christians by ISIS, and their communities are now part of Eastern Christian diaspora churches located in California, Detroit, and Chicago. As Bishop Francis Y. Kalabat, the

[58] Ibid., 183.

[59] Pauly Maniyattu, *Heaven on Earth: The Theology of Liturgical Spacetime in the East Syrian Qurbana* (Rome: Mar Thoma Yogam, 1995), 189–95.

Chaldean Catholic bishop in Detroit, Michigan, has recently said about those Christians being persecuted in Iraq, as part of a slow-motion genocide there and elsewhere in the Middle East today:

> We are called the Church of Martyrs. . . . That's our pain and our saving grace. Our faith isn't a theory. It's not a set of teachings. It's a person and we're called to be like him. When I look at this evil, I want to be Rambo. But that won't do any good. We carry the cross for a reason.[60]

### *3.1.6 The West Syrian and Maronite Rites*

Although among the West Syrian Churches the year is divided into eight rather than nine liturgical seasons, the liturgical year in this rite holds a great deal in common with the East Syrian Rite, and so our presentation here can be much shorter and less detailed. The year begins with the Sunday of the Consecration of the Church, celebrated in the last days of October or the first days of November, a feast no doubt having its origins in the feast of the *Encaenia* (Dedication) of the Holy Sepulchre in Jerusalem.[61] It continues with the following common liturgical seasons organized around the major dominical feasts:[62]

Annunciation-Nativity (roughly eight weeks in length)

Epiphany (Baptism of Jesus); includes Presentation of the Lord on February 2

Great Lent (forty-eight days)

[60] S. G. Freedman, "As Iraqi Christians in U.S. Watch ISIS Advance, They See 'Slow-Motion Genocide,'" *New York Times*, September 6, 2014.

[61] See Matthew Black, "The Festival of Encaenia Ecclesiae in the Ancient Church with special reference to Palestine and Syria," *Journal of Ecclesiastical History* 5 (1954): 78–85; and Bernard Botte, "Les Dimanches de la Dédicace dans les églises syriennes," *L'Orient Syrien* 2 (1957): 65–70.

[62] For these major feasts and their propers both in Syriac and English, see *Ma'de'dono: The Book of the Church Festivals According to the Ancient Rite of the Syrian Orthodox Church of Antioch*, trans. Archdeacon Murad Saliba Barsom, ed. Metropolitan Mar Athanasius Yeshue Samuel (Archbishop of the Syrian Orthodox Church in the United States of America and Canada, 1984). See also Patriarch Afram Barsoum, *The Spiritual Treasure on Canonical Prayer*, trans. V. Rev. Joseph Tarzi (Archdiocese of the Syrian Orthodox Church in the Western US, 1999).

Holy Week

Resurrection and Pentecost (including Ascension on the fortieth day of Easter)

Season of the Apostles, June 29 (Sts. Peter and Paul)

Transfiguration, August 6

Finding or Exaltation of the Cross, September 14

There are a number of feasts of the Blessed Virgin Mary on the calendar, some of which are unique to the West Syrian Rite:

Holy Virgin Mary of the Sowing, January 15

Annunciation, March 25

Holy Virgin Mary of the Harvest, May 15

Assumption, August 15

Nativity of Mary, September 8

Glorification of the Holy Virgin Mary at the Lord's Birth, December 26

Together with the liturgical calendars of the Syrian Catholic Church and the Syro-Malankara Church in India, while at core identical with the pattern outlined above, the Syriac Maronite calendar also contains additional feast days imported from the Roman Catholic liturgical calendar (e.g., the Immaculate Conception on December 8), as is the case with all Eastern Rite Catholic Churches. Unique to the Maronite calendar are, not surprisingly, the Solemnity of St. Maron on February 9 and the universally popular nineteenth-century Lebanese monastic Saint Sharbel Makhlouf on July 23 (July 24 in the Roman Rite). Another unique characteristic of the Maronite Rite is that Easter or Bright Week is called *Hawareyeen*, Week of Apparitions, commemorating the postresurrection appearances of Christ.

Along with the common Wednesday and Friday fast outside the Easter season, West Syrian Christians have five seasons of obligatory fasting. These are as follows: (1) the Fast of Nineveh or the Ninevites (shared, as we have seen, with the Ethiopian and East Syrian Rites); (2) Great Lent (beginning forty-eight days before Easter); (3) Advent;

(4) the Fast of the Apostles (a three-day fast from June 26 to 29); and (5) the Fast of the Virgin Mary (a five-day fast beginning on August 10).[63]

As noted previously, like all of the Eastern Christian rites, West Syrian Christians also know their share of contemporary persecution and martyrdom, especially in the Middle East, as part of that "slow-motion genocide" of Christians referred to by Chaldean Bishop Kalabat above. As Lawrence Cunningham has written in his remarkable study, *A Brief History of Saints*:

> It has been argued by more than one scholar that more Christians died because they were Christians in the twentieth century than all those who died over the course of the three centuries of Roman persecution. The genocidal attacks on the Armenian Christians by the Turkish government, the wholesale disappearance of Christians into the Soviet gulags from the 1920s onwards, the persecution of Christians in the period of National Socialism in Germany, the ruthless suppression of Christians in China after the Communist takeover of that country, and the history of Christian suffering in many Islamic countries which goes on apace, would add up to deaths in the millions.[64]

One of the characteristics of Christian martyrdom today, of course, is its ecumenical nature. Again, Cunningham notes that "Pope John Paul II has argued . . . that the best evidence of Christian ecumenism is to be found in the martyrs of the twentieth century—Catholic, Protestant, and Orthodox—who have given up their lives in defense of the gospel and for the fundamental truths that guarantee the dignity of all people."[65] And more recently, Pope Francis has said on numerous occasions in conversation with various Eastern patriarchs:

> The ecumenism of suffering and the ecumenism of martyrdom, the ecumenism of blood is a powerful call to journey along the road of reconciliation among the Churches, with decision and with trusting

[63] See Ephrem Barsoum Severius, *The Golden Key to Divine Worship: With Commentary on the Ritual of the Syriac Church* (West New York, NJ, 1951).

[64] Lawrence Cunningham, *A Brief History of Saints* (Malden, MA: Blackwell, 2005), 115.

[65] Ibid., 117–18.

> abandonment to the action of the Spirit. . . . When terrorists or world powers persecute Christian minorities or Christians, when they do this, they don't ask: "But are you Lutheran? Are you Orthodox? Are you Catholic? Are you a Reformed Christian? Are you a Pentecostal?" No! "You are a Christian!" They only recognize one of them: the Christian. The enemy never makes a mistake and knows very well how to recognize where Jesus is. This is ecumenism of the blood.[66]

Such situations of persecution and martyrdom, as they have already in the Armenian, Byzantine, and Coptic Rites, are bound to have several liturgical ramifications and expressions in the calendars of saints and martyrs in all of the Eastern Churches, just as contemporary Western martyrs are increasingly included in the calendars of various Churches of the West (e.g., Oscar Romero, Maximilian Kolbe, Dietrich Bonhoeffer, and Miguel Pro).

## 3.2 The Liturgy of the Hours

The Liturgy of the Hours in the Eastern liturgical traditions is still celebrated not just in monasteries but also in parish churches. In the fourth century the cursus of daily prayer found different expressions in cathedrals and city parishes (the cathedral office), desert monasteries (the desert monastic), and city monasteries (urban monastic) with unique characteristics in each geographical locality. The current ritual form of the Liturgy of the Hours in the Eastern liturgical traditions is the result of a long history of evolution, growth, fusion, and adaptation of these expressions to the needs and culture of the daily cursus of each tradition. We even have cases of parallel traditions of monastic and cathedral offices for the Liturgy of the Hours surviving today within the same tradition, such as in the Coptic and the Ethiopian Rites. In all traditions, however, the celebration of the Liturgy of the Hours during the daily cycle of offices is a reminder of Christ's role in our lives and a call to worship God. As an example of this, the ancient hymn of light, *Phōs Hilaron*, sung at Byzantine vespers says:

> O joyous light of the holy glory of the immortal Father, heavenly, holy, blessed Jesus Christ! As we come to the setting of the sun and behold

[66] May 8, 2014, Vatican Radio.

the evening light, we praise you Father, Son and Holy Spirit, God! It is fitting at all times that you be praised with auspicious voices, O Son of God, giver of life. That is why the whole world glorifies you.[67]

And, as Robert Taft has written of the theology of the Liturgy of the Hours:

The Liturgy of the Hours, like all Christian liturgy, is an eschatological proclamation of the salvation received in Christ, and a glorification and thanksgiving of God for that gift. In its original and primitive sense, the Liturgy of the Hours, indeed all liturgy, is beyond time. For the Christian, there is really no sacred space, no sacred persons or times; all are redeemed in Christ, for whom only God is holy and those to whom he has given his sanctification, his saints, that is, his people.[68]

The fourth century marks a turning point in the history of the Liturgy of the Hours, as it is during this century that we observe the gradual formation of the seven liturgical families of Eastern Christianity. The daily office that emerges in this context is the result of the interplay between the monastic practice and the practice of urban churches. The characteristic of monastic practice is the continuous and in-sequence recitation of the psalms, a practice not tied to a specific time of day but striving toward the achievement of continuous prayer. Urban churches, on the other hand, marked morning and evening with liturgical gatherings in which the psalms used were relevant to the time of day, such as Psalm 62 (63) for morning services, Psalm 140 (141) for evening services. The former practice, rooted in the monastic tradition of Egypt, is called monastic office; the latter, rooted in the practice of urban churches, is called cathedral office. The urban monastic office is a hybrid of the above two, where the cathedral practice of morning and evening prayer is complemented by liturgical gatherings between morning and evening prayer, giving rise to the minor hours of the third, sixth, and ninth hours, and compline following vespers and the meal. One could say that the Liturgy

[67] Antonia Tripolitis, "PHOS HILARON: Ancient Hymn and Modern Enigma," *Vigiliae Christianae* 24 (1970): 189–96, here 189.

[68] Robert Taft, "The Theology of the Liturgy of the Hours," in *Handbook for Liturgical Studies*, vol. 5: *Liturgical Time and Space*, ed. Anscar Chupungco (Collegeville, MN: Liturgical Press, 2000), 119–32, here 129.

of the Hours in all Eastern liturgical traditions is the result of the interplay between these three styles of praying the office in the fourth century.

Each of the Eastern Churches has in its liturgical tradition a full cycle of services for the daily office, centered around morning (nocturn-matins-lauds) and evening prayer (vespers) and complemented by the minor hours (third, sixth, ninth, compline), with some particularities in each tradition. In actual practice, however, one could say that morning and evening prayers are the offices most often celebrated, but again the frequency of these celebrations varies from tradition to tradition. Further, within each tradition there is variety of both the frequency and manner of celebration, depending on locality and context. Even in monastic contexts, when one expects to find more rigor, variety of practice exists within each tradition. While these offices exist more or less in all Eastern liturgical traditions, their structure and content vary greatly, in each case the daily office bearing the "footprint" of the history and evolution of each rite and the interplay between cathedral, monastic, and urban monastic liturgy within each tradition. There are traditions whose daily office is predominantly monastic, such as the Coptic; whose daily office is predominantly cathedral, such as the Armenian and East Syrian; and whose office is a hybrid of the two, such as the Byzantine.[69]

[69] Robert Taft, "The Liturgy of the Hours in the East," in *Handbook for Liturgical Studies*, ed. Chupungco, 5:29–57, here 32; Robert Taft, *The Liturgy of the Hours in East and West: The Origins of the Divine Office and Its Meaning for Today*, 2nd rev. ed. (Collegeville, MN: Liturgical Press, 1993) 217. There has been a lot of discussion about the terms "monastic" and "cathedral" liturgy, and their understanding in the Byzantine Rite has been challenged; see Robert Taft, "Cathedral vs. Monastic Liturgy in the Christian East: Vindicating a Distinction," *Bollettino della Badia Greca di Grottaferrata* 2 (2005): 173–219; Stig Simeon R. Frøyshov, "The Cathedral-Monastic Distinction Revisited. Part I: Was Egyptian Desert Liturgy a Pure Monastic Office?," *Studia Liturgica* 37 (2007): 198–216 (part 2 has not been published yet); Stig Simeon R. Frøyshov, "Byzantine Rite," *The Canterbury Dictionary of Hymnology*, Canterbury Press, August 17, 2021, http://www.hymnology.co.uk/b/byzantine-rite; Stefano Parenti, "The Cathedral Rite of Constantinople: Evolution of a Local Tradition," OCP 77 (2011): 449–69. In the Byzantine Rite, one should technically not speak of "cathedral" and "monastic" but "ekklēsiastēs" (the Office of the Cathedral of Hagia Sophia in Constantinople) and "hagiopolitēs" (the Office of the Holy City of Jerusalem as celebrated in the church of the Holy Sepulchre). For the sake of clarity and consistency, however, since we are addressing more than just the Byzantine Rite, we have decided to use this division of "cathedral" and "monastic" liturgy, with the understanding that nuancing is needed in each of the rites discussed.

As many of these offices are quite lengthy and their celebration is not limited to monastics or clergy, one can observe them celebrated in abridged forms not reflected in the official liturgical books. This reality makes the study of the Liturgy of the Hours in these traditions difficult, as many times what one would expect to observe in theory and what one sees in practice can vary greatly. On the other hand, this challenge reflects the very reality that these liturgical traditions are living traditions that are forced to evolve as they face new realities and new challenges and as they adapt to the particularities of each place and community, reflecting what the late Fr. Taft used to say in his lectures: "All liturgy is local."

### *3.2.1 The Psalter*

Foundational to the structure and the celebration of the Liturgy of the Hours among all Eastern Christian traditions is the book of Psalms of the Old Testament, or the Psalter. In fact, the two oldest translations of the Old Testament are in use among Eastern Christians: the Septuagint (LXX) and the Peshiṭta. The former was translated from the Hebrew into Hellenistic Greek originally for use among the Greek-speaking Jews of Alexandria (Egypt) in the third century BC—this is the version that the New Testament authors refer to and that the early Church used.[70] The latter was translated from the Hebrew into Syriac sometime in the second century AD in or around the Syriac city of Edessa.[71] The Old Testament versions in current use by the Armenian, Byzantine, Coptic, and Ethiopian traditions are based on the LXX (each tradition with its own history and particularities), while that of the Syriac-speaking traditions (East Syriac, West Syriac, Maronite) are based on the Peshiṭta. Both in the LXX and the Peshiṭta the psalms have a different numbering, which oftentimes confuses the Western reader. For this reason, we provide the table below that correlates the numbering with the Hebrew version used currently in Western Bibles:[72]

[70] Natalio Fernández Marcos, *The Septuagint in Context: Introduction to the Greek Version of the Bible*, trans. Wilfred Watson (Leiden: Brill, 2000); Martin Hengel, *The Septuagint as Christian Scripture: Its Prehistory and the Problem of Its Canon*, trans. Mark Biddle (Edinburgh: T & T Clark, 2002).

[71] *The Syriac Peshiṭta Bible with English Translation: Psalms*, trans. Richard Taylor, text prepared by George Kiraz and Joseph Bali (Piscataway, NJ: Gorgias Press, 2020), xiii.

[72] Note that the Vulgate numbering of the psalms is the same as in LXX.

| LXX | Peshiṭta | Hebrew |
|---|---|---|
| 1–8 | 1–8 | 18 |
| 9:1-21 | 9 | 9 |
| 9:22-39 | 10 | 10 |
| 10 | 11 | 11 |
| 11–112 | 12–113 | 12–113 |
| 113:1-8 | 114:1-8 | 114 |
| 113:9-26 | 114:9-26 | 115 |
| 114 | 115:1-9 | 116:1-9 |
| 115 | 115:10-19 | 116:10-19 |
| 116 | 116 | 117 |
| 117–145 | 117–145 | 118–146 |
| 146 | 146 | 147:1-11 |
| 147 | 147 | 147:12-20 |
| 148–150 | 148–150 | 148–150 |

Furthermore, the psalms in the Psalter are grouped in different ways among the Eastern Christian traditions, reflecting and facilitating their use in the liturgical context and particularly in the celebration of the Liturgy of the Hours.

The Armenian tradition has its own unique division of the psalter (Psalms 1–147; Psalms 148–150, the lauds, are not included in this division but are used in the office). The Armenian Psalter is divided into eight canons of seven *gobłayk'*. Each *gobłay* is comprised of (usually) three psalms and concludes with the small doxology. Each canon is accompanied by a corresponding Old Testament canticle, which in the Armenian liturgical commentary tradition is understood as the eighth *gobłay*. In this system, each night one canon is recited, thus going through the whole Psalter in eight days.[73]

[73] Michael Daniel Findikyan, *The Commentary on the Armenian Daily Office by Bishop Step'anos Siwnec'i (†735): Critical Edition and Translation with Textual and Liturgical Analysis*, OCA 270 (Rome: Pontificio Istituto Orientale, 2004), 333–37; Gabriele Winkler, "The Armenian Night Office I," *Journal of the Society for Armenian Studies* 1 (1984): 93–113, here 107–8; Gabriele Winkler, "The Armenian Night Office II: The Unit of Psalmody, Canticles, and Hymns with Particular Emphasis on the Origins and Early

The *current* Byzantine Psalter, popularly named "monastic" or, more accurately, *Hagiopolite*, as it reflects the Psalter used in the Holy City of Jerusalem, divides the 150 psalms into twenty *kathismata*. Each *kathisma* is comprised of three *staseis*; and each *stasis* is made up of usually three psalms (depending on the length of the psalms) and each ending with a doxology. Throughout the year, the whole Psalter is recited once a week, with the *kathismata* appointed to vespers and matins of every day. During Great Lent and Holy Week, the Psalter is recited twice a week, when the Psalter is also distributed in the minor hours (first, third, sixth, and ninth). In actual practice, however, the Psalter is rarely recited in parishes, with some exceptions during Great Lent and Holy Week.

The Constantinopolitan Psalter, however, that was used in the Great Church of Christ, Hagia Sophia in Constantinople, was remarkably different in structure and execution from the Hagiopolite Psalter described above and currently used in the churches that follow the Byzantine Rite,[74] reflecting a different office of the Hours. This Constantinopolitan Psalter, reflecting the "*ekklēsiastēs*"[75] or, more popularly, the "cathedral" office of Constantinople, was divided into eight fixed antiphons and sixty-eight variable antiphons. The eight fixed antiphons, a total of ten psalms, were Psalms 85 and 140 in vespers or evening prayer; Psalms 3, 62, 133, 50, and 148–150 in *Orthros* or morning prayer; and Psalm 118 divided into three antiphons for Sunday *Orthros*. The remaining 140 psalms were divided into sixty-eight variable antiphons. The odd-numbered antiphons had "Alleluia" as their response, and the even-numbered antiphons had a three-word response in Greek, built in the following way: a verb in the imperative, a personal pronoun, and the vocative "Lord"; for example, the response to antiphon 2 (Psalms 4–6) was "Have compassion on me, Lord" («Οἰκτήρησόν με Κύριε»). The total number of verses in the cathedral Psalter was 2,542 (roughly half the number of verses in the

Evolution of Armenia's Hymnography," *Revue des études Arméniennes* 17 (1983): 471–551, here 474–75; Taft, *Liturgy of the Hours*, 221.

[74] In the monastic Psalter all 150 psalms are divided into twenty sessions (καθίσματα) and sixty stations (στάσεις), three to each κάθισμα. The whole Psalter is recited once a week, or twice during Lent. The total number of verses is 4,782 or 4,784, arranged by short distinctions of half verses. Therefore, the choirs alternate more frequently; psalms are more often read than chanted; see appendix 1 of *The Festal Menaion*, 530–34.

[75] Parenti, "The Cathedral Rite of Constantinople," 449–69.

monastic Psalter), arranged by whole verses. The psalms were always chanted, in contrast to the Hagiopolite Psalter where they were read.[76]

The sixty-eight variable antiphons (140 psalms) were distributed between vespers and *Orthros* so that all would be chanted in one week (the first week). Then, in the following week (the second week), those antiphons assigned to *Orthros* in the first week would now be chanted in vespers, and those antiphons assigned to vespers in the first week would now be chanted in *Orthros*, thus forming a two-week cycle. This two-week cycle is a characteristic of the cathedral office. A similar two-week cycle is found in the East Syriac tradition (see section 3.2.6). Within this two-week cycle a different response for each day of the week, called *kekragari*, was assigned to Psalm 140 (LXX), a fixed vesperal antiphon, and similarly a different response was assigned for each day of the week, called *pentekostari*, to Psalm 50 (LXX), a fixed matins antiphon.

For a while the two different uses coexisted, with that of Hagia Sophia losing ground. Writing in the thirteenth century, archbishop of Ochrid Demetrios Chomatenos attested to the survival of the Constantinopolitan Liturgy of the Hours in only three churches:

> There are two established practices that contain and dictate the prayers, the hymns and the spiritual odes of the ecclesiastical office [=Liturgy of the Hours]. The one practice, which is also the more perfect one, is predominantly called the sung [office]; it's not widespread but is limited to a small number of places, which we know, that is the great church of the prosperous Constantinople, the famous cathedral of Thessaloniki and the far-famed cathedral of Athens. . . . The second practice, called Hagiopolitis, is common to all, as every church of the orthodox Christians honors it.[77]

In the current Coptic tradition, the Psalter is not divided in any way, and it does not exist as a separate liturgical book; rather, the

[76] This summary description is based on Oliver Strunk, "The Byzantine Office at Hagia Sophia," *Dumbarton Oaks Papers* 9–10 (1956): 177–202, and Miguel Arranz, "La liturgie des heures selon l'ancien Euchologe byzantin," *Studia Anselmiana* 68 (1979): 1–19.

[77] J. Pitra, ed., *Analecta sacra et classica spicilegio solesmensi parata* (Paris, 1888), 619–20; see Stefanos Alexopoulos, "When a Column Speaks: The Liturgy of the Christian Parthenon," *Dumbarton Oaks Papers* 69 (2015): 159–78.

psalms are embedded in the Horologion (the Book of Hours). The vast majority of the psalms are read in the daily cursus of the Liturgy of the Hours in an ascending order, beginning with Psalm 1 in prime. The manuscript tradition, however, reflects a great diversity: some manuscripts witnessing the distribution of all 150 psalms in the daily cursus, and others witnessing the Hagiopolite division of the Psalter into twenty *kathismata*.[78]

The continuous recitation of the Psalter in the Ethiopic tradition occurs during Great Lent, when the full Psalter is to be recited in one week in vespers and matins of Monday through Saturday, excluding Sunday. The Ethiopian Psalter bears the title the Psalms of David or *Mäzmurä Dawit*[79] and is divided into fifteen *neguś*, each *neguś* containing ten psalms. The fifteen *neguś* are sequentially distributed in such a way that, depending on the day, twenty or thirty psalms are recited in vespers and matins combined each day, with all 150 psalms recited by the completion of the cycle.[80]

The Syriac traditions do not share the same division of the Psalter. The East Syriac Psalter today is divided into twenty *hullale*, each having three *marmyata*, each *marmita* consisting of ideally three psalms (depending on their length). It has been suggested that the division of the Psalter into *marmyata* antedates its division into *hullale*. The East Syriac division of the Psalter seems to be modeled after the division of the Hagiopolite Psalter.[81] While closer to Jerusalem, the West Syriac and Maronite traditions do not follow the division of the Hagiopolite Psalter. The psalms are divided into fifteen *marmyata*, and each *marmita* has four *šubḥe*, each *šubḥa* usually consisting of three psalms.

[78] Ugo Zanetti, "La distribution des psaumes dans l'horologion copte," OCP 56 (1990): 323–69. Many thanks to Ramez Mikhail for directing us to this valuable resource.

[79] To be differentiated from the Psalms of the Virgin (Mary) or *Mäzmurä Dəngəl* and the Psalms of Christ or *Mäzmurä Krəstos*; these are hymnological compositions modelled after the Psalms. See *Encyclopaedia Aethiopica* (Wiesbaden: Harrassowitz Verlag, 2008), 3:896–98.

[80] Habtemichael Kidane, *L'ufficio divino della Chiesa etiopica*, OCA 257 (Rome: Pontificio Istituto Orientale, 1998), 173–76.

[81] See Alex Neroth van Vogelpoel, *The Commentary of Gabriel of Qatar on the East Syriac Morning Service on Ordinary Days*, Texts from Christian Late Antiquity 53 (Piscataway, NJ: Gorgias Press, 2018), 102–4.

| Armenian | Hagiopolitēs = Current Byzantine | Ekklēsiastēs = "Cathedral" Byzantine |
|---|---|---|
| Psalms 1–147 divided into eight *kanonk'* | Psalms 1–150 divided into twenty *kathismata* | Psalms 1–150 divided into seventy-six antiphons |
| 1 *kanon* has 7 *gobłayk'* | 1 *kathisma* has 3 *staseis* | 8 fixed antiphons: Pss 85 and 140 at vespers; 3, 62, 133; Ps 50; and Pss 148–150 in *Orthros*, Ps 118 divided into 3 antiphons for Sunday *Orthros* |
| 1 *gobłay* consists generally of 3 psalms (depending on their length) + doxology | 1 *stasis* consists generally of 3 psalms (depending on their length) + doxology | |
| 1 *kanon* has on average 3x7=21 psalms | 1 *kathisma* has on average 3x3=9 psalms | 68 variable antiphons: odd numbered with "alleluia" as response, even numbered with three-word response |
| Psalter recited in nocturns in cycles of 8 days | Psalter recited once a week (vespers and matins), or twice during Great Lent (all offices) | 2-week cycle so that all 68 antiphons are assigned to both vespers and *Orthros* |

The table above summarizes the divisions of the Psalter in the liturgical use of the Eastern Christian traditions.[82]

No matter its manner of division and particular use, the book of Psalms permeates all aspects of the liturgical life and spiritual expressions of the Eastern Christian churches. In the work *On Repentance and the Reading of David*, ascribed to John Chrysostom, the author notes about the importance of the Psalter ("David" in his writing):[83]

> What can I say about the blessed David? That the grace of the Spirit arranged that he be declared every day and every night. . . . At vigils in the church, David is first, middle and last. In the morning hymning, David is first, middle and last. In the funeral processions, David is first,

[82] Adjusted from Winkler, "The Armenian Night Office II," 477; Strunk, "The Byzantine Office at Hagia Sophia," 177–202; Pierre-Edmond Gemayel, "La structure des vêrpes maronites," *L'Orient Syrien* 9 (1964): 105–34, here 111–12 (with many thanks to Prof. Joseph Amar for the reference); Habtemichael Kidane, *L'ufficio divino della Chiesa etiopica*, 173–76.

[83] *De poenitentia et in lectionem de Davide et de uxore Uriae.* PG 64:12–13; translation by the authors.

| East Syrian | West Syrian and Maronite | Ethiopian |
|---|---|---|
| Psalms 1–150 divided into twenty *hullale* | Psalms 1–150 divided into fifteen *marmyata* | Psalms 1–150 divided into fifteen *neguś* |
| 1 *hullala* has 3 *marmyata* | 1 *marmita* has 4 *šubḥe* | Each *neguś* has 10 psalms |
| 1 *marmita* consists generally of 3 psalms (depending on their length) + doxology | 1 *šubḥe* consists generally of 3 psalms (depending on their length) + doxology | M has 3 *neguś* (Ps 1–30)<br>T has 3 *neguś* (31–60)<br>W has 2 *neguś* (61–80)<br>R has 3 *neguś* (81–110)<br>F has 2 *neguś* (111–130)<br>Sat has 3 *neguś* (131–150) |
| 1 *hullala* has on average 3x3=9 psalms | 1 *marmita* has on average 4x3=12 psalms | |
| | Recited throughout the Liturgy of the Hours in one day | Psalter recited once a week in Great Lent, distributed in Vespers and Matins, Monday to Saturday |

> middle and last. In the weaving at the homes of virgins, David is first, middle and last. What wondrous things! Many, not even having received the basics of literacy, learn by heart all of David. But he shines forth in such a way in every circumstance and among all age groups not only in the cities and the churches, but also in the countryside and the desert and the uninhabited earth, where with even greater zeal he lifts up towards God holy choruses. In monasteries a holy chorus of angelic orders, David is first, middle and last. In monasteries of companies of virgins who imitate Mary, David is first, middle and last. In the deserts crucified men converse with God, David is first, middle and last. . . . And David stands alone, and he raises the servants of God to angelic vigils, turning earth into heaven, and making people equal to the angels, adorning in everything our life, and becoming everything to everyone, and in all things making our life angelic.

What is described above reflects all Eastern Christian traditions; the Psalter permeates the liturgical and spiritual life of all faithful, whether lay or clergy or monastics, whether in urban centers or the countryside or the desert, whether in churches or monasteries or secluded areas of asceticism.

### *3.2.2 The Armenian Rite*

The Liturgy of the Hours of the Armenian Rite is found in its Book of Hours (*Žamagirk'*) and contains the following offices:

1. Office of the Night (*Gišerayin žam* = Nocturns)
2. Office of the Morning (*Arawōtean žam* = Matins)
3. Office of Sunrise (*Arewagali žam* = First Hour)
4. Office of the Midday Hours (*Čašu žam* = Third, Sixth, and Ninth Hours)
5. Office of the Evening (*Erekoyan žam* = Vespers)
6. Office of Peace (*Xałałakan žam* = Compline I)
7. Office of Rest (*Hangstean žam* = Compline II)

The Armenian Office is cathedral in character, preserving elements of ancient Jerusalem and Cappadocian liturgy.[84] Noted is the absence of (monastic) continuous psalmody with one exception, nocturns, where, after the recitation of the fixed psalms of the invitatory (Pss 3, 87, 102, 142), continuous psalmody is recited based on the Armenian division of the Psalter.

The main building block or structural unit of the Armenian Liturgy of the Hours, and Armenian liturgy in general, is a liturgical unit named *kanon* (to be distinguished from the *kanon* of the Armenian Psalter), whose origins lie in the ancient stational liturgy of Jerusalem. Every office can be broken down to repetitions of this liturgical unit, which is comprised of (1) psalm(s), (2) hymn or *šarakan* (= troparion),[85] (3) acclamation (optional), (4) diaconal proclamation with optional intercessions, and (5) prayer or acclamation.[86]

[84] Robert Taft, "The Armenian Liturgy: Its Origins and Characteristics," in *Treasures in Heaven: Armenian Art, Religion and Society*. Papers Delivered at the Pierpont Morgan Library at the Symposium Organized by Thomas F. Mathews and Roger S. Wieck, 21–22 May 1994 (New York: Pierpont Morgan Library, 1998), 13–30, here 18.

[85] The collection of these *šarakan* hymns are found in the *Šarakan* or *Šaraknoc'* book structured according to the liturgical year. The *šarakan* hymns have evolved out of the responses to the Psalter and the canticles; Winkler, "The Armenian Night Office II," 517–18 and following; Findikyan, *Commentary*, 435, footnote 86.

[86] Findikyan, *Commentary*, 332.

Armenian Sunday matins contains a liturgical unit that highlights the strong links between the liturgy of the city of Jerusalem in the fourth century and Armenian liturgy. This liturgical unit is the Office of the Oil-Bearing Women, also preserved but to a lesser extent in the Byzantine tradition. Centered on the gospel readings of the resurrection account (Matt 28:1-20; Mark 15:42–16:8; Luke 23:50–24:12; John 19:38–20:18), with its three pre-gospel psalms (Pss 112:1-3; 43:26, 23b; 145:10, 1-2), and the proclamation and acclamation after the gospel hymn, this Office of the Oil-Bearing Women betrays its strong link to the Jerusalem Cathedral Resurrection Office and its point of origin.[87]

The Office of Sunrise, on the other hand, is a latecomer in the history of the Armenian office of the Hours. Devotion to the sunrise at the end of matins, probably of monastic origin in order to pray at the time of the rising of the sun, is clearly witnessed by the tenth century, but not yet as an independent service. Rather, it is appended to the end of matins. By the thirteenth century, however, the Office of Sunrise has its own existence as an independent office. Possibly, the author of this separation and redactor of the very "neat" structure of the Office of Sunrise is St. Nersess Shnorhali.[88]

A similar process of duplication and eventually separation to two offices explains the presence of two different services of compline in the Armenian Liturgy of the Hours: the Office of Peace and the Office of Rest. The latter appears for the first time in the thirteenth century and becomes a standard feature only by the end of the fifteenth century; it became the place for "overflow" material originally appended to the end of vespers. The Office of Peace shares common elements with the Byzantine Office of Compline as presented in the Evergetis Typikon demonstrating, according to Michael Daniel Findikyan, their early common Palestinian roots.[89]

Appearing in early commentaries of the Armenian Liturgy of the Hours one also finds discussion on Sunday Third Hour, which is the Liturgy of the Word of the Eucharistic Synaxis. The placement of this office within the commentaries of the Liturgy of the Hours *and* its

[87] See ibid., 380–404 for a detailed discussion.

[88] See ibid., 405–36 for a detailed discussion.

[89] See ibid., 499–510 for a detailed discussion.

absence from the commentaries of the Divine Liturgy has led scholars to hypothesize about its original function. Robert Taft has suggested that the Liturgy of the Word of the Armenian tradition was originally an Armenian Presanctified, something similar to the Palestinian Office of the *Typika*, in its beginnings a Palestinian monastic presanctified liturgy that later influenced the structure of the Byzantine Liturgy of the Word.[90] There is no evidence, however, for the existence of an Armenian Presanctified.[91]

In current Armenian practice, the offices that are usually celebrated are the Office of the Night (nocturns) and the Office of the Morning (matins), celebrated together in the morning, and the Office of the Evening (vespers), usually celebrated on Saturday evening. During Lent one can also observe the celebration of the Office of Sunrise, the Office of Peace, and the Office of Rest.[92]

The Office of the Night (*Gišerayin žam* = nocturns) has the following structure:[93]

1. Invitatory (doxology, Lord's Prayer, introit [Ps 50:17]), Pss 3, 87, 102, 142, hymns, proclamation and intercessions, hymns, prayer)
2. Monastic psalmody
3. Office of the Dead (post-thirteenth-century addition, conducted only when the Divine Liturgy is celebrated)
4. Canticle (Exod 15) accompanied by a hymn, acclamation, proclamation,[94] and a prayer (liturgical unit of *kanon*)
5. Lord's Prayer

[90] Taft, "The Armenian Liturgy," 18–21.

[91] Findikyan, *Commentary*, 440n14. The only instance is Armenian translation of the Byzantine Presanctified. See Stefanos Alexopoulos, *The Presanctified Liturgy*, 117–18.

[92] Taft, *The Liturgy of the Hours*, 224.

[93] Outline based on Findikyan, *Commentary*, 333–41; Winkler, "The Armenian Night Office I" and "The Armenian Night Office II"; Taft, *The Liturgy of the Hours*, 221; https://www.stnersess.edu/liturgical-services.html.

[94] Proclamation (*karoz*) are biddings, petitions; acclamation (*maght'ank'*) is a short prayer of praise.

Then the Office of the Morning (*Arawōtean žam* = matins) follows, which has the following structure:[95]

1. Invitatory (Lord's Prayer, introit [Ps 89:14-17])
2. *Kanon* of the Three Youths (Dan 3:26-46, 52-58, acclamation, hymn, proclamation, acclamation)
3. *Kanon* of the Magnificat (Luke 1:46-55, 68-69; 2:29-32, hymn, proclamation, and prayer)
4. Office of the Oil-Bearing Women (celebrated only on Sundays—has its roots in the Sunday Resurrection Office of Jerusalem)
5. *Kanon* of Psalm 50 (Ps 50, hymn, proclamation, acclamation)
6. *Kanon* of Psalms 148–150 (Pss 148–150, hymns, acclamation, hymn, proclamation, prayer, *Trisagion*)
7. [Only on Sundays: Sunday Dismissal: Ps 112, gospel, hymn for Sunday, proclamation, prayer, Lord's Prayer—end of Sunday Matins]
8. *Kanon* of Ps 112 (Ps 112, hymn, proclamation, prayer)
9. Dismissal (different on fasting days and on feast days)

The Office of the Evening (*Erekoyan žam* = vespers)[96] has the following structure:

1. Invitatory (doxology, Lord's Prayer, introit [Ps 54:16, 18])
2. Cathedral psalmody (Ps 85, acclamation, Pss 139–141)
3. Lucernarium (*Phos Hilaron* on Saturdays / acclamation on other evenings, proclamation, acclamation, *mesedi* (variable psalmic verse) with Ps 140:2 as response)

[95] Outline based on Findikyan, *Commentary*, 341–404; Taft, *The Liturgy of the Hours*, 221; and https://www.stnersess.edu/liturgical-services.html. For the text, see *The Book of Hours, Or, The Order of Common Prayers of the Armenian Apostolic Orthodox Church: Matins, Prime, Vespers and Occasional Offices* (Evanston, IL: Ouzoonian House, 1964), 3–61.

[96] Outline adjusted from Findikyan, *Commentary*, 472–73; Taft, *The Liturgy of the Hours* 223; and https://www.stnersess.edu/liturgical-services.html. For the text, see *The Book of Hours, Or, The Order of Common Prayers of the Armenian Apostolic Orthodox Church*, 75–99.

4. Evening Prayer (proclamation, prayer, *Trisagion*, invocation of the Mother of God, acclamation, proclamation, doxology)
5. *Kanon* of Ps 120 (Ps 120, hymn, proclamation, prayer)
6. Concluding *Kanon* (different during Lent, days of fasting, feasts, and Saturdays)
7. The Lord's Prayer

Finally, all the minor hours have exactly the same structure, formed by the repetition of the same liturgical unit (*kanon*): psalm, hymn, acclamation, proclamation, prayer.[97]

### *3.2.3 The Byzantine Rite*

The Byzantine rite has had a long history of evolution and synthesis,[98] and the imprint of this evolution and synthesis is dramatically reflected in the Liturgy of the Hours. Cathedral vespers and matins, as they were celebrated at the Great Church of Constantinople (Hagia Sophia), had the following schema:[99]

[97] For the Office of Sunrise (*Arewagali žam* = First Hour), see Findikyan, *Commentary*, 406, and https://www.stnersess.edu/liturgical-services.html. For the text, see *The Book of Hours, Or, The Order of Common Prayers of the Armenian Apostolic Orthodox Church*, 62–74. For the Office of the Midday Hours (*Čašu žam*, Third, Sixth, and Ninth Hours), see https://www.stnersess.edu/liturgical-services.html. The offices of Peace, Rest, and the Sunday Third Hour have more complicated structures. For the Office of Peace (*Xałałakan žam* = Compline I), see https://www.stnersess.edu/liturgical-services.html. For the Office of Rest (*Hangstean žam* = Compline II), see https://www.stnersess.edu/liturgical-services.html; for the text, see *Rest Service of the Armenian Church*, comp. and ed. Archbishop Torkom Manoogian (New York: St. Vartan Press, 1981). Finally, for the Office of the Sunday Third Hour (= Liturgy of the Word of Eucharistic Liturgy), see Findikyan, *Commentary*, 442; for the text see Findikyan, ed., *Divine Liturgy of the Armenian Church*, 10–22.

[98] For a brief overview of this history, see Robert Taft, *The Byzantine Rite: A Short History* (Collegeville, MN: Liturgical Press, 1992).

[99] Miguel Arranz, "L'office de l'Asmatikos Hesperinos ('vêpres chantées') de l'ancien Euchologe byzantin," OCP 44 (1978): 107–30, 391–412; idem, "L'office de l'Asmatikos Orthros ('matines chantées') de l'ancien Euchologe byzantin," OCP 47 (1981): 122–57; for an outstanding detailed study, see Gregor Hanke, *Vesper und Orthros des Kathedralritus der Hagia Sophia zu Konstantinopel*, Jerusalemer Theologisches Forum 21, 2 vols. (Münster: Aschendorff Verlag, 2018).

| **Cathedral Vespers** | **Cathedral *Orthros*** |
|---|---|
| *Part I:*<br>• Ps 85 (fixed antiphon)<br>• Six variable antiphons<br>• Ps 140 (fixed antiphon) with responses and entrance of clergy and laity into the nave (variable antiphons suppressed on big feasts—vespers began on ambo).<br><br>**Each antiphon is accompanied by a prayer* | *Part I:*<br>• Pss 3, 62, 133 (fixed antiphon)<br>• Six variable antiphons<br>• Eighth antiphon (second canticle of three youths, Dan 3:57ff.) with responses and entrance of clergy and laity into the nave (variable antiphons suppressed on big feasts—*Orthros* began on ambo).<br><br>**Each antiphon is accompanied by a prayer* |
| *Part II:*<br>• *Ektenēs* litany with *Great Kyrie Eleison*<br>• Small antiphon 1 (Ps 144 with refrain *Tais presbeiais*<br>• Small antiphon 2 (Ps 115 with refrain Alleluia with *Ho Monogenēs* at the end)<br>• Small antiphon 3 (Ps 116 with refrain the *Trisagion*)—each antiphon with its prayer (for the prayers see Vespers of Pentecost).<br><br>**Each antiphon is accompanied by a prayer* | *Part II:*<br>• *Synaxarion* of the day<br>• *Ektenēs* litany with *Great Kyrie Eleison*<br>• Ps 50 with response and *Ho Monogenēs* at the end<br>• Pss 148–150 (the last antiphon of the Psalter)<br>• *Gloria in excelsis* followed by the *Trisagion*<br>• On Sundays: procession to the altar before the Gloria—after Gloria the Sunday Prokeimenon (Ps 9:33) and the gospel of the resurrection read from the ambo (*Pss 50 and 148–150 accompanied by their respective prayers, not sure about Gloria*) |
| *Part III:*<br>• Prayer and synaptē for catechumens<br>• Two prayers for the faithful<br>• Angel of peace litany and third prayer of the faithful (of dismissal)<br>• Prayer of inclination | *Part III:*<br>• Prayer and synaptē for catechumens<br>• Two prayers for the faithful<br>• Angel of peace litany and third prayer of the faithful (of dismissal)<br>• Prayer of inclination |

The three-antiphon structure observable in part 2 above is at the core of the structure of the minor hours (midnight, first, third, sixth, ninth) in the cathedral rite:[100]

*Three-Antiphon Structure:*

Diaconal Synaptē

Prayer of First Antiphon

Psalm with response

Diaconal Synaptē

Prayer of Second Antiphon

Psalm with response

Diaconal Synaptē

Prayer of Third Antiphon

Psalm with response

Angel of peace litany and prayer of dismissal

Prayer of inclination

The offices of the *current* Liturgy of the Hours of the Byzantine Rite, the outcome of the neo-sabbaitic synthesis (thirteenth century to sixteenth century) have a totally different structure, reflecting great influence from the liturgical tradition of Jerusalem. These are found in the liturgical book called *Horologion* (Book of Hours) and they are:

1. *Mesonyktikon* (Midnight Office)
2. *Orthros* (Matins)
3. *Prōtē Hora* (First Hour)
4. *Tritē Hora* (Third Hour)
5. *Hektē Hora* (Sixth Hour)
6. *Enatē Hora* (Ninth Hour)
7. *Hesperinos* (Vespers)
8. *Apodeipnon* (Compline)

[100] Miguel Arranz, "Les prières presbytérales des Petites Heures dans l'ancien Euchologe byzantin," OCP 39 (1973): 29–82.

*Trithektē* (tersext) is a feature of weekdays of Great Lent (a relic of the cathedral office).[101] On Holy Friday and (by imitation) on the eve of Epiphany and Christmas, the great or royal Hours of the first, third, sixth, and ninth are solemnly celebrated.[102] The Office of the *Typika*, originally a Palestinian monastic presanctified liturgy, which in the Byzantine context lost its eucharistic character,[103] is rarely celebrated in parishes. It is usually attached to the end of the ninth hour if it is a fasting day ("alleluia" was chanted at *Orthros*),[104] or it is attached to the end of the sixth hour if it is not a fasting day ("God is Lord . . ." was chanted at *Orthros*).

As Taft summarizes, Byzantine vespers today is "basically a hagiopolite cathedral lucernarium with Constantinopolitan prayers and litanies, to which a monastic synaxis of continuous psalmody has been prefixed."[105] Remnants of the Constantinopolitan cathedral vespers are the prayers, now grouped together and read silently during Psalm 103, while their doxological conclusions or *ekphōnēseis* are scattered throughout vespers, indicating sometimes the original place of their respective prayers. The outline of the *current* Byzantine vespers is as follows:[106]

1. Opening
2. Psalm 103 (seven vesperal prayers read by priest while reader recites psalm)
3. Great synaptē (petitions)
4. Monastic psalmody (usually omitted at parish contexts)
5. Psalms 140, 141, 129, 116 with hymnody and incensation
6. Entrance with censer and entrance prayer

[101] Miguel Arranz, "Les prières presbytérales de la Tritoekti de l'ancien Euchologe byzantin," OCP 43 (1977): 70–93, 335–54.

[102] Stefanos Alexopoulos, «Οἱ Ἀκολουθίες τῶν Μεγάλων Ὡρῶν» [The Offices of the Royal Hours], *Ἐκκλησία* 92 (2015): 686–701.

[103] Alexopoulos, *The Presanctified Liturgy in the Byzantine Rite*, 80–90.

[104] In the celebration of the Byzantine Liturgy of the Hours, the "alleluia" is a feature of fasting/Lenten days, in contrast to the Roman liturgical tradition.

[105] Taft, *The Liturgy of the Hours*, 227.

[106] Adapted from ibid., 278–79.

7. *Phos Hilaron*[107]
8. *Prokeimenon* (psalmic verses)
9. [Three Old Testament or epistle readings on the eve of dominical, Marian, or other feasts]
10. *Ektenēs* (petitions)
11. Lord, Vouchsafe (prayer)
12. Angel of peace litany (petitions)
13. Peace and prayer of inclination
14. *Aposticha* (hymnody)
15. *Nunc dimittis*
16. *Trisagion* and hymns
17. Dismissal

Matins has a more complicated structure. It is a significantly longer service, a conflation of four originally distinct services: the royal office (originally a brief service for the sovereign used in imperial monastic foundations), monastic nocturns of continuous psalmody, a cathedral vigil of Hagiopolite origin on Sundays and important feasts, and cathedral morning prayer.[108] The great length of this service and its relative complexity have led to the reality that when it is celebrated, it is usually considerably abridged. The outline of the *current* matins is as follows:[109]

[107] On this famous hymn, see Antonia Tripolitis, "ΦΩΣ ΙΛΑΡΟΝ: Ancient Hymn and Modern Enigma," *Vigiliae Christianae* 24 (1970): 189–96; Peter Plank, *Phos hilaron: Christushymnus und Lichtdanksagung der frühen Christenheit* (Bonn: Borengässer, 2001); Graham Field, "Phōs Hilaron," in *Brill Encyclopedia of Early Christianity Online*, ed. David G. Hunter, Paul J. J. van Geest, Bert Jan Lietaert Peerbolte; available online at http://dx.doi.org.ezp-prod1.hul.harvard.edu/10.1163/2589-7993_EECO_SIM_00002749. For the Western reception of this ancient hymn, see Frieder Schulz, "Lumen Christi: Der altkirchliche Vespergesang Phos hilaron Zur westkirchlichen Rezeption: Forschung—Übertragung—Musikfassung," *Jahrbuch für Liturgik und Hymnologie* 43 (2004): 11–48.

[108] Taft, *The Liturgy of the Hours*, 277.

[109] Adapted from ibid., 279–82.

1. Opening
2. Royal Office
   a. Psalms 19 and 20
   b. *Trisagion*
   c. Lord's Prayers
   d. *Ektenēs* (petitions, originally including one for the sovereign)
3. Nocturns
   a. *Hexapsalmos* (six psalms) 3, 37, 62, 87, 102, 142—the twelve matins prayers are read by the priest while the reader recites the psalms
   b. Great synaptē (petitions)
   c. Verses from Psalm 117 and "God is Lord . . ." or Isaiah 26 and "Alleluia" in Great Lent
   d. *Apolytikia* (dismissal hymns of the day or trinitarian during Great Lent)
4. Monastic Psalmody (usually omitted in parishes) in three *staseis*
   a. *Kathismata* (sessional hymns) and small synaptē (petitions) after each *stasis* of the Psalter, usually said even if monastic psalmody is omitted
5. Cathedral Vigil
   a. Psalm 118 or *Polyelaios* (Pss 134–135, plus 136 in Great Lent)—usually omitted in Greek parish use
   b. *Eulogētaria* on Sundays
   c. Small synaptē
   d. *Hypakoē* or sessional hymns
   e. *Anabathmoi* (gradual hymns)
   f. Gospel reading unit (one of eleven resurrection lections on Sundays or lection of feast)
6. Morning Office
   a. Psalm 50 followed by hymns and intercessions

b. Canon(s) (hymnograpahical genre)[110]
c. *Exaposteilarion* (hymn) or *phōtagōgikon* (hymn) in Great Lent
d. Psalms 148–150 with hymnody
e. Great Doxology (chanted on Sundays and feasts, read on ferial days)
f. Intercessions and dismissal (with *aposticha* [hymnody] on ferial days)

In parish use today, vespers and matins are to be celebrated every day,[111] but in many cases, they are not celebrated during weekdays unless the Divine Liturgy is scheduled to be celebrated. The minor hours (midnight, first, third, sixth, ninth, compline) are rarely celebrated outside of Great Lent.[112]

### *3.2.4 The Coptic Rite*

The Coptic Liturgy of the Hours reflects the strong and rich monastic heritage and tradition of Egypt. The monastic praying of the hours in the Egyptian desert has left an indelible mark on the history of the Coptic Liturgy of the Hours. Indeed, more than one cursus of offices has survived in the manuscript tradition, reflecting a variety of uses.[113] The earliest witness to the current practice dates to the thirteenth century and is attested to in the majority of manuscripts sources.[114]

[110] The canon are nine poetic odes (second ode is usually not used) of multiple troparia (hymns) each, originally accompanying but now supplanting the nine biblical canticles. Taft, *The Liturgy of the Hours*, 282–83; *The Festal Menaion*, 546–48.

[111] For an observer's description of the celebration of vespers and matins, see Taft, *The Liturgy of the Hours*, 283–91.

[112] For an excellent overview of the history of these services in the manuscript tradition, see Jeffrey Anderson and Stefano Parenti, *A Byzantine Monastic Office, 1105 A.D.: Houghton Library, MS gr. 3* (Washington, DC: The Catholic University of America Press, 2016), especially part 2, 255–353; for the themes of the minor hours in the Byzantine tradition, see Stefanos Alexopoulos, "Anamnesis, Epiclesis and Mimesis in the Minor Hours of the Byzantine Rite," *Worship* 94 (2020): 228–45.

[113] For another type of Coptic Horologion, see Maged Hanna, «Τὸ Ὡρολόγιον τῆς Κοπτικῆς Ὀρθόδοξης Ἐκκλησίας κατὰ τὸν Codex Parisinus 107 Arabe» (The Horologion of the Coptic Church) (PhD diss., University of Athens, 2005), who publishes the manuscript Paris 107 Arabe.

[114] Ibid., 20n30 notes that Khs-Burmester misread the arabic dating given at the end of the manuscript to 1034, when it should read 1234.

The current Book of Hours (= *Agpyh*)[115] has eight offices:

1. Morning Office (*Salat Baker* = Matins)
2. Third Hour (*Salat el-saah el-thalethah*)
3. Sixth Hour (*Salat el-saah el-sadesah*)
4. Ninth Hour (*Salat el-saah el-taseàh*)
5. Eleventh Hour (*Salat el-ghorob aw Salat el-saàh el-hadyh' asher* = Vespers)
6. Twelfth Hour (*Salat el-nom aw Salat el-saàh el-thany' asher* = Compline)
7. The Veil (*Salat el-setar*)
8. Midnight (*Salat nesfel-lyl* = Nocturns)

The last two offices are unique to the cursus of the Coptic Divine Office and late additions. The Office of the Veil survives in the sources only in Arabic, pointing to its late composition, and is first attested in the fourteenth century (1320s) in the writings of the presbyter Ibn-Kabar as a practice of the monks of the Scete of St. Makarios, prayed the first hour of the night and seems to be a doubling of compline.[116] The Midnight Office is comprised of three watches, each of the same structure.[117]

All of the offices have a shared basic structure, made up of three parts: (1) the opening fixed prayers, common to all; (2) the main body with shared structure among the Hours but with different content

[115] Literally means "the hour." The full title of the Book of Hours is *Kitab el-sabaat salawat el-nahariah wa el-layliah*, that is, the book that contains the seven offices. It is also known as *mazamirel-swaay*, that is the psalms of the Hours; Hanna, "The Horologion of the Coptic Church," 24–25. For the English text of the current Coptic Hours, see under "Agphy" in the mobile application "Coptic Reader," https://suscopts.org/coptic-reader/. See also O. H. E. Khs-Burmester, *The Horologion of the Egyptian Church: Coptic and Arabic Text from a Mediaeval Manuscript* (Cairo: Edizioni del Centro Francescano di Studi Orientali Cristiani, 1973).

[116] Hanna, "The Horologion of the Coptic Church," 69–70; Taft, *The Liturgy of the Hours*, 252.

[117] Hanna, "The Horologion of the Coptic Church," 71–77; Taft, *The Liturgy of the Hours*, 252.

for each; and (3) the dismissal material, common to all (with the exception of the absolution prayer):[118]

1. Opening Fixed Prayers
    a. In the name of the Father . . .
    b. The Lord's Prayer
    c. Prayer of Thanksgiving
    d. Psalm 50
2. Main Body
    a. The opening of the office
    b. Psalms (*different for each Hour*)
    c. Gospel reading (*different for each Hour*)
    d. Hymns (*different for each Hour*)
3. Dismissal Prayers
    a. Lord have mercy forty-one times
    b. Holy, Holy, Holy . . .
    c. The Lord's Prayer
    d. Prayer of Absolution (*different for each Hour*)
    e. Dismissal Prayer: Have mercy on us, O God. . . .

The psalm and gospel readings for each Hour of the day are as given in the table on p. 189.

The core of this structure are the psalms (2b), the gospel reading (2c), and the prayer (3d). Most of the Hours have twelve psalms, an inclusion dating to the early monastic practice of Egypt.[119] In this way, the whole Psalter is recited every day. The offices that have more than twelve psalms are later additions, such as the Veil (added sometime in the thirteenth century), or additional psalms were added to the original twelve, such as in the Midnight Office.[120] Much of the hymnody added to this core is shared with the Byzantine tradition, most

[118] Based on Hanna, "The Horologion of the Coptic Church," 28–29; O. H. E. Khs-Burmester, "The Canonical Hours of the Coptic Church," OCP 2 (1936): 78–100, here 89–100; Khs-Burmester, *The Horologion of the Egyptian Church*.

[119] Khs-Burmester, "The Canonical Hours," 83.

[120] Hanna, "The Horologion of the Coptic Church," 34.

| | 2.b Psalms | 2.c Gospel Reading |
|---|---|---|
| **First** | 1–6, 8, 11–12, 14–15, 18, 24, 26, 62, 66, 69, 112, 142 | John 1:1-17 |
| **Third** | 19, 22–23, 25, 28–29, 33, 40, 42, 44–46 | John 14:26–5:4 |
| **Sixth** | 53, 56, 60, 62, 66, 69, 83–86, 90, 92 | Matt 5:1-16 |
| **Ninth** | 95–100, 109–112, 114–115 | Luke 9:10-17 |
| **Eleventh** | 116–117, 119–128 | Luke 4:38-41 |
| **Twelfth** | 129–133, 136–137, 140–141, 145–147 | Luke 2:25-32 |
| **Veil** | 4, 6, 12, 15, 22, 24, 26, 29, 42, 56, 66, 69, 85, 90, 96, 109, 114–115, 120, 128–133, 136, 140, 145 | John 6:15-23 |
| **Midnight** | *First Watch*: 3, 6, 12, 69, 85, 90, 116, 117, 118<br>*Second Watch*: 119–128<br>*Third Watch*: 129–133, 136, 137, 140, 141, 145–147 | Matt 25:1-13<br>Luke 7:36-50<br>Luke 12:32-46 |

likely not a Byzantine influence on the Coptic Rite but possibly due to a common earlier Greek text that influenced both traditions.[121]

In the Coptic Rite, as in all the Eastern Christian traditions, the themes of each of the minor Hours are usually defined by an event in salvation history, such as the crucifixion. The remembrance of these events serves to edify, educate, and nurture the faith of the believers. For example, the absolution prayer of the sixth Hour presents the recollection of the passion as something that offers comfort and opportunity for prayer while communicating its meaning and significance. The prayer then moves to its epiclesis section, where the petition is made that the faithful are blessed with a transfigured life that is "peaceful," "spotless," and "pleasing" to God. In other words, every occasion is seen as an opportunity for the faithful to renew their commitment and dedication to the Gospel and to be reminded of the eschatological outlook of the Church:

[121] Khs-Burmester, "The Canonical Hours," 84–89.

> We thank You, our King, the Pantocrator, the Father of our Lord God and Savior Jesus Christ, and glorify You, for you have made the times of the passions of your only-begotten Son, to be times of comfort and prayer. Accept unto You our supplication and abolish the handwriting of our sins that is written against us, just as you tore it in this holy hour, by the cross of Your only-begotten Son, Jesus Christ, our Lord and Savior of our souls, this is by which You destroyed all the power of the enemy. Grant us, O God, a glorious time, a spotless conduct, and a peaceful life, so that we may please Your holy and worshipping name, and that, without falling into condemnation, we may stand before the fearful and just throne of Your only-begotten Son Jesus Christ our Lord, and that we, together with all Your saints, glorify You, the Father, who is without beginning, and the Son who is of one essence with You, and the Holy Spirit the Life-Giver, now and forever and unto the ages of all ages. Amen.[122]

### *3.2.5 The Ethiopian Rite*

The eclectic nature of the Ethiopian liturgical tradition is also quite prominent in its Liturgy of the Hours. It has two parallel offices as in the Coptic tradition, cathedral and monastic, but it is also characterized by its complex chant system; the *dɛbtɛra* (church musician) needs to employ a number of different chant books, with often-overlapping genres of hymns and a quite complicated musical system. The primary liturgical books necessary for the celebration of the cathedral office are the *Me'eraf,* which provides the proper elements;[123] the *Dəggʷa,*[124] which provides the antiphons proper to the feast and season; the *Ṣoma Dəggʷa,* which provides antiphons for the season of Great Lent; and the *Qəne,* which consists of improvised liturgical poetry of different types.[125] There are three musical tones or *zema* (lit. a pleasing

[122] "The Sixth Hour" in Coptic Orthodox Diocese of Southern USA, "Coptic Reader."

[123] See Bernard Velat, *Études sur le Me'erāf,* Patrologia Orientalis 33 (Paris: Firmin-Didot et Cie, 1966); *"Me'erāf"* in *Encyclopaedia Aethiopica* (2007), 3:910–11.

[124] See Kay Kaufman Shelemay and Peter Jeffery, *Ethiopian Christian Liturgical Chant: An Anthology,* vols. 1–3 (Madison: A-R Editions, 1993–1997) for presentation and examples. For a summary, see Kay Kaufman Shelemay, Peter Jeffery and Ingrid Monson, "Oral and Written Transmission in Ethiopian Christian Chant," *Early Music History* 12 (1993): 55–117.

[125] Velat, *Études sur le Me'erāf,* 9; Gregory Woolfenden, *Daily Liturgical Prayer: Origins and Theology* (Aldershot, England; Burlington, VT: Ashgate, 2004), 184; Habtemichael Kidane, *L'ufficio divino della Chiesa etiopica,* 189–223.

sound): the *ge'ez zema*, the *ɛraray zema*, and the *'əzl zema*.[126] The execution of hymnody is accompanied by the beating of drums and the shaking of cymbals providing the beat for the movement of the body or what is understood as the "liturgical dance" of the Ethiopian tradition.[127] In current use, the cathedral office is used only on Sundays and important feasts of the liturgical year in parish churches.

The cathedral office is "the most important occasion for music in the Ethiopian liturgy,"[128] is characterized by its length, and is the only one somewhat studied.[129] It is comprised of the following offices:

(1) *wazema*, which is the equivalent to vespers. It starts in early afternoon on the eve of the Sunday or important feast, and it can last up to five hours.

(2) *Mɛwɛddəs* literally means "praise" and is the equivalent of Sunday nocturns. It begins at around one o'clock in the morning (at first cockcrow) and is followed by matins and the Eucharist without interruption.

(3) *Səbh 'ɛtɛ negh* literally means "the glorification of the morning," and it is the equivalent to matins. It is available in several forms depending on the day of the liturgical year.

Finally, (4) *Kəstɛt zɛ'ɛryam* literally means "the revelation of heaven"; it's a unique cathedral office that is celebrated on major feasts of Mary and the saints (thirty in total) and replaces nocturns and matins. It is of considerable length and includes the complete recitation of the Psalter, abundant ecclesiastical poetry, all the Old and New Testament canticles with antiphons, readings from the gospels and a variety of other sources, and a variety of prayers.[130]

The monastic office, on the other hand, is preserved in four different, independent, and competing traditions: (1) The *Sɛ'atat za-Gebs* (the Book of Hours of the Copts) is a translation of the Coptic monastic Book of Hours with the addition of a number of Byzantine elements. It is comprised of all the expected offices (nocturns; matins; third, sixth, ninth Hours; vespers; and compline) with the exception of prime. This office arrived in Ethiopia after 1270 during a period of

[126] Shelemay and Jeffery, *Ethiopian Christian Liturgical Chant*, 1:7–8.

[127] Taft, *The Liturgy of the Hours*, 262.

[128] Shelemay and Jeffery, *Ethiopian Christian Liturgical Chant*, 1:6.

[129] Velat, *Études sur le Me'erāf*; Kidane, *L'ufficio divino della Chiesa etiopica*.

[130] Taft, *The Liturgy of the Hours*, 262–66; Shelemay and Jeffery, *Ethiopian Christian Liturgical Chant*, 1:6; Woolfenden, *Daily Liturgical Prayer*, 189.

**Wazema = Vespers***

| | Festal | Lenten | |
|---|---|---|---|
| Enarxis | Fixed opening prayer<br>Hymn (wazema)<br>Prayer for travelers | Fixed opening prayer<br>Hymn (wazema)<br>Prayer for travelers | |
| Liturgical Unit 1 | Ps 23<br>Proper antiphon<br>Vesper hymn (qəne wazema) 1<br>Prayer for rain | Psalm of day (M: Ps 1; T: Ps 31; W: Ps 63; R: Ps 81; F: Ps 111; Sat: Ps 131)<br>Proper antiphon<br>Prayer for rain | M – Sat = days of the week<br>All nonvariable texts from *Me'eraf* |
| Liturgical Unit 2 | Ps 92<br>Proper antiphon<br>Vesper hymn (qəne wazema) 2<br>Prayer of the sovereign | Psalm of day (M: Ps 2; T: Ps 32; W: Ps 64; R: Ps 82; F: Ps 112; Sat: Ps 132)<br>Proper antiphon<br>Prayer for the sovereign | For Festal Vespers<br>Antiphons, proper antiphons, antiphon of canticle from *Dəgg*$^{w}$*a* |
| Liturgical Unit 3 | Ps 140<br>Proper antiphon<br>Vesper hymn (qəne wazema) 3<br>Prayer of evening thanks | Ps 50<br>Proper antiphon<br>Prayer of evening thanks | Vesper hymns from *Qəne*<br>For Lenten Vespers<br>Proper antiphons from *Ṣoma Dəgg*$^{w}$*a* |

| | | | |
|---|---|---|---|
| Readings | Readings from epistle/Acts<br>Canticle IX (Daniel 3:52-56)<br>Antiphon of canticle<br>Vesper hymn (qəne wazema) 4 or other hymns | Readings from epistle/Acts | <u>Basic structure of Liturgical Unit:</u><br>• Psalm<br>• Antiphon<br>• Hymn<br>• Prayer |
| | Alleluia psalm (mesbak)<br>Gospel<br>3 prayers (Kidan) of evening | Alleluia psalm (mesbak)<br>Gospel<br>3 prayers (Kidan) of evening | |
| Liturgical Unit 4 | Ps 101<br>Antiphon (šalast) | Ps 101<br>Antiphon (šalast) | |
| Liturgical Unit 5 | Ps 84<br>Antiphon (salam ge'ez) | Ps 84<br>Antiphon (salam ge'ez) | |
| | Christ Lord, have mercy on us (x3)<br>Prayer of blessing | Christ Lord, have mercy (x3)<br>Prayer of blessing | |
| Dismissal Rites | Doxology<br>Creed<br>The Lord's Prayer<br>Dismissal | Doxology<br>Creed<br>The Lord's Prayer<br>Dismissal | |

*Adapted from Taft, *The Liturgy of the Hours*, 263; Woolfenden, *Daily Liturgical Prayer*, 185; Kidane, *L'ufficio divino della chiesa Etiopica*, 314–35; Velat, *Études sur le Me'eraf*, 128–29.

| | **Mɛwɛddəs = Nocturns*** | |
|---|---|---|
| Enarxis | Fixed opening prayers<br>*Trisagion*<br>Prayer (Kidan) of the night | |
| Liturgical Unit 1 | 1st Məsbak drawn from Ps 89<br>2nd Məsbak drawn from Ps 71<br>3rd Məsbak drawn from Ps 117 or 106 or 135<br>Prayer of thanksgiving<br>Liton<br>4th Məsbak (variable psalm)<br>Liton<br>Mäzmur<br>Prayer for the sick | Məsbak = sung psalm versicle, comprised of the beginning of the psalm, the thematic link to the feast, and the end of the psalm preceded by a doxology** |
| Liturgical Unit 2 | Pss 62, 3, 5<br>Antiphon ('Arba'et)<br>Prayer for travelers | |
| Liturgical Unit 3 | Ps 39 and Qəne<br>Ps 40 and Qəne<br>Ps 41 and antiphon ('Arba'et)<br>Prayer for rain | |
| Liturgical Unit 4 | Ps 42 and Qəne<br>Ps 43 and Qəne<br>Ps 44 and antiphon ('Arba'et)<br>Prayer for crops | |
| Liturgical Unit 5 | Ps 45 and antiphon ('Arba'et)<br>Ps 46 and antiphon ('Arba'et)<br>Ps 47 and antiphon ('Arba'et)<br>Prayer for the rivers | |

| Liturgical Unit 6 | Ps 48 and antiphon (Bä-ḫammestu)<br>Ps 49 and antiphon (Bä-ḫammestu)<br>Ps 50 and antiphon ('Arba'et)<br>Prayer for the sovereign | |
|---|---|---|
| Liturgical Unit 7 | Ps 117 and antiphon ('Arba'et)<br>Ps 91 and antiphon (Bä-ḫammestu)<br>Ps 92 and Qəne<br>Prayer for peace<br>Invocation: "Christ Lord, have mercy on us" (x3) | |
| Liturgical Unit 8 | 15 canticles of Old and New Testaments<br>Pss 148–150<br>Prayer for the sovereign | |
| Liturgical Unit 9 | Hymns<br>Alleluia psalm (mesbak)<br>Gospel<br>Ps 101<br>Antiphon (šalast)<br>Ps 84<br>Antiphon (salam ge'ez) | |
| Dismissal Rites | Doxology<br>Creed<br>The Lord's Prayer<br>Dismissal | |

*Adapted from Taft, *The Liturgy of the Hours*, 264; Woolfenden, *Daily Liturgical Prayer*, 185; and Kidane, *L'ufficio divino della chiesa Etiopica*, 274–80; Velat, *Études sur le Me'eraf*, 130–32.

**For more, see "Məsbak" in *Encyclopaedia Aethiopica* (2007), 3:939–40.

**Səbhʹɛtɛ negh = Matins***

| | Festal | Ferial | Lenten |
|---|---|---|---|
| | Opening prayer<br>Prayer of absolution | Opening prayer<br>Prayer of absolution | |
| | Antiphon<br>Litany | Antiphon<br>Supplication | Antiphon<br>Litany |
| | Ps 62, 64, 91, 5<br>Hymns<br><br>Prayer of the sick | Ps 62, 64, 91, 5<br>Hymns<br><br>Prayer of the sick | Ps 62 (M: Pss 3–30; T: Pss 33–60;<br>W: Pss 68–80; R: Pss 83–110;<br>F: Pss 113–130; Sat: Pss 133–147)<br>Prayer of the sick |
| | Nunc dimittis (canticle XV)<br>Hymn<br>Prayer for travelers | Ps 50 or a choice of canticles II, IV, XI, XIII, XIV, and XV | Psalmic verses<br><br>Prayer for travelers |
| | Chant<br>Canticle of Dan 3:52-56 (canticle IX)<br>Hymn<br>Antiphon<br>Canticle of Dan 3:57-90 (canticle X)<br>Lauds (Pss 148–150)<br>Antiphon of lauds<br>Hymn<br>Prayer for the sovereign<br>Antiphon<br>Hymn or antiphon<br>Antiphon | <br>Canticle of Dan 3:52-56 (canticle IX)<br>Canticle of Dan 3:57-90 (canticle X)<br><br><br>Lauds (Pss 148–150)<br>Antiphon of lauds<br><br>Prayer for the sovereign<br>Antiphon | <br>Canticle of Dan 3:52-56 (canticle IX)<br>Canticle of Dan 3:57-90 (canticle X)<br><br><br>Lauds (Pss 148–150)<br>Antiphon of lauds |

| | | | |
|---|---|---|---|
| | Alleluia psalm<br>Gospel<br>Prayer | Alleluia psalm<br>Gospel<br>Prayer | Reading from Isaiah<br>Synaxarion<br>Alleluia psalm<br>Gospel |
| | Ps 101<br>Antiphon (šalast) | Ps 101<br>Antiphon (šalast) | Ps 101<br>Antiphon (šalast) |
| | Ps 84<br>Antiphon (salam ge'ez) | Ps 84<br>Antiphon (salam ge'ez) | Ps 84<br>Antiphon (salam ge'ez) |
| | Christ Lord, have mercy (x3)<br>Prayer of blessing | Christ Lord, have mercy (x3)<br>Prayer of blessing | Christ Lord, have mercy (x3)<br>Prayer of blessing |
| Dismissal Rites | Creed<br>The Lord's Prayer<br>Dismissal | Creed<br>The Lord's Prayer<br>Dismissal | Creed<br>The Lord's Prayer<br>Dismissal |

*Adapted from Taft, *The Liturgy of the Hours*, 265; Woolfenden, *Daily Liturgical Prayer*, 195–96; Kidane, *L'ufficio divino della chiesa Etiopica*, 347–49.

Coptic liturgical influence on the Ethiopian liturgical tradition.[131] The *Sɛ'atat za-Gebs* is not the prominent office celebrated in monastic settings anymore;[132] the one in common use is (2) the *Sɛ'atat of Abba Giyoris Saglawi*, an indigenous Book of Hours named after its compiler who died in 1426 and comprised of nocturns, vespers, and the office of the twelfth hour of Marian character. These offices are to be celebrated in a church but do not require the presence of *dɛbtɛra*, and they are celebrated daily. (3) The *Sɛ'atat* of the Psalter has as its characteristic the full recitation of the entire Psalter every day divided in the offices, together with the fifteen biblical canticles. Finally, (4) the manuscript Vatican eth. 21 preserves an office with an Hour for each of the twelve daylight hours plus vespers, nocturns, and matins.[133]

### *3.2.6 The East Syrian Rite*

The office in the East Syrian Office Rite is primarily cathedral in character with monastic "embolisms" as expressed in the various types of monastic vigils (*Lelya*), compline on certain commemorations of saints and feasts, and the survival of the minor hours of terce (*Quta'a*) and sext (*Eddana*) during Great Lent. Vespers (*Ramsa*), vigils for Sundays and feasts (*Quala d'sahra*), and matins (*Ṣapra*) are the offices regularly celebrated, and all are distinctly cathedral. This almost "symbiotic" presence of monastic offices next to the prominent cathedral Hours goes back to the liturgical reform instigated by Catholicos Išo'yahb III[134] in 650 and 651 at the Upper Monastery of Mar Gabriel in Mosul. The reform set the cathedral offices of vespers and matins in the form that they have survived up to today, with the monks adopting their celebration but also having their own night

[131] Taft, *The Liturgy of the Hours*, 266–69.

[132] Adjusted from ibid., 266; Shelemay and Jeffery, *Ethiopian Christian Liturgical Chant*, 1:6–7.

[133] Taft, *The Liturgy of the Hours*, 270–71. See also Alessandro Bausi, "Ethiopian Manuscripts in the Vatican Library," in *Coptic Treasures from the Vatican Library: A Selection of Coptic, Copto-Arabic and Ethiopic Manuscripts; Papers Collected on the Occasion of the Tenth International Congress of Coptic Studies (Rome, September 17th–22nd, 2012)*, ed. Paola Buzi and Delio Vania Proverbio, Studi e Testi 472 (Vatican: Biblioteca apostolica vaticana, 2012), 53–62.

[134] On Išo'yahb III, see entry in *The Blackwell Dictionary of Eastern Christianity* (Oxford: Blackwell Publishers, 2001), 259 and the bibliography cited there.

vigils and minor hours. The minor hours went out of use by the ninth century, with the exception of terce and sext that have survived on weekdays of Great Lent, compline on certain feasts, none in the opening of vespers, and terce in the psalmody at the opening of the Divine Liturgy.[135]

A testimony to the antiquity of the East Syriac office and its cathedral character is the organization of the weekday propers in two weeks or choirs. Each day of the week, Monday through Saturday, has a set of propers for nocturns, matins, and vespers, to be found in the liturgical book called *The Book of Before and After*.[136] This book is named as such by the variable psalm verses with alleluia (*šurraya*) and hymns/responses (*'onita*) that are chanted before (*daqdam*) and after (*d'batar*), framing cathedral structural elements such as Psalm 140 at vespers. Two choirs are responsible for singing at the services in rotation. The "first choir" is responsible for Monday, Wednesday, and Friday of odd weeks (defined as such when the Sunday preceding falls on an odd day in the calendar numbering). The "second choir" is responsible for Tuesday, Thursday, and Saturday of odd weeks. The sequence is reversed of even weeks (defined as such when the Sunday preceding falls on an even day in the calendar numbering).[137]

On the other hand, a "late" addition to the Liturgy of the Hours in the East Syriac tradition is the "responses of the martyrs," added to the end of matins and vespers around the seventh century, originally probably as a processional chant to a martyrium (tomb of a martyr).[138] Another such addition is the introduction of the Lord's Prayer at the beginning and end of services, thus framing their liturgical celebrations. The addition is finalized in the eighth century.[139]

[135] Taft, *The Liturgy of the Hours*, 227; Juan Mateos, *Lelya - Ṣapra: Essai d'interprétation des matines chaldéennes*, OCA 156 (Rome: Pontificium Institutum Orientalium Studiorum, 1959), 27; Juan Mateos, "L'office divin chez les Chaldéens," in *La prière des heures*, Monseigneur Cassien and Dom Bernard Botte, Lex orandi 35 (Paris: Les Éditions du Cerf, 1963), 253–81, here 257–60. For the Liturgy of the Hours in English, see Arthur Maclean, *East Syrian Daily Offices* (London: Rivington, Percival, 1894).

[136] Taft, *The Liturgy of the Hours*, 226–27; Woolfenden, *Daily Liturgical Prayer*, 124; Sylvester Pudichery, *Ramsa: An Analysis and Interpretation of the Chaldean Vespers* (Pachalam: Dharmaram College, 1972), 161–62.

[137] Taft, *The Liturgy of the Hours*, 226.

[138] Neroth van Vogelpoel, *The Commentary of Gabriel*, 92–94; Mateos, *Lelya - Ṣapra*, 79–80.

[139] Neroth van Vogelpoel, *The Commentary of Gabriel*, 95–96.

Central to the understanding of the celebration and ritual movement of East Syriac liturgy in general and the Liturgy of the Hours in particular is the use of the bema, an enclosed platform in the middle of the nave.[140] It is there that the Liturgy of the Hours would be celebrated, beginning with the opening of the altar veil and a procession from the altar to the bema through the enclosed walking space connecting the two. As the bema fell out of use in the fourteenth century this introit procession was suppressed and with it much of the associated ceremonial lost.[141] Another element that has been lost is the actual lamp-lighting that would take place in both the morning and the evening, at matins and vespers, right after the initial psalmody, rooted in the vesperal lucernarium of the Anastasis Church in Jerusalem. In both cases, a candle was lit from the interior lamp, that which was within the veiled altar, and brought out in procession to light the exterior lamp on a lampstand in the nave.[142]

*Laku Mara* is a popular hymn that is chanted twice every day, once at vespers and once in the morning, either at the Divine Liturgy or, if not celebrated, within ferial matins, with a variable verse: "To you, O Lord of All, we give thanks, / And you, Jesus Christ we praise, / For you are the Resurrection of our bodies, / And you are the Savior of our souls." This hymn has its roots in a tradition according to which the cross of Christ was located over the tomb of Adam, who was brought back to life when Christ's blood imbued his bones at the crucifixion.[143]

*Lelya* (nocturns) and *Ṣapra* (matins) are celebrated together on ferial days. On Sundays and feasts *Quala d'sahra*, a vigil, is placed between the two. Vespers is a celebration in the evening on the previous day, opening the liturgical day, as in all Eastern Rites. As there are many variables depending on whether it is a ferial, festal, or Lenten day, what follows is an outline of the services celebrated on a ferial day:

[140] Emma Loosley, *The Architecture and Liturgy of the Bema in Fourth- to Sixth-Century Syrian Churches*, Texts and Studies in Eastern Christianity 1 (Leiden: Brill, 2012); Robert Taft, "Some Notes on the Bema in the East-Syrian Liturgy," OCP 34 (1968): 326–59.

[141] Taft, *The Liturgy of the Hours*, 229–30.

[142] Neroth van Vogelpoel, *The Commentary of Gabriel*, 89–91.

[143] Ibid., 57n75.

vespers, nocturns, and matins (with some selected variables mentioned; all psalms follow the Peshiṭta numbering):[144]

*Ramsa* (Vespers):

1. Initial prayers
2. Psalmody
3. [On Sundays and feasts: hymn of incense, *ayk etra*]
4. *Laku Mara* hymn
5. *Šurraya daqdam* (psalm verses with alleluia "before") + *onyata* (hymns)
6. Vesperal psalms (140, 141, 118:105-12, 116)
7. *Šurraya d'batar* (psalm verses with alleluia "after") + *onyata* (hymns)
8. *Karozutha* (litany)
9. *Trisagion* and prayer (this would be the end of festal vespers, followed by procession to the martyrium)
10. *'Onita d'ramza* (hymn of vespers; variable)
11. *Šurraya* (psalm verses with alleluia; depending on the day of the week and whether it's the first or the second week)
12. *'Onita d'sahade* (hymn of the martyrs; originally accompanied by a procession)
13. *Subba'a* (compline) on some days
14. The Lord's Prayer
15. Final prayers, followed by kiss of peace (and creed in festal vespers)

[144] Outline for nocturns and matins based on Mateos, *Lelya - Ṣapra*, 88–103; Neroth van Vogelpoel, *The Commentary of Gabriel*, 76–77; for a more detailed outline, see 114–21. Outline for vespers based on Pudichery, *Ramsa*, 47–59; Jacob Vellian, *East Syrian Evening Services* (Kottayam: Indian Institute for Eastern Churches, 1971).

*Lelya* (Nocturns):

1. Opening prayers
2. Psalmody: three *hullale* (different choice on each day, in ascending order from Monday through Saturday)[145]
3. *'Onyata d-mawtba* (hymns)
4. *Šubbaḥa* (psalm with response; different psalms on each day of the week)[146]
5. *Tešboḥa* (hymn with theme of forgiveness and healing; different every day of the week)
6. *Karozutha* (litany)

[*Quala d'sahra* (Vigil) only on Sundays and feast days]

*Ṣapra* (Matins):

1. Two opening prayers
2. Nine fixed psalms (100, 91, 104:1-16a, 113, 93, 148, 149 [only on ferias], 150)
3. Hymns (ferial days: *Laku Mara*; festal days: response of the morning *'onita d-ṣapra*)
4. Psalm 51:1-17 (ferias only)
5. Hymns of praise (ferial days: "To you be praise"; festal days: two hymns of light, *Benedicite, Gloria in excelsis* [on Sundays and feasts of the Lord] or a different hymn of praise on memorials)
6. *Trisagion*
7. The Lord's Prayer
8. *'Onita d'sahade* (hymn of the martyrs)
9. Concluding prayers and sealing blessing

[145] Monday, *Hullale* 1–3; Tuesday, 4–6; Wednesday, 7–9; Thursday, 10, 11, 15; Friday, 16–18; Saturday, 19–21; see section 5.2.1

[146] Monday, Ps 12; Tuesday, Ps 27; Wednesday, Ps 66; Thursday, Ps 53; Friday, Psalm variable; Saturday, Ps 150; 116.

Finally, a well-known characteristic of the East Syriac Rite is that many of its prayers are purely doxological; their purpose is solely to offer glory to God without asking anything, as they do not express any petition to be fulfilled by God. An example of such a prayer is the prayer before the procession (recited before the hymn of the martyrs at vespers): "In heaven and on earth blessed is your divinity your adorable Lordship be worshipped and the holy, glorious, high and exalted name of your blessed Trinity be adored at all times, Lord of all, Father, Son and Holy Ghost—Amen."[147] Another example is the prayer that accompanies the *Trisagion* hymn: "O holy one (you) who are by nature holy and glorious in your Being and high and exalted above all by your divinity, a nature holy and blessed forever, we confess, adore and praise you at all times Lord of all Father, Son and Holy Ghost—Amen."[148]

### *3.2.7 The West Syrian Rite*

The West Syriac liturgical tradition has seven canonical Hours of prayer, found in two books: the ferial Book of Hours (*Shimo*)[149] and the festal collection (*Penqitho*).[150] The seven Hours are:

1. Evening Prayer (*Ramsho* = Vespers)
2. Prayer of the End of the Day (*Soutoro* = Compline)
3. Nocturns (*Lilio*)
4. Morning Prayer (*Sapro* = Matins)
5. Third Hour (*Tloth sho'in*)
6. Sixth Hour (*Sheth sho'in*)
7. Ninth Hour (*Tsha' sho'in*)

[147] Pudichery, *Ramsa*, 57.

[148] Ibid., 39.

[149] *Prayer with the Harp of the Spirit: The Prayer of Asian Churches*, vol. 1: *A Weekly Celebration of the Economy of Salvation* (Kerala: Kurisumala Ashram, 1996); *The Book of Common Prayer of the Syrian Church*, trans. Bede Griffiths (Piscataway, NJ: Gorgias Press, 2005). For an online abbreviated version, see http://syriacorthodoxresources.org/Liturgy/SimplePrayer/index.html.

[150] *Prayer with the Harp of the Spirit: The Prayer of Asian Churches*, vol. 2: *The Crown of the Year—Part I* (Kerala: Kurisumala Ashram, 2000); vol. 3: *The Crown of the Year—Part II* (Kerala: Kurisumala Ashram, 2009); vol. 4: *The Crown of the Year—Part III* (Kerala: Kurisumala Ashram, 1986).

In current practice, both in monasteries and in parishes, when celebrated, these offices are usually grouped into two sequences: (1) ninth Hour, vespers, compline; and (2) nocturns, matins, third and sixth Hours. Each Hour of prayer begins with the *Qaumo* that consists of the opening, the *Trisagion*, the Lord's Prayer, and the Hail Mary, and ends with the *Qaumo* and the Nicene Creed.[151]

Ferial vespers is structured in the following way (psalm numbers follow the Hebrew numbering):[152]

1. *Qaumo*
2. [Psalm 51—optional]
3. Introductory prayer
4. Psalms 141, 142, 119:105-12, 117
5. *Eqbo* (hymn)
6. *Proemion* (introduction)
7. *Sedro* (prayer)
8. *Qolo* (hymn, often many strophes)
9. *'Etro* (prayer of acceptance of incense)
10. *Qolo*
11. *Quiqlion* (responsorial psalm)
12. *Eqbo* (hymn)
13. *Proemion*
14. *Sedro*
15. *Qolo*
16. *B'outho* (hymn of supplication)

[151] *The Book of Common Prayer of the Syrian Church*, 1–4; http://syriacorthodox resources.org/Liturgy/SimplePrayer/Qawmo.html.

[152] Outline based on *The Book of Common Prayer of the Syrian Church*, 4–7, 28–39. See also Taft, *The Liturgy of the Hours*, 243 (for festal vespers); Woolfenden, *Daily Liturgical Prayer*, 149–52.

Vespers is followed by compline:[153]

1. Introductory prayer
2. *Proemion* (introduction)
3. *Sedro* (prayer)
4. *Qolo* (hymn)
5. *B'outho* (hymn of supplication)
6. Psalms 91, 121
7. *Qaumo* + creed

Nocturns and matins are celebrated together. A ferial celebration would follow this basic outline:

Nocturns:[154]

1. *Qaumo*
2. Introductory prayer
3. Psalms 134, 119:169-76, 117
4. First *Quamo* (station) of the Mother of God
   a. Introductory prayer
   b. *Proemion*
   c. *Sedro*
   d. *Qolo* (hymn)
   e. *B'outho* (hymn of supplication)
5. Second *Quamo* (station) of the saints
   a. Introductory prayer
   b. *Proemion*
   c. *Sedro*
   d. *Qolo* (hymn)
   e. *B'outho* (hymn of supplication)

[153] Outline based on *The Book of Common Prayer of the Syrian Church*, 7–10, 39–41. Woolfenden, *Daily Liturgical Prayer*, 152–53.

[154] Outline based on *The Book of Common Prayer of the Syrian Church*, 11–21, 42–55. Juan Mateos, "Les matines chaldéennes, maronites et syriennes," OCP 26 (1960): 51–73, here 59–65.

6. Third *Quamo* (station) of repentance
   a. Introductory prayer
   b. *Proemion*
   c. *Sedro*
   d. *Qolo* (hymn)
   e. *B'outho* (hymn of supplication)
7. *Proemion*
8. *Sedro*
9. Song of Mary (*Magnificat*)
10. Psalm and response
11. Psalms 148–150
12. Commemoration of the saint of the day
13. *Proemion*
14. *Sedro*
15. Hymn of angels (*Gloria in excelsis*)

Matins immediately follows:[155]

1. Introductory prayer
2. Psalms 51 with hymnody, 63 with hymnody, 113 with hymnody
3. *Proemion*
4. *Sedro*
5. *Qolo* (hymn)
6. *'Etro* (prayer of acceptance of incense)
7. *Qolo* (hymn)
8. *Quiqlion* (responsorial psalm)
9. *Eqbo* (hymn)

[155] Outline based on *The Book of Common Prayer of the Syrian Church*, 22–25, 55–68; Mateos, "Les matines chaldéennes, maronites et syriennes," 59–65.

10. *Proemion*
11. *Sedro*
12. *Qolo*
13. *B'outho* (hymn of supplication)
14. *Qaumo* + creed

A characteristic of the West Syrian celebration of the Liturgy of the Hours is the abundance of variable hymnology and prayers that present to us a wonderful articulation of West Syriac theology. These hymns and prayers are a great example of catechesis in the context of liturgical celebration—the faithful are taught in the liturgical context both the content of their faith and how to apply it to daily life. For example, in the *sedro* ferial Monday matins we have a summary of Christology, Mariology, the place and role of saints, ecclesiology, and eschatology, presented in a diachronic continuum, reflecting both the antiquity and the continuity of the Syriac tradition:

> Lord, God, everlasting light, who were born at the end of time from the virgin Mary, you who give light to those in heaven and give glory on earth to those who glorify you; you are he who made our fathers great in the beauty of fear and of pure love, and enlightened the prophets by the signs of mysteries and revelations, and magnified the apostles by miracles and the voices of preaching, and honored the martyrs with crowns of victory, and gave wisdom to the doctors and adorned the righteous with love of labors, so that they offered you the fruit of praise; enlighten and instruct your Church with knowledge and good works by the splendor of the saints, even as by their intercession we beseech you to make us imitators of them in faith and hope and love and virtue; that we may come to a blessed end and to the lot which has fallen to them, and we and our faithful departed may be worthy of the heavenly kingdom, and we will offer praise and thanksgiving to you and your Father and your Holy Spirit, now and always and for ever. Amen.[156]

Another characteristic of Syriac hymnody is the use of paradox to speak of the incarnation. For example, in a hymn to the Virgin Mary

[156] *The Book of Common Prayer of the Syrian Church*, 57.

the poet speaks of Christ making a christological confession through paradox using images familiar to the family setting but also alluding to titles and events of the Scriptures: "Behold, he is lulled like a baby, the infant who is older than the ages; and behold, he leaps like a child, before whom John leapt at meeting with him; and behold, he is carried in the arms, the elder who is the ancient of days."[157]

### *3.2.8 The Maronite Rite*

The Liturgy of the Hours in the Maronite liturgical tradition shares the same roots and structures with that of the West Syriac tradition. While the process of Latinization did not affect the structure and content of the Maronite Liturgy of the Hours, it gradually influenced its practice. Although evidence points to the active participation of the laity in the celebration of the Liturgy of the Hours even up to the seventeenth century, it gradually became a clerical obligation, due to Latin influence. Efforts have been made, particularly after Vatican II, to reintroduce the celebration of vespers and matins in the life of the parish,[158] without much success.

The structure of current Maronite *ramsho* (vespers) and *safro* (matins) is very similar, structured around psalmody, the *hoosoyo*, and the readings. The psalmody contains both variable psalms (a remnant of the continuous recitation of the Psalter in one day throughout the Liturgy of the Hours)[159] and invariable psalms associated with each office (Pss 141:1-4; 142; 119:105-12; 117 at vespers; Pss 148; 149:1-6; 150; 117 at matins [Hebrew numbering]). The current *safro* (matins) has undergone considerable abbreviation, if compared to what appears in the manuscript tradition and older printed editions. The service is shortened by eliminating duplications (such as the unit of Pss 148; 149:1-6; 150; 117 that were repeated in different sections) and limiting the number of *hoosoyo* to one, following the completion of

[157] *Qolo* of the Mother of God, for *Sapro* (Matins) on Thursdays; *The Book of Common Prayer of the Syrian Church*, 201.

[158] *The Prayer of the Faithful According to the Maronite Liturgical Year,* Translated and Adapted for Use in the Diocese of St. Maron, USA, from Prière du Croyant Selon l'Année Liturgique Maronite, edited by Boutros Gemayel, 3 vols. (Brooklyn, NY: Diocese of Saint Maron, 1982, 1984, 1985), here 1:ix–xi, xiii; Woolfenden, *Daily Liturgical Prayer*, 149.

[159] Pierre-Edmond Gemayel, "La structure des vêpres maronites," 105–34, here 112.

the psalmody, instead of five throughout the whole service.[160] The abbreviation can be understood in the context of the will to reintroduce the Liturgy of the Hours to parish life and adapt it to the reality of modern Western life rhythms.

| ***Ramsho* (Vespers)** | ***Safro* (Matins)** |
|---|---|
| 1. Introductory rite<br>Doxology<br>Opening prayer (variable)<br>Greeting<br>Praise of the angels | 1. Introductory rite<br>Doxology<br>Opening prayer (variable)<br>Greeting<br>Praise of the angels |
| 2. Psalmody<br>First prayer (variable) by reader<br>Psalm (variable)<br>Second prayer (variable) by reader<br>Pss 141:1-4; 142; 119:105-12; 117<br>*Sooghito* (hymn; variable) | 2. Psalmody<br>First prayer (variable) by reader<br>Psalm (variable) [+hymn]<br>Second prayer (variable) by reader<br>*Nuhro* (hymn of light) [+hymn]<br>Third prayer (variable) by reader<br>Pss 148; 149:1-6; 150; 117<br>[Canticle of three youths, Dan 3:52-90] |
| 3. *Hoosoyo* (variable)—Prayer of forgiveness - Offering of incense<br>*Proemion*<br>*Sedro* (prayer of incense)<br>*Qolo* (hymn of incense)<br>*'Etro* (prayer of acceptance of incense) | 3. *Hoosoyo* (variable)—Prayer of forgiveness - Offering of incense<br>*Proemion*<br>*Sedro*<br>*Qolo*<br>*'Etro* |
| 4. Readings (variable)<br>*Mazmooro* (responsory)<br>*Synaxarion* (commentary on theme of day)<br>Readings | 4. Readings (variable)<br>*Mazmooro*<br><br>Readings |
| 5. Supplication (variable) | |
| 6. *Hootomo* (conclusion)<br>*Trisagion*<br>Lord's Prayer<br>Examination of conscience<br>Dismissal | 6. *Hootomo* (conclusion)<br>Great doxology<br><br>Concluding prayer |

[160] See Mateos, "Les matines chaldéennes, maronites et syriennes," 55–59; compare Schema II on p. 56 with current matins as presented here.

The collection of the various *hoosoyo* used in the Liturgy of the Hours is indeed a treasure trove of Syriac poetry and theology, demonstrating that fine balance between petition and praise, sinfulness and salvation, awareness of the fallen human nature and assuredness of redemption. They are a great source for discovering the theological articulation of the Syriac Christian tradition and realizing their catechetical and formative nature. One such example is the *hoosoyo* for Tuesday matins:

*Proemion*
Praise, glory and honor to the splendid Dawn whose light never fades, the radiant Son whose beams ever shine, the bright Day whose light is unchanging, resplendent Sea of light that illumines all creatures, the hidden Child revealed from the mysterious Father before the star of light. To the Good One is due glory and honor this morning, and all the days of our lives, now and for ever. Amen.

*Sedro*
Be praised and glorified, O God, who created light and dispelled the darkness. You have taken us from the sleep of error and granted us this morning to fill us with joy. You reveal to us the light of your creative power and the sublime grandeur of your wisdom, for you created the heavens and spread the earth over the waters. We beg you to keep us from the places where sin lies in wait to wound the virtues within us. Illumine our souls with the rays of your love and the hope of your glorious manifestation of that great Dawn that will never end. In all our actions and conduct, may the presence of your light and the splendor of your revelation guide us to eternal happiness. Joyfully we shall sing praise to you, O Christ, the light of truth, and to your Father, the Father of mercy, and to your life-giving Spirit, light of all beings, now and for ever. Amen.

*Qolo*
Holy are you, O God, in your compassion you have given life to our corrupt form. Holy are you, O Strong One, in your love you have purified us from our sins, in your mercy you have washed them away. Holy are you, O Immortal One, you have given us

life and purified us from our iniquity. Glory to you because of your love for our human race. In your kindness sinners have obtained the forgiveness of their sins. Unceasingly they adore you and call upon your name. Lord, grant pardon to all the sinners who beg you, in your goodness, to pardon their faults. Make us worthy to stand at your right hand and glorify your grace for ever.

*'Etro*
O incense of sweet aroma and pleasing fragrance, that filled the whole earth with the aroma of your divine gifts, accept the fragrance of this incense (our prayer) which we offer you. Grant that it may bring joy to our souls, pardon of our faults, the forgiveness of our sins, and rest to all the faithful departed. To you be glory for ever. Amen.[161]

## 3.3 Conclusion

It would not be hyperbole to characterize the Liturgy of the Hours in the liturgical life of the Eastern Churches, together with the feasts and seasons of the liturgical year summarized in the first half of this chapter, as constituting a primary catechetical school of spirituality and prayer for their faithful. One's participation in the daily cycle of offices embedded in the various feasts and seasons becomes an opportunity for the Church to preach the Gospel, proclaim the Scriptures, teach the faith, and celebrate salvation in Christ. It is within the Liturgy of the Hours and the liturgical year, especially the great feasts of Pascha and Pentecost, that the faithful learn the language of prayer and are molded in what it means to be a Christian.

This formative nature and power of the liturgy is, however, seriously challenged in the modern world. The current Western rhythm of life that has almost taken over the whole world makes it difficult for the faithful to fully participate in the communal celebration of the Liturgy of the Hours or even the major feast day liturgies on a regular basis. This is particularly true in the diaspora communities where for a variety of practical reasons (such as distance, lack of clergy, isolation)

[161] *The Prayer of the Faithful*, vol. 1 (1982), 81-82.

the full cycle of offices is rarely, if ever, celebrated. The complexity of many of the offices, the inaccessibility to the pertinent liturgical books, and the knowledge necessary to navigate these liturgical books needed for each office has made, until recently, the private recitation of the Hours difficult. Many Eastern Churches, however, are using technology to address this real problem, and the liturgical wealth of the Liturgy of the Hours is becoming more and more accessible and user friendly.[162]

These tools are becoming very popular, allowing for the more frequent celebration of the Liturgy of the Hours, both in public and in private, and enlivening their formative power in the modern age with the assistance of technology. Once again, the liturgical year and the Liturgy of the Hours highlight prayer as an indispensable characteristic of Christian life that is both anamnetic and eschatological; it looks back to and is inspired by the events of salvation history, and it looks forward to the kingdom of God. It is life lived in Christ "between memory and hope,"[163] as Thomas Talley once called it, life in the present between Christ's first coming and his second. Celebrating feasts and seasons and praying at set times throughout each day are constant reminders for continuous prayer, for a life immersed in prayer. Following the weekly and annual cycle of feasts and the daily setting and the rising of the sun in prayer, the faithful make a confession of faith to the Christian God and recognize him as the true light, life, and hope.

[162] See, for example, for the Byzantine tradition, "AGES Initiatives Digital Chant Stand," https://www.agesinitiatives.com/, and "Digital Chant Stand," https://apps.apple.com/us/app/digital-chant-stand/id891132857. For the Coptic tradition, "Coptic Reader." For the West Syriac tradition, http://syriacorthodoxresources.org/Liturgy/SimplePrayer/index.html, and "Qleedo+," https://apps.apple.com/us/app/qleedo-orthodox-prayers/id1015279062.

[163] Thomas Talley, "History and Eschatology in the Primitive Pascha," in *Worship: Reforming Tradition* (Washington, DC: Pastoral Press, 1990), 86.

# *Chapter 4*

# Marriage and Holy Orders

It is common in Western Roman Catholic sacramental theology to refer to the rites of marriage and ordination together as "sacraments of vocation." Hence, it seemed good to us as well to combine them in this chapter. But there are some differences between East and West to be noted here. Unlike the Roman Catholic West, with the understanding, due to the necessity of presbyteral and episcopal celibacy, that not all people can receive both sacraments, this is not the case in the Christian East, where all traditions, including Eastern Catholic rites, admit married men into diaconal and presbyteral orders, although in the West ordination to the permanent diaconate for married men since Vatican II has now also been restored. With regard to marriage it is important to note as well that unlike the Christian West where it is generally understood that the bride and groom are the ministers of marriage, the Christian East views marriage as confected by the words and actions of the priest, who functions, thus, as the real minister of the rite.

Regarding the section on ordination in this chapter, as noted in the introduction, our friend and colleague Paul Bradshaw permitted us to use the chapter "Ordination Rites in the Churches of the East" from his recent study, *Rites of Ordination: Their History and Theology*.[1] Among other numerous details, Bradshaw demonstrates that the phrase "the divine grace . . . ," which appears in numerous Eastern rites, is not, contrary to Bernard Botte's influential assertion, the "formula" for ordination but part of a liturgical bidding to the gathered liturgical

[1] Paul F. Bradshaw, *Rites of Ordination: Their History and Theology* (Collegeville, MN: Liturgical Press, Pueblo, 2013).

assembly.[2] Here also to be noted is that ordination of women as deacons is documented in the Eastern sources with some contemporary use being made of these sources today both in Egypt and Greece.

## 4.1 Rites of Marriage

Among all Eastern Christian traditions, marriage is known as the "crowning" or the "blessing of the crowns," reflecting the understanding that the crowning of the couple is the central ritual action of the marriage liturgy. But the marriage liturgies of the East as we know them today reflect a long process during which local domestic Jewish and Greco-Roman marriage customs, such as the crowning, the joining of hands, rings, and the common cup, became Christianized and then ritualized. Early Christians followed their local domestic customs of betrothal and marriage; the presence and involvement of invited clergy (bishops and/or priests) at these local domestic marriage celebrations were the first steps toward the gradual ritualization of marriage customs and their incorporation in the ecclesial realm.[3] It is in the sixth century that we have the first evidence of a ritual of marriage celebrated by ecclesiastical authorities.[4] Manuscript evidence of the marriage ritual from all Eastern liturgical traditions points to a continuous evolution and enrichment of the marriage rites that attests to the Christianization of local domestic customs and their inclusion in the ecclesial marriage rites but also mutual influence and interchange between traditions. While the printing press brought standardization to the marriage rites of the Eastern Christian Churches, these rites continue to evolve, albeit at a much slower pace.

When comparing the Eastern Christian marriage rites, one can discern what Kenneth Stevenson called their "deep structures"[5]

[2] See below, pp. 254–56.

[3] For the presentation of evidence, see Kenneth Stevenson, *Nuptial Blessing: A Study of Christian Marriage Rites*, ACC 64 (London: Alcuin Club/SPCK, 1982), 3–26; Gabriel Radle, "The History of Nuptial Rites in the Byzantine Periphery," Excerpta ex Dissertatione ad Doctoratum (Rome: Pontificium Institutum Orientalium Studiorum, 2012), 45–56.

[4] The marriage of Byzantine Emperor Maurice; see below section 4.1.2.

[5] Kenneth Stevenson, *To Join Together: The Rite of Marriage*, Studies in the Reformed Rites of the Catholic Church 5 (New York: Pueblo Publishing Company, 1987), 7–10, building on Arnold van Gennep, *Les Rites de Passage* (Paris: Librairie Critique Émile Nourry, 1909). See also Kenneth Stevenson, "The Armenian Rite of Marriage," in

that comprise three originally separate elements: (1) the betrothal, (2) marriage itself, and (3) the removal of the crowns. The betrothal would take place first, followed later by the marriage itself, and seven or eight days later the wedding crowns would be ceremoniously removed. Kenneth Stevenson rightly observes: "The parallel with the Patristic rites of baptism is unmistakable, where enrollment for the catechumenate corresponds with betrothal, baptism with marriage, and removal of the white robe with removal of the crowns."[6]

In all traditions today, all three elements are celebrated as one service. While historically almost all traditions have had the marriage rites linked with the Eucharist (either the full celebration or a presanctified liturgy), the marriage rites today are generally rarely celebrated in the context of a full Divine Liturgy, less so in the Maronite and Coptic traditions. All traditions also envision the possibility of a second (or even third, in some cases) marriage, but that possibility is generally seen as a pastoral concession toward human frailty. The rites of second marriage have not received attention from scholars. The couple is usually not crowned, and the prayers are highly penitential.[7]

### *4.1.1 Armenian Rite*

The Armenian marriage rite is characterized by its eclecticism, synthesizing indigenous practices with Byzantine, East Syrian, and

---

*Crown, Veil, Cross: Marriage Rites*, ed. Jacob Vellian, Syrian Church Series 25 (Kottayam: Jyothi Book House, 1990), 68–74, here 69.

[6] Stevenson, "The Armenian Rite of Marriage," 69.

[7] For the Armenian tradition, Grigoryan Heriknaz, "The Problem of Second and Third Marriage in Armenia" (in Armenian), in *Collection of Scientific Articles of Yerevan State University Student Scientific Society 1.4 (30)* (Yerevan: YSU Press, 2019), 24–33; we would like to thank Fr. Hovsep Karapetian for summarizing it for us; for the Byzantine tradition, see John Meyendorff, *Marriage: An Orthodox Perspective* (Crestwood, NY: St. Vladimir's Seminary Press, 1984), 44–47; Patrick Viscuso, "Late Byzantine Canonical Views on the Dissolution of Marriage," *Greek Orthodox Theological Review* 44 (1999): 273–90; for the Coptic tradition, see Khs-Burmester, *The Egyptian or Coptic Church*, 143–44, and "Second Marriage Prayer" in Coptic Orthodox Diocese of Southern USA, "Coptic Reader"; for the Ethiopian tradition, see Emmanuel Fritsch, "Matrimony," in *Encyclopaedia Aethiopica*, vol. 3 (Wiesbaden: Harrassowitz Verlag, 2007), 869–73, here 871–72; for the West Syrian tradition, see *The Order of Solemnization of the Sacrament of Matrimony According to the Rite of the Syriac Orthodox Church of Antioch*, tr. Murad Barsom, ed. Mor Athanasius Yeshue Samuel, Syriac Liturgies for Worship 5 (New Jersey: Beth Antioch Press, 2014), viii.

Latin usages,[8] thus making it an excellent candidate for a case study on the history of Armenian liturgy. Early Armenian evidence points to marriage celebrated in a domestic setting with the presence of a priest who would bless the crowns used at marriage. The earliest evidence comes from the fourth century, at the time of Nersess the Great (364–372).[9] It was in the eighth century that ecclesiastical marriage became compulsory in Armenia. Canon 15 of the Council of Duin (AD 719) prescribed: "The priest . . . leads those who are to be crowned into the church and . . . conducts over them the order and canon according to Christian regulations."[10] The earliest manuscript evidence of an ecclesiastical marriage ritual dates from the ninth to the twelfth centuries.[11]

The marriage ritual according to this early manuscript evidence consists of a betrothal service probably celebrated separately and earlier than the "Canon of Marriage, " as the liturgy of marriage is called. The structure of the betrothal is very simple, comprised primarily of readings and a prayer. The readings for the betrothal service are Proverbs 3:13-18; Galatians 5:14-18; Psalm 111 (LXX); Matthew 24:30-35.[12] A characteristic of the betrothal service is the exchange of crosses between the couple; in fact, the betrothal is also called "Canon of Making the Exchange of Crosses,"[13] possibly a parallel to the Byzantine exchange of betrothal rings.[14] The prayer of betrothal refers to the cross as protection of the couple and points to their future marriage by a clear reference to their crowning:

[8] M. Daniel Findikyan, "Marriage: Eastern Churches," in *The New Westminster Dictionary of Liturgy and Worship*, ed. Paul F. Bradshaw (Louisville: Westminster John Knox, 2002), 298–300, here 299.

[9] Stevenson, "The Armenian Rite of Marriage," 68.

[10] Findikyan, "Marriage: Eastern Churches," 298.

[11] Stevenson, *Nuptial Blessing*, 104–5. For the texts, see F. C. Conybeare, *Rituale Armenorum, Being the Administration of the Sacraments and the Breviary Rites of the Armenian Church* (Oxford: Clarendon Press, 1905), 108–9 (Betrothal) and 109–14 (Canon of Marriage).

[12] Conybeare, *Rituale Armenorum*, 108; Stevenson, *Nuptial Blessing*, 105. Both identify the psalmic verse "Blessed is the man that feareth the Lord" as Ps 118. But it is verse 1 from Ps 112 (Ps 111 LXX).

[13] Conybeare, *Rituale Armenorum*, 108.

[14] Stevenson, *Nuptial Blessing*, 105.

> Vouchsafe now also, O Lord, this cross for the strength and bulwark of them that take refuge in thee. By means of this all-victorious sign drive away from these persons designs deceitful and froward, and all other knavery. . . . Let the interchange of this cross between them be deemed an inauguration and sure foundation of the base of the edifice of holy matrimony; that they may receive the crown of comeliness upon their heads.[15]

Printed editions of the nineteenth century also included in the betrothal the presentation and blessing of betrothal gifts, the blessing of robes, and the joining of hands.[16]

The current Armenian betrothal service, however, is strikingly different. The readings consist of a text from the Song of Songs;[17] Galatians 4:22-26, 28-31; 5:1a; and Luke 1:26-38.[18] Then a prayer follows pronounced over the couple that asks God to protect the couple and points to their future marriage:

> We beseech Thee, bless these Thy servants, (N) and (N), who are now betrothed in preparation for holy matrimony, and grant unto them in peace and purity and true love to attain to the matrimonial crowning, and becoming united, in fulfillment of Thy divine ordinance, to increase and multiply on earth, and to serve, praise and glorify Thee.[19]

Then the priest blesses the betrothal ring: "This betrothal ring is now being blessed in the name of the Father and of the Son and of the Holy Spirit. Amen." He then gives it to the bridegroom, who places it on "the fourth finger of the right hand of the Bride." Then the priest will "make the sign of the Cross over the Betrothal Veil and shall place it over the head of the Bride."[20] A prayer then follows that

[15] Conybeare, *Rituale Armenorum*, 109.

[16] Stevenson, *Nuptial Blessing*, 107.

[17] "The Lord has made thee, has formed thee, has fashioned thee from the womb, O thou most beautiful amongst women. Thy mother gave birth to thee unblemished." As the note in the Betrothal text indicates, this text is "not found in the ordinary texts of the Bible"; *Wedding Service and Betrothal Ceremony* (New York: St. Vartan Press, 1983), 2.

[18] Ibid., 4–7.

[19] Ibid., 10.

[20] Ibid., 10.

petitions the protection of the cross be bestowed on the couple, echoing the older tradition of the exchange of the crosses:

> O Thou protector and hope of the faithful, Christ our God, guard, protect and bless these Thy newly betrothed servants, (N) and (N), keeping them under the shelter of the holy and precious Cross in peace, and safe from the visible and invisible enemy. And make them worthy with thanksgiving always to serve Thee, and praise and glorify Thee.[21]

Before the wedding, the wedding garments would be brought to the priest to bless them, but this is rarely practiced today.[22] The prayer of the blessing of the wedding garments asks Christ to "bless these wedding garments with a spiritual blessing, so that no evil spirits of demons or swindlers may dare come near them. Fortified, rather, in the power of your holy Cross, may they be delivered from Satan's every trap."[23] Once more the power of the cross is invoked in the protection of the couple against evil powers.

The Armenian marriage ritual in the earliest manuscript witness is quite straightforward. It begins with a series of readings (Ps 20 LXX; Gen 1:26-28; Gen 2:18, 21-23; Isa 61:9–62:5; Eph 5:22-33; Matt 19:1-9; and John 2:1-11) followed by a set of double prayers (the nuptial prayer and its accompanying inclination prayer).[24] Unique to the Armenian marriage rite is the selection of Old Testament readings. In his article on the Old Testament readings of the Armenian marriage liturgy, Findikyan notes that it mirrors the structure of the Liturgy of the Word portion of the Divine Liturgy. The list of Old Testament readings that he provides is almost identical with the list above (Ps 20 LXX; Gen 1:26-27; Gen 2:21-24; Isa 61:9–62:7; Isa 62; Hos 14:5-7).[25] On the seventh day after the wedding, the crowns of the newlyweds

[21] Ibid., 12.

[22] https://www.stnersess.edu/services-of-blessing.html.

[23] https://www.stnersess.edu/uploads/2/3/7/7/23772132/halavorhnek.pdf.

[24] Conybeare, *Rituale Armenorum*, 109–12; it should be noted that there is some variety among the manuscripts. On the structure of the "double prayers," see Michael Daniel Findikyan, "'Double Prayers' and Inclinations in the Liturgy of the Armenian Church: The Preservation and Proliferation of an Ancient Liturgical Usage," *St. Nersess Theological Review* 8 (2004): 117–38.

[25] Michael Findikyan, "Old Testament Readings in the Liturgy of Matrimony of the Armenian Apostolic Orthodox Church," *St. Vladimir's Theological Quarterly* 31 (1989): 86–93.

were ceremoniously lifted; the short service included the reading of John 2:1-11 and a set of two prayers (the main prayer and an inclination prayer).[26]

The current Armenian marriage ritual has expanded by including additional elements, both preceding and following the readings and the set of two prayers. The current rite opens with the joining of hands of the bridegroom and the bride by the priest. The rubrics direct that the priest "taking the right hand of the Bride (her palm open) gives it into the right hand of the Bridegroom."[27] As he joins the hands, he prays:

> Taking the hand of Eve, God gave it into the right hand of Adam, and Adam said: This now is bone from my bones and flesh from my flesh. This shall be called "Woman," for she was taken out of her Man. Therefore, a man shall leave his father and his mother, and shall cleave to his wife, and they shall be one flesh.[28]

What follows the joining of hands is a clear Latin influence, possibly borrowed during the encounter of the Armenians with the Crusaders, and that is the presence of a threefold interrogation confirming the freedom of consent of both parties to the marriage. The earliest testimony of this practice in Armenian weddings dates to the fourteenth century.[29]

Then comes the blessing of the wedding rings: "Bless, O Christ our God, these wedding rings of thy servants (N and N), and grant that in wearing them as tokens of mutual love and fidelity they may together serve Thee, and praise and glorify Thee."[30] The priest then places the rings on "the left ring finger" of the bridegroom and the bride and then he blesses them.[31]

After the joining of the hands and the blessing of the wedding rings, the readings take place; these are very similar to the ones in

[26] Conybeare, *Rituale Armenorum*, 112–14.

[27] *Wedding Service and Betrothal Ceremony*, 16.

[28] Ibid., 16.

[29] Ibid., 18–22; Alphonsus Raes, *Introductio in Liturgiam Orientalem* (Rome: Pontificium Institutum Studiorum Orientalium, 1947), 162 and note 1 on the same page.

[30] *Wedding Service and Betrothal Ceremony*, 24; there is also the option of blessing one ring, in which case the above prayer is adjusted appropriately.

[31] Ibid., 26.

the manuscript tradition: Genesis 1:26-27; Genesis 2:21-24; Isaiah 61:9-11; Ephesians 5:22-33; Matthew 19:3-9.[32] When comparing the two lists, Psalm 20 (LXX) is missing, as is the reading from Hosea, while the Isaiah reading is abbreviated. In fact, it appears that the number of readings range between five and seven in the printed editions.[33] Then the couple recite the creed; at its completion, the priest concludes with a doxology.[34]

Then the "matrimonial crowns" are brought to the priest in a tray. The priest places the crown on the bridegroom's head saying: "Alleluia! The king shall rejoice, O Lord, in the manifesting of Thy strength; in the salvation he shall exceedingly be glad." Placing then the crown on the bride's head, he says: "Alleluia! At his right hand shall stand the Queen, adorned in colorful robes worked with gold." After that, the priest blesses the couple with the sign of the cross reciting the small doxology: "Glory to the Father and to the Son and to the Holy Spirit; now and always and forever and ever. Amen."[35]

The priest then, placing a handheld cross over the heads of the couple, recites the nuptial prayer and its accompanying inclination prayer. This set of double prayers[36] is the euchological "heart" of the Armenian marriage rites. The anamnetic section of the first prayer connects the creation of man and woman (quoting Gen 1:26-27) and the divine order to be fruitful and multiply (Gen 1:28) with salvation history, as it is "through their union [of man and woman] were born patriarchs and kings, priests and prophets," leading to the incarnation that "restored and perfected in us Thine image and likeness."[37] The prayer then refers to "the first of his Messianic signs at the wedding of Cana . . . thus blessing marriage with a new blessing and endowing it with the new purpose of propagating the holy church."[38] Not only is marriage placed squarely within salvation history, but in the epicletic part of the prayer that follows, the couple being married is listed among righteous couples of the Scriptures, thus making the

[32] Ibid., 32–40.

[33] Stevenson, *Nuptial Blessing*, 107.

[34] *Wedding Service and Betrothal Ceremony*, 4–42.

[35] Ibid., 44.

[36] Findikyan, "Double Prayers."

[37] *Wedding Service and Betrothal Ceremony*, 46.

[38] Ibid., 46.

couple part of salvation history and highlighting that the purpose and end goal of marriage is salvation, inclusion in God's kingdom:

> And now, O Beneficent Lord our God and heavenly Father, as thou didst bless the marriage of our holy ancestors, of Abraham and Sarah, of Isaac and Rebecca, of Jacob and Rachel, of Joseph and Asenath, of Joachim and Anna, of Zachariah and Elizabeth, and of all Thy righteous ones, bless likewise, O Lord, the marriage of these Thy servants, N and N, whom Thou hast honored with the holy crown of matrimony. Keep them without blemish in spiritual love and in one accord throughout their life in this world. Bless also, O Lord, their procreation of children, heirs to a virtuous life and the glory of Thy most Holy Name. So that living in Thy peace to a ripe old age in this world they may be worthy to attain to endless joy in the world to come, in the company of all Thy saints.[39]

The inclination prayer that follows petitions that Christ unite the couple, "together joined in the spirit of meekness, loving one another with modesty, pure in spirit and always ready for good works." The prayer continues, asking that the couple may be sheltered "all the days of their lives under the sign of the holy and victorious cross." It concludes with the petition that they may be planted "as a fruitful olive tree in the House of God" and experience a long life with the joy of children and grandchildren, and "be unto Thee a people serving Thee and glorifying Thee."[40]

The removal of the crowns, structurally an appendix to the marriage ritual, takes place following the above inclination prayer. Originally celebrated seven days after the wedding, it consists of a reading (John 2:1-11) followed by a prayer that accompanies the ritual removing of the crowns: "We remove their braided crowns from their heads . . . and we bless them with the sign of the Cross." The prayer then petitions for the spiritual and material well-being of the couple and asks that they "become worthy of Thy heavenly kingdom and for the unfading crowns."[41] It should be noted here that this prayer is different from the double prayers attested in the manuscript tradition.[42]

[39] Ibid., 48.
[40] Ibid., 48.
[41] Ibid., 56.
[42] Conybeare, *Rituale Armenorum*, 112–14.

The final element of the Armenian marriage ritual is the sharing of the common cup. Its place at the end of the service points to it being a late addition. In fact, its place varies in the printed editions of the nineteenth century, in one case even placing it at the home of the newly married.[43] The common cup here may be either a late influence of the Byzantine marriage ritual or a late ritualization of a domestic marriage custom.

### *4.1.2 Byzantine Rite*

The Byzantine marriage rites are divided into three parts, originally celebrated at different times but currently celebrated together in sequence: betrothal, marriage (called crowning), and the removal of the crowns. The present marriage rites are the result of a long process of evolution and cross-fertilization between Constantinople and the Byzantine periphery (Southern Italy, Middle East, Balkans) and became standardized with the dawn of the printing press.

The wedding of Emperor Maurice (582–602) to Constantina in 582 is the earliest evidence that we have of a ritualized wedding, officiated by a clergyman. The imperial wedding was held eight days after the betrothal, it was presided by Patriarch John IV the Faster, and it took place in the imperial hall. The ritual elements of the wedding ceremony included the joining of hands, the crowning of the couple with imperial crowns, and the communion of the couple, most likely from presanctified gifts.[44] Later imperial weddings took place in the oratory of the palace, and the imperial crowns were distinguished from the wedding crowns.[45] Imperial legislation recognized the validity of marriages held in churches in 741,[46] while the *Novella 89* of Emperor Leo VI (886–912) made church marriages obligatory: "We order that marital cohabitation be sanctioned by the witness of the sacred blessing."[47]

[43] Stevenson, *Nuptial Blessing*, 107.

[44] For a detailed description, see Radle, "The History of Nuptial Rites," 64–73.

[45] Ibid., 74–78.

[46] Stefano Parenti, "The Christian Rite of Marriage in the East," in *Handbook for Liturgical Studies*, vol. 4: *Sacraments and Sacramentals*, ed. Ạnscar Chupungco (Collegeville, MN: Liturgical Press, 2000), 255–74, here 257.

[47] Radle, "The History of Nuptial Rites," 60. For more on imperial legislation, see Radle, "The History of Nuptial Rites," 56–62.

The earliest ritual appears in the Euchologion Barberini gr. 336 of the eighth century. The manuscript includes both betrothal and wedding prayers, which are placed right after the prayer for the blessing of a house.[48] The structure of both the betrothal and wedding are quite straightforward, each having a pair of prayers at the center, an epicletic prayer followed by the giving of peace, not in the manuscript but implied by the prayer at the bowing of the heads that follows.[49]

| Prayer for Betrothal (ἐπὶ μνηστείας) | Prayer for Wedding (εἰς γάμους) |
|---|---|
| | Litany |
| Prayer: "Eternal God, who brought into unity . . ." | Prayer: "Holy God, who fashioned man . . ." |
| | Crowning and joining of hands |
| [Peace] | [Peace] |
| Prayer at the bowing of the heads: "Lord, our God, who once betrothed yourself . . ." | Prayer at the bowing of the heads: "Lord our God, who in your saving dispensation . . ." |
| | Prayer of the common cup: "O God, who made all things . . ." |
| | Communion |
| | Dismissal |

The fact that here the prayer of the common cup is placed before communion of the Eucharist (most likely of the presanctified gifts) is an indication that the common cup is not eucharistic; rather, as a recent introduction to the rite, the compiler did not know what to do with it.[50] The question is settled with the marriage ritual as presented in Paris Coislin 213, dated to 1027, a euchologion belonging to Strategios, a presbyter of the Great Church of Constantinople (Hagia Sophia) and thus reflecting the tradition of The City.[51]

[48] Stefano Parenti and Elena Velkovksa, *L'Eucologio Barberini gr. 336*, 2nd ed., Bibliotheca Ephemerides Liturgicae. Subsidia 80 (Rome: C.L.V.-Edizioni Liturgiche, 2000), 185–88, no. 184.1–189.1.

[49] Same structure as in the Armenian rite; see above section 4.1.1 and Findikyan, "Double Prayers."

[50] Radle, "The History of Nuptial Rites," 84–87.

[51] James Duncan, *Coislin 213: Euchologe de la Grande Église* (Rome: Pontificium Institutum Orientale, 1983), vii (f. 211r).

| Betrothal | Marriage/Crowning |
|---|---|
| After the end of the Divine Liturgy (f. 101r) | If they want to be crowned on the same day (f. 102r) |
| | Ps 127 and entry in the church |
| Petitions by deacon | Petitions by deacon |
| Prayer: "Eternal God, who brought into unity . . ." | Prayer: "Holy God, who fashioned man . . ." |
| | Crowning and joining of hands |
| Prayer at the bowing of the head: "Lord, our God, who once betrothed yourself . . ." | Prayer at the bowing of the head: "Lord our God, who in your saving dispensation . . ." |
| Exchange of rings | |
| | Lord's Prayer |
| | Communion from presanctified gifts |
| | Prayer of the common cup: "O God, who made all things . . ." |
| | Reception of the common cup |
| Dismissal—betrothed leave the church | Dismissal |
| | Prayer of the removal of the crowns |

Here we have the first evidence of marriage called crowning in the Byzantine tradition. Crowning was to become "no longer an element within the rite of marriage, but rather *the* defining element of that rite."[52] The communion from the presanctified gifts drew to it the Lord's Prayer as preparation for the reception of the Eucharist; the common cup is blessed and received after the reception of the Eucharist.

Between the eleventh and the fifteenth centuries there is a multiplication and duplication of prayers in the liturgical periphery of Constantinople (Southern Italy, Middle East, Balkans), affecting the structure of the marriage rites, leading to a wide variety of witnesses in the manuscript tradition.[53] By the fifteenth century communion of the Eucharist disappears. It is the printing press in the sixteenth century that quite arbitrarily standardizes the marriage rites to what we observe today.

[52] Radle, "The History of Nuptial Rites," 79.

[53] For a summary, see Parenti, "The Christian Rite of Marriage," 262–68.

| Betrothal | Crowning |
|---|---|
| | Entrance Psalm 127 |
| Opening blessing | Opening blessing |
| Litany | Litany |
| | Prayer: "God most pure . . ." |
| | Prayer: "Blessed are you, Lord our God . . ." |
| Prayer: "Eternal God, who brought into unity" | Prayer: "Holy God, who fashioned man . . ." |
| Peace | Crowning: "N is crowned . . ." |
| Prayer: "Lord, our God, who once betrothed yourself . . ." | Ps 8:6b |
| The placing of the rings: "N is betrothed . . ." | Epistle reading: Eph 5:20-33 |
| Prayer: "Lord our God, you journeyed . . ."[54] | Gospel reading: John 2:1-11 |
| | Litany |
| | Prayer: "Lord our God, who in your saving dispensation . . ." |
| | Litany and Lord's Prayer |
| | Peace |
| | Prayer: "O God, who made all things . . ." (blessing of the common cup) |
| | Reception from the common cup |
| | "I will take the cup of salvation . . ." Ps 115:4 |
| | Ritual dance with three hymns: "Isaiah dance . . . Holy Martyrs . . . Glory to you, Christ God . . ." |
| | Blessings over the couple |
| | Prayer of the lifting of the crowns: "God our God, who were present in Cana of Galilee . . ." |
| | Peace |
| | Final blessing / prayer: "May the Father, Son, and Holy Spirit . . ." |
| | Dismissal[55] |

[54] https://www.goarch.org/-/the-service-of-betrothal; Meyendorff, *Marriage*, 113–17.

[55] https://www.goarch.org/-/the-service-of-the-crowning-the-service-of-marriage; Meyendorff, *Marriage*, 117–31.

The betrothal service, celebrated immediately before the crowning, has basically remained stable throughout the centuries, with the addition of one long prayer following the exchange of rings. The structure of the crowning service, however, has seen many additions and changes. A significant structural change is that the original pair of prayers ("O God who fashioned man . . ." and "Lord our God, who in your saving dispensation . . .") while still present are separated by the readings and do not function anymore as a structural unit. Additional prayers are added to the service, and what is often called a "ritual dance" takes place toward the end, when the couple, led by the priest, processes around the table on the solea three times while hymns are chanted. In fact, it is not a ritual dance but a relic of the procession of the married couple out of the church.[56] Finally, the lifting of the crowns, originally done some days after the wedding, has been incorporated into the service itself. This short but beautiful prayer highlights the eschatological purpose of marriage:

> O God our God, Who were present in Cana of Galilee and blessed the marriage there, do You (✠) also bless these, Your servants, who, by Your Providence, are joined in the community of marriage. Bless their comings-in and their goings-out. Replenish their life with all good things. (Here the priest lifts the crowns from the heads of the bride and groom and places them on the table.) Accept their crowns in Your Kingdom unsoiled and undefiled; and preserve them without offense to the ages of ages.[57]

### *4.1.3 Coptic Rite*

The earliest evidence of Coptic marriage prayers comes from the tenth-century Euchologion of the White Monastery in Egypt.[58] While lacking rubrics, the euchologion provides us with prayers for the blessing of oil, for the blessing of the crowns, for the blessing of oil (a different prayer) for the anointing of the couple, for the blessing

[56] Parenti, "The Christian Rite of Marriage," 270.

[57] https://www.goarch.org/-/the-service-of-the-crowning-the-service-of-marriage.

[58] For the text, see Emmanuel Lanne, *Le grand euchologe du Monastère Blanc*, Patrologia Orientalis 28.2 (Paris: Firmin-Didot, 1958), 392–99; for the dating, see Alin Suciu, "À propos de la datation du manuscrit contenant le Grand Euchologe du Monastère Blanc," *Vigiliae Christinae* 65 (2011): 189–98.

| Betrothal | Marriage |
|---|---|
| [Couple stand apart, each in the men's and women's side, respectively]<br>Triple declaration<br>Thanksgiving prayer<br>Censing | Thanksgiving prayer<br>Censing |
| 1 Cor 1:1-10<br><br>John 1:1-17 | Eph 5:22–6:3<br>Acts 16:13-15<br>Matt 19:1-6 |
| Three intercessory prayers<br>Creed | Litany |
| Three betrothal prayers | Three marriage prayers |
| Thanksgiving | |
| Blessing of robes—clothing of bride<br>Bridegroom approaches the bride and gives her a cross and ring<br>Veiling of bridegroom and bride | Blessing of oil<br>Anointing<br>Blessing of crowns<br>Crowning<br>Blessing of couple |
| Hymn | Hymns<br>[Eucharist] |

of bread, and for the blessing of wine, providing us with a possible ritual outline of the marriage rites. By the thirteenth century, betrothal precedes marriage and includes the dowry and gifts, including a cross and a ring, thus Christianizing local custom. The marriage ritual itself takes place in the ecclesial context and is centered on the crowning and the celebration of the Divine Liturgy.[59] It is not until the fifteenth century, during the time of Gabriel V (1409–1428), that the Coptic marriage liturgy was codified[60] to the form that was used up to the 1990s.

[59] Stevenson, *To Join Together*, 72.

[60] Stevenson, *Nuptial Blessing*, 109.

In this form, an informal engagement[61] would precede these rites, and the removal of the crowns would follow two or seven days after the wedding itself.[62] The betrothal and marriage rites shared a common outline, as can be seen above.[63]

In 1999, the Coptic Synod decided to combine the betrothal and marriage into a single rite. Apparently this had already been decided by Pope Cyril IV (1853–1862) and Pope Cyril V (1874–1927), so the synod was not suggesting something totally new. The decision was also made to eliminate the readings of the betrothal based on the comparison with the Byzantine tradition, which does not have readings at the betrothal. As a result of this merger, a rite of an (informal) engagement was put together by Hegumen Philotheos Ibrahim.[64]

The new marriage rites keep the marriage ritual intact (the 1 Peter and Acts readings are preserved only if the marriage is celebrated during the Divine Liturgy) but insert elements of the betrothal such as the triple declaration, adjusting the wording to reflect the wedding context, the blessing of the vestments, the putting on of the vestments and the rings, and the creed, essentially incorporating the betrothal rite into marriage (incorporated betrothal elements in *italics* in the table on p. 229).

The prayer of the wedding commitment, originally the first of the three betrothal prayers, uses language that alludes to the joining of hands, although the rubrics do not make any such mention. This prayer is actually a doublet, as it repeats the themes of the first of the three marriage prayers that follows later, which itself is textually very close to the Byzantine prayer for the joining of hands, the third and oldest of the three marriage prayers in the Byzantine rite. All three have the same structure of anamnesis–epiclesis–fruits of marriage. The anamnetic part of all three prayers uses Genesis 2:18, 22; the epicletic part of all three prayers talks about "joining" or "adjoining" the groom and the bride, that God is who "joins" the two; and in all three prayers the epiclesis is followed by a fruits-of-marriage part that is quite similar to one another (see table on p. 230).

[61] Khs-Burmester, *The Egyptian or Coptic Church*, 131–32.

[62] Ibid., 140–42; Stevenson, *To Join Together*, 73.

[63] Khs-Burmester, *The Egyptian or Coptic Church*, 132–42; Stevenson, *To Join Together*, 72–73; Stevenson, *Nuptial Blessing*, 109–11.

[64] (Bishop) Mattā'us, *Al-qarārāt al-mağma'iyya al-ḫāṣṣa bi-l-ṭuqūs al-kanasiyya* [The Synodical Decisions Concerned with Ecclesiastical Rites] (Dayr al-Suryān, 2001), 5–6. We owe this precious information and the reference to Ramez Mikhail.

| New Marriage Rites (after 1999)[65] | Marriage (before 1999) |
|---|---|
| Hymns<br>*Triple declaration with signing*[66]<br>Thanksgiving prayer<br>Verses of the cymbals (Hymns)<br>*Prayer of the wedding commitment*<br>*Prayer of the vestments*<br>*Priest gives the vestments and rings to the couple* | <br><br>Thanksgiving prayer<br>Censing |
| Eph 5:22–6:3<br><br><br>Matt 19:1-6 | Eph 5:22–6:3<br>1 Pet 3:5-7<br>Acts 16:13-15<br>Matt 19:1-6 |
| Litanies | Litanies |
| *Creed* | |
| Three marriage prayers | Three marriage prayers |
| Blessing of oil<br>Anointing<br>Blessing of crowns<br>Crowning<br>Blessing of couple | Blessing of oil<br>Anointing<br>Blessing of crowns<br>Crowning<br>Blessing of couple |
| Hymns<br>[Divine Liturgy with added readings: 1 Pet 3:5-7 and Acts 16:13-15] | Hymns<br>[Divine Liturgy] |

[65] Coptic Orthodox Diocese of Southern USA, "Coptic Reader."

[66] "In the name of our Lord, God, and Savior, Jesus Christ, the founder of the statute of perfection and the author of the law of graces, we declare in this orthodox assembly and before the altar of the Lord of hosts the union of possession and the marriage of the blessed Orthodox son (. . .) to his betrothed, the blessed Orthodox daughter (. . .). In the name of the Father and the Son and Holy Spirit."

| Coptic Prayer of the Wedding Commitment (Original First Betrothal Prayer) | Coptic First Marriage Prayer | Byzantine Third Marriage Prayer (Joining of Hands) |
|---|---|---|
| [Anamnesis] | [Anamnesis] | [Anamnesis] |
| O God, who formed man by His own hands, and gave him the woman for his help and strength, | O God, who are eternal and everlasting, who have no beginning, whose wisdom has no limit and whose power has no end, who made man from the earth, and gave him a woman out of his side, and accommodated her for him as a helper fit for him, as it pleases Your Lordship and goodness, because it is not good for a man to be alone. | Holy God, Who fashioned man from the dust, and from his rib fashioned woman, and joined her to him as a helpmate for him, for it was seemly unto Your Majesty for man not to be alone upon the earth, do You Yourself, |
| [Epiclesis] | [Epiclesis] | [Epiclesis] |
| now also, our Master, be a mediator for the groom and his helpmate, adjoin (. . .) and (. . .) through the pledge of fellowship, | We ask You, also, now, O our King, to join Your two servants (. . .) and (. . .) to be united to each other in one body, and to enter into the law of joy, and to abide in Your truthful teachings. | O Sovereign Lord, stretch forth Your hand from Your holy dwelling place, and join together this Your servant (Name) and Your servant (Name), for by You is a wife joined to her husband. |
| [Fruits of Marriage] | [Fruits of Marriage] | [Fruits of Marriage] |
| and grant them the sign of their union, so that, through the bond of love, they may be unified in harmony, and say unto them, "My peace I give you both; My peace I leave with you both." For You are the peace of us all, and unto You do we offer the glory and honor.[67] | Grant them a living fruit out of the womb so that they rejoice in the birth of good children and have quiet and peaceful times. Prepare them for every good work through Christ Jesus our Lord.[68] | Join them together in oneness of mind; crown them with wedlock into one flesh; grant to them the fruit of the womb, and the gain of well favored children, for Yours is the dominion.[69] |

[67] Coptic Orthodox Diocese of Southern USA, "Coptic Reader."

[68] Coptic Orthodox Diocese of Southern USA, "Coptic Reader."

[69] https://www.goarch.org/-/the-service-of-the-crowning-the-service-of-marriage. See also Meyendorff, *Marriage*, 123.

A unique element of the Coptic marriage rites is the blessing of oil and the anointing of the couple, which made its way also in the Maronite marriage rites where it survived up to the sixteenth century (see section 4.1.7). The use of oil in this context allows for a theological understanding of marriage that is linked to the themes of baptism, coronation, and healing.[70] One could see the anointing in the context of marriage as signifying the extension of the baptismal vocation in the context of Christian marriage.[71] By being anointed, the couple is set apart, as kings are by their coronation and anointing, but in the context of marriage they are set apart to live married life as witnesses, "martyrs," of the Gospel. The anointing and crowning have an eschatological theme, as they point to the heavenly kingdom as the final destiny of the couple.

In order, however, for that to be achieved, human nature needs to be healed, and hence the prayer of the blessing of the oil. This particular prayer is based on the blessing of the oil of the sick from the *Apostolic Tradition* with the addition of petitions relevant to marriage.[72] Each petition is followed by the "Amen" of the people, making this prayer very lively. The oil is prayed to be "A weapon of righteousness and justice . . . An anointment of purity and incorruption . . . Light and unfading beauty . . . Joy, ornament, and true comfort . . . Power, salvation, and victory over all the deeds of the adversary . . . Renewal and salvation of their souls, bodies, and spirits . . . Richness with the fruit of good deeds."[73]

The blessing of the crowns is accompanied by a prayer that highlights the eschatological significance of marriage and follows the same format as the prayer for the blessing of the oil. After a short anamnetic section that recalls how God "crowned the saints with unfading crowns and reconciled the heavenly and earthly and united them," God is asked to bless the crowns that are to be placed on the heads of the couple. Then a series of petitions follow, in the same format with the petitions for the oil that preceded, each followed by

[70] Jeanne-Ghislaine van Overstraeten, "Le rite de l'onction des époux dans la liturgie copte du mariage," *Parole de l'Orient* 5 (1974): 49–93.

[71] Kenneth Stevenson, "The Coptic and Ethiopic Rites of Marriage," in Vellian, *Crown, Veil, Cross*, 75–82, here 76–77; see also Stevenson, *To Join Together*, 73; Stevenson, *Nuptial Blessing*, 110–11.

[72] Stevenson, "The Coptic and Ethiopic Rites of Marriage," 76.

[73] Coptic Orthodox Diocese of Southern USA, "Coptic Reader."

the "Amen" of the people. The crowns are to be for the couple "Crowns of glory and honor . . . Crowns of blessing and salvation . . . Crowns of joy and happiness . . . Crowns of jubilation and delight . . . Crowns of virtue and justice . . . Crowns of wisdom and understanding hearts . . . Crowns of comfort and confirmation."[74]

The blessing of the couple at the end of the marriage rites is quite beautiful. After asking that God bless the newlywed couple in line with famous Old Testament couples, the prayer continues:

> May the blessing of the Lord, to His name be the honor, at the wedding of Cana of Galilee, settle upon you and your home, unify you in harmony, create a spiritual love in your hearts, sustain your livelihood, fill your house and grant you a long age and happy life with blessed children. We ask Him to accept from us the prayers of this blessed crowning, reward us with the eternal for the temporal, the heavenly for the earthly, and forgive us our sins.[75]

### *4.1.4 Ethiopian Rite*

The Ethiopian marriage rites are found in the *Mäṣḥafä täklil* (Book of Coronation). They are based on a seventeenth-century translation from Coptic[76] and follow closely the outline of the pre-1999 Coptic marriage rites (see above, section 4.1.3).[77] While the Coptic marriage rites envision celebrating marriage in the context of the Divine Liturgy, they are rarely celebrated as "many people hold that to receive Holy Communion is unattainable since such an awesome sacrament deserves the utmost preparation and, in fact, is tantamount to dying. Because of such beliefs . . . most people do not presume to marry according to Church law and prefer traditional civil marriage."[78] In

[74] Coptic Orthodox Diocese of Southern USA, "Coptic Reader."

[75] Coptic Orthodox Diocese of Southern USA, "Coptic Reader."

[76] Fritsch, "Matrimony," 869–73, here 870; Stefan Weninger, "Täklil: Mäṣḥafä täklil," in *Encyclopaedia Aethiopica*, vol. 4 (Wiesbaden: Harrassowitz Verlag, 2010), 844–45.

[77] For a more detailed outline, see Fritsch, "Matrimony," 871; see also Osvaldo Raineri, "Celebrazione del matrimonio nel rito etiopico," in *La celebrazione Cristiana del Matrimonio: Simboli e Testi*, ed. Giustino Farnedi, Studia Anselmiana 93, Analecta Liturgica 11 (Rome: Pontificio Ateneo S. Anselmo, 1986), 307–41.

[78] Fritsch, "Matrimony," 869; see also Steven Kaplan, "Marriage," in *Encyclopaedia Aethiopica*, 3:793–97; Steven Kaplan, "Wedding(s)," in *Encyclopaedia Aethiopica*, 4:1174–76.

fact, only those who want to be ordained or are respected members of the community or very faithful believers get married in the church.[79] The rite of second marriage is designated for those who have contracted a civil marriage and at some point want to get married in the church.[80]

In 2001, the Ethiopian Church published an English translation of the marriage rites[81] that presents an abridged form of the rites. Surprisingly, it begins with what seems to be a Western importation, an introduction that begins, "Dear brothers and sisters, today we have gathered in this holy place to join our brother . . . and our sister . . . in holy matrimony." Then the priest asks if there are any impediments for the marriage, followed by declarations from both the groom and the bride that there are no impediments. After that, they respond in the affirmative to the priest's question, "Do you wish this woman/man to be your lawful wife/husband?" and they deliver their vows in set texts copying Western paradigms.[82]

The abridged form of the marriage incorporates elements of the betrothal into the marriage rites producing one ritual unit, as can be seen in the following outline:

Prayer of the rings (the prayer speaks of one ring while two rings are blessed)

Placing of the rings

Prayer of matrimony (= Coptic prayer of the wedding commitment)

Prayer over the vestments (= Coptic prayer of vestments)

Prayer over the oil (= Coptic blessing of oil)

Prayer over the crowns (= Coptic blessing of crowns)

[79] Fritsch, "Matrimony," 869.

[80] Ibid., 869, 871–72.

[81] *Matrimony Book: Prayer of the Sacrament of the Matrimony of the Ethiopian Orthodox Tewahido Church* (Addis Ababa: Tensae Publishing House, 2001); we would like to thank Emmanuel Fritsch for making this available to us.

[82] *Matrimony Book*, 2–4. The vows are also present in the 1964 full marriage ritual; they are recited right before the beginning of the betrothal. Many thanks to Emmanuel Fritsch for sharing with us his own translation into English of the 1964 ritual. It is possible that these are inserted so that the ecclesiastical marriage is recognized as valid by the state.

Crowning (followed by a blessing, as in the Coptic tradition)

Prayer of thanksgiving (= Coptic thanksgiving prayer)

Ephesians 5:25-33

Matthew 19:3-9

Litanies

Creed

Exhortation/blessing of couple (= Coptic blessing of couple)[83]

In comparing this Ethiopian marriage rite with the Coptic marriage rite of 1999, the main difference is that the readings in the former case conclude all the betrothal and marriage elements, while in the latter case they divide the betrothal from the marriage elements. In addition, the Ethiopian version does not envision the celebration of the Divine Liturgy. Rather, it ends with the note that "the marriage register may now be signed, and while this is being done the congregation shall sing a suitable hymn."[84] This abridged Ethiopian marriage rite is the product of *Liqä Seltanat* (his title as rector of the Holy Trinity cathedral in Addis Ababa) Häbtä Maryam (his own name) Wärqnäh (his father's name), as a pastoral response to the reality that very few people were married into the church because of the very strict requirements for participation in the Eucharist.[85]

### *4.1.5 East Syrian Rite*

According to Kenneth Stevenson, the East Syrian marriage ritual is "the quaintest of all; its pastoral, theological, and liturgical aspects take us into a very different world, but it is real, authentic, and probably quite ancient."[86] Indeed, not only is it the most extensive and elaborate of all, not only is it rich in theological meaning, but it preserves ancient elements of the domestic marriage rituals. It fact, it seems that the marriage rites moved from the domestic to the eccle-

[83] Summarizing *Matrimony Book*, 4–16.

[84] *Matrimony Book*, 16.

[85] We owe many thanks to Emmanuel Fritsch for this information. See also Fritsch, "Matrimony," 870.

[86] Stevenson, *Nuptial Blessing*, 119.

siastical setting gradually, with concerns regarding the necessary requirements for the validity of a marriage. Addressing such concerns, the thirteenth canon of the Synod of Qatar (676) states: "It is not permitted to a woman to be united with a man without the agreement of her parents, nor without the intervention of the holy cross and of the priest who blesses."[87]

Evidence from the eighth and ninth centuries add, to the presence and blessing of the priest and the cross, the necessary presence of laypeople, the *ḥnānā*,[88] and the ring.[89] There is nothing, however, to indicate that the marriage rites would take place in the church building. It is only in the eleventh century that calls were made for the betrothal to be celebrated in the church building: "The betrothal should be completed in the temple of holiness through the mediation of the priest, deacon, the Christian faithful and through the ecclesiastical ceremony and through prayer, the cross, ring, and *ḥnānā*. Whatever is done contrary to this, but according to the customs of the people in their houses, is invalid."[90] The presence of a priest, however, was not always possible because of the historical context of the Church of the East. 'Abdiš 'o Bar Brika (d. 1318), a canonist of the Church of the East and metropolitan of Nisibis and Armenia, notes in his canonical collection that the "presence of the priest is necessary unless impossible,"[91] pointing to the reality of domestic weddings even in the fourteenth century. It is in the same century that Patriarch Timothy II (1318–1332) lists five elements as necessary for a valid marriage: the priest, the chalice mixed with wine and water, the *ḥnānā* blessed by the priest and shared by the couple, the cross, and the ring.[92]

[87] K. M. Jomon, "*T'AKS'A D-'AL R'AZ'A Q'ADISH'A D-ZUW'AG'A*—A Textual and Theological Analysis of the Order of Marriage in the East Syriac Tradition" (PhD diss., Mahatma Gandhi University, 2014), 13–14; Stevenson, *Nuptial Blessing*, 117.

[88] A uniquely East Syrian practice, *ḥnānā* is dust from a martyr's grave mixed with water and oil and then dried; also used in the anointing of the sick (see section 3.3.6).

[89] Jomon, "Order of Marriage," 14–15.

[90] Ibid., 15; text of Ibn al-Ṭayyab (d. 1043), who served as secretary to Patriarch Mar Elias I (1028–1049).

[91] Ibid., 16–17.

[92] Ibid., 17–18. For a more detailed account, see Pierre Yousif, "La célébration du mariage dans le rite chaldéen," in *La celebrazione Cristiana del Matrimonio*, ed. Farnedi, 217–59, here 218–29.

The East Syrian marriage rites still maintain a strong domestic character, flowing from the domestic setting to the church building and back to the domestic setting and are laced with substantial psalmody and hymnody and extensive prayers. They involve the following parts:

1. The sending of the ring (consent) and the joining of hands of the guardians
2. The betrothal
3. The blessing of the wedding garments and the crowns
4. The crowning
5. The making of the nuptial chamber

Before the betrothal proper begins, the rites are initiated with the "order of carrying the rings and of holding of hand"[93] (part 1), by which the consent of the bride to the wedding is given. The priest sends two women with a ring to the bride's house, who place the ring on the bride's finger, saying that this ring is from "so and so" and continue thus: "If you are pleased in him that he may be your bridegroom keep silence and dwell in peace. And if you are not pleased in him throw the ring from your finger."[94] Her acceptance kicks off the betrothal process. The priest then comes to her house, and after the dowry is agreed upon, the priest joins the hands of the guardians of the bridegroom and the bride and offers a prayer,[95] thus sealing the commitment of the two parties to marry.

The betrothal then follows (part 2), opening with extensive hymnody and psalmody. In one of the hymns, we are provided with an outline of the important elements of the marriage ritual: the cup, the *ḥnānā*, the crowns, the cross, the ring, the wedding garments and ornaments; Christ is asked to bless not just the couple but everyone present and the whole world:

[93] Jomon, "Order of Marriage," 100.

[94] Ibid., 100n9.

[95] Ibid., 100–103; Yousif, "La célébration du mariage," 232–33.

> Our Lord, bless the bridegroom and bride in the likeness of Isaac and his wife Rebecca. Bless our Lord the bridegroom and bride in the likeness of Jacob and his wife Rachael. Bless also our Lord the groomsman like John, the herald of the spirit. Bless our Lord the bride's maid like Elizabeth the kinswoman of Mary. Bless our Lord this cup like that cup which was in the upper room. Bless our Lord this *ḥnānā* like that *ḥnānā* which your hands fashioned. Bless our Lord the crowns of your servants like that crown of Aaron, the priest. Bless our lord this cross like that cross of Constantine. Bless our Lord this ring like the ring of king Solomon. Bless our Lord these ornaments like the ornaments of Sarah and Rebecca. Bless our Lord our honourable shepherd in the likeness of Simeon the head of the disciples. Bless our Lord the group of priests like the company of Aaronite (priests). Bless our Lord the deacons like that troop of Stephen. Bless our Lord our teacher and again the guardian of our feebleness. Bless also our Lord learners (students) and make them wise in spiritual books. Bless our Lord this place and make dwell in it your blessed peace. Bless our Lord this village (city) and encircle it with a strong wall. Bless our Lord the old who are in it (the church) in the likeness of Job your servant whom you chose. Bless also our Lord the young people and adorn them with youthfulness. Bless our Lord the women who are in it (the church) like blessed Saint Mary. Bless also our Lord the boys and guard them by the right hand of your mercy. Bless our Lord all of our assembly as you blessed your twelve. Bless our Lord this house in the likeness of the house of Sakai to where you entered upon. Bless our Lord the food items as you blessed the little bread. Bless our Lord these dresses like the veil (vestments) of Mar Elijah. Bless our Lord this table (altar) like the table of the just Abraham. Bless also our Lord these jars like the water jars of the city of Cana. Bless our Lord all the world and encircle it with a strong wall. Bless our Lord every one of us because you are blessed and son of the blessed. Let us praise your name and your Father and Holy Spirit together for ever and ever.[96]

A long prayer follows that summarizes the meaning of the rituals of the betrothal: The priest is presented "as a mediator, the ring as the truth of promise, and the cup of wine as blood and water from the side of the saviour and the cross the living witness and *ḥnānā* filled with blessings which the gentiles received for absolution."[97] As

[96] Jomon, "Order of Marriage," 109n38.

[97] Ibid., 110.

the priest holds the ring "which was and is the sign of the power of the kingdom"[98] over the cup with wine and water, he recounts all the instances in the Scriptures when a ring was used. The single ring, only for the bride, and the biblical instances of the use of the ring in the prayers show a great affinity to the Jewish tradition and point to an early stage of development.[99] The priest then signs the cup with the ring in the form of the cross and places the ring in the cup. He then blesses the cup with the cross, reciting another prayer, highlighting the importance and meaning of the cross both in Christian history and in the present. After that, he recites another prayer, places the *ḥnānā* in the cup, and says: "This cup of the espousals of these our brothers is set apart, sanctified, accomplished, perfected through the mediation of the glorious Petrinal priesthood, of the ring of Solomon, of the cross of the Lord and of the *ḥnānā* from the relics of the saints, in the name of the Father and of the Son and of the Holy Spirit for ever," uniting once more all the elements of the betrothal together. The cup is then given to the bridegroom, who drinks two-thirds of it, and then to the bride, who drinks the remaining one-third.[100]

In the Indian context, the Syro-Malabar marriage rites have incorporated and Christianized two Hindu practices, the Minnu (Thali) and the Manthrakody or Saree (Veil), originally in place of the giving of the ring. The Minnu is a small golden ornament with a cross on its one side, differentiating it from the Thali of the Hindus, which the bridegroom ties on the neck of the bride. In popular culture, the tying of the Minnu is seen as what constitutes the heart of a marriage ritual.[101]

Then follows the blessing of wedding garments and the crowns (part 3). Accompanied by hymns and psalms, each wedding garment is blessed by a prayer, and finally the crowns are blessed. After the blessing of the wedding garments, the bridegroom and the bride are taken away with the wedding garments to be dressed for the crowning.[102]

[98] Ibid., 112.

[99] Brock, "The Earliest Texts," 383.

[100] Jomon, "Order of Marriage," 113–15, 175–76.

[101] Charles Payngot, "The Syro-Malabar Marriage," in *La celebrazione Cristiana del Matrimonio*, ed. Farnedi, 261–82, here 265–67.

[102] Jomon, "Order of Marriage," 115–22, 176–82.

The crowning (part 4) then takes place, bringing the marriage rites into the ecclesial setting. This part is also packed with hymnody, psalmody, and prayers. The crowns are placed on the heads of the bridegroom and the bride; the priest proclaims: "Give thanks, O queen church, to the son of the king who betrothed you and made you enter into his bridal chamber and gave you the dowry, the blood that shed forth for you from his side and clothed you [in] the robe of magnificent and unceasing light."[103] After the readings (Eph 5:21–6:5 and Matt 19:1-11), the bridegroom, the bride, and the witnesses are blessed.[104]

Finally (part 5), the marriage rites move again back to the domestic setting with the ceremony that accompanies the making of the bridal chamber. This concluding part of the marriage ritual is also full of hymnody, psalmody, and prayers, all wishing the couple well and invoking God's blessings and protection upon them.[105] The final prayer recited by the priest is of particular beauty:

> O God who blessed the forefathers, raised and exalted them, gladdened them and made them fruitful and multiplied them in the world and blessed the pure bed of their marriage and they became loveable and beloved heirs for the inheritance of the son. May you bless this bed of your servants that they may be in love and unity and let them be made worthy to adorn their children and glorify them with good deeds. Thus from us and from them and from the blessed fruits that come from their loins may ascend glory to you, the giver of pure marriage and true communion now and in all times forever and ever.[106]

Bryan Spinks summarizes well the many themes present in the extensive East Syrian marriage rites:

> The texts of the service view marriage as another Cana of Galilee. The imagery of Christ the bridegroom is adopted and amalgamated with the imagery from the Book of Revelation, where the lamb is slain, suggesting that the dowry is a costly sacrifice and demonstration of pure love—the blood of the covenant. The ring is a type of "the ring"

[103] Ibid., 122–30, here 123 and footnote 112, 182–97, here 182.
[104] Ibid., 130–36, 197–210.
[105] Ibid., 136–42, 211–17.
[106] Ibid., 140n172, 214.

which features in salvation history—of Joseph, of Rebecca, and of the Church espoused to Christ. It carries the salvation history of all rings in scripture. The *hnana* is regarded as eschatological drink, appropriate for the eschatological symbolism of human marriage. The crowning represents royal status, and the bridal chamber takes on the role of the heavenly sanctuary.[107]

### *4.1.6 West Syrian*

The earliest manuscript evidence of the West Syrian marriage liturgy dates to the tenth and eleventh centuries and displays both variety but also affinity with all current Syrian liturgical traditions: West Syrian, East Syrian, and Maronite.[108] The modern West Syrian marriage ritual shares the fundamental structures of the ritual of these early witnesses[109] but also demonstrates its ability "to adapt to different circumstances," as Kenneth Stevenson notes.[110] In fact, there is no one universal text used among Syrian Orthodox worldwide; while the structure is common, there is significant variation within the texts[111] and adaptations christianizing local customs.[112]

The formal rites of betrothal and marriage are called "The First Service: The Blessing of the Rings" and "The Second Service: The Blessing of the Crowns," respectively. They were originally celebrated on different days; as in the other rites, they are celebrated together today.[113] The need, however, to have an informal betrothal for the couple before the wedding has led, at least in the North American

[107] Bryan Spinks, "Eastern Christian Liturgical Traditions: Oriental Orthodox," in *The Blackwell Companion to Eastern Christianity*, ed. Ken Parry (Oxford: Wiley-Blackwell), 339–67, here 346. See also Louis Edakalathur, *The Theology of Marriage in the East Syrian Tradition* (Rome: Mar Thoma Yogam, 1994).

[108] Sebastian Brock, "The Earliest Texts of the Syrian Orthodox Marriage Rite," OCP 78 (2012): 335–92, here 382–85.

[109] See table 2 in ibid., 377–89.

[110] Stevenson, *Nuptial Blessing*, 114.

[111] Phillip Tovey, "West Syrian Marriage Rites," *Studia Liturgica* 25 (1995): 192–206. In our presentation, we follow the structure and texts of *The Order of Solemnization of the Sacrament of Matrimony*.

[112] See, for example, C. A. Abraham, "The Sacrament of Matrimony of the Syro-Malankara Church," in Vellian, *Crown, Veil, Cross*, 41–48, here 46.

[113] Stevenson attests to the celebration of the betrothal on the eve of the marriage; Stevenson, *Nuptial Blessing*, 113.

context, to the duplication of the betrothal service; the new service is called either engagement[114] or betrothal.[115] The engagement consists of an opening prayer, the blessing of the rings by the priest, and the placing of the rings by the priest on the fingers of the couple being engaged, followed by the "Service of the Virgin Mary," which consists of hymns to Mary and a concluding prayer for the couple and all gathered for their engagement.[116]

The structure of the two liturgical units called "services" is identical for the most part. Originally two separate services, they are ritually framed by the introductory prayers prefacing the First Service and the concluding prayers closing the Second Service, thus giving the semblance of one service.

Unique to the First Service is the verbal expression of consent of the couple upon their arrival to the church,[117] a foreign element added to the service in the American context. Unique to the Second Service are the readings (absent in the First Service), the admonition to the couple, the prayer for the joining of hands, and the prayer for the removal of the crowns. The last two items seem to be a later addition to the rite, as they follow the admonition to the couple, a kind of ritual homily addressing the couple. We know that the removal of the crowns would take place at a later time, usually seven days after the wedding, as in the other Eastern rites. The joining of hands could be either a Byzantine influence or a late ritualization of a domestic custom. Unique to the Indian context are the Thali and the Saree. Hindu in origin but christianized, the Thali is "tied around the bride's neck by the bridegroom. The Thali is a tiny gold ornament in the shape of a human heart with a cross embossed. . . . The bridegroom covers the bride's head with a Veil or Saree. The hymn sung during the Thali ceremony exalts the cross: 'The cross is the sign of blessing; the sign of Victory. We glory in the cross of Christ.'"[118]

114 *The Order of Solemnization of the Sacrament of Matrimony*, v.

115 Ibid., 1

116 Ibid., 1–8.

117 *The Order of Solemnization of the Sacrament of Matrimony*, 10.

118 Abraham, "The Sacrament of Matrimony," 46.

| The First Service: The Blessing of the Rings | The Second Service: The Blessing of the Crowns |
|---|---|
| Consent [in the American context] | |
| Introductory prayers | |
| Opening prayer | Opening prayer |
| Psalms and hymns<br>Psalm [Ps 51 (LXX 50)]<br>Hymn<br>Psalm 45:1, 2, 9<br>Hymn | Psalms and hymns<br><br>Hymn<br>Ps 20:1-4 (LXX 21) |
| *Ḥusoyo* (prayer of forgiveness)<br>*Proemion* (preface)<br>*Sedro* (prayer)<br>Hymn<br>*'Etro* (prayer of incense) | *Ḥusoyo*<br>*Proemion*<br>*Sedro*<br>Hymn<br>*'Etro* |
| | Readings<br>Ephesians 5:21-23<br>Canticle: Ps 129:8 (LXX 128)<br>Matt 19:3-6<br>Prayer after the gospel |
| Prayer and blessing of rings<br>Giving of rings | Prayer and blessing of crowns<br>Placing of crowns<br>Thali [in the Indian context]<br>Saree [in the Indian context] |
| <br><br>Prayer for the groom and the bride | Prayer to the best man<br>Prayer to the bridesmaid<br>Prayer for the groom and the bride |
| Concluding prayer | |
| Supplication of St. James | Supplication of St. James |
| | Admonition to the couple |
| | Prayer of joining of hands |
| | Prayer upon removal of crowns |
| | Concluding prayers:<br>The Lord's Prayer<br>The Creed<br>Service of the Virgin Mary[119] |

[119] Ibid., 9–22 for the First Service, and 23–47 for the Second Service; Jeanne-Ghislaine van Overstraeten, "Les liturgies nuptiales des églises de langue syriaque et le mystère de l'église-épouse," *Parole de l'Orient* 8 (1977–1978): 235–310, here 244–45; Tovey, "West Syrian Marriage Rites," 194, 199.

While all Eastern rites employ the image of Christ as the bridegroom of the Church provided by Paul in Ephesians 5, the West Syrian rite builds on it greatly and gives its marriage rites a highly christological, soteriological, and ecclesiological emphasis.[120] While the image of Christ as the Bridegroom and the Church as his Bride is used to define the union of the couple being married, it seems as if the marriage of the couple is an opportunity to teach, proclaim, and glorify Christ and what he has done for our salvation. Using bridal language, the prayer texts expand on and explore the image of Christ as the Bridegroom and the Church as his Bride. In the First Service (betrothal), for example, the *Sedro* reads:

> O Lord, full of goodness, fountain of grace and source of blessings, the incorruptible holy Myron (chrism), You adorn with Your diverse gifts, and those who approach You with true faith You then fill with imperishable blessings. By Your coming in the flesh, O Lord, You have filled Your Holy Church with the sweet fragrance of Your divine wisdom and with the finest robes of non-fading glory; and with the crown of righteousness, You adorned and glorified her. From water and spirit, You made her Your glorious betrothed, and my means of the ring, which is Your cross and Your Body and Blood, that You entrusted to her, You manifested Your agreement and unity with her.[121]

The prayer of the blessing of the rings connects the image of Christ as the Bridegroom and the Church as his Bride with the rings in a unique manner, and through the biblical images and examples used it presents the betrothal of the couple in the context of redemption and covenant:

> O Lord, Jesus Christ, Bridegroom of truth and justice, You betrothed to Yourself the Church of the Gentiles and by Your Blood You wrote the deed of dowry, and by Your nails You gave her a ring. As the ring of the Holy Church was blessed, bless now, O Lord, these rings that we give to Your servant N and Your maid N. This is the ring by which Sarah was betrothed to Abraham, Rebecca to Isaac, and Rachel to Jacob. By this ring all the power and authority over Egypt was placed in the hands of Joseph. By its surety Daniel was delivered and became great in the king's presence. By this ring the prodigal son was accepted. By the truth of this ring the just gained victory, and by its fame the

[120] For a detailed analysis, see van Overstraeten, "Les liturgies nuptiales," 257–92.

[121] *The Order of Solemnization of the Sacrament of Matrimony*, 49–50.

> merchants became rich. Great, therefore, is the pledge of this ring. This is the ring which invites the races and generations to the betrothals and wedding feasts and gathers them that are far, and mutual relations are accomplished between them. By this ring women are married to men. By this ring the bridegrooms and brides are joined in marriage. Bless ✠ my Lord these rings that they may become the sign and seal of the true betrothal of our daughter N to our son N. May they receive heavenly blessings and bring forth righteous sons and daughters. By Your grace, O Lord, let their promise come to happy fulfillment.[122]

A similar theological approach is employed in the prayer for the blessing of the crowns. Not only is Christ presented as the one who crowns the couple (typical for Eastern Christianity), but the bridal crowns are seen as a way to make the couple a part of divine economy:

> O Lord, Who did adorn the sky with luminaries: the sun, the moon, and the stars; O God, who did crown the earth with fruits, flowers, and blossoms of all kinds; O Jesus Christ who did crown kings, priests, and prophets; O compassionate One, Who did bestow His triumph upon His worshipers in return for their heroic combat to keep the faith; Lord, Who crowned king David with the crown of victory; O God, Who encircled the ocean like a crown around all the earth; O Good One, Who blessed the year by His grace, put Your right hand, full of mercy and compassion, upon the heads upon which these crowns are placed. Grant them that they may also crown their children with righteousness, justice, and mirth. May Your peace and concord abide with them throughout the days of their lives forever. Amen.[123]

After the crowns are blessed, the priest waves the crowns in the sign of the cross over the head of the bridegroom and the bride, respectively, chanting the following hymn three times in each case: "The crown in our Lord's hand comes and descends from heaven. Fitting to the bridegroom/bride is the crown which the priest places upon his/her head."[124]

[122] *The Order of Solemnization of the Sacrament of Matrimony*, 17–18.
[123] Ibid., 32–33.
[124] Ibid., 34–35.

The crowns take an eschatological meaning in the prayer of the removal of the crowns, where the kingdom, presented as the "heavenly table," is the final goal of marriage, where the participants wear the "everlasting and imperishable crown." Present are also nuances to martyrdom in the reference to Christ's crown of thorns:

> Our Lord Jesus Christ, Who were crowned with a crown of thorns, and destroyed the powers of Satan, bless Your servants as You blessed our father Adam and our mother Eve, and Seth, Noah, Abraham and Sarah, Isaac and Rebecca, Jacob and Rachel, Joseph and Aseneth, and David who was king, prophet, and singer of Your Holy Church. Make them, O Lord, a blessed couple, emulous of good works of righteousness. By laying aside these temporary crowns, make them worthy to be among the guests at Your heavenly table who are worthy of that everlasting and imperishable crown.[125]

What follows the crowning is a typical prayer, a ritual well-wishing of the celebrant to the couple. The prayer asks that God shower the newly crowned couple with every blessing; grant them faith, hope, charity; and bless them with children, "and from among them may there come priests, deacons, and leaders."[126] This last petition, unique to this rite, makes the survival of the priesthood and leadership of the church a crucial matter for every family, sharing with them the responsibility for identifying and cultivating vocations, making them stewards of the survival and growth of the church.

### *4.1.7 Maronite Rite*

The history of the Maronite marriage ritual reflects the adventures of the Maronite Rite over the centuries in trying to find the balance between being faithful to its Syrian heritage and at the same time being Catholic.[127] The current ritual, published in 1942, is due to the

[125] Ibid., 43–44.

[126] Ibid., 37.

[127] *The Mystery of Crowning According to the Maronite Antiochene Church* (Brooklyn, NY: Diocese of St. Maron, 1991), i–ii; van Overstraeten, "Les liturgies nuptiales," 247. See also Michel Aoun, "Le mariage dans l'Église maronite d'après un rituel manuscrit du XVIe siècle," *Parole de l'Orient* 23 (1998): 111–65, here 161.

significant work of Chorbishop Raggi.[128] The rite consists of two parts: the betrothal that takes place at the home of the bride and the crowning that takes place at the church. While this schema preserves the division of time between betrothal and marriage, it also led to the duplication of the betrothal rites and their inclusion in the marriage rites, such as the consent, the joining of hands, and the blessing of rings, as can be seen below.[129]

Both in history and in current practice the Maronite marriage ritual has borrowed elements from both Eastern rites and the Roman Rite. The earliest documented borrowed element was the anointing of the couple after the joining of the hands at betrothal, a Coptic influence through the *Nomocanon* of Al-Assal of the thirteenth century, which in the Maronite tradition assumed a penitential, purificatory, and exorcistic meaning. The anointing, extended to all present, dropped out of use in the sixteenth century.[130] The consent, "found in the betrothal as well as in the crowning is an obvious Latin influence," was decreed by the Synod of Qaunoubine in 1580, and is since present in all Maronite marriage rituals.[131] Another Latin importation is the covering of the joined hands with the priest's stole, both in betrothal and in crowning rites.[132] Finally, it is possible that the use of two rings in both the betrothal and crowning is the result of Byzantine influence.[133]

In spite of the adventures of the marriage ritual of the Maronite tradition, it shares its core elements with that of the West Syrian tradition, both structurally and thematically. The *Ḥusoyo* (prayer of forgiveness) with its constitutive parts (*Proemion*, *Sedro*, Hymn, *'Etro*), together with the common set of readings, the crowning of the couple and the witnesses, and the removal of the crowns are at the heart of the crowning rites, structural elements shared with the West Syrian Rite. Thematically, the predominant theme here too is Christ as the Bridegroom and the Church as the Bride. For example, the *Proemion* of the

[128] *The Mystery of Crowning*, ii. Aoun, "Le mariage," 161–65.

[129] Outline based on *The Mystery of Crowning* (Betrothal, 3–9; and Crowning, 12–51) and van Overstraeten, "Les liturgies nuptiales," 247–48.

[130] *The Mystery of Crowning*, iv; van Overstraeten, "Les liturgies nuptiales," 247, 249; Stevenson, *Nuptial Blessing*, 115.

[131] *The Mystery of Crowning*, iii; one exception is the ritual of 1839; see van Overstraeten, "Les liturgies nuptiales," 248.

[132] *The Mystery of Crowning*, 4 (betrothal) and 21 (crowning); Stevenson, *Nuptial Blessing*, 116.

[133] Stevenson, *Nuptial Blessing*, 115.

| Rite of Betrothal (at the bride's house) | Rite of Crowning (at church) |
| --- | --- |
| | Opening doxology<br>Opening prayer<br>Ps 128 (LXX 127) |
| | *Ḥusoyo* (prayer of forgiveness)<br>*Proemion* (preface)<br>*Sedro* (prayer)<br>Hymn<br>*'Etro* (prayer of incense) |
| | [*Trisagion*]<br>*Mazmooro* (psalm for the readings)<br>Eph 5:22-27 (optional readings also provided)<br>Matt 19:3-6 (optional readings also provided) |
| Consent<br>Joining of hands<br>Blessing of rings<br>Giving of rings<br>Blessing of girdle, clothing, and jewelry<br>Concluding prayer | Litany<br>Hymn<br>Consent<br>Joining of hands<br>Blessing of rings<br>Giving of rings |
| | Blessing of crowns<br>Crowning (groom, bride, witnesses)<br>Hymn |
| | [Celebration of Divine Liturgy] |
| | Removal of crowns |

Ḥusoyo reads: "May we be worthy to offer praise and thanksgiving to Jesus Christ, the heavenly Bridegroom. In his love, he betrothed the Church of all peoples and nations; by his cross he sanctified her and made her a glorious bride."[134] Similarly, the hymn sung before

[134] *The Mystery of Crowning*, 13.

the consent in the marriage ritual proclaims: "Alleluia! The divine Groom has betrothed to himself a bride who is and will be without equal. Her beauty surpasses all, and her Groom is alive forever. With the blood that flowed from his side, he wrote her marriage covenant."[135]

While the presence of the verbal consent is the result of Latin influence, the Maronite marriage ritual preserves the Eastern understanding of God as the celebrant and the one that unites the two in marriage. Marriage is understood not as a covenant between the bride and the groom but between God and the couple. Right after the consent, the couple join their hands on the Bible that has been placed on a table before them; the celebrant covers their joined hands with his stole, holds it in place with his right hand, and proclaims:

> By the hand of God and his holy Word, our son N and our daughter N are joined in marriage in the name of the most Holy Trinity: Father, Son, and Holy Spirit. May their marriage be as firm as the covenant by which heaven and earth were created, and be blessed as was the covenant by which Sarah was joined to Abraham, Rebecca to Isaac, and Rachel to Jacob, so that nothing shall separate them but death.[136]

Both the theme of God being the one that unites the couple and theme of Christ as the Bridegroom of the Church are eloquently brought together in the hymn attributed to St. Ephrem chanted right after the crowning. Especially if this celebratory hymn is indeed of Ephrem, it is possible that it echoes a domestic marriage ritual; notice the mention of banquet, nuptial gifts, hosts, guitars, trumpets, flutes, and flute players in the hymn.

> O Christ, you appeared from Mary and from the seed of your servant David; you clothed yourself with our human flesh and became one of us. O Christ, the Bridegroom, you betrothed the holy and faithful Church; in the upper room you gave her your body and blood and sealed your nuptial covenant with her.
>
> O beautiful One, you invited those endowed with beauty to your wedding banquet; they each brought their fitting nuptial gift. O Lord,

[135] Ibid., 20.
[136] Ibid., 21.

now extend your right hand and bless the bridegroom and the bride; they came to the holy Church to receive the blessing of the priests.

We all proclaim your praise: the Church that blessed their crowning, the priests and congregation that prayed for them, the infants and children, the young men and maidens, the groom, bride and witnesses, the guests and the hosts, and all who are joined here with us now.

The guitars and the trumpets, the flutes and the flute prayers, all the pleasing gifts chant glory to the Trinity, Father, Son and Holy Spirit, One true God. Glory be to you and mercy be upon us, now and at all times. Amen and Amen.[137]

### *4.1.8 Conclusions*

The rites of marriage in all Eastern Christian traditions are rich in symbolism and ritual; their prayers and hymnology convey an "unabashed theological exuberance"[138] and are expressions of communal joy and celebration, transforming the secular into the ecclesial and sacred. This is most evident in the East Syrian marriage rites, where the ritual flows from the domestic (betrothal) to the ecclesial (marriage) and back to the domestic (blessing of the bridal chamber). In all traditions, each with their own expression and emphasis, four themes emerge as common. First, the Christ-Church image from Ephesians 5 emerges as the paradigm for the marital relationship. In most cases, and particularly in the Syrian traditions, the marriage prayers and hymnology become the contexts of christological preaching, highlighting the mysteries of the incarnation and passion as expressions of Christ's love for the Church. Christ's sacrificial love for the Church emerges as the paradigm for the love between the spouses. Second, as Christ blessed with his presence the wedding at Cana (John 2), so does he bless and unite the couple at their wedding. Christ emerges as the celebrant. Third, God blesses the couple in line with other famous Old Testament couples, incorporating the couple in salvation history. Finally, the crowning of the couple, which quickly emerged as the central ritual action of marriage, is not only an expression of joy but also a pointer to the salvation of the couple and their participation in the kingdom of God as the purpose of marriage.

[137] Ibid., 26–27.

[138] Findikyan, "Marriage: Eastern Churches," 298.

## 4.2 Ordination Rites

Like all the other liturgies of the various Eastern churches, the ordination rites of the different traditions have undergone some development and expansion in the course of their history, and because the oldest manuscripts date only from the eighth century onward—and in some traditions are very much later than that[139]—some effort is required to uncover their earlier forms. Here it is also necessary to draw attention to two other Eastern traditions that have not been dealt with in any detail elsewhere in our study: the Melkite and Georgian. While ordination rites in extant manuscripts from both of these traditions, stemming originally from Antioch and Jerusalem, provide helpful details with regard to the historical development of ordination rites in the East, both of these "rites" have been since the Middle Ages so thoroughly Byzantinized and, in the specific case of the Orthodox Church of Georgia, so "Russified" that little of their own indigenous liturgical traditions survive in use, with the notable exception of Georgian chant traditions.[140]

The older manuscripts for the Eastern rites of ordination tend to provide only for bishops, presbyters, deacons, subdeacons, and readers, although some of them lack a rite for a bishop (probably because it was not regularly needed in each diocese but only by the patriarch), and some also include forms for women deacons or "deaconesses" (Armenian, Byzantine, East Syrian, and Georgian) and *chorepiscopoi* (rural bishops; East Syrian, West Syrian, and Maronite). Later pontificals often add rites for appointment to other offices, among them cantors, archdeacons, abbots and abbesses, metropolitans, and patriarchs.[141]

[139] For details of the available sources, see Paul F. Bradshaw, *Ordination Rites of the Ancient Churches of East and West* (New York: Pueblo, 1900), 5–14. For Barberini 336, see *L'Eucologio Barberini gr. 336*, ed. Parenti and Velkovska.

[140] At the same time, Georgian liturgical texts are currently being reedited and published with one of the expressed goals being the restoration of the Georgian Rite itself. Only the first volume of the Euchologion has appeared so far but this volume does contain the rites of ordination. See Edisher Chelidze, ed., *Didni Kurthevani* [Great Euchologion], vol. 1 (Tbilisi: Ahali Ivironi, 2006).

[141] For a study of the Coptic rite for a patriarch, see Emmanuel Lanne, "Dans la tradition alexandrine l'ordination du patriarche," in *Ordination et Ministères: Conférences Saint Serge, XLIIe Semaine d'études liturgiques*, ed. Achille Triacca and Alessandro Pistoia (Rome: C.L.V.-Edizioni Liturgiche 1996), 139–55.

Despite the superficial diversity of the various traditions, they display many similarities of structure and sometimes of text as well. Some of these resemblances are the consequence of the later influence of one tradition upon another, and especially the spread of West Syrian and/or Byzantine features to other churches, which can sometimes be detected by the fact that they duplicate the equivalent indigenous liturgical units. Nevertheless, behind all of this can be seen a common ritual pattern from which they all appear to derive, a pattern that is shared to a great extent by the earliest Western sources too. This widespread convergence inspires confidence that the pattern is ancient and may be traced back to at least the end of the fourth century if not before. The rites for a bishop, a presbyter, and a deacon all once consisted of:

- proclamation of the result of the election, and acclamation of assent by the people
- a bidding, inviting the people to pray for the ordinand
- prayer by the people for the ordinand
- the sign of the cross made on the forehead of the ordinand
- a substantial prayer said by the presiding bishop while laying his hand on the ordinand
- the exchange of a ritual kiss
- the celebration of the Eucharist

In the case of the ordination of a bishop may be added the imposition of the gospel book prior to the imposition of the hand and his solemn seating at the conclusion of the rite. This basic pattern subsequently became obscured by the addition of further elements to the rites, and especially by the tendency to acquire additional ordination prayers and in some cases to associate the imposition of the hand with the proclamation and bidding rather than the prayer (see further below).

### *4.2.1 Proclamation of the Result of the Election and Acclamation of Assent by the People*

The important place accorded to the election of a candidate for ordination in early Christianity should not be understood as pointing to some notion of the ideal of democracy or, at least at first, to the principle that a congregation had the right to choose its own ministers. Nor was it seen as in any way opposed to the divine calling of a minister; on the contrary, it was understood as the means by which God's choice of a person for a particular ecclesiastical office was discerned and made manifest. As both patristic writings and the prayers in the rites themselves make clear, it was always considered that it was God who chose and ordained the ministers through the action of the church. There was thus no dichotomy between actions "from below" and "from above." The church's discernment of God's choice might on occasion even override an individual's own lack of a sense of vocation, and it contrasts with more modern views of the primacy of the "interior call." Once the divine choice had been revealed in this way, then the church might proceed to pray that God would bestow on the one whom he had appointed the requisite qualities for the effective discharge of the office.

As time went by, however, the ritual of prayer and the imposition of the hand came to be thought of as the *real* act of ordination, the means by which the office itself was bestowed on the candidate, with election merely a dispensable preliminary to it. A distinction in terminology, however, still tended to be retained between the ordination of bishops, presbyters, and deacons, on the one hand, and admission to the minor orders, on the other, when they too adopted the imposition of hands, *cheirotonia* being used for the former but *epithesis* for the latter.

Moreover, in spite of the decline of the electoral process, vestiges of the former arrangement can still be detected among the preliminaries of the later ordination rites of the Eastern churches. It appears that originally at the election of a bishop the people had cried out, *Axios*, "Worthy!" because the fifth-century ecclesiastical historian Philostorgius recounts that, when the Arian Demophilos was appointed as bishop of Constantinople in 370 , many of the people shouted, *Anaxios*, "Unworthy!" instead of *Axios*.[142] The oldest manuscript of the Armenian rite for the ordination of deacons and presbyters (ninth/tenth century) preserves a memory of this same procedure for them too. The rite begins with an announcement of the choice of the candidate,

[142] Philostorgius, *Historia ecclesiastica* 9.10 (PG 65:576C).

made by a deacon in the case of an ordination to the diaconate and by a presbyter in the case of an ordination to the presbyterate.

> They call N. from being a clerk to the diaconate of the Lord/from the office of deacon to that of priest, to the service of holy Church, to its ministration, in accordance with the testimony of himself and of the congregation: he is worthy.[143]

The final statement was doubtless originally intended to be a question, to which a congregational response was expected, as it still is, the version in another manuscript probably dating from no later than the thirteenth century:

> Divine and heavenly grace that always fulfills the needs of the holy ministry of the apostolic Church. They call N. from the diaconate to the priesthood for the ministration of the holy Church. According to the testimony of himself and of the congregation, is he worthy?" *And the congregation say three times*: "He is worthy."[144]

Some such formulary was apparently already known to Pseudo-Dionysius in the late fifth or early sixth century, as he refers to an *anarresis*, "proclamation," in his description of the rite of ordination: "The bishop makes the proclamation of the ordinations and the ordinands, the mystery signifying that the consecrator, beloved by God, is the interpreter of the divine choice. He does not lead the ordinand to ordination by his own grace, but he is moved by God for all the consecrations."[145] Other allusions to "the divine grace" in connection with ordination imply that it may have been in use at least in Antioch before the end of the fourth century.[146]

Although the Armenian tradition does not preserve a rite for a bishop in the earliest manuscript, the later episcopal rite also retains the same triple congregational response,[147] and this acclamation of

[143] Bradshaw, *Ordination Rites*, 128–29.

[144] British Museum Add. 19.548; in Conybeare, *Rituale Armenorum*, 237.

[145] Pseudo-Dionysius, *De ecclesiastica hierarchia* 5.3.5 (PG 3:512).

[146] See John Chrysostom, *Sermo cum presbyter fuit ordinatus* 4 (PG 48:700); the reference to his ordination in Theodoret, *Historia ecclesiastica* 5.27.1; and Chrysostom, *De sacerdotio* 4.1, and Gregory Nazianzen, *Oratio* 15.35.

[147] Heinrich Denzinger, *Ritus Orientalium*, vol. 2 (Würzburg: Stahel, 1863 = Graz: Akademische Druck - und Verlagsanstalt, 1961), 361.

assent occurs in other Eastern traditions as well, but now moved to the end of the whole act of ordination, presumably once the people's role in the election itself had disappeared. The earliest example of this switch is in the rite for a bishop in the fifth-century *Testamentum Domini*.[148]

### *4.2.2 The Bidding*

In the early Armenian Rite the formula provided for the announcement of the results of the election was then repeated in a variant form by the bishop but omitted the words "he is worthy" at the end and instead linked to an invitation to pray for the candidate: "I lay hands upon him. Do you all offer up your prayers that he be worthy to serve in the rank of the diaconate before God and the holy altar/in the rank of priesthood without blemish before the Lord all the days of his life." A similar combined proclamation/bidding formulary exists in one form or another in all later Eastern rites for bishops, presbyters, and deacons and in some cases is extended to the minor orders as well.[149] This combination presumably occurred as the result of the displacement of the congregational acclamation of assent to the end of the rite.

Bernard Botte argued that its most primitive version was that in the eighth-century Byzantine Rite, where it is said to be read from a scroll. Its wording is identical in the conferral of all three offices apart from the name of the particular order:

> The divine grace, which always heals that which is infirm and supplies that what is lacking, appoints the presbyter N., beloved by God, as bishop. Let us pray therefore that the grace of the Holy Spirit may come upon him.[150]

But Botte overlooked the probability that it had previously existed as two independent liturgical units and even went on to make the implausible claim that it was intended to be the sacramental form of

[148] See Bradshaw, *Ordination Rites*, 118.

[149] It occurs in relation to the subdeacon in the Coptic and Syrian Orthodox rites, and both the reader and the subdeacon in the East Syrian and Melkite rites: see Bradshaw, *Ordination Rites*, 141, 146–57, 176, 201–3.

[150] Ibid., 133–36.

ordination itself! He admitted that it was pronounced by a deacon in the later Coptic and Syrian Orthodox Rites and so could not have that function there and was also in a preliminary position in the Byzantine rites for the presbyterate and diaconate in the eighth-century Barberini manuscript. But he judged that the Byzantine rite for the episcopate, together with the East Syrian and Maronite rites, had retained the true primitive usage in which the proclamation was made by the presiding bishop during the imposition of the hand. Its apparent relegation to a less central position in the other rites he believed to have been the result of the introduction of secondary elements—a second imposition of the hand in the Syrian Orthodox rite and the ordination prayers themselves in the Byzantine tradition: these tended to push the formulary into the shade.[151]

Most other scholars have rightly rejected Botte's theory.[152] Not only was Botte applying to the rites a completely Western and anachronistic sacramental theology, but he failed to see that the formulary was simply a bidding to which the imposition of the hand had in some traditions later become attached from its proper association with the ordination prayer. Moreover, he was mistaken about the East Syrian rite, as the formulary there is recited *before* the imposition of the hand, as it is also in the eleventh-century Grottaferrata manuscript of the Byzantine rite at the ordination of a bishop as well as in the rites for the presbyterate and diaconate. In that manuscript the version for a bishop contains an opening phrase that strengthens its association with the electoral process: "By the vote and approval of the most divinely-beloved bishops and the most holy presbyters and deacons."[153] It seems highly improbable that this variation could have been a late addition, especially as the election had, in practice, been restricted to the episcopal college alone for many centuries. It is

[151] Bernard Botte, "La formule d'ordination 'La grâce divine' dans les rites orientaux," *L'orient syrien* 2 (1957): 285–96.

[152] Pierre-Marie Gy, "Ancient Ordination Prayers," *Studia Liturgica* 13 (1979): 75. See also Emmanuel Lanne, "Les ordinations dans le rite copte: leurs relations avec les *Constitutions Apostoliques* et la *Tradition* de saint Hippolyte," *L'orient syrien* 5 (1960): 81–106, here at 82–83; Jean Tchékan, "Elements d'introduction à l'étude de la liturgie byzantine des ordinations," *Compagnie de Saint-Sulpice: Bulletin du Comité des Études* 10 (1968): 190–208, here at 201.

[153] *L'eucologio costantinopolitano agli inizi del secolo XI*, ed. Miguel Arranz (Rome: Pontificia Università Gregoriana, 1996), 142.

therefore likely that this is a survival from the more ancient tradition, which had already undergone some modification in the Barberini manuscript.

Although Botte was right that the Byzantine version eventually came to be adopted in one form or another by all other Eastern rites, it is clear that prior to this, various traditions had their own equivalents of it. Thus, while the Coptic rites seem to have inherited the Byzantine formulary through the West Syrian tradition, the rite for a bishop there has an extensive proclamation/bidding of its own. The Georgian rite similarly had a rather lengthy formulary of the same kind, pronounced by a deacon, which was used, with appropriate modifications, in appointment to all three orders. This may have originated in the Jerusalem tradition and has no doubt undergone some expansion and elaboration in the course of its history. It is followed by another formulary, said by the bishop, that has some resemblance to the Byzantine one: "The grace of God heals the sick, satisfies them that are in need: hands are laid on this our child."[154]

This combination of proclamation and bidding created a sort of bridge between the two parts of the ordination process, announcing the result of the election and inviting the congregation to pray for the ordinand. Its wording confirms that the exercise of human choice was thought of as manifesting the divine will and that the ordination was seen as effected by the grace of the Holy Spirit acting in response to the prayer of the church.

### *4.2.3 Prayer of the People for the Ordinand*

One would naturally expect that the prayer of the people, in one form or another, would follow the bidding, and this certainly seems to have been the original practice, but in the course of time the importance of prayer by the whole community in ordination seems to have been lost. In some cases another presidential prayer now intervenes; in others it has fallen out altogether or left only a trace of its former existence.

Thus, in the Barberini manuscript of Byzantine rites, the triple response, "Lord, have mercy," is explicitly mentioned as following the proclamation/bidding only in the case of the episcopate, but it

[154] Bradshaw *Ordination Rites*, 149–50, 166–67.

may also have been practiced in the other rites that employ the same formulary (presbyters, deacons, and deaconesses), even though it is not specified in the rubrics. In every case, however, a litany with appropriate petitions for the ordinands appears, not directly after the bidding, but after the first of two ordination prayers has been said. This unusual arrangement suggests that the first ordination prayer is a later addition to the rites that destroyed the natural liturgical sequence and left the *Kyrie* response high and dry. Though such litanies were normally led by a deacon, in the rite for the episcopate a bishop fulfills this function, and in the rite for the presbyterate it is undertaken by a presbyter.[155]

In the early Armenian rite the litany similarly intervenes between the first and second ordination prayers for deacons and presbyters. This arrangement is very probably the result of Byzantine influence on the structure of the services, not part of the indigenous tradition, and it does not persist in later manuscripts. In the East Syrian rites the ordination prayers follow directly after the biddings, while the Syrian Orthodox rites have only the response, "Lord, have mercy," following the proclamation/bidding, but no litany as such. The Coptic and Maronite rites are similar, except that in the case of the episcopate in the former, a full litany with a special suffrage for the ordinand does still intervene after the bidding.[156]

In the ancient Georgian rite, the deacon who pronounces the bidding is directed to say three times, "Lord, have mercy and make him worthy." This was doubtless originally a congregational response and may be a conflation of two responses that were earlier quite separate, an acclamation of assent to the candidate's worthiness in reply to the announcement of his election and the normal form of supplication. A litany occurs here in the text at the beginning of the whole collection of prayers, but with a rubric that directed it to be used at the ordination of bishops, presbyters, and deacons. Presumably it was intended to be said between the bidding and the ordination prayers. Finally, in the Melkite ritual a threefold "Lord, have mercy" follows the first bidding and then comes the Byzantine proclamation/bidding formulary and a litany, except in the rite for the diaconate, where the litany comes in what was very probably its

[155] Ibid., 133–35.

[156] Ibid., 129, 131, 143, 145, 150, 158, 160, 163, 178, 181, 183, 191, 194, 197.

original position, prior to Byzantine influence, directly after the first bidding. Like that bidding, the litany is said by a presbyter at the ordination of a presbyter and by the chief deacon at other ordinations.[157]

### 4.2.4 *The Imposition of the Gospel Book at the Ordination of a Bishop*

This ceremony, first found in the *Apostolic Constitutions* and other fourth-century sources, occurs in all later Eastern Rites[158] but was performed by one or more of the bishops themselves rather than by deacons, as in the *Apostolic Constitutions*. As it was also deacons who performed it at Rome, however, that seems to confirm that the original custom had been as described in the *Apostolic Constitutions* and that Eastern practice had subsequently changed in order to increase episcopal involvement in the rite. In the Syrian Orthodox and Maronite rites, two bishops hold the book open over the head of the ordinand during the imposition of the hand. In the Byzantine rite it is performed by the archbishop, with the other bishops present also touching the book. Moreover, the open book is here laid on the head *and neck* of the ordinand and apparently understood as symbolizing "the yoke of the Gospel" that the new bishop received, since in later manuscripts of the rite this allusion is incorporated into the first ordination prayer.[159] In the East Syrian rite the archbishop is directed to place the book on the back of the ordinand in such a way that "it faces the one who is to read from it," and a gospel reading from it follows, after which the book is closed and left on the ordinand's back during the imposition of the hand and the prayers.[160] These modifications reinforce the judgment that the real meaning of the ceremony had

[157] Ibid., 166, 206.

[158] Scholars had traditionally thought that in the Coptic rite it was limited to the consecration of the patriarch alone, but see Heinzgerd Brakmann, "Zur Evangeliar-Auflegung bei der Ordination koptischer Bischöfe," in *ΕΥΛΟΓΗΜΑ: Studies in Honor of Robert Taft, SJ*, ed. Ephrem Carr et al., Studia Anselmiana 110 (Rome: Centro Studi S. Anselmo, 1993), 53–69, for a contrary view.

[159] See Arranz, *L'eucologio costantinopolitano*, 143. Although these rites do not specify whether the open book faced up or down, later practice has been that it faces down.

[160] Bradshaw, *Ordination Rites*, 133, 163, 183, 198.

been lost, its form being deliberately altered in order to make it more intelligible.

### 4.2.5 *The Sign of the Cross*

The earliest allusion to the use of the sign of the cross in ordination is found in the fourth-century *Canons of Hippolytus*, where the prayer for a deacon contains the clause "make him triumph over all the powers of the Devil by the sign of your cross with which you sign him."[161] Its existence at Antioch at the ordination of bishops in the fourth century is attested by John Chrysostom,[162] and the "cruciform seal" immediately after the imposition of the hand is mentioned by Pseudo-Dionysius as being common to all the major orders (*De ecclesiastica hierarchia* 5.2), with later Eastern rites confirming this to be the case, except that it normally precedes rather than follows the imposition of the hand. The use of the sign of the cross in early baptismal rituals may have provided the precedent for its adoption in Eastern ordination practice, especially as it is given a similar interpretation: the *Canons of Hippolytus* implies that it was seen as apotropaic, while Pseudo-Dionysius says that it signified "the cessation of all carnal desires and the imitation of the divine life."

### 4.2.6 *The Imposition of the Hand*

As indicated earlier, some Eastern rites display a tendency to associate the beginning of the imposition of the hand (usually specified as the right hand) with the first formula spoken by the presiding bishop, which may be called a prayer in the text even if it is not strictly speaking one, rather than with what appears to have been the original ordination prayer. This is the case in the early Armenian rites for deacons and presbyters, in the eighth-century Byzantine rite for a bishop (but not those for presbyters and deacons), and in the Maronite and Melkite rites, where the imposition of the hand begins at the proclamation/bidding formula.[163]

[161] Ibid., 111.

[162] John Chrysostom, *Adversus Judaeos et Gentiles* 9 (PG 48:826); *Homilia in Matthaeum* 54 (PG 58:537).

[163] Bradshaw, *Ordination Rites*, 128, 130, 133, 191, 194, 197, 206, 209.

In every Eastern rite, however, it is the presiding bishop alone who lays his hand on the ordinand, and only in a few cases are there signs of obviously secondary attempts to associate others with him in this action. In the East Syrian rite for a bishop, the other bishops place their right hands on the ordinand's sides, and in the Coptic rite they lay their hands on the ordinand's arms and not on his head. In the Armenian rite for a presbyter, a rubric directs that after the ordinand kneels down, "the priests lay their hands upon his," leaving where the hands are to be placed unclear. A parallel rubric in the rite for the diaconate specifies that it is on "his hands."[164] Later manuscripts of the presbyteral rite, however, while exhibiting some further confusion over the rubric, seem to agree that it is the ordinand's shoulders on which the other priests are to lay a hand.[165] Both the Syrian Orthodox and Maronite rites display a unique feature in relation to the imposition of the hand for all three orders: the presiding bishop extends his hands over the consecrated bread and wine three times before proceeding to lay his right hand on the ordinand. This ceremony seems to have been introduced in order to express the idea that it was not the presiding bishop himself but Christ who ordained his ministers, and it was his spiritual power that was bestowed on them.[166]

Although no patristic source makes any reference to the posture to be adopted by ordinands during the ordination prayer and imposition of the hand, Pseudo-Dionysius states that candidates for the episcopate and presbyterate were to kneel on both knees, and a candidate for the diaconate on his right knee (*De ecclesiastica hierarchia* 5.2) This is supported by the more extensive rubrics found in some of the later texts, except for the Armenian, which speaks instead of the left knee for a deacon.[167]

### *4.2.7 The Ordination Prayer*

As indicated earlier, there is a common tendency in the Eastern rites for ordination prayers to multiply, either by the addition of what may have been a local alternative to the principal prayer or by the

[164] Ibid., 128, 130, 151, 163.
[165] See Conybeare, *Rituale Armenorum*, 236–37.
[166] Bradshaw, *Ordination Rites*, 178, 181, 183, 191, 195, 197.
[167] Ibid., 128.

incorporation of prayers from foreign sources. Thus, the Byzantine rite has two ordination prayers for each order, one immediately after the bidding and the second, probably more original one, after the litany.[168] The oldest Armenian rites have adopted the same pattern (doubtless from Byzantine influence), although the prayers are different in content and the rite for presbyters has a third prayer after the Liturgy of the Word. The East Syrian rites also have two prayers, the first located even before the bidding itself and identical in every case except for the name of the office being conferred. The Georgian rites had three prayers for each order, one of them drawn from the *Testamentum Domini* and another with parallels to the principal prayer in the East Syrian rite. In the Syrian Orthodox tradition, several preparatory and supplementary prayers have grown up before and after the principal ordination prayer. The Coptic rites combine prayers from this source with material from the *Apostolic Constitutions*. The Maronite rites each have a number of prayers, suggesting a long process of accretion, some of them analogous to prayers in the Syrian Orthodox tradition, others with resemblances to ones in the Melkite tradition, and others with no known parallel. One prayer in the rite for deacons is a version of a Byzantine one, and one in the rite for a bishop is derived from the *Apostolic Constitutions*. Something similar was true of the Melkite rite. Some prayers resemble Georgian texts (which has led to the suggestion that they both derive from Jerusalem[169]), others are similar to Byzantine prayers, others to those in the Maronite rites, and still others have no clear parallels.[170]

#### *4.2.7.1 For a Bishop*

In the case of prayers for a bishop, there is evidence of an even closer literary connection between the different rites. In five of the six traditions that have rites for the episcopate in their oldest manuscripts, there is a substantial amount of common material in one of

[168] For reasons to think that the first prayer is a later composition than the second, see ibid., 51–52, 64–65.

[169] See further Heinzgerd Brakmann, "Die altkirchlichen Ordinationsgebete Jerusalems," *Jahrbuch für Antike und Christentum* 47 (2004): 108–27.

[170] See the table of relationships between the prayers in Bradshaw, *Ordination Rites*, 243.

their prayers. The following is the Byzantine version, the elements common to the other prayers being indicated by the use of italics:

> Lord our *God, who,* because human nature cannot sustain the essence of your divinity, by your dispensation *have established teachers* subject to the same passions as ourselves who approach your throne to offer you sacrifice and oblation for all your people; Lord, *make him* who has been made dispenser of the high-priestly grace *to be an imitator of you, the true shepherd, giving his life for your sheep, guide of the blind, light of those in darkness, corrector of the ignorant, lamp in the world, so that, after having formed* in this present life *the souls who have been entrusted to him, he may stand before your judgment-seat without shame and receive the great reward* which you have prepared for those who have striven for the preaching of your Gospel. For yours are mercy and salvation.[171]

Although part of this is an allusion to John 10:15 and a quotation from Romans 2:19-20, it is inconceivable that each tradition would have lighted upon the latter independently, especially as it is a very strange passage to choose for this purpose, because in its original context it had nothing to do with ordination or ministry but formed part of a critical passage directed toward the Jews. Although the Byzantine version is the shortest of the prayers containing the common material and so might be thought to have been the source of all the others, this is unlikely in its present form, as there are at least two peculiarities that suggest it too has undergone some modification: it is addressed, not to God the Father, but to Christ ("you, the true shepherd"),[172] and its description of teachers as those "who approach your throne to offer sacrifice and oblation" is a strange mixture of images and appears to be a secondary adaptation made in order to incorporate a cultic dimension rather than a part of the primary stratum of the prayer.

[171] Bradshaw, *Ordination Rites*, 134. See the synopsis of the parallels in the prayers, ibid., 246–47, and further discussion of their origin, ibid., 50–55; also Frans van de Paverd, "Ein Gebet zur Bischofsweihe aus dem vorbyzantinischen Jerusalem," in Carr, *Eulogēma*, 511–23, who argues for a Jerusalem origin for the common core.

[172] The same is also true of the second prayer for a deacon. Gy, "Ancient Ordination Prayers," 82, suggested that this was part of a general Byzantine tendency to direct to Christ those prayers that came to be said in a low voice.

The presence of such similar euchological material in very diverse contexts suggests that the nucleus of this prayer is as old as some of our patristic sources and was in established use before the divisions that took place in the Eastern churches during the fifth century. It seems to have been ancient enough to have developed in at least two distinct forms prior to that time, with a Byzantine/Coptic trajectory, on the one hand,[173] and a Georgian/East Syrian (and perhaps Syrian Orthodox) version, on the other. This second strand strengthened the christological dimension of the prayer, introduced an explicit invocation of the Holy Spirit on the ordinand, and added a reference to the healing ministry of the bishop.

Thus, the two images of the episcopal office that seemingly constitute part of the original nucleus of the prayer are those of shepherd (as is true of the patristic sources, but here brought into explicit association with Christ the true shepherd) and teacher/guardian of the truth (a contrast with most patristic texts). Cultic/liturgical imagery seems to have had no place at all in the earliest stratum but to have been gradually introduced at a later stage in the various traditions. In some cases a clumsy fusion of ideas took place, as with the teaching and priestly themes in the opening of the Byzantine prayer noted above, or the notion of the "perfect priest after the example of the true shepherd" in the Georgian version. In other cases, a simple addition was made, such as the insertion of "priests" after the Pauline "apostles, prophets, and teachers" in the East Syrian prayer. In the Syrian Orthodox prayer there was direct substitution, with, for example, "every priestly order" replacing "teachers," which resulted in an all but total obliteration of the earlier themes.

### *4.2.7.2 For a Presbyter*

Although, as we have said, there has obviously been some borrowing from one source to another in the prayers for presbyters, no common nucleus seems to underlie the majority as it did in the case of the prayers for a bishop, but they appear to stem from several quite

[173] Pierre-Marie Gy, "La théologie des prières anciennes pour l'ordination des évêques et des prêtres," *Revue des sciences philosophiques et théologiques* 58 (1974): 599–617, here at 604, considered that the description of God as unknowable at the beginning of the Byzantine version was characteristic of the theology of the Greek fathers at the end of the fourth century.

distinct euchological traditions, no doubt reflecting the considerable regional diversity in early ordination practice.

The second of the two prayers in the Byzantine rite seems to be the earlier. It also displays strong similarities to the first prayer in the Melkite rite and also to a longer prayer in the Syrian Orthodox rite, suggesting a common source for all three.[174] Unlike the equivalent prayers for a bishop and for a deacon, it does have an explicit petition for the gift of the Holy Spirit, but unlike our patristic texts, it does not define the presbyterate by means of biblical typology, probably because nothing could be found that was appropriate to the nature that the office was thought to have.

> O God, great in power and unsearchable in understanding, wonderful in your counsels beyond the sons of men, Lord, fill this man, whom you have willed to undertake the rank of the presbyterate, with the gift of your Holy Spirit so that he may be worthy to stand blamelessly at your altar, to proclaim the Gospel of your salvation, to exercise the sacred ministry of the word of your truth, to offer you gifts and spiritual sacrifices, and to renew your people by the baptism of regeneration; so that, being present at the second coming of our great God and Savior Jesus Christ your only Son, he may receive the reward of the good stewardship of his office in the abundance of your goodness. For blessed and glorified is your most honored and magnificent name.[175]

The presbyterate is not portrayed as a collegial governing body, but instead the prayer employs strictly functional language. The use of the expression "exercise the sacred ministry [*hierourgein*] of the word," echoing Romans 15:16, "exercising the sacred ministry of the Gospel of God," strongly suggests that the priestly dimension of the office was seen as finding its fulfillment at least as much in the preaching of the word as in sacramental functions,[176] and this corresponds to what we know of the nature of the ordained ministry at Antioch in the fourth century, where presbyters took a prominent part in preach-

[174] See Bradshaw, *Ordination Rites*, 64–65, 134, 181, 209.

[175] Ibid., 135.

[176] See also John Chrysostom, *Sermo cum presbyter fuit ordinatus* (PG 48:694, 699), where he said that he had been placed among the priests and that the word was his sacrifice; and *Apostolic Constitutions* 8.16 for the use of the noun *hierourgias*, "holy services," to denote presbyteral functions in its ordination prayer for presbyters.

ing but eucharistic presidency seems still to have been normally an episcopal prerogative.[177] The other versions of this prayer modify the references to proclaiming the gospel and exercising the ministry of the word, because this later ceased to be a function normally exercised by presbyters, and introduce the terms "priest" or "priesthood" instead, since these began to be used unequivocally to denote the presbyterate rather than the episcopate in the East in the fifth century.

The preaching of the word is also given the pride of place in a number of other Eastern ordination prayers. The first Georgian prayer, which parallels the second Melkite prayer, begins by linking the earthly ministry to the ministry of heaven, much as was also done in the prayer for a bishop in the *Testamentum Domini*, but mentions only the function of true teaching in its petition for the ordinand. The same is true of the third Melkite prayer: while it refers in a general way to the discharging of services (*leitourgias*) on behalf of the church and to beseeching God's propitiation for all, the only function explicitly specified is the teaching of God's commandments. The third prayer in the Georgian rite, which occurs in a somewhat longer and apparently later form in the East Syrian rite, asks God to send the Holy Spirit on the ordinand that he may have "the word of teaching, for the opening of his mouth," before going on to mention the ministry of healing and the celebration of the Eucharist. The East Syrian version adds to this the administration of baptism. A similar list of functions also occurs in the fourth Melkite prayer—offering gifts and sacrifices, "utterance in the opening of his mouth," praying for the sick, the administration of baptism, and care of the needy.[178]

Two of the Armenian prayers for a presbyter, like the first Georgian/second Melkite prayer, also begin with a comparison of the heavenly and earthly ministries. The first of these goes on to speak of priests as being "shepherds and leaders" of the congregation, images that elsewhere are used of the episcopal rather than presbyteral order, before specifying the functions of "the word of preaching," the

[177] See *Apostolic Constitutions* 2.57.9, and the evidence of John Chrysostom cited in Frans van de Paverd, *Zur Geschichte der Messliturgie in Antiocheia und Constantinopel gegen Ende des vierten Jahrhunderts*, OCA 187 (Rome: Pontificium Institutum Orientalium Studiorum, 1970), 131. According to the *Itinerarium Egeriae* (25.1; 26.1; 27.6–7; 42.1; 43.2, 3), the same seems to have been true at Jerusalem.

[178] See Bradshaw, *Ordination Rites*, 160–61, 170–71, 210–12.

work of healing, the bestowal of the Spirit in baptism, and the celebration of the Eucharist. The second prayer merely asks for the bestowal of the sevenfold gifts of the Spirit so that the ordinand may teach and shepherd the people. The third Maronite prayer, which has some slight similarity to the first Georgian/second Melkite prayer, compares the heavenly and earthly ministries and refers to priestly, teaching, and governing/shepherding functions.[179]

### *4.2.7.3 For a Deacon*

These prayers display both the same variation as to whether they use the typology of Stephen or not as is evidenced in our patristic sources and also a similar tendency to reticence with regard to the actual functions of the diaconate. Where any details of the ministry are mentioned, they almost always relate to service at the altar rather than to any wider pastoral responsibility.

The first Byzantine prayer asks for the bestowal of the same grace that was given to Stephen but has no explicit invocation of the Holy Spirit on the candidate. On the other hand, it does refer at the beginning to God in his *foreknowledge* sending down the Holy Spirit on those *destined* to be ministers: Is this perhaps a reflection of Acts 6:3 where the assembly are directed to choose men already "full of the Spirit" to be appointed to office? It gives little indication of the nature of the ministry for which the deacon is being ordained, except that it is related to the Eucharist. It speaks of "those destined . . . to serve at your immaculate mysteries" and cites 1 Timothy 3:9, "holding the mystery of faith in a pure conscience," which some commentators have thought may be intended here, though not in its original context, as a reference to the deacon's function of holding the chalice for the distribution of communion.[180] It ends with the quotation from 1 Timothy 3:13—"for those serving well will gain for themselves a good rank"—which is also found in the deacon's prayer in the so-called *Apostolic Tradition*, and here again the reference is not to ecclesiastical preferment but to the deacon's standing on the day of judgment.[181]

[179] Ibid., 130–32, 195.

[180] See, for example, Aimé Georges Martimort, *Deaconesses: An Historical Study* (San Francisco: Ignatius Press, 1986), 156.

[181] Bradshaw, *Ordination Rites*, 136.

The second prayer, like the second prayer for a bishop, is addressed to Christ rather than to God the Father, but this appears to be a secondary development, as a Syrian Orthodox version of it begins in a completely different manner. The Byzantine form does not use the typology of Stephen but in its extended introduction links the diaconate to Christ, not claiming that he directly instituted it, but interpreting his saying in Matthew 20:27 ("whoever wishes to be first among you must be your servant [*doulos*]") as a prophetic word concerning it. The prayer then goes on to ask for the bestowal of appropriate gifts of the Holy Spirit, these being personal qualities rather than the powers to fulfill any specific function. It includes an insistent aside that ordination is indeed effected by the descent of the Spirit and not by the action of the bishop. This has the appearance of a later addition to the original text, though it is ancient enough to have also been included in the Syrian Orthodox version.[182] The inclusion of such a strongly defensive doctrinal statement in the prayer suggests that there was some controversy over the issue, and it may have been added in the late fourth century, since John Chrysostom makes a similar statement in one of his writings: "For this is ordination: the man's hand is imposed, but God does all and it is his hand that touches the ordinand's head when he is rightly ordained."[183]

The Syrian Orthodox version, also found in the Maronite rite, modifies the Byzantine prayer in several ways: it supplies an introduction that sets the ordination of the deacon within an ecclesial framework; it introduces a reference to Stephen, though without the designation "protomartyr"; and it expands the second half of the prayer with petitions for right judgment on the part of those responsible for choosing ordinands. Some of these petitions also occur in the preliminary prayer, "Lord God of hosts . . . ," used in all Syrian Orthodox ordinations from subdeacon upward.[184]

The first ordination prayer for a deacon in the Georgian rite (here described as for an archdeacon) parallels the second prayer in the

[182] But there strangely in the plural—"the imposition of the hands of us sinners." The same phrase also occurs in one of the Maronite ordination prayers.

[183] John Chrysostom, *Homilia in Acta Apostolorum* 14.3 (PG 60:116). He also implies in one of his baptismal homilies that the Antiochene baptismal formula was changed from the active to the passive form at this time in order to make a similar point.

[184] Bradshaw, *Ordination Rites*, 178–79.

Melkite rite. It defines the diaconate neither in relation to Christ, who is mentioned only briefly toward the end of the prayer, nor by the typology of Stephen, but simply as one of a list of diverse ministries bestowed by God on the church—teachers, deacons, presbyters, and ministers. This is an unusual combination of offices: it omits any explicit reference to bishops and does not follow a hierarchical order, nor is it an allusion to any New Testament listing. The Melkite tradition seems to have found it difficult to comprehend and tried to make some sense out of it by arranging the titles in pairs, altering "presbyters" to "priests" in the process. The prayer has no explicit epiclesis, which may be a sign of its antiquity, but, on the other hand, at least in its present form, it speaks of the ordinand's ultimate promotion to a higher rank, which does not seem to belong to the earliest concept of the office.[185]

The third Georgian prayer parallels the East Syrian ordination prayer, following the pattern of the rite for the presbyterate. This sets the creation of the diaconate in the context of the mission of Christ and of the apostles (the latter reference being expanded in the East Syrian prayer to prophets, apostles, priests, and teachers, apparently under the influence of Ephesians 4:11-12) and cites the example of Stephen and his companions. As in the first Georgian prayer, service at the altar is stated to be the principal function of the office, a point further strengthened in the East Syrian version by two additional references to the sacraments. There is, on the other hand, no mention of the ordinand's eventual promotion to a higher rank but merely the petition for a favorable verdict on the day of judgment.[186]

Of the remaining prayers of the Melkite rite, the first has the appearance of being a late composition, since extensive biblical quotation is not a characteristic of more ancient prayers, and it is very much built around Acts 6:5. As well as mentioning service of the altar, however, where it is the only prayer to refer explicitly to the diaconal function of giving communion to the people from the chalice, it also speaks of a ministry to widows and orphans—but has that been introduced simply because of the influence of Acts 6 rather than being a reflection of a genuine ministry of this kind? The position of the fourth prayer, after the bestowal of the symbols of office, suggests

[185] Ibid., 169, 207.

[186] Ibid., 158–59, 170.

that it too is a late addition to the rite, even if it is not itself a late composition. It speaks simply of faithful service at the liturgy and of progress to a higher rank, though whether this is ecclesiastical or eschatological is not entirely clear.[187]

The first of the two Armenian prayers for the diaconate, like two of those in the rite for the presbyterate, uses the comparison of the heavenly and earthly ministries. It goes on to set the diaconal office within an ecclesial context and then prays for the gift of appropriate personal qualities for the ordinand. Service at the altar is again designated as the principal function of the order, and the example of Stephen is invoked: he is here described not only as the first martyr and first deacon and minister of God's worship but also as an apostle! There is no explicit epiclesis, though it prays that the ordinand, "filled with the Holy Spirit, may stand fast" and eventually be worthy of promotion to the priesthood. The second prayer is much shorter and does contain a petition for the gift of the Holy Spirit. Once again, ministry at the holy table is described as the chief function of the office, and the remainder of the prayer seeks God's protection for the new minister. Like the first Armenian prayer, those prayers in the Maronite rite that are without parallel in other traditions also employ the comparison of heavenly and earthly ministries.[188]

### *4.2.8 The Kiss*

The only concluding symbolic ceremony mentioned in the *Apostolic Tradition* and its derivatives was the exchange of a kiss between the assembly and a new bishop, except for the *Apostolic Constitutions*, which included the seating of the new bishop and placed the kiss after that.[189] It does not appear to be merely the kiss of peace that would normally occur within the eucharistic rite, for what evidence there is from the ante-Nicene period suggests that the latter formed the conclusion of the prayers of the faithful rather than the beginning of the eucharistic action.[190] The ordination kiss seems instead to have

[187] Ibid., 206–8.

[188] Ibid., 128–29, 192–93.

[189] Ibid., 108, 110, 114, 119.

[190] See Justin Martyr, *Apology* 1.65.2; Tertullian, *De oratione* 18; Michael Philip Penn, *Kissing Christians: Ritual and Community in the Late Ancient Church* (Philadelphia: University of Pennsylvania Press, 2005).

been intended to express the acceptance by the community of their new relationship with the one ordained.

No indication is given by any of the patristic sources as to whether a similar kiss was also exchanged in the case of the presbyterate and diaconate, with the sole exception of the *Testamentum Domini*, which directs that both "priests and people" are to give the kiss of peace to a newly ordained presbyter.[191] On the other hand, it is a consistent feature of later Eastern rites. Pseudo-Dionysius, for example, describes it as an element common to all the orders and interprets it as symbolizing "the sacred communion of like minds and their loving joy toward one another" (*De ecclesiastica hierarchia* 5.2). By then, however, the ritual had apparently been clericalized: the kiss was given to the newly ordained minister by the bishop and all the clergy, and no reference is made to the laity's involvement in the action.

Although no directions are given about the kiss in the ninth-century Armenian text, the closing prayer in each of the rites does make reference to its existence and describes it as a welcome given by all. Later manuscripts of the rite for the presbyterate, however, while preserving the prayer in this form, direct that the salutation be done only by the bishop and the other priests.[192] In Byzantine practice there was a further development, and participation became restricted to those thought of as effecting the ordination: thus, only the bishops present kiss a newly ordained bishop, and only the presiding bishop kisses a new presbyter or deacon. No mention is made of a kiss in the case of a deaconess or subdeacon in this tradition, but it is recorded in the case of the reader, though here it is differently described, the word "peace" being used.[193] On the other hand, in other traditions the kiss is sometimes described as being given *by* the newly ordained deacon, presbyter, or bishop *to* the other ministers present.

### *4.2.9 Other Concluding Ceremonies*

The only other concluding ceremonial actions in the eighth-century Byzantine rite for a bishop are the bestowal of the *omophorion*, the

[191] Bradshaw, *Ordination Rites*, 119.

[192] See Conybeare, *Rituale Armenorum*, 242.

[193] Bradshaw, *Ordination Rites*, 134, 136–37, 139.

Eastern equivalent of the Western pallium, as a symbol of episcopal office and his seating in the episcopal chair, the one coming before the kiss and the other after. In the Byzantine rite for a presbyter, the bishop similarly vests the newly ordained with the robes of his office, gives him the kiss, and seats him with his fellow presbyters. The same is true in the case of a deacon, except that instead of his being seated with fellow deacons, he is given the fan with which to perform his duty of fanning the eucharistic elements on the altar, and after receiving communion himself, he is given the chalice and assists in giving communion to the people.[194] Similar ceremonies conclude the other Eastern rites, and a number of the later texts—the Coptic, East Syrian, Maronite, Melkite, and Syrian Orthodox—include a solemn declaration that the candidate has been duly ordained to the particular order, as well as adding some unique features. Thus, the East Syrian rite includes the presentation of the book of the epistles to a new deacon, the book of gospels to a new presbyter, and the pastoral staff to a new bishop. In the Syrian Orthodox rite, both deacon and presbyter receive a thurible, and a bishop the pastoral staff. In the Maronite rite a new presbyter performs several actions that symbolize the liturgical duties of his office—incensing and carrying the gospel book and then the paten in procession—and a new deacon reads a passage from the epistles as well as incensing, carrying the epistle book in procession, and waving the chalice veil. In the Melkite rite a presbyter was given the gospel book and read John 1:1-3 and was then given the consecrated bread and proclaimed the invitation to communion, "Holy things for holy people." A deacon was likewise given the gospel book and read the same passage before receiving the eucharistic vessels and the fan. The Byzantine rite itself also gives a distinctive function to the new presbyter in the eucharistic consecration that follows the ordination: he holds one of the pieces of bread in his hands throughout the prayer, bowing over the holy table. Like the Melkite custom, this is obviously intended to give symbolic expression to his new role as a participant in eucharistic presidency.[195]

[194] Ibid., 134, 136–37.

[195] For later developments of this ceremony, see Tchékan, "Elements d'introduction à l'étude de la liturgie byzantine des ordinations," 204–5.

### *4.2.10 The Celebration of the Eucharist*

With the sole exception of the East Syrian tradition, which permits ordinations to take place at any time, Eastern rites consistently locate ordinations within a eucharistic celebration, although the Byzantine and Melkite traditions do allow the diaconate to be conferred during the Liturgy of the Presanctified instead, as the diaconal liturgical function can equally be exercised there. There are differences, however, with regard to the precise point within the Eucharist at which the ordination is to take place. In the Byzantine rite, the ordination of a bishop is located at the very beginning of the Eucharist, and the new bishop is then expected to read the gospel, preach, and offer the oblation; a presbyter is ordained immediately after the entrance of the gifts so that he may then fulfill his new liturgical role by participating in the eucharistic action; and a deacon, at the end of the eucharistic prayer so that he may then fulfill the diaconal function of assisting in the distribution of the consecrated elements to the communicants. The same is true of the Coptic rite, except that a deacon is ordained at the same point in the rite as the presbyter.

In the Maronite and Syrian Orthodox traditions, on the other hand, ordination to all the orders is deferred until the eucharistic consecration has been completed, in order that the consecrated bread and wine may be used in conjunction with the imposition of the hand (see above). In the case of the Maronite tradition, however, the oldest manuscripts suggest that the ordinations once came at an earlier point in the liturgy.[196] In the Syrian Orthodox rite a new bishop is directed to receive Communion and then assume the presidency of the rite for the remainder of the celebration.

### *4.2.11 The Ordination of Women Deacons*

As noted above, the Armenian, Byzantine, East Syrian, and Georgian Rites also include prayers and rubrics for the ordination of women deacons or deaconesses.[197] And of particular interest is the

[196] See Pierre-Edmond Gemayel, *Avant-messe maronite: histoire et structure*, OCA 174 (Rome: Pontificium Institutum Orientalium Studiorum, 1965), 125–33.

[197] Bradshaw, *Ordination Rites*, 88–92, 137–39, 162–63, 168–69. On the ordination of women in both and East and West, see Ute Eisen, *Women Officeholders in Early Christianity: Epigraphical and Literary Studies* (Collegeville, MN: Liturgical Press, 2000);

fact that on February 17, 2017, the Greek Orthodox patriarch of Alexandria, Theodoros II, ordained five African women as "deaconesses" and appointed them to perform various sacramental (e.g., assisting with adult female baptisms) and other ministries (especially to women) as part of the overall mission of the Patriarchate in the Congo.[198] While called "deaconesses" and *not* "sub-deaconnesses," it appears that the rite actually used was more akin to the Byzantine ordination of subdeacons rather than to deacons properly speaking.[199] That is, this particular rite took place in the nave of the church rather than at the altar and included the orarion (stole), handlaying, prayer, and washing of the patriarch's hands. But whether ordained as deacons or subdeacons, the precedent for the restoration of the ordination of women into an official order of ministry has now been set by at least one Greek Orthodox patriarchate.

The Byzantine rite for the ordination of women deacons, however, is clearly an ordination rite parallel to that for deacons, with two ordination prayers separated by a litany. When compared with the extant prayers of the Armenian, Georgian, and East Syrian Rites, it is clear that the first prayer in the Byzantine Rite of Barberini 336 reflects an earlier form of a common tradition underlying all of them.

> *After the holy oblation has been made and the doors are open, before the deacon says,* All the saints . . . , *she who is to be ordained is brought to the bishop. He says aloud,* The divine grace . . . , *and she bows her head, and he lays his hand on her head, and making three crosses, he prays thus:* Holy and

---

Kyriaki Karidoyanes FitzGerald, *Women Deacons in the Orthodox Church* (Brookline, MA: Holy Cross Orthodox Press, 1999); Valerie Karras, "Female Deacons in the Byzantine Church," *Church History* 73 (2004); idem, "The Liturgical Functions of Consecrated Women in the Byzantine Church," *Theological Studies* 66 (2005): 96–116; Kevin Madigan and Carolyn Osiek, *Ordained Women in the Early Church: A Documentary History* (Baltimore: Johns Hopkins University Press, 2005); Martimort, *Deaconesses: An Historical Study*; Roger Gryson, *The Ministry of Women in the Early Church* (Collegeville, MN: Liturgical Press, 1976); Cypriano Vaggagini, *Ordination of Women to the Diaconate in the Eastern Churches*, ed. Phyllis Zagano (Collegeville, MN: Liturgical Press, 2013); Phyllis Zagano, ed., *Women Deacons? Essays with Answers* (Collegeville, MN: Liturgical Press, 2016).

[198] See Petros Vassiliadis, "The Revival of the Order of Deaconess by the Patriarchate of Alexandria," *Public Orthodoxy* (Fordham University, November 17, 2017) at https://publicorthodoxy.org/2017/11/17/support-alexandria-deaconess/.

[199] See Bradshaw, *Ordination Rites*, 139.

> almighty God, who through the birth of your only-begotten Son and our God from the Virgin according to the flesh sanctified the female, and not to men alone but also to women bestowed grace and the advent of your Holy Spirit; now, Lord, look upon this your servant and call her to the work of your diaconate, and send down upon her the abundant gift of your Holy Spirit; keep her in orthodox faith, in blameless conduct, always fulfilling her ministry according to your pleasure; because to you is due all glory and honor.[200]

After the short litany and the second ordination prayer, belonging to a later stratum in the development of the rite, the following rubric directs:

> *And after the "Amen," he places the diaconal orarion* [stole] *around her neck under the maphorion* [veil], *bringing forward the two ends. And then standing in the ambo, [the deacon] says,* Having commemorated all the saints. . . . *After she has received the holy body and the precious blood, the archbishop gives her the holy cup, which she receives and places on the holy table.*[201]

The fact that she receives and then immediately places the holy cup on the table certainly suggests that the distribution of the cup was no longer part of the woman deacon's liturgical ministry at the time of the eighth-century Barberini 336. But the fact that she is handed the cup by the archbishop in the first place, *after* having received Holy Communion, along with the rite itself, clearly demonstrates that at one time the liturgical ministries of deacons and deaconesses were deemed equivalent.

The ordination of women as "deacons" in the Greek Orthodox Patriarchate of Alexandria is not really the first time that women have been ordained as deacons in the modern Greek Orthodox Church. It is well known that Bishop St. Nektarios, using the rite in Barberini 336, ordained two women as deacons in 1911 to serve at Holy Trinity Monastery, which he had established on the island of Aegina. Nektarios was followed in 1986 by Metropolitan Christodoulos at Demetrias, later the archbishop of Athens, who ordained at least one

[200] Ibid., 137–38.
[201] Ibid., 138.

woman using what he referred to as the "ritual of St. Nektarios."[202] It is too soon to tell whether the action of the Alexandrian patriarch and these Greek precedents will serve as a catalyst for similar developments in the Christian East elsewhere.

[202] Phyllis Zagano, "Grant Her Your Spirit (On the Female Diaconate)," *America*, February 7, 2005, www.americamagazine.org.

# *Chapter 5*

# Anointing of the Sick and Christian Burial

Illness, death, and their relationship to the meaning of life are central to any existential reflection, no matter one's faith tradition or philosophy of life. In the Christian response to these questions, illness and death are intimately connected to sin, the result of the Fall, the disobedience toward God of Adam and Eve, representing the whole of humanity. In the person of Christ the relationship between God and humanity is restored (hence he is often called the "second Adam"); sin, death, and evil are defeated; and life is restored. Christ's earthly ministry is filled with numerous healing miracles, occasions where life is restored to those already dead, and ultimately the victory of life over death through Christ's own resurrection. In this chapter, we will examine how the Eastern Christian Churches answer the existential questions regarding illness and death through their own liturgical rites of the anointing of the sick and burial.

## 5.1 Healing

As a reality of the human condition, illness is addressed in different contexts and in a variety of ways within the Eastern Christian liturgical traditions. Such contexts include the anointing of the sick, petitions and prayers for the sick in the context of the eucharistic liturgy, and other occasional prayers of healing. The liturgical treatment of illness and the petitions for healing link physical with spiritual health and thus connect the petition for health with the petition for forgiveness of sins. This approach is rooted in the healing ministry of Christ, in the healing ministry of the apostles, and in the healing ministry in the apostolic community, with James 5:14-15 seen as the origin of what becomes later the mystery/sacrament of unction:

> Are any among you sick? They should call for the *elders* of the church and have them *pray over them, anointing them with oil in the name of the Lord*. The prayer of faith will *save* the sick, and the Lord will *raise them up*; and anyone who has committed *sins will be forgiven*. (emphasis added)

Here are the ritual roots of the unction of the sick, especially the tradition among Eastern Christians to have more than one priest (ideally) celebrate the sacrament, centered on praying over the sick and anointing them with oil. While in the New Testament the majority of healing incidents take place by the laying on of hands, anointing with oil is clearly mentioned in the context of healing in Mark 6:13. Another notable element is the connection between illness and sin highlighted in verse 15 above, a constant in the ensuing theological and liturgical traditions of the Eastern Churches regarding the anointing of the sick.

### *5.1.1 The Early Evidence*

Early Christian evidence points to a variety of healing prayers, many involving the blessing of oil for the sick, others the laying on of hands, and others giving no indications of any accompanying ritual action. In most cases regarding the blessing of oil for the sick, that blessing takes place in the context of a eucharistic celebration. So, for example, we read in the Latin version of the so-called *Apostolic Tradition* 5:

> If anyone offers oil, let him render thanks according to the offering of bread and wine—and let him say [it] not word for word but to similar effect—saying: "As, sanctifying this oil, you give, God, health to those using and receiving [it], whence you have anointed kings, priests, and prophets, so also may it afford strengthening to all tasting [it] and health to all using it."[1]

[1] Paul Bradshaw, Maxwell Johnson, and L. Edward Phillips, *The Apostolic Tradition* (Minneapolis: Fortress Press, 2002), 50. For a commentary, see ibid., 49. See also Eric

A similar prayer is provided in *The Prayers of Sarapion of Thmuis* 5. It is also prayed in the context of a eucharistic celebration; it calls for the consumption of the blessed oil and, in this case, the blessed water; and it adds an exorcistic element to the petition of the prayer:

> We bless these creatures through the name of the only-begotten Jesus Christ. Upon this water and upon this oil we name the name of the one who suffered, who was crucified and raised up, and who is seated at the right hand of the uncreated. Graciously give healing power to these creatures so that through eating and drinking every fever and every demon and every disease may be cured, and so that the participation of these creatures may become a healing medicine and a medicine of wholeness in the name of your only-begotten Jesus Christ, through whom (be) to you the glory and power to all the ages of ages. Amen.[2]

The laying on of hands as a ritual healing gesture is noted in *The Prayers of Sarapion of Thmuis* 30. The prayer itself is titled "Laying on of Hands of the Sick," and it is followed by a rubric possibly placing it in the eucharistic celebration by noting that it is to be "accomplished before the prayer of offering." The prayer itself is as follows:

> Lord God of compassion, stretch out your hand and graciously grant healing to all the sick. Graciously make them worthy of health. Release them from the sickness which lies upon them. Let them be healed in the name of your only-begotten. Let his holy name come to be in them a medicine for health and wholeness. For through him (be) to you the

Segelberg, "The Benedictio Olei in the Apostolic Tradition of Hippolytus," *Oriens Christianus* 48 (1964): 268–81. For similar prayers in other early Church sources, see *The Prayers of Sarapion of Thmuis* 17 in Maxwell Johnson, *The Prayers of Sarapion of Thmuis: A Literary, Liturgical, and Theological Analysis*, OCA 249 (Rome: Pontificio Istituto Orientale, 1995), 66–67 for the text, 143–47 for commentary; *The Canons of Hippolytus* 3 in Paul Bradshaw, *The Canons of Hippolytus*, AGLS 2, GLS 50 (Bramcote, Nottingham: Grove Books, 1987), 13; *Testamentum Domini* 1.24 in Grant Sperry-White, *The Testamentum Domini: A Text for Students, with Introduction, Translation, and Notes*, AGLS 19, GLS 66 (Bramcote, Nottingham: Grove Books, 1991), 20. On the scholarly debate regarding the authorship, date, and provenance of the *Apostolic Tradition*, see Paul Bradshaw, *The Search for the Origins of Christian Worship* (New York: SPCK, 2002), 80–83; Alistair Stewart-Sykes, *Hippolytus: On the Apostolic Tradition; An English Version with Introduction and Commentary* (Crestwood, NY: St. Vladimir's Seminary Press, 2001); John Baldovin, "Hippolytus and the *Apostolic Tradition*: Recent Research and Commentary," *Theological Studies* 64 (2003): 520–42.

[2] Johnson, *The Prayers of Sarapion*, 52–53 for the text, 121–23 for commentary.

> glory and power in holy Spirit both now and to all the ages of ages. Amen.[3]

The only case where the blessing of oil for the sick is not clearly defined by a eucharistic context is *Apostolic Constitutions* 8.29.1-3:

> 1. Concerning water and oil, I, Matthew, command [thus]: 2. Let the bishop bless the water or the oil; however, if he is absent, let the presbyter bless [them], the deacon assisting. But if the bishop is there, let the presbyter and the deacon assist. 3. Let him say thus: O Lord of hosts, the God of powers, creator of the waters and provider of the oil, [you who are] compassionate and the lover of mankind, the giver of water for drinking and for cleansing, and of oil that cheers [man's] countenance for joy and gladness; do you yourself now, through Christ, sanctify this water and this oil, in the name of him or her that has brought [them], and grant [them] the power to restore health, to drive away diseases, to put demons to flight, to protect the household, [and] to put to flight all snares [of the enemy], through Christ our hope, through whom, in whom, in the Holy Spirit, glory, honour and worship [be] to you for ever. Amen.[4]

In this prayer, both water and oil are sanctified for the purpose of healing and protection from evil. The phraseology of the prayer in its references to water and oil ("for cleansing . . . for gladness") reminds one of baptism. Prayer 17 from *The Prayers of Sarapion of Thmuis*, titled "Prayer for Oil of the Sick or for Bread or for Water," has an even stronger exorcistic emphasis:

> Father of our Lord and Savior Jesus Christ, having all authority and power, the savior of all people, we call upon you and implore you that healing power of your only-begotten may be sent out from heaven upon this oil. May it become to those who are anointed (or to those who receive of these your creatures) for a rejection of every disease and every sickness, for an amulet warding off every demon, for a departing of every unclean spirit, for a taking away of every evil spirit, for a driving away of all fever and shiverings and every weakness, for good grace and forgiveness of sins, for a medicine of life and salvation, for health and wholeness of soul, body, spirit, for perfect strength.

[3] Ibid., 80–81 for the text, 182–83 for commentary.

[4] W. Jardine Grisbrooke, ed. and trans., *The Liturgical Portions of the Apostolic Constitutions: A Text for Students*, AGLS 13–14, GLS 61 (Bramcote, Nottingham: Grove Books, 1990), 91.

> Master, let every satanic energy, every demon, every plot of the opposite one, every blow, every lash, every pain, or every slap in the face, or shaking, or evil shadow be afraid of the only-begotten; and let them depart from the inner and the outer parts of these your servants so that the name of Jesus Christ, the one who was crucified and risen for us, who took to himself our diseases and weaknesses, and is coming to judge the living and the dead, may be glorified. For through him (be) to you the glory and the power in holy Spirit both now and to all the ages of ages. Amen.[5]

While healing is asked for here ("for a driving away of all fever and shiverings and every weakness . . . for health and wholeness of soul, body, spirit, for perfect strength"), the largest part of the text is exorcistic, accompanied by a request "for good grace and forgiveness of sins." The observation that many of these prayers include the blessing of water and that, together with the bidding for healing, petitions for the forgiveness of sins are provided and are in varying levels exorcistic may point to the liturgical context of baptism as the place of thematic inspiration and possible origin of these prayers.

Another striking observation, which may reflect the antiquity of the above prayers, is the absence of a pneumatic epiclesis, or even the mention of the Holy Spirit in the context of the blessing of the oil for healing. This is not so in the prayer preserved in *Testamentum Domini* 1.24-25, a prayer said over oil but also over water in the context of a eucharistic celebration:

> If there is oil for the healing of those who suffer, let it be sanctified in the following way. Let him say quietly, setting the vessel before the altar: Lord God, you who bestowed on us the Spirit, the Paraclete: Lord, [whose] name is salvific and unshaken, hidden to the foolish but revealed to the wise: Christ, you who have sanctified and made wise in your mercy us your servants whom you in your wisdom have chosen, who sent the knowledge of your Spirit to us sinners through your holiness, when you bestowed the power of the Spirit upon us, you are the healer of all who are ill and all who suffer. You who gave the gift of healing to those deemed worthy of this [gift]: send the deliverance of your compassion upon this oil which is a type of your richness, that it may deliver those who are diseased, and [that] it may heal the sick and sanctify those who return, as they draw near to your

[5] Johnson, *The Prayers of Sarapion*, 66–67 for the text, 143–47 for commentary.

> faith. For you are powerful and glorious for ever and ever. People: Amen. Similarly, the same [prayer] over water.[6]

There might also be a connection to reconciliation in this prayer, as the phrase "and sanctify those who return, as they draw near to your faith" may reflect the use of this oil for the reconciliation of penitents.[7] Another unique characteristic of this prayer is how emphatic it is in its effort to demonstrate that the ministry of healing is a prerogative of the clergy granted by God ("us your servants whom you in your wisdom have chosen . . . You who gave the gift of healing to those deemed worthy of this [gift]"). While in all the prayers presented the rubrics and/or the setting make it clear that clergy bless the oil (and water) of healing, the effort to justify the divine origin of the gift of healing that the clergy possess is also to be noted.

Visiting the sick was a significant ministry of the early church. *Canons of Hippolytus* 21 provides us with a glimpse into the early church's pastoral ministry to the sick. It notes: "the sick also, it is a healing for them to go to the church to receive the water of prayer and the oil of prayer, unless the sick person is seriously ill and close to death: the clergy shall visit him each day, those who know him."[8] *Didascalia Apostolorum* 16 relegates the ministry of the sick to the diaconate. In particular, when discussing the function of women deacons it states: "for a deaconess is needed . . . to visit those who are sick, ministering to them in whatever way they require, and to bathe those who have begun to recover from sickness."[9]

In the emerging liturgical rites of the East after the fourth century, ministry to the sick by means of praying over them and anointing them with blessed oil evolved into what we commonly call the sacrament of unction. In all traditions, the relationship between the anointing of the sick and the forgiveness of sins is always present, to the point where in popular piety unction is oftentimes seen as a way to avoid confession. The language of forgiveness of sins in the prayers has led in some cases to the common celebration of the anointing of the sick and reconciliation.

[6] Sperry-White, *The Testamentum Domini*, 20.

[7] Ibid., 20n5.

[8] Bradshaw, *The Canons of Hippolytus*, 26.

[9] Sebastian Brock and Michael Vasey, *The Liturgical Portions of the Didascalia*, GLS 29 (Bramcote, Nottingham: Grove Books, 1982), 23.

With the exception of the Armenian and East Syriac traditions, which will be examined below, all other traditions share the presence of a sevenfold structure (epistle reading, gospel reading, prayer), adapted to each respective liturgical tradition, pointing to a possible common source of influence. While this common sevenfold structure is seen as "more or less dependent on the Byzantine"[10] ritual and, hence, as a result of Byzantine influence, both early Byzantine and Hagiopolite sources do *not* reflect a sevenfold structure, making it unlikely that a *later* Byzantine structure exerted such influence on so many rites. It remains though that the Byzantine, Coptic, Ethiopian, West Syriac, and Maronite traditions share this sevenfold structure, a fact that "is of interest for comparative liturgy"[11] and invites further study.

### *5.1.2 Hagiopolite*

Manuscript Sinai georg. 12 of the tenth century preserves a Georgian translation of the original Greek euchological tradition of Jerusalem before its Byzantinization.[12] According to the text, the priest first censes over the sick person, blesses him or her with the sign of the cross and then prays over him or her, petitioning that God, "the physician of souls and bodies . . . strengthen and vivify, raise and restore" the sick person. A series of psalms follows (LXX 60, 19, 142, 85, 90). Then a prayer is read over the sick person that requests that God deliver the sick person from the "affliction of the devil . . . and this evil illness." Another pair of prayers follows, headed by a rubric that identifies the source of illness as the "evil, unclean spirits." The priest is directed to incense the person, bless him or her with the sign of the cross, and recite an excorcistic prayer. Then a series of psalms is recited (LXX 12, 101, 53, 30 or 70, 63, 69). The prayer that follows petitions that God cleanse the ill person "from evil and unite him/her with your holy church and remove from him/her every evil

[10] A. G. Martimort, *The Church at Prayer*, vol. 3: *The Sacraments*, new ed. (Collegeville, MN: Liturgical Press, 1987), 124.

[11] Stefano Parenti, "Care and Anointing of the Sick in the East," in *Handbook for Liturgical Studies*, vol. 4: *Sacraments and Sacramentals*, ed. Anscar Chupungco (Collegeville, MN: Liturgical Press, 2000), 161–69, here at 166.

[12] Tinatin Chronz, *Die Feier des Heiligen Öles nach Jerusalemer Ordnung*, Jerusalemer Theologisches Forum 18 (Münster: Aschendorff Verlag, 2012), 40–41.

creature that harms him/her with the power of the Holy Spirit." This is indeed the first instance of an invocation to the Holy Spirit in these prayers. Then another exorcistic prayer follows. Then, "when the evil spirit has departed," the priest prays one more prayer, addressed this time to Christ: "We all who stand here beseech you, Lord Jesus Christ, spread over him/her the Holy Spirit, the Spirit of wisdom and understanding, the spirit of knowledge and piety, the Spirit of counsel and strength, and the fear of God. For you are the God of mercy, and to you is due glory." This prayer is followed by the prayer of the fervent litany.[13] Sickness is understood here as the outcome of being overpowered by the devil, and healing is seen as delivery from the grasp of evil powers. The last prayer asks for the restoration of the Holy Spirit's presence in the healed person's life, echoing a return to the grace accomplished at baptism and chrismation.

While in all the above prayers there is no mention of the blessing of oil or of anointing the sick with oil, they are followed by a seemingly independent prayer that calls for the blessing of both oil and water. The rubric that precedes directs as follows: "But for the sick, pure water is sanctified in a pure vessel. The pure water is placed upon the altar, prayers are made for the person, and then it is sanctified." While the rubrics make mention of water only, the title of the prayer, "Consecration of the Water and Oil," and the prayer itself refer to *both* water and oil being sanctified:

> God, in your mercy you have visited us and blessed us with the spirit of salvation and care, kind One, you who are hidden from the unreasonable and revealed to the wise, Christ, who through your Holy Spirit sanctified us and made us wiser and renewed us your servants, whom you have chosen in your wisdom; you who sent the knowledge of the Holy Spirit upon us sinners in your goodness, grant to this oil and water your sanctification, your grace and the power of the Holy Spirit. Bless us, who are doctors of all diseases and afflictions, with the grace of healing, and let all be worthy of them through you. Grant the gift of mercy to this oil and water, which are types of your abundance, and mercy, so that we the burdened may be redeemed and the defiled cleansed and the diseases healed and the repentant who sacrifice to you sanctified, for you are the God of mercy, and praise is due to you,

[13] Ibid., 82–91 for the Georgian text and German translation.

to the Father and the Son and the Holy Spirit now and always and for all time and eternity. Amen.[14]

This prayer preserves the practice attested to in the early church documents of sanctifying *both* water and oil for the sick, is strikingly similar to that of *Testamentum Domini*,[15] and is also part of the reconciliation office for apostates, called in the Hagiopolite tradition *hilasmos* (mercy),[16] another example of the close connection between healing and forgiveness. Based on hagiographical evidence, a possible ritual context of a general anointing from a vessel containing oil that is placed on the altar (as in our prayer) is vespers on Sunday evening during the singing of the vesperal hymns, where the priest, standing inside the altar barrier, would extend his hand and with his finger anoint all the faithful approaching him.[17]

### *5.1.3 Byzantine*

The history and evolution of the ritual celebration of unction in the Byzantine tradition remains to be fully explored.[18] Part of the challenge is that from the earliest manuscript evidence from the eighth century (Barberini gr. 336) to the current practice we observe a variety of structures and practices. Even today, no two priests celebrate this sacrament the same way, even if the printed books imply a liturgical uniformity. In this case we have an example of Byzantine liturgical

[14] Translation from the German of the authors.

[15] Tinatin Chronz and Heinzgerd Brakmann, "Fragmente des Testamentum Domini in georgischer Übersetzung," *Zeitschrift für Antikes Christentum* 13 (2009): 395–402; Chronz, *Die Feier des Heiligen Öles*. To compare, see above, section 5.1.2.

[16] Chronz, *Die Feier des Heiligen Öles*, 42, and footnote 21.

[17] Ibid., 41, and footnote 20 for the Greek text.

[18] The most complete study in English is Paul Meyendorff, *The Anointing of the Sick*, Orthodox Liturgy Series 2 (Crestwood, NY: St. Vladimir's Seminary Press, 2009); Panayiotis Skaltsis, «Ἱστορικὴ Ἐξέλιξις τῆς Ἀκολουθίας τοῦ Εὐχελαίου» [Historical Evolution of the Service of Unction], in *Τὸ Ἱερὸν Μυστήριον τοῦ Εὐχελαίου* [The Holy Mystery of Unction] (Drama: Holy Metropolis of Drama, 2000), 27–101. This volume is significant as it includes scholarly articles on various aspects of the sacrament of unction (historical, theological, pastoral) by faculty of the School of Theology of the University of Thessaloniki. Fr. Victor Gorodenchuk is currently writing a dissertation under the direction of Fr. Dominic Serra at The Catholic University of America on the topic.

creativity in continuity at its fullest. The evolution of the Byzantine unction, literally the prayer of/over the oil, could be outlined in four phases.

Phase 1 represents the first attestation of unction in the earliest surviving Byzantine Euchologion, Barberini gr. 336 of the eighth century.[19] Here we find a total of six prayers: three for the sick, two over the oil for the anointing, and one for a "sick ascetic."[20] The presence of a diaconal litany associated with the blessing of the oil[21] alludes to some kind of ritual context, although unknown to us. The appropriate place and time for the celebration of this ritual is not mentioned, nor is there any direction regarding the number of priests involved; presumably one priest would celebrate this rite. The prayers ask for the "healing of body and soul," and their purpose is to restore the sick person to the worship life of the Church. As Stefano Parenti notes, "The anointing does not presuppose the sick person's reconciliation but rather obtains it, seeing that sin—even grave sin—is part of the spiritual sickness that must be treated."[22]

Phase 2 is characterized by the emergence of the sevenfold structure of the sacrament of unction indicated by the stipulation that seven priests celebrate the sacrament. While prayers are now multiplied, we do not yet have seven sets of epistle and gospel readings.

Paris Coislin gr. 213, dated to 1027, belonged to Strategios, a presbyter of Hagia Sophia in Constantinople[23] and thus reflects Constantinopolitan usage. According to this witness, seven presbyters would repeat on seven consecutive days the following: the preparation rites (*prothesis*) for the Divine Liturgy would include seven loaves of bread (*prosphora*), the oil would be blessed in turn by all seven priests, and then the Divine Liturgy would take place. Then, all seven priests would read the prayer and anoint not just the sick person but everyone in the household, including the house itself. After the anointing

[19] Stefano Parenti and Elena Velkovska, eds., *L'Eucologio Barberini gr. 336*, Bibliotheca Ephemerides Liturgicae. Subsidia 80, 2nd rev. ed. (Rome: C.L.V.-Edizioni Liturgiche, 2000).

[20] Ibid., 192–94.

[21] Ibid., 248.

[22] Parenti, "Care and Anointing of the Sick," 163.

[23] James Duncan, *Coislin 213: Euchologe de la Grande Église* (Rome: Pontificium Institutum Orientale, 1983). On how the redactor of this manuscript reworked material from Barberini gr. 336, see Stefano Parenti, "Towards a Regional History of the Byzantine Euchology of the Sacraments," *Ecclesia Orans* 27 (2010): 109–21, here 117–18.

was completed, a dismissal would take place in the house that included the reading of Luke 19:1-10,[24] and then they would proceed to the private chapel for the dismissal of the Divine Liturgy.[25] It is obvious that this could take place only at the residence of a wealthy person who would have a private chapel on his or her property and also could afford to invite seven priests to be there for seven consecutive days.

Constantinopolitan lectionaries of the eleventh century also attest to the very beginnings of the sevenfold structure as a Constantinopolitan feature. One such example is the eleventh-century gospel lectionary Benaki gr. 107 (TA316). At the end of the manuscript a list of readings for various occasions is provided. This section is headed by the following rubric, common among luxury gospel lectionaries from Constantinople,[26] which identifies the given readings with the liturgical practice of the cathedral of Hagia Sophia: "Gospels read on various commemorations and processions and liturgies and vigils that the Great Church celebrates" (f. 295r). Anointing of the sick is included in this list, identified by the following header, also common among luxury Constantinopolitan gospel lectionaries: "For the sick

[24] The choice of reading is interesting, as the host of this service is obviously quite wealthy.

[25] For a full outline, see Meyendorff, *The Anointing of the Sick*, 43–45; Skaltsis, «Ἱστορικὴ Ἐξέλιξις», 59–67. For the text, see Miguel Arranz, *L'eucologio costantinopolitano agli inizi del secolo XI* (Rome: Pontificia Università Gregoriana, 1996), 380–82. St. Petersburg gr. 226 of the tenth century, f. 121v–126r provides us with less information but confirms that seven priests are to take part, that the oil is prayed over before the Divine Liturgy, and that the sick person is anointed after the liturgy. Seven prayers are provided as alternate prayers, the first one being for a priest. According to Parenti these prayers are to be understood as formulas of anointing; Parenti, "Care and Anointing of the Sick," 163. Two South Italian manuscripts, Grottaferrata Γ.β.IV of the tenth century and Grottaferrata Γ.β. X of the tenth/eleventh century, witness a certain diversity between Constantinople and the periphery. In these cases, seven priests again take part, the blessing of the oil can take place either in the evening or in the morning, blessed in turn by each of the seven priests, the Divine Liturgy takes place with James 5:13-20 and John 4:46-54 as the readings. After the Divine Liturgy each priest prays the prayer over the oil again, and the sick person comes forward to be anointed. The manuscript provides three prayers for the blessing of the oil; see Parenti, "Care and Anointing of the Sick," 163–64.

[26] Characterized as "luxury" because of their high quality and decoration. On luxury gospels, see Kathleen Maxwell, "The Textual Affiliation of Deluxe Byzantine Gospel Books," in *The New Testament in Byzantium*, ed. Derek Krueger and Robert Nelson (Washington, DC: Dumbarton Oaks Research Library and Collection, 2016), 33–85.

and upon the oil of the sick of the seven presbyters" (f. 297v) and directing one to Mark 6:7-13 for the gospel reading (found on f. 295v).[27] While only one reading is indicated, significantly seven priests are mentioned. Alternate gospel readings in Constantinopolitan gospel lectionaries "for the sick" are Matthew 10:1-5, 8; Luke 9:1-6; and John 4:46-54. Matthew 8:14-23 (the healing of Peter's mother-in-law) is designated for ill women.[28] Constantinopolitan Praxapostolos lectionaries[29] of the eleventh century pair the one gospel reading of the anointing of the sick with James 5:10-16. Alternate readings for the sick are Romans 15:1-7 and Romans 6:18-23.[30]

Phase 3 represents an era of great diversity and ritual expansion in the celebration of the euchelaion (this is the first time this word appears) in the Byzantine tradition. A common characteristic is that its celebration is preceded by a vigil and followed by the celebration of the Divine Liturgy. Regarding the former, Parenti notes: "There are many possibilities for celebrating the vigil part of the service. Their structure reflects the contemporary superposition of the monastic Liturgy of the Hours on the cathedral Office as well as Middle Eastern influences on the Constantinopolitan tradition."[31]

The fullest expansion of the rite in this phase is represented by the twelfth-century Sinai gr. 973.[32] The euchelaion would be celebrated on seven consecutive days. On each day, seven presbyters would serve vespers, a vigil (*pannychis*), and matins together, and then each presbyter would celebrate the Divine Liturgy at a different church. They would then all come together and celebrate a very elaborate blessing of the oil, where each priest would in turn bless the oil with

[27] f. 295r: «Εὐαγγέλια ἀναγινωσκόμενα εἰς διαφόρους μνήμας καὶ λιτὰς καὶ λειτουργίας καὶ παννυχίδας ἃς ποιεῖ ἡ μεγάλη ἐκκλησία»; f. 297v: «Εἰς ἀσθενοῦντας καὶ ἐπὶ ἐλαίου ἀρρώστου τῶν ζ΄ πρεσβυτέρων». Heinzgerd Brakmann, "Literaturbericht: Der Gottesdienst der Östlichen Kirchen," *Archiv für Liturgiewissenschaft* 53 (2011): 138–270, here at 215. Many thanks to Tinatin Chronz for bringing these to our attention. The whole manuscript can be viewed at https://www.benaki.org/index.php?option=com_collections&view=writings&lang=el. See also Chronz, *Die Feier des Heiligen Öles*, 366–70.

[28] Ibid., 368–69.

[29] Samuel Gibson, *The Apostolos: The Acts and Epistles in Byzantine Liturgical Manuscripts*, Texts and Studies 18 (Piscataway: Gorgias Press, 2018).

[30] Chronz, *Die Feier des Heiligen Öles*, 367.

[31] Parenti, "Care and Anointing of the Sick," 165.

[32] For the full outline, see Meyendorff, *The Anointing of the Sick*, 46–51. For the Greek text, see Dmitrievsky, *Opisanie liturgicheskikh rykopisei*, vol. 2 (Kiev: Tip. Universiteta sv. Vladimira, 1895–1901; Petrograd: Tip. V. F. Kirshbauma, 1917), 101–9.

a prayer framed by Psalm 50, an antiphon, penitential hymns, and the lighting of his oil lamp. Then, the Eucharist would follow. Before the dismissal, again each priest would recite one prayer, framed by Psalm 50 and the putting out of his oil lamp. Finally, the sick person would be anointed, followed by all present. After the dismissal, the sick person would be taken home where the home itself was anointed and Luke 19:1-10 was read. The sick person was to prepare for the anointing by confessing his or her sins and washing, and he or she was not to wash for seven days after the anointing.

Such a complex ritual, and the requirement for a week-long celebration of daily Divine Liturgies, made the celebration of euchelaion in such a way impractical. The thirteenth century, marking the fourth phase, points to its consolidation. The connection with the Eucharist is eventually lost,[33] and the sevenfold structure is highlighted by the emergence of seven pairs of epistle and gospel readings, each pair coupled with a distinct prayer. It is possible that this sevenfold structure of epistle, gospel, prayer reflects the adjustment from celebrating the Divine Liturgy seven days in a row in the context of the euchelaion to the euchelaion being celebrated on only one day.[34]

The current rite has its roots in the thirteenth century and the reform of the euchelaion attributed to Patriarch Arsenios of Constantinople (1255–1260), who edited the prayers so that there are seven prayers of equal length.[35] By the fourteenth century a prayer of absolution was read at the end of the service while the gospel book was held open over the head of the sick person,[36] making the connection between unction and penance even more pronounced. The last of the Byzantine liturgical commentators, Symeon of Thessaloniki, who died in 1429, dedicates part of his liturgical commentary to the euchelaion.[37] The lack of priests in the last century of the Byzantine Empire and the ensuing Ottoman era allowed for the celebration of

[33] This was a gradual process rather than a rupture; manuscripts up to the sixteenth century still attest to the connection between the euchelaion and the celebration of the Divine Liturgy. See Skaltsis, «Ἱστορικὴ Ἐξέλιξις», 73–76.

[34] Miguel Arranz, "Le preghiere degli infermi nella tradizione bizantina, (I sacramenti della restaurazione dell'antico Eucologio costantinopolitano: II-5)," OCP 62 (1996): 295–351, here at 350.

[35] Skaltsis, «Ἱστορικὴ Ἐξέλιξις», 72.

[36] Parenti, "Care and Anointing of the Sick," 166.

[37] *Διάλογος*, PG 155:516B–536B. For a summary, see Skaltsis, «Ἱστορικὴ Ἐξέλιξις», 80–91.

the euchelaion by three, two, or, in necessity, one priest,[38] which is now the practice in most Orthodox churches.

While today the euchelaion is not celebrated in a eucharistic context, there remains a connection to the celebration of the Divine Liturgy. A bowl containing wheat flour is offered during the celebration of the sacrament, which holds up seven candles that are lit during the service, one for each gospel reading. At the conclusion of the service, the flour is made into a *prosphoron* (bread offering) that is brought to the church and is used for the Divine Liturgy. The sick person and the family, after the proper preparation including confession, receive the Eucharist.

The euchelaion as currently used has the following structure:

Part 1: Vigil with elements of matins

Part 2: The blessing of the oil

1. Litany
2. Prayer of blessing the oil
3. Hymns

Part 3: Anointing (repeated sevenfold)

1. Epistle and gospel reading
    a. James 5:10-16 and Luke 10:27-37
    b. Romans 15:1-7 and Luke 19:1-10
    c. 1 Corinthians 12:27–13:8 and Matthew 10:1, 5-8
    d. 2 Corinthians 6:16–7:1 and Matthew 8:14-23
    e. 2 Corinthians 1:8-11 and Matthew 25:1-13
    f. Galatians 5:22-6:2 and Matthew 15:21-28
    g. 1 Thessalonians 5:14-23 and Matthew 9:9-13
2. Fervent litany
3. Prayer (seven different prayers, one for each time)
4. Anointing prayer (same prayer repeated each time) and anointing (although in current practice, not recorded in the rubrics, there is only one anointing at the end of the service, when this prayer is said)

[38] Skaltsis, «Ἱστορικὴ Ἐξέλιξις», 80–81n165.

Part 4: Absolution

1. Open gospel book placed over the head of the sick person
2. Prayer of absolution

Part 5: Dismissal

At the heart of the modern celebration of the euchelaion remain two ancient prayers already attested to in Barberini gr. 336, the earliest Byzantine Euchologion. The first of the two is the prayer for the blessing of the oil (part 2.2):[39]

> O Lord, in your mercy and compassion, you heal the afflictions of our souls and bodies: sanctify now this oil, O Master, that it may bring healing to those who are anointed with it, relief from every passion, from every sickness of flesh and spirit, and from all evil; and so that your holy name may be glorified, of the Father, and of the Son, and of the Holy Spirit, now and ever, and unto ages of ages. Amen.[40]

In this prayer healing is defined as the relief from passions, sickness of flesh and spirit, and all evil, and the purpose of healing is to enable the sick person to once again glorify God. In other words, the human person is approached in a holistic way, as body, as soul, as spirit, whose destiny is to glorify God.

The second prayer that is also attested to in Barberini gr. 336[41] is the anointing prayer (part 3.4). It identifies God the Father as the "Physician of souls and bodies," a topos in healing prayers of Eastern Christianity. Christ is presented as the agent of healing and the deliverer from death. The prayer asks that the sick person not only be healed from the sickness of body and soul but also be "enlivened" with Christ's grace, in other words restored to the life of the church:

> O holy Father, Physician of souls and bodies, who sent your only-begotten Son, our Lord, Jesus Christ, who heals every infirmity and delivers from death: heal you servant (name) from the infirmities of body and soul which afflict him/her, and enliven him/her with the grace of your Christ; through the prayers of our most holy Lady, the Theotokos and ever-virgin Mary, through the intercessions . . . [list

[39] Parenti and Velkovska, *L'Eucologio Barberini gr. 336*, prayer 199.2 on 193.

[40] Translation from Meyendorff, *The Anointing of the Sick*, 130.

[41] Parenti and Velkovska, *L'Eucologio Barberini gr. 336*, prayer 196.2 on 192.

> of saints] . . . and of all the saints. For you are the fountain of healing, O our God, and to you we give glory, to the Father, and the Son, and the Holy Spirit, now and ever, and unto the ages of ages. Amen.[42]

In today's Orthodox world, the churches influenced by the Greek practice make frequent use of the euchelaion in a communal setting, such as on Holy Wednesday, and in private settings, both in cases of illness but also as spiritual preparation during Lenten periods (such as Great Lent, Christmas lent, Holy Apostle's fast, Dormition fast).[43] On the other hand, the celebration of euchelaion is not that frequent in churches following the Slavic practice, which continue to hold on to the stipulation that seven priests are to celebrate the sacrament. In addition, it is usually reserved for cases of severe illness, closer to the "extreme unction" of the Roman Catholic Church, an effect of Latin theological influence in Russian Christianity in and after the seventeenth century.[44]

### *5.1.4 Coptic and Ethiopian*

In the Coptic tradition today the unction for the sick is called *Ṣalāt al-Qandīl* (Prayer of the Lamp) or *Ṣalāt Masḥat al-Marḍah* (Prayer of the Anointing of the Sick).[45] It is characterized by a sevenfold structure comprised of seven liturgical units called "prayers," each organized around a set of readings and a prayer. Its public celebration takes place once a year on the Friday before Lazarus Saturday, between the morning offering of incense and the celebration of the Divine Liturgy; it presupposes confession, and all present are anointed.[46]

[42] Translation from Meyendorff, *The Anointing of the Sick*, 138–39.

[43] See Basilius (Bert) Groen, *Ter genezing van ziel en lichaam: De viering van het oliesel in de Greeks-Orthodoxe Kerk* (Kampen, Netherlands: J. H. Kok Publishing House, 1990); idem, "The Anointing of the Sick in the Greek Orthodox Church," in *Pastoral Care of the Sick*, ed. Mary Collins and David Power (London: SCM Press, 1991), 50–59; Meyendorff, *The Anointing of the Sick*, 56–59.

[44] Meyendorff, *The Anointing of the Sick*, 59–61.

[45] We owe these to Dr. Ramez Mikhail (private communication).

[46] For an outline of the service, see O. H. E. Khs-Burmester, *The Egyptian or Coptic Church: A Detailed Description of Her Liturgical Services and the Rites and Ceremonies Observed in the Administration of Her Sacraments* (Cairo: Publications de la Société d'Archéologie Copte, 1967), 144–51. For the full text in English, see Coptic Orthodox Diocese of Southern USA, "Coptic Reader."

This sevenfold structure is attested in the Coptic tradition as early as the fourteenth century. Yūḥanā ibn Sibā‘, an otherwise unknown author of the fourteenth century, makes clear reference to the sevenfold unction of the sick. He uses James 5:14-15 as the scriptural foundation of the sacrament. The service is made up of seven prayers, each of the prayers has its epistle reading from the letters of Paul, its psalm, and its gospel reading. It is celebrated by seven priests and gives witness to the practice of placing the gospel book over the head of the sick at the end of the service. He also notes that this service is performed for three categories of people: for the sick, those who seek forgiveness, and those who are in distress, imprisoned, or in debt.[47] Gabriel V, eighty-eighth pope of Alexandria, is a fifteenth-century witness to the same sevenfold structure of the anointing of the sick.[48] He provides a detailed outline of the first prayer, and then notes that the other six follow the same pattern. He makes a point to identify the unique prayers recited for each of the seven prayers (i.e., the seven liturgical units that comprise the rite). He also attests the placing of the gospel book over the sick person's head at the end of the service.[49]

The current rite reflects the same schema. Each of the seven prayers (the seven liturgical units that comprise the rite) share the same structure. The first prayer has incorporated in its beginning the opening elements of the rite, including the blessing of the oil, and the seventh prayer includes additional prayers, the anointing, and the dismissal. These can be seen in the following schema:

[47] Vincentio Mistrih, *Yūḥannā ibn Abī Zakarīā: Pretiosa Margarita de Scientiis Ecclesiasticis* (Cairo: Edizioni del Centro Francescano di Studi Orientali Cristiani, 1966), 585–86 (Latin translation). We are grateful to Ramez Mikhail for bringing this text to our attention and making it available to us and for checking the Arabic text for us.

[48] Alfonso Abdallah, *L'ordinamento liturgico di Gabriele V* (Cairo: Edizioni del Centro Francescano di Studi Orientali Cristiani, 1962), 345–47. We would like to thank Ramez Mikhail for making this text available to us.

[49] Abdallah, *L'ordinamento liturgico di Gabriele V*, 345–46. Ernst Suttner, "Die Krankensalbung (das 'Öl des Gebetes') in den altorientalischen Kirchen," *Ephemerides Liturgicae* 89 (1975): 371–96, here at 372.

## The Structure of the Prayers in the Coptic Prayer of the Lamp

| First Prayer | Second–Sixth Prayers | Seventh Prayer |
|---|---|---|
| Lighting of the lamp | Lighting of the lamp | Lighting of the lamp |
| Introductory elements | | |
| Prayer of thanksgiving | | |
| Prayer of incense | | |
| Psalm 50 | | |
| Intercessory prayer for (1) the sick | Intercessory prayer (2) for the travelers; (3) for the waters; (4) for the civil authorities; (5) for the departed; (6) for the offerings | Intercessory prayer for (7) the catechumens |
| Litany | | |
| Prayer for the blessing of the oil | | |
| Readings | Readings | Readings |
| (1) Jas 5:10-20 and Jn 5:1-17 | (2) Rom 15:1-7 and Luke 19:1-10<br>(3) 1 Cor 12:28–13:8 and Matt 10:1-8<br>(4) Rom 8:14-21 and Luke 10:1-9<br>(5) Gal 2:16-10 and John 14:1-19<br>(6) Col 3:12-17 and Luke 7:36-50 | (7) Eph 6:10-18 and Matt 6:14-18 |
| The three great prayers (intercessory) and their litanies for peace, for the patriarch, and for the assemblies | | Prayers<br>"Again we ask you, Lord of Hosts . . ."<br>"O Lord, the merciful and manifold in mercy . . ."<br>"O God . . . the physician of our bodies and souls . . ." |
| | | Anointing of the sick person |
| | | Doxology |
| | | Lord's Prayer |
| Creed | | Creed |
| Prayer 1 | Prayers 2–6 | Prayer 7 of absolution |
| | | People present anointed |

A number of prayers in the Coptic rite of unction correspond with prayers from the Byzantine euchelaion. In his presentation of the Coptic rite of unction, O. H. E. Khs-Burmester identifies these prayers.[50] Of these common prayers, two are highlighted here. First, the prayer for the blessing of the oil:

> O Lord the Merciful, the Healer of affliction of our souls and bodies, sanctify this oil that it may become a means of healing to all those who are anointed therewith from the pollutions of the soul and the sufferings of the body, that in this also Your name may be glorified. For to you belongs glory and salvation; and to You we offer up glory, O Father, Son and Holy Spirit, now and forever and unto the ages of all ages. Amen.[51]

In the Coptic tradition, this prayer is to be read inaudibly by the priest.

The second prayer is prayed right before the anointing of the sick person:

> O God, the good Father, the Physician of our bodies and our souls; who sent Your only-begotten Son Jesus Christ to heal all sickness, and to save from death. Heal Your servant (. . .) from his bodily sickness; and give unto him renewed life, that he may glorify Your greatness and that he may give thanks for Your graciousness, that he may fulfill Your will through the grace of Your Christ, and the intercessions of the Theotokos, and the prayers of the Your saints. For You are the Fount of healing; and to You we offer up glory and honour together with Your only-begotten Son and the Holy Spirit. Now and ever and to the ages of all ages. Amen.[52]

The Byzantine text includes a longer list of saints in the intercessions, not just the Theotokos and general invocation of all the saints appearing here.

[50] Khs-Burmester, *The Egyptian or Coptic Church*, 145–51. Only the fifth and sixth prayers (liturgical units) do not have prayers that are in common with the Byzantine rite.

[51] Coptic Orthodox Diocese of Southern USA, "Coptic Reader." To compare with the prayer in the euchelaion, see section 5.1.4.

[52] For the prayer in the Byzantine *Euchelaion*, see Meyendorff, *The Anointing of the Sick*, 138–39.

As in all the other Eastern liturgical traditions, the emphasis in the Coptic prayer of the lamp is not just the healing from sickness but a holistic recovery of the human person, which necessarily includes the forgiveness of sins and the renewed commitment to a Christian life. The prayer of the first prayer (structural unit) blends these two themes. What is unique in this prayer is that the possibility of death is clearly mentioned with the petition that the sick person may be taken to paradise (that portion of prayer is indicated by *italics*):

> Master, Lord Jesus Christ, King of the ages, who brought all things into existence out of nothing, both the visible and the invisible. Who came of His own will and His great mercy according to the economy, to save us from the death of sin and the victories of the adversary; You, Doer of good with alacrity, longsuffering, who show much care for the good; remember, O Lord, Your mercies, and turn not away Your gracious countenance from us, who have been called by Your Goodness; but give ear to our prayer and to the poor supplication of us, Your sinful servants, and give healing to Your servant (. . .) who has fled under the shadow of Your wings, for You are the lover of Mankind, and forgive him those things which are against him, which he has committed during all his life; and forgive him his transgressions which he has committed willingly or unwillingly, whether of his own motion, or that of any other; whether in thought or in deed against Your good pleasure. As You have forgiven, O Master, the debtor of the talents which he owed You, forgive this, Your servant the things which are against him and pardon him all his transgressions. And as you cleansed the leper by Your word, and took away the leprosy from his body according to Your will; so again take away the sickness from the body of this Your servant (. . .) and sanctify him. You who healed the daughter of the woman from Canaan at once at her mother's prayer, so again at the prayers of Your priests, even us who do not presume the confidence in ourselves, but in Your grace towards us, deliver this Your servant from all assaults and all the works of the devil. You raised up the son of the widow, and the daughter of the ruler from death; and commanded them to rise up; and raised up Lazarus after he had been dead four days from Hades by the authority of Your Godhead; raise up this Your servant from the death of sin, and if You bid him to rise again, give unto him help and assistance that he may please You in his living all the days of his life. *And if you bid his soul be taken, grant that by the hands of angels of light he may have power that will save him from the demons of darkness. Translate him into the paradise of joy, that he may*

*be with all the saints;* through Your blood which was shed for our salvation, and with which you purchased us; for You are the hope of Your servants. Through the intercessions of the Virgin the Theotokos, and the prayers of all the saints; for glory and honour and worship are due to the Father and the Son and the Holy Spirit, now and ever, and unto the age of all ages. Amen.[53]

This extensive and beautiful prayer is built around two petitions, that Christ may heal and forgive, grounded on salvation history as the justification of these two petitions. Together with displaying confidence in Christ's all-encompassing love, the anamnetic sections of this prayer, interspersed with petitions ("as you did . . . do now") make references to a number of events in the life of Christ that deal with both forgiveness and healing, and one notes here a progression from forgiveness, such as the debtor of the talents (Matt 25:14-30); to healing of illnesses that are not immediately life-threatening, such as the leper (Matt 8:1-4; Mark 1:40-45; Luke 5:12-16); to releasing from the demons, such as the daughter of the woman from Canaan (Matt 15:21-28); to raising from the dead, such as the son of the widow of Nain (Luke 7:11-17), the daughter of the ruler (Jairus; Matt 9:18-26; Mark 5:21-43; Luke 8:40-56), and Lazarus (John 11:1-44). The prayer acknowledges the real possibility of death and includes a petition asking that, if that is the case, the person be led to paradise. Possibly as a pastoral sensitivity to the family of the sick person so as to give them hope for healing, the rubrics indicate that this portion of the prayer (in *italics* above) is read silently by the priest.

The Ethiopian liturgical tradition apparently did not know of the sacrament of the anointing of the sick prior to the fifteenth century.[54] Apparently, and in order to root out magical practices related to healing, but also to enable the penance of sick people, Emperor Zär᾽a Ja῾eqob (1434–1468), composed a rite of unction for the sick sometime between 1441 and 1443 that was titled *Mäṣḥafä baḥrəy* (Book of Essence).[55] The rite is quite simple in structure. After the recitation

[53] Coptic Orthodox Diocese of Southern USA, "Coptic Reader."

[54] Ugo Zanetti, "Unction of the Sick," in *Encyclopaedia Aethiopica*, vol. 4 (Wiesbaden: Harrassowitz Verlag, 2010), 1020–21.

[55] Getatchew Haile, "Baḥrəy: Mäṣḥafä baḥrəy," in *Encyclopaedia Aethiopica*, vol. 1 (Wiesbaden: Harrassowitz Verlag, 2003), 446–47; Zanetti, "Unction of the Sick," 1020;

of the creed, a series of scriptural readings follow: Genesis 1:1-2; Matthew 6:7-13; Mark 6:12-13; Mark 16:12-20; Luke 1:46-55; John 1:1-5; and James 5:10-20. Then two prayers for the blessing of the oil are recited, followed by an absolution. This rite is to take place in a domestic setting and confession is to precede, hence the absolution at the end of the rite.[56]

A century later, this rite was replaced by *Mäṣḥafä qändil* (Book of the Lamp). It is a ritual imported from the Coptic tradition, translated into Geʿez in the sixteenth century, and adopted by Ethiopian liturgical usage with small changes.[57] It is almost identical to the Coptic parent version both in structure and in content, with some small differences. One such difference is the presence of a long prayer full of scriptural allusions that is not found in the Coptic version.[58]

### *5.1.5 West Syrian*

Anointing of the sick with oil is attested in the West Syriac tradition already by the sixth century. It is associated with both healing and the forgiveness of sins and is sometimes identified with the baptismal oil of the catechumens.[59] The West Syriac rite of anointing of the sick is known as the Rite of the *Qandilo*.[60] Unique to this tradition is that the rite is made up of a fivefold structure (five services), each

---

Suttner, "Die Krankensalbung," 377–78; Anaïs Wion, "Onction des malades, funérailles et commémorations: pour une histoire des textes et des pratiques liturgiques en Éthiopie chrétienne," *Afriques* 3 (2011), URL: http://journals.openedition.org/afriques/921; DOI : https://doi.org/10.4000/afriques.921. For the text and Latin translation, see Marius Chaîne, "Le rituel éthiopien – Rituel de l'extrême-onction," *Bessarione* 29 (1913): 420–51; 30 (1914): 12–41, 213–31, here at 30 (1914), 213–31.

[56] Wion, "Onction des malades, funérailles et commemorations"; Haile, "Baḥrəy: Mäṣḥafä baḥrəy," 447; Chaîne, "Le rituel éthiopien – Rituel de l'extrême-onction," 30 (1914): 224–31.

[57] Ugo Zanetti, "Qändil. Mäṣḥafä qändil," in *Encyclopaedia Aethiopica*, 4:259–60. For the text and a Latin translation, see Chaîne, "Le rituel éthiopien – Rituel de l'extrême-onction," 29 (1913): 420–51; 30 (1914): 12–41.

[58] Zanetti, "Qändil," 260.

[59] For the evidence, see Wilhelm de Vries, *Sakramententheologie bei den Syrischen Monophysiten*, OCA 125 (Rome: Pontificium Institutum Orientalium Studiorum, 1940), 211–17; Suttner, "Die Krankensalbung," 380–91.

[60] For an ET of the rite, see https://dss-syriacpatriarchate.org/church-rites/anointing-of-the-sick-qandilo/the-service-of-qandilo/?lang=en. All references and texts of the Rite of the *Qandilo* are quoted from here.

## Structure of the Rite of the *Qandilo*

| First Service | Second Service | Third Service | Fourth Service | Fifth Service |
|---|---|---|---|---|
| Opening Prayer | Opening Prayer | Opening Prayer | Opening Prayer | Opening Prayer |
| Psalm 50 | | | | |
| *Proemion* (Preface) | *Proemion* | *Proemion* | *Proemion* | *Proemion* |
| *Sedro* (Prayer) | *Sedro* | *Sedro* | *Sedro* | *Sedro* |
| *'Etro* (Prayer of Incense) | *'Etro* | *'Etro* | *'Etro* | *'Etro* |
| Rom 15:1-7 | Jas 5:10-20 | 1 Cor 6:1-5 | Rom 13:11-14 | Eph 6:10-20 |
| Luke 18:35-43 | Luke 10:25-37 | Matt 9:36–10:4 | Matt 15:21-31 | Matt 9:18-26 |
| Litany | Litany | Litany | Litany | Litany |
| | | | | Anointing of the sick person |
| Concluding prayer | Concluding prayer | Concluding prayer | Concluding prayer | Concluding prayer |
| | | | | Anointing of everyone present |

structurally identical and complete.[61] Dough is placed in a dish and immersed in oil, as in the Maronite tradition. Five wicks in the form of the cross are placed in the oil. The rubrics explain the fivefold structure as a reference (1) to the five wise virgins of the parable of the ten virgins (Matt 25:1-13) and (2) to the five senses, which will be anointed at the end of the rite. Interestingly, the gospel reading of the parable of the ten virgins is not one of the five gospel readings of the Rite of the *Qandilo* but is the one gospel reading of the shorter version examined above. While the rubrics indicate that priests in plural celebrate the rite, their number is not specified. The structure of the five liturgical units, called "services," are identical, with the following exceptions: Psalm 50 is recited in the first service, and the anointing takes place in the fifth service.

The possible connection of the oil of the sick with the prebaptismal oil of gladness is confirmed by the content of the *'Etro* of the first service, which is almost identical to the prayer of blessing the prebaptismal oil (the oil of gladness) in the Byzantine Rite (common texts are *italic* in the table below).

The relationship between the two prayers is rather obvious, both structurally and content-wise; they are the same prayer. The *'Etro* prayer, while technically a prayer of incense, is really a prayer over the oil; it seems like the offering of the incense in the first line is there just to make it fit the genre of the *'Etro* prayers.

Possibly because of their common Antiochene roots, the Rite of the *Qandilo* and the Byzantine Rite have additional common elements. The second service of the Rite of the *Qandilo* shares with the Byzantine euchelaion the blessing of the oil for the anointing of the sick:

> Lord God, who by your abundant mercies heal the infirmity of the souls and bodies, bless this oil, that it may become for those who are anointed with it healing and redemption from all evil passions and sickness, and defilements of the soul and body, and deliverance from every evil. May Your most holy name be glorified.[62]

[61] Suttner, "Die Krankensalbung," 381.

[62] To compare with the prayer in the euchelaion, see section 5.1.3.

## A Comparison between the *'Etro* Prayer of the First Service and the Oil of Gladness Prayer in the Byzantine Rite

| ***'Etro* of the First Service** | **Oil of Gladness Prayer—Byzantine Rite** |
|---|---|
| Receive this incense from our hands, O Lord God, | Sovereign Lord and Master, God of our Fathers, |
| and sanctify this oil and make it a sign of your ineffable grace, | |
| so that it may become for all those who are anointed with it, healing of the soul and the body and for the redemption from "the deluge of sin," *as it happened for those who were in the ark of Noah the Just, who sent a dove, which returned with an olive leaf in its beak, as the promise of reconciliation and perfect redemption from the deluge and the sign of grace.* You who bring forth the fruits of Olive for the perfection of your divine and holy mysteries, | *Who did send to them in the Ark of Noah a dove bearing a twig of olive in its beak as a sign of reconciliation and salvation from the Flood, and through these things prefigured the Mystery of Grace;* and thereby have filled them that were under the Law with the Holy Spirit, and perfected them that are under Grace: do You Yourself |
| *bless this oil by the power and the overshadowing of your Holy Spirit, that it may become incorruptible grace, sign of victory, renewal of the soul and the body, deliverance from every demonic operation and protection from evil for those who are anointed with it in faith, or receive from it,* | *bless this Oil by the power and operation and descent of the Holy Spirit that it may become an anointing of incorruption, a shield of righteousness, a renewal of soul and body, and averting of every operation of the devil, to the removal of all evils from them that are anointed with it in faith, or that are partakers of it.* |
| Father, Son, and the Holy Spirit, now and always forever and ever. | To Your Glory, and to that of Your only-begotten Son, and of Your All-holy, Good, and Life-creating Spirit, both now and ever, and to the ages of ages.[63] |

[63] The ET is from https://www.goarch.org/-/the-service-of-holy-baptism.

In addition, the pair of readings in the second service of the Rite of the *Qandilo* (Jas 5:10-20 and Luke 10:25-37) is identical with the first pair of readings from the euchelaion. We noted above how in the euchelaion this prayer of blessing the oil and this set of readings comprise the oldest stratum of the service. The presence of the same prayer for the blessing of the oil and the set of readings together in the second service of the Rite of the *Qandilo* may point to a common early liturgical unit. There are more common elements: the concluding prayer of the first service is similar to the second part of the second prayer in the euchelaion,[64] the concluding prayer of the third service and the third prayer of the euchelaion share the same opening,[65] and in both rites the gospel is placed over the head of the sick person while the prayer of forgiveness is read.[66]

While references to healing are present throughout the Rite of the *Qandilo,* the emphasis is on the forgiveness of sins; it is clearly a penitential rite. In the concluding prayer of the second service we read:

> Our Lord, God and savior Jesus Christ, by your abundant mercies, you have healed our pains and infirmities of the souls and the bodies. Stretch forth your mighty right hand and bless this oil and those who are anointed with it. Heal this your servant from all illness and infirmities of the soul and the body. Forgive all his faults and offences by word, deed or thought and purify him from all sinful defilements and iniquities. Deliver him all the days of his life from all incidents that are harmful and causing temptations. Make him one who obeys your commandments and fulfills your laws. Do not leave him that his enemies may rejoice over him. By your grace heal all those who are anointed with this oil. May we all find your compassion on the great day of your coming, by your grace and mercies, now and forever and ever. Amen.

The healing of body and soul is presented in this prayer as the first of a number of steps that lead to a life aligned with the Gospel. The epicletic verbs used in this prayer present the sequence of every step—"heal . . . forgive . . . deliver . . . make him one who obeys . . . do not leave him"—and the prayer ends with a strong eschato-

[64] For the text, see Meyendorff, *The Anointing of the Sick*, 143.

[65] For the text, see ibid., 148.

[66] In the Rite of the *Qandilo* this is the concluding prayer of the fifth service, after the anointing of the sick person has taken place. For the *Euchelaion*, see Meyendorff, *The Anointing of the Sick*, 170.

logical outlook. The concluding prayer of the fourth service presents a similar sequence that begins with the plea for forgiveness and ends with a petition of eschatological communion with the saints: "*Absolve*, O Lord, their debts and *forgive* their sins. . . . *Purify* them from all defilements of the soul and the body. *Sanctify* them by the power of your Holy Spirit. *Enlighten* their minds with the splendor of your divine knowledge. *Make them worthy* of the delights of your kingdom with all your saints."

The emphasis on the forgiveness is also highlighted in the formula that is used for the anointing that lacks any reference to physical healing: "May you be purified and sanctified, and may your debts and sins that you have committed voluntarily or involuntarily, with knowledge or without knowledge be forgiven, and may all evil thoughts and satanic acts be blotted out from you, in the name of the Father and of the Son and of the Holy Spirit for eternal life."

Finally, there is also a shorter version of the anointing of the sick in use that is apparently a more recent redaction, as, according to Wilhelm de Vries, it does not appear in the manuscript tradition.[67] Its structure is simple, with an opening prayer, followed by a long penitential prayer that highlights the themes of forgiveness and vigilance. In the context of the latter and as an example to be avoided, the prayer makes reference to the five foolish virgins from the parable of the ten virgins, linking this prayer with the gospel reading. The prayer is followed by the readings, James 5:7-20 and Matthew 25:1-13 (the parable of the ten virgins). Then another penitential prayer is read, followed by the anointing of the five senses plus the feet with variations in the opening of the following formula: "May the Lord God have mercy on you, and through his great mercy forgive you everything that you have sinned against."[68]

### 5.1.6 *Maronite*

The history of the Maronite anointing of the sick is defined by a process of intense Latinization between the sixteenth and nineteenth centuries and an effort to reclaim its Syriac heritage in the twentieth

[67] de Vries, *Sakramententheologie bei den Syrischen Monophysiten*, 217; Suttner, "Die Krankensalbung," 381–82.

[68] https://dss-syriacpatriarchate.org/church-rites/anointing-of-the-sick-qandilo/?lang=en.

century.[69] The Synod of Mount Lebanon in 1736 led to the full adoption of the Latin rite of extreme unction for the anointing of the sick, with the oil blessed by a bishop on Holy Thursday; a modified form of the Rite of the Lamp, understood as nonsacramental, was limited to an annual celebration on Holy Wednesday.[70] The current rite is based on the 1942 ritual and reflects the effort of the Maronite Church to balance this long process of Latinization with a return to its own traditions as reflected in the manuscript tradition.[71]

According to the 2001 American edition and translation of the ritual,[72] the Rite of the Lamp (*qindil*)[73] takes place on Holy Wednesday evening. According to the rubrics accompanying the rite, a bowl containing a ball of dough immersed in oil, as in the West Syriac tradition, is placed on a table. Seven wicks are placed in the dough, which are lit during the service.[74] The service begins with the (1) preparatory rites, which include a doxology, an opening prayer, Psalm 50 (51), a prayer of forgiveness, and a hymn.[75] (2) The readings follow, James 5:13-18 and Luke 10:25-37.[76] Then (3) the litanies and the lighting of the seven wicks ensue. This is a liturgical unit repeated seven times, reflecting the presence of the sevenfold structure in the sacrament of unction in the Maronite tradition. Each liturgical unit, repeated seven times, has the following structure:[77]

[69] For a summary, see Claude Franklin, "Oil of Gladness: The Historical Origins of the Maronite Rite of Lamp," Licentiate Thesis (Rome: Pontificium Institutum Orientalium Studiorum, 2005), 61–102. I would like to thank Fr. Claude for making his thesis available to us.

[70] Franklin, "Oil of Gladness," 5–9, 65–68.

[71] Ibid., 76–100, where the manuscripts used are identified. The tables are very useful in identifying how the manuscript tradition was used in the compilation of the 1942 ritual.

[72] *The Passion Week According to the Antiochene Syriac Maronite Church* (Brooklyn, NY: St. Maron Publications, 2001), 2:43–90. A new translation is in preparation.

[73] For the history of the Rite of Lamp in the Maronite tradition, see Ziad Sacre, "Le rite de la lampe et l'onction des malades dans l'église maronite: Traduction et étude historique, liturgique et théologico-spirituelle" (diss., Sorbonne University-Paris IV, 1996). Unfortunately, we were not able to consult this work.

[74] *The Passion Week According to the Antiochene Syriac Maronite Church*, 45.

[75] Ibid., 45–55.

[76] Ibid., 55–63.

[77] Ibid., 63–81.

1. Litany by the deacon
2. The lighting of one wick
3. Hymn (*Qolo*)

After the completion of the seventh unit, (4) the blessing of the oil takes place with the following prayer:

> O Lord God, in the abundance of your mercy, you cure the infirmity of our soul and body. Bless this oil. For those who are anointed with it, may it be a cure and a salvation from all sufferings, ill and malice; may your holy name be glorified through it. You are our all-merciful and compassionate Savior, our Lord and God, Jesus Christ. To you, to your Father and to your Holy Spirit be glory and thanksgiving, for ever.[78]

This prayer is identical to the Byzantine prayer of blessing the oil[79] and is followed by the hymn: "We praise you; we bless you; we adore you; we acknowledge and ask you: have mercy on us, O Lord, and hear us." Then (5) an epicletic prayer is offered, asking for the Holy Spirit to come upon the oil:

> May your Holy and living Spirit, O Lord, come and bless this oil. May your divinity abide in it, so it may become, in the Holy Spirit, the oil of joy—a regenerating oil, a consecrated oil, an angelic shield against the power of the adversary. May it become a joy and eternal happiness to those who believe in it, so that it may protect those who are anointed by it. Because it is for them the oil of a new life, may they shine like heavenly stars, in purity and holiness, on the day in which the Just will radiate like the sun in the Kingdom of their Father. With them and among them, we will offer glory to you, for ever.[80]

This prayer has similarities in content to the second part of prayer one in the Byzantine tradition[81] and contains baptismal echoes. The

[78] Ibid., 81–82.

[79] See above section 5.1.3.

[80] *The Passion Week According to the Antiochene Syriac Maronite Church*, 83.

[81] See Meyendorff, *The Anointing of the Sick*, 138: "Let this oil, Lord, become the oil of gladness, the oil of sanctification, a royal robe, an armor of might, the averting of every work of the devil, an unassailable seal, the joy of heart, and eternal rejoicing. Grant that those who are anointed with the oil of regeneration may be fearsome to

fact that it is preceded by the hymn "We praise you" quoted above reflects the celebration of the Divine Liturgy, where this same hymn always precedes the eucharistic epiclesis.[82] These elements definitely place the Rite of the Lamp with the core of the sacramental life of the church, being a link between baptism and the Eucharist. The (6) anointing then takes place with the formula "For the forgiveness of your sins and faults and for the healing of your body and soul" while a penitential hymn is sung,[83] followed (7) by a christological *Trisagion* ("Holy are you, O God; Holy are you, O Strong One; Holy are you, O Immortal One. O Christ, who was crucified for us, have mercy on us"), the Lord's Prayer, and a concluding prayer.[84]

The Rite of the Lamp has very clear penitential overtones; one could say the emphasis is on spiritual healing and the forgiveness of sins. For example, in the hymn of the first of seven liturgical units of litanies and the lighting of the wicks (3.3 above), we are offered a link to baptismal anointing by an embedded theological commentary regarding the parts of the body that were historically anointed, although today only the forehead is anointed:

> O good Shepherd, you came to seek the lost sheep. Call us now, O Lord, that we may be sheep of your flock. O good One, you open the door to the sinners. Open to us the door of your mercy, that we may come to you.
>
> With the sign of your cross, mark, Lord, all the members of our body and protect them from all harm. Do not let evil and his inclinations dominate at will: our eyes, that they may look to you with a pure look; our ears, that they may be inclined to listen to your word; our lips, that they may sing the glory of your name; our breath, that it may breathe the fragrance of eternal life; our hands, that they may keep knocking at your door; and our feet, that they may walk on the path leading to the temple of your divinity. Our soul then, Lord, will be able, with our five senses, to raise glory to your Holiness. From the treasury of your

their adversaries, and that they may shine with the radiance of your saints, having neither stain nor defect, and that they may attain your everlasting rest and receive the prize of their high calling."

[82] *Qurbono: The Book of Offering: The Service of the Holy Mysteries According to the Antiochene Syriac Maronite Church; Season of the Glorious Birth of the Lord* (Brooklyn, NY: St. Maron Publications, 1993), 127 (Anaphora of the Twelve Apostles), 147 (Anaphora of James), 175 (Anaphora of St. Mark).

[83] Ibid., 85–87.

[84] Ibid., 87–89.

kindness, grant pardon to all the sins we committed with the senses of our body and soul. Amen.[85]

Very clearly the emphasis here is on restoring the health of one's spiritual life so that a person may continue to offer glory to God. This hymn presents Christian life as a journey toward God and the anointing of the five senses as protection against evil, a reminder of one's calling, an encouragement in one's life struggles, and trust in God's love. This latter point is made even more clear in the hymn of the second liturgical unit of litanies (3.3 above) where the Christian asks: "Take me under your winds, that evil may not harm me."[86] The hymn of the fifth liturgical unit of litanies is even more penitential: "Grant us, now, mercy and compassion and pardon our sins. Make us worthy to take refuge in the contrition of heart."[87] The few instances where bodily health is mentioned is in the petitions, but always in the context of spiritual healing and health. For example, we read in the petitions of the first liturgical unit of litanies: "For the medicine that we receive and the healing of our soul and body, let us pray to the Lord."[88] Or among the petitions of the second liturgical unit of litanies: "For the perfect health of our soul and body, let us pray to the Lord."[89] The following petition of the seventh liturgical unit of litanies, "For this oil, that it may be consecrated and for our sins and faults, that they may be forgiven, let us pray to the Lord,"[90] summarizes the penitential aspect of the anointing of the sick in the Maronite liturgical tradition.

Two traditions that stand apart are the Armenian and the East Syriac traditions. In both, the anointing of the sick with blessed oil is attested historically but has fallen out of use. And in both traditions the use of oil has been replaced by another material medium to signify healing: blessed water in the Armenian tradition, *ḥnānā*[91] in the East Syriac tradition.

[85] Ibid., 65–66.

[86] Ibid., 69.

[87] Ibid., 75.

[88] Ibid., 63.

[89] Ibid., 67.

[90] Ibid., 79.

[91] A uniquely East Syrian practice, *ḥnānā* is dust from a martyr's grave mixed with water and oil and then dried; see section 5.1.8. It is also used in the marriage ritual; see section 4.1.6.

### *5.1.7 Armenian*

The earliest theological articulation regarding unction comes from a sixth-century Armenian *Scholium* on a Greek commentary on the Epistle of James 5:14-15.[92] It calls for the elders to pray over the sick person; it connects sin with illness and makes the confession of sins a necessary part of the healing process that leads to the anointing with oil. It then explains the necessity of the anointing with oil as something sensible that points to the spiritual reality, drawing a parallel between unction of the sick, baptism, and the Eucharist:

> But if the power of prayer works this (cure), why do those who are cured need an anointing with oil? It is evident that in our being composed of two parts, anything palpable is, therefore, intermediary of the spiritual welfare for our complex nature: thus, water and Spirit, bread and God. You will understand, in the same way, the fact of being anointed with some oil. For it impresses the grace of cure for the body.[93]

From this *Scholium*, the following ritual schema emerges:

1. Elders (in plural) gather
2. Prayer recited over the sick person
3. Confession of sins
4. Anointing with oil

While the use of unction for the sick is attested in the Armenian tradition,[94] its practice declined after the fifteenth century. While anointing the sick with oil is not practiced today, prayers of healing accompanied with the blessing of water has replaced the oil of the sick. The outline of this service is as follows:[95]

1. Introduction
2. Psalm 6

[92] Edward Kilmartin, "The Interpretation of James 5:14-15 in the Armenian Catena on the Catholic Epistles: Scholium 82," in OCP 53 (1987): 335–64.

[93] For an ET of the Scholium, see ibid., 341.

[94] See the nonliturgical sources listed in ibid., 363–64.

[95] Diocese of the Armenian Church of America (Eastern), *Prayers for Healing* (n.p.: St. Vartan Press, n.d.).

3. Prayer
4. *Trisagion*
5. Hymn
6. Prayer 41 of St. Gregory of Narek
7. Readings:
   a. 2 Kings 2:19-22
   b. James 5:13-16
   c. John 7:37-39
8. Diaconal proclamation and priestly prayer + blessing
9. Diaconal proclamation and priestly prayer
10. Conclusion
11. Reception of holy water

Psalm 6 recited by the deacon and the faithful at the beginning of the service sets the tone, a balance between acknowledging one's sins but also expressing one's confidence in God's deliverance. The prayer that follows (no. 3 above) reiterates this same theme: "O great God, worker of miracles, you keep your promises and grant mercy and forgiveness of sins to those you love through your holy Son Jesus Christ, who renewed us from the mortality of our sins . . . look upon your servants, so that redeemed from sin, they may be made right with you and may be clothed in our Lord Jesus Christ."[96] The beautiful prayer of St. Gregory of Narek (no. 6 above) affirms in a poetic way Christ's transformative power under which the faithful place themselves:

> Son of the living God, blessed in all things, unfathomable offspring of the awesome Father, for whom nothing is impossible—when the radiant light of your merciful glory dawns, sin melts away. Demons are driven out. Wrongs are erased. Handcuffs are snapped. Chains are severed. The dead return to life. Injuries are treated. Wounds are healed. Diseases are cured. Sadness leaves. Sighs are cut short. Misery flees. The fog lifts. The haze recedes. Gloom dissipates. Obscurity

[96] Ibid., 7–8.

> wears out. Darkness vanishes. Night departs. Anguish is ejected. Evil deeds are annihilated. Depression is banished. And your all-powerful hand reigns, O Redeemer of all. You did not come to kill human spirits, but to breathe life into them. Forgive my countless misdeeds in your bountiful mercy. For you alone are beyond words in heaven, and beyond contemplation on earth, existing in matter and to the extreme ends of the world. The Beginning of everything, and within everything. Utterly blessed are you in the heights, and to you with the Father and the Holy Spirit glory forever. Amen.[97]

The petition for forgiveness of sins in this prayer is placed in the context of the total psychosomatic healing that Christ's reign brings forth, rooted in the saving event of the incarnation, and displays a total trust in Christ's restorative power.

The blessing and use of water instead of oil possibly influenced the choice of 2 Kings 2:19-22 and John 7:37-39 as two of the three readings, while James 5:13-16 connects the current practice with the older blessing of oil and anointing. The readings are followed by a series of diaconal proclamations and prayers that echo the "double prayer" structure of the Armenian rite[98] without, however, the presence of the giving of the peace and the diaconal invitation to bow the heads between the two prayers.

After the anamnesis section, the consecratory prayer moves to the epiclesis of the Holy Spirit upon the water with a threefold invocation of the power of the holy cross, each accompanied by a petition, followed by a triple blessing of the waters and concluding with the petition for health (numbering added):

> [Epiclesis] And now, good Lord, send the grace of the Holy Spirit on this water and bless it with your invisible right arm, [1] and by the power of your all-conquering Cross. [1a] Give it the grace to heal the infirmities and relieve the pains of all who drink it. [2] Lord, bless this water by the power of your holy Cross [2a] so that those who drink it may be free of pain. [3] Lord, bless this water by the sign of this holy

[97] Armenian Church of America (Eastern), *Prayers for Healing*, 13–15. See also St. Grigor Narekatsi, *Speaking with God from the Depths of the Heart: The Armenian Prayer Book of St. Gregory of Narek* (Yerevan, 2016), 187–88.

[98] Michael Daniel Findikyan, "'Double Prayers' and Inclinations in the Liturgy of the Armenian Church: The Preservation and Proliferation of an Ancient Liturgical Usage," *St. Nersess Theological Review* 8 (2004): 117–18.

> Cross [3a] so that by this priest and the prayers of these people, wherever it is sprinkled may be even more fruitful for humanity's gain. . . .
>
> [Blessing] May this water be blessed and sanctified by the sign of this holy Cross, and by this holy Gospel and by the grace of this day. . . . (x3)
>
> [Petition] Dispel the pain and heal the sickness of Your people, Lord our God, and grant to all perfect health by the sign of Your all-conquering Cross through which You removed the weakness of mankind and condemned the enemy of our life and salvation. You are our life and salvation, beneficent and all-merciful God, Who alone can forgive us our sins and remove diseases and sickness from us, to Whom are known our needs and necessities. Bestower of gifts, grant Your bounteous mercy to Your creatures according to their individual needs, through whom Your Holy Trinity is always glorified and praised, now and forever and unto the ages of ages. Amen.[99]

At the conclusion of the service, holy water is distributed in small containers for the faithful to take home. The frequency of the celebration of this healing service varies depending on particular circumstances. The blessed water is distributed in small containers to the faithful to drink or transport to the sick. During the coronavirus pandemic (2020), it was being conducted daily in Holy Etchmiadzin in Armenia, the seat of the Armenian Katholicos, while it was celebrated weekly at St. Vartan Cathedral in New York.[100]

### *5.1.8 East Syrian*

The earliest attestation to the use of oil for the sick in the East Syrian Rite is in a canon from the Synod of 554 that addresses the manner of reconciliation for those who have fallen into magic. The canon notes that, among other things, they are to be anointed with the oil for the sick.[101] The East Syriac tradition also attests to the laying-on of hands for the healing of the sick.[102] The most unique

[99] Armenian Church of America (Eastern), *Prayers for Healing*, 19–21.

[100] I owe this information to Fr. Hovsep Karapetian (e-mail correspondence, June 11, 2020).

[101] Wilhelm de Vries, *Sakramententheologie bei den Nestorianern*, OCA 133 (Rome: Pontificium Institutum Orientalium Studiorum, 1947), 281–82.

[102] Ibid., 282.

feature, however, of this tradition is the mixture called *ḥnānā*, which literally means mercy;[103] it is used in both the healing and the marriage rituals of the Church of the East.[104] The *ḥnānā* is made by mixing dust from a martyr's grave with oil and water. The mixture then is molded into threads and dried. Over the threads, dust from the tomb of St. Thomas is sprinkled by forming the sign of the cross and the following blessing is said: "This *ḥnānā* is sanctified by the grace of St. Thomas the Apostle for the health and healing of body and soul in the name of the Father."[105] The use of *ḥnānā* is attested in East Syriac literature, such as the ninth-century Chronicle of *Siirt*, where it is used for healing, when it is given to a sick person to drink it, and for protection, when it is worn or carried as a talisman.[106] The use of *ḥnānā* in the East Syriac tradition echoes the practice of pilgrims to tombs of saints where they would fill flasks or ampullae (eulogiae) with sand, oil, or blessed water from the saint's tomb and use it both for healing and for protection purposes,[107] and this practice reflects a strong link with and awareness of martyrdom.

### *5.1.9 Conclusions*

Prayer for healing is not limited to the sacrament of unction. As noted above, the sick are included in the intercessions section of almost all of the Eastern eucharistic prayers. For example, the intercessions of the Armenian Divine Liturgy (*Badarak*) pray for "a speedy recovery to those who are afflicted with diverse diseases."[108] Simi-

[103] K. M. Jomon, "*T'AKS'A D-'AL R'AZ'A Q'ADISH'A D-ZUW'AG'A*—A Textual and Theological Analysis of the Order of Marriage in the East Syriac Tradition" (PhD diss., Mahatma Gandhi University, 2014), xxiii.

[104] For the use of *Ḥnānā* in marriage, see section 4.1.6.

[105] de Vries, *Sakramententheologie bei den Nestorianern*, 283, quoting I. M. Vosté, *Pontificale iuxta ritum Ecclesiae Syrorum Orientalium id est Chaldaeorum*, 4 vols. (Vatican: S. Congregazione «Pro Ecclesia Orientali», 1937–1938), 4:399.

[106] de Vries, *Sakramententheologie bei den Nestorianern*, 282–83, referring to Addai Scher and Robert Griveau, "Histoire Nestorienne (Chronique de Séert)," Patrologia Orientalis 13 (Paris: Firmin-Didot, 1919), 449, 588, 593.

[107] Kurt Weitzmann, ed., *Age of Spirituality: Late Antique and Early Christian Art, Third to Seventh Century* (New York: The Metropolitan Museum of Art, 1979), no. 515, 576; see also Gary Vikan, *Byzantine Pilgrimage Art* (Washington, DC: Dumbarton Oaks, 1982), 13–27.

[108] Findikyan, ed., *The Divine Liturgy of the Armenian Church*, 35.

larly, the celebrant in the Divine Liturgy of St. James as used by the Syrian Orthodox Church prays in the intercessions: "Also, remember our brethren: the prisoners, the sick, the infirm, the afflicted and those who are tormented by evil spirits."[109] A more extensive reference to the sick is present in the Coptic Divine Liturgy of Cyril (Mark). The intercessions include a litany for the sick prayed by the deacon: "Pray for our fathers and our brethren who are sick with any sickness, whether in this place or in any place, that Christ our God may grant us, with them, health and healing, and forgive us our souls" with the priest following by saying, "Take away from them, and from us, every sickness and every malady; the spirit of sickness, chase away. Those who have lain in maladies, raise up and comfort."[110] Prayers for the sick are also to be found among the so-called occasional prayers[111] of all Eastern Christian liturgical traditions. Finally, healing scrolls, expressing a marginal but popular liturgico-magical approach to illness and healing, are known to be used in the Armenian, Ethiopian, and even Greek traditions.[112]

[109] Phillip Tovey, *The Liturgy of St. James as Presently Used*, AGLS 40 (Cambridge: Grove Books, 1998), 19.

[110] Coptic Orthodox Diocese of Southern USA, "Coptic Reader." The intercessions are not as extensive in the Greek version of Mark; see Geoffrey Cuming, *The Liturgy of Mark: Edited from the Manuscripts with a Commentary*, OCA 234 (Rome: Pontificium Institutum Studiorum Orientalium, 1990), 23–24.

[111] The Euchologia Project of the Byzantine Division of the Austrian Academy of Sciences under the leadership of Professor Claudia Rapp studies these occasional prayers in the Byzantine tradition. See https://www.oeaw.ac.at/en/imafo/research/byzantine-research/communities-and-landscapes/euchologia-project. See also Claudia Rapp, Eirini Afentoulidou, Daniel Galadza, Ilias Nesseris, Giulia Rossetto, and Elisabeth Schiffer, "Byzantine Prayer Books as Sources for Social History and Daily Life," *Jahrbuch der Österreichischen Byzantinistik* 67 (2017): 173–211.

[112] On Armenian healing scrolls, see Frédéric Feydit, *Amulettes de l'Arménie chrétienne* (Venise: St.-Lazare, 1986). On Ethiopian healing scrolls, see Kristen Windmuller-Luna, "Ethiopian Healing Scrolls" (2015), https://www.metmuseum.org/toah/hd/heal/hd_heal.htm. There is one published example of a fourteenth-century Greek healing scroll, shared among two American libraries, University of Chicago Library ms 125 and Pierpont Morgan Library ms 499; see Glenn Peers, *Orthodox Magic in Trebizond and Beyond: A Fourteenth-Century Greco-Arabic Amulet Roll* with a contribution by Barbara Roggema (Seyssel: La Pomme d'or, 2018); http://goodspeed.lib.uchicago.edu/ms/index.php?doc=0125&view=description and https://www.themorgan.org/manuscript/85705 for manuscript images.

## 5.2 Rites for Christian Burial

Dealing with the reality of death, its meaning, and what lies after it is at the heart of Christian faith. It is not a coincidence that the Easter hymn of the Orthodox tradition connects the resurrection of Christ with the fate of those in the tombs: "Christ is risen from the dead, trampling death down by death, and to those in the tombs bestowing life." The various funeral rites of the Eastern Christian traditions make use of the reality of death and the mourning of their relatives as an opportunity to proclaim the hope of the resurrection and preach a loving and forgiving God, who died on the cross and rose for the dead, granting life to all and promising life in the kingdom. At the same time, effort is made to console the bereaved and to remind them of the reality and inevitability of death. How these themes come together varies from tradition to tradition. Michael Daniel Findikyan notes: "Funerals in the Christian East are remarkably diversified and complex because, more than other liturgical services, they are conditioned by local and cultural factors. Societal attitudes toward death and bereavement naturally inspired the theology and spirituality of funeral texts."[113] In all Eastern Christian traditions, the funeral rites involve rituals at the home of the deceased, the church, and the burial site; in some cases, the procession from one place to the other is included.

### *5.2.1 Armenian*

The Canon of Burial, as the funeral rite is called in Armenian, appears in the *Maštocʿ*, the liturgical book containing the sacramental rites and occasional prayers and offices of the Armenian church,[114] similar to the Byzantine Euchologion. The ninth-century *Maštocʿ* manuscript Venice arm. 457 together with the tenth- to eleventh-

[113] M. Daniel Findikyan, "Funerals: Eastern Churches," in *The New Westminster Dictionary of Liturgy and Worship*, ed. Paul F. Bradshaw (Louisville: Westminster John Knox, 2002), 215–17, here at 215.

[114] Michael Daniel Findikyan, "An Armenian Funeral Prayer Attributed to Bishop Stepʿanos of Siwnikʿ and the Prayer for the Blessing of Water," in *CYNAΞIC KAΘOΛIKH: Beiträge zu Gottesdienst und Geschichte der fünf altkirchlichen Patriarchatae für Heinzgerd Brakmann zum 70. Geburtstag*, ed. Diliana Atanassova and Tinatin Chronz, Orientalia – Patristica – Oecumenica 6.1 (Wein: Lit Verlag, 2014), 197–212, here 197–98n4.

century *Maštoc'* Yerevan 1001 preserve the earliest full funeral rituals of the Armenian tradition.[115] Already in the ninth-century manuscript there are separate funeral rites for the clergy (priest, bishop, patriarch), for the monastics, and for laymen and laywomen.[116] The core structural unit in these earliest complete Armenian funeral rites (ninth century), also present in the current Armenian rite, is as follows:[117]

- Psalmody
- Reading
- Intercessions
- Prayer

This structure is actually characteristic of the Armenian liturgical tradition and "is ubiquitous in the Daily Hours, in the sacraments, and in occasional offices such as the Blessing of a Church. There can be little doubt that the Armenians inherited the structure from Jerusalem."[118] The growth of the funeral ritual throughout the centuries can be understood as the result of the accumulation of additional material, such as hymnody, around this core liturgical unit. Another liturgical unit characteristic of the Armenian tradition that we see time and again throughout the Canon of Burial is the following: prayers, peace, prayer of inclination.[119]

[115] Andrea Schmidt, *Kanon der Entschlafenen: Das Begräbnisrituale der Armenier: Der altarmenische Bestattungsritus für die Laien*, Orientalia Biblica et Christiana 5 (Wiesbaden: Harrassowitz Verlag, 1994), 75–76, 173–76. For a review of this work, see Michael Daniel Findikyan, "Armenian Funeral Rites: An Assessment of a Recent Study," *St. Nersess Theological Review* 2 (1997): 95–101.

[116] Schmidt, *Kanon der Entschlafenen*, 77–78. For ET of these texts, see F. C. Conybeare, *Rituale Armenorum, Being the Administration of the Sacraments and the Breviary Rites of the Armenian Church* (Oxford: Clarendon Press, 1905), 119–35 (for laity), 161–65 (for monastic), 243–76 (for priests), and 276–93 (for children). Regarding the latter, Schmidt notes that the text that Conybeare provides is an artificial text of his own composition from a variety of sources. The earliest manuscript that contains a funeral rite for children dates to AD 1296. See Schmidt, *Kanon der Entschlafenen*, 78n4.

[117] Schmidt, *Kanon der Entschlafenen*, 154. For a comparative table identifying this unit both in the ninth-century ritual and the current Armenian funeral rites, see 155.

[118] Findikyan, "Armenian Funeral Rites," 97–98.

[119] Findikyan, "Double Prayers."

As in all funeral rites, the Canon of Burial for a layman or laywoman begins at the home of the deceased and is comprised of the following elements:[120]

- Alleluia
- Doxology
- Psalm 50
- Petition and doxology
- Psalmody (Pss 34:1-7; 35:6-13 with 35:5 as a response)
- Petition and doxology
- Isaiah 38:10 as response
- Hymnology
- Doxology
- Litany of petitions
- Prayer: "Eternal God, without beginning . . ."
- Peace
- Prayer of inclination: "Our Father, who are in heaven . . ."
- Alleluia
- 2 Corinthians 1:3-11
- John 5:19-23
- Litany of petitions
- Prayer: "O God of souls and creator of bodies . . ."
- Peace
- Inclination prayer: "Almighty Lord, through your beneficence . . ."
- Hymn
- Intercession
- Petitions

[120] Outline based on Schmidt, *Kanon der Entschlafenen*, 150, and the ET of the Canon Burial kindly provided by Fr. Hovsep Karapetian of Washington, DC.

- Prayer
- The Lord's Prayer

Central to the rites celebrated at the home of the deceased are two prayers. The first prayer, "Eternal God, without beginning," includes a long recollection of salvation history, beginning with creation and ending with redemption and the promise of the resurrection, very similar to the anamnesis section of the eucharistic liturgy. It then moves to the epicletic section, which in this case is related to the departed:

> And now, O beneficent and compassionate God, receive the soul of this your servant [name] who has completed his/her time of sojourn on earth, and is now free from all the toils and deceptions of this world. Count him/her among your saints in your heavenly kingdom, where pain and suffering are excluded, and all your chosen ones rejoice, always shining with endless happiness from the sight of your divine glory. Count among them the soul of this departed one, that together with him/her we will glorify you, O Father, with the Son and the Holy Spirit, now and always and forever and ever. Amen.[121]

The second prayer is the Armenian recension of the well-known Byzantine prayer:

> O God of souls and creator of bodies, who abolished death and trampled upon Satan and granted life to the world. Rest the soul of this your servant [name] in a place of light and in a place of rest from where all afflictions, sorrow and lamentations are far removed. And may you forgive all the sins that he/she has committed, either in word, deed, or thought. As a beneficent and merciful God who loves mankind, pardon him/her. For who is the human who lives and does not sin? For you alone are without sin, and your kingdom is an eternal kingdom that does not pass away. Your words are true, and you are the life and resurrection for all who are asleep [in you]. And to you with the Father and the Holy Spirit is befitting glory, dominion and honor, now and always, and forever and ever. Amen.[122]

[121] ET of the Canon Burial kindly provided by Fr. Hovsep Karapetian of Washington, DC. See also Conybeare, *Rituale Armenorum*, 121.

[122] ET of the Canon Burial kindly provided by Fr. Hovsep Karapetian of Washington, DC. See also Conybeare, *Rituale Armenorum*, 122.

This ancient prayer is considered a loan from the Byzantine tradition,[123] but that is the only point of connection between the Armenian and Byzantine funeral rites. As Andrea Schmidt writes and Findikyan affirms, this common element with the Byzantine funeral rites is the only one between the two, as both their structure and content are fundamentally different, and thus the two are independent traditions.[124]

In the series of hymns comprising the hymnology there is a beautiful trinitarian hymn that in each short strophe addresses each of the three persons of the Holy Trinity, and each strophe has a very clear anamnesis-epiclesis structure:

> Father without beginning / Benevolent lover of humanity! / You are the Creator of souls and bodies, / Remember our departed / And give them rest with Your saints.
>
> Only begotten Son, / You are compassionate to all, / And by your Cross and blood you redeemed your people, / Remember those purchased at the cost of your blood, O Lord, / And give them rest with Your saints.
>
> True Spirit, / Inexhaustible fountain and fulfiller of all blessings / Remember our departed / And give them rest with your saints.

The body then of the deceased is taken to the church and the Canon of Burial continues:[125]

- Hymns
- Alleluia
- 1 Thessalonians 4:13-18
- Alleluia
- John 12:24-26
- Litany of petitions
- Prayer: "O Christ, God and eternal king . . ."

[123] On this prayer and comparative tables, see Schmidt, *Kanon der Entschlafenen*, 109–15.

[124] Schmidt, *Kanon der Entschlafenen*, 117; Findikyan, "Armenian Funeral Rites," 98.

[125] Outline based on Schmidt, *Kanon der Entschlafenen*, 151, and the ET of the Canon Burial kindly provided by Fr. Hovsep Karapetian of Washington, DC.

- Peace
- Prayer of inclination: "O compassionate God, who love mankind . . ."
- Petitions
- Prayer
- Lord's Prayer

Then the body is taken in procession to the cemetery for the burial. During the procession resurrection hymns are sung. As they approach the cemetery, the procession pauses for a station, where Matthew 11:25-30 is read, followed by petitions and the prayer "O Christ, Son of God, forbearing and compassionate." The procession then continues while hymns are sung.[126]

Upon arrival, Psalm 114 is sung, and then the readings of 1 Corinthians 15:12-24 and John 5:24-30 are said. A litany of petitions follows, most of which ask for the Lord's protection of the living from the evil one. For example, the petitions ask that "he may drive away from us all the deceptions of the evil one . . . that he may keep us under the shadow of his almighty hand . . . that he may instantly crush the adversary under our feet, let us beseech the Lord." One petition involves the departed: "For the souls of those that are at rest and have fallen asleep in Christ and in the true light and right faith, let us beseech the Lord." Then a prayer follows, "O God of souls and Creator of bodies," followed by the peace and the prayer of inclination: "Now, O King of kings and Lord of lords." After that the priest takes soil in his hand, blesses it and drops the soil in the grave, saying, "May the divine blessing descend upon the remains of the deceased and make it sprout again on the last day." This is followed by a hymn and then by Psalm 22. Then the prayer "O Christ our God, source of life," the peace, and the inclination prayer "You are blessed, O Lord God our Savior" are prayed, and the priest once again drops soil over the body in the grave, repeating three times, "May the blessed earth descend into his/her grave and make it sprout on the last day."[127]

[126] Outline based on Schmidt, *Kanon der Entschlafenen*, 151, and the ET of the Canon Burial kindly provided by Fr. Hovsep Karapetian of Washington, DC.

[127] Outline based on Schmidt, *Kanon der Entschlafenen*, 152, and the ET of the Canon Burial kindly provided by Fr. Hovsep Karapetian of Washington, DC.

As the grave is filled with soil, hymns are sung that affirm the faith of the departed in the resurrection, such as the following: "O Jesus, preserve this soul that you have given, for it believed in Your Cross and Resurrection, O Heavenly King; Give it rest, bearing in mind its faith." Other hymns have the departed speak in the first person petitioning that the Lord remember him or her at the second coming. For example, "My mortal body has drawn near to the earth from which you created me, and my soul has gone forth from me; Lord, at Your Second Coming remember me who have taken refuge in you." An extensive litany of petitions follows, then the prayer "Blessed are you, O Lord our God,"[128] the peace, and the inclination prayer "Our Lord and Savior Jesus Christ, Son of the living God."[129] Then, after hymns, petitions, and a short prayer ("O Christ, Son of God, forbearing and compassionate") the priest seals the tomb once at each of three sides of the grave, saying, "May the grave and the bones of this servant of God be blessed and remain sealed by the sign of the holy Cross and by the word of the Holy Gospel, in the name of the Father, of the Son and of the Holy Spirit." On the fourth side he then prays, "May the seal of the Lord remain unbroken on the tomb of this servant of God until the Second Coming of Christ, who, coming again, will renew it in glory, to the glory of the Father and of the Holy Spirit. Amen."[130]

The funeral rites at the burial site conclude with the Lord's Prayer but continue at the home of the departed. After the Alleluia, Psalm 43:18-27 is said, followed by a litany and a prayer of consolation, this time addressing the pastoral reality of the pain of loss of the bereaved:

> O Father of compassion and God of all consolation, you console us in all our afflictions. You afflict and you heal, and you never let go of your creatures. Grant them, O Lord, a tempered and consoled spirit. Console through yourself those that are afflicted in heart and cure the wounds of sorrow. So that cured from the grief of their sorrow by the firm hope

[128] See also Conybeare, *Rituale Armenorum*, 127–28.

[129] See also ibid., 128–29.

[130] Outline based on Schmidt, *Kanon der Entschlafenen*, 153, and the ET of the Canon Burial kindly provided by Fr. Hovsep Karapetian of Washington, DC; on these prayers see Findikyan, "Armenian Funeral Prayer."

of your glory they may glorify your great dominion, now and always and forever and ever. Amen.[131]

Another set of petitions follows, completed with the prayer "O Christ, Son of God, forbearing and compassionate." The funeral rites end with the Lord's Prayer.[132] Psalm 118, hymns, readings (2 Thess 2:13-16; Luke 21:34-38), and prayers are recited on the following day at the gravesite.[133]

### 5.2.2 *Byzantine*

As in the other Eastern liturgical traditions, the Byzantine tradition knows of a variety of funeral rites depending on one's ecclesiastical status (clergy, monastics), gender, and age. Modern studies on the funeral rites in the Byzantine tradition[134] have allowed for a better understanding of their history and evolution. Summarizing their findings, we could divide the history of the funeral rites in six phases.

The first phase coincides with our earliest manuscript witnesses (eighth to tenth centuries). During this phase we cannot speak of a funeral liturgy per se, but we have elements that point to a ritual

[131] See also Conybeare, *Rituale Armenorum*, 129–30.

[132] Outline based on Schmidt, *Kanon der Entschlafenen*, 153, and the ET of the Canon Burial kindly provided by Fr. Hovsep Karapetian of Washington, DC.

[133] Outline based on Schmidt, *Kanon der Entschlafenen*, 154.

[134] See, for example, Stefanos Alexopoulos, "Ἀκολουθία Νεκρώσιμος εἰς Μοναχοὺς καὶ Ἱερεῖς" [The Funeral Service of Monks and Priests], in *Τὸ Μυστήριον τοῦ Θανάτου εἰς τὴν Λατρείαν τῆς Ἐκκλησίας. Πρακτικά τοῦ Θ΄ Πανελληνίου Λειτουργικοῦ Συμποσίου* (Athens: Church of Greece, 2009), 401–72; Vitaliano Bruni, *I Funerali di un Sacerdote nel Rito Bizantino* (Jerusalem: Franciscan Printing Press, 1972); Themistocles Christodoulou, *Ἡ Νεκρώσιμη Ἀκολουθία κατὰ τοὺς Χειρόγραφους Κώδικες 10ου-12ου Αἰώνος* [The Funeral Service According to the Manuscripts of the Tenth-Twelfth Centuries] (Thera: Thesbites Edition, 2005); Peter Galadza, "The Evolution of Funerals for Monks in the Byzantine Realm—10th to 16th Centuries," OCP 70 (2004): 225–57; Panayiotis Skaltsis, "Θεολογικὲς Προϋποθέσεις καὶ Ἱστορική Ἐξέλιξη τῆς Ἐκκλησιαστικῆς Κήδευσης" [Theological Conditions and Historical Evolution of Ecclesiastical Burial], in *Νεκρώσιμα Τελετουργικά* (Drama, Greece: Holy Metropolis of Drama, 2001), 45–183; Elena Velkovska, "Funeral Rites in the East," in *Sacraments and Sacramentals*, ed. Chupungco, 345–54; Elena Velkovska, "Funeral Rites according to the Byzantine Liturgical Sources," *Dumbarton Oaks Papers* 55 (2001): 21–51.

structure unfortunately unknown to us.[135] So in this period we cannot speak of funeral rites but only of funeral prayers.[136] The following liturgical elements can be identified:[137]

- Readings
- Litany for the deceased
- Prayer one
- Peace
- Bowing of heads
- Prayer two (of inclination)
- Prayer at the tomb

While the readings would possibly be read in the context of the Divine Liturgy, the rest of the elements comprise a liturgical unit whose elements are constant, regardless of who was buried. Actually there is a theological link between prayer one and prayer two, as "the first prayer is destined for the dead, the second is an invocation for the mourners present, asking for relief of their pain at the loss of their loved one."[138] While the structure would remain the same, depending on who was buried (clergy, monastic, infant, etc.), prayer one and the prayer at the tomb would be the two places that alternative prayers provided in the manuscripts that reflected the status, gender, or age of the deceased could be used.[139]

The second phase (tenth to twelfth centuries) sees the emergence of a full funeral rite in the proper sense. The earliest Byzantine funeral rite appears in the tenth- to eleventh-century manuscript Grottaferrata Γ.β. X from southern Italy. The funeral rite here is comprised of

[135] There is disagreement among scholars what this ritual structure is. Miguel Arranz, "Les prières presbytérales de la «Pannychis» de l'ancien Euchologe byzantin et la «Panikhida» des défunts," OCP 40 (1974): 314–43; 41 (1975): 119–39 argues that the Pannychis is the ritual structure, a claim that Elena Veklovska challenges: Velkovska, "Funeral Rites according to the Byzantine Liturgical Sources," 30, 34–35.

[136] Velkovska, "Funeral Rites according to the Byzantine Liturgical Sources," 30.

[137] Alexopoulos, "Ἀκολουθία Νεκρώσιμος," 406–7.

[138] Velkovska, "Funeral Rites according to the Byzantine Liturgical Sources," 23.

[139] For the evidence both from the Byzantine periphery and Constantinople, see ibid., 22–29.

three liturgical units: (1) Studite monastic matins, (2) cathedral stational liturgy, and (3) burial rites. This funeral rite is a witness to a very dynamic period in Byzantine liturgy as the first liturgical unit (Studite monastic matins) emerges out of the post-iconoclastic Studite synthesis, while the second liturgical unit reflects the influence of the Hagiopolite cathedral liturgy on the Byzantine liturgical tradition of southern Italy.[140] This funeral rite is common for all faithful, with only minor variations in the opening psalmody (the hexapsalmos if the person is lay, Ps 90 if he or she is a monastic), the hymnody (its place is indicated in the manuscript but the full texts are not provided), and the final prayer at burial where options are provided for the burial of an abbot, a bishop, a monk, a deacon, and a child.[141]

Phase 3 (twelfth to fourteenth centuries) is marked by the appearance of funeral rites designated for monastics, in parallel to the common funeral ritual for clergy, monastics, and laity. Such was the creativity of this period that Peter Galadza identifies eighteen (!) different schemata of monastic funeral rites.[142] Phase 4 (fifteenth to sixteenth centuries) saw the emergence of a separate funeral ritual for clergy. This is not a new creation but rather an adaptation of elements and structures already present in the monastic funeral rites.[143] Phase 5 (sixteenth to nineteenth centuries) is marked by the emergence of the printing press and thus the eventual standardization of use. This is reflected, for example, in printed editions of the Euchologion where one encounters funeral rites for laity, for monks, for clergy, for men, and for infants.[144] Phase 6 was inaugurated in the nineteenth century among the Orthodox churches that follow the liturgical practices of the Ecumenical Patriarchate with the publication of the liturgical typikon (ordo) of Georgios Violakes. This typikon, reflecting

[140] Ibid., 30–36; for the Greek text see 46–51.

[141] For an outline of the rite, see ibid., 30–36; Alexopoulos, "Ἀκολουθία Νεκρώσιμος," 446–47. At the burial, the deceased is anointed with oil, which is blessed with the same prayer as the oil of gladness in the baptismal rites, and during the anointing a triple Alleluia is sung, as baptism when the oil of gladness is poured in the font.

[142] Galadza, "The Evolution of Funerals for Monks," 225–57; Velkovska, "Funeral Rites according to the Byzantine Liturgical Sources," 36–39; Alexopoulos, "Ἀκολουθία Νεκρώσιμος," 409–23.

[143] Bruni, *I Funerali di un Sacerdote*, 124–27; Skaltses, "Θεολογικὲς Προϋποθέσεις," 131; Alexopoulos, "Ἀκολουθία Νεκρώσιμος," 424–25, 454–55.

[144] Alexopoulos, "Ἀκολουθία Νεκρώσιμος," 401–2. For a comparative table of these rites, see 428–45.

the use of the Ecumenical Patriarchate, notes that the funeral service is common "for all the deceased, kings, patriarchs, bishops, priests, men, women, older and younger alike, and even infants. . . . For you are all one in Christ Jesus."[145]

The liturgical practice of the Ecumenical Patriarchate today knows of three funeral rites: the common funeral service for all; the funeral service for infants, which is an abbreviation and adaptation of the full funeral rite; and the funerals during Bright Week, where the funeral ritual is comprised exclusively of paschal hymnology.[146] What follows is an outline of the common funeral service. It should be noted, however, that in actual practice the service is abbreviated in many different ways, depending on the context and the celebrant, abbreviations that are not reflected in the published texts.

As with all liturgical traditions, the funeral rites begin with the preparation of the body at the house of the deceased. The priest is invited and celebrates a funeral *Trisagion*, a short rite that first appears in the second half of the twelfth century and has the following structure:[147]

- Initial blessing
- *Trisagion* prayers (Holy God . . . [x3], small doxology, All Holy Trinity . . ., small doxology, the Lord's Prayer)
- Four funeral troparia
- Litany
- Prayer: "O God of Spirits . . ."
- Dismissal
- Chanting of "Eternal Memory"

[145] Georgios Violakes, *Τυπικὸν τῆς τοῦ Χριστοῦ Μεγάλης Ἐκκλησίας* (Athens: Saliveros, n.d.), 439. For comments on this common funeral service, see 434–39.

[146] The official text as found in *Εὐχολόγιον τὸ Μέγα* (Athens: Papademetriou, 2014), 379–457 offers funeral rites for laity, for monks, for priests, for men, and for infants; for an ET of the common funeral service, see https://www.goarch.org/-/funeral-service; for the funeral service of an infant, see https://www.goarch.org/-/funeral-service-for-infants; for the funeral service during Bright Week, see https://www.goarch.org/-/funeral-service-during-renewal-week.

[147] Velkovska, "Funeral Rites according to the Byzantine Liturgical Sources," 40; for an ET, see https://www.goarch.org/-/the-trisagion-service.

While originally the body would be washed, be prepared, and remain at home while the family would keep vigil over the body, today in most cases this is done by the funeral home, and the priest usually performs the *Trisagion* service either at the home (with or without the body) or, in the United States, at the wake at the funeral home.[148]

On the day of the funeral, the body is brought into the church with the singing of "Holy God . . .," a remnant of the funeral procession from the home of the deceased to the church, and in current practice the body is placed in the nave. The full funeral service has the following outline (in brackets are comments reflecting usual practice in Greek-speaking parishes):

- Opening
- Psalm 90 in three stations, each with its response, every station ends with a litany and prayer [most often only a selection of a few verses of each station are said]
- Funeral *eulogētaria*
- Psalm 50 [omitted]
- Funeral canon with *kontakion* and litany after sixth ode [canon omitted, only *kontakion* is sung]
- Funeral hymns in all eight tones
- Beatitudes [they are sung in the Church of Greece, but not the Ecumenical Patriarchate]
- *Prokeimenon*
- Epistle reading (1 Thess 4:13-18)
- Gospel reading (John 5:24-30)
- Litany
- Prayer: "O God of Spirits . . ."
- Farewell kiss with hymnody

[148] In case of clergy, the preparation of the body of the deceased priest is overseen (ideally prepared) by two or three clergy; see https://www.goarch.org/-/funeral-for-clergy.

- Funeral *Trisagion* [omitted]
- Dismissal

The body is then taken to the cemetery with the singing of "Holy God." At the burial site, soil and oil[149] are poured over the deceased, and after the burial the funeral *Trisagion* is said. In current practice, however, the sequence is inverted: the funeral *Trisagion* is said, soil and oil are poured over the deceased, and the dismissal takes place. The burial usually takes place after everyone leaves. The deceased are then commemorated on the following anniversaries with memorial services built around the heart of the funeral *Trisagion* on the third, ninth, and fortieth days, and then on the sixth month and annual commemorations. In addition to these days, the Byzantine liturgical week celebrates the commemoration of the dead every Saturday, especially on the two Saturdays of the souls, the Meatfare Saturday (which has extended to the following two Saturdays, Cheesefare Saturday and first Saturday of Great Lent) and the Saturday before Pentecost.[150] Finally, the faithful are invited to submit the names of their deceased (together with the names of the living) to be commemorated at the *prothesis* (preparation) rites of every Divine Liturgy.[151]

At the heart of the funeral rites in the Byzantine tradition is the following prayer:

> O God of spirits and of all flesh, You trampled upon death and abolished the power of the devil, giving life to Your world. Give rest to the

[149] The anointing of the deceased with oil was once common to all Eastern Christian funeral rites, and among the Armenian, Byzantine, East Syriac, and West Syriac liturgical traditions it was known as funerary unction. The earliest attestation is in the work of Pseudo-Dionysius the Areopagite, who already knows of the practice as "ancient." Findikyan, "Armenian Funeral Rites," 99. For the Byzantine traditions, see the study by Demetrios Tzerpos, *Ἡ Ἀκολουθία τοῦ Νεκρωσίμου Εὐχελαίου κατὰ τὰ Χειρόγραφα Εὐχολόγια τοῦ ΙΔ΄-ΙΣΤ΄ Αἰῶνος*, Λατρειολογήματα 1 (Athens: Institute for Byzantine Musicology, 2000).

[150] Velkovska, "Funeral Rites according to the Byzantine Liturgical Sources," 41–42.

[151] On the Prothesis Rites in the Byzantine Tradition, see Stelyios Muksuris, *Economia and Eschatology: Liturgical Mystagogy in the Byzantine Prothesis Rite* (Brookline, MA: Holy Cross Orthodox Press, 2013) and Georgios Keselopoulos, *Η Πρόθεση: Μελέτη Λειτουργική, Ιστορική – Θεολογική (8ος -15ος Αιώνας)*, 2 vols. (Nicosia: Center for Studies of the Holy Monastery of Kykkos, 2018).

> soul of Your departed servant (*Name*) in a place of light, in a place of green pasture, in a place of refreshment, from where pain, sorrow, and sighing have fled away. As a good and loving God, forgive every sin he (*she*) has committed in word, deed, or thought, for there is no one who lives and does not sin. You alone are without sin. Your righteousness is an everlasting righteousness, and Your word is truth. For You are the resurrection, the life, and the repose of Your departed servant (*Name*), Christ our God, and to You we offer glory, with Your eternal Father who is without beginning and Your all-holy, good, and life-creating Spirit, now and forever and to the ages of ages.[152]

While the prayer here is addressed to Christ, originally, as attested in the earliest Byzantine Euchologion Barberini gr. 336, it was addressed to the Holy Trinity.[153] The presiding clergy, and with him all the faithful, address both the reality of sin but also an unwavering trust in God's goodness and love, such that the prayer ends with a confession of faith in the resurrection and life in Christ for the faithful departed: "For You are the resurrection, the life, and the repose of Your departed servant." This prayer is indeed ancient, attested on papyri and in epigraphical evidence already by the sixth and seventh centuries,[154] and is also found in the Armenian and Coptic traditions.

Much of the funeral service hymnody is addressed not to the deceased whose funeral is celebrated but to the people attending the funeral service, reminding them of the proper priorities in life. In the funeral hymn of the third tone the following is sung:

> Vanity are all the works and quests of man, and they have no being after death has come; our wealth is with us no longer. How can our glory go with us? For when death has come all these things are vanished clean away. Wherefore to Christ the Immortal King let us cry, "To him (her) that has departed grant repose where a home is prepared for all those whose hearts You have filled with gladness."[155]

In fact, in one of the hymns chanted during the farewell kiss, the poet has the deceased person address the people present and say:

[152] ET from https://www.goarch.org/-/funeral-service with adjustments by authors.
[153] Velkovska, "Funeral Rites according to the Byzantine Liturgical Sources," 44.
[154] Ibid., 23–24.
[155] https://www.goarch.org/-/funeral-service.

> Looking on me as I lie here prone before you, voiceless and unbreathing, mourn for me, everyone; brethren and friends, kindred, and you who knew me well; for but yesterday with you I was talking, and suddenly there came upon me the fearful hour of death: therefore come, all you that long for me, and kiss me with the last kiss of parting. For no longer shall I walk with you, nor talk with you henceforth: for to the Judge I go, where no person is valued for his (her) earthly station: Yea, slave and master together stand before Him, king and soldier, rich man and poor man, all accounted of equal rank: for each one, according to his (her) own deeds shall be glorified, or shall be put to shame. Therefore I beg you all, and implore you, to offer prayer unceasingly for me to Christ our God, that I be not assigned for my sins to the place of torment; but that He assign me to the place where there is Light of Life.[156]

Commenting on the content of the hymnography of the funeral rite, Elena Velkovska writes:

> In the hymnography all the Hellenistic uncertainty about the hereafter, conceived as a place of turbulence and discomfort rather than as a place of quiet and peace, lives on. But what is still more surprising is the total lack of any allusion to the paschal death of Christ illumined by the resurrection: because of the dynamics of the risen Christ's victory over death, it provides *the* classic Christian typology of the Christian's transition to the other life.[157]

It is particularly because of the content of the hymnography that there are calls for a reform or renewal of the funeral rites in the Byzantine tradition.[158]

### *5.2.3 West Syrian*

The West Syrian funeral rites are known as *tekso d'oufoyo*, or the order of enshrouding, stemming from the preparation of the body of the deceased. There is a multiplicity of funeral rites, depending on

[156] https://www.goarch.org/-/funeral-service.

[157] Velkovska, "Funeral Rites according to the Byzantine Liturgical Sources," 43.

[158] Velkovska, "Funeral Rites in the East," 352–53; Peter Galadza, "Lost and Displaced Elements of the Byzantine Funeral Rites: Towards a Pastoral Re-appropriation," *Studia Liturgica* 33 (2003): 62–74; Stelyios Muksuris, "Revisiting the Orthodox Funeral Service: Resurrecting a Positive Thematology in the Rite for the Dead," *Greek Orthodox Theological Review* 61 (2016): 141–67.

the age, gender, and ecclesiastical status of the deceased (male, female, monastic, child, deacon, priest, bishop, patriarch).[159] All of these rites, however, share the same structure. The funeral rites for lay men, women, children, deacons, and nuns are comprised of three units called "services," while those for priests and bishops are comprised of four "services." These have the following structure (items in bold are the variable elements, which are different in each case, depending on the gender, age, and ecclesiastical status of the deceased):

- *Trisagion* (only in first service)
- Lord's Prayer (only in first service)
- **Opening prayer**
- Psalm 50
- **Hymns/Psalm**
- ***Eqbo* (concluding prayer)**
- *Husoyo* (prayer of absolution)
- ***Proemion* (preface)**
- ***Sedro* (prayer)**
- **Hymns**
- ***'Etro* (prayer of incense)**
- **Hymns**
- *Trisagion* (only in first service)
- Lord's Prayer (only in first service)

After the third service in the case of the funeral of men, women, children, deacons, and nuns, a Liturgy of the Word follows. The readings for men and deacons are 1 Thessalonians 4:13-18 and John 5:24-29; for women, 2 Corinthians 5:1-10 and Matthew 25:1-13; for children,

[159] Mor Athanasius Yeshue Samuel, ed., and Murad Saliba Barson, trans., *The Order for the Burial of the Dead According to the Ancient Rite of the Syrian Orthodox Church of Antioch* (Lebanon, 1974), 3; Mor Athanasius Yeshue Samuel, ed., and Murad Saliba Barson, trans., *The Book of the Order for the Burial of the Clergy According to the Ancient Rite of the Syrian Orthodox Church of Antioch* (Teaneck, NJ: The Archdiocese of the Syrian Orthodox Church for the Eastern United States, 2003), vi.

1 Corinthians 15:12-27 and Luke 7:11-17. Funeral rites for nuns have three readings, Acts 9:36-43; 2 Corinthians 5:1-13; and Matthew 25:1-13; with the exception of the Acts reading, they are identical with the reading for women. In the case of funerals for priests and bishops, and after the fourth service, there are a total of six readings: Genesis 49:33–50:14; Numbers 20:23-30; Job 7:1-7; 2 Peter 3:8-18; 1 Corinthians 15:34-57; and Matthew 24:45-51; 25:14-30. Following the readings, a litany is said, its petitions adapted to the gender and ecclesiastical status of the deceased.

Then, in the case of funerals for clergy only, a procession takes place, carrying the deceased clergyman head first to the altar, where the priest, censing his body, on behalf of the deceased, and in dialogue with the deacons present, bids goodbye to the altar, the church, the clergy, the faithful. If the deceased clergyman is a priest, after the body is taken to the altar and the aforementioned farewell dialogue takes place, the body is then processed to the west side of the church, where the farewell dialogue continues.[160] If the deceased is a bishop, his body is processed around the whole church with stations at each of the four sides:

> Then they carry the body and place it before the altar and the hierarch or one of the priests waves the censer over the body, saying:

| | |
|---|---|
| *Hierarch:* | Farewell, O holy altar |
| *Priests and Deacons:* | Depart in peace, O honorable prelate |
| *Hierarch:* | Farewell, O holy church |
| *Priests and Deacons:* | Depart in peace, O modest prelate |
| *Hierarch:* | Farewell, O holy bishops |
| *Priests and Deacons:* | Depart in peace, O pious prelate |
| *Hierarch:* | Farewell, O heads of the churches |
| *Priests and Deacons:* | Depart in peace, O our beloved father |
| *Hierarch:* | Farewell, O heads of the monasteries |

[160] *The Book of the Order for the Burial of the Clergy*, 35 (for deacons); 121–23 (for priests).

*Priests and Deacons:* Depart in peace, O our blessed father

*Hierarch:* Farewell, O noble priests

*Priests and Deacons:* Depart in peace, O true shepherd

Then they shall take the body to the west side of the church and say:

*Hierarch:* Farewell, O pure deacons

*Priests and Deacons:* Depart in peace, O wise leader

*Hierarch:* Farewell, O all clergy

*Priests and Deacons:* Depart in peace, O our holy father

*Hierarch:* Farewell, O my beloved ones and friends

*Priests and Deacons:* Depart in peace, O our righteous father

Then they shall take the body to the north side of the church and say:

*Hierarch:* Farewell, O monastery and its dwellers

*Priests and Deacons:* Depart in peace, O teacher of truth

*Hierarch:* Farewell, O city and its inhabitants

*Priests and Deacons:* Depart in peace, O eminent prelate

*Hierarchs:* Farewell, O my fellow mortals

*Priests and Deacons:* Depart in peace, O our true prelate

Finally, they shall take the body to the south side of the church and say:

*Hierarch:* Farewell, O church and its children

*Priests and Deacons:* Depart in peace, O preacher of truth

*Hierarch:* Give me peace and may you live in peace
This peace that you give me is hence forever

*Priests and Deacons:*

Depart in peace, O respected prelate
May our Lord receive you in the blessed mansions

May Christ, who took you away, make us worthy to see you in the new life that will shine forth from heaven. Glory to you, O Jesus our Savior, in Whose hands is death and Whose will is life.

*Hierarch:* May tranquility dwell in the church which you served

*Priests and Deacons:*
Kyrie-eleison. Kyrie-eleison. Kyrie-eleison.

Then they shall return the body to the front of the altar.[161]

Following the readings in the case of the laity, or the ritual farewell in the case of the priests, hymns are sung, and then oil is blessed to be used for the anointing of the deceased. The prayer of the oil is common to all:

> O Lord God, by Whose Godhead's command and Lordship's authority this Your servant (name) has departed from this temporal life, send to him/her from above the help of your angelic hosts, and by means of this oil, which is to be poured on his/her body, grant that he/she may become slippery and unrestrainable by the adverse powers and the host of enemies who lie in wait in the air to wage war against the souls of men. Bring him/her safe to the heavenly abodes of light and exultation among the saints so that, rejoicing and exceedingly glad, he/she may offer You glory and give thanks to You, Father, Son and Holy Spirit, now and forever.[162]

The deceased is then anointed with the sign of the cross and in the name of the Holy Trinity on the face, the chest, and the knees.

After the body is anointed, Psalm 50 is sung antiphonally, where each verse of Psalm 50 has a different poetic antiphon. This section is common to all funerals. The first of these responses has the deceased bid goodbye to the members of the community: "Farewell, my brethren, pray for me, and whenever you continue to pray, re-

[161] *The Book of the Order for the Burial of the Clergy*, 215–17.

[162] See, for example, *The Order for the Burial of the Dead*, 50 (funeral of males). The text above is from the funeral of a bishop, adjusted. *The Book of the Order for the Burial of the Clergy*, 219–21.

member me."[163] A procession to the cemetery then starts, with the singing of hymns. When they reach the grave and right before the burial, "the priest shall take some soil in his right hand and cast it on the departed in the form of a cross, saying: Your will, O Lord, has been fulfilled as you have decreed, saying: Dust you are, and to dust you shall return and again you shall be restored." Hymns are then sung, followed by the great doxology, the *Trisagion*, the Lord's Prayer, the creed, and psalmic verses.[164]

Memorials are celebrated on the third and the fortieth days after the passing away of the deceased, as well as on the one-year anniversary of his or her death. The structure of the memorial services are common to all categories of deceased, but with the exception of the *Husoyo*, all other elements are specific to the age, sex, and ecclesiastical status. The memorial service is comprised of the following elements:

1. Opening prayer
2. Psalm
3. Concluding prayer
4. *Husoyo*
5. *Proemion*
6. *Sedro*
7. Hymns
8. Readings[165]
9. Supplication

10 *Hoothomo* (prayer of conclusion)[166]

[163] *The Order for the Burial of the Dead*, 50; see 50–56 for all the antiphons.

[164] *The Book of the Order for the Burial of the Clergy*, 47.

[165] 1 Cor 15:50-58 and Luke 16:19-31 for men and deacons; 2 Cor 5:1-10 and Matt 25:1-13 for women and nuns; 1 Cor 15:50-58 and John 5:24-2

[166] *The Order for the Burial of the Dead*, 66–77 (men), 122–29 (women), 172–74 (children); *The Book of the Order for the Burial of the Clergy*, 49–60 (deacons), 137–48 (priests and bishops, see note on 229), 281–90 (nuns).

### 5.2.4 Maronite

The funeral rites of the Maronite tradition are contained in the Book of *Ginnazat*.[167] As in the other Eastern Christian traditions, there are funeral services for men, women, and priests, and a common service is primarily used as a memorial service of more than one person.[168]

A short rite is celebrated at the home of the deceased, a rite that is common to men and women. The clergy and the people gather around the body. Then the presiding clergy burns incense and says the prayer: "May the most Holy Trinity be blessed with the fragrance of this incense as we offer now for the rest and pardon of the Lord's servant (name) and for our parents, brothers and sisters, relatives and benefactors, and all the departed. In the name of the Father, and of the Son, and of the Holy Spirit. Amen."[169] An incense hymn then is chanted, built around two themes: the hope in the resurrection and the petition for forgiveness of the deceased.[170] The concluding prayers follow that express the petition and hope that the deceased "may participate in the company of your [the Lord's] saints in everlasting happiness" and that he or she may be showered with "the dew of your [the Lord's] eternal mercy."[171] This short service ends with the recitation of the Lord's Prayer.

If the deceased is clergy, the rite is longer and has a different structure:

- Opening doxology
- Opening prayer
- Hymns
- *Hoosoyo* (rite of incense)
    - *Proemion* (preface)
    - *Sedro* (prayer)
    - Hymn

[167] *Book of Ginnazat: Order of Christian Funerals According to the Rites of the Maronite Antiochene Church* (San Antonio, TX: Diocese of St. Maron, 1988).

[168] *Book of Ginnazat*, 6.

[169] Ibid., 25.

[170] Ibid., 25–28.

[171] Ibid., 28.

- Readings
    - 1 Corinthians 15:50-57
    - Matthew 24:45-51
- Concluding hymns[172]

When the time for the funeral comes, the body of the deceased is taken in procession to the church. During the procession, Psalms 148–150 and 117 are sung. It is noted in the rubrics that the chanting of these psalms is "a recent tradition."[173] When the body arrives at the church, it is received by the clergy at the entrance with incense, and the body is led to the front of the church, while the following entrance hymn is chanted:

> Open your gates, O heavenly Jerusalem; / let our prayers stand before the throne of Christ / and our petitions obtain mercy and forgiveness.
>
> O Lord, through the intercession of your Mother and all your saints, heed our supplications and be compassionate to us.
>
> O Lord, grant rest in your blissful kingdom / to those who have entrusted their lives to you / in the hope of their resurrection.[174]

When the body is brought in the church, if the deceased is clergy, the body is placed in such a way that the head is toward the altar; if a layperson, the body is placed with the feet toward the altar,[175] reflecting the orientation of the body (facing the people if clergy, facing the altar if lay) during their participation in the liturgical life of the community.

Then the funeral rites begin. While all have the same structure, the prayers, hymns, and readings are different for a male, a female, and a priest. There is also a common service, regardless of gender or ecclesiastical status, but even there the readings vary depending on the gender and age of the deceased.[176] The common structure is comprised of the following elements:

[172] Ibid., 31–36.
[173] Ibid., 39–43; the rubric is on 39.
[174] Ibid., 47.
[175] Ibid., 7.
[176] Ibid., 101–4.

- Opening doxology
- Opening prayer
- Psalmody
    - Psalm 50 (LXX 50)
    - Prayer of the first psalm
    - Psalm 103 (LXX 102) with antiphons
    - Prayer of the second psalm
    - Psalm 130 (LXX 129) with antiphons
    - Prayer of the third psalm
    - Psalm 63 (LXX 62) with antiphons
- Canticle
- *Hoosoyo* (rite of incense)
    - *Proemion* (preface)
    - *Sedro* (prayer)
    - *Qolo* (hymn)
    - *'Etro* (prayer of incense)
- Readings
    - 1 Corinthians 15:35-49 and Mark 13:32-37 (men)
    - Romans 6:3-14 and John 5:19-29 (women)
    - 1 Thessalonians 4:13-18 and Mark 13:32-37 (common service); 1 Thessalonians 4:13-18 and Luke 7:1-10 (if a boy); 1 Corinthians 15:51-57 and Luke 8:49-56 (if a girl)
- Supplication
- Concluding prayers[177]

Unique to the funeral rites of a priest are the "beatitudes" that are placed between the epistle and gospel readings. These are not the biblical beatitudes but a hymn to the priesthood:

> Blessed is the priesthood, for it attained virtue.
> Blessed is the priesthood, for it loved repentance.
> Blessed is the priesthood, for it crucified the body.

[177] Ibid., 51–69 (male); 70–88 (female); 90–106 (common service); 107–31 (for priests).

Blessed is the priesthood, for it rejected vengeance.

Blessed is the priesthood, for it encouraged alms.

Blessed is the priesthood, for it hated greed.

Blessed is the priesthood, for it loved the holy ones.

Blessed is the priesthood, for its way of life is pure.

Blessed is the priesthood, for it deserved the kingdom.

Blessed is the priesthood, for it is accepted by the Lord.[178]

At the end of the funeral service, the celebrant approaches the deceased and proclaims: "For those who believed in the Father, Son, and Holy Spirit, death becomes, as they taste it, eternal life. For those who believe in Christ, the Son of God, death becomes, as they taste it, eternal life. For those who believe in the mystery of the Trinity, death becomes, as they taste it, eternal life."[179]

The hymn that follows has the deceased say, "I prayed in the holy temple and, behold, I am going out to journey on that road taken by all generations. O priests, remember me in the sanctuary and your deacons, before the altar. Pray for me, O people, that his grace may be my companion, and his mercy may be upon me."[180] In the case of clergy, the body of the deceased is carried around the altar or the church three times while a hymn is sung. The hymn has the deceased clergy bid goodbye to the altar with references to the celebration of the Eucharist: "As I carried your holy body in procession and distributed life to mortals, behold, I have died in the grave; make me worthy to enter your dwelling place."[181] Then the body is placed before the altar and the clergy bid him farewell while another hymn is sung. Then the body is taken out of the altar, a cross is placed on the deceased person's chest, if he is a priest, or his right hand, if he is a bishop, and the people then approach and kiss the cross while a hymn is sung, which again has the deceased bid goodbye to the altar, the church, and the community, asking for their prayers.[182] Then, while the body is taken to the cemetery, hymns are sung.[183]

[178] Ibid., 124.
[179] Ibid., 136.
[180] Ibid., 136.
[181] Ibid., 136.
[182] Ibid., 137–38.
[183] Ibid., 141–42.

In the funeral of a layperson, the deceased is greeted at the gravesite while a hymn is sung, again having the deceased addressing the faithful gathered, greeting them, and asking for their prayers.[184] Another hymn is sung while the body is placed in the grave, and another while the grave is sealed.[185] Then the concluding prayer is recited: "O Lord, grant rest and consolation to your servant/handmaiden (name). He/she worshiped you, and with true faith sleeps in your hope. May he/she stand at your right on the day of your divine manifestation, and with her the righteous and the just offer you praise."[186] A hymn follows and the rite ends with the Lord's Prayer.

Memorials are held on the third, the ninth, and the fortieth days after a person's death and on the one-year anniversary of their death. According to Patriarch Ad-Doueihi, these are celebrated

> on the third day, because the Lord rose from the dead on the third day, thus becoming the first-born and head of those who fell asleep; on the fortieth day, because he ascended into heaven after forty days; on the ninth day, because the departed become "companions" of the nine choirs of the angels, and mostly because the Lord sent the Spirit Paraclete to his apostles nine days after his ascension; that he might lift up their spirits and give them courage; last, at the end of the year: as we commemorate, each year, the feast (literally, birth) of the saints, the departed are remembered because they share with them everlasting life.[187]

While rarely celebrated today, a thirty-day memorial imitating the people of Israel who mourned Moses (Deut 34:8) is also known in the Maronite tradition.[188]

### *5.2.5 East Syrian*

The East Syrian tradition is unique in that, while, as in other rites, it has different formularies depending on the gender, age, clerical rank, and social status of the deceased (and adds to the list burial for an unbaptized child), it is only the clergy who are designated as "the

[184] Ibid., 145.
[185] Ibid., 145–48.
[186] Ibid., 149.
[187] Ibid., 7–8.
[188] Ibid., 8.

sons of the Church" and whose funerals take place in the church; for the laity, who are designated "sons/daughters of the world," the funeral service begins at home and proceeds directly to the cemetery of burial. And since the laity are not brought in the church, their funeral rites include readings only from the Old Testament and the Acts of the Apostles; in the East Syriac tradition the gospel and epistle readings may not be read publicly outside the church and hence are only read at funerals of clergy since only they take place in the church.[189]

A central liturgical unit of the East Syriac funeral liturgy is the *Kathisma*. The structure of the *Kathisma* is as follows:[190]

- Prayer
- Portion of a psalm (*shurraya*)
- Prayer
- Portion of a psalm (*shurraya*)
- Hymns
- Prayer
- [Psalmic verses (*subbaḥa*)—only for clergy]
- Prayer
- Hymns

The prayers of the *kathismata* are typical of the East Syriac tradition that offer pure praise and glory to God, without expressing any petition at all. One such prayer reads as follows: "We confess your grace which created us, and we praise your compassion which cares for us, and we worship your greatness which makes our race glad in the two worlds that you have created, Lord of our death and of our life."[191] The last part of the prayer, "in the two worlds . . . our life," is a phrase that appears in the conclusion of almost every prayer and

[189] Findikyan, "Funerals: Eastern Churches," 215. Douglas Webb, "The Funeral Services of the Nestorian Church," in *Temple of the Holy Spirit: Sickness and Death of the Christian in the Liturgy; The Twenty-First Liturgical Conference Saint-Serge*, trans. Matthew O'Connell (New York: Pueblo Publishing Company, 1983), 285–99, here at 285–87.

[190] Webb, "The Funeral Services of the Nestorian Church," 289.

[191] Ibid., 289; translation adapted.

highlights God's rule both in this life ("our death") and the life to come ("our life").[192] The hymns generally address the themes of death and resurrection. The hypothesis has been made that the hymns that are responsorial (led by a cantor with a chorus singing the response) were a "liturgical substitute for professional female mourners."[193]

The funeral rituals begin with the washing of the body of the deceased. Clergy are dressed with their vestments, laypeople are dressed "in white garments as on the day of his wedding," according to the directions in a printed edition of 1954.[194] While there is an indirect link to the white baptismal garments, the emphasis here is eschatological and celebratory. The process of washing the body of the deceased is accompanied by a vigil that is made up of the *kathismata* mentioned in the previous paragraph. The amount of the *kathismata* performed depends on whether the deceased is a layperson, clergy and his rank, or an unbaptized infant. Three *kathismata* are done if the deceased is a man, a woman, or a baptized child; a total of four for a monastic; five for a deacon; six for a priest; eight for a bishop; and up to ten for a patriarch.[195] Regarding unbaptized infants, these prescriptions are to be followed: "If a child shall live to be six months old without receiving baptism, and his mother shall have partaken of the life-giving Body and Blood, which shall have mingled with the milk which he has sucked, one *kathisma* shall be said over him, and, in consideration of his parents, one priest shall attend his funeral."[196] The unbaptized infant here is seen as already being in a way part of the church as through his mother's milk it has already partaken of the life-giving mysteries and therefore deserves an ecclesiastical funeral.

As laypeople are not taken to church, the readings are done at the domestic setting before the procession to the burial site. The choice of readings differs between men and women. For men they are Isaiah 38:10-20 and Ezekiel 37:1-14; for women they are Genesis 28:1-19 and Acts 9:36-42.[197] The distinction in the readings is a result of a "creative

[192] Ibid., 287.

[193] Ibid., 289.

[194] Ibid., 288.

[195] Ibid., 288. The number of *kathismata* for the clergy vary in the manuscript tradition.

[196] Ibid., 289.

[197] Ibid., 292.

tendency, rooted in pastoral sensitivity,"[198] to pick readings appropriate for each situation. The readings designated for deceased women, for example, present the death and burial of Sarah (the Genesis reading) and the raising of Tabitha (the Acts reading).

In the case of clergy, after the recitation of the appropriate number of *kathismata*, they are taken to the church for the celebration of the Divine Liturgy. The readings for the Divine Liturgy funeral of a priest are Numbers 20:22-29 (the death of Aaron); Acts 20:17-38 (Paul's farewell to the church of Ephesus); 1 Corinthians 15:34-38 (declaration of the resurrection); and John 5:19-30 (resurrection and judgment).[199] Appropriate prayers and hymns intermingle with the readings, and then the eucharistic liturgy takes place. After Communion, the deceased is carried around the church with four stations (bema, entrance of the altar, nave, door of the church) while the following hymn is sung, a kind of farewell of the deceased to the church but also a witness to the hope of paradise: "Rest in peace, O Church, for I am going away: may those who remain in righteousness pray for me. O my brethren and companions and beloved, keep my memory in remembrance, for I am now separated from you forever, and pray for me. I am going away, yet I am not afraid, for my Lord is calling me, and will place a crown of praise upon my head, and will refresh me."

Then the deceased is carried in procession to the grave (the procession starts from the church in the case of the clergy, from the home in the case of the laity). Hymns are chanted by two choirs on the way. An anonymous commentator of the ninth or tenth century described the joyful character of the funeral procession in the following way:

> They go forth praising and honoring the deceased as though accompanying him to the kingdom; and they doubt not that he is an heir to the heavenly mansions. Because he has lived in the faith which is written in the holy books and which was signified by the Old and New Testaments, and was signed in baptism and sanctified by the Body and Blood of Christ, and has obtained the forgiveness of sins, he is worthy of the heavenly kingdom. And because he is worthy, they attend him with honors: neither do they lament, because he is freed from sorrow

[198] Findikyan, "Funerals: Eastern Churches," 215.
[199] Webb, "The Funeral Services of the Nestorian Church," 293.

> and has attained the joys which he desired. For our Christian home is in heaven.[200]

More hymns are then sung and prayers are read at the graveside, some depending on whether the deceased is clergy or laity. When the time to lower the body has come, a "farewell" homily is chanted in three sections, usually a selection from the homilies of Narsai. In the case of clergy, a "procession of peace" is formed, when all present greet the deceased priest by touching his hands with theirs and then placing their hands on their lips.[201] After the body is lowered into the grave and the singing of hymns, the priest holding soil in his hands prays the following prayer:

> God, the maker of all, who has decreed unto our mortal nature, that dust are you, and unto dust you shall return: may he raise you up therefrom, rejoicing in the glory of the resurrection: and may the holy mysteries, which you have received plead for you, and be to you for pardon in the fearful judgement of righteousness, when the righteous shall receive the recompense of their labors, and the just their reward. Then may you meet Christ with open face, and lift up praise and render glory to the Father, Son, and Holy Spirit, Amen.[202]

Then the priest scatters the soil over the body in the grave in the form of a cross, a long chant follows, then Psalm 90 (LXX 89) followed by a concluding prayer.[203]

### *5.2.6 Coptic*

Early evidence regarding funeral practices in Egypt come from the prayer collection attributed to Sarapion of Thmuis, from papyri, from epigraphical evidence, and from Pachomian monasticism. Sarapion's Prayer 18 is titled "Prayer for the One Who Has Died and Is Carried

[200] R. H. Connolly, *Anonymi Auctoris Expositio Officiorum Ecclesiae Georgio Arbelensi Vulgo Adscripta, II. Accedit Abrahae bar Lipheh interpretatio officiorum [II]*, Corpus Scriptorum Christianorum Orientalium, Scriptores Syri, 2nd ser., vol. 92 (Rome and Paris: Peeters, 1915), 134; translation from Webb, "The Funeral Services of the Nestorian Church," 296.

[201] Webb, "The Funeral Services of the Nestorian Church," 298 and 336, note 31.

[202] Ibid., 298–99.

[203] Ibid., 299.

Out."[204] A comparison between this prayer and the prayer "O God, the Eternal, who know the hidden things" of the Coptic funeral rites (see below) shows a certain influence[205] and therefore a possible link between this prayer and the Coptic funeral euchological tradition. Papyrological evidence suggests that the funeral was possibly called "service of the clothes,"[206] a reference to the ritual cleansing and dressing of the body of the deceased with funeral garments. In Pachomian monasticism, the deceased monastic would be brought into the church on the day he or she passed away, and a vigil would take place involving psalms and hymns. The following morning, after morning prayer, the body of the deceased monastic would be washed and prepared. The Divine Liturgy would then be offered for the deceased. Then he or she would be processed to the burial grounds to be buried.[207] Later epigraphical evidence from epitaphs quote psalms and prayers of the Coptic funeral rites[208] and can be valuable sources for the study of their history and evolution. Finally, epigraphical evidence from Nubia attests to the use of a Nubian version of the Byzantine prayer "O God of spirits and of all flesh."[209]

The funeral rites begin at the house of the deceased with the preparation of the body by washing and clothing it. If the deceased is clergy, he is dressed with the vestments of his office, and the Psalter and hymns are recited over his body throughout the night. A priest is invited to the house, where he recites the prayer of thanksgiving. When the body is taken out of the house, the deacons chant, "Lord, remember me in your kingdom" (Luke 23:42) or "Christ is risen" if

[204] Johnson, *The Prayers of Sarapion*, 68–69.

[205] Johnson, *The Prayers of Sarapion*, 167; for the discussion on this prayer, see 163–67.

[206] Ágnes Mihálykó, *The Christian Liturgical Papyri: An Introduction*, Studien und Texte zu Antike und Christentum 114 (Tübingen: Mohr Siebeck, 2019), 18n52.

[207] Armand Veilleux, *La liturgie dans le cénobitisme Pachômien au quatrìeme siècle* (Rome: Libreria Herder, 1968), 371–79; Mihálykó, *The Christian Liturgical Papyri*, 72–73, 148.

[208] See, for example, Maher Eissa and Renate Dekker, "The Latest Known (Bohairic) Coptic Epitaphs (NMEC 46 and 47)," *Journal of Coptic Studies* 20 (2018): 57–79.

[209] Heinzgerd Brakmann, "Defunctus adhuc loquitur": 300–310; for the Nubian redaction of the prayer (and comparison with the Byzantine version in the eighth-century Barberini gr. 336), see 306. Many thanks to Ramez Mikhail for bringing this article to our attention. See also Adam Łajtar, "A Greek Inscription from el-Chandaq, Nubia," in *Zeitschrift für Papyrologie und Epigraphik* 94 (1992): 217–20.

during the Paschal season, followed by the *Trisagion* (Holy God, Holy Mighty). An elaborate procession then takes place, processing the deceased body from his home to the church. Upon arrival, the body is placed in the middle of the nave.[210]

The Coptic tradition knows of eleven different funeral rites (for men, women, women who died at delivery, boys, girls, deacons, priests, monk-priests, bishops, monks, and nuns). All share the same structure, with only certain elements that are variable, such as a selection of psalms, the readings, and the concluding prayer. The memorial services on the third and fortieth days also follow the same structure.

- Introductory elements
- Thanksgiving prayer
- Psalm 50
- Selection of psalms
- Readings
- Funeral exposition
- Three great litanies (for peace, for the fathers, for the assemblies)
- Creed
- Litany of the departed
- Prayer: "Graciously, O Lord"
- Concluding prayer
- Lord's Prayer
- Prayer of submission to the Son
- Prayer of absolution to the Son
- Concluding rites[211]

[210] Khs-Burmester, *The Egyptian or Coptic Church*, 201–2.

[211] Coptic Orthodox Diocese of Southern USA, "Coptic Reader." See also Khs-Burmester, *The Egyptian or Coptic Church*, 201–16; Woolley, *Coptic Offices*, 109–54.

The variable elements, depending on the age, gender, and ecclesiastical status of the deceased, are the selection of psalms, the readings, and the concluding prayer. These are presented in the table below.

The concluding prayer in the funeral rites for men provides a valuable insight into the history of the funeral rites. The elements it shares with Prayer 18 from the *Prayers of Sarapion* and the place of the prayer in the rite itself point to the continuous use of this prayer in the Coptic tradition.

Central to the Coptic funeral rites is the prayer that follows the litany of the departed and is common to all funeral rites:

> Graciously, O Lord, repose all their souls in the bosom of our holy fathers Abraham, Isaac, and Jacob, and sustain them in a green pasture, beside still waters in the Paradise of joy, the place out of which grief, sorrow, and groaning have fled away in the light of Your saints. Raise up their bodies also on the day which You have appointed, according to Your true promises which are without lie. Grant them the good things of Your promises—that which an eye has not seen nor ear heard, neither have come upon the heart of man—the things which You, O God, have prepared for those who love Your holy name. For there is no death of Your servants, but a departure. Even if any negligence or heedlessness has overtaken them as men, since they were clothed in flesh and dwelt in this world, O God, as a Good One and Lover of Mankind, graciously accord, O Lord, to repose and forgive them, Your servants, the orthodox Christians who are in the whole world from the east to the west and from the north to the south, each one according to his name and each one according to her name. For no one is pure and without blemish, even though his life on earth be a single day. As for those, O Lord, whose souls You have taken, repose them, and may they be worthy of the kingdom of the heavens. As for us all, grant us our Christian perfection that would be pleasing to You, and give them and us a share and inheritance with all Your people.[212]

[212] Coptic Orthodox Diocese of Southern USA, "Coptic Reader"; see also Khs-Burmester, *The Egyptian or Coptic Church*, 203n4.

## The Variable Elements in the Coptic Funeral Rites

(Psalm numbers are all LXX.)

| | Selection of Psalms | Readings | Concluding Prayer |
|---|---|---|---|
| *Men* | Ps 138:7-10<br>Ps 118:175-176<br>Ps 113:16-18<br>Ps 114:1-9 | 1 Cor 15:1-23<br>John 5:19-29 | "O God the Eternal" |
| *Women* | Ps 102:1-4<br>Ps 113:16-18<br>Ps 118:174-175 | 1 Cor 15:39-50<br>Matt 26:6-13 | "Truly the multitude of your abundant" |
| *Women who died at delivery* | **Exception**<br>Is 26:9-20 | Rom 5:1-16<br>John 16:20-23 | "Truly the multitude of your abundant" |
| *Boys* | Ps 26:9, 10, 13<br>Ps 64:4, 5<br>Ps 114:3-5 | 1 Thess 4:13-18<br>Luke 7:11-16 | "O true God and Logos" |
| *Girls* | Ps 33:4-5<br>Ps 61:1, 2, 5<br>Ps 88:73-76<br>Ps 118:73-76 | 1 Cor 15:50-58<br>Matt 9:18-26 | "O Beneficent Savior" |
| *Deacons* | Ps 65:16-20<br>Ps 118:105-112<br>Ps 134:13, 14, 19-21 | 1 Cor 15:23-38<br>John 12:20-26 | "Again, let us ask God the Pantocrator" |
| *Priests* | Ps 134:1-5<br>Ps 107:31, 32, 41, 42, 43<br>Ps 118:25-30 | 2 Cor 4:10–5:1<br>Matt 25:14-23 | "How great are Your works" |
| *Monk-Priests* | Ps 33:10-14<br>Ps 118:121-128<br>Ps 54:4-8 | Rom 8:2-11<br>2 Cor 4:10–5:1<br>Luke 20:27-38<br>John 17:1-12 | "O God who are without beginning" |
| *Bishops* | Ps 117:1-5<br>Ps 118:33-40<br>Ps 138:11-13 | Heb 13:7-21<br>Luke 22:24-30 | "O Master, Lord Jesus Christ, Co-Creator of all creation" |
| *Monks* | Ps 33:10-14<br>Ps 118:121-128<br>Ps 54:4-8 | Rom 8:2-11<br>2 Cor 4:10–5:1<br>Luke 20:27-38<br>John 17:1-12 | "O God who are without beginning" |
| *Nuns* | Ps 12:1-4<br>Ps 118:161-168<br>Ps 15:7-11 | 2 Cor 5:11-17<br>Luke 10:38-42 | "God of spirits and Lord of all flesh, who according to Your hidden counsel" |
| *Third and Fortieth Days* | Ps 68:1-3, 7, 8<br>Ps 118:17-20<br>Ps 68:13-18 | Rom 5:6-17<br>John 11:38-45 | "We thank You, Lord Pantocrator" |

## Coptic Concluding Prayer and Prayer 18 of the *Prayers of Sarapion*

### Concluding Prayer, Coptic Funeral Ritual

[Last prayer of the funeral rites for men]

O God, the Eternal, who know the hidden things before they are, who know all things, who brought all things into being out of non-existence, *in whose hands is the authority over life and death. Who descend into the gates of Hades, and bring up. A mystery of Yours is the creation of man, O our master, and the dissolution of Your temporal creation and their eternal resurrection.* You are He to whom is rendered thanksgiving for all things, and for entry into the world, and for his departure out of it in hopes of the resurrection, we bless the coming of Your Christ, and the sonship which You have given us in Him, who condescended to our passions and did raise us with Him into freedom from passion. *Receive, our Master, in holy charge, this soul of Your servant (. . .), and keep him in repose until the resurrection and the manifestation of Your Christ, in the bosom of our holy fathers, Abraham, Isaac and Jacob,* the place out of which grief, sorrow and groaning have fled away. *And if he has committed any sins against You as a man, forgive and pardon him, and let all his chastisements pass away,* for You did not form man unto corruption but unto life. And repose him in that place; and we, who are in this place have mercy on us, and make us worthy to serve You, free from care. *Those who mourn, give them comfort.* Those who survive, console. Those who are orphaned, sustain them. And those who are gathered together and share in their sorrow, have mercy on them and bless them. Give unto them a heavenly reward in the age to come and forever and ever. For You are a merciful and compassionate God, and unto You we send up glory and honor and worship, O Father, Son, and Holy Spirit, now and ever.[213]

### Prayer 18, *Prayers of Sarapion*

Prayer 18: Prayer for the One Who Has Died and Is Carried Out

*God, you have the power of life and death,* God of the spirits and Master of all flesh, *God of the dead and of the living. You lead down to the doors of Hades and you lead up. You create the human spirit in a person and take the souls of the saints and give them rest.* You, who alone are incorruptible and unchangeable and eternal, are the one who changes and turns and transforms your creatures as it is right and beneficial. We pray to you for the sleep and rest of this your (male or female) servant.

*Give rest to his soul,* his spirit, in green pastures, *in the inner rooms of rest with Abraham, Isaac, and Jacob and all your saints.* And raise (his) body on the appointed day according to your truthful promises so that you may give to him according to the worthy inheritance(s) in your holy pastures. *Do not remember his transgressions and his sins,* but make his departure to be peaceful and blessed.

*Heal the griefs of those who carry (him) with a spirit of consolation* and give us all a good end.

Through your only-begotten Jesus Christ, through whom (be) to you the glory and the power in the holy Spirit to the ages of ages. Amen.[214]

[213] Coptic Orthodox Diocese of Southern USA, "Coptic Reader"; see also Khs-Burmester, *The Egyptian or Coptic Church*, 203.

[214] Johnson, *The Prayers of Sarapion*, 68–69.

While not identical to the Byzantine prayer "O God of spirits and of all flesh," it shares similar phraseology and similar themes, such as that the souls of the departed rest in "green pasture" where "the place out of which grief, sorrow, and groaning have fled away" and the petition that God "as a Good One and Lover of Mankind" forgive their sins" for "no one is pure and without blemish." It is very possible that a common ancestor lies between this prayer and the Byzantine prayer "O God of spirits and of all flesh."[215]

Each of the variable concluding prayers addresses the particulars of the deceased person's situation (depending on his gender, age, and ecclesiastical status) and in certain cases tries to relate with and appease the feelings of loss of the survivors. For example, in the case of the funeral rites for a boy, the petition part of the concluding prayer ("O true God and Logos") reads as follows:

> Therefore, we ask and entreat You, O Lover of Mankind, in mercy and pardon and repose to receive this sinless charge of Your child (. . .); who has not finished his life on earth, nor has enjoyed good things, nor has received, nor given; but has lived in milk without guile, and beauty without blemish, and virginity without spot. . . . For You blessed children with Your good mouth, giving commandment concerning children, saying, "Take heed that you do not despise one of these little ones [Matt 18:10] for I say to you that in heaven their angels always see the face of My Father who is in heaven." If thus this great blessing from heaven is theirs, count Your servant (. . .) in the number of the children who have gone before him, those who are gathered into the places of repose, in Your kingdom, the one hundred and forty-four thousand [Rev 14:3-5]. Clothe him with them in the spotless raiment and unfading beauty in the tabernacles of light, the place which You have appointed for them that please You. . . . On behalf of Your servants his father and mother, whose great sorrow and heartache reaches unto You in tears and mourning. You as the Good One and a Lover of Mankind, went into the city of Nain, and raised the son of the widow unto her, living and incorrupt [Luke 7:11-17]. To these others then, O Lord, raise up other seed in place of him that they may rejoice in place of their mourning.[216]

[215] For the full text of the Byzantine "O God of spirits and of all flesh . . .," see section 5.5.2.

[216] Coptic Orthodox Diocese of Southern USA, "Coptic Reader"; see also Khs-Burmester, *The Egyptian or Coptic Church*, 206.

This prayer is a remarkable example of euchological creativity, where theology, psychology, and culture are intertwined masterfully. The prayer works at different levels simultaneously. It acknowledges the brevity of the deceased boy's life and all those things that the boy did not experience, but with an emphasis on the youthfulness that did not have the time or opportunity to sin. The prayer reminds the mourners of Matthew 18:10, that the children belong to heaven, and identifies these children with the spotless ones of Revelation 14:3-5. The prayer then addresses the real and hard pain of loss that the parents feel, recalls the miracle of the raising of the son of the widow of Nain, and asks that the grieving parents are soothed by the birth of another child that would replace their pain of loss with the joy of new life.

While these are prayed for a deceased boy, the prayer for a deceased girl has a different emphasis, revealing the cultural context of these prayers. The petition part of the concluding prayer ("O our beneficent Savior") reads as follows:

> We pray to You, O Lover of Mankind and lover of Your creation, for this Your handmaid, the young maiden, the virgin (. . .); who has departed from the body, like all her forefathers, and has come to You, the God of truth. May her passing to You be bright like an unquenchable lamp. Count her with her fellow virgins who have gone before her at Your great supper, with the unspeakable joy of them that rejoice. And raise her up again according to Your true and unfailing promises at the resurrection of the just; that she may receive a share and an inheritance in the kingdom of Your Christ, Jesus our Lord.[217]

While theologically it is a soothing prayer that affirms the hope and joy of the resurrection, from the cultural point of view there is no mention of the mourning of the parents or the things in life that the young girl did not have the opportunity to enjoy, as in the case of the prayer for a deceased boy.

During Holy Week, prayers for the dead are not permitted and therefore the funeral services have a different structure; they are comprised of an Old Testament reading, a psalm verse, and a gospel

[217] Coptic Orthodox Diocese of Southern USA, "Coptic Reader"; see also Khs-Burmester, *The Egyptian or Coptic Church*, 208.

reading, the selection depending on the age, gender, and ecclesiastical status of the departed. As prayers for the dead are not permitted during Holy Week, after the Divine Liturgy on Palm Sunday, and "in anticipation" for those that may die during Holy Week, a memorial service is celebrated.[218] Finally, memorial services take place on the third day at the home of the deceased and on the fortieth day, the sixth month, and the year at the church.[219]

### *5.2.7 Ethiopian*

The funeral rites are found in the *Mäṣḥafä gənzät*, or "The Book of the Wrapping" (of the body),[220] and central to it is the *fətḥat*, or the absolution. While the origins of the *Mäṣḥafä gənzät* are not known, it seems that it combines early Greek and Coptic texts in translation synthesized with local traditions.[221] The manuscript tradition, which begins in the fifteenth century, presents a huge variety, diversity, and flexibility in texts and rituals within the rite that reaches some kind of standardization only in the twentieth century with the use of the printing press.[222]

Both the shrouding and the absolution are ritual and theological highlights of the funeral service, respectively: the former to highlight in an extensive and elaborate ritual the preparation of the body; the latter "to absolve, to set free, to let loose or to release the dead person

[218] Khs-Burmester, *The Egyptian or Coptic Church*, 214–16.

[219] Ibid., 216–18.

[220] Tedros Abraha, "Gənzät: Mäṣḥafä gənzät," in *Encyclopaedia Aethiopica*, vol. 2 (Wiesbaden: Harrassowitz Verlag, 2005), 748–49, here at 748. See also Richard Pankhurst, "Funerals," in *Encyclopaedia Aethiopica*, 2:587–91. For the full text in Geʿez with a German translation, see Friedrich Erich Dobberahn, "Der äthiopische Begräbnisritus," in *Liturgie im Angesichts des Todes: Judentum und Ostkirchen*, ed. Hansjakob Becker and Hermann Ühlein, Pietas liturgica 9–10 (Sankt Ottilien: EOS Verlag, 1997), 1:137–316, 657–84; 2:859–1036; 3:1397–1432.

[221] Abraha, "Gənzät: Mäṣḥafä gənzät," 748.

[222] Wion, "Onction des malades, funérailles et commemorations." The variety in the manuscript witnesses of the funeral rites can also be attributed (especially for later manuscripts) to a theological controversy regarding the question of whether communion should be given to the dead. See Getatchew Haile, "The Mäṣḥafä Gənzät as a Historical Source Regarding the Theology of the Ethiopian Orthodox Church," *Scrinium* 1 (2005): 58–76, here at 60.

from the bondage of his/her sins."[223] The emphasis on the shrouding has its roots in a tradition that maintains that St. Helen, who found the cross, also found "the hidden or lost funeral ritual, which Joseph of Arimathea and Nicodemus used for shrouding Our Lord." It was Benjamin I of Alexandria (623–662?) who discovered the ritual and sent a copy to the Ethiopians.[224]

The funeral itself consists of four parts. The first part takes place in the house of the deceased and involves prayers of absolution and a watch over the deceased, the preparation of the body, and the shrouding. The prayers vary depending on the gender, age, clerical rank, and social status of the deceased.[225] In a ritual published by Getatchew Haile, the directives are given for this first part of the funeral rite taking place in the domestic setting. It directs that prayers of absolution and the whole Psalter with additional texts included in the Ethiopic Psalter are read. Then water is blessed by reading over it the whole Gospel of John. This water is then used to bathe the deceased. The term used for the bathing is "baptism," and the formula "In the name of the Father, the Son, and the Holy Spirit" is proclaimed while bathing ("baptizing") the dead person and providing him or her with a cross. Then they are shrouded with new clothes, "that it may signal with this that they have new clothes in the kingdom of heaven, as the Apostle Paul has said: 'As we are clothed in the image of the earthly, likewise we shall be clothed in the image of the heavenly [1 Cor 15:49].'"[226] Then they "perform for the dead seven shroudings, setting for them seven crosses—one at the head side, one at the feet side, one at the right, one at the left, and three on them. Let them also kindle twelve lamps for a priest, seven for a deacon, and four for laypeople. Putting on lights for them is for the recognition of their translation from the world of darkness to the world of light." Then they begin reciting the beginning of Psalm 118, as the transition to the funeral procession from the house to the church, prayers are read over salt and water, and the house is sprinkled.[227]

[223] Haile, "The Mäṣḥafä Gənzät," 58.

[224] Ibid., 59.

[225] Abraha, "Gənzät: Mäṣḥafä gənzät," 748.

[226] Haile, "The Mäṣḥafä Gənzät," 71.

[227] Ibid., 71.

The second part of the funeral rites involves an elaborate procession of the deceased from his or her home to the church for the funeral Divine Liturgy. This procession, led by clergy in full vestments, is structured around a division of Psalm 118 in seven sections, each section ending with a station when the casket is lowered, readings are proclaimed, and prayers are read. These stations are possibly "a practice that appears to be a ritualization of the need for the pallbearers to rest."[228]

The third part of the funeral rites takes place in the church and involves the full celebration of the Divine Liturgy for all deceased, regardless of gender, age, clerical rank, and social status.[229] Where they are placed in the church, however, depends on which space they would occupy when they lived, according to their rank: "And let them lie down according to their ranks. If it is a priest, let them bring him in, inside the curtain, before the altar. But if it is a deacon, a monk, a nun, or a layman, outside the sanctuary, according to the directive."[230] At the end of the liturgy the farewell kiss is given to the deceased, first by the head priest and then by all present, and oil is poured over the deceased.[231]

The fourth part of the funeral rites takes place over the grave and "entails an inclination prayer, numerous intercessions, two prayers for the imposition of hands, a litanic prayer attributed to Abba Sälama II (d. 1388), and a series of seven dismissal benedictions."[232] Following the burial and as part of the absolution granted to the deceased, alms are given on behalf of the deceased "to the poor, the wretched, the elderly, and the orphans or to the church."[233] The Ethiopian tradition also has a high number of *täzkar* or commemoration days after the death and burial: the third, the seventh, the twelfth, the thirteenth, the fortieth, the sixtieth, and eightieth days, as well as the six-month

[228] Findikyan, "Funerals: Eastern Churches," 216.

[229] Ibid.

[230] Haile, "The Mäṣḥafä Gənzät," 72.

[231] Some manuscript witnesses, such as the one published by Getatchew Haile, also attest to the controversial practice of giving communion to the dead person. Haile, "The Mäṣḥafä Gənzät," 60, 72 and note 10 on the same page.

[232] Findikyan, "Funerals: Eastern Churches," 216.

[233] Haile, "The Mäṣḥafä Gənzät," 73.

and year anniversary.[234] Mention should also be made of mourning practices that run parallel to the official funeral rites.[235]

Many manuscripts of *Mäṣḥafä gənzät* include the text of the *Ləfafä ṣədək*, a collection of magical prayers in either scroll or book form that is buried with the deceased. In these prayers the Virgin Mary plays a central role as one who "takes on the role of intercessor for those who are damned in hell, and obtains from God, with Jesus Christ's help, the secret Book of Life. Being a copy of the celestial Book of God, the L.s. [*Ləfafä ṣədək*] has the power to protect the soul after death on its journey to the afterworld, the heavenly realm." These texts, either in scroll or in booklet form, can be worn as prophylactic during one's life but also are buried with the deceased; if in scroll format, it is extended over the whole body, from head to toe.[236] The *Ləfafä ṣədək* has been purged from printed editions of the funeral rites, in the effort of the Ethiopian church to circumvent magical practices.

### *5.2.8 Conclusions*

Each of the funeral rites examined here bears the imprint of the theological reflection and cultural context in which they were formed and developed. All traditions, however, highlight the importance and centrality of the resurrection as the victory of life over death. In its own way, each tradition also addresses the pastoral challenge of offering solace to the bereaved family and friends, allowing for

[234] "If it is possible for them, let them absolve and celebrate the Eucharist 40 days. If it is impossible for them, (let them do it) on the third day, as the Resurrection of the Word; then on the seventh day, for his soul reaches (on that day) the seventh heaven, before the throne of the glory of God, whether righteous or sinful. Then also on the twelfth day, let them read at the tomb seven times during the day and seven times during the night. . . . Let them raise incense, reciting the Prayer of Incense. Let them again perform (the ritual) on the thirtieth day and fortieth day, because Our Lord had ascended the heavens on the fortieth day." Haile, "The Mäṣḥafä Gənzät," 73; Abraha, "Gənzät: Mäṣḥafä gənzät," 749. But these could be expensive; see Pankhurst, "Funerals," 590.

[235] Pankhurst, "Funerals," 588–90; see also Roger Cowley, "Attitudes to the Dead in the Ethiopian Orthodox Church," *Sobornost* 6 (1972): 241–56.

[236] Bogdan Burtea, "Ləfafä ṣədək," in *Encyclopaedia Aethiopica*, vol. 3 (Wiesbaden: Harrassowitz Verlag, 2007), 542–3; Wion, "Onction des malades, funérailles et commemorations."

expressions of grief conditioned by the cultural context but defined by the central Christian belief in the resurrection and life after death. The funeral rites would be an excellent case study to examine the dynamic and relationship between official liturgy and local culture it its expression of grief.

These mourning, funeral, and burial rituals and practices of the Eastern Christian churches do not go unchallenged in the modern world. For example, the practices of the family of preparing the body of the deceased, of gathering around the deceased in a domestic setting with family and friends and mourning, are replaced by the services of the funeral homes, where one observes a growing distance from the experience of death and a certain beautification of death. Another example is the manner in which each Eastern Christian church deals with the practice of cremation, as most do not accept the practice and do not perform a funeral service for those cremated. But they are faced with the question of what to do when the cremation was not the result of the will of the deceased but the decision of his or her family for financial reasons (usually). Finally, the length of the funeral rites places a big challenge on their celebration in the modern Western world, forcing clergy to abbreviate the funeral services. A systematic study of the funeral services in each tradition with an eye to the modern challenges they face is called for.

## *Chapter 6: Conclusion*

# The Ethos of Eastern Christian Worship and Liturgical Spirituality

As we have seen repeatedly in this work, all Eastern Christian traditions are highly liturgical, for, indeed, liturgy is at the heart of the life of these churches and their faithful. And it is certainly not hyperbole to say so. Whether under the cupola of a magnificent domed church adorned with splendid iconography, or the roof of a humble chapel with only a couple of portable icons of Christ and the Virgin Mary, or even with no icons at all, the liturgy celebrated in every church lies at the center of life of the Christians of the East. From their pre-baptismal rites to their funeral and memorial services, every aspect of their life is marked by ritual, petitions, prayers, and hymns. It is in liturgy that they learn the language of prayer, the articulation of their beliefs, the appropriate manner of worshiping God, and the applicability of faith in their daily lives. Their identities are formed in liturgical celebrations filled with the sweet-smelling incense, surrounded by the melodies of their cantors and choirs chanting hymns, and gazing at the images of Christ, the Virgin Mary, and the saints painted on portable icons or the walls of their church. Eastern Christians have strong bonds to their liturgical traditions as throughout the centuries in the many times of distress, repression, persecution, and expulsion, it was in the liturgical life of their traditions that they found consolation, peace, strength, and courage; many becoming neo-martyrs,[1] giving their life for Christ by refusing to

[1] Neo-martyr means "new" martyr, to distinguish from the martyrs of the early Church during the Roman persecutions. Neo-martyrs are those who gave their lives

abandon their faith. For this reason, Eastern Christians have a strong sense of tradition and ownership of that tradition and feel that they are responsible to hand on that tradition to their children and grandchildren, even if many times they do not understand aspects of it. They feel obliged to preserve and pass on what they received.

While the Eastern Christian traditions are not identical with one another, and each has its own emphasis defined by its history, culture, and theological approach, all share in what we would call a common liturgical ethos and spirituality, a certain common denominator that unites these traditions in spite of their different liturgical traditions, history, and culture. This liturgical ethos and spirituality is now tested as all Eastern Christian Churches have communities in the Western world, forced out of their homelands because of financial hardship, persecution, and genocide. What follows is a brief encounter with a selection of some characteristics of this common liturgical ethos and spirituality and a discussion of some of the common challenges they face in the twenty-first century.

## 6.1 Liturgy and Faith

The Eastern Christian traditions have suffered divisions among themselves for many centuries, going all the way back to the christological controversies of the fifth and sixth centuries and the (ecumenical) councils of Ephesus (431) and Chalcedon (451). Recent theological dialogue among the Eastern Christian communions, however, has shown that while each communion's expression of Christian faith is conditioned by historical, cultural, and linguistic particularities, they all share the same faith. Sebastian Brock puts it well when he says:

> One of the most important findings of recent ecumenical dialogue on the topic of Christology has been the realization that, in cases where verbally conflicting doctrinal statements are to be found (such as "two natures" or "one nature" in the incarnate Christ), it is not a question of one being right and the other wrong; rather, both should be seen as

---

for the faith under Islam and communism. See, for example, Nomikos Michael Vaporis, *Witnesses for Christ: Orthodox Christian Neomartyrs of the Ottoman Period, 1437–1860* (Crestwood, NY: St. Vladimir's Seminary Press, 2000).

> right. In order to perceive that this is so, it is essential to realize that the verbally conflicting formulations have arisen because each side understood the key terms, or phrases, in a different way. Only when one explores beneath the surface of the verbal conflict, does it become clear that the underlying understanding of each side is in fact essentially the same, even though expressed in a different way.[2]

In fact, the dialogue among the Eastern Christian churches is a great example of the success of the ecumenical movement, where the churches moved beyond polemics to recognize their common faith in the tradition and practices of their fellow Eastern Christians with whom they have been separated for fifteen centuries.[3] The realization that a common faith is shared emerges not only in the official theological consultations but also in the systematic study of the liturgical texts of the Eastern Christian traditions. Liturgy emerges as the authentic expression of faith articulated, prayed, lived, and taught in each tradition. The liturgical scholar and bishop of the Armenian Church M. Daniel Findikyan accurately notes:

> It could be said that what the Church declares to God in the inspired words of her liturgy is a more authentic and accurate gauge of her orthodoxy than the stark conciliar statements and synthetic dogmatic definitions on which we are accustomed to focus our attention in our efforts to ascertain the "official" teaching of this or that Church. . . . It is precisely in the Church's liturgy, her Spirit-driven "Abba, Father!" [Gal. 4:6] that the Church's most instinctive and genuine confession of faith resides. There it is lived, learned, transmitted and, most importantly, is solemnly and officially confessed to God in prayer.[4]

[2] Sebastian Brock, "The Origins of the Qanona 'Holy God, Holy Mighty, Holy Immortal' According to Gabriel of Qatar (Early 7th Century)," A Review of Syriac and Oriental Studies, *The Harp (Volume 21): Festschrift: Rev. Fr. Emmanuel Thelly*, ed. Geevarghese Panicker, Rev. Jacob Thekeparampil, and Abraham Kalakudi (Piscataway, NJ: Gorgias Press, 2011), 173–86, here 173.

[3] For an overview of the dialogue, see Sebastian Brock, "The Syriac Churches and Dialogue with the Catholic Church," *Heythrop Journal* 45 (2004): 466–76; Christine Chaillot, ed., *The Dialogue between the Eastern Orthodox and Oriental Orthodox Churches* (Volos: Volos Academy Publications, 2016).

[4] Michael Daniel Findikyan, "Christology and the Armenian Holy Sacrifice (*Soorp Badarak*)," in Chaillot, *The Dialogue*, 378–86, here 379–80.

Looking at the liturgical texts of the Eastern Christian traditions as sources and expressions of their theological heritage has proven to be quite valuable. For example, Bishop Mar Awa Royel of the Church of the East points out:

> At the heart of the Church's christological expression is the mystery of the Incarnation—that the Son of God became Man for our salvation. The Assyrian Church of the East ardently holds to the duality of natures in Christ—the divinity and the humanity—yet clearly expressed the unity of the natures in the singularity of the person of Christ the Son. . . . The main liturgical formulary of the Church of the East, the *Khudra*, is replete with christological expressions that demonstrate the orthodoxy of her faith.[5]

In his famous article where he addresses the validity of the ancient eucharistic prayer of Addai and Mari of the Church of the East, Robert Taft set the proper framework for understanding different *expressions* of the Christian faith in the liturgical context: He writes:

> By way of conclusion, then, I believe one can say there *are* irreducible local differences in the *liturgical expression* of what I would take to be fully reconcilable *teaching* of both East and West on the Eucharist: that the gifts of bread and wine are sanctified via a prayer, the anaphora, which applies to the present gifts of bread and wine that Jesus handed on. *How* the individual anaphoras express this application has varied widely depending on local tradition, particularly history, and the doctrinal concerns of time and place. In my view these differences *cannot* with any historical legitimacy be seen in dogmatic conflict with parallel but divergent expressions of the same basic realities in a different historico-ecclesial milieu.[6]

To cite another example, a whole series of dissertations completed at the theological faculties of the Universities of Athens and Thessaloniki in Greece, all directed under different professors, points to the unity of the faith between the Orthodox and the Coptic traditions.

[5] Mar Awa Royel, "A Survey of the Christology of the Assyrian Church of the East as Expressed in the *Khudra*," unpublished paper, available at https://www.academia.edu/12388876/A_Survey_of_the_Christology_of_the_Assyrian_Church_of_the_East_as_Expressed_in_the_Khudra.

[6] Robert Taft, "Mass Without the Consecration?": 506–7; emphasis in the original.

More particularly, they demonstrate that the Eutychian monophysitism condemned at Chalcedon in 451 is absent from the liturgical texts of the Coptic Church.[7] Such studies are very promising as they cultivate the mutual knowledge of liturgical traditions of each church, confirm the unity of faith, appease those that question the theological agreement reached in the context of dialogue, and help lead the implementation of the liturgical implications of ecclesial reconciliation that is called for by the agreed statements of the dialogue between the Orthodox and Oriental Orthodox. Similarly, the invaluable work of Sebastian Brock has shown that the liturgical tradition of the Church of the East does not reflect a "Nestorian" theology[8] but is a revered and, in fact, an ancient expression of Syriac Christianity that uniquely complements the puzzle that is called Eastern Christianity.

This rapprochement among Eastern Christians is also encouraged by the tragic reality of persecution in many areas of the Middle East that forces Christians to work together, pray together, and share the sacraments. In their dwindling numbers and under the pressure of persecution, they find solace and strength in one another. The desperate situation in the Middle East has led thousands of Eastern Christians to flee to the West and live in safety, but many times at a distance from their own communities. In such cases there has been an unofficial intercommunion between Eastern Christians, where eucharistic hospitality is offered by an Eastern Christian community to another in the absence of their own communities. It is everyone's hope that the leadership of the Eastern Christian churches will work together toward an official full intercommunion, "translating" the theological agreements into action.

## 6.2 Hymnology

Hymns are at the heart of the liturgical life of all the Eastern Christian churches. It is through the hymns that God is praised and the

[7] See, for example, Stefanos Alexopoulos, "Greek Scholarship on the Coptic Liturgical Tradition: An Assessment," in *CYNAΞIC KAΘOΛIKH: Beiträge zu Gottesdienst und Geschichte der fünf altkirchlichen Patriarchate für Heinzgerd Brakmann zum 70. Geburtstag*, ed. Diliana Atanassova and Tinatin Chronz, (Wien: Lit Verlag, 2014), 1–11.

[8] Sebastian Brock, "The 'Nestorian' Church: A Lamentable Misnomer," *Bulletin of the John Rylands Library* 78 (1996): 23–35.

faithful are taught their faith. There are multiple genres of hymns in each tradition, continually embellished with new compositions, particularly as the liturgical year of each tradition is embellished with feasts of newly declared saints. At the same time, ancient hymns are in continuous use for centuries, loved and revered, demonstrating the sense of tradition and continuity that permeates the Eastern Christian churches.

An example of such an ancient hymn, which also embodies the movement from division toward unity among the Eastern Christian churches, is the *Trisagion* hymn. This hymn is common among all Eastern Christian churches, but with a different theological interpretation that once divided them but now highlights the unity in diversity. There are two versions and two basic interpretations of the *Trisagion* hymn: christological and trinitarian. The christological version, probably the older version of the two,[9] understands the hymn as addressed to Christ, hence its christological ending, depending on the liturgical season: "Holy God, Holy Mighty, Holy Immortal, who was . . . [born/baptized/crucified] . . . for us, have mercy on us." The non-Chalcedonian churches use the christological *Trisagion*. The trinitarian version simply does not have a christological ending: "Holy God, Holy Mighty, Holy Immortal, have mercy on us." The Chalcedonian churches (Byzantine tradition) understand the *Trisagion* as being trinitarian in the following way: "Holy God" refers to the Father, "Holy Mighty" to the Son, and "Holy Immortal" to the Holy Spirit. The Church of the East also understands the *Trisagion* hymn as being trinitarian, but sees the hymn as addressed to the Holy Trinity as a whole, not to each person of the Trinity separately, as is the case in the Byzantine understanding. Current historical and theological research has shown that these versions and interpretations are not contradictory; rather, they reflect the diversity of expression of the one common faith.[10]

[9] See above, p. 76.

[10] Sebastià Janeras, "Le trisagion: Une formule brève en liturgie comparée," in *Comparative Liturgy Fifty Years after Anton Baumstark (1872–1948)*, ed. Taft and Winkler, 495–562; Brock, "The Origins of the Qanona," 173–85; Kazimierz Ginter, "The *Trisagion* Riots (512) as an Example of Interaction between Politics and Liturgy," *Studia Ceranea* 7 (2017): 41–57.

Common to the liturgical spirituality and outlook of all Eastern Christians is the centrality of the resurrection. Not only is the annual celebration of Easter considered to be the "crown" of feasts of the liturgical year, but every Sunday's Eucharist is also a celebration of the resurrection of Christ. This is reflected (1) in the hymnody chanted at vespers on Saturday evening and at matins on Sunday morning; (2) in a series of resurrection gospel readings proclaimed at Sunday matins, continuing an ancient Jerusalem tradition; (3) in the colors of vestments, as penitential colors such as purple or black are never worn on Sundays, even in Great Lent; (4) in the body posture of the celebrant and the faithful by following the canonical legislation of the First Ecumenical Council of Nicaea (AD 325), which forbids kneeling on Sundays (see section 6.7 below).

The hymnody of the Eastern Churches deals with the topic of the resurrection in many different ways. For example, in one of the hymns (*qolo*) sung at vespers on Saturday night in the West Syriac tradition, the poet addresses the importance of the resurrection with a series of questions that highlight the centrality of the resurrection for Christian faith:

> If there is no resurrection, what did the martyrs gain by death? And if there is no other world, why did the righteous labor? And if the resurrection is not true, even Christ did not rise from the dead. You dead, await the Son, for the hope of his promise is sure, when he said in his Gospel, that in the hour, when the dead hear the living voice of God, the graves shall be opened and they shall come forth to meet him when he comes.[11]

A Sunday hymn from the East Syriac tradition is a wonderful expression of the triumph of life over death and the ensuing joy of the whole creation: "Rejoice, take heart, O mortals: the reign of Death is ended! Christ crushed it by his passion; made life reign by his rising! Earth and heaven rejoice now, and angels sing together: praise him who, by his rising, raised up our race which was lost."[12]

[11] *The Book of Common Prayer of the Syrian Church*, trans. Bede Griffiths (Piscataway, NJ: Gorgias Press, 2005), 315–16.

[12] *Emmanuel: That Is, the Book of Public Prayer* (San Diego: Chaldean Catholic Diocese of St. Peter the Apostle, 2013), 88.

The Byzantine tradition links the eleven resurrection gospel readings[13] with eleven *exaposteilaria* and *doxastica* (hymn genres), which narrate in poetical form the story of each resurrection gospel. Each is called *eothinon* to define it as the Sunday *morning* gospel reading. Below, for example, one can see the correlation between the second *eothinon* (morning) gospel reading and the relevant second *eothinon exaposteilarion* and second *eothinon doxastikon.*[14]

The Ethiopian tradition has an extremely rich corpus of hymns, which are executed uniquely in this tradition accompanied by the beating of drums, the rattling of sistrums, and the rhythmic swaying of the prayer staff, joined by hand clapping and the movement of the body following the tune and rhythm of the melody sung.[15] These features enable the active and lively participation of the faithful in the singing of the hymns, as they join the choir by swaying their body, clapping their hands, and singing when the hymn is familiar. This engagement of the faithful also enhances the formative nature of these hymns, as their function is also to teach the faith to the faithful. In the following paschal hymn, a summary of salvation history is provided together with a presentation of the christological teaching regarding the person of Christ:

> He said to our father Adam, "I shall be born from your daughter and become a child for your sake in order that My mercy might be revealed unto you. I shall make you glorious and exalt your name more than the heavenly angels. For I fashioned you with My hands in the likeness of My Son. I created you in the light of My glory for the inheritance of My Kingdom. I will raise you up from the dead with the power of My resurrection. For your sake and for the sake of those like you, I descended into Hades with the authority of My Father in heaven." Having seen the majesty of His divinity, the angel of death cried, as it was written, "For he shatters the doors of bronze" and thereby unbound the bondage of death. And thus we believe that He has neither a mother in

[13] (1) Matt 28:16-20; (2) Mark 16:1-8; (3) Mark 16:9-20; (4) Luke 24:1-12; (5) Luke 24:12-35; (6) Luke 24:36-53; (7) John 20:1-10; (8) John 20:11-18; (9) John 20:19-31; (10) John 21:1-14; (11) John 21:14-25.

[14] English from Digital Chant Stand of the Greek Orthodox Archdiocese of America, https://dcs.goarch.org/goa/dcs/dcs.html.

[15] Andualem Dagmawi Gobena, "Soteriology in the Ethiopian *Täwaḥədo* Church as Reflected in the Liturgical Hymns of the *Dəggʷa* of Yared" (PhD diss., University of St. Michael's College, Toronto, 2019), 64–66.

| **Second *Eothinon* Gospel (Mark 16:1-8)** | **Second *Eothinon* *Exaposteilarion*** | **Second *Eothinon* *Doxastikon*** |
|---|---|---|
| When the Sabbath was past, Mary Magdalene, and Mary the mother of James and Salome, bought spices, so that they might go and anoint Jesus. And very early on the first day of the week they went to the tomb when the sun had risen. | | The women with their ointments went with Mary to the tomb, |
| And they were saying to one another, "Who will roll away the stone for us from the door of the tomb?" | | and they wondered how they would attain what they desired. |
| And looking up, they saw that the stone was rolled back—it was very large. And entering the tomb, they saw a young man sitting on the right side, dressed in a white robe; and they were amazed. And he said to them, | The women with the myrrh rejoiced when they saw that the great stone had from the tomb been rolled away. For they had seen a young man sitting within on the right side. And he addressed them, saying: | Then they saw that the stone was rolled back, and also a godly young man who tried to quiet the disturbance of their souls. For he said, |
| "Do not be amazed; you seek Jesus of Nazareth, who was crucified. He has risen, He is not here; see the place where they laid Him. But go, tell His disciples and Peter that He is going before you to Galilee; | "Lo, Christ has risen from the dead. Go and tell His disciples and Peter too, to proceed to Galilee on the mountain. | "The Lord Jesus has risen. Therefore, preach it to His Disciples and preachers, that they should go quickly to Galilee; |
| there you will see Him, as He told you." And they went out and fled from the tomb, for trembling and astonishment had come upon them; and they said nothing to anyone, for they were afraid. | For He will there appear to you His friends, as He foretold you." | and you will see Him, risen from the dead, as the Giver of Life and Lord." |

heaven nor a father on earth. He is God and Human in His essence. They condemned Him without sin. His side was struck without pain for His divinity was impassible. Our Lord Jesus has borne all these. He took on the earthly flesh and with this flesh, He descended into Hades where He unbound the bondage of death saying, "Come and get out from there you that were imprisoned." And He said to those

> who were in the darkness, "See the light." He rebuked the angel of death saying, "Where, O death, is your victory? Where, O death, is your sting?"[16]

In this one hymn, salvation history, Christology, soteriology, and eschatology all come together, a kind of a theological treatise in poetical form that communicates and makes accessible fundamental Christian teachings through the medium of poetry; theology celebrated, theology taught, in a liturgical context!

## 6.3 The Biblical Nature of Eastern Christianity

The fact that liturgy is at the heart of all Eastern Christian traditions does not mean that they place less emphasis on the Scriptures, that they are not scriptural, as sometimes is thought. On the contrary, the Scriptures, the Old and the New Testaments, are central to the faith, worship, and life of all Eastern Christian traditions. In fact, Scripture defines all aspects of their life, and their liturgical traditions are imbued with Scripture. The emphasis is not on the memorization of Scripture but on living the Scriptures in one's daily life. Scripture for the most part is proclaimed and exegeted in the context of worship: in the celebration of the liturgical year, where the major events of salvation history are celebrated; in liturgical prayer, which is laced with scriptural quotations and allusions; with the readings from Scripture, that are ever present in almost all liturgical celebrations; with hymnography, that offers both exposure to and commentary on the Scriptures; with iconography, which creates a visual text that allows the worshiper to "read" the scriptural narratives on the walls of churches and portable icons.

Eastern Christian liturgies are not only laced with scriptural readings, citations, and allusions, but the "Gospel" itself, the lectionary that contains the gospel readings for the liturgical year, is highly honored. It is "enthroned" on the Holy Table, it is processed with great honor, it is venerated as the Word of God, and it is often highly adorned as a proclamation of that which it points to, that which it reveals, the mystery of Christ. Architectural features such as the ambo

[16] Gobena, "Soteriology in the Ethiopian *Täwaḥədo* Church," 146.

in the Byzantine tradition[17] or the bema in the East Syriac tradition[18] provide a privileged space for the proclamation of the gospel.

Further insight in how the Eastern Churches understand and exegete Scripture can be gained by looking at the "prayer of the gospel" that is recited before the reading of the gospel in the Divine Liturgy. For example, in the Byzantine tradition the celebrant prays the following prayer:

> Shine in our hearts, O Master Who love mankind, the pure light of Your divine knowledge, and open the eyes of our mind that we may comprehend the proclamations of Your Gospels. Instill in us also reverence for Your blessed commandments so that, having trampled down all carnal desires, we may lead a spiritual life, both thinking and doing all those things that are pleasing to You. For You, Christ our God, are the illumination of our souls and bodies, and to You we offer up glory, together with Your Father, Who is without beginning, and Your all-holy, good, and life-creating Spirit, now and forever and to the ages of ages. Amen.[19]

This prayer, originating in the liturgical tradition of Jerusalem, outlines a movement in four parts in one's effort to approach, understand, and apply the Scriptures in one's life: inspiration, comprehension, transformation, action. It provides a particular hermeneutic approach characteristic of Eastern Christianity. The beginning point is faith; that is how it is received and understood, so its interpretation depends on God's inspiration—the prayer asks that the Lord "shine in our hearts" and "open the eyes of our mind." Then that leads to our comprehending the message effecting a transformation of self, demonstrated in action: "having trampled down all carnal desires, we may lead a spiritual life, both thinking and doing all those things that are pleasing to You." All liturgical action is directly related to this movement of inspiration, comprehension, transformation, action. The celebration of liturgy, and the Divine Liturgy in particular, not only

[17] Stephen Xydis, "The Chancel Barrier, Solea, and Ambo of Hagia Sophia," *The Art Bulletin* 29 (1947): 1–24.

[18] Emma Loosley, *Architecture and Liturgy of the Bema*; Robert Taft, "On the Use of the Bema in the East-Syrian Liturgy."

[19] https://www.goarch.org/-/the-divine-liturgy-of-saint-john-chrysostom.

embodies this movement but allows for the community's initiation, participation, and growth into the salvific message of the Gospel.[20]

## 6.4 The Centrality of the Cross

While all Eastern Christian traditions reserve a special place for the resurrection of Christ in the weekly (Sunday) and annual (Easter) cycles of liturgical celebrations, it is viewed and understood in the context of the crucifixion; the one event cannot be understood without the other. In fact, their constant experience of persecution and martyrdom makes these churches crucifixional—because of their suffering, the cross is very relevant and relatable to their own experience, and it makes sense only in relation to the resurrection that is to follow. The cross is amply used, both as a symbol and as an action—Eastern Christians are well known for crossing themselves numerous times throughout services and in private prayer. A cross is given to them to wear for life at their baptism, and priests and bishops bless the faithful with a cross—in almost all the Eastern Christian traditions the cross is always held in the hand by the clergy. These crosses are usually empty crosses (without the body of Christ on them) pointing to the resurrection. Parents and grandparents bless their children and grandchildren with the sign of the cross; people express their joy and thanks by signing themselves with the cross; when in fear or anguish, they sign themselves with the cross; the cross is almost second nature to Eastern Christians!

The Armenian tradition is known for its *khachkars*, monumental stone crosses carved on upright slabs. These have been associated with commemorations of events (battles, building of bridges, donations to monasteries); they mark tombs, act as landmarks, are expressions of gratitude, are believed to have protective powers, and more recently are set up as commemorations for the victims of the Armenian Genocide.[21] The Armenian tradition also knows of an office for the

[20] Adapted from Stefanos Alexopoulos, "The Gospel Narrative in Byzantine Liturgy," in *History and Theology in the Gospels*, ed. T. Nicklas, K.-W. Niebuhr, and M. Seleznev (Tübingen: Mohr Siebeck, 2020), 235–46.

[21] Colum Hourihane, "Cross," *The Grove Encyclopedia of Medieval Art and Architecture* (New York: Oxford University Press, 2012); https://www-oxfordreference-com.ezp-prod1.hul.harvard.edu/view/10.1093/acref/9780195395365.001.0001/acref-9780195395365-e-656.

"Consecration of a Cross." The cross to be consecrated is brought into the church and is washed with water and wine, and a series of psalms, prayers, and readings are performed. The prayers offer a summary of salvation history, as the undoing of Adam's disobedience:

> But he [Adam] from lust of things unattainable was in his ignorance tricked by the deceiver intro transgressing the commandment, and was undone by the bitter tasting of the tree of knowledge. And forfeiting the godlike commandment, he became heir to a life on which a curse was laid and to death. Then you did relent in your fatherly care and compassion; and sent from your bosom your only-begotten Son, our Lord Jesus Christ, the Savior, who fashioned us, and renewed us grown old by a second and divine quickening of life; *whereby he transfigured all that is ours by making it his own* in an economy, enduing us with the same grace unto the glory of his father's will. He was crucified on the tree of life, and withal fastened to the cross along with himself the old man in us. To us he vouchsafes the same cross . . . faith in our participation in the cross, and an ascent on high in glory . . . by spreading abroad his divine creative arms thereon, your only begotten gathered together them that were scattered into reconciliation with you, abolishing among us death and corruption, by means of this divine emblem, which you have provided for the salvation of them that fear you by the sight of the rainbow.[22]

Another prayer places before our eyes the various challenges faced by the people, their fears and hopes:

> Endue with the grace of your holy Spirit this emblem which we have set up in your name. Grant it to be a guardian of souls and bodies for all who shall put their trust in your Son crucified, and who bow down and adore this emblem, which we have raised in your name. And to each that asks for justice and righteousness, do hear him and have mercy, and graciously grant his petitions. And may they who shall see it afar, and seal themselves with the emblem of your cross, be saved by you in all their straits. And if enemies assault any man, of if he be oppressed by foul spirits, Lord, help and save any such. And if any be afflicted with diverse diseases, and fall to praying before the cross,

[22] Adapted from F. C. Conybeare, *Rituale Armenorum, Being the Administration of the Sacraments and the Breviary Rites of the Armenian Church* (Oxford: Clarendon Press, 1905), 39–53 for the whole office, here 41.

> hear and help them. . . . And if there be astir clouds or wrath laden with hail, or parching winds, or angry storm or frozen rain, or blight or locust or caterpillar, and any other edict or wrath, and if men come and pray to you before your cross, hear such and forgive, and avert the wrath of punishment. And heal murrain and all diseases of our cattle, and all disasters of fire and water. And grant us the emblem of your cross as a trophy and talisman.[23]

Feasts of the cross are part of the liturgical calendar of all Eastern Christian churches, the most important, and common to all, being the Feast of the Exaltation of the Holy Cross on September 14, or September 27 on the Coptic and Ethiopic calendars. The hymns of this day are, of course, permeated with references to the cross. For example, on this day even the *Trisagion* hymn is replaced in the Byzantine tradition by another hymn that highlights the strong link between the cross and the resurrection: "We venerate your Cross, Master; and we glorify Your Holy Resurrection." Similarly, a hymn from the Coptic tradition sings praises to the places associated with the salvific events: "Hail to the cross. Hail to the city of the Only-Begotten. Hail to the tomb of Christ. Hail to the place of the resurrection."[24] The entrance hymn of this day in the Maronite tradition offers both a theological understanding of the meaning of the cross and a glimpse in the soul of Eastern Christians who hold the cross dearly in their hearts:

> Alleluia! Lord, your cross was taken from the tree in Eden, and your death upon the cross has granted new life to all the world. In its shadow refuge can be found for the rich and poor. All the prophets and the martyrs sing its praises. On this day we join them in giving glory. Alleluia! The cross is our light!
>
> Alleluia! When they crucified the Lord, our great Redeemer, and he died upon the cross for our salvation, all was fulfilled. Joseph, his disciple, with great love came to bury him. He beheld and touched the body of the Savior. On this day we join with him in giving glory. Alleluia! The cross is our light!
>
> Alleluia! With the cross we bless ourselves for Christ's protection. When the Tempter comes to us with his deception and sees the cross;

[23] Ibid., 50.

[24] "Feast of the Cross," Coptic Orthodox Diocese of Southern USA, "Coptic Reader."

> far from it he flees and hides himself in the darkest depths, for the holy cross is mighty and defends us. On this day we raise it up in exaltation. Alleluia! The cross is our light![25]

The cross as a symbol of hope and salvation, and a sign of Christ's presence and protection, plays a very significant role in the spirituality of Eastern Christians. The reality and experience of persecution and martyrdom throughout the centuries has led Eastern Christians to view these through the lenses of the redemption offered through the cross. In another hymn from the Coptic tradition, it is declared: "The Cross is our weapon, the Cross is our hope, the Cross is our salvation, the Cross is our pride. Alleluia, Alleluia, Alleluia."[26]

## 6.5 The Monastic Perspective

All Eastern Christian traditions bear the imprint, to a greater or lesser extent, of the monastic heritage. Rooted as far back as the fourth-century monastic movement in the deserts of Egypt and Palestine, they all have active monastic communities seen as spiritual centers and authentic expressions of the faith. The high regard of monasticism is due not only to the ascetic way of life and prophetic outlook of monastics but also to the role of monasteries at times of distress and persecution. Monasteries, built in remote and secluded areas, became worship centers for the persecuted Eastern Christians, educational hubs where their children would learn how to read and write using liturgical books as textbooks, and repositories of knowledge by maintaining and building libraries with impressive holdings of both religious and nonreligious material. It was in monasteries that in many cases faith, language, and culture were preserved.[27]

Monasticism's impact is definitive and multifaceted. Not only did it influence liturgy—monastic practices of liturgical life were, and still are, in varying degrees adopted and adapted to parish life—but

[25] *Book of Offering: According to the Rite of the Antiochene Syriac Maronite Church* (Bkerké: Maronite Patriarchate, 2012), 606–7.

[26] "Feast of the Cross," Coptic Orthodox Diocese of Southern USA, "Coptic Reader."

[27] See, for example, Sebastian Brock, ed., *The Hidden Pearl: The Syrian Orthodox Church and Its Ancient Aramaic Heritage*, vol. 2: *The Heirs of the Ancient Aramaic Heritage* (Rome: Trans World Film Italia, 2001), 134–66; vol. 3: *At the Turn of the Third Millennium; The Syrian Orthodox Witness* (Rome: Trans World Film Italia, 2001), 121–22.

it also affected theological reflection. Until quite recently, the totality of the theological production among Eastern Christians under oppressive rule has traditionally been by educated monastics, often but not necessarily ordained, who studied their theological heritage, engaged with the world they lived in, and composed new theological works.

The monastic context cultivated not only theological reflection but also practices such as spiritual discipleship and fasting. The relationship between the master and the disciple in the monastic context is mirrored in the relationship between the spiritual adviser (who can also be the father confessor) and the faithful. The practice of fasting is imbued in the liturgical cycles of the liturgical year, in some cases covering two-thirds of the whole year. For example, in the Byzantine tradition, fasting periods and days include Great Lent and Holy Week before Easter, the Apostle's fast, the Dormition Fast, the Christmas Fast, Wednesdays and Fridays of (almost) every week, and certain feast days, such as the Exultation of the Cross on September 14, the decapitation of John the Baptist on August 29, and the eve of Epiphany on January 5. In today's world, plagued by consumerism and individualism (among other things), the monastic tradition stands as a pillar reminding us of the centrality of God in our life, of our calling to be Christian in every aspect of our life, and to be witnesses to the Gospel by our way of life. This is eloquently and beautifully summarized in the prayer that is recited every day during the Great Lent in the Byzantine tradition, accompanied by full prostrations, ascribed to St. Ephrem the Syrian:

> O Lord and Master of my life!
>
> Take from me the spirit of sloth,
> faint-heartedness, lust of power, and idle talk.
>
> But give rather the spirit of chastity,
> humility, patience, and love to Your servant.
>
> Yes, Lord and King! Grant me to see my own errors
> and not to judge my brother,
>
> for You are blessed unto the ages of ages. Amen.[28]

[28] Adapted from https://www.goarch.org/-/lenten-prayer-of-st-ephrem-the-syrian.

The calendars of the Eastern Christian traditions are filled with commemorations of monastic figures; early monastic pioneers such as Antony and Macarius are almost universally celebrated, while all traditions continue to honor their own monastic saints. Let us not forget that one of the Eastern Christian churches, the Maronite Church, is named after a monastic, St. Maron! In fact, many of the modern saints recently canonized are monastics who have had a great impact on the spiritual lives not only of monastics but also of the faithful and are very popular, such as the recently canonized Saints Paisios and Porphyrios in the Greek Orthodox Church. These canonizations have led to a flurry of new liturgical compositions as new hymns dedicated to these saints are written to be used in the Liturgy of the Hours.

Indeed, monasteries today play a significant role in the spiritual life of the Eastern Christian churches, and in many cases monasteries are at the center of movements of liturgical research, revival, and renewal through the digitization of their manuscript collections, the generous hosting of scholars for the study of these manuscripts, the publication of scholarly studies (such as the Monastery of St. Katherine on Sinai and Vatopedi Monastery on Mount Athos), and in some cases the experimental implementation of liturgical reform. Monasteries are also more popularly known for their revival and cultivation of the traditional liturgical arts such as music (Simonos Petra and Vatopedi Monasteries on Mount Athos) and iconography (such as Xenophontos Monastery on Mount Athos), which are becoming more and more appealing. For example, the iconography of the St. Nicholas Shrine that is being built on Ground Zero in New York will be executed by a monk-iconographer belonging to the monastic brotherhood of Xenophontos Monastery on Mount Athos.[29]

## 6.6 Sacraments or Mysteries? The Sacramental Understanding of the World

While the Eastern Churches have come to accept the scholastic numbering of the seven sacraments, due to Western influence in different phases of their histories, they universally call the sacraments "mysteries" and hold a wider understanding of what these are. When

[29] See https://usa.greekreporter.com/2020/09/04/mt-athos-monks-to-decorate-nycs-st-nicholas-shrine/.

not captive by scholastic definitions of sacraments, the mysteries are understood as those liturgical celebrations that make present the mystery of God through which salvation is communicated to the faithful participants. According to the Syriac Father Theodore of Mopsuestia (350–428), "The Mysteries of the church are not isolated rites of passages, rather they are a shadow of the heavenly realities and at the same time pledge and foretaste of the future glory of heaven."[30] It is through the celebration of and participation in the mysteries that the faithful become part of salvation history and are included in the Divine Economy and Christ is made present and active in every aspect of their lives.

While in all traditions a place of primacy is given to the mysteries of baptism, chrismation, and the Eucharist, historically the mysteries were not limited to the known seven (baptism, chrismation, Eucharist, orders, marriage, reconciliation, unction); lists vary, sometimes significantly in both number and content. Liturgical celebrations often understood as mysteries include monastic tonsure, church consecration, and funeral. Unique to these lists are the *Malkā*[31] and the sign of the cross[32] in the East Syriac tradition.

Nicholas Cabasilas, a fourteenth-century spiritual author of the Byzantine tradition, wrote a treatise titled *The Life in Christ* where he explores the relationship between the spiritual life and the sacramental life. He understands that union with Christ necessarily involves two elements:

[30] Jose Kochuparampil, "Theology of *'Rāzē*: The Mysteries of the Church in the East Syriac Tradition," in *East Syriac Theology: An Introduction*, ed. Pauly Maniyattu (Satna: Ephrem's Publications, 2007), 248–77, here 252.

[31] Holy Leaven; it is believed to be handed over from St. Thomas and the disciples of Christ to the Church as a sign of ecclesial communion and continuity with the uninterrupted tradition of the Church. Kochuparampil, "Theology of *'Rāzē*," 253–54, 263. See also Bryan Spinks, "The Mystery of the Holy Leaven (*Malka*) in the East Syrian Tradition," in *Issues in Eucharistic Praying in East and West: Essays in Liturgical and Theological Analysis*, ed. Maxwell Johnson (Collegeville, MN: Liturgical Press, 2010), 63–70; Mar Awa Royel, "The Sacrament of the Holy Leaven (*Malkā*) in the Assyrian Church of the East," in *The Anaphoral Genesis of the Institution Narrative in Light of the Anaphora of Addai and Mari*, ed. Cesare Giraudo, OCA 295 (Rome: Edizioni Orientalia Christiana, 2013), 363–86.

[32] "The periodic signing of the cross in the celebration of the mysteries thus functions as a constant reminder that Christ, the principle protagonist of the Mysteries, operates and perfects all the services of the Church." Kochuparampil, "Theology of *'Rāzē*," 265–66.

> There is an element which derives from God, and another which derives from our own zeal. The one is entirely His work, the other involves striving on our part. However, the latter is our contribution only to the extent that we submit to His grace and do not surrender the treasure nor extinguish the torch when it has been lighted.[33]

We see here the principle of synergy, that our salvation necessitates our own response to God's invitation; and in the Eastern Churches that response primarily takes place within the liturgical life and experience. The outcome of this synergy is newness of life, unity with Christ, becoming one with Christ. And this is lived and experienced in the sacramental life. Cabasilas expresses this in the following way:

> In the sacred Mysteries, then, we depict His burial and proclaim his death. By them we are begotten and formed and wondrously united to the Savior, for they are the means by which, . . . "in him we live, we move, and have our being" (Acts 17:28). Baptism confers being and in short, existence according to Christ. It receives us when we are dead and corrupted and first leads us into life. The anointing with Chrism perfects him who has received new birth by infusing into him the energy that befits such a life. The Holy Eucharist preserves and continues this life and health. It is therefore by this Bread that we live and by the chrism that we are moved, once we have received being from the baptismal washing.[34]

And the purpose of sacramental participation is salvation:

> What then could be a greater proof of kindness and benevolence than that He who washes with water should set the soul free from uncleanness? Or that He by anointing it with chrism should grant it to reign in the heavenly kingdom? Or that He as the Host of the banquet should provide His own Body and Blood? And moreover, that men should become Gods (cf. Jn 10:35) and sons of God (cf. Rom 8:14). And that our nature should be honoured with God's honour, and that dust should be raised to such a height of glory as to become equal in honour and dignity to the divine nature?[35]

[33] Nicholas Cabasilas, *The Life in Christ* (New York: St. Vladimir's Seminary Press, 1974), 48–49.

[34] Ibid., 49–50.

[35] Ibid., 51–52.

A hymn composed by the fourth-century Saint Ephrem the Syrian, who is held in high esteem by all Eastern Christian churches for his beautiful theological expression in poetry, reminds us that it is the same Holy Spirit that was active in the incarnation, in Christ's baptism, and in the Christian sacraments, thus bringing into salvation history the sacraments of initiation and therefore making every Christian a part of Divine Economy:

> See, Fire and Spirit are in the womb of her who bore You;
> see, Fire and Spirit are in the river in which You were baptized.
> Fire and Spirit are in our baptismal font,
> in the Bread and the Cup are Fire and Holy Spirit.[36]

Participation in the Eucharist is central to the sacramental understanding of Eastern Christians and fundamental in their understanding of salvation. Sacramental life is the process through which a Christian grows into the mystery of God and allows himself or herself to be assumed by that mystery that can be approached only by faith, and eucharistic participation is the apex of this process. A tenth-century Coptic author wrote about the Eucharist, not only in terms of the passion but also in terms of the incarnation; in fact, the reception of the Eucharist is seen as an incarnational experience where our body and blood are assumed by Christ's body and blood, and thus participate in Divine Life, that is, salvation:

> When he wanted to redeem us through himself and to raise us up to heaven, he established for us an economy [*dabbara lanā tadbī ran*], so that he would remain with us forever, just as he was with his disciples. He commanded us to take the bread (from which comes our flesh as well as his flesh) and the water and wine (from which comes our blood as well as his blood), to raise them up on the holy altar, and to ask him in his name for what he taught us, so that he might descend upon them through his Holy Spirit, through whom he descended upon the flesh and blood of Mary, and so that he might transform them into his body and blood. (He did this) so that he might truly come to be with us in a visible, comprehensible, and tangible way, just as he was with the

[36] Sebastian Brock, *The Luminous Eye: The Spiritual World Vision of Saint Ephrem*, 2nd ed. (Kalamazoo, MI: Cistercian Publications, 1992), 108. We are grateful to Alex Neroth van Vogelpoel for bringing this hymn to our attention.

> apostles—so that he might die for our sakes, just as he died for the people at that time; that he might be twisted up by being torn and discarded on the plate, just as he was wrapped up in linen bands and discarded in the tomb, and that he might pour out his blood for our sake in the cup, just as he poured out his blood on Golgotha.[37]

Saint Ephrem the Syrian notes the following about the meaning of the Eucharist:

> In a new way his body has been fused with our bodies,
> and his pure blood has been poured into our veins.
> His voice, too, is in our ears and his splendor in our eyes.
> The whole of him with the whole of us is fused by his mercy.
> And because he loved his Church greatly, he did not give her the manna of her rival;
> He became the Bread of Life for her to eat him.

The next strophe connects chrismation and baptism with the Eucharist, but through the created order; by referring to wheat, olive, and grape, he highlights the sacramental potential of all creation and its participation in the economy of salvation:

> Wheat, olive and grape that were created for our use,
> these three in three ways serve you in symbol.
> With three medicines you have cured our sickness;
> humanity was weak, suffering and failing;
> you have strengthened it with your blessed Bread,
> you have consoled it with your sober Wine,
> and you have given it joy with your holy Anointing.[38]

In this great gift of the Eucharist, Eastern Christians participate with a deep sense of their personal unworthiness but also with a profound faith in God's loving-kindness and forgiveness. Saint Gregory of

[37] From Pseudo-Sāwīrus ibn al-Muqaffa's *The Book of Elucidation*, as presented in Stephen Davis, *Coptic Christology in Practice: Incarnation and Divine Participation in Late Antique and Medieval Egypt* (Oxford: Oxford University Press, 2008), 298. We are grateful to Ramez Mikhail for bringing this text to our attention.

[38] Adapted from Robert Murray, *Symbols of Church and Kingdom: A Study in Early Syriac Tradition* (London: Cambridge University Press, 1975), 77. We are grateful to Alex Neroth van Vogelpoel for bringing this hymn to our attention.

Narek, an Armenian theologian and poet of the tenth century, expresses this eloquently in his "Prayer 47." In this prayer, St. Gregory parallels himself with the prodigal son from the well-known parable of Christ (Luke 15:11-32), confessing his sinfulness and asking for God's mercy. He ends the prayer in the following way:

> And even though I am wanting in virtue, you sacrifice the fatted calf of heaven, your only begotten Son, out of love for mankind. Your blessed Son who is always offered and yet remains whole, who is sacrificed continuously upon innumerable altars without being consumed, who is all in everyone and complete in all things, who is in essence of heaven and in reality of earth, who is lacking nothing in humanness and without defect in divinity, who is broken and distributed in individual parts, that all may be collected in the same body with him as head. Glory to you with him, Father most merciful. Amen.[39]

The reception of the Eucharist is understood among Eastern Christians not as an entitlement but as a privilege, a continuous call to holiness, a constant reminder of God's call for a journey toward a lived and transfigured life defined by Christ. An Armenian eucharistic hymn articulates beautifully this call to holiness:

> The Medicine of Life flew from on high to reside in those worthy of it.
> Let us make holy our souls and thoughts in honor of His glory.
> We hold God in our hands: let there be no blemish in our bodies.
> Once He has entered, He takes up residence with us,
> so let us make ourselves holy within.[40]

## 6.7 Sacred Space, Liturgical Posture, and Iconography

Eastern Christians understand liturgical space as sacred space. Their church buildings are set apart not only by their use but also by dedication rites celebrated by a bishop. These dedication rites carry

[39] St. Grigor Narekatsi, *Speaking with God from the Depths of the Heart: The Armenian Prayer Book of St. Gregory of Narek* (Yerevan, 2016), 205; see also Michael Daniel Findikyan, "St. Gregory of Narek's Book of Prayers and the Eucharist: Another Holy Communion," *Revue Théologique de Kaslik* 3–4 (2009–2010): 291–311.

[40] Brock, *The Luminous Eye*, 112–13.

strong baptismal themes laced with eschatological overtones. As the human person is baptized, is chrismated, and through the Eucharist becomes one with Christ, so is the space set apart in which the community gathers. That space too is washed and anointed, so that the Eucharist can be celebrated on its altar within its walls.[41] It is not that God is brought down in the consecrated space; rather, by the celebration of the Eucharist on the holy altar the worshiping community is elevated before the very throne of God. The second consecratory prayer of the altar in the Byzantine tradition petitions: "Fill this temple built for your hymning with glory, and make this altar Holy of Holies; so that, standing in front of it, as standing in front of your awesome throne of your Kingdom, we may blamelessly worship you." But these rites of consecration are at the same time a continuous reminder to the Christian community gathered in worship of their calling to renewal, to living the Gospel:

> Be renewed, brothers, and having put aside your old man, conduct yourselves in the newness of life, having overpowered your passions, which lead to death. Let us educate all the members, so they can hate the taste of evil. For this reason only let us remember to avoid the old customs. In this way, man is renewed, in this manner we honor the day of the Consecration.[42]

Central to every Eastern Christian church is the holy altar, which is considered the most holy place in the church building. The first prayer of the dedication service in the Armenian tradition explains why this is so:

> Lord God almighty, who hast established the heaven with its firmament, and alone hast created hosts many. Thou Lord of all the earth

[41] On rites of consecration in the Eastern Christian traditions, see René-George Coquin, "La consécration des églises dans le rite copte; ses relations avec les rites syrien et byzantin," *L'Orient Syrien* 9 (1964): 149–87; M. Daniel Findikyan, "The Armenian Ritual of the Dedication of a Church: A Textual and Comparative Analysis of Three Early Sources," OCP 64 (1998): 75–121; Youhanna Youssef, "The Rite of the Consecration of the Church of Koskam," *Ancient Near Eastern Studies* 46 (2009): 72–92 (Coptic tradition); Vitalijs Permjakovs, "Make This the Place Where Your Glory Dwells: Origins and Evolution of the Byzantine Rite for the Consecration of a Church" (PhD diss., University of Notre Dame, 2012).

[42] Second Sticheron (hymn) of Vespers of Consecration.

> hast made strong thy holy church, and commanded us to establish an altar therein, and to offer reasonable sacrifices and burnt offerings, that are presented without blood in thy name, for the life and salvation of mankind. In like wise also now, Lord, send thy spirit holy that maketh holy, and hallow this altar unto the hope of the faithful, unto the life and salvation of all who stand in the presence of thy great glory, unto the renewing of spirits and approbation of thy will, who alone art God merciful, long-suffering, and plenteous in mercy. For thy name, of Father and Son and holy Spirit, is praised and blessed now and ever.[43]

The language of such prayers highlights the continuity and discontinuity with the ritual of the temple of Solomon in Jerusalem. The language of sacrifice and burnt offerings is ever present but with the significant clarification that these are "reasonable" and "without blood," pointing to the celebration of the Eucharist as that which replaced the sacrifices of the Old Testament. The paradigm, however, of the temple of Solomon as sacred space inspires the Eastern Christian understanding of the sacredness of a Christian church building.

The Ethiopian tradition in its understanding of church space highly pronounces this relationship of sacredness between the temple of Solomon and the church building. The temple of Solomon

> was constructed within a courtyard, and the edifice itself had a threefold structure: a vestibule, then a nave, and then the innermost chamber, the holy of holies (Hebrew: *Qodesh Ha-Qodashim*), which contained the ark of the covenant and which only the High Priest could enter, and then only on the Day of Atonement. Every church in Ethiopia (usually erected within a compound) must contain a replica of one of the tablets of the ark of the covenant, called a *tabot*, which is kept in a box, or it is not a church. . . . Like the temple, each church in Ethiopia is tripartite in form, with a vestibule (*qene mahlet*); a nave (*qeddest*), where communion is given; and a sanctuary (*maqdas*) or holy of holies (*qeddesta qeddusan*), in which the *tabot* is located and on which the priest prepares communion. Also similar to the temple in Jerusalem is the inaccessibility of the holy of holies to nonclerical believers.[44]

[43] Conybeare, *Rituale Armenorum*, 5.

[44] Philip Esler, *Ethiopian Christianity: History, Theology, Practice* (Waco, TX: Baylor University Press, 2019), 172–73.

In a hymn of the East Syriac tradition, the altar in particular, and the church building in general, assumes an ecclesiological meaning as the place where the whole church gathers, and by participation in the Holy Eucharist the broken humanity is healed and restored: "How right is it to glorify within this one, holy house, where are prophets, apostles, martyrs and priests and teachers, where the sacred table is, which forgives all Adam's sons."[45]

In all Eastern Christian traditions the space of the altar is clearly demarcated—usually by a screen or a wall with icons (Byzantine, Coptic, Ethiopic traditions),[46] by height (the altar area is raised like a stage) and a curtain (Armenian), or by a raised platform that is one to three steps higher than the nave (Syriac traditions). In some traditions the clergy wear liturgical slippers/shoes (Armenian and Syriac) when they are in the altar area and serve, while in other traditions all faithful remove their shoes upon entering (Ethiopian), as they consider the ground they are stepping on holy (but also following cultural norms).

The traditional posture of prayer for Eastern Christians is standing, particularly on Sundays. While kneeling is seen as a penitential posture, reserved for periods of fasting, standing is considered an expression of the belief in the resurrection and the joy in its celebration on Sundays, as every Sunday celebration is centered on the theme of the resurrection of Christ.[47] Free-standing chairs and pews are a relatively new phenomenon in Eastern Christian churches, first appearing in the diaspora communities, influenced by Catholic and Protestant seating arrangements. While the presence of chairs and pews makes attending services more comfortable for the modern person, it is not conducive to active participation, as it promotes a static approach to liturgy; movement is hindered as it makes it difficult to join processions in the church, to make full prostrations, to move around, and to venerate icons.

[45] Hymn "Before" sung at Vespers on Wednesday of the Second Week, *Emmanuel: That Is, the Book of Public Prayer*, 44.

[46] Sharon Gerstel, *Thresholds of the Sacred: Architectural, Art Historical, Liturgical, and Theological Perspectives on Religious Screens, East and West* (Washington, DC: Dumbarton Oaks Research Library and Collection, 2006).

[47] Gabriel Radle, "Embodied Eschatology: The Council of Nicaea's Regulation of Kneeling and Its Reception across Liturgical Traditions," *Worship* 90 (2016): 345–71, 433–61.

Conducive to the understanding of sacred space is the tradition, historically among all Eastern Christian traditions, of iconography. The walls of the church building, in varying degrees, are adorned with cycles of images depicting events from the life of Christ (dominical cycle), events from the life of the Virgin Mary (Marian cycle), images of saints (sanctoral cycle), and images related to the celebration of the Divine Liturgy (liturgical cycle), such as the "Communion of the Apostles" scene. Images have a multifaceted role: they decorate the space, reflecting the cultural context of each community; they educate by presenting salvation history (the Gospel) in images; they project the heroes of the Christian faith who lived out the Gospel and are set as examples; and they visualize the belief that the whole Church gathers when the community comes together to celebrate, particularly the Divine Liturgy. Images are touched, kissed, censed, and processed (portable icons) in the church—they are integrated in the liturgical life of the community. Smaller-sized portable images are part of the private piety and prayer life of the faithful.[48]

## 6.8 Challenges Facing the Eastern Christian Churches

The Eastern Christian churches have miraculously survived and even flourished under very difficult circumstances throughout the centuries. Their liturgical life and tradition offers a unique ritual expression of the Gospel. They have a unique ethos and liturgical spirituality. But these Eastern Christian churches are now called to make their presence visible and engage with the modern Western world, become dialogue partners, and offer their unique perspectives and contributions. In order to be successful at this, however, they need to address certain challenges that they face. Here we identify and briefly discuss the three challenges that we think are the most important.

(1) Eastern Christian churches need to define their identity, especially the relationship between religion and nation. Fr. Armando Elkhoury, a Maronite priest and scholar, poignantly notes:

[48] See George Galavaris, *The Icon in the Life of the Church* (Leiden: Brill, 1981); Léonide Ouspensky, *Theology of the Icon*, 2 vols. (Crestwood, NY: St. Vladimir's Seminary Press, 1992); Christoph Schönborn, *God's Human Face: The Christ-Icon* (San Francisco: Ignatius Press, 1994); Maximos Constas, *The Art of Seeing: Paradox and Perception in Orthodox Iconography* (Alhambra, CA: Sebastian Press, 2014).

> The Maronite Church is going through an identity crisis. In fact, this is a worldwide phenomenon and not specific to the United States. Is the Maronite Church an ethnic Church? Is it a Lebanese Church or an Arabic Church? Does the Maronite Church serve only those who come from Lebanon or the Middle East and by extension those who are married into a Lebanese or Middle Eastern family? Or is it the Church of Christ, in which there is no distinction between Lebanese and non-Lebanese?[49]

In fact, the above statement is true for all Eastern Christian churches; one has just to substitute the ecclesial, geographical, and linguistic terms, and it will be applicable to every tradition. It is true that the Eastern Christian churches played a very significant role in preserving the unique identities of their faithful, often understood also in ethnic and national terms, but sometimes to the detriment of the Gospel. A bishop of the Greek Orthodox Church, the late Metropolitan of Kozani Dionysios, wrote in a memo to the members of the Holy Synod of the Church of Greece the following:

> We carry the burden of a bad inheritance. . . . It is our national inheritance, which is tightly associated with the life of the Church. So in all circumstances we forget that we are not ethnarchs any more but hierarchs, bishops and shepherds of the Church. We do not forget the fact that we are Greeks, but we must also not forget that Greeks are not the only Orthodox Christians. In this way we adulterate our priestly conviction when we preach the divine word, we demean ourselves with cheap national talk, and in the end have our conscious calm that we did our duty. But we should not forget that the Church has already served the Nation enough, has paid others' sins, and has emptied herself for the sake of Hellenism. Now, without denying our ethnicity, we need to know that above all we are shepherds of the Church.[50]

This is particularly challenging in the diaspora communities, where church leaders try to strike a balance between maintaining the

[49] https://thehiddenpearl.org/2013/02/12/crisis-in-the-life-of-the-maronite-church/.

[50] Stefanos Alexopoulos, "The Orthodox Church in Greece and the Challenges of Secularization, Immigration, and EU Enlargement," in *Religion: Problem or Promise? The Role of Religion in the Integration of Europe*, ed. Šimon Marinčák, Orientalia et Occidentalia 4 (Košice: Michael Lacko Center, 2009), 201–6, here 205.

ethnic and religious identity, on the one hand, and opening the doors of their communities to "outsiders" who are very much interested in the religious identity but do not share the ethnic identity.[51]

Nationalism has been a real danger, particularly for the Orthodox people of Eastern Europe for the last two centuries. It is nationalism that led to the creation of national Orthodox Churches in the East, enacting a "local church ecclesiology according to *secular* paradigms of 'locality,'" to borrow a phrase from Peter Galadza.[52] This situation forced the Ecumenical Patriarchate to issue a conciliar encyclical in 1872 condemning nationalism, phyletism as it was called then, in very strong terms. It states: "We renounce, censure, and condemn racism, that is racial discrimination, ethnic feuds, hatreds and dissensions within the Church of Christ, as contrary to the teaching of the Gospel and the holy canons of our blessed fathers."[53]

The Eastern churches can overcome the danger of nationalism by rediscovering their missionary identity and calling for and embarking on an outward approach to the preaching of the Gospel. While the challenges that they have faced (and many still face) have forced them to look inward and function in a "survival mode," the revival of their missionary outlook will enable them to share with the world their own riches. The Christianization of the Slavs by the Byzantines and the missionary outreach as far as China and Korea by the Church of the East demonstrates that mission is part of the heritage and tradition of the Eastern churches and only needs to be revitalized and energized. The well-known liturgical theologian Fr. Alexander Schmemann has written:

> To recover the missionary dimension of the Church is today's greatest imperative. We have to recover a very basic truth: that the Church is *essentially* Mission, that the very roots of her life are in the commandment of Christ: "Go Ye therefore and teach all nations" (Matt. 28:19).

[51] For a case study from the Ukrainian Greek Catholic Church in Canada, see Christopher Guly, *Strangers in a Strange Church: New Faces of Ukrainian Catholicism in Canada* (Ottawa: Novalis, 2019). We are grateful to Daniel Galadza for bringing this book to our attention.

[52] Peter Galadza, "The Structure of the Eastern Churches: Bonded with Human Blood or Baptismal Water," *Pro Ecclesia* 17 (2008): 373–86, here 375.

[53] Maximos, Metropolitan of Sardes, *The Oecumenical Patriarchate in the Orthodox Church: A Study in the History and Canons of the Church*, Analecta Vlatadōn 24 (Thessaloniki: Patriarchal Institute for Patristic Studies, 1976), 308–9.

> A Christian community that would lose this missionary zeal and purpose, that would become selfish and self-centered, that would limit itself to "satisfying the spiritual needs of its members," that would identify itself completely with a nation, a society, a social or ethnic group—is on its way to spiritual decadence and death, because the essential spiritual need of a Christian is precisely that of sharing the life and the Truth with as many men as possible and ultimately with the whole world. Mission thus is the organic need and task of the Church in the world, the real *meaning* of Church's presence in history between the first and the second advents of her Lord, or, in other terms, the meaning of Christian history. Obviously not all members of the Church can go and preach in the literal sense of the word. But all can have a concern for the missionary function of the Church, feel responsible for it, help and support it. In this respect each diocese, each parish and each member of the Church are involved in the missionary ministry.[54]

In this missionary outlook, the liturgical tradition of each Eastern church is to play a significant role, as it did in the past. The well-known report of the envoy of Vladimir, the prince of Kiev, regarding the celebration of the Eucharist in the Great Church of Holy Wisdom (Hagia Sophia) in Constantinople, is telling: "We knew not whether we were in heaven or on earth, for surely there is no such splendor or beauty anywhere on earth. We cannot describe it to you; we only know that God dwells there among men and that their Service surpasses the worship of all other places."[55]

(2) Eastern Christian churches need to promote the study of their own liturgical traditions. While there is almost universal acknowledgment that their liturgical heritages are treasure troves of theology,

[54] Alexander Schmemann, "Orthodoxy and Mission," *St. Vladimir's Seminary Quarterly* 3, no. 4 (1959): 41–42. Also available at https://www.schmemann.org/byhim/orthodoxyandmission.html. On this topic, see also Alexander Schmemann, "The Missionary Imperative," in *Church, World, Mission: Reflections on Orthodoxy in the West* (Crestwood, NY: St. Vladimir's Seminary Press, 1979), 209–16; Pantelis Kalaitzidis, "New Trends in Greek Orthodox Theology: Challenges in the Movement towards a Genuine Renewal and Christian Unity," *Scottish Journal of Theology* 67 (2014): 127–64, here 143–45.

[55] Samuel Cross and Olgerd Sherbowitz-Wetzor, eds. and trans., *The Russian Primary Chronicle: Laurentian Text* (Cambridge, MA: Medieval Academy of America, 1953), 110–11.

spirituality, and ritual, they have not been adequately studied.[56] Their study will not only enhance our academic knowledge about the history, structures, and evolution of the various Eastern liturgical rites; they will also unveil a rich theological expression and a ritual with tremendous formative power.[57] The study of liturgy will also offer a corrective to the popular perception that Eastern liturgy is static or unchanging. On the contrary, the history of each of the Eastern liturgical rites is indeed one of conserving and changing, borrowing and adapting, expanding and abridging, defined by historical circumstances and pastoral realities. This knowledge of the history of each liturgical tradition can protect each tradition from two extremes in the approach to liturgy:

> (1) on the one hand, seeing *all* current practices as normative, normal, and historical, clothing them with the romantic veil of "changelessness" and branding them "traditional," even if they reflect very recent changes in worship; or (2) seeing *no* practice as normative, normal, and historical but rather seeking to change, alter, and reform worship so that it fits the tastes, trends, and whims of any individual or group, so that worship may become "relevant," whatever that might mean.[58]

[56] The Byzantine liturgical tradition is the best studied so far, thanks to the pre-1917 Russian liturgical scholarship; to Juan Mateos, Robert Taft, and Miguel Arranz at the Oriental Institute in Rome; and to the revival of liturgical studies in Greece, Serbia, and Russia. See Michael Zheltov, "Православная литургика" [Orthodox Liturgics], in *Pravoslavnaia Entsyklopediia* (Moscow: Pravoslavnaia Entsyklopediia, 2000–2018), 41:220–25; I would like to thank Vitaly Permiakov for bringing this to our attention. Taft and Winkler, eds., *Comparative Liturgy Fifty Years After Anton Baumstark (1872–1948)*. Stefanos Alexopoulos, "The State of Liturgical Studies and Liturgical Research in Greece Today," in *Inquiries into Eastern Christian Worship: Selected Papers of the Second International Congress of the Society of Oriental Liturgies, Rome, 17–21 September 2008*, ed. Bert Groen, Steven Hawkes-Teeples, Stefanos Alexopoulos, Eastern Christian Studies 12 (Leuven: Peeters, 2012), 375–92; in the same volume, Nina Glibetić, "Liturgical Renewal Movement in Contemporary Serbia," 393–414; Hlib Lonchyna, "Metropolitan Andrew Sheptytsky and Liturgical Reform: A Case Study," 367–73 (for the Ukrainian Greek Catholic Church). See also Peter Galadza, *The Theology and Liturgical Work of Andrei Sheptytsky (1865–1944)*, OCA 272 (Rome: Pontificio Istituto Orientale, 2004).

[57] On the formative power of liturgy, see Derek Krueger, *Liturgical Subjects: Christian Ritual, Biblical Narrative, and the Formation of the Self in Byzantium* (Philadelphia: University of Pennsylvania Press, 2014).

[58] Stefanos Alexopoulos, "Ὅλοι Μαζί: Liturgical Practice and Liturgical History," in *A Living Tradition: On the Intersection of Liturgical History and Pastoral Practice*, ed. David A. Pitt, Stefanos Alexopoulos, and Christian McConnell (Collegeville, MN: Liturgical Press, 2012), 256–70, here 256.

The knowledge of the history of one's liturgical tradition contributes greatly to the recognition and preservation of the authenticity of a rite, the study and unpacking of an unchanging core (Tradition with a capital "T"), and the articulation of that unchanging core in diverse ways that reflect the tradition and authenticity of each rite.[59] A study of the history and worship of the Eastern Christian churches can only enhance the understanding of liturgy, its function, and its role in the life of the Eastern churches. The function of liturgical revitalization and liturgical renewal is "to lead to a personal and communal renewal in Christ through a deeper knowledge, greater appreciation and more conscious participation in the worship of the Church. After all, liturgy is not just texts, rites and rituals; it is the encounter with the mystery of God, the now-and-not-yet of the Christian experience, the visible expression of faith."[60] In fact, the study of liturgy of each tradition and the ensuing liturgical revitalization and renewal is the guarantor of each liturgical tradition. On the one hand, it highlights the necessity for the study of the history of liturgy; on the other hand, it encourages the development of a theology of worship that is based on the actual liturgical texts. Or, to put it in a different way, we need to know the history of what we celebrate and why we celebrate and use the liturgical texts as a hermeneutic tool when doing liturgical theology. Liturgical renewal, then, is not a break from tradition. On the contrary! Liturgical renewal safeguards liturgical tradition; liturgical renewal points and leads to the restoration of proper liturgical practice; and liturgical renewal allows us to rediscover the catechetical and formative power of liturgy.[61] The

[59] Alexander Rentel, "Byzantine and Slavic Orthodoxy," in *The Oxford History of Christian Worship*, ed. Geoffrey Wainwright and Karen Westerfield Tucker (Oxford: Oxford University Press, 2006), 254–306, here 299.

[60] Adapted from Stefanos Alexopoulos, "Liturgical Renewal in the Church of Greece: Past, Present, Future?," *Greek Orthodox Theological Review* 61 (2016): 209–23, here 210.

[61] Alexopoulos, "Liturgical Renewal in the Church of Greece," 214; on the topic of liturgical reform in the Byzantine tradition, see Paul Meyendorff, *Russia, Ritual, and Reform: The Liturgical Reforms of Nikon in the 17th Century* (Crestwood, NY: St. Vladimir's Seminary Press, 1991); Thomas Pott, *Byzantine Liturgical Reform: A Study of Liturgical Change in the Byzantine Tradition* (Crestwood, NY: St. Vladimir's Seminary Press, 2010). For a study and presentation of contemporary efforts toward liturgical reform in the Greek and Russian Orthodox traditions, see Nicholas Denysenko, *Liturgical Reform after Vatican II: The Impact on Eastern Orthodoxy* (Minneapolis: Fortress Press, 2015).

criteria of historical basis, theological depth, and pastoral sensitivity should govern any effort of liturgical revitalization and renewal.

Particular for the Eastern Catholic churches, the question of liturgical renewal needs to be discussed together with the Latinization, in some cases dramatic, that they have undergone. The Second Vatican Council (1962–1965) has indeed been an important turning point, as it signified a change of policy in the Roman Catholic Church, by encouraging the Eastern Catholic churches to return to the liturgical practices of their original traditions and revise their rites accordingly.[62] Since the Second Vatican Council, "de-Latinization" has been taking place among Eastern Catholic churches in various degrees, involving not just liturgical practice but also church architecture and iconography. As an example of the latter, we would like to single out the work accomplished by Fr. Abdo Badwi who reintroduced iconography back to the Maronite church, based on the venerable Syriac iconographic tradition.[63]

(3) Eastern Christian churches need to engage with Western culture and the modern world. The modern world is rapidly evolving and changing, oscillating between fundamentalism and traditionalism, on the one hand, and untrammeled freedom, a globalization of values, where individualism, self-centeredness, narcissism, and immediate gratification have become standards of success, on the other. The Eastern churches and their communities are forced to emerge from a premodern context, without the experience (for the most part) of the Enlightenment, the Reformation, the Counter-Reformation, the French Revolution, the Industrial Revolution, and the various emancipation and equality movements of the nineteenth and twentieth centuries, which lie at the foundations of the modern world. Are the Eastern Christian churches willing to engage with modernity and all that it entails, offering their unique contribution and constructive criticism to its accomplishments, or will they retreat toward an inward

[62] The *Instruction for Applying the Liturgical Prescriptions of the Code of Canons of the Eastern Churches* (Vatican: Libreria Editrice Vaticana, 1996) summarizes all Roman Catholic documents relating to the call for liturgical renewal among the Eastern Catholic Churches. We are grateful to Daniel Galadza for bringing this to our attention.

[63] Abdo Badwi, *The Liturgical Year Iconography of the Syro-Maronite Church* (Kaslik: Publications de l'Université Saint-Esprit de Kaslik, 2006).

approach defined by a certain nostalgia for the "old way of life" and structures and forms of their past?

Modern society is multicultural, where identities are moving from being something compact and unique to a paradigm of multiple diverse identities. Responding to this paradigm shift, Eastern Christian traditions need to develop a theology of otherness and identity.[64] First steps have been made toward this direction, for example, in the theological reflection of the Greek Orthodox Metroplitan John Zizioulas: "Identity includes otherness, for otherness is part of what makes unity, and otherness, far from being a threat to unity, is its condition *sine qua non*, and because otherness is part of what makes unity, not its result."[65]

The important questions of identity and unity are very relevant in the ecumenical movement and dialogue, in which all the Eastern Christian churches are called to participate to move toward a common Eastern Christian witness to the world, healing their divisions, at times polemical. The reality of living side by side, facing the same challenges, and dealing with the same problems can only encourage the dialogue and rapprochement among them and the other Christian traditions, Roman Catholic, Anglican, and Protestant, that need to be studied from the theological, historical, and liturgical point of view. Eastern Christians, particularly in the diaspora, need to be aware of who their neighboring fellow Christians are, what they believe, and how they celebrate what they believe. Unfortunately, the knowledge that Eastern Christians have of Western Christians (with the possible exception of Eastern Catholics) is at best outdated, and often biased and erroneous. If Eastern Christianity is to remain relevant and contribute to the making of our modern world and offer their unique Eastern Christian witness as an option, they need to learn the "language" of the other, understand the other, and engage with the other, without fear of losing their identity.

Against all odds in many cases, the Eastern Christian churches have survived repression, persecution, expulsion, and martyrdom. In these trials, their liturgical life has been one of the pillars that has kept them standing and going, enduring and persevering, suffering

[64] Pantelis Kalaitzidis, "Challenges of Renewal and Reformation Facing the Orthodox Church," *The Ecumenical Review* 61 (2009): 136–64, here 162.

[65] As presented by Kalaitzidis, "Challenges of Renewal," 163.

and hoping, surviving into the modern era. But now modernity poses a new set of challenges to the Eastern Christian churches, and their survival depends on how they choose to respond to these. Once again, we believe that their liturgical traditions, these ritual expressions of the Christian faith, these ritual celebrations of the Gospel of Christ, with their distinct Eastern theological expression and flavor, can carry them through this new challenge. They can indeed offer the modern world a different and unique response to the core questions of life, they can speak to the hearts and minds of people who strive for a better world, and they can offer meaning and purpose to the modern person.

# Bibliography According to Rite


## General Resources

Atiya, Aziz, ed. *The Coptic Encyclopedia.* 8 vols. New York: Macmillan, 1991.

Bradshaw, Paul F., ed. *The New Westminster Dictionary of Liturgy and Worship.* Louisville: Westminster John Knox, 2002.

Cabrol, Fernand, and Henri Leclercq, eds. *Dictionnaire d'archéologie chrétienne et de liturgie.* 15 vols. Paris: Letouzey et Ané, 1907–1953.

Fink, Peter, ed. *The New Dictionary of Sacramental Worship.* Dublin: Gill and Macmillan, 1990.

Kazhdan, Alexander, and Alice-Mary Talbot, eds. *The Oxford Dictionary of Byzantium.* 3 vols. New York: Oxford University Press, 1991.

Parry, Ken, ed. *The Blackwell Companion to Eastern Christianity.* Oxford: Wiley-Blackwell, 2007.

Wainwright, Geoffrey, and Karen Westerfield Tucker, eds. *The Oxford History of Christian Worship.* Oxford: Oxford University Press, 2006.

## Periodicals

*Archiv für Liturgiewissenschaft*

*Bolletino della Badia Greca di Grottaferrata*

*Bulletin de la Société d'Archéologie Copte*

*Byzantinische Zeitschrift*

*Byzantion*

*Coptic Church Review*

*Dumbarton Oaks Papers*

*Ecclesia Orans*

*Echos d'Orient*

*Ephemerides Liturgicae*

*Greek Orthodox Theological Review*

*Jahrbuch für Antike und Christentum*

*Jahrbuch für Liturgik und Hymnologie*

*Journal of Coptic Studies*
*Journal of Early Christian Studies*
*Liturgy Digest*
*Maison-Dieu, La*
*Muséon, Le*
*Oriens Christianus*
*Orientalia Christiana Periodica*
*Orient syrien, L'*
*Ostkirchliche Studien*
*Parole de l'Orient*
*Prôche-Orient chrétien*
*Questions Liturgiques / Studies in Liturgy*
*Revue de l'Orient chrétien*
*Revue des études arméniennes*
*Revue des études byzantines*
*St. Nersess Theological Review*
*St. Vladimir's Theological Quarterly*
*Studia Liturgica*
*Studia Patristica*
*Studi sull'oriente Cristiano*
*Vigiliae Christiana*
*Worship*
*Θεολογία*
*Σύναξη*

## Monograph Series

Alcuin/GROW Liturgical Study
Analecta Liturgica
Anaphorae Orientales
Anaphorae Syriacae
Corpus Scriptorum Christianorum Orientalium
Eastern Christian Studies
Liturgia Condenda
Liturgiewissenschaftliche Quellen und Forschungen
Orientalia Christiana Analecta
Patrologia Orientalis
Sources chrétiennes
Λειτουργικὰ Βλατάδων
Ποιμαντική Βιβλιοθήκη

## Collections of Texts


Bradshaw, Paul F. *Ordination Rites of the Ancient Churches of East and West.* New York: Pueblo, 1990.

Denziger, Henricus. *Ritus orientalium coptorum, syrorum, et armenorum in administrandis sacramentis.* Graz: Akademische Druck - und Verlagsanstalt, 1961.

Hammond, C. E., and F. E. Brightman, eds. *Liturgies, Eastern and Western: Being the Texts, Original or Translated.* Vol. 1: *Eastern Liturgies.* Oxford: Clarendon Press, 1896; repr. Piscataway, NJ: Gorgias Press, 2002.

Hänggi, Anton, and Irmgard Pahl, eds. *Prex Eucharistica.* Vol 1: *Textus e Variis Liturgiis Antiquioribus Selecti.* Spicilegium Friburgense 12. Freiburg: Universitätsverlag Freiburg, 1998.

Jasper, R. C. D., and G. J. Cuming, eds. *Prayers of the Eucharist: Early and Reformed.* 4th ed., edited by Paul F. Bradshaw and Maxwell E. Johnson. ACC 94. Collegeville, MN: Liturgical Press Academic, 2019.

Renaudot, Eusèbe. *Liturgiarum Orientalium collectio.* 2 vols. Frankfurt: Joseph Baer, 1847.

Stavrinos, Ambrosios. *Αἱ ἀρχαιόταται καὶ αἱ σύγχρονοι λειτουργίαι τῶν κυριωτέρων τοῦ Χριστοῦ Ἐκκλησιῶν.* Λειτουργικὰ Βλατάδων 4. 2nd ed. Thessaloniki: Patriarchal Institute for Patristic Studies, 2001.

Whitaker, E. C. *Documents of the Baptismal Liturgy.* 3rd rev. and exp. ed., edited by Maxwell E. Johnson. ACC 79.Collegeville, MN: Liturgical Press, Pueblo, 2003.


## General Bibliographies


Brakmann, Heinzgerd. "Literaturbericht: Der Gottesdienst in den östlichen Kirchen (Teil I)." *Archiv für Liturgiewissenschaft* 53 (2011): 140–271.

———. "Literaturbericht: Der Gottesdienst in den östlichen Kirchen (Teil II)." *Archiv für Liturgiewissenschaft* 57 (2015[2017]): 117–285.

Janeras, Sebastià. *Bibliografia sulle liturgie orientali (1961–1967).* Rome: Pontificium Institutum Liturgicum Anselmianum, 1969.

Sauget, J. M. *Bibliographie des liturgies orientales (1900–1960).* Rome: Pontificium Institutum Orientalium Studiorum, 1962.


## General Introductions


Aßfalg, Julius, and Paul Krüger. *Kleines Wörterbuch des Christlichen Orients.* Wiesbaden: Otto Harrassowitz, 1975.

Attwater, Donald. *Eastern Catholic Worship*. New York: Devin-Adair Company, 1945.

Chaillot, Christine. "The Ancient Oriental Churches." In *The Oxford History of Christian Worship*, edited by Wainwright and Westerfield Tucker, 131–69.

Dalmais, Irénée-Henri. *Liturgies d'orient: rites et symboles*. Paris, Les Éditions du Cerf, 1980. English translation: *Eastern Liturgies*. Translated by Donald Attwater. Twentieth Century Encyclopedia of Catholicism. Vol. 112. New York: Hawthorn Books, 1960.

Fahey, Michael. "Sacraments in the Eastern Churches." In *The New Dictionary of Sacramental Worship*, edited by Fink, 1123–30.

Fink, Peter. "Traditions, Liturgical, in the East." In *The New Dictionary of Sacramental Worship*, edited by Fink, 1255–72.

Finn, Edward. *These Are My Rites: A Brief History of the Eastern Rites of Christianity*. American Essays in Liturgy. Collegeville, MN: Liturgical Press, 1980.

Groen, Basilius, and Christian Gastgeber, eds. *Die Liturgie der Ostkirche. Ein Führer zu Gottesdienst und Glaubensleben der orthodoxen und orientalischen Kirchen*. Freiburg: Herder, 2012.

Janin, R. *Les églises orientales et les rites orientaux*. 4th ed. Paris: Letouzey & Ané, 1955.

Liesel, Nicholas. *The Eastern Catholic Liturgies: A Study in Words and Pictures*. Westminster, MD: Newman Press, 1960.

Oeldemann, Johannes. *Die Kirchen des christlichen Ostens: Orthodoxe, orientalische und mit Rom unierte Ostkirchen*. Kevelaer: Verlagsgemeinshcaft Topos Plus, 2006.

Raes, Alphonsus. *Introductio in Liturgiam Orientalem*. Rome: Pontificium Institutum Orientalium Studiorum, 1947.

Rentel, Alexander. "Byzantine and Slavic Orthodoxy." In *The Oxford History of Christian Worship*, edited by Wainwright and Westerfield Tucker, 254–306.

Roccasalvo, Joan. *The Eastern Catholic Churches: An Introduction to Their Worship and Spirituality*. American Essays in Liturgy. Collegeville, MN: Liturgical Press, 1992.

Salaville, Sévérien. *An Introduction to the Study of Eastern Liturgies*. Translated by John Barton. London: Sands and Co. Publishers, 1938.

Spinks, Bryan D. "Eastern Christian Liturgical Traditions: Oriental Orthodox." In *The Blackwell Companion to Eastern Christianity*, edited by Parry, 339–67.

Taft, Robert. *The Byzantine Rite: A Short History.* American Essays in Liturgy. Collegeville, MN: Liturgical Press, 1992.

Trempelas, Panayiotis. *Λειτουργικοὶ Τύποι Αἰγύπτου καὶ Ἀνατολῆς*. 2nd ed. Athens: Soter, 1993.

Winkler, Gabriele. "Über die Kathedralvesper in den verschiedenen Riten des Ostens und Westens." *Archiv für Liturgiewissenschaft* 16 (1974): 53–102.

Woolfenden, Gregory. "Eastern Christian Liturgical Traditions: Eastern Orthodox." In *The Blackwell Companion to Eastern Christianity*, edited by Parry, 319–38.

## General Studies: Collected Papers

*Acts of the First International Congress of the Society for Oriental Liturgies (SOL) Held at Collegium Orientale, Eichstätt, Bavaria, Germany, 23–28 July, 2006.* Published in *Bollettino della Badia Greca di Grottaferrata* 4 (2007) and 5 (2008).

Atanassova, Diliana, and Tinatin Chronz, eds. *CYNAΞIC KAΘOΛIKH. Beiträge zu Gottesdienst und Geschichte der fünf altkirchlichen Patriarchate für Heinzgerd Brakmann zum 70. Geburtstag.* Wein: Lit Verlag, 2014.

Baumstark, Anton. *Die Messe im Morgenland.* Sammlung Kösel 8. Kempten: J. Kösel, 1906.

Bradshaw, Paul F., and Maxwell E. Johnson. *The Eucharistic Liturgies: Their Evolution and Interpretation.* ACC 87. Collegeville, MN: Liturgical Press, Pueblo, 2012.

Carr, Ephrem, S. Parenti, A.-A. Thiermeyer, and E. Velkovska, eds. *EYΛOΓHMA: Studies in Honor of Robert Taft, S.J.* Studia Anselmiana 110. Analecta Liturgica 17. Rome: Pontificio Ateneo S. Anselmo, 1993.

Feulner, Hans-Jürgen, Elena Velkovska, and Robert Taft, eds. *Crossroad of Cultures: Studies in Liturgy and Patristics in Honor of Gabriele Winkler.* OCA 260. Rome: Pontificio Istituto Orientale, 2000.

Findikyan, Michael Daniel, Daniel Galadza, André Lossky, eds. *Sion, mère des Églises: Mélanges liturgiques offerts au Père Charles Athanase Renoux.* Münster: Aschendorff Verlag, 2016.

Galadza, Daniel, Nina Glibetić, and Gabriel Radle, eds. *TOΞOTHΣ: Studies for Stefano Parenti.* Ἀνάλεκτα Κρυπτοφέρρης 9. Grottaferrata: Monastero Esarchico, 2010.

Groen, Bert. "Liturgical Language and Vernacular Tongues in Eastern Christianity." In *Sanctifying Texts, Transforming Rituals: Encounters in Liturgical Studies*, edited by Paul van Geest, Marcel Poorthuis, and Els Rrse, 407–24. Leiden: Brill, 2017.

Groen, Bert, Daniel Galadza, Nina Glibetić, Gabriel Radle, eds. *Rites and Rituals of the Christian East: Proceedings of the Fourth International Congress of the Society of Oriental Liturgy, Lebanon 10–15 July 2012*. Eastern Christian Studies 22. Leuven: Peeters, 2014.

Groen, Bert, Daniel Galadza, Nina Glibetić, Gabriel Radle, eds. *Studies in Oriental Liturgy: Proceedings of the Fifth International Congress of the Society of Oriental Liturgy, New York, 10–15 June 2014*. Eastern Christian Studies 28. Leuven: Peeters, 2019.

Groen, Bert, Steven Hawkes-Teeples, and Stefanos Alexopoulos, eds. *Inquiries into Eastern Christian Worship: Selected Papers of the Second International Congress of the Society of Oriental Liturgies, Rome, 17–21 September 2008*. Eastern Christian Studies 12. Leuven: Peeters, 2012.

Hawkes-Teeples, Steven, Basilius J. Groen, and Stefanos Alexopoulos, eds. *Studies on the Liturgies of the Christian East: Selected Papers from the Third International Congress of the Society of Oriental Liturgy, Volos, May 26–30, 2010*. Eastern Christian Studies 18. Leuven: Peeters, 2013.

Johnson, Maxwell E., ed. *Between Memory and Hope: Readings on the Liturgical Year*. Collegeville, MN: Liturgical Press, Pueblo, 2000.

———. *Issues in Eucharistic Praying in East and West: Essays in Liturgical and Theological Analysis*. Collegeville, MN: Liturgical Press, Pueblo, 2010.

———. *Living Water, Sealing Spirit: Readings on Christian Initiation*. Collegeville, MN: Liturgical Press, Pueblo, 1995.

———. *Praying and Believing in Early Christianity: The Interplay between Christian Worship and Doctrine*. Collegeville, MN: Liturgical Press, Michael Glazier, 2013.

———. *The Rites of Christian Initiation: Their Evolution and Interpretation*. Rev. and exp. ed. Collegeville, MN: Liturgical Press, Pueblo, 2007.

Lüstraeten, Martin, Brian Butcher, and Steven Hawkes-Teeples, eds. *LET US BE ATTENTIVE! Proceedings of the Seventh International Congress of the Society of Oriental Liturgy, Prešov (Slovakia), 9–14 July 2018*. Studies in Eastern Christian Liturgies 1. Münster: Aschendorff, 2020.

Macomber, William. "A Theory of Origins of the Syrian, Maronite, and Chaldean Rites." OCP 39 (1973): 235–42.

Meyendorff, Paul. "Origins of the Eastern Liturgies." *St. Nersess Theological Review* 1 (1996): 213–22.

Spinks, Bryan D. *Do This in Remembrance of Me: The Eucharist from the Early Church to the Present Day*. London: SCM Press, 2013.

———. *Early and Medieval Rituals and Theologies of Baptism: From the New Testament to the Council of Trent*. Aldershot, England: Ashgate, 2005.

Spronk, Klaas, Gerard Rouwhorst, Stefan Royé, eds. *A Catalogue of Byzantine Manuscripts in Their Liturgical Context: Challenges and Perspectives; Collected Papers Resulting from the Expert Meeting of the Catalogue of Byzantine Manuscripts Programme Held at the PThU in Kampen, the Netherlands on 6th–7th November 2009*. CBM-Subsidia 1. Turnhout: Brepols, 2013.

Taft, Robert. *Beyond East and West: Problems in Liturgical Understanding*. 2nd rev. and enl. ed. Rome: Pontifical Oriental Institute, 1997.

———. *The Liturgy of the Hours in East and West: The Origins of the Divine Office and Its Meaning for Today*. 2nd rev. ed. Collegeville, MN: Liturgical Press, 1993.

Taft, Robert, and Gabriele Winkler, eds. *Comparative Liturgy Fifty Years after Anton Baumstark (1872–1948): Acts of the International Congress, Rome, 25–29 September 1998*. OCA 265. Rome: Pontificio Istituto Orientale, 2001.

Vellian, Jacob, ed. *Crown, Veil, Cross: Marriage Rites*. Syrian Churches Series 25. Kottayam: Jyothi Book House, 1990.

Woolfenden, Gregory. *Daily Liturgical Prayer: Origins and Theology*. Aldershot, England; Burlington, VT: Ashgate, 2004.

## The Liturgies of Jerusalem and Palestine

### *Texts*

Ajjoub, Maxime Leila. *Livre d'heures du Sinai (Sinaiticus Graecus 864)*. SC 486. Paris: Les Éditions du Cerf, 2004.

Black, Matthew. *A Christian Palestinian Syriac Horologion (Berlin MS. Or. Oct. 1019*. Cambridge: Cambridge University Press, 1954.

*Cyrille de Jérusalem: Catéchèses Mystagogiques*. Edited by A. Piédagnel. Translated by Pierre Paris. SC 126. Paris: Les Éditions du Cerf, 1966.

Johnson, Maxwell E. *Lectures on the Christian Sacraments: The Procatechesis and the Five Mystagogical Catecheses Ascribed to St. Cyril of Jerusalem: Text, Translation and Introduction*. Popular Patristic Series 57. Yonkers: St. Vladimir's Seminary Press, 2017.

Kazamias, Alkiviadis. *Λειτουργία τοῦ Ἁγίου Ἰακώβου τοῦ Ἀδελφοθέου καὶ τὰ Νέα Σιναϊτικὰ Χειρόγραφα*. Thessaloniki: Patriarchal Institute for Patristic Studies, 2006.

Mateos, Juan. "Un Horologion inédit de Saint-Sabas: Le codex sinaitique grec 863 (IXe siècle)." In *Mélanges Eugène Tisserant III*, 47–76. Studi e Testi 233. Vatican: Biblioteca apostolica vaticana, 1964.

McGowan, Anne, and Paul F. Bradshaw. *The Pilgrimage of Egeria: A New Translation of the* Itinerarium Egeriae *with Introduction and Commentary*. ACC 93. Collegeville, MN: Liturgical Press, Pueblo, 2018.

Mercier, Dom B.-Ch. *La liturgie de Saint Jacques, Édition critique du texte grec avec traduction latine.* Patrologia Orientalis 26.2. Paris: Firmin-Didot, 1946.

Papadopoulos-Kerameus, A. "Τυπικὸν τῆς ἐν Ἱεροσολύμοις Ἐκκλησίας (Cod. XLIII S. Crucis)." In *Ἀνάλεκτα Ἱεροσολυμιτικῆς Σταχυολογίας,* 1–254. Vol. 2. St. Petersburg, 1891.

Renoux, Athanase. *Le codex arménien Jérusalem 121.* Vol. 1: *Introduction.* Patrologia Orientalis 35, no. 1. Turnhout: Brepols, 1969. Vol. 2: *Édition.* Patrologia Orientalis 36, no. 2 Turnhout: Brepols, 1971.

Tarchnischvili, Michel. *Le grand lectionnaire de l'Église de Jérusalem Ve–VIIIe siècle.* Corpus Scriptorum Christianorum Orientalium 188–89, 204–5. Louvain: Secrétariat du CSCO, 1959–1960.

Terian, Abraham. *Macarius of Jerusalem: Letter to the Armenians, AD 335.* AVANT: Treasures of the Armenian Christian Tradition 4. Crestwood, NY: St. Vladimir's Seminary Press/St. Nersess Armenian Seminary, 2008.

Verhelst, Stéphane, et al. *Liturgia Ibero-Graeca Sancti Iacobi. Editio – Translatio – Retroversio – Commentarii.* Jerusalemer Theologisches Forum 17. Münster: Aschendorff, 2011.

*Studies*

Baldovin, John. *Liturgy in Ancient Jerusalem.* AGLS 9. Bramcote, Nottingham: Grove Books, 1989.

———. *The Urban Character of Christian Worship: The Origins, Development, and Meaning of Stational Liturgy.* OCA 228. Rome: Pontificium Institutum Studiorum, 1987.

Brakmann, Heinzgerd. "Die altkirchlichen Ordinationsgebete Jerusalems. Mit liturgiegeschichtlichen Beobachtungen zur christlichen Euchologie in Palaestina, Syria, Iberia und im Sasanidenreich." *Jahrbuch für Antike und Christentum* 47 (2004): 108–27.

Chronz, Tinatin. *Die Feier des Heiligen Öles nach Jerusalemer Ordnung.* Jerusalemer Theologisches Forum 18. Münster: Aschendorff Verlag, 2012.

Cuming, Geoffrey J. "Egyptian Elements in the Jerusalem Liturgy." *Journal of Theology Studies* 25 (1974): 117–24.

Cutrone, E. J. "Cyril's *Mystagogical Catecheses* and the Evolution of the Jerusalem Anaphora." OCP 44 (1978): 52–64.

Day, Juliette. *Baptism in Early Byzantine Palestine 325–451.* AGLS. Cambridge: Grove Books, 1999.

———. *The Baptismal Liturgy of Jerusalem: Fourth- and Fifth-Century Evidence from Palestine, Syria and Egypt.* Liturgy, Worship and Society. Aldershot, England: Ashgate, 2007.

———. "The Catechetical Lectures of Cyril of Jerusalem: A Source for the Baptismal Liturgy of Mid-Fourth Century Jerusalem." In Paul F. Bradshaw and Juliette Day, *Further Essays in Early Eastern Initiation: Early Syrian Baptismal Liturgy*, 24–56. AGLS 78. Norwich, Norfolk, UK: Hymns Ancient and Modern, 2014.

Doval, A. *Cyril of Jerusalem, Mystagogue: The Authorship of the Mystagogic Catecheses*. Patristic Monograph Series 17. Washington, DC: The Catholic University of America Press, 2001.

Fenwick, John R. K. *The Anaphoras of St. Basil and St. James: An Investigation into Their Common Origin*. OCA 240. Rome: Pontificium Institutum Orientale, 1992.

Frøyshov, Stig Simeon R. "The Early Development of the Liturgical Eight-Mode System in Jerusalem." *St. Vladimir's Theological Quarterly* 51 (2007): 139–78.

Galadza, Daniel. "Liturgical Byzantinization in Jerusalem: Al-Bruni's Melkite Calendar in Context." *Bollettino della Badia Greca di Grottaferatta*. 3rd series, 7 (2010): 69–85.

———. *Liturgy and Byzantinization in Jerusalem*. Oxford Early Christian Studies. Oxford: Oxford University Press, 2018.

Johnson, Maxwell E. "Baptismal Liturgy in Fourth-Century Jerusalem in Light of Recent Scholarship" in *Inquiries into Eastern Christian Worship*, edited by Groen, Hawkes-Teeples, and Alexopoulos.

Leeb, Helmut. *Die Gesänge im Gemeindegottesdienst von Jerusalem vom 5 bis 8 Jahrhundert*. Vienna: Herder, 1970.

Morozowich, Mark. "A Palm Sunday Procession in the Byzantine Tradition? A Study of the Jerusalem and Constantinopolitan Evidence." OCP 75 (2009): 359–83.

———. "Jerusalem Celebration of Great Week Evening Services from Monday to Wednesday in the First Millennium." *Studi sull'Oriente Cristiano* 14 (2010): 99–126.

Petrin, Anna Adams. "The Egyptian Connection: Egyptian Elements in the Liturgy of Jerusalem Revisited." PhD dissertation, University of Notre Dame, 2018.

Ray, Walter D. "August 15 and the Development of the Jerusalem Calendar." PhD dissertation, University of Notre Dame, 2000.

Spinks, Bryan D. "The Jerusalem Liturgy of the *Catecheses Mystagogicae*: Syrian or Egyptian?" *Studia Patristica* 18, no. 2 (1989): 391–96.

Tarby, André. *La prière eucharistique de l'Église de Jerusalem*. Théologie historique 17. Paris: Beauchesne, 1972.

Verhelst, Stéphane. "La déposition des oblats sur l'autel en Syrie-Palestine: contribution à l'histoire de la prothesis." *Oriens Christianus* 82 (1998): 184–203.

———. "Les présanctifiés de saint Jacques." OCP 61 (1995): 381–405.

———. "The Liturgy of Jerusalem in the Byzantine Period." In *Christians and Christianity in the Holy Land: From the Origins to the Latin Kingdoms*, edited by Ora Limor and Guy G. Stroumsa, 421–62. Turnhout: Brepols, 2006.

Winkler, Gabriele. *Die Jakobus-Liturgie in ihren Überlieferungssträngen. Edition des Cod. arm 17 von Lyon, Übersetzung und Liturgievergleich.* Anaphorae Orientales 4. Anaphorae Armeniacae 4. Rome: Pontificio Istituto Orientale, 2013.

———. "Preliminary Observations about the Relationship between the Liturgies of St. Basil and St. James." OCP 76 (2010): 5–55.

Zerfass, Rolf. *Die Schriftlesung im Kathedraloffizium Jerusalems*. Münster: Aschendorff, 1968.

## The Armenian Rite

### *Texts*

Catergian, Joseph, and Joseph Dashian. *Die Liturgien bei den Armeniern. Fünfzehn Texte und Untersuchungen.* Vienna: Mxit'arean Tparan, 1897.

Conybeare, Frederic Cornwallis. *Rituale Armenorum, Being the Administration of the Sacraments and the Breviary Rites of the Armenian Church.* Translated by A. J. Maclean. Oxford: Clarendon Press, 1905; repr. Hildesheim: Olms, 2004.

Rücker, Adolf, Peter Ferhat, and Anton Baumstark. *Denkmäler altarmenischer Meßliturgie.* Analecta Gorgiana 448. Piscataway, NJ: Gorgias Press, 2010.

### *Studies*

Feulner, Hans-Jürgen. *Die armenische Athanasius-Anaphora. Kritische Edition, Übersetzung und liturgievergleichender Kommentar.* Anaphorae Orientales 1. Anaphorae Armeniacae 1. Rome: Pontificio Istituto Orientale, 2001.

———. "Die Vernetzung der armenischen Athanasius-Anaphora mit den benachbarten Liturgiebereichen." In *The Christian East: Its Institutions and Its Thought; A Critical Reflection. Papers of the International Scholarly Congress for the 75th Anniversary of the Pontifical Oriental Institute, Rome, 30 May–5 June 1993*, edited by Robert Taft, 43–64. OCA 251. Rome: Pontificio Istituto Orientale, 1995.

———. "On the 'Preparatory Rites' of the Armenian Divine Liturgy: Some Remarks on the Ritual of Vesting." In *Worship Traditions in Armenia and the Neighboring East*, edited by Roberta Ervine, 93–117. AVANT: Treasures of the Armenian Christian Tradition 3. Crestwood, NY: St. Vladimir's Seminary Press; St. Nersess Armenian Seminary, 2006.

Findikyan, M. Daniel. "Armenian Hymns of the Holy Cross and the Jerusalem *Encaenia*." *Revue des études armeniennes* 32 (2010): 25–58.

———. "The Armenian Ritual of the Dedication of a Church: A Textual and Comparative Analysis of Three Early Sources." OCP 64 (1998): 75–121.

———. *The Commentary on the Armenian Daily Office by Bishop Step'anos Siwnec'i (†735): Critical Edition and Translation with Textual and Liturgical Analysis.* OCA 270. Rome: Pontificio Istituto Orientale, 2004.

———. *From Victims to Victors: The Holy Martyrs of the Armenian Genocide.* New York: Diocese of the Armenian Church of America (Eastern), 2015.

———. "St. Gregory of Narek's Book of Prayers and the Eucharist: Another Holy Communion." *Revue théologique de Kaslik* 3–4 (2009–2010): 291–311.

Johnson, Maxwell E., and M. Daniel Findikyan. "Toward the Restoration of Pre-baptismal Anointing in the Armenian Rite of Baptism." In Armenian Liturgy Seminar, Society of Oriental Liturgy, Etchmiadzin, Armenia, September 13, 2016, in the *Acta* of the Congress, edited by Nina Glibetić and Gabriel Radle. Forthcoming.

Renoux, Charles (Athanase). *Initiation chrétienne: Rituels arméniens du baptême.* Paris: Les Éditions du Cerf, 1997.

———. *Le lectionnaire de Jérusalem en Arménie: le Čašoc.* Patrologia Orientalis 44.4. Turnhout: Brepols, 1989.

———. *Un rite pénitentiel le jour de la Pentecôte? L'office de la génuflexion dans la tradition arménienne.* Wien: Mechitharisten-Buchdruckerei, 1973.

Schmidt, Andrea. *Kanon der Entschlafenen: Das Begräbnisrituale der Armenier: Der altarmenische Bestattungsritus für die Laien.* Orientalia Biblica et Christiana 5. Wiesbaden: Harrassowitz, 1994.

Taft, Robert. "The Armenian Liturgy: Its Origins and Characteristics." In *Treasures in Heaven: Armenian Art, Religion, and Society.* Papers Delivered at the Pierpont Morgan Library at the Symposium Organized by Thomas F. Mathews and Roger S. Wieck, 21–22 May 1994, 13–30. New York: Pierpont Morgan Library, 1998.

———. "The 'Holy Sacrifice' (*Surb Patarag*) as a Mirror of Armenian Liturgical History." In *The Armenian Christian Tradition: Scholarly Symposium in Honor of the Visit to the Pontifical Oriental Institute, Rome, of His Holiness Karekin I, Supreme Patriarch and Catholicos of All Armenians, December 12,*

*1996*, edited by Robert Taft, 175–97. OCA 254. Rome: Pontifical Oriental Institute, 1997. Reprinted in Robert Taft, *Divine Liturgies—Human Problems in Byzantium, Armenia, Syria and Palestine*. Variorum Collected Studies Series. Aldershot, England: Ashgate, 2001.

Winkler, Gabriele. *Das armenische Initiationsrituale. Entwicklungsgeschichtliche und liturgievergleichende Untersuchung der Quellen des 3. bis 10. Jahrhunderts*. OCA 217. Rome: Pontificio Istituto Orientale, 1982.

———. "Der armenische Ritus: Bestandsaufnahme und neue Erkenntnisse sowie einige kürzere Notizen zur Liturgie der Georgier." In *The Christian East: Its Institutions and Its Thought; A Critical Reflection. Papers of the International Scholarly Congress for the 75th Anniversary of the Pontifical Oriental Institute, Rome, 30 May–5 June 1993*, edited by Taft, 265–98. OCA 251.

———. *Die Basilius-Anaphora. Edition der beiden armenischen Redaktionen und der relevanten Fragmente, Übersetzung und Zusammenschau aller Versionen im Licht der orientalischen Überlieferungen*. Anaphorae Orientales 2. Anaphorae Armeniacae 2. Rome: Pontificio Istituto Orientale, 2005.

———. *Die Jakobus-Liturgie in ihren Überlieferungssträngen. Edition des Cod. arm 17 von Lyon, Übersetzung und Liturgievergleich*. Anaphorae Orientales 4. Anaphorae Armeniacae 4. Rome: Pontificio Istituto Orientale, 2013.

———. "On the Formation of the Armenian Anaphoras: A Completely Revised and Updated Overview." *Studi sull'Oriente Cristiano* 11, no. 2 (2007): 97–130.

———. "Preliminary Observations about the Relationship between the Liturgies of St. Basil and St. James." OCP 76 (2010): 5–55.

## The Byzantine Rite

### *Texts*

AGES Initiatives. "Digital Chant Stand." https://www.agesinitiatives.com/dcs/public/dcs/dcs.html.

Anderson, Jeffrey, and Stefano Parenti. *A Byzantine Monastic Office, 1105 A.D.: Houghton Library, MS gr. 3*. Washington, DC: The Catholic University of America Press, 2016.

Arranz, Miguel. *L'eucologio costantinopolitano angli inizi del secolo XI*. Rome: Pontificia Università Gregoriana 1996.

———. *Le typicon du Monastère du Saint-Sauveur à Messine. Codex Messinensis GR 115 A.D. 1131*. OCA 185. Rome: Pontificium Institutum Orientalium Studiorum, 1969.

Cabasilas, Nicholas. *A Commentary on the Divine Liturgy*. Translated by J. M. Hussey and P. A. McNulty. London: SPCK, 1983.

———. *The Life in Christ*. Translated by Carmino deCatanzaro. Crestwood, NY: St. Vladimir's Seminary Press, 1974.

Dmitrievsky, A. *Opisanie liturgicheskikh rykopisei*. 3 vols. Kiev: Tip. Universiteta sv. Vladimira, 1895–1901; Petrograd: Tip. V. F. Kirshbauma, 1917.

Engberg, G., C. Høeg, and G. Zuntz, eds. *Prophetologium*. Monumenta Musicae Byzantinae, Lectionaria. Copenhagen: Munksgaard, 1939–1981.

Goar, Jacques. *Euchologion sive rituale Graecorum*. 2nd ed. Venice, 1730; repr. Graz: Akademische Druck - und Verlagsanstalt, 1960.

Greek Orthodox Archdiocese of America. «Ἑλληνικὰ Λειτουργικὰ Κείμενα τῆς Ὀρθόδοξης Ἐκκλησίας.» http://glt.goarch.org/.

Hawkes-Teeples, Steven, ed. and trans. *St. Symeon of Thessalonika: The Liturgical Commentaries*. Studies and Texts 168. Toronto: Pontifical Institute of Medieval Studies, 2011.

Jordan, Robert. *The Synaxarion of the Monastery of the Theotokos Evergetis*. [I] *September to February* [II] *March-August: The Moveable Cycle*. Belfast Byzantine Texts and Translations 6.5/6.6. Belfast: Institute of Byzantine Studies the Queen's University of Belfast, 2000–2005.

Mateos, Juan. *Le Typicon de la Grande Église*. OCA 165–166. Rome: Pontificio Istituto Orientale, 1962–1963.

Meyendorff, Paul. *St. Germanus of Constantinople on the Divine Liturgy*. Crestwood, NY: St. Vladimir's Seminary Press, 1984.

Mother Mary and Kallistos Ware, trans. *The Festal Menaion*. London: Faber and Faber, 1969.

———. *The Lenten Triodion*. Boston: Faber and Faber, 1978.

Parenti, Stefano, and Elena Velkovska. *L'Eucologio Barberini gr. 336*. Bibliotheca Ephemerides Liturgicae. Subsidia 80. 2nd ed. Rome: C.L.V.-Edizioni Liturgiche, 2000.

Thomas, John, and Angela Constantinides Hero, eds. *Byzantine Monastic Foundation Documents: A Complete Translation of the Surviving Founder's Typika and Testaments*. 5 vols. Washington, DC: Dumbarton Oaks Research Library and Collection, 2000.

Trempelas, Panayiotis. *Αἱ τρεῖς Λειτουργίαι κατὰ τοὺς ἐν Ἀθῆναις κώδικας*. 2nd ed. Athens: Soter, 1982.

## *Studies*

Alexopoulos, Stefanos. "Gestalt und Deutung der christlichen Initiation im mittelalterlichen Byzanz." In *Die Taufe: Einführung in Geschichte und Praxis*, edited by Christian Lange, Clemens Leonhard, and Ralph Olbrich, 49–66. Darmstadt: WBG, 2008.

———. *The Presanctified Liturgy in the Byzantine Rite: A Comparative Analysis of Its Origins, Evolution, and Structural Components*. Liturgia Condenda 21. Leuven: Peeters, 2009.

———. "When a Column Speaks: The Liturgy of the Christian Parthenon." *Dumbarton Oaks Papers* 69 (2015): 159–78.

Alexopoulos, Stefanos, and Annewies van den Hoek. "The Endicott Scroll and Its Place in the History of Private Communion Prayers." *Dumbarton Oaks Papers* 60 (2006): 145–88.

Alexopoulos, Stefanos, and Dionysios Bilalis Anatolikiotes. "Towards a History of Printed Liturgical Books in the Modern Greek State: An Initial Survey." *Ecclesia Orans* 34 (2017): 421–60.

Arranz, Miguel. "Evolution des rites d'incorporation et de réadmission dans l'église selon l' Euchologe byzantin." In *Gestes et paroles dans les diverses familles liturgiques: Conférences Saint-Serge, XXIVe Semaine d'études liturgiques, Paris, 28 juin-1er juillet 1977*, edited by A. Pistoia and A. Triacca, 31–75. Rome: Centro liturgico vincenciano, 1978.

———. "Les grandes étapes de la liturgie byzantine: Palestine-Byzance-Russie. Essai d'aperçu historique." In *Liturgie de l'Église particulière et liturgie de l'Église universelle: Conférences Saint-Serge, XXIle Semaine d'études liturgiques, Paris, 30 juin–3 juillet 1975*, 43–72. *Bibliotheca Ephemerides Liturgicae. Subsidia* 7. Rome: C.L.V.-Edizioni Liturgiche, 1976.

———. "Les Sacraments de l'ancien Euchologe constantinopolitain" (10 articles). 1, OCP 48 (1982): 284–335. 2, OCP 49 (1983): 42–90. 3, OCP 49 (1983): 284–302. 4, OCP 50 (1984): 43–64. 5, OCP 50 (1984): 372–97. 6, OCP 51 (1985): 60–86. 7, OCP 52 (1986): 145–78. 8, OCP 53 (1987): 59–106. 9, OCP 55 (1989): 33–62. 10, OCP 55 (1989): 317–38.

Bertonière, Gabriel. *The Historical Development of the Easter Vigil and Related Services in the Greek Church*. OCA 193. Rome: Pontificio Istituto Orientale, 1972.

———. *The Sundays of Lent in the Triodion: The Sundays Without a Commemoration*. OCA 253. Rome: Pontificio Istituto Orientale, 1997.

Bornert, René. *Les commentaires byzantins de la Divine Liturgie du VIIe au XVe siècle*. Archives de l'Orient Chrétien 9. Paris: Institut Français d'Études Byzantines, 1966.

Denysenko, Nicholas. *The Blessing of Waters and Epiphany: The Eastern Liturgical Tradition*. Farnham, Surrey, England; Burlington, VT: Ashgate, 2012.

———. *Liturgical Reform after Vatican II: The Impact on Eastern Orthodoxy*. Minneapolis: Fortress Press, 2015.

Engberding, Hieronymus. *Das eucharistische Hochgebet der Basileiosliturgie. Textgeschichtliche Untersuchungen und kritische Ausgabe*. Theologie des christlichen Ostens 1. Münster: Aschendoff, 1931.

Engberg, Sysse. "The Greek Old Testament Lectionary as a Liturgical Book." *Cahiers de l'Institut du Moyen Âge Grec et Latin* 54 (1987): 39–48.

———. "The Needle in the Haystack: Searching for Evidence of the Eucharistic Old Testament Lection in the Constantinopolitan Rite." *Bollettino della Badia Greca di Grottaferrata* 13 (2016): 47–60.

———. "The *Prophetologion* and the Triple-Lection Theory: The Genesis of a Liturgical Book." *Bollettino della Badia Greca di Grottaferrata* 3 (2006): 67–91.

Frøyshov, Stig Simeon R. "Byzantine Rite." *The Canterbury Dictionary of Hymnology*. Canterbury Press, August 17, 2021. http://www.hymnology.co.uk/b/byzantine-rite.

———. "The Cathedral-Monastic Distinction Revisited: Part I: Was Egyptian Desert Liturgy a Pure Monastic Office?" *Studia Liturgica* 37 (2007): 198–216.

———. "Greek Hymnody." *The Canterbury Dictionary of Hymnology*. Canterbury Press, August 17, 2021. http://www.hymnology.co.uk/g/greek-hymnody.

———. "Rite of Constantinople." *The Canterbury Dictionary of Hymnology*. Canterbury Press, August 17, 2021. http://www.hymnology.co.uk/r/rite-of-constantinople.

Galadza, Peter. "The Evolution of Funerals for Monks in the Byzantine Realm—10th to 16th Centuries." OCP 70 (2004): 225–57.

Glibetić, Nina. "A New, Eleventh-Century Glagolitic Liturgical Fragment from St. Catherine's Monastery on the Sinai: The Oldest Slavic Horologion." *Archeographical Papers* 37 (2015): 11–47.

———. "An Early Balkan Testimony of the Byzantine Prothesis Rite: The Nomocanon of St. Sava of Serbia (†1236)." In *CYNAΞIC KAΘOΛIKH. Beiträge zu Gottesdienst und Geschichte der fünf altkirchlichen Patriarchate für Heinzgerd Brakmann zum 70. Geburtstag*, edited by Atanassova and Chronz, 239–48.

Hanke, Gregor. *Vesper und Orthros des Kathedralritus der Hagia Sophia zu Konstantinopel*. Jerusalemer Theologisches Forum 21. 2 vols. Münster: Aschendorff Verlag, 2018.

Janeras, Sebastià. *Le Vendredi-Saint dans la tradition liturgique byzantine. Structure et histoire de ses offices*. Studia Anselmiana 99. Analecta Liturgica 13. Rome: Pontificio Anteno S. Anselmo, 1988.

Kaleodis, Patrikios. *Κώδιξ Εἰδικῶν Θεμάτων Ἐκκλησιαστικῆς Τάξεως καὶ Ἐκκλησιαστικῆς Ἐθιμοτυπίας*. 3rd rev. ed. Athens: Apostoliki Diakonia, 2012.

Larin, Vassa. *The Byzantine Hierarchal Divine Liturgy in Arsenij Suxanov's Proskinitarij*. OCA 286. Rome: Pontificio Istituto Orientale, 2010.

———. "Feasting and Fasting According to the Byzantine Typikon." *Worship* 83 (2009): 133–48.

Mateos, Juan. *La célébration de la parole dans la liturgie byzantine: Étude historique*. OCA 191. Rome: Pontificium Institutum Studiorum Orientalium, 1971. English translation: *A History of the Liturgy of St. John Chrysostom*. Vol. 1: *The Liturgy of the Word*. Translated by Steven Hawkes-Teeples. Fairfax: Eastern Christian Publications, 2016.

Mathews, Thomas. *The Early Churches of Constantinople: Architecture and Liturgy*. University Park: Pennsylvania State University Press, 1971.

Milosevic, Nenad. *To Christ and the Church: The Divine Eucharist as the All-Encompassing Mystery of the Church*. Los Angeles: Sebastian Press, 2012.

Morozowich, Mark. *Holy Thursday in Jerusalem and Constantinople: The Liturgical Celebrations from the Fourth to the Fourteenth Centuries*. OCA. Rome: Pontificio Istituto Orientale, forthcoming.

Muksuris, Stelyios. *Economia and Eschatology: Liturgical Mystagogy in the Byzantine Prothesis Rite*. Brookline, MA: Holy Cross Orthodox Press, 2013.

Parenti, Stefano. *L'Anafora di Crisostomo: Testo e contesti*. Jerusalemer Theologisches Forum 36. Münich: Aschendorff Verlagen, 2020.

———. "The Cathedral Rite of Constantinople: Evolution of a Local Tradition." OCP 77 (2011): 449–69.

———. "*'Misericordia, pace, sacrificio di lode'*. Le disavventure vechie e nuove di una locuzione liturgica." *Ecclesia Orans* 37 (2020): 237–71.

———. "Towards a Regional History of the Byzantine Euchology of the Sacraments." *Ecclesia Orans* 27 (2010): 109–21.

Parenti, Stefano, and Robert Taft. *Storia della Liturgia di S. Giovanni Crisostomo* II: *Il Grande Ingresso*. Edizione italiana rivista, ampliata e aggiornata. Ἀνάλεκτα Κρυπτοφέρρης 10. Grottaferrata: Monastero Esarchico, 2014.

Parenti, Stefano, and Elena Velkovska. *Mille anni di "Rito Greco" alle porte di Roma: Raccolta di saggi sulla tradizione liturgica del Monastero italo-bizantino di Grottaferrata*. Ἀνάλεκτα Κρυπτοφέρρης 4. Grottaferrata: Monastero Esarchico, 2004.

Parpulov, Georgi. *Toward a History of Byzantine Psalters ca. 850–1350 A.D.* Plovdiv, 2014.

Pott, Thomas. *Byzantine Liturgical Reform: A Study of Liturgical Change in the Byzantine Tradition*. Translated by Paul Meyendorff. The Orthodox Liturgy Series 2. Crestwood, NY: St. Vladimir's Seminary Press, 2010.

Radle, Gabriel. "The Byzantine Tradition of Marriage in Calabria: Vatican *reginae svecorum gr. 75* (a. 982/3)." *Bollettino della Badia Greca di Grottaferrata* III 9 (2012): 221–45.

———. "Embodied Eschatology: The Council of Nicaea's Regulation of Kneeling and Its Reception across Liturgical Traditions." Part 1 in *Worship* 90 (2016): 345–71. Part 2 in *Worship* 90 (2016): 433–61.

———. "The History of Nuptial Rites in the Byzantine Periphery." Excerpta ex Dissertatione ad Doctoratum. Rome: Pontificium Institutum Orientalium Studiorum, 2012.

———. "The Liturgical Ties between Egypt and Southern Italy: A Preliminary Investigation." In *CYNAΞIC KAΘOΛIKH. Beiträge zu Gottesdienst und Geschichte der fünf altkirchlichen Patriarchate für Heinzgerd Brakmann zum 70. Geburtstag*, edited by Atanassova and Chronz, 617–32.

Rapp, Claudia. "Spiritual Guarantors at Penance, Baptism, and Ordination in the Late Antique East." In *A New History of Penance*, edited by Abigail Firey, 121–48. Leiden: Brill, 2008.

Rapp, Claudia, Eirini Afentoulidou, Daniel Galadza, Ilias Nesseris, Giulia Rossetto, Elisabeth Schiffer. "Byzantine Prayer Books as Sources for Social History and Daily Life." *Jahrbuch der Österreichischen Byzantinistik* 67 (2017): 173–211.

Rentel, Alexander. "Byzantine and Slavic Orthodoxy." In *The Oxford History of Christian Worship*, edited by Wainwright and Westerfield Tucker, 254–306.

Roosien, Mark. "'Slighter than a Spider's Web': Earthquakes, Liturgy, and the Making of Imperial Christianity in Late Antique Constantinople 330–660." PhD dissertation, University of Notre Dame, 2018.

Schulz, Hans-Joachim. *The Byzantine Liturgy: Symbolic Structure and Faith Expression*. New York: Pueblo, 1986.

Schmemann, Alexander. *The Eucharist: Sacrament of the Kingdom*. Crestwood, NY: St. Vladimir's Seminary Press, 1988.

———. *For the Life of the World: Sacraments and Orthodoxy*. Crestwood, NY: St. Vladimir's Seminary Press, 1973.

———. *Great Lent: Journey to Pascha*. Rev. ed. Crestwood, NY: St. Vladimir's Seminary Press, 1974.

———. *Introduction to Liturgical Theology*. 2nd ed. Crestwood, NY: St. Vladimir's Seminary Press, 1975.

———. *Of Water and Spirit: A Liturgical Study of Baptism*. Crestwood, NY: St. Vladimir's Seminary Press, 1974.

Sheerin Daniel. "The Anaphora of the Liturgy of St. John Chrysostom: Stylistic Notes." In *Language and the Worship of the Church*, edited by David Jasper and R. C. D. Jasper, 44–81. London: The Macmillan Press, 1990.

Strunk, Oliver. "The Byzantine Office at Hagia Sophia." *Dumbarton Oaks Papers* 9–10 (1956): 175–202.

Stuhlman, Byron David. *The Initiatory Process in the Byzantine Tradition: Texts in Translation from Early Manuscripts of the Euchology and Typikon of the Hagia Sophia in Constantinople, with a Brief Commentary*. Gorgias Eastern Christian Studies 18. Piscataway: Gorgias Press, 2009.

Taft, Robert. "The Authenticity of the Chrysostom Anaphora Revisited: Determining the Authorship of Liturgical Texts by Computer." OCP 56 (1990): 5–51.

———. *The Byzantine Rite: A Short History*. Collegeville, MN: Liturgical Press, 1992.

———. *The Great Entrance: A History of the Transfer of Gifts and Other Pre-anaphoral Rites of the Liturgy of St. John Chrysostom*. OCA 200. Rome: Pontificio Istituto Orientale, 1978.

———. *A History of the Liturgy of St. John Chrysostom*. Vol. 4: *The Diptychs*. OCA 238. Rome: Pontificio Istituto Orientale, 1991.

———. *A History of the Liturgy of St. John Chrysostom*. Vol. 5: *The Precommunion Rites*. OCA 261. Rome: Pontificio Istituto Orientale, 2000.

———. *A History of the Liturgy of St. John Chrysostom*. Vol 6: *The Communion, Thanksgiving, and Concluding Rites*. OCA 281. Rome: Pontificio Istituto Orientale, 2008.

———. "Holy Week in the Byzantine Tradition." In *Between Memory and Hope: Readings on the Liturgical Year*, edited by Johnson, 155–82.

———. "In the Bridegroom's Absence: The Paschal Triduum in the Byzantine Church." In *La celebrazione del Triduo pasquale: anamnesis e mimesis. Atti del III Congresso Internazionale di Liturgia, Roma, Pontificio Istituto Liturgico, 9–13 maggio 1988*, 71–97. Analecta Liturgica 14. Studia Anselmiana 102. Rome: Pontifico Ateneo S. Anselmo, 1990.

———. "The Liturgy of the Great Church: An Initial Synthesis of Structure and Interpretation on the Eve of Iconoclasm." *Dumbarton Oaks Papers* 34–35 (1980–1981): 45–75.

———. "Marian Liturgical Veneration: Origins, Meaning, and Contemporary Catholic Renewal." In *Orientale Lumen III Conference. Proceedings—1999. June 15–18, 1999, at The Catholic University of America, Washington, DC*, 91–112. Fairfax, VA: Eastern Churches Publications, 1999.

———. "Mount Athos: A Late Chapter in the History of the Byzantine Rite." *Dumbarton Oaks Papers* 42 (1988): 179–94.

———. "A Tale of Two Cities: The Byzantine Holy Week Triduum as a Paradigm of Liturgical History." In *Time and Community: In Honor of Thomas J. Talley*, edited by J. Neil Alexander, 21–41. Washington, DC: Pastoral Press, 1990.

———. *Through Their Own Eyes: Liturgy as the Byzantines Saw It*. Patriarch Athenagoras Orthodox Institute: The Paul G. Manolis Distinguished Lectures 2005. Berkeley, CA: InterOrthodox Press, 2006.

———. "'What Shall We Call You?' Marian Liturgical Veneration in the Byzantine Tradition." In *Úcta ku presvätej Bohorodičke na kresťanskom Východe*, 121–40. Medzinárodná vedecká konferencia 25.–26. novembra 2005, Teologická fakulta Trnavskej univerzity/Centrum spirituality Východ-Západ Michala Lacka, vedeckovýskukmné prackovisko Teologickej fakulty TU. Košice, 2005.

van de Paverd, Frans. *Zur Geschichte der Messliturgie in Antiocheia und Konstantinopel gegen Ende des vierten Jahrhunderts*. OCA 187. Rome: Pontificium Institutum Orientalium Studiorum, 1970.

Velkovska, Elena. "Funeral Rites according to the Byzantine Liturgical Sources." *Dumbarton Oaks Papers* 55 (2001): 21–51.

Zheltov, Michael. "The Moment of Eucharistic Consecration in Byzantine Thought." In *Issues in Eucharistic Praying in East and West*, edited by Johnson, 219–62.

## The Coptic Rite

*Bibliographies*

Brakmann, Heinzgerd. "Neue Funde und Forschungen zur Liturgie der Kopten (1984–1988)." In *Actes du IVe Congrès Copte, Louvain-la-Neuve, 5–10 septembre 1988*, edited by Marguerite Rassart-Debergh and Julien Ries, 2:419–35. Louvain-la-Neuve: Institut Orientaliste, 1992.

———. "Neue Funde und Forschungen zur Liturgie der Kopten (1988–1992)." In *Acts of the Fifth International Congress of Coptic Studies, Washington [DC], 12–15 August 1992*, edited by Tito Orlandi, 1:9–32. Rome: Centro Italiano Microfiches, 1993.

———. "Neue Funde und Forschungen zur Liturgie der Kopten (1992–1996)." In *Ägypten und Nubien in spätantiker und christlicher Zeit. Akten des 6. Internationalen Koptologenkongresses, Münster, 20.–26. 1996*, edited by Stephen Emmel et al., 1:451–64. Wiesbaden: Reichert, 1999.

———. "Neue Funde und Forschungen zur Liturgie der Kopten (1996–2000)." In *Coptic Studies on the Threshold of a New Millennium: Proceedings of the Seventh International Congress of Coptic Studies. Leiden, August 27–September 2, 2000*, edited by M. Immerzeel and J. van der Vliet, 1:575–606. Leuven: Peeters, 2004.

———. "Neue Funde und Forschungen zur Liturgie der Kopten (2000–2004)." In *Actes du huitème Congrès international d'études coptes (Paris, 28 juin–3 juillet 2004)*. Vol. 1: *Bilans et perspectives 2000–2004*, edited by A. Boud'hors and D. Vaillancourt, 127–49. Cahiers de la Bibliothèque copte 15. Paris: De Boccard, 2006.

———. "New Discoveries and Studies in the Liturgy of the Copts (2004–2012)." In *Coptic Society, Literature and Religion from Late Antiquity to Modern Times: Proceedings of the Tenth International Congress of Coptic Studies, Rome, September 17th–22th 2012, and Plenary Reports of the Ninth International Congress of Coptic Studies, Cairo, September 15th–19th, 2008*, edited by Paola Buzi, Alberto Camplani, and Federico Contardi, 1:457–81. Orientalia Lovaniesnia Analecta 247. Leuven: Peeters, 2016.

## *Texts*

Coptic Orthodox Diocese of Southern USA. "Coptic Reader." Apple App Store, Vers. 2.84 (2020). https://apps.apple.com/us/app/coptic-reader/id649434138.

Khs-Burmester, O. H. E. *The Egyptian or Coptic Church: A Detailed Description of Her Liturgical Services and the Rites and Ceremonies Observed in the Administration of Her Sacraments*. Cairo: Publications de la Société d'Archéologie Copte, 1967.

———. *The Horologion of the Egyptian Church: Coptic and Arabic Text from a Mediaeval Manuscript*. Cairo: Edizioni del Centro Francescano di Studi Orientali Cristiani, 1973.

Lanne, Emmanuel. *Le grand euchologe du Monastère Blanc*. Patrologia Orientalis 28.2. Paris: Firmin-Didot, 1958.

Newman, Nicholas. *The Liturgy of Saint Gregory the Theologian: Critical Text with Translation and Commentary*. Belleville, IL: Saint Dominic's Media, 2019.

## *Studies*

Bradshaw, Paul F. "The Barcelona Papyrus and the Development of Early Eucharistic Prayers." In *Issues in Eucharistic Praying in East and West*, edited by Johnson, 129–38.

Brakmann, Heinzgerd. "Typologie des manuscrits liturgiques coptes." In *Les manuscrits liturgiques, cycle thématique 2003–2004 de I'IRHT*, edited by Olivier Legendre and Jean-Baptiste Lebigue. Ædilis, Actes. Séminaires et tables rondes, 9. Paris-Orléans: IRHT, 2005.

Budde, Achim. *Die ägyptische Basilios-Anaphora. Text-Kommentar Geschichte.* Münster: Aschendorff, 2004.

Chase, Nathan. "Rethinking Anaphoral Development in Light of the Barcelona Papyrus." PhD dissertation, University of Notre Dame, 2020.

Cody, Aelred. "Calendar, Coptic." In *The Coptic Encyclopedia*, edited by Atiya, 2:433–36.

Cuming, Geoffrey J. *The Liturgy of St. Mark.* OCA 234. Rome: Pontificium Institutum Orientalium Studiorum, 1990.

Farag, Mary. "Δύναμις Epicleses: An Athanasian Perspective." *Studia Liturgica* 39 (2009): 63–79.

———. "The Anaphora of St. Thomas the Apostle: Translation and Commentary." *Le Muséon* 123, 3–4 (2010): 317–61.

Gerhards, Albert. *Die griechische Gregoriosanaphora: Ein Beitrag zur Geschichte des Eucharistischen Hochgebets.* Liturgiewissenschaftliche Quellen und Forschungen 65. Münster: Aschendorff, 1984.

Hammerstaedt, Jürgen. *Griechische Anaphorenfragmente aus Ägypten und Nubien.* Sonderreihe Papyrologica Coloniensia 28. Opladen/Wiesbaden: Westdeutscher Verlag, 1999.

Ishaq, Emil Maher. "Festal Days, Monthly." In *The Coptic Encyclopedia*, edited by Atiya, 4:1111–12.

Johnson, Maxwell E. "Interrogatory Creedal 'Formulae' in Early Egyptian Baptismal Rites: A Reassessment of the Evidence." *Questions Liturgique* 101 (2021): 75–93.

———. *Liturgy in Early Christian Egypt.* AGLS 33. Bramcote, Nottingham: Grove Books, 1995.

———. *The Prayers of Sarapion of Thmuis: A Literary, Liturgical, and Theological Analysis.* OCA 249. Rome: Pontificio Istituto Orientale, 1995.

Khs-Burmester, O. H. E. "The Baptismal Rite of the Coptic Church: A Critical Study." *Bulletin de la Société d'Archéologie Copte* 11 (1945): 27–86.

———. "The Canonical Hours of the Coptic Church." OCP 2 (1936): 78–100.

———. *The Egyptian or Coptic Church: A Detailed Description of Her Liturgical Services and the Rites and Ceremonies Observed in the Administration of Her Sacraments.* Cairo: Publications de la Société d'Archéologie Copte, 1967.

———. "The Greek Kirugmata, Versicles and Responses, and Hymns in the Coptic Liturgy." OCP 2 (1936): 363–94.

———. "The Turuhat of the Coptic Church." OCP 3 (1937): 78–109, 505–49.

———. "Vesting Prayers and Ceremonies of the Coptic Church." OCP 1 (1935): 305–14.

Malak, Hanna. "Les Livres Liturgiques de l'Église Copte." In *Mélanges Eugène Tisserant*, 1–35. Vol. 3. Studi e Testi 233. Vatican: Biblioteca apostolica vaticana, 1964.

McGowan, Anne Vorhes. "The Basilian Anaphoras: Rethinking the Question." In *Issues in Eucharistic Praying in East and West*, edited by Johnson, 219–62.

Mihálykó, Ágnes. *The Christian Liturgical Papyri: An Introduction*. Studien und Texte zu Antike und Christentum 114. Tübingen: Mohr Siebeck, 2019.

Mikhail, Ramez. "The Evolution of Lent in Alexandria and the Alleged Reforms of Patriarch Demetrius." In *Copts in Context: Negotiating Identity, Tradition, and Modernity*, edited by Nelly van Doorn-Harder, 169–80, 252–58. Columbia, SC: University of South Carolina Press, 2017.

———. "The Presanctified Liturgy of the Apostle Mark in Sinai Arabic 237: Text and Commentary." *Bollettino della Badia Greca di Grottaferrata* 12 (2015): 163–214.

———. *The Presentation of the Lamb: The Prothesis and Preparatory Rites of the Coptic Liturgy*. Studies in Eastern Christian Liturgies 2. Münster: Aschendorff Verlag, 2020.

———. "'We Will Enter into His Dwelling Place': Reconstructing the History of the Chants at the Transfer of the Gifts in Egypt." In *LET US BE ATTENTIVE! Proceedings of the Seventh International Congress of the Society of Oriental Liturgy Prešov (Slovakia), 9–14 July 2018*, edited by Lüstraeten, Butcher, and Hawkes-Teeples, 173–87.

Russo, Nicholas. "The Origins of Lent." PhD dissertation, University of Notre Dame, 2009.

Wassef, Cérès Wissa. "Calendar, Seasons, and Coptic Liturgy." In *The Coptic Encyclopedia*, edited by Atiya, 2:443–44.

———. "Le calendrier copte, de l'antiquité à nos jours." *Journal of Near Eastern Studies* 30 (1971): 1–48.

Winkler, Gabriele. *Die Basilius-Anaphora. Edition der beiden armenischen Redaktionen und der relevanten Fragmente, Übersetzung und Zusammenschau aller Versionen im Licht der orientalischen Überlieferungen*. Anaphorae Orientales 2. Anaphorae Armeniacae 2. Rome: Pontificio Istituto Orientale, 2005.

Youhanna, Youssef, and Ugo Zanetti. *La consecration du Myron par Gabriel IV, 86e patriarche d'Alexandrie en 1374 A.D.* Jerusalemer Theologisches Forum 20. Münster: Aschendorff, 2014.

Zanetti, Ugo, and Heinzgerd Brakmann. *La liturgie de Saint Marc dans le Sinaii arabe 237: Èdition et traduction annotèe*. Münster: Aschendorff Verlag, 2021.

Zheltov, Michael. "The Anaphora and the Thanksgiving Prayer from the Barcelona Papyrus: An Underestimated Testimony to the Anaphoral History in the Fourth Century." *Vigiliae Christianae* 62 (5): 467–504.

### *Nubian Rite*

Brakmann, Heinzgerd. "Defunctus adhuc loquitur. Gottesdienst und Gebetsliteratur der untergegangenen Kirche in Nubien." *Archiv für Liturgiewissenschaft* 48 (2006): 283–333.

———. "La Nubie chrétienne et ses prières liturgiques grecques." In *La liturgie - témoin de l'église. Conférences Saint-Serge. 57e Semaine d'études liturgiques. Paris, 28 juin–1er juillet 2010*, edited by André Lossky and Manlio Sodi, 285–92. Città del Vaticano, 2012.

Frend, William. "A Eucharistic Sequence from Qasr Ibrim." *Jahrbuch für Antike und Christentum* 30 (1987): 90–98.

———. "Nubian Liturgy." In *The Coptic Encyclopedia*, edited by Atiya, 6:1816–17.

Frend, William, and I. A. Muirhead. "The Greek Manuscripts from the Cathedral of Qasr Ibrim." *Le Muséon* 89 (1976): 43–49.

Hammerstaedt, Jürgen. *Griechische Anaphorenfragmente aus Ägypten und Nubien.* Sonderreihe Papyrologica Coloniensia 28. Opladen/Wiesbaden: Westdeutscher Verlag, 1999.

Kubínska, J. "Prothesis de la Cathédrale de Faras. Documents et recherches." *Revue des Archéologues et Historiens d'Art de Louvain* 9 (1976): 7–37.

Łajtar, A. "Greek Inscriptions from the Monastery on Kom H in Old Dongola." In *The Spirituality of Ancient Monasticism: Acts of the International Colloquium Cracow-Tyniec, 16–19.11.1994*, edited by M. Starowieyski, 47–61. Cracow: Wydawnictwo Benedyktynow, 1995.

## The Ethiopian Rite

### *Bibliographies*

Kidane, Habtemichael. *Bibliografia della liturgia etiopica*. OCA 280. Rome: Pontificio Istituto Orientale, 2008.

### *Texts*

*Book of Baptism*. Addis Ababa: Tensae Publishing House, 2001.

Daoud, Marcos, and H. E. Blatta Marsie Hazen. *The Liturgy of the Ethiopian Church*. Originally published in 1959; reprinted Kingston, Jamaica: Ethiopian Orthodox Church, 1991; reedited 2006. http://www.ethiopianorthodox.org/english/church/englishethiopianliturgy.pdf.

Harden, J. M. *The Anaphoras of the Ethiopic Liturgy*. London: SPCK, 1928.

*Matrimony Book: Prayer of the Sacrament of the Matrimony of the Ethiopian Orthodox Tewahido Church*. Addis Ababa: Tensae Publishing House, 2001.

*Studies*

Euringer, Sebastian. *Die Äthiopischen Anaphoren des hl. Evangelisten Johannes des Donnersohnes und des hl. Jacobus von Sarug*. OCA 33. Rome: Pontificium Institutum Orientalium Studiorum, 1934.

Fritsch, Emmanuel. "The Anaphoras of the Geʿez Churches: A Challenging Orthodoxy." In *The Anaphoral Genesis of the Institution Narrative in Light of the Anaphora of Addai and Mari*, edited by Giraudo, 275–315.

———. "The Liturgical Year and the Lectionary of the Ethiopian Church." *Warszawskie Studia Teologiczne* 12, no. 2 (1999): 71–116.

———. *The Liturgical Year of the Ethiopian Church*. Ethiopian Review of Cultures Special Issue 9–10. Addis Ababa, Ethiopia: Master Printing Press, 2001.

———. "New Reflections on the Image of Late Antique and Medieval Ethiopian Liturgy." In *Liturgy's Imagined Past/s: Methodologies and Materials in the Writing of Liturgical History Today*, edited by Teresa Berger, 39–92. Collegeville, MN: Liturgical Press, Pueblo, 2016.

Glenday, David K. "Mary in the Liturgy: An Ethiopian Anaphora." *Worship* 47 (1973): 222–26.

Gobena, Andualem Dagmawi. "Soteriology in the Ethiopian *Täwaḥədo* Church as Reflected in the Liturgical Hymns of the *Dəggʷa* of Yared." PhD dissertation, University of St. Michael's College, Toronto, 2019.

Haile, Getachew. "A Hymn to the Blessed Virgin from Fifteenth-Century Ethiopia." *Worship* 65 (1991): 445–50.

———. "On the Identity of Silondis and the Composition of the Anaphora of Mary Ascribed to Hereyaqos of Behensa." OCP 49 (1983): 366–89.

Hammerschmidt, Ernst. *Studies in the Ethiopic Anaphoras*. Äthiopistische Forschungen 25. 2nd ed. Stuttgart: Franz Steiner Verlag Wiesbaden, 1987.

Kidane, Habtemichael. "La celebrazione della Settimana Santa nella Chiesa Etiopica." In *Hebdomadae sanctae celebratio: Conspectus historicus comparativus*, edited by Antonius Georgius Kollamparampil, 93–134. *Bibliotheca Ephemerides Liturgicae. Subsidia* 93. Rome: C.L.V.-Edizioni Liturgiche, 1997.

———. "Ethiopian (or Geʿez) Worship." In *The New Westminster Dictionary of Liturgy and Worship*, edited by Bradshaw, 169–72.

———. *L'ufficio divino della Chiesa etiopica*. OCA 257. Rome: Pontificio Istituto Orientale, 1998.

Macomber, William. "Ethiopian Liturgy." In *The Coptic Encyclopedia*, edited by Atiya, 2:987–90.

Priess, Maija. *Die äthiopische Chrysostomos-Anaphora*. Äthiopistische Forschungen 68. Wiesbaden: Harrassowitz Verlag, 2006.

Winkler, Gabriele. "A New Witness to the Missing Institution Narrative." In *Studia Liturgica Diversa: Essays in Honor of Paul F. Bradshaw*, edited by Maxwell E. Johnson and L. Edward Phillips, 117–28. Portland: Pastoral Press, 2004.

———. *Das Sanctus: Über den Ursprung und die Anfänge des Sanctus und sein Fortwirken*. OCA 267. Rome: Pontificio Istituto Orientale, 2002.

## The East Syrian Rite

### *Bibliographies*

Yousif, Pierre. *A Classified Bibliography on the East Syrian Liturgy*. Rome: Mar Thoma Yogam, 1990.

The Center for the Study of Christianity, The Hebrew University of Jerusalem. "A Comprehensive Bibliography on Syriac Christianity." http://www.csc.org.il/db/db.aspx?db=SB.

### *Texts*

*Emmanuel: That Is, the Book of Public Prayer*. San Diego, CA: Chaldean Catholic Diocese of St. Peter the Apostle, 2013.

Gelston, Antony. *The Eucharistic Prayer of Addai and Mari*. Oxford: Clarendon Press, 1992.

Maclean, Arthur John. *East Syrian Daily Offices*. London: Rivington, Percival, 1894.

Neroth van Vogelpoel, Alex. *The Commentary of Gabriel of Qatar on the East Syriac Morning Service on Ordinary Days*. Texts from Christian Late Antiquity 53. Piscataway, NJ: Gorgias Press, 2018.

Spinks, Bryan D. *Addai and Mari—The Anaphora of the Apostles: A Text for Students*. GLS 24. Cambridge: Grove Books, 1980.

———. *Mar Nestorius and Mar Theodore the Interpreter: The Forgotten Eucharistic Prayers of East Syria*. AGLS 45. Cambridge: Grove Books, 1999.

### *Studies*

Badger, George Percy. *The Nestorians and Their Rituals*. 2 vols. London: Joseph Masters, 1852.

Chalassery, Joseph. *The Holy Spirit and Christian Initiation in the East Syrian Tradition*. Rome: Mar Thoma Yogam, 1995.

Codrington, Humphrey William. "The Chaldean Liturgy." In *Studies of the Syrian Liturgies*, 60–85. London: Geo. E. J. Coldwell, 1952.

de Vries, Wilhelm. *Sakramententheologie bei den Nestorianern*. OCA 133. Rome: Pontificium Institutum Orientalium Studiorum, 1947.

Edakalathur, Louis. *The Theology of Marriage in the East Syrian Tradition*. Rome: Mar Thoma Yogam, 1994.

Giraudo, Cesare, ed. *The Anaphoral Genesis of the Institution Narrative in Light of the Anaphora of Addai and Mari*. OCA 295. Rome: Edizioni Orientalia Christiana, 2013.

Jammo, Sarhad. "The Anaphora of the Apostles Addai and Mari: A Study of Structure and Historical Background," OCP 68 (2002): 5–35.

———. "L'office du soir chaldéen au temps de Gabriel Qatraya." *L'Orient Syrien* 12 (1967): 187–210.

———. *La structure de la Messe chaldéene du début jusqu'à l'Anaphore. Étude historique*. OCA. Rome: Pontificium Institutum Orientalium Studiorum, 1979.

Jomon, K. M. "*T'AKS'A D-'AL R'AZ'A Q'ADISH'A D-ZUW'AG'A*—A Textual and Theological Analysis of the Order of Marriage in the East Syriac Tradition." PhD dissertation, Mahatma Gandhi University, Kottayam, Kerala, 2014.

Kannookadan, Pauly. *The East Syrian Lectionary: An Historico-Liturgical Study*. Rome: Mar Thoma Yogam, 1991.

Macomber, William. "A Theory on the Origins of the Syrian, Maronite, and Chaldean Rites." OCP 39 (1973): 235–42.

Maniyattu, Pauly, ed. *East Syrian Theology: An Introduction*. Satna, India: Ephrem's Publications, 2007.

———. *Heaven on Earth: The Theology of Liturgical Spacetime in the East Syrian Qurbana*. Rome: Mar Thoma Yogam, 1995.

Mateos, Juan. *Lelya - Ṣapra. Les offices chaldéens de la nuit et du matin*. OCA 156. Rome: Pontificium Institutum Orientalium Studiorum, 1972.

Pudichery, Sylvester. *Ramsa: An Analysis and Interpretation of the Chaldean Vespers*. Pachalam: Dharmaram College, 1972.

Royel, Mar Awa. "The Sacrament of the Holy Leaven (*Malkā*) in the Assyrian Church of the East." In *The Anaphoral Genesis of the Institution Narrative in Light of the Anaphora of Addai and Mari*, edited by Giraudo, 363–86.

Russo, Nicholas. "The Validity of the Anaphora of *Addai and Mari*: Critique of the Critiques." In *Issues in Eucharistic Praying in East and West: Essays in Liturgical and Theological Analysis*, edited by Johnson, 21–62.

Spinks, Bryan D. "The Mystery of the Holy Leaven (*Malka*) in the East Syrian Tradition." In *Issues in Eucharistic Praying in East and West*, edited by Johnson, 63–70.

———. *Worship: Prayers from the East*. Washington, DC: Pastoral Press, 1993.

Taft, Robert. "Mass Without the Consecration? The Historic Agreement on the Eucharist between the Catholic Church and the Assyrian Church of the East Promulgated 26 October 2001." *Worship* 77, no. 6 (2003): 482–509.

———. "On the Use of the Bema in the East-Syrian Worship." *Eastern Churches Review* 3 (1970): 30–39.

Vellian, Jacob. *East Syrian Evening Services*. Kottayam: Indian Institute for Eastern Churches, 1971.

Yousif, Pierre. *L'eucharistie chez saint Éphrem de Nisibe*. OCA 224. Rome: Pontificium Institutum Orientalium Studiorum, 1984.

## The West Syrian Rite

### *Bibliographies*

The Center for the Study of Christianity, The Hebrew University of Jerusalem. "A Comprehensive Bibliography on Syriac Christianity." http://www.csc.org.il/db/db.aspx?db=SB.

### *Texts*

*Anaphoras: The Book of the Divine Liturgies According to the Rite of the Syrian Orthodox Church of Antioch*. Translated by Murad Saliba Barsom. Edited by Mar Athanasius Yeshue Samuel. Lodi, NJ: Mar Athanasius Yeshue Samuel, 1991.

*The Book of Common Prayer of the Syrian Church*. Translated into English by Bede Griffiths. Piscataway, NJ: Gorgias Press, 2005.

Codrington, Humphrey William. "The Syrian Liturgies of the Presanctified." *Journal of Theological Studies* 4 (1903): 69–82; 5 (1904): 369–77 and 535–45.

Connolly, R. H., and H. W. Codrington, eds. *Two Commentaries on the Jacobite Liturgy, by George, Bishop of the Arab Tribes and Moses Bar Kepha: Together with the Syriac Anaphora of St. James and a Document Entitled "The Book of Life."* London: Williams and Norgate, 1913.

*Ma'de'dono: The Book of the Church Festivals According to the Ancient Rite of the Syrian Orthodox Church of Antioch*. Translated by Archdeacon Murad

Saliba Barsom. Edited and published by Metropolitan Mar Athanasius Yeshue Samuel, Archbishop of the Syrian Orthodox Church in the United States of America and Canada, 1984.

Malankara Archdiocese of the Syriac Orthodox Church in North America. "Qleedo+ (Orthodox Prayers)." Apple App Store, Vers. 4.8.5 (2020), https://apps.apple.com/us/app/qleedo-orthodox-prayers/id1015279062.

Syrian Orthodox Patriarchate of Antioch. "Department of Syriac Studies." https://dss-syriacpatriarchate.org/patriarchal-library/?lang=en.

*Studies*

Aydin, Mor Polycarpus Augin. *The Syriac Order of Monastic Profession and the Order of Baptism: Common Structure, Imagery and Theological Themes.* Gorgias Eastern Christian Studies 47. Piscataway, NJ: Gorgias Press, 2017.

Black, Matthew. "The Festival of Encaenia Ecclesiae in the Ancient Church with Special Reference to Palestine and Syria." *Journal of Ecclesiastical History* 5 (1954): 78–85.

Botte, Bernard. "Les Dimanches de la Dédicace dans les églises syriennes." *L'Orient Syrien* 2 (1957): 65–70.

———. "Le rite de baptême dans l'Église syrienne." *L'Orient Syrien* 1 (1956): 137–55.

Brock, Sebastian. *Fire from Heaven: Studies in Syriac Theology and Liturgy.* Variorum Collected Studies Series 863. Aldershot, England: Ashgate, 2006.

———. *Holy Spirit in the Syrian Baptismal Tradition.* 2nd ed. The Syrian Churches Series 9. Kottayam, India: Anita Printers, 1979).

———. "Some Early Baptismal Commentaries." OCP 46 (1980): 20–61.

———. *Studies in Syriac Spirituality.* The Syrian Churches Series 13. Kottayam, India: Jyothi Book House, 1988.

———. "Studies in the Early History of the Syrian Orthodox Baptismal Liturgy." *Journal of Theological Studies* 23 (1972): 16–64.

Codrington, Humphrey William. "The Syrian Liturgy." In *Studies of the Syrian Liturgies*, 1–47.

de Vries, Wilhelm. *Sakramententheologie bei den Syrischen Monophysiten.* OCA 125. Rome: Pontificium Institutum Orientalium Studiorum, 1940.

Gogan, Brian. "Penance Rites of the West Syrian Liturgy: Some Liturgical and Theological Implications." *The Irish Theological Quarterly* 42 (1975): 182–96.

Jarjour, Tala. *Sense and Sadness: Syriac Chant in Aleppo*. Oxford: Oxford University Press, 2018.

Macomber, William. "A Theory on the Origins of the Syrian, Maronite, and Chaldean Rites." OCP 39 (1973): 235–42.

Spinks, Bryan D. "The Anaphora of Severus of Antioch: A Note on its Character and Theology." In *Θυσία αἰνέσεως. Mélanges liturgiques offerts à la mémoire de l'archevêque Georges Wagner (1930–1993)*, edited by Job Getcha and André Lossky, 345–51. Analecta Sergiana 2. Paris: Presses Saint-Serge, 2005.

Tovey, Phillip. *Essays in West Syrian Liturgy*. Kottyam: Oriental Institute of Religious Studies, 1997.

———. *The Liturgy of St. James as Presently Used*. AGLS 40. Cambridge: Grove Books, 1998.

Varghese, Baby. *The Syriac Version of the Liturgy of St. James: A Brief History for Students*. AGLS 49. Cambridge: Grove Books, 2001.

Winkler, Gabriele. *Die Jakobus-Liturgie in ihren Überlieferungssträngen. Edition des Cod. arm 17 von Lyon, Übersetzung und Liturgievergleich*. Anaphorae Orientales 4. Anaphorae Armeniacae 4. Rome: Pontificio Istituto Orientale, 2013.

### The Maronite Rite

*Bibliographies*

The Center for the Study of Christianity, The Hebrew University of Jerusalem. "A Comprehensive Bibliography on Syriac Christianity." http://www.csc.org.il/db/db.aspx?db=SB.

*Texts*

*Anaphora Book of the Syriac-Maronite Church of Antioch*. Translated by Joseph P. Amar. Youngstown, OH: The Liturgical Commission, Diocese of St. Maron, USA, 1978.

Diocese of St. Maron, USA. *Mysteries of Initiation: Baptism, Confirmation, Communion, According to the Maronite Antiochene Church*. Washington, DC: Diocesan Office of Liturgy, 1987.

Elkhoury, Armando. "The Hidden Pearl—Resources." https://thehiddenpearl.org/resources/.

*Fenqitho: A Treasury of Feasts According to the Syriac-Maronite Church of Antioch*. Brooklyn, NY: Diocese of St. Maron, 1982.

*The Maronite Liturgical Year*. 3 vols. Brooklyn, NY: Diocese of St. Maron, 1982.

*Studies*

Badwi, Abdo. *The Liturgical Year Iconography of the Syro-Maronite Church.* Kaslik, Liban: Université Saint-Esprit, 2006.

Bonian, Stephen. "Themes from the Maronite Liturgical Seasons." *Diakonia* 22 (1988–1989): 169–84.

Codrington, Humphrey William. "The Maronite Liturgy." In *Studies of the Syrian Liturgies*, 48–59.

Franklin, Claude. "Oil of Gladness: The Historical Origins of the Maronite Rite of Lamp." Licentiate Thesis, Rome: Pontificium Institutum Orientalium Studiorum, 2005.

Gemayel, Boutros. "The Maronite Divine Liturgy." *Eastern Churches Journal* 9 (2002): 33–62.

Gemayel, Pierre-Edmond. *Avant-messe maronite: histoire et structure*. OCA 174. Rome: Pontificium Institutum Orientalium Studiorum, 1965.

Hadaya, Marcelle. *L'office maronite du samedi saint: traduction et étude liturgico-théologique*. Kaslik, Liban: Université Saint-Esprit, 1995.

Hayek, Michel. *Liturgie Maronite: Histoire et textes eucharistiques*. Tours, France: Mame, 1964.

Heinz, Andreas. *Die Heilige Messe nach dem Ritus der Syrisch-maronitischen Kirche*. Sophia: Quellen östlicher Theologie 28. Trier: Paulinus Verlag, 1996.

Khawand, Louis. *Le pardon dans la messe maronite*. Kaslik, Liban: Université Saint-Esprit, 1988.

Macomber, William. "A Theory on the Origins of the Syrian, Maronite, and Chaldean Rites." OCP 39 (1973): 235–42.

———. "The Maronite and Chaldean Versions of the Anaphora of the Apostles." OCP 37 (1971): 55–84.

Mouhanna, Augustin. "Le rite du pardon dans l'Église Maronite." *Parole de l'Orient* 6–7 (1975–1976): 309–24.

———. *Les rites de l'initiation dans l'Église maronite*. OCA 212. Rome: Pontificium Institutum Orientalium Studiorum, 1980.

———. "La troisième anaphore de Saint Pierre Apôtre, dite *Šarrar*, en usage dans l'Église Maronite." In *The Anaphoral Genesis of the Institution Narrative in Light of the Anaphora of Addai and Mari*, edited by Giraudo, 237–58.

Naaman, Abbot Paul. *The Maronites: The Origins of an Antiochene Church—A Historical and Geographical Study of the Fifth to the Seventh Centuries*. Cistercian Studies 243. Collegeville, MN: Cistercian Publications, 2011).

Sacre, Ziad. "Le rite de la lampe et l'onction des malades dans l'église maronite: Traduction et étude historique, liturgique et théologico-spirituelle." PhD dissertation, Sorbonne University–Paris IV, Paris, 1996.

Spinks, Bryan D. "A Tale of Two Anaphoras; Addai and Mari and Maronite Sharar." In *The Anaphoral Genesis of the Institution Narrative in Light of the Anaphora of Addai and Mari*, edited by Giraudo, 359–74.

Tabet, Jean. *L'office commun maronite; étude du lilyō et du ṣafrō*. Kaslik, Liban: Université Saint-Esprit, 1972.

Van Rompay, Lucas. "Excursus: The Maronites." In *The Oxford History of Christian Worship*, edited by Wainwright and Westerfield Tucker, 170–74.

# Index